Mauritius, Réunion & Seychelles

Sarina Singh
Deanna Swaney
Robert Strauss

Mauritius, Réunion & Seychelles

3rd edition

Published by
 Lonely Planet Publications
 Head Office: PO Box 617, Hawthorn, Vic 3122, Australia
 Branches: 150 Linden St, Oakland, CA 94607, USA
 10a Spring Place, London NW5 3BH, UK
 1 rue du Dahomey, 75011 Paris, France

Printed by
 Craft Print Pte Ltd, Singapore

Photographs by

Olivier Cirendini	Paul Piaia	Sepp Seufzenecker
Shoot	Sarina Singh	Julian Smith
Robert Strauss	Deanna Swaney	Robert Willox

Front cover: The tamarillo *(tomate arbuste)* is a sweet tree tomato found in Réunion (Olivier Cirendini)

First Published
 December 1989

This Edition
 February 1998

National Library of Australia Cataloguing in Publication Data

Singh, Sarina, 1968-.
    Mauritius, Réunion & Seychelles.

3rd ed.
includes index
ISBN 0 86442 498 1.

1. Mauritius – Guidebooks. 2. Réunion – Guidebooks. 3. Seychelles – Guidebooks. I. Swaney, Deanna.
II. Strauss, Robert. III. Title.

916.9804

text & maps © Lonely Planet 1998
photos © photographers as indicated 1998
climate chart of St-Denis compiled from information supplied by Patrick J Tyson, © Patrick J Tyson, 1998

Sarina Singh

A passionate traveller ever since she can remember, Sarina took the plunge and bought a one-way ticket to India after completing a business degree (majoring in Hotel Management) in Melbourne, Australia. She did a marketing executive traineeship with Sheraton Hotels in New Delhi, but later drifted into journalism. Writing mainly about India, assignments also lead her to the Middle East, Nepal, Kenya, Zanzibar and Pakistan where she interviewed a notorious Mujahideen warlord at his clandestine headquarters near the Afghanistan border.

After 3½ years in India Sarina returned to Australia, did a post-graduate journalism course and then wrote two television documentary scripts. Other Lonely Planet titles she has worked on are *Africa*, *Rajasthan* and *India*. She is currently writing a book about a prominent polo player.

Deanna Swaney

After completing university studies, Deanna Swaney made a shoestring tour of Europe and has been addicted to travel ever since. Despite an erstwhile career in computer programming, she managed intermittent forays away from encroaching yuppiedom in midtown Anchorage, Alaska, and at first opportunity, made a break for South America where she wrote Lonely Planet's *Bolivia*. Subsequent travels led through an erratic circuit of island paradises – Arctic and tropical – and resulted in three more guides: *Tonga*, *Samoa* and *Iceland, Greenland & the Faroe Islands*.

She returned to dry land for the *Zimbabwe, Botswana & Namibia* guide and has since co-authored the second editions of *Brazil* and *Mauritius, Réunion & Seychelles*, updated the second edition of *Madagascar & Comoros* and contributed to the shoestring guides to Africa, South America and Scandinavia.

Robert Strauss

Robert was born in England. In the early 1970s he took the overland route to Nepal

and then studied, taught and edited in England, Germany, Portugal and Hong Kong. For Lonely Planet he has worked on travel survival kits to China, Tibet, Japan, Brazil, and Bolivia and contributed to shoestring guides for South America, North-East Asia and Europe. He has also written the Trans-Siberian Rail Guide (Compass Publications, UK).

From Sarina

On my journey through Mauritius, Réunion and the Seychelles, I met some incredibly helpful and hospitable people. In Mauritius, thanks to Joy and Sheena Joymungul for wholeheartedly welcoming me into their family; Abeydin Jaulim for making sure I never got lost; Ramesh and Shyama Lutchmun for their kindness; and Louis Hein de Charmoy for his comprehensive insights on Mauritius. Thanks also to Sandrine Lincoln, Ricardo Lacour, Mr Bissoondoyal, Suchita Ramdin and Raymond Duvergé. On Rodrigues, thanks to Jean-Marc Begue for showing me the island in a style all of his own.

Réunion just would not have been the same without Carl Houart, a goldmine of information and delightful person – thanks. Thanks also to Chris Verboven for giving me the cutting edge on a few contemporary

French phrases, and also Laure Dupont, François Gillet, Richard Stratford, Sudha Souprayen and Gilles Le Cointre.

In the Seychelles, I'd like to thank the effervescent Alain and Ginette St Ange, Pat McGregor and Jean François Ferrari for their prolific assistance. Thanks also to Basil Ferrari, Wix Nibourette and the insouciant George Julienne – my cycling companion on La Digue.

At Lonely Planet, I'd like to give special thanks and credit to Justin Flynn for being such a proficient and supportive editor. Thanks also to Sam Carew, Greg Herriman, Cathy Lanigan, Janet Watson, and the staff at the LP Paris and London offices – for their much appreciated assistance. I'd like to especially thank French author, Olivier Cirendini, for his terrific contribution to the Réunion section.

A personal vote of thanks to med students extraordinaire – Ajeet Singh and Justin Dwyer – for helping me with Japanese Yen conversions and some speedy reading. And to my parents – for their generosity in all respects.

This Book
The 1st edition of Mauritius, Réunion & Seychelles was written by Robert Willox in 1989. The 2nd edition was updated by Robert Strauss and Deanna Swaney. This edition was fully updated by Sarina Singh. Olivier Cirendini researched and wrote the Trekking in Réunion chapter.

From the Publisher
This edition was edited at the Lonely Planet office in Australia by Justin Flynn. Anne Mulvaney, David Andrew and Martin Hughes all came off the bench at various stages of the game to lend a helping hand with editing and proofing. Janet Watson slaved over the mapping and was ably assisted by Trudi Canavan, Paul Piaia and Lyndell Taylor. Glenn Beanland and Janet took care of the designing while layout was completed by Glenn Beanland and Andrew

Smith. Trudi, Janet and Margie Jung provided the illustrations. David Kemp and Margie were responsible for the cover design. Thanks to the staff at Lonely Planet's French office for their valuable assistance.

Thanks
Many thanks to the travellers who used the last edition and wrote to us with helpful hints, useful advice and interesting anecdotes. Your names follow:

Liam and Vicky, Steve and Alicia, Alan Aitchison, Dr Bernhard Assmus, Joshua Berry, Piet Bommer, A and M Boudry, Bruce Cockroft, Katie Cooke, Sharon Croome, Hannah de Angelis, Dave Dubyne, Brian Ellis, Carrie Garavan, Robert Garnett, Mark Grice, Robyn Griffith, Jean Hendry, Sam Kimber, William McEwan, Vinod Persand, Angela Pistoia, Diane Porter, Dr M S Smith, Joanne Tzzo, Erik Wilbers.

Warning & Request
Things change – prices go up, schedules change, good places go bad and bad places go bankrupt – nothing stays the same. So, if you find things better or worse, recently opened or long since closed, please tell us and help make the next edition even more accurate and useful.

We value all of the feedback we receive from travellers. Julie Young coordinates a small team who read and acknowledge every letter, postcard and email, and ensure that every morsel of information finds its way to the appropriate authors, editors and publishers.

Everyone who writes to us will find their name in the next edition of the appropriate guide and will also receive a free subscription to our quarterly newsletter, *Planet Talk*. The very best contributions will be rewarded with a free Lonely Planet guide.

Excerpts from your correspondence may appear in new editions of this guide; in our newsletter, *Planet Talk*; or in updates on our Web site – so please let us know if you don't want your letter published or your name acknowledged.

Contents

Map Legend

BOUNDARIES

- ━━━━━━━ ....International Boundary
- ━━·━·━·━ ....Provincial Boundary
- ━ ━ ━ ━ ━ .... Disputed Boundary

ROUTES

- ═══A25═══ ..... Freeway, with Route Number
- ═══════ ....Major Road
- ═══════ ....Minor Road
- ══════════ .... Minor Road - Unsealed
- ═══════ ....City Road
- ═══════ ....City Street
- ═══════ ....City Lane
- - - - - - - - - ....Ferry Route
- - - - - - - - - ....Walking Track

AREA FEATURES

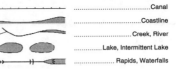

- ....Building
- .... Christian Cemetery
- ....Beach
- ....Market
- .... Park, Gardens
- ....Pedestrian Mall
- .... Urban Area

HYDROGRAPHIC FEATURES

- ....Canal
- ....Coastline
- .... Creek, River
- .... Lake, Intermittent Lake
- .... Rapids, Waterfalls

SYMBOLS

✈ ....Airfield	← ....One Way Street	
✈ ....Airport	▣ ....Parking	
☉ ....Bank	)(.........................Pass	
⚲ ....Beach	▨ ....Picnic Area	
☌ ....Bird Sanctuary	○ ....Point of Interest	
⌒ ....Cave	☗ ....Petrol Station	
▤ ☗ ....Cathedral, Church	★ ....Police Station	
⌢⌢⌢ ....Cliff or Escarpment	✉ ....Post Office	
◎ ....Embassy	∴ ....Ruins	
▇ ....Fort	♠ ....Shelter	
✿ ....Garden	⚓ ....Shipwreck	
⋈ ....Gate	❖ ....Shopping Centre	
⌐ ....Golf	◎ ....Spring	
▥ ....Hindu Temple	血 ....Stately Home	
✚ ....Hospital	✦ ....Surf Beach	
☀ ....Lighthouse	▭ ....Swimming Pool	
⚑ ....Monument	☎ ....Telephone	
◖ ....Mosque	▣ ....Tomb	
▲ ....Mountain or Hill	❶ .....Tourist Information	
血 ....Museum	◔ ....Transport	
☂ ....National Park	⚑ ....Volcano	

CAPITAL ....National Capital
CAPITAL ......Provincial Capital
CITY ....City
Town .... Major Town
Town ....Town
Village ....Village

- ■ ....Place to Stay
- Å .... Camping Ground
- ⌂ ....Hut or Chalet
- ▼ .... Place to Eat
- ⊌ .... Pub or Bar

Note: not all symbols displayed above appear in this book

Introduction

The islands of the Indian Ocean are just as interesting, exhilarating and beautiful as the South Pacific islands, yet it's the South Pacific that gets the sizzling romances, the riveting adventure stories and the news headlines. The fact is, the Indian Ocean islands are somewhat shrouded in intrigue – perhaps because they tend to lie hidden in the shadow of East Africa, and are sometimes wrongly labelled as African. Even some intrepid travellers cannot place them on a map and may confuse them with Fiji, Tahiti or Hawaii, because they can't place Mauritius or the Seychelles and have never heard of Réunion. The French, however, are generally *au fait* with the Indian Ocean region, because France once controlled it.

The British ended up with most of it in 1814 as a prize for defeating Napoleon. They dutifully, stiffly, almost reluctantly, governed Mauritius and the Seychelles, but did little to alter the implanted French language or influence the evolving Créole culture.

Both Mauritius and the Seychelles have been independent nations for some time now, and are doing well considering the fate of their liberated big cousins in Africa. Réunion has stuck relatively comfortably with France and is today governed as a French overseas *département*.

The beauty of these Indian Ocean islands, is that each has a personality all its own. If you're searching for *the* ultimate tropical paradise, you can't beat the Seychelles, with its magical beaches and lagoons. Indeed, the Seychelles boasts some of the most striking islands on the planet and offers sensational diving and snorkelling. Mauritius also has its fair share of idyllic beaches as well as various plateau attractions. Of the three islands it is the cheapest to visit, which largely explains the steady rise in tourism. Réunion is the surprise package, with a live volcano and awesome alpine scenery. It offers world-class trekking with a luscious tropical twist. Often referred to as 'France's best kept secret', the island is virtually unexplored by all but the French.

Apart from their natural wonders, the three islands also have a vibrant cultural mix. Each has developed differently and each is a country of contrasts in itself – they're fascinating melting pots of races, religions and cultures. The mixes on all three islands are similar, but they vary in degree. In Mauritius, Indian culture dominates; a Créole identity has been valiantly forged in the Seychelles; and Réunion follows European ways. The result – a flamboyant potpourri of people, cuisines, languages, traditions and beliefs.

Facts about the Region

ECOLOGY & ENVIRONMENT

Most of the coastlines of Mauritius, the Seychelles, and the west coast of Réunion are fringed by coral reefs, fragile environments of calcareous deposits secreted by tiny marine animals known as coral polyps. The glorious white sand beaches of the Indian Ocean islands are composed of dead coral, shells and marine algae; without reefs, the beaches will erode and disappear. The reefs also provide shelter and habitat for numerous fish, shells, crustaceans, sea urchins and other marine life which in turn provide a food source for larger fish as well as humans, both directly and indirectly.

In order to protect the marine environment we strongly urge you not to buy anything made of turtle shell nor to buy or take shells from the beach. Stocks of turtles and many of the most beautiful shells have been cleared in many areas and some are actually endangered. Governments are trying to curb trade in and export of tortoiseshell, coral, shells and other natural products; please don't contribute to the problems by providing market incentives for the collectors.

SOCIETY & CONDUCT
Dos and Don'ts

Religious Etiquette Particular care should be taken if you attend a religious place (shrine, temple, mosque) or event. Dress and behave appropriately – don't wear singlet tops, shorts or mini-skirts, and refrain from holding hands or smoking. Holy places such as temples and mosques require that you remove your shoes

---

Considerations for Responsible Diving

The popularity of diving is placing immense pressure on many sites. Please consider the following tips when diving and help preserve the ecology and beauty of reefs.

- Do not use anchors on the reef, and take care not to ground boats on coral. Encourage dive operators and regulatory bodies to establish permanent moorings at popular dive sites.
- Avoid touching living marine organisms with your body or dragging computer consoles and gauges across the reef. Polyps can be damaged by even the gentlest contact. Never stand on corals, even if they look solid and robust. If you must secure yourself to the reef, only hold fast to exposed rock or dead coral.
- Be conscious of your fins. Even without contact the surge from heavy fin strokes near the reef can damage delicate organisms. When treading water in shallow reef areas, take care not to kick up clouds of sand. Settling sand can easily smother the delicate organisms of the reef.
- Practise and maintain proper buoyancy control. Major damage can be done by divers descending too fast and colliding with the reef. Make sure you are correctly weighted and that your weight belt is positioned so that you stay horizontal. If you have not dived for a while, have a practice dive in a pool before taking to the reef. Be aware that buoyancy can change over the period of an extended trip: initially you may breathe harder and need more weight; a few days later you may breathe more easily and need less weight.
- Take great care in underwater caves. Spend as little time within them as possible as your air bubbles may be caught within the roof and thereby leave previously submerged organisms high and dry. Taking turns to inspect the interior of a small cave will lessen the chances of damaging contact.
- Resist the temptation to collect or buy corals or shells. Aside from the ecological damage, taking home marine souvenirs depletes the beauty of a site and spoils the enjoyment of others. The same goes for marine archaeological sites (mainly shipwrecks). Respect their integrity; they may even be protected from looting by law.
- Ensure that you take home all your rubbish, and any litter you may find as well. Plastics in particular are a serious threat to marine life. Turtles can mistake plastic for jellyfish and eat it.
- Resist the temptation to feed fish. You may disturb their normal eating habits, encourage aggressive behaviour or feed them food that is detrimental to their health.
- Minimise your disturbance of marine animals. In particular, do not ride on the backs of turtles as this causes them great anxiety. ■

before entering – there's often a sign indicating where to leave your shoes. Don't touch a carving or statue of a deity. At some Hindu temples (such as the one in St-Denis), you also need to remove leather items such as belts. At mosques, you usually have to cover your head in certain areas, so remember to take along a scarf. If at anytime you're unsure about protocol, ask somebody.

Photographic Etiquette In many temples and mosques, photography is not allowed (such as the Hindu temple and Grande Mosquée in St-Denis). You should always be sensitive about taking photos of people, especially women, who may find it offensive – ask first. It may also be insensitive to take photos at certain religious ceremonies – again, it's best to ask first.

LANGUAGE

Créole is a blend of French and assorted African languages and is spoken on Mauritius, Réunion and the Seychelles. However, there are variations in the Créole dialect between these three countries. For instance, Seychelles Créole is fairly similar to that of Mauritius, but differs significantly from the Créole spoken in Réunion. For further details and some useful Créole words, see under Language in the individual country sections.

Along with local and Créole dialects, French is spoken on all three islands. You'll often find that menus in the Indian Ocean are mostly in French, with Créole variations in some cases.

Remember that an important distinction is made in French between *tu* and *vous*, which both mean 'you'. *Tu* is only used when addressing people you know well, children or animals. When addressing an adult who is not a personal friend, *vous* should be used unless the person invites you to use *tu*. Generally, younger folk insist less on this distinction, and they may use *tu* from the beginning of an acquaintance.

French

The following list contains French words which may come in handy. Get hold of Lonely Planet's *French phrasebook* for a comprehensive list of French words and phrases, as well as useful tips on grammar, pronunciation and much more.

Basics

Yes.	*Oui.*
No.	*Non.*
Maybe.	*Peut-être.*
Please.	*S'il vous plaît.*
Thankyou (very much).	*Merci (beaucoup).*
You're welcome.	*Je vous en prie.*
Excuse me.	*Excusez-moi.*
I'm sorry/Forgive me.	*Pardon.*
with	*avec*
without	*sans*
How?	*Comment?*
Why?	*Pourquoi?*
Where?	*Où?*
When?	*Quand?*
Who?	*Qui?*
What?	*Quoi?*
Which?	*Quel* (m)/*Quelle* (f)*?*

Greetings & Civilities

Hello/Good morning.	*Bonjour.*
Good evening.	*Bonsoir.*
Goodbye.	*Au revoir.*
How are you? (formal)	*Comment allez-vous?*
How are you? (informal)	*Comment ça va?/Ça va?*
I'm fine, thanks.	*Bien, merci.*
Madam/Mrs	*Madame*
Ms/Miss	*Mademoiselle*
Sir/Mr	*Monsieur*

Small Talk

What's your name?	*Comment vous appelez-vous?*
My name is ...	*Je m'appele ...*
Where/What country are you from?	*De quel pays êtes-vous?*
I'm from ...	*Je viens de ...*

Language Difficulties

Do you speak English?	*Parlez-vous anglais?*

I understand.	*Je comprends.*
I don't understand.	*Je ne comprends pas.*
Could you please write it down?	*Est-ce que vous pouvez l'écrire?*

Getting Around

I want to go to …	*Je voudrais aller à …*
What time does the … leave/arrive?	*À quelle heure part/arrive …?*
aeroplane	*l'avion*
bus	*le bus*
next	*prochain*
first	*premier*
last	*dernier*
ticket	*billet*
timetable	*horaire*
How long does the trip take?	*Combien de temps durera le trajet?*
I'd like to hire a …	*Je voudrais louer …*
bicycle	*un vélo*
car	*une voiture*
motorcycle	*une moto*

Directions

Where is …?	*Où est …?*
How do I get to …?	*Comment dois-je faire pour arriver à …?*
Is it near/far?	*Est-ce prés/loin?*
Go straight ahead.	*Continuez tout droit.*
Turn left/right.	*Tournez à gauche/droite.*
at the next corner	*au prochain carrefour*
behind	*derrière*
in front of	*devant*
towards	*vers*
left	*à gauche*
right	*à droite*
on	*sur*
under	*sous*
between	*entre*
north/south	*nord/sud*
east/west	*est/ouest*

Around Town

I'm looking for …	*Je cherche …*
a bank	*une banque*
an exchange office	*un bureau de change*
the … embassy	*l'ambassade de …*
my hotel	*mon hôtel*
the police	*la police*
the post office	*la poste*
a public telephone	*une cabine téléphonique*
the tourist information office	*l'office de tourisme*
the beach	*la plage*
a church	*une église*
the hospital	*l'hôpital*
a library	*une bibliothèque*
the museum	*le musée*
the park	*le parc*
a pub/bar	*un bar*
a travel agency	*une agence de voyages*
I'd like to make a telephone call.	*Je voudrais téléphoner.*
I'd like to change some money/travellers cheques.	*Je voudrais changer de l'argent /des chèques de voyage.*

Accommodation

I'm looking for …	*Je cherche …*
the youth hostel	*l'auberge de jeunesse*
the camping ground	*le camping*
a hotel	*un hôtel*
I'm going to stay …	*Je resterai …*
one night	*un jour*
two nights	*deux jours*
a week	*une semaine*
How much is it per day/ per week/ per month?	*Quel est le prix pour par jour/ par semaine / par mois?*

I would like ... *Je voudrais ...*
a single room *une chambre*
(air-conitioned) *simple*
(climatisée)
a double room *une chambre*
double
a bedroom *une chambre*
a double bed *un grand lit*
twin beds *lits jumeaux*
an extra bed *un lit*
supplémentaire
a bathroom *une salle de bain*
a shower *une douche*
a washbasin *un lavabo*
hot water *eau chaude*
a balcony *un balcon*
a window *une fenêtre*
a terrace *une terrace*
a sea view *une vue sur la mer*
full board *pension*
complète
half board *demi-pension*

facilities *facilités*
dining room *salle à manger*
kitchen *cuisine*
television *télévision*
swimming pool *piscine*
towels *serviettes*
(not) included *(non) compris*
on request *sur demande/*
commande
price/tariff *prix/tarif*

Food
breakfast *petit déjeuner*
lunch *déjeuner*
dinner *dîner*
meal *repas*
the daily special *le plat du jour*
the bill *l'addition*

Seafood
crayfish *langouste*
fish *poisson*
lobster *homard*
octopus *poulpe*

prawn, shrimp *crevette*
seafood *fruits de mer*
sea urchins *ourites*
squid *calmar*
trout *truite*
tuna *thon*

Meat
meat (generic) *viande*
bacon *lard*
beef *bœuf*
chicken *poulet*
duck *canard*
goat *chèvre*
ham *jambon*
mutton *mouton*
pork *porc*
rabbit *lapin*
hare *lièvre*
mixed grill *grillades*

Vegetables
avocado *avocat*
beans *haricots*
cabbage *chou*
carrot *carotte*
cassava *manioc*
cauliflower *chou fleur*
chips *pommes frites*
cucumber *concombre*
eggplant *aubergine*
lentils *lentilles*
lettuce *laitue*
onion *oignon*
peas *petits pois*
potato *pomme de terre*
salad *salade*
sweet potato *patate douce*
tomato *tomate*
vegetables *légumes*

Fruit
apple *pomme*
apricot *abricot*
banana *banane*
coconut *noix de coco*
custard apple *corossol*
fruit *fruit*
grapefruit *pamplemousse*

guava	*goyave*
lemon	*citron*
mango	*mangue*
orange	*orange*
passionfruit	*grenadelle*
peach	*pêche*
pear	*poivre*
pineapple	*ananas*
star fruit	*carambol*

Desserts

cake	*gâteau*
chocolate	*chocolat*
cream	*crème*
dessert	*dessert*
ice cream	*glace*
jam	*confiture*
pancake; crêpe	*crêpe*
pastries	*pâtisseries*
sugar	*sucre*

Drinks

beer	*bière*
brandy	*cognac*
coffee	*café*
drinks	*boissons*
fruit juice	*jus de fruit*
hot chocolate	*chocolat chaud*
lemonade	*limonade*
milk	*lait*
mineral water	*l'eau minérale*
tea	*thé*
wine	*vin*

Condiments

chilli	*piment*
curry	*carri*
ginger	*gingembre*
mustard	*moutarde*
pepper	*poivre*
salad dressing	*vinaigrette*
salt	*sel*
sweet and sour	*aigre-doux*
vinegar	*vinaigre*

Miscellaneous

bread	*pain*
butter	*beurre*

cheese	*fromage*
cup	*tasse*
eggs	*oeufs*
fork	*fourchette*
glass	*verre*
jam	*confiture*
knife	*couteau*
napkin	*serviette*
noodles	*nouilles*
pasta	*pâtes*
plate	*assiette*
rice	*riz*
spoon	*cuiller*
thick soup	*potage*
vegetarian	*végétarien*

Shopping

How much is it?	*C'est combien?*
Can I look at it?	*Est-ce que je peux le/la voir?*
Do you accept credit cards?	*Est-ce que je peux payer avec ma carte de crédit?*
It's too big/small.	*C'est trop grand/petit.*
more/less	*plus/moins*
cheap/cheaper	*bon marché/moins cher*
I'm looking for …	*Je cherche …*
a grocery shop	*une épicerie*
a supermarket	*un supermarché*
the market	*le marché*
a pharmacy	*une pharmacie*
a bookshop	*un librairie*
hat	*chapeau*
matches	*alumettes*
soap	*savon*
toothpaste	*dentifrice*
sunblock	*crème haute protection*
condoms	*préservatifs*
toilet paper	*papier hygiénique*
sanitary napkins	*serviettes hygiéniques*
disposable nappies	*couches coulottes*

Time & Dates

What time is it?	*Quelle heure est-il?*
It's ... o'clock.	*Il est ... heures.*
today	*aujourd'hui*
tomorrow	*demain*
yesterday	*hier*
the/this morning	*le/ce matin*
the/this afternoon	*l'/cet après-midi*

Days

Monday	*lundi*
Tuesday	*mardi*
Wednesday	*mercredi*
Thursday	*jeudi*
Friday	*vendredi*
Saturday	*samedi*
Sunday	*dimanche*

Months

January	*janvier*
February	*février*
March	*mars*
April	*avril*
May	*mai*
June	*juin*
July	*juillet*
August	*août*
September	*septembre*
October	*octobre*
November	*novembre*
December	*décembre*

Health

I'm ...	*Je suis ...*
diabetic	*diabétique*
epileptic	*épilectique*
asthmatic	*asthmatique*
anaemic	*anémique*
I'm allergic ...	*Je suis allergique ...*
to antibiotics	*aux antibiotiques*
to penicillin	*à la penicilline*
to bees	*aux abeilles*

Numbers

0	*zéro*
1	*un*
2	*deux*
3	*trois*
4	*quatre*
5	*cinq*
6	*six*
7	*sept*
8	*huit*
9	*neuf*
10	*dix*
11	*onze*
12	*douze*
13	*treize*
14	*quatorze*
15	*quinze*
16	*seize*
17	*dix-sept*
18	*dix-huit*
19	*dix-neuf*
20	*vingt*
21	*vingt-et-un*
22	*vingt-deux*
30	*trente*
40	*quarante*
50	*cinquante*
60	*soixante*
70	*soixante-dix*
80	*quatre-vingts*
90	*quatre-vingt-dix*
100	*cent*
1000	*mille*
one million	*un million*

Emergencies

Call a doctor/ ambulance!	*Appelez un médecin/ une ambulance!*
Call the police!	*Appelez la police!*
Help!	*Au secours!*
I've been robbed.	*On m'a volé.*

Marine Life in the Indian Ocean

The Indian Ocean is a fascinating place for anybody with an interest in marine life. Coral reefs provide a home and shelter for an enormous variety of life. Most evident are, of course, the often fantastically colourful reef fish – but fish are only one of a host of species to be seen. Glass-bottom or semi-submersible boat trips, snorkelling or, best of all, scuba diving, will all help to open the door to the magical world below the surface.

A number of reef species engage in interesting symbiotic relationships, where two unrelated species get together in some activity for their mutual good.

The best recorded and, to the casual onlooker, most visible of these relationships is probably that of the anemone fish and the anemone. The brightly coloured anemone fish are a type of damselfish which have become acclimatised to living among the stinging tentacles of anemones. The bright orange clown anemone with its white vertical stripes edged with black is one of the most instantly recognisable fish on the reef. A typical group of anemone fish will consist of several males and one larger female fish. They spend their entire life around the anemone, emerging briefly to feed then diving back into the protective tentacles at the first sign of danger. Anemone fish are not naturally immune to the anemone's sting – it is thought they gradually acquire immunity by repeatedly brushing themselves against the tentacles. Possibly they coat themselves with a layer of the anemone's mucus and the anemone does not sting the fish, just as its tentacles avoid stinging one another.

The relationship between anemone fish and the anemone is probably somewhat one-sided. The anemone fish may attract other fish within the anemone's grasp but an anemone can live without the anemone fish, the anemone fish are never seen without a protective anemone nearby.

Cleaner fish have another interesting reef relationship. The small cleaner wrasse performs a service on larger fish. They set themselves up at 'cleaner stations' and wait for customers. The cleaners perform a small 'dance' to indicate they're ready for action and then zip around the larger fish nibbling off fungal growth, dead scales, parasites and the like. They will actually swim right into the mouth of larger fish to clean their teeth! Obviously this must be a tempting opportunity for the larger fish to get a quick free meal but cleaner fish are not threatened while they're at work.

Top Right: Starfish are a common and often colourful sight in the Indian Ocean.

Right: The sea anemone and feeder fish enjoy a harmonious relationship.

Sex & Coral

Corals' sex life may be infrequent (it only happens once a year) but when it does it's certainly spectacular. Some coral polyps are all male or all female, while other colonies' polyps are hermaphrodite, that is they are both male and female. In a few types of coral these polyps can produce their own young which are released at various times over the year. In most cases, however, a hermaphrodite polyp's sperm cannot fertilise its own eggs or other eggs from the same colony.

Although the mass spawning which creates new coral only takes place once a year, the build-up to the big night lasts for six months or more. During that time the polyps ripen their eggs which are initially white but then change to pink, red, orange and other bright colours. At the same time the male testes form in the polyps and develop the sperm.

The big night comes in late spring or early summer, beginning a night or two after a full moon and building to a crescendo on the fourth, fifth and sixth nights. At this time the water temperature is right and tidal variation is at a minimum. Within the coral the eggs and sperm are formed into bundles and a half hour before spawning time the bundles are 'set', that is they are held ready at the mouth of the polyp, clearly visible through the thin tissue. Then these tiny bundles are released and float towards the surface.

The remarkable thing is that all over the reef this spawning takes place at the same time. Different colonies release their egg and sperm bundles, single sex polyps eject their sperm or their eggs, everything floats up. The egg and sperm bundles, big enough to be seen with the naked eye, are a spectacular sight. It's been described as looking like a fireworks display or an upside down snowstorm and since the event can be so accurately predicted divers are often able to witness it.

Once at the surface the bundles break up and the sperm swim off to find eggs of the same coral type. Obviously corals of the same type have to spawn at the same time in order for sperm from one colony to reach eggs from another, but the phenomenon is in all the corals spawning at once. It's far from easy for an individual sperm to find the right egg when the water is swarming with them but scientists think that by all spawning at once they reduce the risk of being consumed by the many marine creatures that would prey on them. By spawning soon after the full moon the reduced tidal variation means there is more time for fertilisation to take place before waves and currents sweep them away.

Once fertilisation has taken place the egg cells begin to divide, and within a day have become swimming coral larvae known as *planulae*. These are swept along by the sea but after a few days the planulae sink to the bottom and if the right spot is found, the tiny larvae become coral polyps and a new coral colony is begun. ∎

The cleaner stations are an important part of reef life; some fish will regularly travel considerable distances for a clean and brush up and experimental removal of the cleaner fish from a section of reef has resulted in an increase in diseased and unhealthy fish and a fall in the general fish population. Certain varieties of shrimps also act as fish cleaners but in nature every situation presents an opportunity for some other creature and the reef also has false cleaners. These tiny fish masquerade as cleaners and then quickly take a bite out of the deceived larger fish. They've been known to take a nip at swimmers!

Even coral itself takes part in a symbiotic relationship. Within the cells of coral polyps are tiny single cell plants known as *zoocanthellae*. Like other plants they utilise sunlight to create energy and consume carbon dioxide produced by the coral. Their presence enables coral to grow much faster.

Throughout much of the Indian Ocean, coral is being decimated by a plague of the crown of thorns starfish and the blame has been placed on the decimation of the starfish's primary natural enemy, the lovely – and popular – triton's trumpet shell.

Coral

Coral is highly varied in its types but almost all the polyp skeletons are white – it's the living polyps which give coral its colourful appearance. During the day most polyps retract to the protection of their hard skeleton, so it's only at night that the full beauty of the hard corals can be seen. Hard coral is, however, only half the story. There is an equally varied assortment of soft corals. Like hard corals they are animals which gather in colonies but they do not have the hard lime skeleton of their reef-building relations. For more information, see the Sex & Coral boxed text in this section.

Fish

The Indian Ocean has several thousand species of fish and this remarkable variety includes everything from tiny diamond fish, the smallest backboned animals, to huge whale sharks. Some fish are seen in the day while others shelter in crevices and caverns in the coral and only emerge at night. Some are grazers, others are hunters. Some huddle together in groups for protection while others move around by themselves. There are territorial species, guarding their own patch of reef fiercely, while others are free ranging.

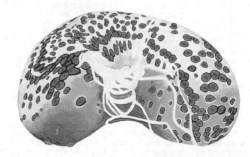

Right: Leopard sea cucumber or bêche-de-mer is a close relative of the starfish.

Sponges

Sponges are among the most primitive of multi-celled creatures, and in fact reefs were probably formed from sponge skeletons long before coral took over the reef construction business. Sponges still play a part in the growth of a reef as they bore into the coral and are a major factor in breaking down the limestone in a reef to eventually form the sand which can grow into a coral cay.

Sponges feed by filtering bacteria out of the water, which they do in amazing volume and with phenomenal efficiency. A sponge can typically handle their own volume of water every five to 20 seconds, and continue doing that 24 hours a day. As the water passes through their body, up to 99% of the bacteria is filtered out.

Despite this efficiency sponges have to look for additional ways to handle the nutrition they need. Some sponges have a form rather like a chimney and passing currents draw water up through the sponge. Most sponges also act as a home to blue-green algae, which pay rent by providing the host sponge with a share of their photosynthetic nutrient production. Other less welcome tenants also find that sponges make a good home – small crabs, shrimps, worms and even brittle stars often take up residence in a sponge's tubes and passages. ■

Starfish

Starfish, *asteroids* or sea stars, are the most visible members of the very large group known as *echinoderms*. There are five distinct types of echinoderms including sea urchins, from which the group's name is derived. The other four are starfish, brittle stars, feather stars and sea cucumbers or bêche-de-mer. It is difficult to believe that creatures as different looking as the starfish and the sea cucumber are closely related but the group all share three distinct characteristics. These are a five-armed body plan, a skeleton of plates and tube feet which are operated by hydraulic pressure. The five-armed plan of the starfish is easy to see and the sea cucumber has the same plan.

Starfish are bottom dwellers, like most echinoderms, and are very visible as they are often brightly coloured, do not move rapidly and in many cases don't hide away during the day. Generally they have five distinct arms, although some may have more – crown-of-thorns starfish usually have 15 or 16 but may have even more. In other starfish, like the rotund pincushion-looking sea star, the arms are not distinct at all but the five-cornered shape is still immediately apparent.

The five arms of a starfish each contain the full quota of organs for respiration, digestion, motion and reproduction. Along the underside of each arm is a groove from which emerge the tiny tube feet. These hydraulically operated feet are the starfish's actual means of locomotion, not the much larger arms. The starfish's mouth, with a surprisingly complex jaw, is at the bottom centre but some starfish, including the crown-of-thorns, can also consume their prey by a method known as 'stomach eversion'. The stomach is pulled out through the mouth and wrapped over the prey which is digested before the stomach is pulled back inside. Most starfish are carnivorous and can even force open the shells of a bivalve like an oyster, then evert their stomach into the opening to digest the bivalve.

Echinoderms in general have strong powers of regeneration and can often regenerate the entire creature from a single broken off arm. A regenerating starfish is known as a comet, since the newly regenerated parts do indeed look like a small star trailing a long, comet-like tail – the original larger arm. ∎

Left: The Yellow-red vasi-form sponge can filter its own volume of water every five to 20 seconds.

Right: The feather star, like most echinoderms, have strong powers of regeneration.

Echinoderms

The widely varied group of creatures known as echinoderms includes sea urchins, starfish or sea stars, brittle stars, feather stars and sea cucumbers. It appears to be a curiously diverse group but they all share basic structural similarities.

Starfish are highly visible since they have few natural enemies and do not hide away during daytime. Sea cucumbers, also known as bêche-de-mer, are also easy to see.

Crustaceans

Hard-shelled crabs, shrimps, prawns and lobsters form another colourful and diverse group of reef creatures. The variety of shrimps is particularly large and many of them engage in the symbiotic relationships which are of such interest on the reef. Several types of shrimps act as cleaners, removing parasites, dead tissue and other waste matter from fish.

Molluscs

Like the echinoderms, molluscs include members that scarcely seem to bear any relationship to each other. Molluscs include a variety of shelled creatures or gastropods, the oysters, scallops and clams known as bivalves and also the cephalopods, a group which includes octopus and squid.

The mollusc family includes the many clams which appear to be embedded in the coral. Their fleshy mantles are seen in a spectacular array of colours.

Nudibranchs, or sea slugs, are snails which have abandoned their shells and put on their party clothes. They're some of the most colourful and graceful reef creatures you can see.

While some of the shells found in the Indian Ocean are incredibly beautiful there are some varieties, such as the cone shell, which can fire out a deadly poisonous barb.

Whales & Dolphins

Fish are not the only creatures to be seen swimming around the waters of the Indian Ocean. The inviting waters are home to dolphins which can sometimes be seen sporting around boats. After decades of being hunted almost to extinction, whales are returning to the region in increasing numbers. The shy and homely dugong is also found in shallow waters around reefs but it's a rare and now protected creature.

Turtles

Several types of turtle are found in the Indian Ocean and although they are no longer present in the huge numbers of the past, there are a number of islands where they still come ashore to lay their eggs. Sea snakes, such as the yellow-bellied sea snake, are also present, but they're rarely seen by divers.

Other Reef Life

Like coral, sponges are an animal and their basic form has changed very little over hundreds of millions of years. The Indian Ocean hosts a variety of worms, many of them colourful and strangely shaped creations totally unlike the typical terrestrial worm. Also found in the region are jellyfish, which are coelenterates and thus belong to the same family as coral and anemones.

Marine Turtles

Throughout the Indian Ocean marine turtles still occur, albeit in dwindling numbers. Marine turtle species found in the ocean include the logger-head turtle (*Caretta caretta*), the green turtle (*Chelonia mydas*), the leatherback turtle (*Dermochelys coriacea*) and the hawksbill turtle (*Eretmochelys imbricata*).

The downfall of many of these turtle species has been their edible flesh (and eggs), highly prized by local fishermen, and their carapace (tortoiseshell), which humans turn into fashionable ornaments. According to CITES (Convention on International Trade & Endangered Species), marine turtles are among the most endangered species, threatened by pollution and human exploitation.

You can play a positive role in ensuring that marine turtles have a future. If you visit a country where sea turtle products are available or where sea turtles nest, please do not eat turtle meat or soup; do not buy any sea turtle product souvenirs, such as hawksbill shell (commonly known as 'tortoiseshell') jewellery, ornaments, or stuffed turtles; take care not to disturb turtles or hatchlings and avoid using white light (for example, car headlights or torches) which can frighten nesting females and attract hatchlings away from the safety of the sea; and never throw plastic litter into the sea or coastal waterways because some turtles eat plastic bags (mistaking them for jellyfish) and suffer fatal intestinal problems as a result.

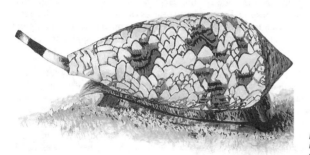

Left: The cone shell's sting is extremely dangerous and can even be fatal.

Regional Facts for the Visitor

PLANNING
When to Go

For all three countries you are advised to make your travel arrangements well in advance, especially if you intend visiting around the busy Christmas/New Year period when hotels can fill up in a flash. Airline reservations may also be difficult to get at this time, so book well ahead to avoid disappointment. Keep in mind that many hotels hike their room rates during the peak seasons.

Weather is another important consideration. For instance, if you're planning a trekking trip to Réunion, the best time is during the dry season from around April to September. Sporting and leisure may also play a part in when you intend to visit. See individual country chapters for details about the best time to visit.

What to Bring

The happiest travellers are those who pack lightly. If you plan to use buses in Mauritius or Réunion, remember there's little space to stow luggage.

Backpacks with detachable daypacks make a versatile combination. Travel packs are backpacks which can be converted into more civilised-looking suitcases. They are cleverly compartmentalised, and have internal frames and special padding.

Clothes Keep clothing light and in cotton wherever possible; this applies especially to socks if you intend to do lots of tramping.

Anything as formal as a suit is unnecessary, but it's good to have a smart shirt and pair of trousers, or a dress or skirt for dinners out; don't forget a pair of good shoes too. Such an outfit can also help at customs and immigration, when entering or leaving a country. If nothing else, it makes you feel more respectable and authoritative (and thus respected) if trouble arises, than you would feel in shorts, T-shirt and thongs (flip-flops).

Make sure you have protection from the sun. Bring a hat, sunglasses and an appropriate-strength sun block. Take it easy to begin with when you go about exposing yourself to the fiery elements. It's so easy to get badly burnt, even when it's overcast, because you don't notice the damage until it's too late. Lip balm is especially good on the beach, where the sun can really pack a punch. To avoid doing a lobster impersonation, the golden rule is to be sun smart.

At the other extreme, a light wrap-up plastic cape or mac will stop a downpour from ruining the odd day or week. It's a must during the wet season. Also, remember to take precautions to keep your camera equipment and personal gear dry – for more tips, see Photography & Video later in this chapter.

At night it cools down a bit on the coast, but not enough to need woolly blankets and thick jumpers. It's a different story on the plateau around Curepipe in Mauritius or high in the cirques of Réunion. The temperature can sometimes drop to freezing and you'll need warm clothing at night. Also, intending trekkers should bring good, strong footwear.

Emergency Kit If you're going to be roughing it away from the resort accommodation you may like to bring a torch (with spare batteries), a small mirror, a Swiss Army-type multi-purpose knife, a first aid kit (for information on a basic medical kit see Health in this chapter), a sewing kit, safety pins and a small padlock (for locking rooms or luggage). That doesn't add up to much extra weight; if you're looking to save weight, bring only a thin towel.

A sheet can come in handy in budget accommodation places, especially if you're particularly fussy about hygiene. A sarong is a good alternative, as it can be used on the beach and also as a sheet or emergency towel. It's not a bad idea to pack insect repellent, especially if you intend staying in budget accommodation, where the mozzies can be tenacious.

VISAS & DOCUMENTS
Passport
You must have a passport with you wherever you go; it's the most basic travel document. Make sure that your passport will be valid for the entire period you intend to remain overseas. If your passport is lost or stolen, immediately contact your country's embassy or consulate (see Facts for the Visitor under individual countries for addresses).

Visas
There are no visa requirements for Mauritius or the Seychelles, but only some countries are exempt from obtaining a visa for Réunion. It will be much easier to get one before you leave home (for further details, see Visas & Documents in the Réunion Facts for the Visitor chapter). If you're planning to visit Madagascar or the Comoros as well, bring along a stock of passport-size photos which are required for visa applications.

For further information about visas, see the Facts for the Visitor chapters in individual country sections.

Photocopies
It's a good idea to carry photocopies of your important travel documents, which obviously should be kept separate from the originals in the event that these are lost or stolen.

Take a photocopy of the first page of your passport (with your personal details and photograph), as well as a copy of the page with your visa (if applicable). A photocopy of your travel insurance policy is also wise. Keep a record of travellers cheques you have exchanged, where they were encashed, the amount and the serial number. Encashment receipts should also be kept separate from your travellers cheques. Photocopy your airline ticket and credit card. Finally, leave copies of your important travel documents with a relative or friend back home – for your peace of mind if nothing else!

Onward Ticket
Apart from a valid passport, Mauritius, Réunion and the Seychelles require visitors to have an onward ticket, which is taken as sufficient evidence that you intend to leave the country. Customs officials may also want to know where you will be staying during your stay. See individual country sections for further details.

Travel Insurance
A travel insurance policy to cover theft, loss and medical problems is a good idea. The policies handled by STA Travel and other student travel organisations are usually good value. Some policies offer lower and higher medical-expense options; the higher ones are chiefly for countries such as the USA which have extremely high medical costs. There is a wide variety of policies available so check the small print.

Some policies specifically exclude 'dangerous activities' which can include scuba diving, motorcycling, even trekking. A locally acquired motorcycle licence is not valid under some policies.

You may prefer a policy which pays doctors or hospitals direct rather than you having to pay on the spot and claim later. If you have to claim later make sure you keep all documentation. Some policies ask you to call back (reverse charges) to a centre in your home country where an immediate assessment of your problem is made.

Check that the policy covers ambulances or an emergency flight home.

EMBASSIES
For information about embassies and consulates, see individual countries, under the Facts for the Visitor chapter.

MONEY
Costs
Preparing a guide to the Indian Ocean islands can feel like writing about Beverly Hills or St-Tropez. If you don't want to live in budget accommodation, and intend to indulge in lots of water activities, come with a decent budget. Remember, if you intend staying at the more upmarket hotels, it's best to take advantage of package rates by booking from overseas.

As in many other facets of life, travelling cheaply can depend on who you know and independent travellers will generally have much greater opportunities to meet and get to know the local people than will packaged tourists whose itineraries are pre-set.

You can survive comfortably on a low budget – around US$25 per day – in Mauritius, but not in the Seychelles or Réunion, primarily due to the lack of truly inexpensive accommodation. It's easier to get around the problem in Réunion, where you can head into the hills and camp or stay in mountain huts or *chambres d'hôte* (family-run B&Bs) – in fact it would be a waste not to since most of Réunion's interest lies in its wilderness. If you stay in budget accommodation, you should be able to keep total costs down to about US$30 per day, even a little less. For more information, see Accommodation in the Réunion Facts for the Visitor chapter.

In the Seychelles it's more difficult because accommodation is regulated by the tourist board; camping is forbidden and prices, availability and the standard of accommodation are fixed. If you keep to the less expensive guesthouses, you should manage to get by on around US$55 per day. Of course, water activities will cost extra.

For more information about costs, see the individual country sections.

Carrying Money

Various types of money belts are available to be worn around the waist, neck or shoulder; and leather or cotton material is more comfortable than synthetics. Such belts are only useful if worn *under* clothing – money belts worn outside clothing are easy prey and attract attention. Some travellers prefer a pouch attached to a string which is worn around the neck, with the pouch against the chest concealed beneath clothing. These days you can also buy innocuous looking leather belts from travel goods suppliers, which have a secret compartment in which you could hide your 'emergency stash'.

Get used to keeping small change and a few banknotes in a shirt pocket so that you can pay bus tickets and small expenses without extracting large amounts of money which could quickly attract attention.

Don't keep all your valuables together: distribute them about your person and baggage to avoid the risk of losing everything in one foul swoop.

Travellers Cheques

Travellers cheques in any of the major currencies may be changed without ado in Mauritius, Réunion and the Seychelles, although French francs are probably the best, especially for Réunion.

A few simple measures should be taken to facilitate the replacement of travellers cheques, should they be stolen or lost. Remember to keep a record of travellers cheques you have exchanged, where they were encashed, the amount and the serial number. Encashment receipts should also be kept separate from your travellers cheques.

See also Stolen Travellers Cheques in the Dangers & Annoyances section later in this chapter.

Credit Cards

Credit cards are widely accepted on Mauritius, Réunion and the Seychelles. Cards are useful in emergencies and for regular purchases. Make sure you know the number to call if you lose your credit card and be quick to cancel it if it's lost or stolen. It's a good idea to make a habit of checking each day that your credit card is with you.

New-style credit card coupons do not have carbon paper inserts and offer more protection against misuse. If you sign an old-style coupon, be sure to ask for the carbon inserts and destroy them after use. Similarly, destroy any coupons which have been filled out incorrectly. These are worthwhile precautions against unwanted duplication of your credit card.

Currency Exchange

See under individual countries Facts for the Visitor chapter for information on currency and exchange rates.

BOOKS
Lonely Planet

Lonely Planet's *Africa on a shoestring*, the

all-time classic budget guide to the continent, contains chapters on Mauritius, Réunion and the Seychelles.

French is the official language of Réunion and is also widely spoken on Mauritius and the Seychelles. For a comprehensive list of French words and phrases, get a copy of Lonely Planet's *French phrasebook*.

General

If you intend to do a lot of reading, bring paperbacks from home and hope you can swap. There is a fairly good range of somewhat expensive paperbacks on sale in the Seychelles and Mauritius. On Réunion, however, you'll find English-language books are rare, but magazines such as *Time* and *Newsweek* are normally available in bookshops *(librairies)*.

See the Facts for the Visitor chapter of each country for a rundown of reading suggestions. Note that most books are published in different editions by different publishers in different countries. As a result, a book might be a hardcover rarity in one country while it's readily available in paperback in another. Fortunately, bookshops and libraries search by title or author, so your local bookshop or library is best placed to advise you on the availability of the recommendations given in the individual country chapters in this book.

ONLINE SERVICES

There are a handful of online services relevant to Mauritius, Réunion and the Seychelles, but services tend to come and go with some frequency. For up-to-date information about online services check the Lonely Planet home page on the Internet (http://www.lonelyplanet.com).

PHOTOGRAPHY & VIDEO
Photography

Points worth remembering include the heat, humidity, very fine sand, tropical sunlight, equatorial shadows and the great opportunities for underwater photography. If you're shooting on beaches, it's important to adjust for glare from water or sand; and keep sand

and salt water well away from your equipment. Don't leave your camera for long in direct sunlight and don't store used film for long in the humid conditions, as it will fade.

The best times to take photographs on sunny days are the first two hours after sunrise and the last two before sunset. This brings out the best colours. At other times, the harsh sunlight and glare washes everything out, though you can use filters to counter the glare.

Equipment

A UV filter permanently fitted to your lens will not only cut down ultraviolet light, but will protect your lens. Other useful accessories include a small flash, a cable release, a lens cleaning kit, and silica-gel packs to protect against humidity. Also, remember to take spare batteries for cameras and flash units. Serious photographers should consider bringing a tripod. Make sure your equipment is insured.

Protecting Your Film & Camera

Film manufacturers warn that, once exposed, film should be developed as quickly as possible. If you're going to be carrying exposed film for a long time, consult a specialist photography handbook about ways of enhancing preservation. Pack everything in plastic bags before you leave home. Try to keep you film cool, and protect it in waterproof and air-proof containers. Silica-gel packs distributed around your gear will assist in absorbing moisture. Always try to keep your camera and film in the shade. Black camera bags tend to absorb heat faster than white or other light-coloured surfaces.

Finally, if you are worried about x-ray security machines at airports ruining your film, despite assurances that they won't, simply remove your camera and film stock from your luggage and take them through separately for inspection.

Underwater Photography

Of course the urge to take underwater photographs is going to affect many Indian Ocean snorkellers and divers. In recent years underwater photography has become much easier. At one time it required complex and expensive equipment, whereas now there are a variety of reasonably priced and easy to use underwater cameras available. It's possible to rent cameras, including underwater video cameras, from some diving operators.

As with basic cameras above surface level the best photos taken with the simplest underwater cameras are likely to be straightforward snapshots. You are not going to get superb photographs of fish and marine life with a small, cheap camera but on the other hand, photos of your fellow snorkellers or divers can often be terrific.

More than with other types of photography the results achieved underwater can improve dramatically with equipment expenditure, particularly on artificial lighting. As you descend natural colours are quickly absorbed, starting with the red end of the spectrum. You can see the same result with a picture or poster that has been left in bright sunlight for too long: soon the colours fade until everything looks blue. It's the same underwater – the deeper you go the more blue things look. Red has virtually disappeared by the time you're 10m down.

The human brain fools us to some extent by automatically compensating for this colour change, but the camera doesn't lie. If you are at any depth your pictures will look cold and blue.

To put the colour back in you need a flash and to work effectively underwater it has to be a much more powerful and complicated flash than above water. Thus newcomers to serious underwater photography soon find that having bought a Nikonos camera they have to lay out as much money again for flash equipment to match. With the right experience and equipment the results can be superb.

Generally the Nikonos cameras work best with 28mm or 35mm lenses. Longer lenses do not work so well underwater. Although objects appear closer underwater with these short focal lengths you have to get close to achieve good results. Patience and practice will enable you to move in close to otherwise wary fish. Underwater photography opens

up whole new fields of interest to divers and the results can often be startling. Flash photography can reveal colours which simply aren't there for the naked eye.

One traveller suggests that a cheaper (but obviously less sophisticated) alternative to an underwater camera, is a special plastic bag which has been designed for normal cameras so they can be taken underwater. The bag is resistant to water and can travel to a depth of approximately 10m. Ask a camera specialist for further details.

Restrictions & Photographing People

Don't take photographs of airports or anything that looks like police or military equipment or property. Photography is sometimes prohibited at temples and mosques – usually there is a sign warning against photography. If you're unsure, don't be afraid to ask somebody.

When taking photographs of people, it's best to ask their permission first. People react differently to a camera – some are happy to be photographed, while others are not, particularly women. If in doubt, it's best to ask. A zoom is a less intrusive means of taking portraits – even if you have obtained permission to take a portrait, pushing a lens in your subject's face can be disconcerting. A reasonable distance between you and your subject may help to reduce your subject's discomfort, and should result in more natural shots.

Video

Properly used, a video camera can give a fascinating record of your holiday. As well as videoing the obvious things – sunsets, spectacular views – remember to record some of the ordinary everyday details of life in the country. Often the most interesting things occur when you're actually intent on filming something else. Remember too that, unlike still photography, video 'flows' – so, for example, you can shoot scenes of countryside rolling past the bus window, to give an overall impression that isn't possible with ordinary photos.

Video cameras these days have amazingly sensitive microphones, and you might be surprised how much sound will be picked up. This can also be a problem if there is a lot of ambient noise – filming by the side of a busy road might seem OK when you do it, but viewing it back home might simply give you a deafening cacophony of traffic noise. One good rule to follow for beginners is to try to film in long takes, and don't move the camera around too much. Otherwise, your video could well make your viewers seasick! If your camera has a stabiliser, you can use it to obtain good footage while travelling on various means of transport, even on bumpy roads. Remember, you're on holiday – don't let the video take over your life, and turn your trip into a Cecil B de Mille production.

Make sure you keep the batteries charged, and have the necessary charger, plugs and transformer for the country you are visiting. In most countries, it is possible to obtain video cartridges in large towns and cities, but make sure you buy the correct format. It is usually worth buying at least a few cartridges duty free to start off your trip.

Finally, remember to follow the same rules regarding people's sensitivities as for still photography – having a video camera shoved in their face is probably even more annoying and offensive for locals than a still camera. Always ask permission first.

HEALTH

Travel health depends on your predeparture preparations, your daily health care while travelling and how you handle any medical problem that does develop. While the potential dangers can seem quite frightening, in reality few travellers to Mauritius, Réunion and the Seychelles experience anything more than perhaps an upset stomach. Travellers should discuss with their physician the most up-to-date methods used to prevent and treat the threats to health which may be encountered.

Predeparture Planning

Immunisations For travellers to Mauritius, Réunion and the Seychelles, few vaccinations are officially required. However, many doctors recommend that travellers get Hep-

atitis A and B jabs just to be on the safe side. A yellow fever vaccination and related documentation is only necessary if you arrive from an infected area.

Plan ahead for getting your vaccinations: some of them require more than one injection, while some vaccinations should not be given together. It is recommended you seek medical advice at least six weeks before travel. Be aware that there is often a greater risk of disease with children and in pregnancy.

Record all vaccinations on an International Health Certificate, available from your doctor or government health department.

You're advised to discuss with your doctor the vaccinations you will need for your trip, as he/she will have the most up-to-date information. Vaccinations you should discuss further with your doctor for this trip include:

- **Hepatitis A** The most common travel-acquired illness after diarrhoea which can put you out of action for weeks. Havrix 1440 is a vaccination which provides long-term immunity (possibly more than 10 years) after an initial injection and a booster at six to 12 months.
  Gamma globulin is not a vaccination but is a ready-made antibody collected from blood donations. It should be given close to departure because, depending on the dose, it only protects for two to six months.
- **Typhoid** This is an important vaccination to have where hygiene is a problem. Available either as an injection or oral capsules.
- **Diphtheria & Tetanus** Diphtheria can be a fatal throat infection and tetanus can be a fatal wound infection. Everyone should have these vaccinations. After an initial course of three injections, boosters are necessary every 10 years.
- **Meninogococcal Meningitis** Healthy people carry this disease; it is transmitted like a cold and you can die from it within a few hours. There are many carriers and vaccination is recommended for travellers to certain parts of Asia, India, Africa and South America. It is also required of all Haj pilgrims entering Saudi Arabia. This vaccination is not officially required for travellers to Mauritius, Réunion and the Seychelles – but it may be worth discussing this further with your doctor, particularly if you intend travelling to certain parts of Africa as well. A single injection will give good protection for three years. The vaccine is not recommended for children under two years because they do not develop satisfactory immunity from it.

Everyday Health
Normal body temperature is up to 37°C or 98.6°F; more than 2°C (4°F) higher indicates a high fever. The normal adult pulse rate is 60 to 100 per minute (children 80 to 100, babies 100 to 140). As a general rule the pulse increases about 20 beats per minute for each 1°C (2°F) rise in fever.

Respiration (breathing) rate is also an indicator of illness. Count the number of breaths per minute: between 12 and 20 is normal for adults and older children (up to 30 for younger children, 40 for babies). People with a high fever or serious respiratory illness breathe more quickly than normal. More than 40 shallow breaths a minute may indicate pneumonia. ■

- **Hepatitis B** This disease is spread by blood or by sexual activity. Travellers who should consider a Hepatitis B vaccination include those visiting countries where there are known to be many carriers, where blood transfusions may not be adequately screened or where sexual contact is a possibility. It involves three injections, the quickest course being over three weeks with a booster at 12 months.
- **Polio** Polio is a serious, easily transmitted disease, still prevalent in many developing countries. Everyone should keep up to date with this vaccination. A booster every 10 years maintains immunity.
- **Yellow Fever** Yellow fever is now the only vaccine which is a legal requirement for entry into many countries, usually only enforced when coming from an infected area.
  Protection lasts 10 years and is recommended where the disease is endemic, eg Africa and South America. For travellers to Mauritius, Réunion and the Seychelles, a yellow fever vaccination and related documentation is only necessary if you arrive from an infected area. You usually have to go to a special yellow fever vaccination centre. Vaccination poses some risk during pregnancy but if you must travel to a high-risk area it is advisable; also people allergic to eggs may not be able to have this vaccine. Discuss with your doctor.
- **Cholera** Despite its poor protection, in some situations it may be wise to have the cholera vaccine, eg for the trans-Africa traveller. Very occasionally travellers are asked by immigration officials to present a certificate, even though all countries and the WHO have dropped a cholera immunisation as a health requirement. This vaccination is not required for travellers to Mauritius, Réunion or the Seychelles, but may be needed if you intend hopping over to Africa. You might be able to get a certificate without having the injection from a doctor or health centre sympathetic to the vagaries of travel in Africa.

Malaria Medication Antimalarial drugs do not prevent you from being infected but kill the malaria parasites during a stage in their development and significantly reduce the risk of becoming very ill or dying.

There is no malaria in Réunion or the Seychelles, but most doctors recommend antimalarial drugs for Mauritius. Expert advice on medication should be sought, as there are many factors to consider, including the area to be visited, the risk of exposure to malaria-carrying mosquitoes, the side effects of medication, your medical history and whether you are a child or adult or pregnant. Travellers to isolated areas in high-risk countries may like to carry a treatment dose of medication for use if symptoms occur.

Health Insurance See Travel Insurance under Visas & Documents, earlier in this chapter.

Travel Health Guides If you are planning to be away or travelling in remote areas for a long period of time, you may like to consider taking a more detailed health guide.

Staying Healthy in Asia, Africa & Latin America, Dirk Schroeder, Moon Publications, 1994. Probably the best all-round guide to carry; it's compact, detailed and well organised.
Travellers Health, Dr Richard Dawood, Oxford University Press, 1995. Comprehensive, easy to read, authoritative and highly recommended, although it's rather large to lug around.
Where There is No Doctor, David Werner, Macmillan, 1994. A very detailed guide intended for someone, such as a Peace Corps worker, going to work in an underdeveloped country.
Travel with Children, Maureen Wheeler, Lonely Planet Publications, 1995. Includes advice on travel health for younger children.

There are also a number of excellent travel health sites on the Internet. From the Lonely

Medical Kit Check List
Consider taking a basic medical kit including:

☐ **Aspirin** or **paracetamol** (acetaminophen in the USA) – for pain or fever.
☐ **Antihistamine** (such as Benadryl) – useful as a decongestant for colds and allergies, to ease the itch from insect bites or stings, and to help prevent motion sickness. Antihistamines may cause sedation and interact with alcohol so care should be taken when using them; take one you know and have used before, if possible.
☐ **Antibiotics** – useful if you're travelling well off the beaten track, but they must be prescribed; carry the prescription with you.
☐ **Loperamide** (eg Imodium) or Lomotil for diarrhoea; prochlorperazine (eg Stemetil) or metaclopramide (eg Maxalon) for nausea and vomiting.
☐ **Rehydration mixture** – for treatment of severe diarrhoea; particularly important if travelling with children.
☐ **Antiseptic** such as povidone-iodine (eg Betadine) – for cuts and grazes.
☐ **Multivitamins** – for long trips when dietary vitamin intake may be inadequate.
☐ **Calamine lotion** or **aluminium sulphate spray** (eg Stingose) – to ease irritation from bites or stings.
☐ **Bandages** and **Band-aids**.
☐ **Scissors, tweezers** and a **thermometer** (note that mercury thermometers are prohibited by airlines).
☐ **Cold and flu tablets** and **throat lozenges**.
☐ **Pseudoephedrine hydrochloride** (Sudafed) may be useful if flying with a cold to avoid ear damage.
☐ **Insect repellent, sunscreen, chap stick** and **water purification tablets**.
☐ A couple of **syringes**, in case you need injections in a country with medical hygiene problems. Ask your doctor for a note explaining why they have been prescribed. ■

Planet home page there are links (http://www.lonelyplanet.com/weblinks/wlprep.htm) to the World Health Organisation and the US Center for Diseases Control & Prevention.

Other Preparations Make sure you're healthy before you start travelling. If you are going on a long trip make sure your teeth are OK. If you wear glasses take a spare pair and your prescription.

If you require a particular medication take an adequate supply, as it may not be available locally. Take part of the packaging showing the generic name, rather than the brand, which will make getting replacements easier. It's a good idea to have a legible prescription or letter from your doctor to show that you legally use the medication, to avoid any problems.

Basic Rules
Food There is an old colonial adage which says: 'If you can cook it, boil it or peel it you can eat it ... otherwise forget it'. Vegetables and fruit should be washed with purified water or peeled where possible. Beware of ice cream which is sold in the street or anywhere it might have been melted and refrozen; if there's any doubt (eg a power cut in the last day or two) steer well clear. Shellfish such as mussels, oysters and clams should be avoided as well as undercooked meat, particularly in the form of mince. Steaming does not make shellfish safe for eating.

If a place looks clean and well run and the vendor also looks clean and healthy, then the food is probably safe. In general, places that are packed with travellers or locals will be fine, while empty restaurants are questionable. The food in busy restaurants is cooked and eaten quite quickly with little standing around and is probably not reheated.

Water The number-one rule is *be careful of the water* and especially ice. If you don't know for certain that the water is safe assume the worst. Reputable brands of bottled water or soft drinks are generally fine, although in some places bottles may be refilled with tap water. Only use water from containers with a serrated seal – not tops or corks. As a general rule, tap water in Mauritius, Réunion and the Seychelles is safe to drink, but care should be taken immediately following a cyclone or bad cyclonic storm. Take care with fruit juice, particularly if water may have been added. Milk should be treated with suspicion as it is often unpasteurised, though boiled milk is fine if it is kept hygienically.

Nutrition

If your food is poor or limited in availability, if you're travelling hard and fast and therefore missing meals, or if you simply lose your appetite, you can soon start to lose weight and place your health at risk.

Make sure your diet is well balanced. Cooked eggs, tofu, beans, lentils and nuts are all safe ways to get protein. Fruit you can peel (bananas, oranges or mandarins for example) is usually safe (melons can harbour bacteria in their flesh and are best avoided) and a good source of vitamins. Try to eat plenty of grains (including rice) and bread. Remember that although food is generally safer if it is cooked well, overcooked food loses much of its nutritional value. If your diet isn't well balanced or if your food intake is insufficient, it's a good idea to take vitamin and iron pills.

In hot climates make sure you drink enough – don't rely on feeling thirsty to indicate when you should drink. Not needing to urinate or small amounts of very dark yellow urine are all danger signs. Always carry a water bottle with you on long trips. Excessive sweating can lead to loss of salt and therefore muscle cramping. Salt tablets are not a good idea as a preventative, but in places where salt is not used much adding salt to food can help. ■

Tea or coffee should also be OK, since the water should have been boiled.

Water Purification The simplest way of purifying water is to boil it thoroughly. Vigorously boiling should be satisfactory; however, at high altitude water boils at a lower temperature, so germs are less likely to be killed. Boil it for longer in these environments.

Consider purchasing a water filter for a long trip. There are two main kinds of filter. Total filters take out all parasites, bacteria and viruses, and make water safe to drink. They are often expensive, but they can be more cost effective than buying bottled water. Simple filters (which can even be a nylon mesh bag) take out dirt and larger foreign bodies from the water so that chemical solutions work much more effectively; if water is dirty, chemical solutions may not work at all. It's very important when buying a filter to read the specifications, so that you know exactly what it removes from the water and what it doesn't. Simple filtering will not remove all dangerous organisms, so if you cannot boil water it should be treated chemically. Chlorine tablets (Puritabs, Steritabs or other brand names) will kill many pathogens, but not some parasites like giardia and amoebic cysts. Iodine is more effective in purifying water and is available in tablet form (such as Potable Aqua). Follow the directions carefully and remember that too much iodine can be harmful.

Medical Problems & Treatment

Self-diagnosis and treatment can be risky, so you should always seek medical help. Although we do give drug dosages in this section, they are for emergency use only. Correct diagnosis is vital.

An embassy, consulate or five star hotel can usually recommend a good place to go for advice. In some places standards of medical attention are so low that for some ailments the best advice is to get on a plane and go somewhere else. Antibiotics should ideally be administered only under medical supervision. Take only the recommended dose at the prescribed intervals and use the whole course, even if the illness seems to be cured earlier. Stop immediately if there are any serious reactions and don't use the antibiotic at all if you are unsure that you have the correct one. Some people are allergic to commonly prescribed antibiotics such as penicillin or sulpha drugs; carry this information when travelling, eg on a bracelet.

Environmental Hazards

Altitude Sickness Lack of oxygen at high altitudes (over 2500m) affects most people to some extent. The affect may be mild or severe and occurs because less oxygen reaches the muscles and the brain at high altitude, requiring the heart and lungs to compensate by working harder. Symptoms of Acute Mountain Sickness (AMS) usually develop during the first 24 hours at altitude but may be delayed up to three weeks. Mild

OLIVIER CIRENDINI

Traditional Créole architecture decorates many rooftops in Réunion and Mauritius.

OLIVIER CIRENDINI

ROBERT STRAUSS

JULIAN SMITH

OLIVIER CIRENDINI

Flora & Fauna
Top: Hikers will come across plenty of chameleons around Ste-Rose, Réunion.
Middle left: Once close to extinction, the Aldabra tortoise is making a comeback in the Seychelles.
Middle right: Tiny lizards are a common sight for hikers in Mauritius.
Bottom: Dragons de feu are a common sight along roads or in front of Créole houses in Réunion.

symptoms include headache, lethargy, dizziness, difficulty sleeping and loss of appetite. AMS may become more severe without warning and can be fatal. Severe symptoms include breathlessness, a dry, irritative cough (which may progress to the production of pink, frothy sputum), severe headache, lack of coordination and balance, confusion, irrational behaviour, vomiting, drowsiness and unconsciousness. There is no hard-and-fast rule as to what is too high: AMS has been fatal at 3000m, although 3500m to 4500m is the usual range.

Treat mild symptoms by resting at the same altitude until recovery, usually a day or two. Paracetamol or aspirin can be taken for headaches. If symptoms persist or become worse, however, *immediate descent is necessary*; even 500m can help. Drug treatments should never be used to avoid descent or to enable further ascent.

The drugs acetazolamide (Diamox) and dexamethasone are recommended by some doctors for the prevention of AMS, however their use is controversial. They can reduce the symptoms, but they may also mask warning signs; severe and fatal AMS has occurred in people taking these drugs. In general we do not recommend them for travellers.

To prevent Acute Mountain Sickness:

- Ascend slowly – have frequent rest days, spending two to three nights at each rise of 1000m. If you reach a high altitude by trekking, acclimatisation takes place gradually and you are less likely to be affected than if you fly directly to high altitude.
- It is always wise to sleep at a lower altitude than the greatest height reached during the day if possible. Also, once above 3000m, care should be taken not to increase the sleeping altitude by more than 300m per day.
- Drink extra fluids. The mountain air is dry and cold and moisture is lost as you breathe. Evaporation of sweat may occur unnoticed and result in dehydration.
- Eat light, high-carbohydrate meals for more energy.
- Avoid alcohol as it may increase the risk of dehydration.
- Avoid sedatives.

Fungal Infections Fungal infections occur more commonly in hot weather and are usually found on the scalp, between the toes or fingers, in the groin and on the body (ringworm). You get ringworm (which is a fungal infection, not a worm) from infected animals or other people. Moisture encourages these infections.

To prevent fungal infections wear loose, comfortable clothes, avoid artificial fibres, wash frequently and dry carefully. If you do get an infection, wash the infected area at least daily with a disinfectant or medicated soap and water, and rinse and dry well. Apply an antifungal cream or powder like tolnifate (Tinaderm). Try to expose the infected area to air or sunlight as much as possible and wash all towels and underwear in hot water, change them often and let them dry in the sun.

Heat Exhaustion Dehydration and salt deficiency can cause heat exhaustion. Take time to acclimatise to high temperatures, drink sufficient liquids and do not do anything too physically demanding.

Salt deficiency is characterised by fatigue, lethargy, headaches, giddiness and muscle cramps; salt tablets may help, but adding extra salt to your food is better.

Anhydrotic heat exhaustion, caused by an inability to sweat, is quite rare. It is likely to strike people who have been in a hot climate for some time, rather than newcomers.

Heat Stroke This serious, occasionally fatal, condition can occur if the body's heat-regulating mechanism breaks down and the body temperature rises to dangerous levels. Long, continuous periods of exposure to high temperatures and insufficient fluids can leave you vulnerable to heat stroke.

The symptoms are feeling unwell, not sweating very much (or at all) and a high body temperature (39°C to 41°C or 102°F to 106°F). Where sweating has ceased the skin becomes flushed and red. Severe, throbbing headaches and lack of coordination will also occur, and the sufferer may be confused or aggressive. Eventually the victim will become delirious or convulse. Hospitalisation is essential, but in the interim get victims out of the sun, remove their clothing, cover them with a wet sheet or towel and then fan continually. Give fluids if they are conscious.

Hypothermia Too much cold can be just as dangerous as too much heat. If you are trekking at high altitudes (such as in Réunion) or simply taking a long bus trip over mountains, particularly at night, be prepared.

Hypothermia occurs when the body loses heat faster than it can produce it and the core temperature of the body falls. It is surprisingly easy to progress from very cold to dangerously cold due to a combination of wind, wet clothing, fatigue and hunger, even if the air temperature is above freezing. It is best to dress in layers; silk, wool and some of the new artificial fibres are all good insulating materials. A hat is important, as a lot of heat is lost through the head. A strong, waterproof outer layer (and a 'space' blanket for emergencies) are essential. Carry basic supplies, including food containing simple sugars to generate heat quickly and fluid to drink.

Symptoms of hypothermia are exhaustion, numb skin (particularly toes and fingers), shivering, slurred speech, irrational or violent behaviour, lethargy, stumbling, dizzy spells, muscle cramps and violent bursts of energy. Irrationality may take the form of sufferers claiming they are warm and trying to take off their clothes.

To treat mild hypothermia, first get the person out of the wind and/or rain, remove their clothing if it's wet and replace it with dry, warm clothing. Give them hot liquids – not alcohol – and some high-kilojoule, easily digestible food. Do not rub victims, instead allow them to slowly warm themselves. This should be enough to treat the early stages of hypothermia. The early recognition and treatment of mild hypothermia is the only way to prevent severe hypothermia, which is a critical condition.

Jet Lag Jet lag is experienced when a person travels by air across more than three time zones (each time zone usually represents a one hour time difference). It occurs because many of the functions of the human body (such as temperature, pulse rate and emptying of the bladder and bowels) are regulated by internal 24-hour cycles. When we travel long distances rapidly, our bodies take time to adjust to the 'new time' of our destination, and we may experience fatigue, disorientation, insomnia, anxiety, impaired concentration and loss of appetite. These effects will usually be gone within three days of arrival, but to minimise the impact of jet lag:

- Rest for a couple of days prior to departure.
- Try to select flight schedules that minimise sleep deprivation; arriving late in the day means you can go to sleep soon after you arrive. For very long flights, try to organise a stopover.
- Avoid excessive eating (which bloats the stomach) and alcohol (which causes dehydration) during the flight. Instead, drink plenty of noncarbonated, nonalcoholic drinks such as fruit juice or water.
- Avoid smoking.
- Make yourself comfortable by wearing loose-fitting clothes and perhaps bringing an eye mask and ear plugs to help you sleep.
- Try to sleep at the appropriate time for the time zone you are travelling to.

Motion Sickness Eating lightly before and during a trip will reduce the chances of motion sickness. If you are prone to motion sickness try to find a place that minimises movement – near the wing on aircraft, close to midships on boats, near the centre on buses. Fresh air usually helps; reading and cigarette smoke don't. Commercial motion-sickness preparations, which can cause drowsiness, have to be taken before the trip commences. Ginger (available in capsule form) and peppermint (including mint-flavoured sweets) are natural preventatives.

Prickly Heat Prickly heat is an itchy rash caused by excessive perspiration trapped under the skin. It usually strikes people who have just arrived in a hot climate. Keeping cool, bathing often, drying the skin and using a mild talcum or prickly heat powder or resorting to air-conditioning may help.

Sunburn Mauritius, Réunion and the Seychelles lie within the humid tropics, where the sun's rays are more direct and concentrated than in temperate zones. Even in the cooler highland areas, everyone will be susceptible to hazardous UV rays.

In the tropics you can get sunburnt surprisingly quickly, even through cloud. Use a sunscreen, hat, and barrier cream for your nose and lips. Calamine lotion or Stingose are good for mild sunburn. Protect your eyes with good-quality sunglasses, particularly if you will be near water or sand.

Infectious Diseases
Diarrhoea Simple things like a change of water, food or climate can all cause a mild bout of diarrhoea, but a few rushed toilet trips with no other symptoms is not indicative of a major problem.

Dehydration is the main danger with any diarrhoea, particularly in children or the elderly as dehydration can occur quite quickly. Under all circumstances *fluid replacement* is the most important thing to remember. Weak black tea with a little sugar, soda water, or soft drinks allowed to go flat and diluted 50% with clean water are all good. With severe diarrhoea a rehydrating solution is preferable to replace minerals and salts lost. Commercially available oral rehydration salts (ORS) are very useful; add them to boiled or bottled water. In an emergency you can make up a solution of six teaspoons of sugar and a half teaspoon of salt to a litre of boiled or bottled water. You need to drink at least the same volume of fluid that you are losing in bowel movements and vomiting. Urine is the best guide to the adequacy of replacement – if you have small amounts of concentrated urine, you need to drink more. Keep drinking small amounts often. Stick to a bland diet as you recover.

Lomotil or Imodium can be used to bring relief from the symptoms, although they do not actually cure the problem. Only use these drugs if you do not have access to toilets, eg if you *must* travel. For children under 12 years Lomotil and Imodium are not recommended. Do not use these drugs if the person has a high fever or is severely dehydrated.

In certain situations antibiotics may be required: diarrhoea with blood or mucus (dysentery), any fever, watery diarrhoea with fever and lethargy, persistent diarrhoea not improving after 48 hours and severe diarrhoea. In these situations gut-paralysing drugs like Imodium or Lomotil should be avoided.

A stool test is necessary to diagnose which kind of dysentery you have, so you should seek medical help urgently. Where this is not possible the recommended drugs for dysentery are norfloxacin 400mg twice daily for three days or ciprofloxacin 500mg twice daily for five days. These are not recommended for children or pregnant women. The drug of choice for children would be co-trimoxazole (Bactrim, Septrin, Resprim) with dosage dependent on weight. A five day course is given. Ampicillin or amoxycillin may be given in pregnancy, but medical care is necessary.

Amoebic dysentery is more gradual in the onset of symptoms, with cramping abdominal pain and vomiting less likely; fever may not be present. It will persist until treated and can recur and cause other health problems.

Giardiasis is another type of diarrhoea. The parasite causing this intestinal disorder is present in contaminated water. The symptoms are stomach cramps, nausea, a bloated stomach, watery, foul-smelling diarrhoea and frequent gas. Giardiasis can appear several weeks after you have been exposed to the parasite. The symptoms may disappear for a few days and then return; this can go on for several weeks. Tinidazole, known as Fasigyn, or metronidazole (Flagyl) are the recommended drugs. Treatment is a 2gm single dose of Fasigyn or 250mg of Flagyl three times daily for five to 10 days.

Hepatitis Hepatitis is a general term for inflammation of the liver. It is a common disease worldwide. The symptoms are fever, chills, headache, fatigue, feelings of weakness and aches and pains, followed by loss of appetite, nausea, vomiting, abdominal pain, dark urine, light-coloured faeces, jaundiced (yellow) skin and the whites of the eyes may turn yellow. **Hepatitis A** is transmitted by contaminated food and drinking water. The disease poses a real threat to the western traveller. You should seek medical advice, but there is not much you can do apart from resting, drinking lots of fluids, eating lightly and avoiding fatty foods. People who have had hepatitis should avoid alcohol for some time after the illness, as the liver needs time to recover.

Hepatitis E is transmitted in the same way, and can be very serious in pregnant women.

There are almost 300 million chronic carriers of **Hepatitis B** in the world. It is spread through contact with infected blood, blood products or body fluids, eg through sexual contact, unsterilised needles and blood transfusions, or contact with blood via small breaks in the skin. Other risk situations include having a shave, tattoo, or having your body pierced with contaminated equipment. The symptoms of type B may be more severe and may lead to long-term problems. **Hepatitis D** is spread in the same way, but the risk is mainly in shared needles.

Hepatitis C can lead to chronic liver disease. The virus is spread by contact with blood usually via contaminated transfusions or shared needles. Avoiding these is the only means of prevention.

HIV & AIDS HIV, the Human Immunodeficiency Virus, develops into AIDS, Acquired Immune Deficiency Syndrome, which is a fatal disease. HIV is a major problem in many countries. Any exposure to blood, blood products or body fluids may put the individual at risk. The disease is often transmitted through sexual contact or dirty needles – vaccinations, acupuncture, tattooing and body piercing can be potentially as dangerous as intravenous drug use. HIV/ AIDS can also be spread through infected blood transfusions; some developing countries cannot afford to screen blood used for transfusions.

If you do need an injection, ask to see the syringe unwrapped in front of you, or take a needle and syringe pack with you.

Fear of HIV infection should never preclude treatment for serious medical conditions.

Intestinal Worms These parasites are most common in rural, tropical areas. The different worms have different ways of infecting people. Some may be ingested on food including undercooked meat and some enter through your skin. Infestations may not show up for some time, and although they are generally not serious, if left untreated some can cause severe health problems later. Consider having a stool test when you return home to check for these and determine the appropriate treatment.

Sexually Transmitted Diseases Gonorrhoea, herpes and syphilis are among these diseases; sores, blisters or rashes around the genitals, discharges or pain when urinating are common symptoms. In some STDs, such as wart virus or chlamydia, symptoms may be less marked or not observed at all, especially in women. Syphilis symptoms eventually disappear completely but the disease continues and can cause severe problems in later years. While abstinence from sexual contact is the only 100% effective prevention, using condoms is also effective. The treatment of gonorrhoea and syphilis is with antibiotics. The different sexually transmitted diseases each require specific antibiotics. There is no cure for herpes or AIDS.

Prostitution in Mauritius is not rife, but there are some young girls who choose to supplement the family income in that manner and may appear a little over-hospitable at the disco. The unofficial red light district for Mauritius is at Pointe aux Sables. Tourists are not encouraged there.

Some pensions, or boarding houses, rent out rooms to couples for a 'little rest', but these are not to be seen as bring-your-own brothels. As families are usually big, unmarried couples have nowhere to go to get better acquainted. Travellers staying in such a place should check the bed linen.

Typhoid Typhoid fever is a dangerous gut infection caused by contaminated water and food. Medical help must be sought.

In its early stages sufferers may feel they have a bad cold or flu on the way, as early symptoms are a headache, body aches and a fever which rises a little each day until it is around 40°C (104°F) or more. The victim's pulse is often slow relative to the degree of fever present – unlike a normal fever where the pulse increases. There may also be vomiting, abdominal pain, diarrhoea or constipation.

In the second week the high fever and slow pulse continue and a few pink spots may appear on the body; trembling, delirium, weakness, weight loss and dehydration may occur. Complications such as pneumonia, perforated bowel or meningitis may occur.

The fever should be treated by keeping the victim cool and giving them fluids as dehydration should also be watched for. Ciprofloxacin 750mg twice a day for 10 days is good for adults.

Chloramphenicol is recommended in many countries. The adult dosage is two 250mg capsules, four times a day. Children aged between eight and 12 years should have half the adult dose; and younger children one-third the adult dose.

Insect-Borne Diseases
Filariasis, leishmaniasis and typhus are all insect-borne diseases, but they do not pose a great risk to travellers to Mauritius, Réunion and the Seychelles.

Malaria Opinions vary as to the prevalence of malaria on Mauritius, but malaria prophylaxis is generally advised. At present, there is no malaria on Réunion and the Seychelles. This serious and potentially fatal disease is spread by mosquito bites. If you are travelling in endemic areas it is extremely important to avoid mosquito bites and to take tablets to prevent this disease. Symptoms range from fever, chills and sweating, headache, diarrhoea and abdominal pains to a vague feeling of ill-health. Seek medical help immediately if malaria is suspected. Without treatment malaria can rapidly become more serious and can be fatal.

If medical care is not available, malaria tablets can be used for treatment. You need to use a malaria tablet which is different to the one you were taking when you contracted malaria. The treatment dosages are mefloquine (two 250mg tablets and a further two six hours later), fansidar (single dose of three tablets). If you were previously taking mefloquine then other alternatives are halofantrine (three doses of two 250mg tablets every six hours) or quinine sulphate (600mg every six hours). There is a greater risk of side effects with these dosages than in normal use.

Travellers are advised to try and avoid mosquito bites at all times. The main messages are:

- wear light-coloured clothing
- wear long pants and long-sleeved shirts
- use mosquito repellents containing the compound DEET on exposed areas (prolonged overuse of DEET may be harmful, especially to children, but its use is considered preferable to being bitten by disease-transmitting mosquitoes)
- avoid highly scented perfumes or aftershave
- use a mosquito net impregnated with mosquito repellent (permethrin) – it may be worth taking your own
- impregnating clothes with permethrin effectively deters mosquitoes and other insects

Cuts, Bites & Stings
Rabies is passed through animal bites. See Less Common Diseases for details.

Bedbugs & Lice Bedbugs live in various places, but particularly in dirty mattresses and bedding, evidenced by spots of blood on bedclothes or on the wall. Bedbugs leave itchy bites in neat rows. Calamine lotion or Stingose spray may help.

All lice cause itching and discomfort. They make themselves at home in your hair (head lice), your clothing (body lice) or in your pubic hair (crabs). You catch lice through direct contact with infected people or by sharing combs, clothing and the like. Powder or shampoo treatment will kill the lice and infected clothing should be washed in very hot, soapy water and left in the sun to dry.

Insect Bites & Stings Bee and wasp stings are usually painful rather than dangerous. However in people who are allergic to them severe breathing difficulties may occur and require urgent medical care. Calamine lotion or Stingose spray will give relief and ice packs will reduce the pain and swelling.

Certain cone shells can sting dangerously or even fatally. There are various fish and other sea creatures which can sting or bite dangerously or which are dangerous to eat. Seeking local advice is the best suggestion.

Cuts & Scratches Wash well and treat any cut with an antiseptic such as povidone-iodine. Where possible avoid bandages and Band-aids, which can keep wounds wet. Coral cuts are notoriously slow to heal and if they are not adequately cleaned small pieces of coral can become embedded in the wound. Avoid coral cuts by wearing shoes when walking on reefs, and clean any cut thoroughly with an antiseptic. Severe pain, throbbing, redness, fever or generally feeling unwell suggest infection and the prompt need for antibiotics, as coral cuts may result in serious infections.

Jellyfish Local advice is the best way of avoiding contact with these sea creatures which have stinging tentacles. Dousing in vinegar will de-activate any stingers which have not 'fired'. Calamine lotion, antihistamines and analgesics may reduce the reaction and relieve the pain.

Leeches & Ticks Leeches may be present in damp rainforest conditions; they attach themselves to your skin to suck your blood. Trekkers often get them on their legs or in their boots. Salt or a lighted cigarette end will make them fall off. Do not pull them off, as the bite is then more likely to become infected. Clean and apply pressure if the point of attachment is bleeding. An insect repellent may keep them away.

You should always check all over your body if you have been walking through a potentially tick-infested area as ticks can cause skin infections and other more serious diseases. If a tick is found attached, press down around the tick's head with tweezers, grab the head and gently pull upwards. Avoid

pulling the rear of the body as this may squeeze the tick's gut contents through the attached mouth parts into the skin, increasing the risk of infection and disease. Smearing chemicals on the tick will not make it let go and is not recommended.

Snakes To minimise your chances of being bitten always wear boots, socks and long trousers when walking through undergrowth where snakes may be present. Don't put your hands into holes and crevices, and be careful when collecting firewood.

Snake bites do not cause instantaneous death and antivenenes are usually available. Immediately wrap the bitten limb tightly, as you would for a sprained ankle, and then attach a splint to immobilise it. Keep the victim still and seek medical help, if possible with the dead snake for identification. Don't attempt to catch the snake if there is a possibility of being bitten again. Tourniquets and sucking out the poison are now comprehensively discredited.

Women's Health
Gynaecological Problems Sexually transmitted diseases are a major cause of vaginal problems. Symptoms include a smelly discharge, painful intercourse and sometimes a burning sensation when urinating. Male sexual partners must also be treated. Medical attention should be sought and remember, in addition to these diseases, HIV or Hepatitis B may also be acquired during exposure. Besides abstinence, the best thing is to practise safe sex using condoms.

Antibiotic use, synthetic underwear, sweating and contraceptive pills can lead to fungal vaginal infections when travelling in hot climates. Maintaining good personal hygiene, and wearing loose-fitting clothes and cotton underwear will help to prevent these infections.

Fungal infections, characterised by a rash, itch and discharge, can be treated with a vinegar or lemon-juice douche, or with yoghurt. Nystatin, miconazole or clotrimazole pessaries or vaginal cream are the usual treatment.

Pregnancy It is not advisable to travel to some places while pregnant as some vaccinations normally used to prevent serious diseases are not advisable in pregnancy, eg yellow fever. In addition, some diseases are much more serious for the mother (and may increase the risk of a stillborn child) in pregnancy, eg malaria.

Most miscarriages occur during the first three months of pregnancy. Miscarriage is not uncommon, and can occasionally lead to severe bleeding. The last three months should also be spent within reasonable distance of good medical care. A baby born as early as 24 weeks stands a chance of survival, but only in a good modern hospital. Pregnant women should avoid all unnecessary medication, vaccinations and malarial prophylactics should still be taken where needed. Additional care should be taken to prevent illness and particular attention should be paid to diet and nutrition. Alcohol and nicotine, for example, should be avoided.

Less Common Diseases

The following diseases pose a small risk to travellers, and so are only mentioned in passing. Seek medical advice if you think you may have any of these diseases.

Cholera This is the worst of the watery diarrhoeas and medical help should be sought. Outbreaks of cholera are generally widely reported, so you can avoid such problem areas. *Fluid replacement is the most vital treatment* – the risk of dehydration is severe as you may lose up to 20L a day. If there is a delay in getting to hospital then begin taking tetracycline. The adult dose is 250mg four times daily. It is not recommended for children under nine years nor for pregnant women. Tetracycline may help shorten the illness, but adequate fluids are required to save lives.

Rabies Rabies is a fatal viral infection found in many countries. Many animals can be infected (such as dogs, cats, bats and monkeys) and it is their saliva which is infectious.

Any bite, scratch or even lick from a warm-blooded, furry animal should be cleaned immediately and thoroughly. Scrub with soap and running water, and then apply alcohol or iodine solution. Medical help should be sought promptly to receive a course of injections to prevent the onset of symptoms and death.

Tetanus Tetanus occurs when a wound becomes infected by a germ which lives in soil and in the faeces of horses and other animals. It enters the body via breaks in the skin. All wounds should be cleaned promptly and adequately and an antiseptic cream or solution applied. Use antibiotics if the wound becomes hot, throbs or pus is seen. The first symptom may be discomfort in swallowing, or stiffening of the jaw and neck; this is followed by painful convulsions of the jaw and whole body. The disease can be fatal.

Tuberculosis (TB) TB is a bacterial infection usually transmitted from person to person by coughing but may be transmitted through consumption of unpasteurised milk. Milk that has been boiled is safe to drink, and the souring of milk to make yoghurt or cheese also kills the bacilli. Travellers are usually not at great risk as close household contact with the infected person is usually required before the disease is passed on.

Typhus Typhus is spread by ticks, mites or lice. It begins with fever, chills, headache and muscle pains followed a few days later by a body rash. There is often a large painful sore at the site of the bite and nearby lymph nodes are swollen and painful. Typhus can be treated under medical supervision. Seek local advice on areas where ticks pose a danger and always check your skin (including hair) carefully for ticks after walking in a danger area such as a tropical forest. A strong insect repellent can help, and serious walkers in tick areas should consider having their boots and trousers impregnated with benzyl benzoate and dibutylphthalate.

Yellow Fever This viral disease is endemic in many African countries but is not present in Mauritius, Réunion or Seychelles. It is transmitted by mosquitoes. The initial symptoms are fever, headache, abdominal pain and vomiting. Seek medical care urgently.

WOMEN TRAVELLERS

As Mauritius, Réunion and the Seychelles predominantly attract couples and families, women travelling alone may get some incredulous stares – particularly in hotels and restaurants. Thanks to the popularity of western videos, women of European origin may be expected to behave like the glamorous and morally questionable characters portrayed on the small screen. Of the three countries covered in this book, Mauritius is probably the most difficult for solo women travellers, but it isn't nearly as bad as India or Latin America.

In the eyes of some male Mauritians (particularly youths) who've had little contact with other facets of western culture, female travellers who don't seem to be the property of any man may be regarded as a candidate for romantic attention.

Having said that, things are unlikely to go beyond long stares (dark glasses can help here), passing comments or catcalls. Usually, an inquisitive *bonjour* is all you'll probably get, leaving you to make the decision whether you wish to engage in conversation. Keep in mind that getting involved in inane conversations with men may be considered as a turn-on. If you get the uncomfortable feeling he's encroaching on your space, the chances are that he is. A polite, yet firm request to keep away is usually enough.

Conservative dress is a good idea. Ways of blending into the background include avoiding sleeveless shirts, shorts, skirts that are too short and, of course, the bra-less look. It's best to restrict wearing your swimsuit to hotels or on the beach.

Women are advised never to hitch or walk alone after dark.

GAY & LESBIAN TRAVELLERS

On all three islands, homosexuality is generally low profile. Réunion is the most liberal when it comes to homosexuality, and follows French law whereby the age of consent for both gays and heterosexuals is 15 years. The gay male scene is more developed than the lesbian one. Although France may be one of Europe's most liberal countries when it comes to homosexuality, Réunion is not. Overt displays of affection between members of the same sex may still be viewed with disdain, particularly away from the capital city.

Mauritius is still conservative when it comes to homosexuality. Open affection is likely to attract stares and even jeers. Although the gay scene is low-key, homosexuality seems to be slowly becoming more open among local Mauritians. In the Seychelles, homosexuality is illegal.

DISABLED TRAVELLERS

All three countries are not particularly well equipped for disabled people: kerb ramps are few and far between, and older buildings and bottom-end hotels often lack lifts and wheelchair access. There are only a handful of public toilets that accommodate wheelchairs. However, most top-end hotels are designed to provide facilities for disabled people, such as wheelchair access, lifts and special bathrooms. It's a good idea to verify the facilities provided when making your hotel reservation.

SENIOR TRAVELLERS

Mauritius, Réunion and the Seychelles are all popular holiday spots with senior travellers. Most tend to stay in the more upmarket hotels which cater well for those who don't want to 'rough it'. These hotels have comfortable rooms including air-conditioning (a lifesaver for those unaccustomed to the heat), an array of facilities, and can arrange many travel arrangements, saving you the hassle.

Mauritius and the Seychelles have traditionally been favourite destinations with senior travellers and Réunion is becoming increasingly popular. While Mauritius and the Seychelles focus on water activities, Réunion has an emphasis on trekking. Tourism authorities are promoting Réunion as a trekkers' paradise for the novice and experienced hiker alike. Apart from a number of challenging treks, there are also plenty of short walks, suitable for older travellers. Discuss the options with someone at Maison de la Montagne in St-Denis or Cilaos (see Information in the Trekking in Réunion chapter for more details).

It may be helpful to discuss your proposed trip with your local doctor before setting off, especially if you plan on trekking, diving or taking on any other energetic activities.

TRAVEL WITH CHILDREN

Children can enhance your encounters with local people, as they often possess little of the self-consciousness and sense of the cultural differences which can inhibit interaction between adults. Admittedly, travelling with children can be challenging at times, and ideally the burden needs to be shared between two adults.

The upmarket hotels usually have babysitting services and can organise supervised water and land activities for the little ones. It's worthwhile asking about the extent of facilities offered when making your hotel reservation.

Remember to bring along plenty of sun protection for your kids and keep in mind that children are likely to be more affected by unaccustomed heat, and need time to acclimatise and extra care to avoid sunburn. Be prepared also for minor effects often brought on by a change of diet or water, disrupted sleep patterns, or even just being in a strange place. Avoid giving your children street food, as it can sometimes bring on tummy upsets.

Nappies, lotions and baby foods are available, but the choice is somewhat limited, especially in Mauritius and the Seychelles. If there is a particular brand you swear by, it's a good idea to bring it along with you.

On the financial side, quite a few hotels, tour operators etc offer discounts for children – usually around 50% of the adult rate for children under 12 years of age; those below two years of age are often not charged at all.

For practical advice and information on how to make travel as stress-free as possible, for both children and parents alike, get hold of Lonely Planet's *Travel with Children* by Maureen Wheeler.

DANGERS & ANNOYANCES
Theft
Don't ever leave the most important valuables (passport, airline tickets, money) in your room; they should be with you at all times or in a hotel safe deposit box. Keep photocopies of important documents – see Photocopies in the Visas & Documents section, earlier.

When travelling on public transport, keep your gear near you. Be extra careful in crowded places (such as the market in Port Louis), and avoid walking around with valuables casually slung over your shoulder.

If you do have something stolen, you should report it to the police. You'll also need a statement proving you have done so if you want to claim on insurance.

Stolen Travellers Cheques If you're unlucky enough to have things stolen, some precautions can ease the pain. All travellers cheques are replaceable, although this does you little immediate good if you have to go home and apply to your bank. What you want is instant replacement. If you don't have the receipt you were given when you bought the cheques, rapid replacement may be more difficult. It's wise to keep an emergency cash-stash in a totally separate place. In that same place you should keep a record of cheque serial numbers, proof of purchase slips and your passport details. The receipt should always be kept separate from the cheques, and a photocopy in yet another location is a good idea. Chances are you'll be able to get a limited amount of funds on the spot, and the rest will be available when the bank has verified your initial purchase of the cheques.

Security Precautions in Hotels & on Beaches Don't leave vital documents, money or valuables in your room. If you consider your hotel to be reliable, place valuables in its safe and get a receipt. Make sure you package your valuables in a small, double-zippered bag which can be padlocked, or use a large envelope with a signed seal which will easily show any tampering. Count money and travellers cheques before and after retrieving them from the safe – this should quickly identify any attempts to extract single bills or cheques which might otherwise go unnoticed.

Don't take any valuables to the beach – and never tempt a passing thief by leaving your belongings unattended. Just take the minimum: swimsuit, towel, hat, T-shirt, sunscreen lotion and enough money for a meal and drinks.

Marine Dangers

Don't touch the coral, shells or fish – some of them sting, cut and occasionally kill. In particular, watch out for sea urchins; the gaudy and easily recognisable lionfish with its poisonous spined fins; and cleverly camouflaged – and exceptionally poisonous – stonefish. Make sure you wear full-shoe fins when diving; and sailing shoes or other suitably tough footwear when windsurfing, snorkelling etc.

Don't swim or let yourself drift too far away from the boat or shore in case you get caught in a strong current. Keep away from the surf breaking on the reef edge or anywhere else for that matter. One big wave and you could be fish fodder. Although shark attacks are few and far between do exercise caution, especially outside the lagoons. There have been some fatal shark attacks, particularly in Réunion (for more information, see the Shark Alert boxed text under Activities in the Réunion Facts for the Visitor chapter). It's probably safest to make a habit of seeking 'shark advice' from the locals, before plunging into the sea.

Coconut Trees

Take care when walking under coconut trees and don't lie beneath them: in recent years there have been some tragic accidents with plummeting coconuts.

LEGAL MATTERS

If you find yourself in a sticky legal predicament, contact your embassy. You should carry your passport with you at all times and keep a photocopy of the first page of your passport (with your personal details and photograph), as well as a copy of the page with your visa (if applicable).

ACTIVITIES

On all three islands you can indulge in a variety of both land and water activities. Naturally water activities are the focus on Mauritius and the Seychelles, while trekking is Réunion's forte. For detailed coverage of the activities available on each island, see Activities in the Facts for the Visitor chapter under individual countries.

Surfing

Some of the surfing spots around Tamarin in Mauritius have been described as 'the perfect set up', with up to 2m waves. Other good surfing locations are near the Baie du Cap; 'Lefts and Rights', which is further south by Ilot Sancho; and one opposite the public gardens in Souillac. The surfing season is from around June to August.

The best surf spots in Réunion are around St-Gilles-les-Bains and St-Leu. The most popular spot and surfing centre is Roches Noires beach at St-Gilles-les-Bains itself.

Diving & Snorkelling

Diving The Seychelles has the best diving locations and schools. Scuba is also popular in Mauritius and Réunion but not so much for the serious diver as for casual or learning divers.

Most of the instructors are members of the US-based Professional Association of Diving Instructors (PADI) and provide safety and tuition of a high standard. Another major diving organisation is the Federation of Australian Underwater Instructors (FAUI). If the school does not possess qualifications, then you may be taking a risk with instruction and equipment.

As well as successfully completing the course remember that your ability, health and qualifications should be checked before any operator sells you courses or takes you out on an introductory dive. This is done through a check in a swimming pool or lagoon. All beginners must be able to swim at least 200m before proceeding. Certain medical conditions, such as asthma (or having a cold), do not go with diving. Also, you must remember that you should allow at least 24 hours between doing a dive and taking a flight.

Don't let having a certificate lull you into thinking that you know everything. Like any activity, experience is vitally important. As well as your diving certificate every diver has a log book in which they should record every dive they make. If a proposed dive is deep or difficult a good dive operator should check your log book to ensure experience is sufficient. A high proportion of diving accidents happen to inexperienced divers getting out of their depth.

More details of sites, schools and courses may be found under each country.

Snorkelling For those who are content with snorkelling, watch out for sunburn, especially on your back. Wear a light T-shirt and slop on the water-resistant sun block creams and lotions. Make sure your kids are equally well protected from the sun.

Deep-Sea Fishing
Tourist bodies and beach hotels of each country continue to expand and heavily promote opportunities for deep-sea angling. This has become a popular attraction for tourists to all three islands. For those who enjoy this activity, information has been provided where appropriate in individual countries.

Other Activities
Other water sports, such as windsurfing, water-skiing, kayaking, pedalos etc, are offered by the main beach hotels and often made available to nonresidents for a price.

See the Facts for the Visitor chapter of each country for lists of clubs and organisations that can help with information, hire equipment and marine recreation for visitors.

See individual countries' Activities sections in the Facts for the Visitor chapter for information on land activities such as mountain bike riding, golf, horse riding, abseiling and rock climbing. For a detailed coverage of Réunion's sensational trekking options, see the Trekking in Réunion chapter. Tennis courts are available at most of the major hotels (some are open to nonresidents for a fee).

ACCOMMODATION
Although this is an expensive region to visit, it's also a great chance to play jetsetter! There is certainly a tantalising array of swanky hotels and resorts, especially in Mauritius and the Seychelles. Indeed Mauritius and the Seychelles have traditionally been playgrounds of the rich and famous, who come here to live in style and indulge in the tempting range of water activities. But if the jetsetter scene is not for you, there are also cheaper accommodation alternatives.

Mauritius and Réunion offer cheaper accommodation options than the Seychelles. However, the standard of facilities and service can be variable at the cheaper places. Apart from a plethora of luxury hotels, Mauritius also has a number of exceedingly cheaper guesthouses and self-catering apartments and bungalows.

There are only a few really upmarket hotels in Réunion, and they are no match for those in Mauritius or the Seychelles. However, Réunion does have a good selection of budget accommodation, including camp sites, youth hostels, gîtes de montagne (mountain lodges), private gîtes, chambres d'hôte and pensions de famille.

The Seychelles has no rock-bottom accommodation, as the tourist industry is heavily controlled by the government.

Many of the mid and top-end hotels on all three islands charge different room tariffs according to the high/low season. Be warned that it can be difficult finding accommodation in the high season – book well ahead to avoid disappointment. If you intend staying in upmarket hotels, take advantage of package rates by booking from overseas.

Hotels offering full-board include all three meals; half-board includes breakfast and one other meal.

Getting There & Away

This chapter provides some general information on how to reach the Indian Ocean area. For much more detail, see the individual country Getting There & Away chapters.

However you're travelling, it's worth taking out travel insurance. Work out what you need. You may not want to insure that grotty old army surplus backpack – but everyone should be covered for the worst possible case: an accident, for example, that will require hospital treatment and a flight home. It's a good idea to make a copy of your policy, in case the original is lost. If you are planning to travel for a long time, the insurance may seem very expensive – but if you can't afford it, you certainly won't be able to afford to deal with a medical emergency overseas. For more information see Visas & Documents in the Regional Facts for the Visitor chapter.

AIR
Buying Tickets
The plane ticket will probably be the single most expensive item in your budget, and buying it can be an intimidating business. There is likely to be a multitude of airlines and travel agents hoping to separate you from your money, and it is always worth putting aside a few hours to research the current state of the market. Start early: some of the cheapest tickets have to be bought months in advance, and some popular flights sell out early. Talk to other recent travellers – they may be able to stop you making some of the same old mistakes. Look at the ads in newspapers and magazines (not forgetting the press of the ethnic group whose country you plan to visit), consult reference books and watch for special offers. Then phone travel agents for bargains. (Airlines can supply information on routes and timetables; however, except at times of inter-airline war they do not supply the cheapest tickets.) Find out the fare, the route, the duration of the journey and any restrictions on the ticket.

(See Restrictions in the Air Travel Glossary.) Then sit back and decide which is best for you.

You may discover that those impossibly cheap flights are 'fully booked, but we have another one that costs a bit more...' Or the flight is on an airline notorious for its poor safety standards and leaves you in the world's least favourite airport in mid-journey for 14 hours. Or they claim only to have the last two seats available for that country for the whole of July, which they will hold for you for a maximum of two hours. Don't panic – keep ringing around.

Use the fares quoted in this book as a guide only. They are approximate and based on the rates advertised by travel agents at the time of going to press. Quoted airfares do not necessarily constitute a recommendation for the carrier. If you are travelling from the UK or the USA, you will probably find that the cheapest flights are being advertised by obscure bucket shops whose names haven't yet reached the telephone directory. Many such firms are honest and solvent, but there are a few rogues who will take your money and disappear, to reopen elsewhere a month or two later under a new name. If you feel suspicious about a firm, don't give them all the money at once – leave a deposit of 20% or so and pay the balance when you get the ticket. If they insist on cash in advance, go somewhere else. And once you have the ticket, ring the airline to confirm that you are actually booked onto the flight.

You may decide to pay more than the rock-bottom fare by opting for the safety of a better-known travel agent. Firms such as STA Travel, who have offices worldwide, Council Travel in the USA or Travel CUTS in Canada are not going to disappear overnight, leaving you clutching a receipt for a nonexistent ticket, but they do offer good prices to most destinations.

Once you have your ticket, write its number down, together with the flight number and other details, and keep the information somewhere separate. If the ticket is lost or stolen, this will help you get a replacement. It's sensible to buy travel insurance as early as possible. If you buy it the week before you fly, you may find, for example, that you're not covered for delays to your flight caused by industrial action.

Round the World Tickets

Round the world (RTW) tickets have become very popular in the last few years. The airline RTW tickets are often real bargains, and can work out no more expensive or even cheaper than an ordinary return ticket. Prices start at about US$1300.

The official airline RTW tickets are usually put together by a combination of two airlines, and permit you to fly anywhere you want on their route systems so long as you do not backtrack. Other restrictions are that you (usually) must book the first sector in advance and cancellation penalties then apply. There may be restrictions on how many stops you are permitted and usually the tickets are valid for 90 days up to a year. An alternative type of RTW ticket is one put together by a travel agent using a combination of discounted tickets.

Travellers with Special Needs

If you have special needs of any sort – you've broken a leg, you're vegetarian, travelling in a wheelchair, taking the baby, terrified of flying – you should let the airline know as soon as possible so that they can make arrangements accordingly. You should remind them when you reconfirm your booking (at least 72 hours before departure) and again when you check in at the airport. It may also be worth ringing round the airlines before you make your booking to find out how they can handle your particular needs.

Airports and airlines can be surprisingly helpful, but they do need advance warning. Most international airports will provide escorts from check-in desk to plane where needed, and there should be ramps, lifts, accessible toilets and reachable phones. Air-craft toilets, on the other hand, are likely to present a problem; travellers should discuss this with the airline at an early stage and, if necessary, with their doctor.

Guide dogs for the blind will often have to travel in a specially pressurised baggage compartment with other animals, away from their owner; though smaller guide dogs may be admitted to the cabin. All guide dogs will be subject to the same quarantine laws (six months in isolation etc) as any other animal when entering or returning to countries currently free of rabies such as the UK or Australia.

Deaf travellers can ask for airport and in-flight announcements to be written down for them.

Children under two travel for 10% of the standard fare (or free, on some airlines), as long as they don't occupy a seat. They don't get a baggage allowance either. 'Skycots' should be provided by the airline if requested in advance; these will take a child weighing up to about 10kg. Children between two and 12 can usually occupy a seat for half to two-thirds of the full fare, and do get a baggage allowance. Push chairs can often be taken as hand luggage.

Warning

The information in individual Getting There & Away country chapters is particularly vulnerable to change: prices for international travel are volatile, routes are introduced and cancelled, schedules change, special deals come and go, and rules and visa requirements are amended. Airlines and governments seem to take a perverse pleasure in making price structures and regulations as complicated as possible. You should check directly with the airline or a travel agent to make sure you understand how a fare (and ticket you may buy) works. In addition, the travel industry is highly competitive and there are many lurks and perks.

The upshot of this is that you should get opinions, quotes and advice from as many airlines and travel agents as possible before you part with your hard-earned cash. The details given in this book regarding airfares should be regarded as pointers and are not a substitute for your own careful, up-to-date research. ■

Air Travel Glossary

Apex Apex ('advance purchase excursion') is a discounted ticket which must be paid for in advance. There are penalties if you wish to change it.

Baggage Allowance This will be written on your ticket: usually one 20kg item to go in the hold, plus one item of hand luggage.

Bucket Shop An 'unbonded' travel agency specialising in discounted airline tickets.

Bumped Just because you have a confirmed seat doesn't mean you're going to get on the plane (see Overbooking).

Cancellation Penalties If you have to cancel or change an Apex ticket there are often heavy penalties; insurance can sometimes be taken out against these penalties. Some airlines impose penalties on regular tickets as well, particularly against 'no-show' passengers.

Check In Airlines ask you to check in a certain time ahead of the flight departure (usually two hours on international flights). If you fail to check in on time and the flight is overbooked the airline can cancel your booking and give your seat to somebody else.

Confirmation Having a ticket written out with the flight and date you want doesn't mean you have a seat until the agent has checked with the airline that your status is 'OK' or confirmed. Meanwhile you could just be 'on request'.

Discounted Tickets There are two types of discounted fares – officially discounted (see Promotional Fares) and unofficially discounted. The lowest prices often impose drawbacks like flying with unpopular airlines, inconvenient schedules, or unpleasant routes and connections. A discounted ticket doesn't necessarily have to save you money – you may be able to pay Apex prices without the associated Apex advance booking and other requirements. Discounted tickets only exist where there is fierce competition.

Full Fares Airlines traditionally offer 1st class (coded F), business class (coded J) and economy class (coded Y) tickets. These days there are so many promotional and discounted fares available from the regular economy class that few passengers pay full economy fare.

Lost Tickets If you lose your airline ticket an airline will usually treat it like a travellers cheque and, after enquiries, issue you with another one. Legally, however, an airline is entitled to treat it like cash and if you lose it then it's gone forever. Take good care of your tickets.

No-Shows No-shows are passengers who fail to show up for their flight, sometimes due to unexpected delays or disasters, sometimes due to simply forgetting, sometimes because they made more than one booking and didn't bother to cancel the one they didn't want. Full-fare passengers who fail to turn up are sometimes entitled to travel on a later flight. The rest of us are penalised (see Cancellation Penalties).

The USA

The *New York Times*, the *LA Times*, the *Chicago Tribune* and the *San Francisco Examiner* all produce weekly travel sections in which you'll find any number of travel agents' ads. Council Travel and STA Travel have offices in major cities nationwide. The magazine *Travel Unlimited* (PO Box 1058, Allston, Mass 02134) publishes details of the cheapest airfares and courier possibilities for destinations all over the world from the USA.

Canada

Travel CUTS has offices in all major cities.

The *Toronto Globe & Mail* and the *Vancouver Sun* carry travel agents' ads. The magazine *Great Expeditions* (PO Box 8000-411, Abbotsford BC V2S 6H1) is useful.

Australia

STA Travel and Flight Centres International are major dealers in cheap airfares. Check the travel agents' ads in the Yellow Pages and ring around.

There are convenient direct Air Mauritius flights between Melbourne/Perth and Mauritius. There are of course other alternatives – discuss these with your travel agent. See

On Request An unconfirmed booking for a flight (see Confirmation).

Open Jaw A return ticket where you fly out to one place but return from another. If available, this can save you backtracking to your arrival point.

Overbooking Airlines hate to fly empty seats and since every flight has some passengers who fail to show up (see No-Shows), airlines often book more passengers than they have seats. Usually the excess passengers balance those who fail to show up, but occasionally somebody gets bumped. If this happens guess who it is most likely to be? The passengers who check in late.

Promotional Fares Officially discounted fares like Apex fares which are available from travel agents or direct from the airline.

Reconfirmation At least 72 hours prior to departure time of an onward or return flight you must contact the airline and 'reconfirm' that you intend to be on the flight. If you don't do this the airline can delete your name from the passenger list and you could lose your seat. You don't have to reconfirm the first flight on your itinerary or if your stopover is less than 72 hours. It doesn't hurt to reconfirm more than once.

Restrictions Discounted tickets often have various restrictions on them – advance purchase is the most usual one (see Apex). Others are restrictions on the minimum and maximum period you must be away, such as a minimum of 14 days or a maximum of one year (see Cancellation Penalties).

Standby A discounted ticket where you only fly if there is a seat free at the last moment. Standby fares are usually only available on domestic routes.

Tickets Out An entry requirement for many countries is that you have an onward or return ticket – in other words, a ticket out of the country. If you're not sure what you intend to do next, the easiest solution is to buy the cheapest onward ticket to a neighbouring country or a ticket from a reliable airline which can later be refunded if you do not use it.

Transferred Tickets Airline tickets cannot be transferred from one person to another. Travellers sometimes try to sell the return half of their ticket, but officials can ask you to prove that you are the person named on the ticket. This is unlikely to happen on domestic flights; on an international flight tickets may be compared with passports.

Travel Agencies Travel agencies vary widely and you should ensure you use one that suits your needs. Some simply handle tours, while full-service agencies handle everything from tours and tickets to car rental and hotel bookings. A good one will do all these things and can save you a lot of money, but if all you want is a ticket at the lowest possible price, then you really need an agency specialising in discounted tickets. A discounted ticket agency, however, may not be useful for other things, like hotel bookings.

Travel Periods Some officially discounted fares, Apex fares in particular, vary with the time of year. There is often a low (off-peak) season and a high (peak) season. Sometimes there's an intermediate or shoulder season as well. At peak times, when everyone wants to fly, not only will the officially discounted fares be higher but so will unofficially discounted fares, or there may simply be no discounted tickets available. Usually the fare depends on your outward flight – if you depart in the high season and return in the low season, you pay the high-season fare. ■

individual country chapters for more detailed flight information.

New Zealand
As in Australia, STA Travel and Flight Centres International are popular travel agents. Also look through newspapers for special deals being offered.

The UK
Trailfinders in west London produces a lavishly illustrated brochure which includes airfare details. STA Travel also has branches in the UK. Look in the listings magazine *Time Out* plus the Sunday papers and *Exchange & Mart* for ads. Also look out for the free magazines widely available in London – start by looking outside the main railway stations.

Most British travel agents are registered with ABTA (Association of British Travel Agents). If you have paid for your flight to an ABTA-registered agent who then goes out of business, ABTA will guarantee a refund or an alternative. Unregistered bucket shops are riskier but also sometimes cheaper.

The Globetrotters Club (BCM Roving, London WC1N 3XX) publishes a newsletter called *Globe* which covers obscure destinations and can help in finding travelling companions.

Air Mauritius operates weekly flights between Mauritius and London. For details on other flights between the UK and Mauritius and the Seychelles, see the individual country Getting There & Away chapters.

Continental Europe
There are numerous flights between Mauritius and Europe, especially France. Air Mauritius operates weekly flights to many European destinations including Paris, Zürich, Geneva, Rome, Munich, Frankfurt, Brussels and Vienna (the number of flights usually varies according to low/high season). Air France operates nine to 12 flights weekly between *la métropole* (mainland France) and Réunion and the trip takes about 12 hours. There are also flights between the Seychelles and France. For more information see the country Getting There & Away chapters.

There are lots of bucket shops in Paris, Amsterdam, Brussels, Frankfurt and a few other places. However, don't take the advertised fares as gospel truth.

The newsletter *Farang* (La Rue 8a, 4261, Braives, Belgium) deals with exotic destinations, as does the magazine *Globe-Trotters*, published by Aventure au Bout du Monde (ABM, 7 Rue Gassendi, 75014, Paris, France; ☎ 01 43 35 08 95).

Africa
You can fly to Mauritius direct from Johannesburg, Cape Town or Durban (South Africa), Harare (Zimbabwe), Antananarivo (Madagascar), Moroni (Comoros), Nairobi (Kenya) or the Seychelles. Airlines offer different fares and packages – for details, contact a travel agent.

For details about flights between Africa and Réunion and the Seychelles, see the individual country Getting There and Away chapters.

Asia
Various airlines operate flights between Mauritius and Mumbai (Bombay), New Delhi, Jakarta, Kuala Lumpur, Singapore and Hong Kong. To get to Réunion, you have to go via Mauritius or the Seychelles.

Hong Kong is the discount plane-ticket capital of the region. Its bucket shops are at least as unreliable as those of other cities. Ask the advice of other travellers before buying a ticket.

Other Indian Ocean Countries
Once you get into the region, the island-hopping, if that's not too light a term in this case, becomes easier and cheaper. The best way of covering all three islands is with a round-trip air ticket using several airlines. The only condition is that you must continue the route in a circle; ie you can't double back. This means you can also take in Madagascar, Comoros and Kenya. These round-trip air tickets are good bargains if you have the time.

Make all inquiries and bookings through a major tour operator or travel agent such as Rogers & Co Aviation in Port Louis, Mauritius, or Bourbon Voyages in St-Denis, Réunion, but not directly through the airlines. You'll have a better shot at a good deal. The same applies in your own country.

Refer to the individual country Getting There & Away chapters for costs and more specific details of air travel.

SEA
Opportunities for sea travel to Mauritius, the Seychelles and Réunion are limited to passing cruise liners, yachts and the very occasional cargo-passenger ship. The cost is high, unless you can work your way as crew. The cruise liners usually only stop for a day or two. Sea travel between the Seychelles, Mauritius and Réunion is out of the question unless you have your own yacht or enough money and time to charter one.

If you want to try crewing onto a yacht, it is possible but your chances are slim. Remember that even if you do strike it lucky and find someone who is looking for crew, they'll be very fussy about whom they'll take.

Yacht skippers normally look for someone with a bit of cash money as well as sailing experience. There is no such thing as a free ride, unless you come across a rich playboy or playgirl who likes the cut of your jib. You must also have the right temperament, as conditions are difficult aboard a yacht. There's no privacy, nowhere to escape to if tension breaks and no buts about it – the skipper is boss.

Cruising time between the island countries varies depending on the weather conditions and the direction you're heading in. About 160km in 24 hours is a rough rule of thumb. There is generally no long-distance sailing between or around Mauritius and Réunion during the cyclone season. The Seychelles lies outside the cyclone zone.

Mauritius

Facts about Mauritius

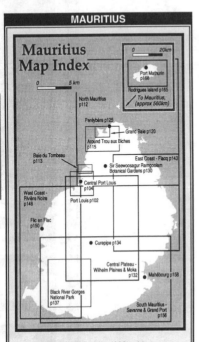

MAURITIUS

Mauritius
Map Index

Port Mathurin p168
Rodrigues Island p165
/ To Mauritius,
(approx 560km)

North Mauritius p112

Pereybère p125

Grand Baie p120

Around Trou aux Biches p115

Baie du Tombeau p113

East Coast - Flacq p143

Sir Seewoosagur Ramgoolam Botanical Gardens p130

Central Port Louis p104

West Coast - Rivière Noire p148

Port Louis p102

Flic en Flac p150

Curepipe p134

Central Plateau - Wilhelm Plaines & Moka p132

Mahébourg p158

Black River Gorges National Park p137

South Mauritius - Savanne & Grand Port p156

Official Name: Republic of Mauritius
Area: 1865 sq km
Population: 1.1 million
Population Growth Rate: 0.9%
Capital: Port Louis
Head of State: President Cassam Uteem
Official Languages: English, French
Main Religion: Hinduism
Currency: Mauritian rupee
Exchange Rate: Rs 20 = US$1
Per Capita GNP: US$3200
Inflation: 10%
Time: UTC +4

Highlights

- Plenty of picturesque beaches and water activities, especially at the northern end of the island
- A colourful mélange of cultures, reflected in festivals, dress, language and cuisine
- The beautiful Sir Seewoosagur Ramgoolam Botanical Gardens at Pamplemousses

If you're searching for a tropical paradise where you can laze away the days on sun-kissed beaches, indulge in wild and wonderful water activities and treat yourself to a delicious range of culinary creations, Mauritius fits the bill.

This beautiful island, about 1600km east of Madagascar, has endless sugar cane plantations, dramatic mountains, a vibrant cultural mix and some of the finest beaches and aquamarine lagoons in the Indian Ocean. Although impressive, Mauritius' beaches are no match to those of the Seychelles and its mountains are not nearly as spectacular as those of Réunion. Mauritius is also heavily populated and has a more commercial ambience than the Seychelles and Réunion. On the plus side, it's considerably cheaper to stay, eat and get around in Mauritius than in Réunion or the Seychelles. For the cost of a week in Réunion, you can stay three weeks in Mauritius. This makes it an excellent destination for the traveller and largely accounts for its increasing appeal to tourists from around the world.

Most visitors tend to stay in the deluxe beach hotels and only venture out on occasional sightseeing or shopping trips. If your budget does not permit the luxury of up-market hotels, don't despair – there are plenty of far cheaper guesthouses and apartments scattered around the island. Similarly, when eating out there are places to suit all pockets, from simple sidewalk cafés to swanky seaside restaurants. The diversity of cuisine – from French to Créole – reflects the rich cultural blend of the island (see the Delicious Mauritius boxed text in the Mauritius Facts for the Visitor chapter).

With more than half the population Hindu, the island has a distinct Indian flavour. Indians first came to Mauritius as indentured labourers, brought to work on the sugar cane fields. The Mahatma Gandhi Institute in Moka has been established to preserve and promote Mauritian Indian history and heritage (for more details see the Mahatma Gandhi Institute boxed text in the Central Mauritius chapter). The island's Indian presence is perhaps most vividly highlighted during the many festivals celebrated throughout the year (see Public Holidays & Special Events in the Mauritius Facts for the Visitor chapter). The remainder of Mauritius' population is predominantly made up of African, Chinese, French and British elements. Each group plays a part in the economy, society and administration of the country, which is structured on the British model.

HISTORY
Mauritius has a colonial history. It has experienced four changes of 'ownership' and name between being first inhabited, in 1598, and independence, in 1968.

Following the liberation of African slaves in 1835, the Indians were brought by the British to Mauritius, along with the Chinese, as cheap labour for the sugar cane plantations.

The Portuguese & the Dutch
Arab traders knew of Mauritius as early as the 10th century. They called the uninhabited island Dinarobin, but did not settle it.

Nor did the Portuguese naval explorers settle Mauritius when they discovered it in the wake of Vasco da Gama's famous trip around the Cape of Good Hope in 1498, though they are credited with the first European landing. Instead, they continued on to the east coast of Africa, Indonesia and India to establish colonies.

Domingo Fernandez dropped anchor in Mauritius in 1511. He named the island Ilha do Cerne (Swan Island); perhaps this was the name of his ship or he might have been referring to the native dodo, which he took to be a sort of swan.

Rodrigues Island, 560km to the northeast, takes its name from another navigator, Don Diego Rodrigues, who called by in 1528. Together with Réunion, the two islands were named the Mascarenes, after Portuguese admiral Don Pedro Mascarenhas. Apart from introducing pesky monkeys, rats and other animals, the Portuguese did little to Mauritius. That was left to the next wave of maritime supremos, the Dutch.

In 1598, Vice Admiral Wybrandt van Warwyck landed on the south-east coast of the island, claimed it for the Netherlands and named it Mauritius, after his ruler, Maurice, Prince of Orange and Count of Nassau. It was another 40 years before the Dutch decided to try settling the country, preferring to use it as a supply base for Batavia (Java). When they did settle in Mauritius, it was around their original landing spot. Settlement ruins can be seen opposite the church at Vieux Grand Port, near Mahébourg.

The colony never really flourished and the Dutch departed for good in 1710, leaving their mark behind. They are held to blame for the extinction of the dodo and the introduction of slaves from Africa, deer from Java, wild boar, tobacco and, above all, sugar cane. In 1642 they also sent Abel Tasman off from the island to discover Tasmania, Fiji and New Zealand.

The French
Five years later Captain Guillaume Dufresne d'Arsal sailed across from Réunion, then called Bourbon, and claimed the island for France. It was renamed Île de France and given over to the Compagnie des Indes Orientales (French East India Company) to run as a trading base.

The French decided they would stay for good, and settlement began in 1721. Not until 1735 did things start moving under the governorship of Bertrand François Mahé de La Bourdonnais, Mauritius' first hero. Under his leadership, port facilities were expanded, the first sugar mill and hospital were built and a road network was established. Also during his administration, Mauritius' best known historic event occurred – the St Géran tragedy.

In 1744, the *St Géran* was wrecked during a storm off Île d'Ambre, near the north-east coast, while waiting to enter Port Louis to unload machinery for the new sugar mill. The event inspired Bernardin de St Pierre's romantic novel *Paul et Virginie*, an early best

MAURITIUS

MAURITIUS

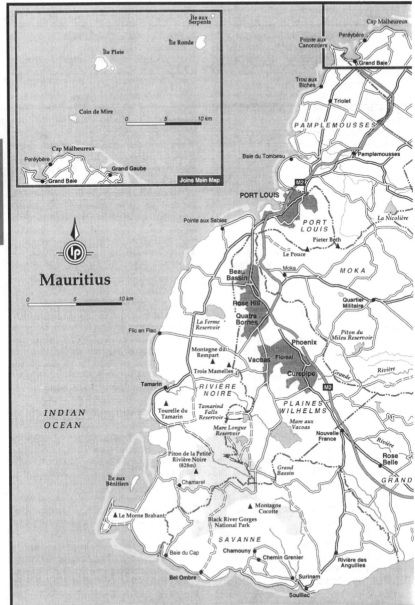

Mauritius

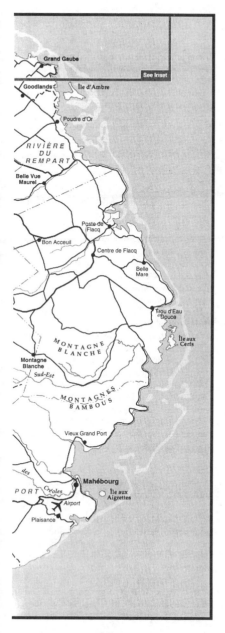

seller. A few years later, La Bourdonnais went off to help fight the British in India and ended up in the Bastille, after falling out with his own side. He was released and his name eventually cleared.

As the English gained the upper hand in the Indian Ocean during the second half of the 18th century, the Compagnie des Indes Orientales collapsed and the sugar industry strengthened. Port Louis became a free trading base and a haven for corsairs – mercenary marines paid by a country to prey on the ships of its enemy. The most famous Franco-Mauritian corsair was Robert Surcouf. Freebooting English, American and French pirates, who had been operating so successfully out of Madagascar towards the end of the 17th and beginning of the 18th centuries, gave way to these licensed and semirespectable pirates.

In 1789 the French colonialists in Mauritius recognised the revolution in France and got rid of their governor. But they refused to get rid of their slaves when the abolition of slavery was decreed in Paris in 1794.

The British

In 1810, during the Napoleonic Wars, the British moved in on the corsairs and on Mauritius. At first, they were defeated at the Battle of Vieux Grand Port, the only French naval victory inscribed on the Arc de Triomphe in Paris. Later, they landed at Cap Malheureux on the north coast and took over the island.

The Treaty of Paris in 1814 gave Île de France, along with Rodrigues and the Seychelles, to the British. They changed its name back to Mauritius, but allowed the Franco-Mauritians to retain their language, religion, Napoleonic Code legal system and sugar cane plantations. In 1835, the slaves were freed and replaced or supplemented by imported labour from India and China.

The British opened up an international market for Mauritian sugar and it became the island's *raison d'être* for the next 150 years. Indian workers continued to be indentured in their thousands. The Franco-Mauritian families produced wealthy sugar barons, and indeed continue to do so to the present day. Through strength of numbers, the Indian workforce gradually achieved a greater say in the running of the country. The Indian political and spiritual leader, Mahatma Gandhi, visited Mauritius in 1901 to push for civil rights.

The island remained relatively unscathed during WWI and WWII. The greatest upheavals to the country and its one-crop economy were caused by cyclones, malaria epidemics (one in 1867 killed half the population of Port Louis), slumps and booms in the world sugar market, and the decline of the country as a maritime trade centre.

The Labour Party was founded in 1936 to fight for the labourers, and did so on the streets the following year. After the war, when a new constitution gave the vote to anyone over 21 who could write their name, the Labour Party gained support.

Under the leadership of Dr Seewoosagur Ramgoolam, who was later knighted, the Labour Party grew in strength during the 1950s. Direct opposition came from the Parti Mauricien Social Démocrate (PMSD), which represented the white and Créole populations.

Independence

Mauritius was granted independence on 12 March 1968. Sir Seewoosagur Ramgoolam was elected prime minister and remained in office for the next 13 years, eventually in coalition with the PMSD. Sir Seewoosagur continued to command reverence as a grand leader until his death in 1986, at the age of 86. His name has now been added to a host of public buildings and places.

In 1982 a coalition of the leftist Mouvement Militant Mauricien (MMM), led by Franco-Mauritian Paul Bérenger, and the Parti Socialiste Mauricien, led by Anerood Jugnauth, gained power. Jugnauth became prime minister. Bérenger became finance minister and, perhaps surprisingly, adopted a strictly monetarist policy which led to the abandonment of promised welfare measures. He also promoted South African investment in Mauritian hotels, which was opposed by Jugnauth. The resulting tensions, and the

personality clash between Jugnauth and Bérenger led to the resignation of Bérenger and a split in the party. Jugnauth broke from Bérenger's MMM, but remained prime minister by teaming up with the Labour Party, the PMSD (under the flamboyant former mayor of Curepipe and Port Louis, Sir Gaetan Duval) and two other parties.

In August 1983, another election gave the five-party coalition victory and the chance to try to please everybody, including South Africa, with less radical policies. Jugnauth continued as prime minister and Bérenger was out in the cold.

All seemed to be going well until 1986, when three Mauritian MPs were caught at Amsterdam airport with heroin in their suitcases. The resulting inquiry opened a can of worms, implicating other politicians in drug money. The deputy prime minister, Harish Boodhoo, first resigned from office and later resigned his seat. Sir Gaetan replaced Boodhoo and went on to compound his playboy image by declaring he was bisexual.

Bérenger was back in contention and his MMM forced Jugnauth to go to the polls on 30 August 1987. Jugnauth won, capturing 39 of the 62 contested seats. In the 1991 general election, a renewed alliance of Bérenger, leading the MMM, and Jugnauth, heading the MSM (Mouvement Socialiste Mauricien), won a landslide victory. They governed the country until 1995, when Jugnauth lost the election to Navin Ramgoolam, son of former prime minister Sir Seewoosagur Ramgoolam. Mauritius officially became a republic in 1992.

GEOGRAPHY

Mauritius is a volcanic island, 58km from north to south and 47km from east to west. It lies roughly 220km from Réunion and 800km from Madagascar to the west; 5854km from Perth (Australia) to the east; and is on the same latitude as Rio de Janeiro (Brazil), Harare (Zimbabwe) and Rockhampton (Australia).

The country includes the inhabited island of Rodrigues, 560km to the north-east, and other scattered coral atolls such as Cargados Carajos and Agalega.

GEOLOGY

Mauritius is thought to be the peak of an enormous sunken volcanic chain which stretches from the Seychelles to Réunion. The island rises steeply in the south to a central plateau which, beyond the mountains behind Port Louis, slopes gently down to the northern coast. The mountains are noted more for gaunt and unusual shapes than for height. The Piton de la Petite Rivière Noire is the highest peak at 828m.

Unlike Réunion, Mauritius has no active volcanoes, though remainders of volcanic activity abound. Extinct craters and volcanic lakes, such as the Trou aux Cerfs crater in Curepipe and the Grand Bassin holy lake, are good examples. Millions of lava boulders, further reminders of volcanic activity, cover the island. Hundreds of little pyramids of these rocks, which had to be gathered to clear the land for sugar cane, can be seen dotting the cane fields.

Mauritius is surrounded by a coral reef which provides several long stretches of white coral sand beaches. The reef is broken in many places. Between Souillac and Le Bouchon, on the southern coast, the sea crashes through the largest break in the reef and against the black cliffs, creating a rugged, wild coastline. There is a similar, though not so spectacular, break in the reef above Flic en Flac on the west coast.

CLIMATE

The Mauritian climate is a mixed affair. Different regions of Mauritius are affected in different ways. Up on the plateau around Curepipe, temperatures average 5°C cooler than on the coast. It can be raining up there while it's clear around the coast, and vice versa. Similarly, east coast weather differs from that of the west coast. The east coast is also much drier during January and February when the prevailing winds drive in from the east, hit the mountains, and dump rain on central and western Mauritius.

The hottest months are from January to April, when temperatures range from 25°C to 35°C. It's nice to get away from the northern hemisphere winter, but it can prove too

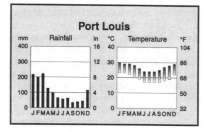

hot and humid for some. This is also the cyclone season and although a direct hit only happens about once every 15 years, the island still suffers days of squally depression from the several cyclones that occur in the region each year. During these times, there are usually several days of heavy rain, which force most holiday-makers to stay cooped up in their hotel rooms.

There are no distinct monsoons. It can rain any and every day of the year. When it's not blowing from the north, the breeze comes from the south-east, courtesy of the regular trade winds.

The depths of a Mauritian 'winter' occur from July to September when temperatures average a chastening 24°C during the day and 16°C at night. This can be more pleasant. There is less rain and humidity, and less chance of frying yourself.

ECOLOGY & ENVIRONMENT

Tourism has become one of Mauritius' major economic pillars. The expansion of tourist facilities, however, has strained the island's infrastructure and has caused all sorts of problems, including environmental degradation and excessive demand on electricity, water, telephone and transport services.

Conservationists are campaigning to protect the fragile marine environment, which has suffered widespread damage over the past few decades. Some of the causes include disturbance from motor boats, fishermen and divers, as well as a proliferating level of pollution.

Collection of shells and coral for commercial purposes has also been detrimental to the marine environment. We strongly urge you

MAURITIUS

not to buy anything made out of turtle shell nor to buy or take any shells from the beach. Governments are trying to do something about it; please don't contribute to the problems by providing the incentive to continue the practices. If you do come across a shop or beach vendor selling shells, coral or turtle shell products, remember that these are banned by the Mauritian government.

Tourists who illegally possess or transport these items should also be aware that the items are liable to confiscation on leaving Mauritius, and to combined fines and confiscation by customs officials in most western countries which have signed agreements on endangered species.

FLORA & FAUNA

It's easy to think that as a result of the extinction of the dodo we are now sadder and wiser, but there's a lot of evidence to suggest that we are merely sadder and better informed.
Last Chance to See by Douglas Adams & Mark Carwardine

Together with the Seychelles and Madagascar, Mauritius is a haven for the botanist, biologist, zoologist, ornithologist and other '-ologists'. Mauritius is, or rather was, the home of the dodo. The funny, fat, flightless bird was wiped out not long after the island was first settled by the Dutch. The poor things were defenceless against humans and their pets or pests – dogs, monkeys, pigs and rats.

Several other species disappeared forever, including the black, flightless parrot, rails (small wading birds) and the giant Mauritian tortoise. Some unique, if less unusual, species survived. The same applies to the natural forests and vegetation, much of which was cleared or altered with the spread of sugar cane fields and the introduction of other plants and trees.

To experience most of what the island has to offer in the way of flora and fauna, the visitor must go to the Sir Seewoosagur Ramgoolam and Curepipe Botanical Gardens, Casela Bird Park near Flic en Flac, Domaine du Chasseur near Mahébourg, Le Val Nature Park, Île aux Aigrettes, Black River Gorges National Park, La Vanille Crocodile Farm near Souillac and, for stuffed replicas, to the Mauritius Institute in Port Louis. These places are covered in more detail in their respective area sections in this book.

For details about flora and fauna on Rodrigues, refer to the Rodrigues & the Outer Islands chapter.

Information

The best source of information on Mauritian wildlife is the Mauritius Wildlife Appeal Fund (MWAF), which was founded in 1984 as a charity to protect and manage the rare birds, plants, reptiles and mammals of Mauritius. MWAF is vigorously supporting the creation of national parks; projects to restore populations of endangered bird species (Mauritius kestrel, pink pigeon, echo parakeet, Mauritius white eye and fody); programmes to restore and conserve endemic vegetation (including Round Island and Île aux Aigrettes); and the monitoring of whales, dolphins and turtles around Mauritius.

The appeal fund is always in need of donations or sponsors, for example, for their 'Sponsor a Kestrel Nestbox' scheme which provides safe nest sites (monkey proof and cyclone proof) for breeding kestrels. The Wildlife Supporters Club, a support group for MWAF, produces a newsletter several times a year and helps with projects. Inquiries about MWAF or the Wildlife Supporters Club should be made to the following address (enclose return postage): Mauritius Wildlife Appeal Fund (MWAF) (☎ 2112228), Public Relations Officer, Edith Cavell St, Port Louis.

The Mauritius Marine Conservation Society and Mauritius Underwater Group (☎ 6965368), Railway Rd, Phoenix, are campaigning to stop the pollution and destruction of the coral reefs around Mauritius. Efforts are being made to tackle reef degradation and to control pollution and the effects of fertiliser application on land. In the early 1990s, MMCS launched a successful pressure campaign to enact a new law against driftnetting and published a booklet called *Whales & Dolphins of Mauritius*. The society is also working on projects to build artificial reefs using appropriate materials; conducting surveys on the occurrence and status of whales and dolphins in Mauritius; making underwater videos of pristine and damaged reef areas for public viewing; and publishing articles on conservation and the marine environment. ∎

Mangroves

The Collins English dictionary defines mangroves as 'any tropical evergreen tree or shrub of the genus *Rhizophora*, having stilt-like intertwining aerial roots and forming dense thickets along coasts'. They are a much maligned species; the word that usually follows *mangrove* is *swamp* and the image is of something dark, muddy, smelly, full of insects and generally most unattractive.

In actual fact mangroves are an extremely interesting plant with a vital environmental importance which has only been recognised comparatively recently. Mangroves are the advance troops, the first plants to reclaim land from the sea, and they are able to do this because of their remarkable resistance to saltwater. Saltwater will kill most plants but mangroves thrive in it. They can either restrict its entry through their roots or expel excess salt through their leaves. Their remarkable adaptation to a hostile environment can also be seen in their extensive root system, which enables them to grow in unstable tidal mud.

Gradually mangroves create new land, but in the process they provide an environment for a host of other living things from oysters, crabs and snails to the mudskipper fish that prefer to scamper around on top of mangrove mud rather than swim in water, like any normal fish. ■

MAURITIUS

Flora

Almost one-third of the 900 plant species of Mauritius occur only on this island. Many of these indigenous plants have fared poorly in competition with introduced plants, especially guava and privet, and have been depleted by introduced animals, such as deer, pigs and monkeys. General forest clearance and the establishment of crop monocultures have exacerbated the problem, so that Mauritius now possesses less than 1% of intact, original forest. One of the best places to see the island's endemic flora is at the Sir Seewoosagur Ramgoolam Botanical Gardens at Pamplemousses (see the Pamplemousses section in the North Mauritius chapter).

To research and conserve native species, the government Forestry Service together with the Mauritian Wildlife Appeal Fund (MWAF) and Royal Society of Arts and Sciences has set aside special vegetation plots which are protected from animal depredation and carefully weeded to remove the much faster growing introduced species. Rare species are propagated in government nurseries and then planted in these plots where they have a better chance of survival and regeneration. It is hoped that these areas will provide an added bonus by attracting and supporting rare Mauritian bird species, such as the echo parakeet, pink pigeon, and Mauritian cuckoo-shrike. Similar work is also being done on Île aux Aigrettes, Round Island and Rodrigues Island (see the respective sections of this book for more information).

For a tropical island, Mauritius is not big on coconut palms. Instead, casuarinas fringe most of the best beaches. These tall, slim trees look like limp-wristed pines, but although they cast needles galore, they are not members of the pine species at all. The casuarinas, which are also known as *filaos* from the Portuguese, act as useful windbreaks and grow well in sandy soil. They may not be as visually appealing as palms, but they are more aurally pleasing when you listen to the wind whistling through the branches.

Along with casuarinas, eucalyptus trees have been widely planted to make up for the decimation of the original forests. These included the tambalacoque tree, which is also known as the dodo tree and is not far from extinction itself. You'll find it, with the services of a guide, only in the forests south of Curepipe and Mare aux Vacoas. It's a tall tree with a silver trunk and a large, strange-looking, brown seed that is half smooth and half rough. Scientists are sceptical about the rumour that the dodo acted as a germinator, feeding on the tough seed which germinated easily after being passed through the bird's stomach.

Other impressive trees, which you don't have to go off the beaten track to see, are the giant Indian banyan and the brilliant red-flowering flamboyant.

Staying with shades of red, one flower you will see in abundance is anthurium, with its single, glossy petal and protruding yellow spadix. The flower, which at first sight you'd swear was synthetic, can last up to three weeks after being cut and is therefore a popular display plant. Now grown in commercial quantities for export, it is used to spruce up hotel and business rooms and public meeting places. The flower originated in South America and was introduced to Mauritius at the end of the last century.

Fauna

The first animal any visitor to Mauritius is likely to meet is the domestic dog – although there's nothing domesticated about it! Every second family seems to have a dog for 'security' purposes. *Chien méchant* (vicious dog) is a common notice on house gates. Although the dogs' bark is generally worse than their bite, walking along some streets in the dark can be a nightmare.

From the roadside you may also catch glimpses of the mongoose, crossing from cane field to cane field, and Java deer, which were first imported by the Dutch for fresh meat.

You must venture further into the wild, particularly around the Rivière Noire (Black River) gorges, to come in contact with wild pigs and bands of macaque monkeys. You'll see little else and there are no dangerous animals.

Marine Life The rich tapestry of amazing fish and shells that you will see around all the Indian Ocean islands is also found in Mauritius. A survey conducted by MWAF showed that whales (finback, pilot, beaked, and sperm), dolphins (spinner and bottlenosed) and turtles (green and hawksbill) are relatively common off the shores of Mauritius.

Game fishing is flourishing, but the subaqua set is not as well catered for, naturally or commercially, as it is in the Maldives or the Seychelles.

Sex & Fish

Nobody ever told reef fish those nice straightforward 'birds and the bees' stories – a high proportion of the fish you see around the Indian Ocean reefs are able to change their sex at some time in their life! Some of them are protandry (they start as males then switch to become females), others are protogyny (they start as females and switch to become males). Some of these fish are monandrous, that is they are all born one sex and only switch to the other sex later. Other species may be born either sex but some of them may later change sex.

The tiny angelfish is an example of protogyny. These fish normally live in small groups of four to seven which control a territory of several square metres. The group usually consists of one larger dominant male with a 'harem' of female fish, although there may sometimes be a smaller 'bachelor' male fish present. The dominant male guards the group's territory and warns off any intruding angelfish. At mating time the male mates with all the females in the group. If the dominant male dies the largest female changes sex and takes over. It appears to be the dominant male which prevents females from changing sex earlier. The male 'dominates' and harasses the larger females and somehow this affects their hormone balance and prevents them changing sex. As soon as the male is removed the largest and most aggressive female is able to switch sexes and start in on dominating her sisters!

The opposite situation can be observed in the familiar clown anemone fish. The small group which shelters around a protective anemone usually consists of a large adult female and a group of smaller males. The female mates with only one of the males and this mature male fish keeps all the other 'bachelor' anemone fish in line. If something happens to the female then the chief male switches sex and becomes the new female, while the most dominant and aggressive of the other males takes over as the new chief male.

Scientists have postulated a number of reasons for this strange state of affairs. Life on the reef is dangerous and very much dog eat dog. If changing sex were not possible and the sole male or female fish in the group died then the group could not reproduce. As it is there's just a quick change of sex on the part of one fish and life continues as normal! Competition is fierce and by staking out their own small territory and defending it against any intruders the small groups of reef fish ensure their own survival. ■

A group of underwater sports enthusiasts and conservationists has formed the Mauritius Marine Conservation Society (MMCS) (☎ 6965368) and the associated Mauritius Underwater Group (MUG) to campaign against pollution and destruction of the coral reefs around Mauritius.

A MMCS report called for marine biologists and fisheries experts to assess and evaluate the long-term effects on the marine environment of the increasing population of Mauritius, the growth of industry, and the use of chemical fertilisers in agriculture.

In the last two decades some divers have been greatly concerned by the decline in the marine resources of the island and the widespread death of corals. Some of the causes already identified include indiscriminate fishing with spearguns, and the collection of shells. This has made coastal waters less attractive to tourist and resident divers and less productive as a source of food.

In the past, the frequent use of explosives to harvest fish was a wasteful and dangerous fishing method which destroyed many reef ecosystems. Damage is caused to corals by anchors and through removal by tourists and local snorkellers. The wholesale removal of sea sand for building destroys an important lagoon ecosystem and causes erosion of beaches. The increasing use of the lagoons for recreation and tourism has considerably reduced the pristine areas of shoreline and coast.

The quality of the marine environment is further impaired by disturbance from motor boats, fishermen, divers and others. Whales, dolphins and turtles are harassed and killed, and even the gazetted 'fishing reserves' are not respected. Increasing pollution of the coastal waters by river-borne refuse, sewerage outfalls and waste from fishing boats has also been noticed.

It is also an unfortunate fact that existing legislation which forbids the use of explosives, spearfishing, collecting of corals and shells, and fishing in some areas and in certain periods, appears quite difficult to enforce.

MMCS has issued a recommended code of conduct to respect the lagoons and reefs of Mauritius:

1. Take care not to remove or break any living corals.
2. Do not buy any shells, corals or preserved fish, turtles etc from hawkers or tourist shops (even if the seller insists that the objects are not from Mauritius or that he/she has a permit).
3. Do not litter the beaches and lagoons with plastic, paper etc.
4. Commend hotel/lodgings management on any special consideration given to the beach, lagoon or reef, for example, conservation posters in reception, replanting of coastal vegetation etc.

One traveller made the following observations about snorkelling and the condition of the coral:

From what I could gather from a local diving specialist, and also from my own experience, snorkelling within the reef (near Grand Baie and Trou aux Biches) is not that great.

The reason for this is that the coral has been removed both by tourists and, presumably, by local traders, in order to make coral necklaces. Also guilty are some of the big hotels which have sent mechanical diggers into the sea to smash and remove coral in order to provide bathing areas for their residents – all the best swimming areas in Mauritius are off public beaches where hotels cannot be built.

Endangered Species
Birdlife The best known representative of Mauritian birdlife was the dodo, a large, plump, flightless dove which found its docility rewarded with extinction in the late 17th century. Although the dodo has since become a stereotype for extinction, few people realise that Mauritius still possesses several incredibly rare bird species in minute numbers which are as doomed as the dodo if the present efforts at conservation cannot be sustained.

The Mauritius kestrel suffered a massive decline in numbers as a result of habitat destruction, pesticide poisoning, and hunting. The Mauritius Kestrel Conservation Program, started in 1973, has used captive breeding followed by release and management of the birds in the wild to produce an amazing recovery.

The echo parakeet is the world's rarest parakeet. Since 1985, MWAF has been running

MAURITIUS

Going, going, gone?
Many of Mauritius' endangered species of fauna and flora are making a slow recovery. Unlike the dodo, which became extinct in the late 1950s, species such as the Mauritius kestrel, pink pigeon and echo parakeet are out of immediate danger, but have not yet won the war of survival.

In 1974 only four Mauritius kestrels existed, making it the rarest bird on earth. Today there are more than 350 birds in the wild thanks to an intensive program of captive breeding, although the bird is still on the endangered species list.

The pink pigeon was once found all over Mauritius but now its habitat is restricted to the wet upland forests of the south-west. Feral cats, monkeys and rats brought about the demise of this tame and vulnerable bird. The wild population of the pink pigeon is currently greater than 250 after it fell to about a dozen in 1985.

In the early 1990s there were only about 20 to 25 echo parakeets (the world's rarest parrot) in Mauritius. Today that figure has risen to about 40 but there needs to be 500 before it can be considered safe from extinction.

Mauritius' flora is also classified as endangered. Today, indigenous forests make up 3% of the island, with only 1% in good condition.

Rodrigues Island has three endangered species: the fruit bat, fody and warbler. The flora has also taken a pounding, with man destroying all original plant groups in almost three centuries.

Justin Flynn

---

a project to protect wild parakeets and boost their numbers through captive breeding.

The pink pigeon, the largest of all the pigeons and doves found on Mauritius, is another highly endangered species. Impediments to progress include poor nesting results due to predation from monkeys and rats, and what one might term a public relations problem – released birds ending up in local casseroles.

The native songbirds of Mauritius, such as the Mauritius cuckoo-shrike, Mauritius black bulbul, Mascarene paradise flycatcher, Mauritius fody, and Mauritius olive white-eye are also threatened. Many of these species are already down to a couple of hundred birds.

The predominant species include many introduced songbirds, such as the little red Madagascar fody, the Indian mynah with yellow beak and feet which make it look like it's just stepped out of a cartoon, the village weaver, and the most common bird on Mauritius – the red-whiskered bulbul.

National Parks
Since 1988, several international organisations have been working with the government to set up national parks in Mauritius. Given the fact that the island now possesses less than 1% of intact, original forest, it is clear why the establishment of this national park commands the highest priority.

The largest reserve is the Black River Gorges National Park, in the south-west of the island. It covers some 3600 hectares and there are plans for further expansion.

Other nature reserves in Mauritius include Le Pouce, Île Ronde, Île aux Serpents, Île aux Aigrettes and Bois Sec (near Grand Bassin).

Île Cocos and Île aux Sables (small islands off Rodrigues), are home to a large bird population (for further details, see the Rodrigues & the Outer Islands chapter).

Several maps of Mauritius show proposed 'nature reserves' which have not yet been officially delineated. Visitor access is (or will be) restricted in many of these reserves, most of which are tiny in size, since they enclose the last vestiges of rare species which are highly sensitive to disturbance.

GOVERNMENT & POLITICS
Mauritius became a republic in March 1992 and the role of the former governor general was changed to that of a president. The National Assembly consists of the speaker, elected and additional members. The Cabinet has about 25 ministers, including the prime minister. General elections are usually held every five years.

ECONOMY

Despite its colourful politics, isolation and population problems, Mauritius achieved a minor economic miracle in the 1980s. Unemployment is still minimal, and the rate of inflation has been dramatically reduced from 42% in 1980 to around 10% at the time of writing. Exports have been steadily increasing over the past few years.

The Export Processing Zone (EPZ), often described as the 'powerhouse of the Mauritian economy', was set up in 1970 to diversify the economy, which had become too dependent on the sugar industry. Today, there are approximately 600 export-oriented companies with more than 100,000 employees.

Sugar

Until recently, the Mauritian economy could be summed up in one word – sugar. It represented more than 90% of exports, covered most of the fertile land in the country and employed most of the people. Now, because of full employment, there is somewhat of a shortage of labour.

The state of the nation depended solely on the sugar harvest and sales. Every so often, a bad cyclone would decimate the cane crop or a sharp drop in sugar prices would have bitter consequences.

A big sugar plantation ranges from 250ha to 1000ha; a small one starts at 10ha. A cane field is productive for between five and 10 years before it must be cleared and replanted. The cane work is mostly seasonal. The harvest is between June and September; all the cane-cutting is done by hand.

In many towns or villages you will see a SILWF building. This is the Sugar Industry Labour Welfare Fund centre, which acts as health clinic, family planning institute, and provides other social services. Health treatment is free, but there are no welfare payouts. Schemes are being considered to introduce mechanisation without causing unemployment.

Other Crops

Since independence, the government has tried to wean the economy away from its dependence on sugar by introducing and encouraging other crops and industries.

Tea, although cultivated since the first settlements, has become the second crop to sugar. It is grown mostly around Curepipe on the central plateau and is used in blending. Tobacco, potatoes, tomatoes, corn and fruit are also being encouraged as alternative crops. The export of fruit and vegetables is still modest.

Industries

Although surrounded by thousands of km of ocean, the Mauritian fishing industry has never been developed on a large scale. It remains primarily the domain of Créoles, leaving room for expansion. A fair amount of fish is imported from the Seychelles to satisfy local demand.

The real successes since the early 1970s have been the development of knitwear, textiles, footwear manufacturing and tourism. Pierre Cardin, Lacoste, Calvin Klein, Marks & Spencer and other famous brands are manufactured in Mauritius. There are also lots of cheap imitations of noted designer labels.

Today, clothing is one of Mauritius' major exports. The amount of foreign investment in the industry has been remarkable. Hong Kong has supplied almost all the foreign investment in textiles. Mauritius now ranks as one of the largest exporters of woollen knitwear in the world. However, the rise of this industry has given the island some major pollution problems.

Tourism

Most of the 390,000 or so yearly visitors to Mauritius come from France and nearby Réunion. South Africans and Germans are the next most frequent visitors, followed by Italians, British and Malagasy. Australia and Japan are expanding markets. Most tourists stay on the island for an average of two weeks.

Tourism is a major revenue earner, which accounts for the ever-increasing number of hotels, apartments, guesthouses, restaurants and water activities.

There are numerous upmarket and budget

hotels, with new ones constantly springing up. In addition, several side industries supporting tourism have taken off – most notably model-boat building (see Things to Buy in the Mauritius Facts for the Visitor chapter).

POPULATION & PEOPLE

Mauritius has an estimated population of 1.1 million. With around 600 people per square km, it has one of the greatest population densities in the world.

Well over half the people are Hindus (both Tamil and non-Tamil), and approximately another 180,000 are Muslims; both these segments of the population are descended from the labourers who were brought to the island to work the cane fields. Only a small percentage of the 30,000 Chinese or Sino-Mauritians came to the country as indentured labourers, most arrived as self-employed entrepreneurs. The remaining population are mainly Créoles, descendants of African slaves, and the ever-diminishing Franco-Mauritians, the original European settlers of the island.

Mauritius is often cited as an example of racial and religious harmony, and compared to most other countries it is. On the surface, there are few signs of intimidation or conflict. However, racial divisions are still apparent and adhered to, more so than in the Seychelles or Réunion. There is little intermarriage or social mixing between the racial communities.

Because Hindus are a majority and Mauritius is a democracy, the Indians always win control at the elections.

The Franco-Mauritians, who make up about 2% of the population, often have wealth as a buffer. Generally, they live up on the cooler heights around Curepipe and have holiday homes on the coast. Since they own the sugar mills and run other big businesses, they can afford to live well in Mauritius or migrate to South Africa and France, as many did after independence.

The Chinese are involved mostly in commerce. Most villages have one or two Chinese stores and there is a large Chinese quarter in Port Louis.

Another small group you might come across are the Chagos islanders, the *ilois* as they are called in Mauritius. As inhabitants of the Chagos Islands of the British Indian Ocean Territory, they were evicted from their homes and resettled in Mauritius between 1965 and 1973 by the UK, when Diego García was leased to the Americans as a military base (see the Rodrigues & the Outer Islands chapter). The British paid UK£1.25 million in compensation directly to the Ilois in 1979, and moved them into housing estates in the northern districts of Port Louis.

The Mauritian government has adopted their cause and is seeking their repatriation to the Chagos Islands, as well as the removal of the US forces.

EDUCATION

The government provides free education at both primary and secondary level. Further training is provided at special schools, technical institutes, handicraft training centres, and teacher training centres.

Several thousand students attend the University of Mauritius at Le Réduit. The Mahatma Gandhi Institute in Moka was established in 1970 to preserve and promote Indian heritage. It offers secondary and tertiary education, as well as courses for younger children (for further details see the boxed text in the Central Mauritius chapter).

ARTS
Dance

If you were to pick one art form to represent Mauritius, it would be the Créole *séga*. It was through this dance that the African slaves would let down their hair at the end of a hard day in the cane fields. Couples danced the séga around campfires on the beach to the accompaniment of drums.

Because of the sand there could be no fancy footwork. So today, when dancing the séga, the feet never leave the ground and must shuffle back and forth. The rest of the body makes up for it and the result, when the fire is hot, can be extremely erotic. In the rhythm and beat of séga, you can see or hear connections with the Latin American salsa,

Delicious Mauritius

SARINA SINGH

One of the joys of travelling in Mauritius is the magnificent variety of cuisines on offer. The predominant cuisines on the island are Créole, European, Chinese and Indian. Some restaurants specialise in one particular cuisine, while others offer the whole bang lot. You'll find that most places, no matter how cheap or expensive, offer seafood as the speciality – prepared in innovative and mouth-watering ways. However, the range of fish in Mauritius is not as large or varied as in the Seychelles.

While in Mauritius, you should sample Créole food. Traditionally, Créole cooking is fairly basic fare, propped up with mountains of rice and designed to fill the belly rather than excite the tastebuds. However, many restaurants have made creative additions to jazz up old recipes. At its best, Créole food is spiced up French cuisine that depends almost entirely on the sauce. It looks exciting and exotic in the tourist-oriented cookbooks, but you'll only really come close to this at the best hotels and restaurants.

Mauritian Créole cooking is best appreciated in the home; an invitation won't be long in coming once you have made friends with a Mauritian. Common dishes are *rougaille*, a Mediterranean-type dish based on tomatoes, onions and garlic, which can contain any kind of meat or fish; *daube*, a Mediterranean type of octopus stew; and chicken curry.

'Mauritian' cuisine is essentially a blend of different cuisines – reflecting an explosion of diverse culinary styles, adapted in a way which makes the most of

SARINA SINGH

the island's natural resources (especially seafood). Main dishes tend to be dominated by meat or seafood, with vegetables as a side dish. At a 'Mauritian' buffet, you'll usually find elements of Indian, Créole, Chinese and French food, prepared according to individual chef's whims. For example, a 'Mauritian' buffet may offer a Muslim biryani, Indian chicken curry, Chinese pork dish, Créole roast beef and French-style vegetables. The presentation of food also often represents a combination of cultures – such as Indian pickles served in a small Chinese porcelain dish, accompanying a traditional Créole curry. Boiled rice forms the base of most Mauritian meals.

Box: The blending of different cuisines is well illustrated in **octopus masalé**. *The main focus of the dish is Créole-style boiled octopus, which is complemented with Indian-style lentils, Chinese-style spinach and plain boiled rice.*

Above Left: Seafood dominates many Mauritian dishes and is prepared in a tantalising range of ways. **Poisson à la Créole** *comprises fried fish smothered in a rich tomato sauce – flavoured with garlic, ginger and a variety of fragrant spices. It's served with a cabbage and carrot pickle which has been marinated in saffron and mustard sauce.*

Left: The tasty Mauritian speciality, **Chicken and shrimp curry** *is sometimes featured as a highlight on menus in the more upmarket hotels and restaurants. It's a grilled prawn topped with a mild chicken and coriander curry, accompanied by a bed of boiled rice, crisp papadam and refreshing tomato chutney.*

SARINA SINGH

Maha Shivaratri

This celebration occurs over three days in February/March and is the largest and most important Hindu festival held outside India. One of the days over which it is held is a public holiday.

Most of the island's Hindu population make the pilgrimage to the holy volcanic lake, Grand Bassin (see description in the West Coast chapter) in honour of Lord Shiva. Many pilgrims, dressed in white, start walking in groups from their village a day or two beforehand, depending on how far they have to travel. They carry a *kanvar*, a light wooden frame or arch decorated with paper flowers. The majority of pilgrims, however, arrive in buses for a day trip. A constant stream of contract buses leaves from Bonne Terre (between Quatre Bornes and Vacoas). The queues are long but move quite quickly.

At the lake, some pilgrims perform a *puja* by making food sacrifices in the water or at various shrines, others bathe, and many take sacred water home. Events are much the same as those which take place on the banks of the Ganges in India.

On the return journey from the lake, the pilgrims who are walking or riding are given fruit and drinks by people in the villages they pass through.

Above Right: Hindus of all ages and various social backgrounds gather at the Maha Shivaratri festival to pay homage to Lord Shiva.

Below Right: The festival brings the entire family together to celebrate.

the Caribbean calypso, and the African origins of the people.

Séga parties spontaneously combusting on the beaches are a thing of the past and you must now go to the big luxury hotels to see a well-choreographed show. There is about one a week and you can usually slip in to watch if you are not a resident.

Smaller hotels also endeavour to put on a 'cultural show'. But the séga groups tend to be amateurs going through the motions for a bit of extra money. There's nothing worse than a lifeless séga – especially when the participants feel obliged to ask you to join in.

Séga variations to Créole pop music are reasonably popular in the discos and are sometimes more authentic than the hotel displays.

Music

Western pop music is popular and has given rise to Michael Jackson lookalikes in some hotel cabarets. But there are a number of good Créole groups and singers, such as Roger Clency and Jean Claude-Monique. For a séga group with politically radical lyrics, try Larmoni. Ras Natty Baby and Les Natty Rebels is perhaps the island's top group for seggae, a musical style which blends reggae and séga.

Ti-Frère, the most popular séga singer in the country, died in 1992. He is credited with reviving séga during the early 1950s, and his song 'Anita' has become a classic. In 1991, Radio France Internationale recorded a special Ti-Frère CD – highly recommended for séga fans.

Literature

Mauritius' most famous contribution to world literature to date – one which has become entangled in the island's history – is the romantic novel *Paul et Virginie* by Bernardin de St Pierre, which was first published in 1788. The French author based the love story on incidents which happened during the wreck of the *St Géran* off Ile d'Ambre, on 18 August 1744. Editions de L'Océan Indien (EOI) has published an English paperback

edition of the novel, translated by Raymond Hein. Read it for interest's sake rather than pleasure. A French TV adaptation of the novel also sank by all accounts.

Those who want to read a 20th century Mauritian novel should read something by the well-known Mauritian author, Malcom de Chazal, whose most famous work is probably *Petrusmok* (1951). Other works written by him include *Sens Plastique* (1948), *Sens Magique* (1956), *Poèmes* (1959) and *Sens Unique* (1974). Malcom de Chazal was known as quite a character. The Swedish author, Bengt Sjögren, met the author and later described him as an eccentric recluse who sat writing all day at the Hotel National in Port Louis, except for the walk that he took by the seaside every morning to cogitate and watch the mighty ocean. However, according to the locals, it was not de Chazal who contemplated the sea, it was the sea that contemplated him.

Other writers well known in Mauritius are Robert Edward Hart, Edouard Maunick, the Masson brothers (Loys & André) and Léoville L'Homme. The Mauritian humourist, Yvan Lagesse, has written a wry assessment of Mauritian life in *Comment vivre à l'île Maurice en 25 leçons* (How to live in Mauritius in 25 lessons).

Since the 1970s, literature has also been published in Créole. Some examples are *Quand Montagne Prend Difé* by René Asgarally; *La Mare Mo Mémoire* (poems) by Ramesh Ramdoyal; and *La Fimé da Lizié* by Dev Virahsawmy.

Mark Twain, Joseph Conrad and Charles Baudelaire all visited the island. Joseph Conrad set a short story, *A Smile of Fortune*, in Mauritius, if you care to look for it in a collection of his works. His novel, *Twixt Land and Sea*, is based on a love story in Port Louis. Baudelaire's first poem, *A une Dame Créole*, was written in Pamplemousses.

Another adventure based around naval history is Patrick O'Brian's *The Mauritius Command*, about a Napoleonic swashbuckler. For more details about recommended titles, see Books in the Mauritius Facts for the Visitor chapter.

MAURITIUS

Sculpture & Painting

Unlike in the Seychelles, the works of Mauritius' artists are not widely displayed or available, which is a shame considering some of the beautiful landscapes you'd like to see painted.

There are plenty of 18th and 19th century prints of such scenes, but the originals must have gone back to France and Britain years ago. For contemporary paintings and sculpture, there is the Max Boullé Gallery at Rose Hill, and the Port Louis Art Gallery.

The Naval Museum in Mahébourg has a selection of lithographs depicting local views and scenes from Bernardin de St Pierre's novel, *Paul et Virginie*. The statue of the famous couple in the small park outside Curepipe town hall and one of King Edward VII in the Champ de Mars, Port Louis, were both created by Mauritius' best known sculptor, Prosper d'Epinay.

SOCIETY & CONDUCT

The island's Indian community maintains many aspects of its culture. The Mahatma Gandhi Institute in Moka was established in 1970 to actively preserve and promote Indian heritage (for more information see the Mahatma Gandhi Institute boxed text in the Central Mauritius chapter).

Dos & Don'ts

Although beachwear is fine for the beaches, you may cause offence or invite pestering if you dress skimpily elsewhere. One traveller has commented that his Mauritian friends did not consider someone stripped to the waist or wearing shorts should be taken seriously; in fact, they used the 'foo-soo-koor' rule to judge such persons. According to this rule, such a person appearing in public must be either *fou* (mad), *saoul* (drunk) or *dans son cour* (inside a personal garden or backyard). Nude bathing is forbidden on Mauritius.

Mauritius has a number of mosques and temples – if you wish to visit, do so with respect (see Society & Conduct in the Facts about the Region chapter at the beginning of this book).

RELIGION

Like India, Hinduism is the main religion on Mauritius. Hinduism is one of the oldest extant religions, with roots extending back to beyond 1000 BC. Today, there are more than 150 temples in Mauritius. After Hindus, the greater part of the population is made up of Catholics, and then Muslims. Protestants constitute only a small proportion of the population. Mosques, churches and Hindu temples can be found within a stone's throw of each other in many parts of Mauritius.

The Sino-Mauritians are less conspicuous in their worship. Many have turned to Roman Catholicism, but there are a few pagodas and Buddhist temples in Port Louis.

The Catholic church still seems to be active in Mauritius despite the comparatively low number of Christians. Many Christians pray at the shrine of Père Laval, in the Port Louis suburb of Ste-Croix. Père Jacques Laval (1803-64), a French missionary, is said to have converted more than 67,000 people to Christianity during his 23 years in Mauritius. His shrine is described in the Port Louis chapter.

LANGUAGE

It is said that when Mauritians have a community meeting, the people speak Créole, take minutes in English and discuss the outcome with government officials in French.

The official languages are English and French. English is used mainly in government and business literature. French is the spoken language in educated and cultural circles, and is used in newspapers and magazines. You'll probably find that most people will first speak to you in French and only switch to English once they realise you don't understand a word they are saying.

Créole, the common bond, derives from French and has similarities with the Créole spoken elsewhere. Ironically, the Mauritian and the Seychelles Créoles are more comprehensible to French people than the patois of Réunion, a thoroughly French department. Most Indo-Mauritians speak Bhojpuri, derived from a Bihari dialect of Hindi.

French

French is widely spoken and understood on Mauritius and in most parts of the Indian Ocean. Most people also speak English, so non-French speakers will not be left incommunicado. However, it's not a bad idea to pick up Lonely Planet's *French phrasebook*, especially if you intend to visit Réunion as well.

For a list of useful words and phrases, see Language in the Facts about the Region chapter at the beginning of this book.

Créole

There are major differences between the pronunciation and usage of Créole and standard French. If you don't speak French in the first place, you're doubly disadvantaged. Editions de L'Océan Indien (EOI) book centres on Mauritius sell publications, such as *Parlez Créole (Guide Pratique pour Touristes)/Speak Créole (A Tourist Guide)*, *English-Créole Phrasebook*, and *Diksonyer Kreol/Anglé (Prototype Mauritian Créole/English Dictionary)*. For more details see Books in the Mauritius Facts for the Visitor chapter.

Créole is a vibrant, direct language. For starters, you might want to try the following Créole phrases:

How are you?	*Ki manière?*
Fine, thanks.	*Mon byen, mersi.*
I don't understand.	*Mo pas comprend.*
OK.	*Correc.*
Not OK.	*Pas correc.*
he, she, it	*li*

Do you have...?	*Ou éna...?*
I'd like...	*Mo oulé...*
I'm thirsty.	*Mo soif.*
Phoenix beer	*la bière zarnier*
(literally 'spider beer' – the label looks like one)	
Cheers!	*Tapeta!*
Great!	*Formidabe!*

Language Trends

Mikael Parkvall, a Swedish traveller with an interest in language research, supplied the following information on language trends in Mauritius:

Asian languages are diminishing. English is fairly stable, whereas Créole becomes more and more popular all the time. The number of francophones has also declined, mostly due to emigration to South Africa. The major languages spoken on Mauritius (in order of popularity) include Créole, Bhojpuri, French, Tamil, Urdu, Telugu, Marathi, Hakka, English, Gujarati, Mandarin and Cantonese. Languages spoken by less than 100 speakers include Polish (!), Punjabi, Sindhi, Bacha, Italian, German and Russian.

It is a myth that Hindi is spoken in Mauritius. Those who, according to the census, speak either Hindi or Bhojpuri are all Bhojpuri speakers. Bhojpuri is a sort of Créole Hindi, and the relationship between these two languages is similar to that between French and Créole, the difference being that whereas French is spoken by at least some Mauritians, Hindi is spoken by none. Bhojpuri lacks prestige, and for all official purposes – as, for example, is the case with the Mauritius Broadcasting Corporation – Hindi is used. Although Bhojpuri is also spoken in India, this Indian version is unintelligible to Mauritians, partly due to the massive influence of French and Créole on Mauritian Bhojpuri. *All* the numerals, for example, are in French.

MAURITIUS

Facts for the Visitor

PLANNING

When To Go

Apart from the Christmas and New Year period, Mauritius doesn't really have high and low seasons. The situation varies throughout the year and is more dependent on outside factors, such as the Réunion holiday period, than on the weather. Consequently, factors other than the climate could determine the best time to visit.

Sporting and leisure considerations may play a part in when you choose to visit. December to March is best for diving, as the water is said to be clearer; June to August is best for surfing along the south coast; and October to March is best for big-game fishing, when the large predators feed closer to shore.

Maps

The map of Mauritius published by the French mapping agency, Institut Géographique Nationale (IGN), is one of the most detailed maps on the market and costs Rs 175. Also very good is the Globetrotter travel map for Rs 155. Globetrotter provides a user-friendly map of the island and also has a number of excellent little insets of various regions, including Port Louis, Curepipe, the east/north/west coasts, Rodrigues Island and Sir Seewoosagur Ramgoolam Botanical Gardens at Pamplemousses. MacMillan has published a map of Mauritius, including a small inset for Rodrigues Island and Port Louis, which is adequate for orientation, but less detailed than the IGN map. It costs Rs 100. Editions de L'Océan Indien (EOI) has published a free-of-charge map booklet with insets of Mauritius, Port Louis, Quatre Bornes, Curepipe, Vacoas, Grand Baie, Rose Hill, the south/west coasts and Rodrigues Island. There are also a few more basic and cheaper maps available. You can pick up maps at most bookshops and supermarkets.

Hikers requiring more detailed information should contact the Ministry for Rodrigues (☎ 2088472; fax 2126329) at the Fon Sing building, 5th floor, Edith Cavell St, Port Louis, or visit the Ministry's office (☎ 8311590) in Port Mathurin, Rodrigues.

The Mauritius Tourism Promotion Authority (☎ 2011703; fax 2125142), on the ground floor of the Emmanuel Anquetil building on Sir Seewoosagur Ramgoolam St in Port Louis, supplies basic maps of the island and town plans of Curepipe and Port Louis in its brochures.

What to Bring

For details, see What to Bring in the Regional Facts for the Visitor chapter at the beginning of this book.

HIGHLIGHTS

For most visitors, the highlight of Mauritius is obviously the beaches. The following suggestions are by no means exhaustive, but may provide indications of less obvious attractions:

Beaches

Pointe aux Roches (surf viewing); Flic en Flac (swimming); Belle Mare (swimming).

Historical Settings & Museums

Eureka House (near Moka); Naval Museum (Mahébourg).

Scenery

Black River Gorges National Park; Domaine du Chasseur; Chamarel Falls; the mellow island of Rodrigues (560km to the north-east of Mauritius).

Markets

Port Louis market.

Gardens

Sir Seewoosagur Ramgoolam Botanical Gardens (Pamplemousses).

TOURIST OFFICES
Local Tourist Offices

Independent travellers in Mauritius are not common. This probably accounts for the dearth of tourist offices on the island. You'll find most shopkeepers, bus drivers, police officers, bar staff etc very helpful without making a fuss.

The Mauritius Tourism Promotion Authority (☎ 2011703; fax 2125142) in Port Louis provides basic tourist information and has a handful of promotional literature.

At SSR airport, the Mauritius Chamber of Commerce & Industry (MCCI) operates a free accommodation information service (☎ 6374100).

Air Mauritius also seeks to promote tourism, but has only limited information at local and overseas offices. You'll probably find that the staff are too busy to devote much time to tourists – unless it's got something to do with an airline booking, of course.

Tourist Offices Abroad

Mauritius Tourism offices around the world include:

France
   Bureau d'Information de l'Île Maurice, 120 Avenue Charles de Gaulle, 92200 Neuilly Cedex (☎ 01 46 40 37 47; fax 01 46 40 11 23)
Germany
   Mauritius Informationsbüro, Postfach 101846, 60018 Frankfurt (☎ (06171) 980354; fax 980652)
Hong Kong
   Mauritius Tourist Information Bureau, Suite A2, 1st floor, Eton building, 288 Des Voeux Road Central (☎ (0852) 2851 1036; fax 2805 2416)
Italy
   Ufficio del Turismo delle Isole Mauritius, BMK SAS Publiche Relazioni, Foro Buonaparte 46, 20121 Milan (☎ (02) 865984)
Japan
   Mauritius Tourist Information Bureau, Ginza Stork building 5F, 1-22-1 Ginza, Chuo-Ku, Tokyo 104 (☎ (03) 5250 0175; fax 5250 1076)
Switzerland
   Mauritius Tourist Information Service, Kirchenweg 5, CH-8032 Zurich (☎ (01) 383 8788; fax 383 5124)
UK
   32/33 Elvaston Place, London SW7 5NW (☎ (0171) 584 3666; fax 225 1135)

USA
   Mauritius Tourist Information Service, 15 Penn Plaza, 415 Seventh Ave, New York, NY 10001 (☎ (212) 239 8367)

VISAS & DOCUMENTS
Visas

You don't need a visa to enter Mauritius if you are a citizen of the UK, Ireland, Australia, USA, Canada, Japan, New Zealand, the European Union (EU) and a number of other countries. Initial entry is granted for a maximum of three months.

Visa Extensions Extensions for a further three months as a tourist are available. To apply for an extension, you must go to the Passport & Immigration Office (☎ 2081212; fax 2122398), Line Barracks (near the Victoria Square bus station) in Port Louis.

Applications must be submitted with one form, two passport-size photos, your passport, an onward ticket and proof of finances. Two letters – one by the applicant explaining why he or she wants to stay longer and one by a local 'sponsor' (it can be someone providing accommodation) – may also be necessary. Some travellers claim they were able to extend their visa without a 'sponsor's' letter.

Providing you can satisfy these demands there should be no further problems, but since the police are responsible for passport control and quite a few Indian visitors overstay their entry permits, there are 'get tough' periods.

Visas for Réunion, Madagascar & India

It's best to apply for any visa in your own country, as the process is usually quicker and sometimes cheaper. Most visa applications require at least two passport photos, so have some handy.

If you apply for a visa for Réunion in Mauritius, the process takes up to three weeks and costs Rs 750 (US$38). The visa section of the French embassy is open Monday, Wednesday and Friday from 9 to 11 am. For further details about visa requirements for Réunion, see the Réunion Facts for the Visitor chapter.

MAURITIUS

The Madagascar embassy is open Monday to Friday from 9 am to 4 pm. Visas take around three days to process. Contact the embassy for further details (for its address see Foreign Embassies in Mauritius below).

In Mauritius, the Indian embassy's visa section is open Monday to Friday from 9.30 am to noon. A visa (valid for one month) costs Rs 300 (US$15) and takes around four days to process.

Onward Ticket

You must have an air ticket out of the country, which you'll be asked to show at customs (so have it handy). If you do not have an onward ticket, you could be invited to buy one, on the spot, from Air Mauritius.

Immigration authorities will probably also ask you to supply the name of your intended accommodation in Mauritius – if you have not booked anything, just have a name in your head and hope it hasn't closed down! You could even be asked to show proof of sufficient finances on arrival.

Travel Insurance

Travellers to Mauritius are advised to carry medical/travel insurance. For more details, see Travel Insurance in the Regional Facts for the Visitor chapter at the beginning of this book.

EMBASSIES
Mauritian Embassies Abroad

Australia
    2 Beale Crescent, Deakin, Canberra, ACT 2600 (☎ (06) 282 4436; fax 282 3235)
Belgium
    68 Rue des Bollandistes, Etterbrek, 1040 Brussels (☎ (02) 733 9988; fax 734 4021)
Egypt
    No 5, 26th of July St, Lebanon Square, Mohandessine, Cairo (☎ (202) 3470929; fax 3452425)
France
    127 Rue de Tocqueville, 75017 Paris (☎ 01 42 27 30 19; fax 01 40 53 02 91)
India
    5 Kautilya Marg, Chanakyapuri, New Delhi 110021 (☎ (011) 301 1112/3; fax 301 9925)
Madagascar
    Route Circulaire, Anjanahary BP 6040, Antananarivo 101 (☎ (02) 32157; fax 21939)

Malaysia
    Suite ABC, 14th floor, Bangunan Angkasa Raya, Jalan Ampangh, 50450 Kuala Lumpur (☎ (603) 2411870; fax 2415115)
Pakistan
    House No 27, Street No 26, Sector F-6/2, Islamabad (☎ (051) 210145; fax 210076)
South Africa
    1163 Pretorius St, Hatfield, Pretoria (☎ (012) 342 1283; fax 342 1286)
UK
    32/33 Elvaston Place, London SW7 5NW (☎ (0171) 581 0294/5; fax 823 8437)
USA
    Suite 441, 4301 Connecticut Ave NW, Washington DC 20008 (☎ (202) 244 1491; fax 244 492)

Foreign Embassies in Mauritius

Rogers House, situated at 5 President John Kennedy St, Port Louis, is home to many of the airlines and several of the diplomatic missions in Mauritius.

The building contains the US embassy (☎ 2082347) and the Australian High Commission (☎ 2081700), which also represents Australian interests in the Seychelles, Madagascar and the Comoros. Other countries with diplomatic representation in Mauritius include:

Canada
    18 Jules Koenig St, Port Louis (☎ 2080821)
France
    14 St George St, Port Louis (☎ 2084103)
India
    LIC building, 6th floor, Port Louis (☎ 2083775)
Madagascar
    Queen Mary Ave, Floreal (☎ 6973476)
UK
    Les Cascades Building, Edith Cavell St, Port Louis (☎ 2111361)

CUSTOMS

Airline passengers aged 16 years and over may import duty-free goods: 250 cigarettes or 250g of tobacco; 1L of spirits; 2L of wine, ale or beer; 250ml of eau de toilette; and a quantity of perfume not exceeding 10 centilitres.

Visitors may import Mauritian currency notes up to a maximum of Rs 700, and take out Rs 350. Duty-free items must be bought with foreign currency.

MAURITIUS

If you bring in plants or plant material you must have obtained a plant permit from the Ministry of Agriculture (☎ 2127931 or 6373194). An import permit (from the same ministry) and a sanitary certificate of country of origin are required for all imported animals and animal material.

The Customs & Excise Department (☎ 2409702; fax 2400434) is in the IKS building, Farquhar St, Port Louis.

MONEY
Costs

Along with Madagascar, Mauritius is among the cheapest places in the Indian Ocean for visitors. However, the last few years have seen an increase in prices for visitors, and there are official aspirations to turn the island into a luxury destination for affluent tourists. Thankfully that has not happened, which means travellers are able to keep costs down by staying in budget accommodation, such as guesthouses and self-catering apartments.

The tourist bodies concentrate on promoting big, fancy beach hotels and tours that cater for the exclusive jet set, the honeymooners and other once-in-a-lifetime sprees, leaving the other end of the market to find its own level.

Independent tourist service operators that cater for individual travellers and day or weekend visitors are concentrated at Grand Baie, Peréybère and Flic en Flac. Unlike in the Seychelles and Réunion, there are no set standards or regulations to follow. Private enterprise is given a free hand. While this means that prices are competitive, it can also mean that service is variable. Just make sure you know exactly what you are getting for your money before paying.

Costs in the lower range of the market have remained reasonably low for several years. The beauty is, the longer you stay in one place, the cheaper the rate should be for the room or apartment – and it is possible to see all of Mauritius by basing yourself in one place. In terms of transport, to save money you should travel by bus as taxis can gobble up your precious rupees. Try to limit yourself to using a taxi only when travelling to/from

the airport – split the cost by sharing with other people.

There are no private beaches in Mauritius, so you are free to share the good hotel beaches and, at a reasonable cost in some cases, water-sports facilities.

Please note that prices given in this book for accommodation, restaurants and some other services may have risen by about 10% to 15% since the time of writing.

Currency

The Mauritian unit of currency is the rupee (Rs), which is divided into 100 cents (c). There are coins of 5, 10, 20, 25 and 50 cents, and Rs 1 and 5. The bank note denominations are 10, 50, 100, 200, 500 and 1000 rupees. There is no problem tendering old and battered notes.

Currency Exchange

Australia	A$1	=	Rs 16.01
Britain	UK£	=	Rs 33.00
France	FF1	=	Rs 3.41
Germany	DM1	=	Rs 12.05
Japan	¥100	=	Rs 19.00
Singapore	S$1	=	Rs 16.00
USA	US$1	=	Rs 20.00

Changing Money

All rates of exchange are set by the government and there is no difference from bank to bank. Banks charge a transaction fee of Rs 50 for one to 10 travellers cheques and Rs 5 for each additional cheque. Don't forget to take along your passport when changing money. And make sure you hang onto the encashment form, which will have to be presented if you want to change Mauritian rupees back into foreign currency. There is no black market in Mauritius.

Travellers cheques bring a better rate than cash, and there are no problems with the major currencies. Personal cheques on the Eurocheque system can also be cashed, but there is a hefty commission. Avoid changing money at hotels, as many charge an additional service commission.

There are increasing numbers of foreign-exchange counters around the island and the

MAURITIUS

banks at SSR airport are open for the arrival and departure of international flights.

Banking hours are from 9.15 am to 3.15 pm on weekdays, 9.15 to 11.15 am on Saturdays.

No restrictions apply on the amount of foreign currency you can bring in and out of the country, providing you declare it and the amount taken out does not exceed the amount brought in.

Credit Cards

Most major credit cards (such as Visa, MasterCard and American Express) are widely accepted. Cash advances on credit cards are available from most of the major banks, such as the Mauritius Commercial Bank, Barclays Bank, State Commercial Bank and the Shanghai Banking Corporation.

Tipping & Bargaining

Tipping is not compulsory. In any case, most of the upmarket hotels and restaurants will include a charge on the bill for government tax and service. In budget hotels and restaurants it's not necessary to tip, although there's nothing to stop you giving something if the service was particularly good. In major tourist areas, such as Grand Baie, there's an annoying tendency for some waiters (usually those whose service is least appreciated) to try to automatically extract tips, eg by not returning change. If you use the services of an airport porter, make sure you give a small tip (around Rs 10).

Bargaining is very much part of life on Mauritius. Daily accommodation rates at most places should drop by around 20% to 30% if you stay for more than a week, and further discounts are usual for off-season or long-stay occupancy.

Taxi rates should always be negotiated before you hop into the car. For more details, see Taxi in the Mauritius Getting Around chapter. You should ask for a discount on car, motorcycle or bicycle rental if you hire for more than a couple of days.

Consumer Taxes

At most of the cheaper *pensions* or local cafés, there are no service charges or taxes on top of your bill. Restaurants and hotels in the middle to top end of the market add 15% government tax to the bill.

POST & COMMUNICATIONS

The postal service is widespread, efficient and reliable. Even the tiniest village has its own post office. Because of the rare Mauritian Blue stamp, the island is well known within world philatelic circles.

Most post offices are open from 8.15 to 11.15 am and noon to 4 pm on weekdays, 8.15 to 11.45 am on Saturdays. The last 45 minutes before closing are for stamp sales only.

There is a small post office in the departure section of the airport, which has different opening hours for almost every day of the week: Monday from 2.30 to 6 pm; Tuesday, Thursday and Friday from 2 to 6 pm; Wednesday from 2 to 4 pm; Saturday from 3.30 to 6 pm; and Sunday from 4.30 to 6.30 pm.

Postal Rates

Air-mail letters are about Rs 10 to Europe, the USA or Australia. Small/large postcards to most countries cost around Rs 4/9.

Receiving Mail

Most post offices have a reliable poste restante service which is free of charge. The maximum period they hold letters is around three months (if you want to extend this, speak to the postmaster). You must show some identification when collecting mail.

Telephone

In the last few years, the telephone service has been modernised so that most subscribers now have seven-digit numbers and international direct dialling (IDD) facilities. There are still a few hitches and glitches with wrong numbers, but the service has vastly improved.

National Calls The good news is that it is only Rs 1 for a local call anywhere on the island. The bad news is that there are very few public phones and even fewer that work.

First check at the local post office, then go to the police station. They are usually helpful to visitors. Failing that, shopkeepers and garages should let you use their phones for a charge. There are no regional area codes for Mauritius. For directory inquiries call ☎ 90.

International Calls International calls can be made from a private or public phone using IDD. Alternatively, you can use the Overseas Telecommunications Service (OTS) office in Port Louis. Call ☎ 2081036 for inquiries.

The rate for a call to Australia or Europe is around Rs 30 per minute. A call to the USA is about Rs 35 per minute. These rates are reduced by around 25% from noon on Saturday until midnight on Sunday. The international dialling code for Mauritius is ☎ 230.

Some useful international dialling codes are: Australia 61; Comoros 269; France 33; India 91; Italy 39; Madagascar 261; New Zealand 64; Réunion 262; Seychelles 248; South Africa 27; UK 44; and the USA 1. For international directory assistance call ☎ 10090; for international operator assistance call ☎ 10091.

Fax & Telegraph
Hotels have fax machines for guests' use, and charge a small increment on the phone rates. Telex and telegraph services are available at the OTS office in Port Louis.

BOOKS
For coverage of Mauritius' literary works and details of recommended authors, see Literature in the Facts about Mauritius chapter.

History
Without a doubt, *the* historian of Mauritius and the Indian Ocean was Dr Auguste Toussaint, who wrote books on the pirates in general, the Surcouf brothers in particular, and the history of Port Louis – *Port Louis: A Tropical City*. He is best known for *The History of the Indian Ocean*. He died at his Forest Side home in February 1987.

For comparison, there is *A New History of Mauritius* by John Addison & K Hazaree-singh, *The Truth about Mauritius* by Basdeo Bissoondoyal and the *Historical Dictionary of Mauritius* by Lindsay Riviere. For a study of the British presence, you might like to dip into *British Mauritius 1810-1948* by Dayachand Napal.

In *Prisoners in Paradise*, Sheila Ward recounts the lives of five personalities who were imprisoned on Mauritius prior to Independence. The chosen characters cover an interesting historical and political span, including the British explorer Matthew Flinders; the Malagasy Prince, Ratsitatane; Ehelepola, the Kandyan chief from Sri Lanka; Reza Khan Pahlavi, the Shah of Iran; and Dr Stoyanovitch, a former prime minister of Yugoslavia.

For a more detailed account of Flinders, pick up a copy of *In the Grips of the Eagle: Matthew Flinders at Île de France* by Huguette Ly-Tio Fane Pineo.

Another interesting roundup of visitors to the island is *They Came to Mauritius* by Derek Hollingworth. It's out of print, but should be available through libraries.

For detailed information about Indian immigration to Mauritius, there's *Select Documents on Indian Immigration* by Saloni Deerpalsingh & Marina Carter.

Rodrigues
The Island of Rodrigues by Alfred North-Coombes is out of print, but check second-hand bookstores and libraries. If you read French, a very useful publication is *À La Découverte de Rodrigues* by Chantal Moreau.

Tropical Flora & Fauna
For advanced reading on tropical fish, refer to either *A Field Guide to the Coral Reef Fish of the Indian & West Pacific Oceans* by RH Carcasson, or *A Guide To Common Reef Fish of the Western Indian Ocean* by KR Bock. For a look at Mauritian birdlife, you could try *Birds of Mauritius* by Claude Michel. For more reading about plants and animals, there's *Fauna of Mauritius and Associated Flora* by France Staub.

You can read about Mauritian wildlife in

naturalist Gerald Durrell's *Golden Bats & Pink Pigeons*. It's a funny and informative book. Durrell spent lots of time on Île Ronde (Round Island), off the north coast of Mauritius, where the country's only snakes (boas) live. Also recommended is *Last Chance to See* by Douglas Adams & Mark Carwardine. The authors manage to maintain a fine sense of humour while wandering round the globe in search of species faced with imminent extinction. The chapter entitled 'Rare or Medium Rare' deals with Mauritius.

Créole Books

Ledikasyon pu Travayer has reprinted Charles Baissac's 1888 Créole folk tale collection, *Sirandann Sanpek: Zistwar an Créole*, which includes parallel English translations, and has compiled a *Diksyoner Kreol-Anglé (Prototype Mauritian Créole-English Dictionary)*.

Another source is Editions de L'Océan Indien (EOI), a publishing company with several outlets on the island. It distributes several Créole titles, including Charles Baissac's *Le Patois Créole*, Goswami Sewtohul's *Petit Dictionnaire Français Créole* and the popular *Parlez Créole* by James Burty David, Lilette David & Clarel Seenyen.

For more details about Créole language, see Language in the Facts about Mauritius chapter.

Cookery

An enduring title is *A Taste of Mauritius* by Paul Jones & Barry Andrews, which portrays in mouthwatering colours what island cooking could be like. *The Best of Mauritian Cooking* by Barry Andrews, Paul Jones & Gerald Gay, and *Genuine Cuisine of Mauritius* by Guy Félix, are also well worth a look.

Other Books

Robert Marsh's *Mountains of Mauritius: A Climber's Guide* is now out of print, but several travellers have been able to arrange (for a nominal charge) for photocopies to be made by staff at the Carnegie library in Curepipe, where many of the rarer books on Mauritius can be found. This guide is a must for the more adventurous and can provide a unique perspective of the island, away from the beaches and tourist trails. Alexander Ward's *Climbing & Mountain Walking in Mauritius* (out of print) predates Marsh's book and is less comprehensive – a copy is held at the Carnegie library.

If you are interested in colonial and early Créole architecture, there is *Maisons Traditionelles de l'Île Maurice* by Jean-Louis Pagès. It will give you an idea of the best Créole houses in Mauritius.

Travel guides in English include *Visitor's Guide to Mauritius, Rodrigues & Réunion* by Katerina & Eric Roberts and *Guide to Mauritius* by Royston Ellis.

Festivals of Mauritius by Ramesh Ramdoyal is an attractive hardback which provides a description of the various festivals celebrated on the island.

For those interested in political reading, there's *Untold Stories* by Sir Satcam Boolell QC, which has a collection of socio-political essays, or *Parliament in Mauritius* by Hansraj Mathur.

For information about diving and snorkelling, you should get a copy of *The Dive Sites of Mauritius* by Alan Mountain, which is comprehensive and well presented.

Bookshops

There are several bookshops *(librairies)* catering for the large residential area between Curepipe and Port Louis.

The best place to pick up the latest titles is at Book Court at Le Caudan Waterfront complex in Port Louis.

A wide selection of books on Mauritius in French and English is available from Editions de L'Océan Indien (EOI) (☎ 4646761) in Rose Hill. It also has an outlet in Curepipe (☎ 6749065). The UK agent for EOI is Nautilus Publishing Company (☎/fax (0181) 947 1912), PO Box 4100, London SW20 OXN – titles are available by mail order. The EOI agent in France is L'Harmattan (☎ 01 40 46 79 11), 16 Rue des Écoles, 75005 Paris.

Libraries

The Mauritius Institute (☎ 2120639) in Port Louis has a library on the 1st floor behind the Natural History Museum. It is open from 9 am to 4 pm on weekdays (except Wednesday) and on weekends from 9 am to noon. The most amenable is the Carnegie Library in Curepipe.

NEWSPAPERS & MAGAZINES

The main daily papers are *L'Express* and *Le Mauricien*, both in French, with the occasional article in English. Each costs Rs 7. Other newspapers include *Le Quotidien*, *Mauritian Times*, *News on Sunday*, *Le Socialiste*, *The Sun*, *The New Nation*, *La Vie Catholique*, *The Star* and *Revi Lalit*.

Weekly magazines include *Cinq Plus*, *Cinq Plus Dimanche* and *Weekend Scope*, all concentrating on cinematic and political glitterati.

There's a good monthly magazine which is worth picking up if your knowledge of French is good enough. *La Gazette des Îles* contains articles on aspects of Mauritian history and that of other islands in the Indian Ocean. It is a touch heavy for the average visitor, but a boon to students of the relevant subjects.

A limited range of foreign newspapers and magazines is available at some bookshops and at a handful of upmarket hotels.

There are two useful publications produced in the UK. Both have news reports and advertisements. *Mauritius News* is published monthly and can be obtained by contacting Mauritius News (☎ (0171) 703 1071), PO Box 26, London SE17 1EG. *Mauritian International* is published quarterly and is available from Nautilus Publishing Company (☎/fax (0181) 947 1912), PO Box 4100, London SW20 OXN.

RADIO & TV

There are three channels on Mauritian TV. The Mauritius Broadcasting Corporation (MBC) comes on from 7 am until late evening and covers important daily events. Most of the transmission is in French, with some English and Hindi segments. See newspapers for programme schedules.

The alternative is the RFO station beamed across from Réunion. The presentation is slicker and it's all in French. There are also several Pay TV stations.

MBC operates a radio service which broadcasts in French, Créole, Hindi, Chinese and English. You can also tune in to the BBC World Service.

PHOTOGRAPHY

There is a plentiful supply of film at reasonable prices around the island. The best processing outlets are in Port Louis.

The main photographic shops in the centre of Port Louis are: Mimosa (Agfa), which also does passport pictures and photocopying; Kwon Pak Lin (Ilford), opposite Mimosa at the top of Sir William Newton St; Prophoto (Kodak), on Chaussée, opposite the Company Gardens; and Scott & Co (Fuji), further along the same road into Barracks St.

Colour developing and printing can be done in one hour at many places and costs around Rs 25 for processing plus Rs 4.50 per print. Agfa print film costs Rs 69/92 for 24/36 exposures. For slide film, prices are around Rs 180 for Agfa (36 exposures). Slide processing usually takes several days and costs Rs 210 for processing (including mounting).

TIME

Daylight hours last from around 5.30 am to 7 pm in summer, 6 am to 6 pm in winter.

Mauritius time is four hours (three hours during the European summer) ahead of Greenwich Mean Time (GMT) and Universal Time Coordinated (UTC), one hour ahead of Madagascar time and two hours ahead of South African time. So when it is noon in Mauritius it is midnight in San Francisco; 3 am in New York and Toronto; 8 am in London; 6 pm in Sydney or Melbourne; and 8 pm in New Zealand.

ELECTRICITY

The power supply throughout the country is 220V. Continental two-pin plugs are the most common, but you could come across square three-pins. If you need to link up with electricity on the island, play safe and take a travel plug.

Many parts of the island experience the occasional blackout – most hotels/guesthouses have torches or candles, but if you're staying in an apartment it's not a bad idea to buy a candle or two.

LAUNDRY

Laundry services are available at most guesthouses, bungalows and hotels. The upmarket hotels naturally incur a higher charge than the more modest places. Quite a few hotels/guesthouses/apartments provide an iron for their guests' use (free of charge). In the larger towns such as Port Louis and Curepipe, there are a number of public self-service laundries which provide washing machines and dryers for a reasonable charge.

WEIGHTS & MEASURES

The metric system has taken over from British standards, but you may see the occasional signpost in miles. For a conversion chart, see the inside back cover of this book.

HEALTH

For a rundown of possible health problems you may encounter in Mauritius, see Health in the Regional Facts for the Visitor chapter.

Hospitals & Clinics in Mauritius

Should you get ill, the public health service is free to residents and visitors alike, but there may be a long wait for a consultation. The main hospitals are the Jeetoo Hospital (☎ 2123201), Volcy Pougnet St, Port Louis; the Princess Margaret Orthopaedic Hospital (☎ 4253031) in Candos; the Sir Seewoosagur Ramgoolam National Hospital (☎ 2434661) at Pamplemousses; and the Jawaharlal Nehru Hospital (☎ 6276181) at Rose Belle. The Moka Eye Hospital (☎ 4334015) is in Moka.

A better, but more expensive alternative, is a private clinic. Among those which have been recommended are the Clinique Darné (☎ 6862307) in Floreal; the Clinique Mauricienne (☎ 4543061), between the university and the governor's residence in Le

Réduit; and Med Point Clinic (☎ 4267777 or 4268888), on Sayed Hossen Rd in Phoenix.

DANGERS & ANNOYANCES
Emergency Phone Numbers

For the police or ambulance, call ☎ 999 and ask to be connected with the required service. Call ☎ 995 for fire.

Stolen Travellers Cheques

For information on what to do if your travellers cheques are stolen/lost, see Dangers & Annoyances in the Regional Facts for the Visitor chapter.

Security

For information on security in Mauritius, see Dangers & Annoyances in the Regional Facts for the Visitor chapter.

Drugs

Drug scandals involving politicians rocked all levels of Mauritian society some years back, so it would not be wise to declare or pursue an interest. Drugs are illegal and there are stiff penalties for offenders.

Exclusion from Beaches

There have been complaints from several travellers about nonresidents being discouraged from entering hotel beach areas. The law is quite clear that there are no private beaches, but some hotels fence in land adjoining the beach and post guards at beaches. Although the ostensible aim of this security is to keep undesirables out, it does seem as if hotels are assuming de facto ownership of 'their' beach and it is becoming increasingly common for foreign visitors who are nonresidents to be faced with bossy, gruff guards. The best approach is to calmly state that the beach is public property and you are legally entitled to use it.

One traveller offers the following advice:

The approach to many beaches is inhibited by 'Private' or 'Keep Out' notices, as well as uniformed hotel security guards. Mauritians, however, are well aware of the law which states that the strip of beach between high and low tide is public property with free access, and the uniformed guards on beaches in front of the hotels will not interfere when you exercise this right. In fact, it's part of the Mauritian character that officials are generally unofficious, unaggressive and willing to concede if you stand your ground, but if it doesn't work every time, don't blame me!

Shower Devices

In some budget accommodation the shower plumbing – often of Brazilian origin – can pose 'shocking' problems to the uninitiated. Some explanation and instruction for use may be helpful.

Hot, or tepid, showers are produced by a frightening and deadly-looking device that attaches to the shower head and electrically heats the water as it passes through. You may see bare wires running into the shower head.

On the wall, you will find a lever that looks suspiciously like an ancient electro-cutioner's switch. You have to flip the switch after the water is running (yes, really), so it's best to leave your shoes or flip-flops on and not get wet until this is done.

When the heater is activated, it will begin to emit an electrical humming sound and the lights in the room may dim or even go out al-together. This is because the heater requires a great deal of electricity to operate effectively.

The temperature of the water can then be adjusted by increasing or decreasing the flow. A larger volume of water cannot be adequately heated in the time it takes to pass through the shower head, so a shower of a bearable temperature may become nothing but a pressureless drip.

When it's time to turn the water off, don't touch the controls until you've dried off and have your footwear on. This may be tricky, especially if the shower stall is small. Before turning the water off, flip the switch on the wall.

A hotel in Port Louis encapsulated instructions for this type of shower with a pithy notice: 'open the tap first, then you press the button, if not you may be electrocuted!'

LEGAL MATTERS

See Legal Matters in the Regional Facts for the Visitor chapter.

BUSINESS HOURS

Office hours are between 9 am and 4 pm Monday to Friday (private businesses are usually open from 8.30 am to 4.30 pm on weekdays and 8.30 am to noon on Satur-days). Most shops and cafés open at 9 am and close between 3 and 6 pm. On Saturdays many close at noon. In Curepipe and Rose Hill, the shops are open an hour longer during the week, but close on Thursday and Saturday afternoons. Check restaurant times before arranging evening meals, as several are only open for lunch or take last orders by a certain time. (See the Money and Post & Communications sections in this chapter for bank and post office hours.)

PUBLIC HOLIDAYS & SPECIAL EVENTS

The following public holidays are observed in Mauritius.

New Year – 1 & 2 January
Independence/Republic Day – 12 March
Labour Day – 1 May
All Saints' Day – 1 November
Christmas Day – 25 December

Apart from the above holidays, there are also a handful of holidays during religious festi-vals; the dates vary each year. With such a full range of beliefs and customs, hardly a week goes by without some celebration.

You can usually find out about the latest *cavadee, teemeedee* or other ceremonies from Mauritius Tourism Promotion Author-ity (☎ 2011703; fax 2125142) in Port Louis.

Hindu

Cavadee The cavadee is a wooden arch decorated with flowers and palm leaves, with pots of milk *(sambos)* suspended from each end of the base. Devotees carry the cavadee from the bank of a river to a temple in order to fulfil a vow in honour of Subramanya, the second son of Lord Shiva, and to pay penance and cleanse their soul. Before the procession commences, skewers are threaded through the tongues and cheeks of devotees. Custom dictates that a reasonable pace be maintained because the milk in the sambo must not have curdled by the time it reaches the temple.

The major Thaipoosam Cavadee takes place in January/February each year at most Hindu temples throughout the island. This is a public holiday. Small cavadees are scheduled once or twice during the rest of the year at selected temples.

Teemeedee This is a Hindu and Tamil fire-walking ceremony in honour of various gods. The ceremonies occur throughout the year, but mostly in December and January. After fasting and bathing, the participants walk over red-hot embers scattered along the ground. The Hindu temples at Camp Diable, The Vale and Quatre Bornes are noted for this event. A feat along similar lines is sword climbing, seen mostly between April and June. The best demonstrations occur at Solitude, Triolet and Mt Choisy, in the northwest.

Other Hindu Festivals Hindus celebrate the victory of Rama over the evil deity Ravana during Diwali, which falls in October or November. To mark this joyous event, countless candles and lamps are lit, to show Rama (the seventh incarnation of Vishnu) the way home from his period of exile.

Holi, the festival of colours, is known for the exuberant throwing of coloured powder and water. The festival symbolises the victory of divine power over demonic strength. On the night before Holi, bonfires are built to symbolise the destruction of the evil demon Holika. This festival is held in February or March.

During Pongal, a Tamil thanksgiving in January/February, food is offered to the gods. The festival marks the end of the harvest season, with various traditional festivities such as the boiling-over of a pot of *pongal* (mixture of rice, sugar, milk and dhal) and the decoration of cows which are then fed the pongal.

Chinese
The Chinese New Year falls around the end of January, or the beginning of February, celebrated in the Chinese Spring Festival. On the eve of the event, homes are spring-cleaned and decked in red, the colour of happiness, and firecrackers are let off to ward off evil spirits. On the following day, wax cakes made of rice flour and honey are given to family and friends. No scissors or knives may be used. There is always a public holiday at this time.

Christian
Père Laval Feast Day, in September, is the anniversary of the Catholic priest's death. Pilgrims from around the world come to his shrine at Ste-Croix to pray for miracle cures. For more details see the Port Louis chapter.

Muslim
Muslims celebrate Id-el-Fitr to mark the end of the fasting month of Ramadan, which is the ninth month of the lunar year. Id-el-Fitr day is always a public holiday (see table below).

ACTIVITIES
Water Activities
Many hotels offer water activities or can arrange them for their guests. Most of the major hotels provide windsurfers, kayaks etc, for guests' use. Some are made available to nonresidents (for a charge). Ask at your hotel about glass-bottom boat trips for sightseeing on the reef.

Table of Islamic Holidays					
Hijra Year	New Year	Prophet's Birthday	Ramadan begins	Eid al-Fitr	Eid al-Adha
1418	09.05.97	17.07.97	31.12.97	29.01.98	08.04.98
1419	28.04.98	06.07.98	19.12.98	18.01.99	28.03.99
1420	17.04.99	26.06.99	09.12.99	08.01.00	16.03.00
1421	06.04.00	14.06.00	27.11.00	27.12.00	06.03.01

For those who fancy a stroll underwater, Scaphandre (☎ 2637820; fax 2636847) organises 'undersea walks' inside the reef, near Grand Baie. After donning lead boots and helmet (Jules Verne fans will enjoy this), you descend a ladder to a platform and stroll along the seabed to feed the fish. The price is Rs 600 per person. Bookings can be made either at the office (on the roundabout junction of the Mon Choisy-Grand Baie road), through tour operators, or at hotels. Some travellers rate this underwater experience as a highlight of their visit to Mauritius.

For something different, there's *Le Nessee*, an air-con Australian-made semi-submersible boat – sort of like a submarine. It allows you to get a closer look at marine life than glass-bottom boats. The charge is Rs 400 for adults, Rs 200 for children under 12 years, free for children under two. The trip lasts for about one hour. For more information/bookings, call ☎ 6743695; fax 6743720, or inquire at your hotel.

Below are some places that offer an array of water activities, or can arrange them for you. Most places are concentrated around the touristy areas, such as Grand Baie. Remember that facilities can vary from one place to another, so before coughing up the cash for anything make sure you know exactly what you're getting for your money.

In Grand Baie, Libellule Travel Agent Tours Ltd (☎ 2636156; fax 2635352) is run by Kalam Azad Joomun and offers a range of water activities at reasonable prices. Ten minutes of paragliding costs Rs 600 per person, scuba diving is Rs 650 per person, deep-sea fishing is Rs 2000 per person for a full day and a glass-bottom boat trip is Rs 150 per person. Another similarly priced possibility is Ebrahim Travel & Tours (☎ 263-7845; fax 2638564) in Grand Baie. Also in Grand Baie, at Le Mauricia Hotel, is Mautourco (☎ 2637800; fax 2637888). This slick organisation can arrange various water activities, including scuba diving, deep-sea fishing and undersea walks.

Centre Nautique (☎ 2638017; fax 2637479) at the Sunset Boulevard complex in Grand Baie, organises glass-bottom boat tours (Rs 150 per person), undersea walks (Rs 600 per person), scuba diving (Rs 600 per dive) and deep-sea fishing (Rs 7500/9000 for a half/full day), and also hires out windsurfers (Rs 100/400 per hour/day). Windsurfing lessons cost Rs 100, kayak hire is Rs 50/200 per hour/day and water-skiing lessons cost Rs 250/650/1250 per 10 minutes/half hour/one hour.

Flambeau Ltd (☎ 2657894; fax 2616361), in Trou aux Biches, can also arrange a number of water activities, including undersea walks, fishing trips, catamaran tours and scuba diving.

Surfing A wave of Aussie and South African surfies built up in the 1970s around Tamarin. A surfing movie called The Forgotten Island of Santosha was also made. But the wave crashed and wiped out interest in surfing during the 1980s. The increasing cost of air travel to Mauritius didn't help.

In the 1990s, the low cost of self-catering accommodation at Tamarin and better air travel opportunities brought another swell of enthusiasm, especially in the south-west part of the island. Tim Williams, of Durban, South Africa, has described some of the surfing spots around Tamarin as 'the perfect set up', with up to 2m waves.

Top of his list are Le Morne and One Eye's (named after the one-eyed owner of Le Morne estate), both off the beaches in front of the two hotels. Other good surfing locations are near the Baie du Cap, 'Lefts and Rights', which is further south by Îlot Sancho, and one opposite the public gardens in Souillac.

The surfing season is from around June to August.

Diving & Snorkelling Mauritius is not really the place for a diving holiday. Diving around the island is not as deeply interesting as around the Seychelles and nothing like the Maldives. The exception would be on the outer isle of Cargados Carajos (also known as St Brandon), but that's a long way away and there are no organised trips there. Spear fishing and the collection of shells, coral and

MAURITIUS

fish are prohibited (see Ecology & Environment in the Facts about Mauritius chapter). Using spearguns is illegal.

Most of the large hotels either have centres to provide diving instruction or can arrange diving trips for guests.

Places to buy underwater equipment include Quay Stores (☎ 2121043), 3 John Kennedy St, Port Louis, and Gaz Industriels (☎ 2121453), Grande Rivière Nord-Ouest.

A great place for diving on Mauritius is near Flic en Flac on the west coast. Several of the hotels in this area have a diving school. The main diving attraction off the coast at Flic en Flac is the cave known as the Cathedral.

Other dive sites include Whale Rock, which can be reached from either Grand Baie or Trou aux Biches, and Roche Zozo, an underwater pinnacle of rock (accessible by boat only during the summer) off the southeast coast. The submerged crater near Île Ronde is a popular dive site accessible from tourist centres in the north, such as Grand Baie.

Snorkelling is a better proposition. There are over-the-side boat trips running from the major beach hotels and from Grand Baie beach. For those who don't want to get wet, there are fleets of glass-bottom boats. The reef off Peréybère beach is said to be good for viewing.

Blue Water Diving Centre (☎ 2657186; fax 2656267), adjacent to Le Pescatore restaurant in Trou aux Biches, is run by the friendly Hugues Vitry. Travellers have recommended this centre for diving and snorkelling trips. For Rs 650 per dive you are taken to shallow but excellent sites and may even be introduced to 'Monika', a tame moray eel who is happy to give divers a 'kiss'! If there are spare places in the boat, snorkellers can negotiate a price to join a diving group and benefit from the better snorkelling out on the reef. Ask Hugues about other diving options – he has plenty of good advice. Another good option is the Atlantis Diving Centre (☎ 2657172; fax 2637859), also in Trou aux Biches, which charges Rs 500 per person per dive.

Other diving centres around the island include:

Canonnier Diving Centre
    Pointe aux Canonniers (☎ 2637995; fax 2637864)
Diveplan Ltd
    Le Morne (☎ 6836775; fax 6836786)
Neptune Diving Centre
    Belle Mare (☎ 4151518; fax 4151993)
Odysee Diving Centre
    Rivière Noire (☎ 6836503; fax 6836318)
Paradise Diving
    Grand Baie (☎ 2637220; fax 2638534)
Sofitel Diving Centre
    Wolmar (☎ 4538700; fax 4538320)

Deep-Sea Fishing October to April is the prime time to catch record-size blue marlin. One of the world's top fishing spots is a couple of km off Le Morne. Here the bottom plunges 700m and the currents attract small fish pursued by huge predators. Marlin, sailfish, barracuda, wahoo, tuna and shark are common.

Anglers' Paradise

Serious anglers will love the superb deep-sea fishing in Mauritius. Big-game fishing is available all year round, although the best opportunities are from October to April.

The water around Mauritius supports a healthy population of blue and black marlin. Shoals of yellowfin tuna (65kg-90kg) move into Mauritian waters in March and April while wahoo, said to be the fastest swimming fish in the sea, are prominent in September.

Other challenges for anglers are the spectacular sailfish (around 45kg), which flies through the air when hooked in an acrobatic display of anger; bonito, a small species of tuna; and blue, hammerhead, mako, tiger and black and white fin shark.

You can book deep-sea fishing boats through most hotels. Boats are equipped with a radio and trolling equipment for live bait and artificial lures. Large fleets are based at the Corsaire Club at Trou aux Biches, the Hotel Club Centre de Pêche and Le Morne Anglers Club, both in Black River.

Justin Flynn

Most of the big hotels run boats and there are several Mauritian boat clubs. Visitors can also hire cheaper local fishing boats if they're not too fussy about where they sling their hooks.

Some outfits have a minimum hire time of around six hours and each boat can normally take five to six anglers. Expect to pay around Rs 9000 per boat (for a full day) when hiring from upmarket fishing centres or hotels, but local operators may drop to 50% of this price or less if approached directly (such as Libellule Travel Agent Tours Ltd (☎ 263-6156; fax 2635352) or Ebrahim Travel & Tours (☎ 2637845; fax 2638564), both in Grand Baie). Before grabbing a cheaper deal, however, make sure you know *exactly* what you will be getting for your money. Most operators lay claim to all fish caught on their boat, but will usually give you a small share of your catch.

Ask your hotel to recommend a reputable big-game fishing organisation, or contact one of the following:

Centre de Pêche de l'Île Maurice
    Rivière Noire (☎ 6836522; fax 6836318)
Beachcomber Fishing Club
    Le Morne (☎ 6836775; fax 6836786)
Black River Sport Fishing Organisation
    Rivière Noire (☎ 6836547)
Organisation de Pêche du Nord
    Trou aux Biches (☎ 2616209; fax 2616267)
La Pirogue Big Game Fishing
    Flic en Flac (☎ 4538441; fax 4538449)
Sofitel Imperial Big Game Fishing
    Wolmar (☎ 4538700; fax 4538320)
Sport Fisher
    Grand Baie (☎ 2638358; fax 2636309)
Surcouf
    Trou d'Eau Douce (☎ 4193198; fax 4193197)

Yacht Cruises You can charter a yacht or join a sailing tour – ask your hotel or a tour operator. Yacht Charters (☎ 2638395; fax 2637814), on Route Royale (Royal Road) in Grand Baie, may also be able to suggest yachting possibilities.

A yacht day trip with lunch costs around Rs 1200 per person. Only day cruises are generally run in the cyclone season between December and April. Longer cruises are left to the rest of the year when gales are rare.

Mautourco (☎ 6743695; fax 6743720), Forest Side, offers a northern or southern island cruise for Rs 1150 per person, including meals and drinks. They can also organise a 'sunset cruise' or 'starlight dinner cruise' – contact them for prices etc. Advance bookings for all yacht tours are essential. Mautourco also has an office at Le Mauricia Hotel in Grand Baie – ☎ 2637800; fax 2637888.

Grand Baie Travel & Tours (☎ 2638771; fax 2638274), on Route Royale, Grand Baie, runs a day trip on the *Isla Mauritia* schooner for Rs 1275 per person, including lunch. Children are charged Rs 630. Centre Nautique (☎ 2638017; fax 2637479), also based in Grand Baie, rents out catamarans for around Rs 250 per hour.

Land Activities

Golf There are golf courses at some of the major beach hotels, but they are designed more for the beach-bored holiday-maker than the enthusiast. The Paradis hotel at Le Morne and the Belle Mare Plage hotel on the east coast both have 18 hole golf courses. The Trou aux Biches Hotel (☎ 2656562; fax 2656611) in the north also has a good golf course.

To give some idea about costs, the Trou aux Biches Hotel charges Rs 500/800 for nine/18 holes; equipment rental is Rs 375.

Tennis Tennis courts at some of the luxury hotels are open to nonresidents (for a charge of course). However, during peak tourist season, when hotels book out, this service may not be available to nonresidents.

Cycling Surprisingly, few visitors seem to realise that cycling is an enjoyable way of seeing the island. Some hotels can arrange bicycle hire. Alternatively, some tour operators rent out bikes, especially around the Grand Baie area. Be extra careful when cycling on the major roads, as the traffic can be very fast and erratic.

Activities continued on page 86

MAURITIUS

Hiking & Trekking in Mauritius

Promoted primarily as a 'beach' destination, few people are aware of the attractions of walking, trekking or rambling around the island's interior. Only a handful of travellers choose to incorporate trekking in their holiday, accounting for the lack of books and information available. Tour operators may be able to offer some advice or recommend somebody who knows about trekking opportunities on the island. One traveller has recommended a private mountain guide, Jean Alain Hervel (☎ 4651508), who speaks English and French.

Information

The tourist office in Port Louis has little information about hiking and trekking. Serious hikers and climbers should try to obtain a copy of *Mountains of Mauritius: A Climber's Guide* (see Books, earlier in this chapter) by Robert Marsh. Marsh writes: 'Obviously the opportunities to enjoy the usual (but for many the unusual) activities of the beautiful seaside must not be missed, but as the locals know, there is a lot of pleasure to be found simply in walking, scrambling and climbing among the bush-clad hilly areas that add so much to the attractiveness of the country'.

The book, which due to the diminutive size of the Mauritian mountains is better suited to hikers and trekkers than to climbers, details 27 routes around and up such landmarks as Le Pouce (the thumb), Deux Mamelles (two breasts or udders), Pieter Both (the peak with an egg-shaped boulder balancing precariously on top), Lion Mountain, Le Morne Brabant and Snail Rock. Marsh includes route maps with each and adds that, scenically, 'the most dramatic and spectacular' regions of Mauritius lie in the western half of the island.

The book also recommends a trek up to Le Piton Grand Bassin: 'It is a must on the itinerary of visitors, and the Piton, which is simply a high point on the rim of the crater in which the Bassin lies, will take only a few minutes easy scrambling to reach'.

Another particularly appealing little book which is unfortunately also hard to come by, is *Climbing and Mountain Walking in Mauritius* (subtitled 'Particularly for those who would like to climb the Mauritius Mountains but who do not know the way') by Alexander Ward. This book provided the inspiration for Marsh's book and Ward is clearly on close terms with his subject matter. He speaks warmly of the mountains he climbs and provides potential trekkers with a great deal of friendly motivation. Copies of these books should be available at Carnegie Library in Curepipe.

A drawback with both of these books is the age of the information. Some things have changed since they were written; some of the trips on private property are now closed to the public while others have been rendered unappealing by growth and development. Areas that are private property are usually marked with signs – if you're unsure about where you should and shouldn't walk, it's best to heed local advice.

Maps

The IGN map (see Maps earlier in this chapter) shows most of the tracks and footpaths, although a few are outdated. The 'yellow roads' indicated are generally just rough vehicle tracks, sometimes passable only to 4WD vehicles, and therefore may double as walking tracks. They're all easy enough to follow, but some smaller tracks (shown on the IGN map as dashed lines) are more difficult and some which are overgrown would require a great deal of bush-bashing to follow.

The IGN map will be adequate for most hikers but those in search of greater detail should apply to the Ministry of Housing, which produces detailed maps suitable for serious, off-the-beaten-track walking.

Getting Started

Most people head for the *Réserve Forestière Macchabée* (Macchabée Forest Reserve), or Black River Gorges National Park (see the map in the Central Mauritius chapter). This mountainous area provides the bulk of the wild walks on the island.

Curepipe is the best base for trekkers and for stocking up before your walk, and Curepipe market has one of the island's best selections of fruit. Due to a dearth of public transport over mountain roads in the island's south-western corner, access to most trailheads will require private transport or a taxi ride.

For lowland walking, take into account the heat and humidity. If you prefer walking on the highland plateau, come prepared for rain at any time of year, especially from October to March. Tropical downpours, frequently lasting for hours, will soak you to the skin. Even during the winter 'dry' season, the high plains trap clouds and moisture from the sea; it may be sunny in Curepipe and bucketing down on the Plaine Champagne. Since rainfall is most likely in the afternoon and public transport is more readily available along the coastal roads, your best option is to walk from inland *towards* the coast. This also provides the added benefit of net altitude loss!

Some trekking options on the island are described below.

Le Pétrin to Grande Rivière Noire This is a superb hike which traverses some of the finest and most scenic countryside on Mauritius. It begins at the junction of the Grand Bassin and Curepipe-Chamarel roads at Le Pétrin. The track is easy to follow through the Black River Gorges National Park, with tiny pockets of indigenous vegetation dispersed through acacia and other introduced forest.

Stage one is an easy level walk which follows the forestry road west from Le Pétrin along the ridge through the forests. It affords splendid views into the Grande Rivière Noire and if it's been raining, there will be good views of waterfalls. The road ends at a picnic site on a fantastic viewpoint.

The route then descends precipitously along a track which is exceptionally steep in parts and often as slippery as soap, so it's not a good idea after heavy rain. After about 1km, the worst of it is over and you emerge on a road which is just passable for 4WD vehicles.

The road drops steeply to the river and the route becomes a flat easy stroll along the river valley, passing sections of forest hideously disfigured by clearing and wood cutting. Eventually, it issues into cane fields. Turn left at the T-junction and continue along the road strewn with sugar cane detritus to the coast road at Grande Rivière Noire.

Much of the land along the lower part of this route is through private property but travellers seem to have had no problem passing through.

Return to Curepipe by bus either via Souillac (change necessary at Baie du Cap) or via Quatre Bornes. Reasonably fit walkers should allow four to five hours to do this wonderful walk.

Le Pétrin to Tamarind Falls This trip begins as for the trek from Le Pétrin to Grande Rivière Noire. Follow the forestry road for just over 2km.

Take the right fork and continue for another 500m or so to a second fork in the road. To reach Tamarind Falls, you must follow the left fork (the right will lead you to the road which connects the Curepipe-Chamarel road with Mare Longue reservoir).

The route is easy throughout, with no steep or tricky bits, often following a scenic ridge. It's mostly forest along the way, with good views, then it descends into more open terrain near the reservoir. A detour at the end around the Seven Waterfalls of Tamarin is fun – there is a trail which drops down to the base of the falls, but people will have to explore for themselves to find it. If you have the energy, it's a fabulous finale to the walk.

For this walk, allow around three hours, more if you want to explore the falls area.

Plaine Champagne to Bel Ombre (South Coast) The trailhead for this walk is the Plaine Champagne viewpoint on the Curepipe-Chamarel road which lies about 2km past (ie toward Chamarel) the radio tower at the highest point on the road (744m). The trail heads due south to Bel Ombre, passing en route a succession of wonderful views through some lovely mixed forests and plantations. The finish meanders along some rather confusing cane field tracks, but a reasonable sense of direction will get you to the coast road without too much difficulty. From Bel Ombre, there are buses to Souillac (change there for Curepipe) and to Tamarin via Baie du Cap. Allow about four hours for this fairly easy walk.

Plaine Champagne to Bassin Blanc & Chemin Grenier This walk begins about 3km south of Le Pétrin along the road towards Plaine Champagne. Heading south, look for the spot where the road makes a sharp turn to the right and two trails branch off to the left. The left fork goes to Piton Savanne and the right goes to Montagne Cocotte and Bassin Blanc.

Follow the track on the right. Although it's shown on the IGN map as a dotted line, it is actually paved for much of its length. The route is fairly open, passing through a variety of landscapes before emerging at Bassin Blanc, a classic crater lake surrounded by forest – a really idyllic spot. Although the IGN map shows a break in the route here, it does in fact continue to meet the yellow road which descends to Chamouny and Chemin Grenier. Return from Chemin Grenier to Curepipe via Souillac, where you'll have to change buses.

Allow two to three hours for this easy walk, plus several hours for the bus trip back to Curepipe.

If you want to make a longer day of it, get an early start and take a side trip to the summit of Montagne Cocotte. At the trailhead, also begin by taking the right fork. After about 1.2km, there'll be a rough and boggy route taking off to the right. When this route crosses a stream, bear to the right and follow the clear path to the forested summit of Montagne Cocotte.

Grande Case Noyale to Chamarel & the Terres de Couleur Start at Grande Case Noyale and continue up the Chamarel road. Although this route is all on normal tarmac roads, there is not much traffic. It's well worth the effort for the scenery and views of the mountains and the coast.

Domaine du Chasseur & Les Montagnes Bambous (Bambous Mountains) Your best chance of exploring these beautiful hills, some of which are crossed by inviting trails but almost free of roads, is to visit Domaine du Chasseur. This private estate has rough 4WD tracks which double as walking tracks open to visitors. They are superb, if a little steep, and they offer magnificent views across forests and down to the coast. For further details, see Domaine du Chasseur in the South Mauritius chapter.

Le Pouce Le Pouce, the prominent thumb-shaped peak which towers over Port Louis and Moka, is an easy climb and makes a great introduction to walking in Mauritius. To reach the trailhead from Port Louis, follow St George St (which changes to Pandit Nehru St and then Mahatma Gandhi St), turn right into St-Denis St and continue past Ste-Anne chapel. Below is one traveller's account of this walk:

We speak very little French, but by walking towards the hill through Port Louis wearing backpacks, and staring, puzzled, towards the hills, people regularly volunteered the necessary directions unbidden. However, if you follow the roads in Port Louis at the base of Signal Hill, you will cross a dry creek bed, and with little prompting find yourself on a gentle grassy incline walking along a 4WD track.

Once you are abreast of the sheer granite escarpment on your right – watch to see when the conspicuous topknot on the escarpment is abreast of you – then take the first path leading sharply upwards to your right. The path is very narrow and the leaves deposit a lot of moisture on hikers and equipment if unprotected.

This narrow path opens onto a grassy plateau where the path becomes less distinct in places. Resist the great temptation to follow numerous goat tracks leading directly to the final granite cone. The true path circles behind the cone almost passing it, when it follows a cleft up the back side of the cone to the most magnificent view imaginable of Pieter Both, Port Louis and the interior.

We had a rain squall catch us at the top, but there was a little shelf to leeward that provided reasonable protection in the whiteout conditions which brought swirling clouds, giving ever-changing glimpses of the surrounding peaks. Very much like a Japanese painting.

We shared the peak with a school class, including very small children. Except for caution at the very summit of the cone, there is no danger in the climb, and we (not very fit 40 year olds) made the climb in 2½ very leisurely hours. We wore flip-flops and basketball shoes. The paths do get very slippery in the rain, so old clothes and the ability to sustain a few quick sitdowns are recommended.

For anyone even remotely inclined to hiking it would be a shame to miss the glorious views from the top.

Barbara Dressler, UK

Railway Walking For something a little different, you could hike along Mauritius' system of defunct railways.

The IGN map still shows bits of the old Mauritian railway system. Yes, Mauritius had a railway system. It stretched from Souillac and Mahébourg to Curepipe, down to Port Louis, swung north to Terre Rouge, Mapou, Poudre d'Or and Rivière du Rempart; then curved east and south to Centre de Flacq; and terminated at Grande Rivière du Sud Est where you can still take the 'free' public ferry – a pirogue poled across the bay to the other side, from where you can either walk or take a bus back to Mahébourg.

The north-east section (Mapou to Grande Rivière du Sud Est) is easy to follow as the line is built up and the foundations are clearly visible. As you walk through farms and land covered by crops, the people are very accommodating. Literally all the old bridges still exist and most of the post offices you see en route were the beautifully constructed train stations.

Mountain climbing apart, this is a top trek and you do meet people. Yes, take a good water bottle. Even today, be prepared to be seen as a 'madman'!

Ralph Watson, Australia

Activities continued from page 81

Horse Riding Horse riding opportunities are at Domaine Les Pailles (☎ 2124225; fax 2124226), an estate run as a tourist attraction – see the Central Mauritius chapter for further details. Some hotels (particularly the upmarket ones) may also be able to arrange horse treks.

WORK
It is not easy getting a work visa unless you are sponsored by a company. For further details, write to the Permanent Secretary, Ministry of Employment, Port Louis, Mauritius. Alternatively, contact your country's Mauritian embassy.

ACCOMMODATION
Mauritius offers the full range of accommodation from budget rooms to super-luxury suites. The main categories are camping, *pensions de famille* (boarding houses), small Indian or Chinese-run hotels, bungalows or apartments, guesthouses and luxury beach hotels. The smarter guesthouses and beach hotels add a 15% government tax to the bill; the others tend not to. Be aware that many advertised tariffs do not include the tax, leaving you to find out about it only when it comes to paying the bill. To avoid confusion, it's best to ask if the room rate includes tax when you make your reservation.

At the budget end of the market the most important thing to remember is: the more of you are there and the longer you stay, the cheaper the rates per person. It is possible to base yourself in one place and see all of Mauritius, especially if you hire a car.

There are regular busy and quiet periods, but no separate high and low seasons. December, January, July and August are usually the busiest months, and some of the top hotels implement a hefty hike in rates at this time. When it is quiet, most places will offer cheaper rates – you may even be able to slash these discounted rates. Half-board is commonly available and includes breakfast and dinner.

One source for accommodation options and rates is the Mauritius Chamber of Commerce & Industry (MCCI), which operates a free information service from a counter (☎ 6374100) at SSR airport. It's usually open for each flight arrival.

The Mauritius Tourism Promotion Authority (☎ 2011703; fax 2125142) in Port Louis issues a list of accommodation tariffs. There are also several local magazines which contain accommodation listings (see Information under Grand Baie in the North Mauritius chapter).

Camping
There is little assistance offered to campers. By the same token, there are few hassles. There are no official camp sites and no restrictions, within reason, about where you can camp on public land. Few shoestring travellers or outdoor enthusiasts bring a tent, but the opportunity to use one exists. The favoured sites are the public beaches such as Blue Bay near Mahébourg, Flic en Flac, Pointe des Puits near Belle Mare, Mon Choisy, and past Le Morne village in front of Baie du Cap estate on the south-west tip. Casuarina trees provide shade and shelter. There are public toilets on some beaches, but many are in a dismal state.

The main drawback, apart from the lack of facilities, is the lack of security. A good idea is to camp as close to the police station as possible, and ask them to keep an eye on your tent. The police on the island are generally very helpful. Several budget guesthouses accept small numbers of campers and charge them a modest fee.

There are plenty of long stretches of quiet beach, but you'd be lucky to find a deserted beach. There are just too many people.

Guesthouses
Guesthouses provide intimate surroundings and are a popular budget choice. Most are near the beach and offer rooms in a family home. Guesthouses are a good alternative to hotels, as you can learn a lot about local life through the owners – the atmosphere tends also to be more down-to-earth. To satisfy

tourist demand, there are more and more guesthouses springing up in Mauritius, particularly around the popular northern part of the island.

Pensions de Famille

These budget boarding houses come in all sorts, sizes and prices. Like guesthouses, they provide much cheaper accommodation than the hotels.

Pensions are concentrated in Mahébourg and Curepipe, with one or two at Peréybère, Quatre Bornes and Rose Hill. A few are small family affairs and offer meals. Others are loosely run by a young caretaker and rent out rooms on an hourly basis for the love trysts of frustrated local couples. Some are clean, some are grubby, but none are the absolute pits. Many have communal toilets and showers. For the sort of price they charge, you can't afford to be fussy. It's not a bad idea to take an inner sheet sleeping bag if you intend staying in pensions or cheap hotels.

Bungalows & Apartments

There are bungalows and apartments around the coast, including seemingly hundreds of them in Grand Baie. You may have to go looking for others, as they are not listed with any organisation or agency. Most will have a sign at the gate or nailed to a tree by the roadside saying *Bungalow à louer* or *Campement à louer* (Bungalow for rent), often with a telephone number. The Friday edition of *L'Express* has a page or two of *petites annonces* (classified advertisements) where you can usually find bungalows and apartments in the columns entitled *à louer* (rental).

Units range from complete bungalows, with up to four bedrooms, to small one and two-bedroom studios with a kitchenette and bathroom. They are usually fully furnished and equipped with fridges. The more expensive ones will have a TV, washing machine and sometimes air-con. Their interior is also more appealing.

For two to four people staying a fortnight or month, bungalows are the best bargains. The proprietor should reduce the daily rate if you stay a week or more – ask for a discount

if it is not offered. Many of the places rely on return visits by guests. Some may ask for a deposit when you make your booking. A maid/cook is sometimes included in the price or can be arranged for an additional charge – inquire when making your booking.

If possible, try to see the apartment/bungalow before booking. Some places are poorly maintained, noisy and provide limited cooking facilities. And a word of advice: make sure you check out the bed – some mattresses are positively lumpy and bumpy, leaving you grumpy in the morning after a dreadful night's sleep! Finally, if you quiver at the thought of sharing the place with creepy crawlies, come armed with a can of insect spray – cockroaches and spiders are not unusual, especially in the cheaper places.

Hotels

Mauritius mainly has middle and top-end hotels, especially around the beach areas. The standard of service varies wildly and, unfortunately, many places have lost the personal touch as they've expanded over the years. Staff at some hotels are eager to please, whereas at other places they can be downright rude.

Cheap Hotels Most of the cheap hotels are in Port Louis, with a couple in Curepipe. However, they are generally poor value for money.

Rates are equivalent to the pensions and meals, if available, are extra. Many of these hotels are used by Indians from South Africa, or local businesspeople.

Beach Hotels Tucked away on the island's best beaches, a room in a beach hotel is considerably more expensive than other accommodation options. Tariffs are usually fixed at daily rates and the price drops if you book a fortnightly package. Given the large number of beach hotels competing for customers, you should have no qualms about shopping around for the best deals and requesting discounts if you stay longer than a week.

The Sun group of hotels offers guests a special Suncard; and the Beachcomber group offers guests a similar deal with its Beachcomber Card.

The Suncard, which every guest receives on registration, entitles the holder to free transfers between St Géran and Le Touessrok hotels; free boat transfer to and from Île aux Cerfs; free use of many sports facilities; some free casino chips; a discount at various shops and boutiques, and discounted rental of certain sports facilities, such as scuba diving. It also lets holders interchange accommodation with other hotels in the group – subject to availability.

The Beachcomber Card, which every guest receives on registration, entitles the holder to free use of many sports facilities; some free casino chips; and discounted rental of certain sports facilities, such as scuba diving.

For advice on problems with hotel security guards and exclusion of nonresidents from public beaches, see Dangers & Annoyances earlier in this chapter.

Urban Hotels There are a few undistinguished urban hotels in and around Port Louis and Curepipe. They are mainly used by travelling salespeople, visiting sports or cultural teams and people attending conferences. The facilities and service at most of these places is lacklustre. Most holidaymakers stay closer to the beach.

FOOD

Despite the dominant Indian flavour of Mauritius, there are only a handful of Indian restaurants. The Chinese are the main caterers and are good at blurring the lines between the various cooking traditions.

If you want lunch or dinner at a pension or guesthouse, you must let the manager know in advance so that sufficient supplies can be obtained. Some places only offer breakfast, so you'll have no choice but to go out for other meals.

Snacks

Mauritians are big on snacks and you can buy samosas, rotis, curried rolls, meatballs, noodle specials, soups and a variety of other basic fare from street vendors in Port Louis, for between Rs 5 and Rs 20. Most smaller towns have a stall or two selling the same. These can be a cheap alternative to the restaurants, but if you do eat here try to select food that has been freshly cooked, not reheated (to avoid a tummy upset).

There are a handful of fast-food joints in Mauritius, mainly in Port Louis and the larger towns. These include KFC and Pizza Hut.

Vegetarian

Most restaurants offer a selection of vegetarian dishes, however seafood/meat seem to dominate the menus. This can leave little choice for vegetarians – even the salads often have a sprinkling of seafood in them.

Vegetarians are probably best sticking to à la carte menus, as buffets are invariably dominated by seafood and meat dishes (unless of course you come across a veg buffet). Indian restaurants offer perhaps the widest variety of vegetarian dishes, such as dhal and a range of curried vegies. And you can always get a veg soup and stir-fried vegetables at Chinese restaurants. For the greatest versatility, it's not a bad idea to stay in self-catering accommodation.

Self-Catering

Prices of tinned or packaged food (much of it imported from South Africa) and household goods are marked in most stores – the merchants don't surreptitiously increase prices for tourists. To give self-caterers an idea of prices, a 100g jar of Nescafe coffee is Rs 110; a 250g tin of milo is Rs 44; a small jar of honey is Rs 26; a carton of long-life skim milk is Rs 16.50; a small block of chocolate is around Rs 24; and a packet of biscuits costs upwards of Rs 8. A packet of spaghetti costs around Rs 25.

The biggest and best markets for fruit and vegetables are in Port Louis, Curepipe and the bigger towns such as Mahébourg and Centre de Flacq. The self-catering accommodation areas around Flic en Flac and Grand Baie are served by well-stocked supermarkets.

Fruits and vegetables are seasonal, and prices vary accordingly. Mauritius has pretty much the same variety as the other Indian Ocean islands, but seems to get more excited over lychees (July) and longans (February). To make sure you pay a fair price for your produce at the market, watch a local person buying the same, or compare the rates of several sellers.

Heart of palm (for which the palm tree is sacrificed) is regarded as a rare delicacy. Unless you've got the money to be extravagant, it's not worth pining over. It's like tasteless coconut flesh and relies on vinaigrette or other dressings to give it flavour. In the Seychelles you are quite likely to get it served up without ceremony at a guesthouse, but not in Mauritius.

To buy fish, go to the fish-landing station in each coastal village and deal directly with the fishermen. In Grand Baie fish is about Rs 100 per kg.

DRINKS

The price of all drink, be it cola, beer, rum or wine, purchased in bottles, usually includes a deposit for the bottle. Remember to take along the empties when replenishing supplies.

Nonalcoholic Drinks

Tea & Coffee Tea and coffee are hit-or-miss affairs. They're never purely Mauritian, as the local crop is used for blending. The tea is likely to be white and sweetened by condensed milk, unless you specify otherwise. While here, you should sample the local speciality – vanilla tea.

Instant coffee costs about the same as in the UK or Australia, but sugar and powdered milk are cheaper. For a decent cappuccino or espresso, try one of the upmarket hotels or restaurants.

Soft Drinks Soft drinks are numerous and are consumed copiously by Mauritians. Pepsi Cola, affectionately referred to as the national drink of Mauritius, is by far the most popular soft drink. The islanders are also fond of locally and commercially made yoghurt drinks. One of the most popular of these is *lassi*, a refreshing yoghurt and iced-water drink. There's also *alouda*, a syrupy brew of agar (china grass), milk and flavouring, which is sold on the streets and at some Hindu festivals.

If you don't trust the local water supply, there are plenty of bottles of mineral water – a 1L bottle is around Rs 8 at the shops, more in hotels.

Alcohol

Beer and rum are potent, plentiful, and cheap but not nasty. Locally brewed Guinness is popular, at Rs 8.50 a bottle. Phoenix pilsner beer, which takes its name from the town where it's brewed, costs Rs 7.50 for a small bottle. At upmarket establishments or discos, the same bottle can cost between Rs 35 and Rs 55!

There is a variety of rum. The best known is Green Island, but Power's No 1 and Anytime are among the most popular brands with the Mauritians. A shot of the latter at a bar costs Rs 5, or you can buy a 750ml bottle for Rs 50 at the store and get an Rs 5 refund on the bottle.

French wine is expensive and most Mauritians drink South African wines, which cost between Rs 85 and Rs 230 a bottle in shops. The cheapest wines are Mauritian-bottled whites and reds for around Rs 32 over the counter. The origin could be a tankerload of table wine surplus from France or imported crystals watered down. It's just about palatable, though.

Tapeta! is Créole for 'Cheers'!

ENTERTAINMENT
Cinemas

Cinemas on Mauritius are fighting a losing battle with dozens of video rental shops which have sprung up in most villages and towns. Mauritians are big film buffs. There are usually two general categories – sex and violence.

Most films are in French. However you can catch an English-language film at Le Caudan Waterfront in Port Louis, which has the best cinema complex on the island (see Entertainment in the Port Louis chapter for further details).

Séga Dances, Discos & Jazz

For details about séga performances, ask at the tourist office or hotels. For further information about séga, see Arts in the Facts about Mauritius chapter and the boxed text in the North Mauritius chapter. Most major hotels lay on at least one séga night per week. Tickets to these events usually cost between Rs 300 and Rs 600 and include a buffet dinner.

Apart from the hotels, the main local jive shops are Sam's Disco (☎ 6865370) on Royal Rd, Vacoas; Palladium (☎ 4546168) in an isolated setting on the Port Louis-Quatre Bornes trunk road; Melody's (☎ 4644097) at the Commercial Centre in Rose Hill and Saxophone (☎ 4653021) in Beau Bassin.

Grand Baie has several discos, including Speedy's and Dream On. Admission to discos usually costs at least Rs 100, and you'll rarely pay less than Rs 30 for a beer.

Casinos

Roulette, blackjack, baccarat and slot machines are some of the after-dinner diversions available for tourists at the casinos in the big beach hotels and at the plush casino at Le Caudan Waterfront in Port Louis. If you intend going to a casino, tidy dress is expected (no thongs, T-shirts etc).

The Chinese casino, L'Amicale Chinese Gaming House, offers something a little different from the hotel casinos (see Entertainment in the Port Louis chapter for more information).

Theatres

There are two main theatres in Mauritius. One is next to Government House in Port Louis and the other is in Rose Hill. They are used mostly for local amateur productions, but host the occasional troupe from overseas. See Entertainment in the Port Louis chapter for more information.

SPECTATOR SPORT
Soccer

Soccer is the national sport, and the King George V Stadium in Curepipe is the main venue. Every town and village seems to have a sporting club based on soccer. Around Mahébourg, the clubs are mainly named after British soccer teams.

Basketball and volleyball are growing in popularity with young locals.

Horse Racing

Mauritius has a busy horse-racing programme from around May to the end of November at the Champ de Mars racecourse in Port Louis. The big race is the Derby, held at the end of August.

Entry into the stands costs Rs 100, but admission to the central area is usually free and you get the chance to mix with thousands of betting-crazy locals.

There are plans to open a racecourse at Domaine Les Pailles (see the Central Mauritius chapter).

THINGS TO BUY

Some prime buys for souvenirs are: model ships, clothing, Indian fabrics, footwear, basket work and embroidery. The best places to shop for them are Curepipe, Rose Hill and Port Louis.

See Ecology & Environment in the Facts about Mauritius chapter for important information about shells, coral and turtle shell products which should not be purchased. Given the wide choice of other things to buy in Mauritius, there is no reason to purchase items made from endangered species.

Model Ships

It is unlikely you will come away from Mauritius without seeing or buying a model ship. Small-scale shipbuilding has become big business during the past few years, after someone carved a model just for fun in 1968.

Magnificently intricate miniature replicas of *The Bounty, Victory, Endeavour, Cutty Sark, Golden Hind* and even the *Titanic* can be bought off the shelf or made to order from a range of small factories. Few of the famous ships made ever visited Mauritius, but there are models of vessels such as the *Confiance*, a 1792 corsair of 26 guns captained by the privateer Robert Surcouf, which featured in the island's history.

An intricate model of the British warship HMS *Victory*.

The models are made out of lintels (teak) or cheaper camphor wood, and larger ships take up to 400 hours to complete. The sails and rigging are dipped in tea to give them a weathered look. Shop around for price comparisons. Prices begin at around Rs 2400 for a small model of a 19th century cutter and average Rs 8500 for a 118cm-long model of the 18th century French vessel *Superbe*.

Many visitors take the models aboard the plane as hand luggage. Sturdy, specially made boxes are usually supplied by the manufacturer. If your boat is boxed, some airlines may charge around Rs 325 per kg.

Make sure you supervise the packing of the model you've chosen – it's not worth the disappointment of unpacking your box at home and finding you've got the wrong model. Also, get a bill of sale and a valid certificate which is recognised by EU countries and western nations, to save paying duty on arrival home.

One of the best places to buy a model ship is Voiliers de L'Océan (☎/fax 6766986) on Sir Winston Churchill St, in Curepipe, which employs about 35 people; the men work on the structure and the women do the rigging and sails. The director Mr K Singh, and his staff, will be glad to show you around the small factory without any pressure to buy. The shop is open every day from 7.30 am to 6.30 pm. Another outlet you could take a look at is Comajora (☎/fax 6751644) in Forest Side.

The biggest factory is Historic Marine (☎ 2839404), St Antoine Industrial Estate, Goodlands, in the north of the island. It is open Monday to Friday from 8 am to 5 pm, Saturdays from 8 am to noon.

Several art and souvenir shops have models for sale, sometimes at reasonable prices. However, the choice is usually limited.

Clothing

Hardcore shoppers in search of bargain prices for swimwear, knitwear, sportswear, T-shirts etc head for the many shops in Rose Hill and Curepipe. Watch out for cheap imitations of noted designer labels. The open-air market held on Saturdays in the centre of Quatre Bornes is also considered a good source of inexpensive clothing.

For more upmarket shopping, there's Le Caudan Waterfront complex in Port Louis, which has a collection of attractive clothing shops selling trendy beachwear, casual gear and slinky lingerie. The Sunset Boulevard complex at Grand Baie also has some fancy clothing shops with fancy prices to match!

Since Mauritius has now become a major clothing exporter, there are bargains to be found in designer goods obtained directly from factory outlets (such as the Phoenix Factory shop, not far from the Phoenix Brewery roundabout in Phoenix). Prices tend to be higher in the fashion boutiques at beach hotels or in beach resorts such as Grand Baie.

Indian Fabrics

The government-authorised Handloom House at the Bank of Baroda building in Sir William Newton St, Port Louis, has a fair range of Indian garments and fabrics.

You can buy dresses, scarves and shirts. Cotton saris are around Rs 500 and kurta

MAURITIUS

MAURITIUS

shirts are Rs 600, but you may be able to bargain these down. Silk fabric is around Rs 450 per metre.

Footwear
You can buy good-quality fashionable shoes or have them made for between Rs 150 and Rs 450. Try the shopping arcade beside the Curepipe bus station.

If you buy flip-flops (thongs), chances are they will have red soles with blue straps. Look at the number of people wearing them. This particular brand is almost part of the national dress. Wear them in Réunion or Madagascar and people will know you've been to Mauritius.

Stamps
Mauritius, like many island nations, prides itself on its colourful stamps and postal history. It was perhaps a stamp more than anything else which first brought the island to the notice of the rest of the world.

The Mauritian Blue, featuring Queen Victoria's head, was a 'Post Paid' stamp, but the engraver made it a 'Post Office' stamp by mistake. Quite a number were printed and posted before the error was discovered. The few that are left are now worth millions. If you're interested in buying collector stamps, inquire at the Mauritius Postal Museum (see the Port Louis chapter).

Handicrafts & Souvenirs
For those not going to Madagascar, there are a number of shops specialising in Malagasy handicrafts, including leather belts and bags, semiprecious-stone solitaire sets, and hats and baskets. There is a plethora of stalls in cramped aisles at the market in Port Louis pushing these products at browsing busloads of tourists (see the Port Louis Market boxed text in the Port Louis chapter for more details).

In the souvenir shops is a range of objects featuring the coloured earths of Chamarel. They'll scream from anyone's mantelpiece. Not so distinctive, but just as earthy, are the dried-flower decorated stationery, bookmarks and picture frames from Fantasies Florales at Peréybère, north of Grand Baie. These gifts don't go with the tropical image of the country, but are more representative of the actual flora.

The Societé des Petites Entreprises Specialisées (SPES) showroom on Labourdonnais Ave, Quatre Bornes, sells 'chunky African-style metal jewellery', coral jewellery, papier mâché animals, embroidery, pottery, paintings, baskets and carpets. The goods are made by a nonprofit organisation which employs disabled people.

At Cheshire Home Boutique, another charitable group, in Tamarin, the residents make baskets, clothes, shell boxes and other items.

Getting There & Away

General information on travel options to and from the Indian Ocean are given in the Regional Getting There & Away chapter at the beginning of this book.

AIR

Apart from the handful of people who sail in by yacht and those who arrive with the occasional cruise liner, all visitors to Mauritius fly into the country. You must have a return or onward ticket before arriving in Mauritius, which you should reconfirm a week prior to departure.

Expensive flights have always been the biggest deterrent to travellers. As with the Seychelles and the Maldives, the only way to cut the cost of flights is to take a package deal with hotel accommodation, or to include Mauritius in a round-the-world (RTW) or other circular fare. Mauritius, following the Seychelles, is now beginning to offer better deals to Europe and the UK. Most airlines offer cheaper low-season fares (the period differs from airline to airline).

The UK

Mauritius News and *Mauritian International* are two useful publications produced in the UK. Both have news reports and plenty of ads from travel agencies specialising in Mauritius. *Mauritius News* is published monthly and can be obtained by contacting Mauritius News (☎ (0171) 703 1071), PO Box 26, London SE17 1EG. *Mauritian International* is published quarterly and is available from Nautilus Publishing Company (☎/fax (0181) 947 1912), PO Box 4100, London SW20 0XN.

The Globetrotters Club (BCM Roving, London WC1N 3XX) publishes *Globe*, a newsletter for members which covers obscure destinations and can help find travelling companions.

Several airlines operate flights between London and Mauritius, including Air Mauritius and British Airways. Air Mauritius charges around UK£595 for an excursion return fare while British Airways charges UK£755.

Europe

Air Mauritius operates weekly flights to many European destinations including Paris, Zürich, Geneva, Rome, Munich, Frankfurt, Brussels, Vienna and London (the number of flights usually varies according to low/high season). Air Mauritius (☎ 01 44 51 15 55), 11 bis Rue Scribe, 75009, Paris, charges around FF6000/8000 in the low/high season for a return ticket between Paris and Mauritius; it operates about five direct flights per week. Air France and British Airways also have flights between France and Mauritius – they both offer competitive fares.

Apart from holiday packages, look for bargain flights offered by Nouvelles Frontières or Air France which will take you from Paris to Réunion; you could then take a cheap return flight to Mauritius from Réunion.

Africa

You can fly to Mauritius direct from Johannesburg, Cape Town or Durban (South Africa), Harare (Zimbabwe), Antananarivo (Madagascar), Moroni (Comoros), Nairobi (Kenya) or the Seychelles. Airlines offer different fares and packages – for details, contact a travel agent.

Asia

Various airlines operate flights between Mauritius and Mumbai (Bombay), New Delhi, Jakarta, Kuala Lumpur, Singapore and Hong Kong.

Australia

Air Mauritius operates flights between Melbourne/Perth and Mauritius. The cheapest return flight from Melbourne costs A$1695 from 1 July to 30 November; A$1940 from 1 December to 31 January. From Perth it is approximately A$300 cheaper.

Alternatively, you can fly to either Singapore or Kuala Lumpur and then take a connecting Air Mauritius flight on to Mauritius.

USA

All flights from New York or Los Angeles to Mauritius go via Europe (ie New York-Paris-Mauritius). From Los Angeles to London costs US$480/755 return in the low/high season and from New York to London costs US$400/540 return in low/high season.

Réunion

A return fare (valid for one month) between Mauritius and Réunion costs Rs 2635. The flight takes around 40 minutes and is popular with visitors from Réunion in search of a cheap holiday on Mauritius. This might explain why the same return excursion fare purchased in Réunion is around 50% higher.

SEA
Réunion

The MV *Mauritius Pride* operates several times monthly between Mauritius and Réunion. For information contact Mauritius Shipping Corporation Ltd (☎ 2412550; fax 2425245), Nova building, 1 Military Rd, Port Louis. In Réunion call Scoam (☎ 42 19 45; fax 43 25 47) at Le Port.

The return fare between Mauritius and Réunion is Rs 1600/1900 in the low/high season (in seats); Rs 2400/2700 in the low/high season (in cabins). Children below 12 years of age are charged half price. The one-way trip takes about 12 hours.

Cargo Ships

Although there is still a fair amount of maritime trade to and from Mauritius, very few cargo ships take passengers. To inquire about sailings and possible bookings, contact the Shipping Division (☎ 2083241), Ireland Blyth Ltd, Port Louis.

Yachts

Several yachts call at Mauritius during the non-cyclone season through June to November. They berth at Grand Baie or in Port Louis.

On average, it takes a day to sail to Réunion and two days to return; five days to Madagascar and seven back; and 10 days to the Seychelles and two weeks back. Rodrigues, 560km to the north-east, is a seven day sail.

It is possible to hitch a ride on a yacht if you are willing to pay expenses and can crew, but the opportunities are rare. Check the noticeboard at Grand Baie Yacht Club. Alternatively, there is the remote chance of a charter, but it will be very expensive.

LEAVING MAURITIUS

There is a Rs 300 airport tax on international departures. There are a handful of duty-free shops at the airport and items must be purchased with foreign exchange; a 1L bottle of blended whisky costs around Rs 495.

Apart from shops, the airport departure area also has a post office (for opening hours, see Post & Communications in the Mauritius Facts for the Visitor chapter) and a no-frills restaurant. There's also a small stand-up bar; a coffee costs Rs 30, a small bottle of coke is Rs 35 – or if you're feeling really blue about leaving the sunny shores of Mauritius, a scotch on the rocks is Rs 80.

Getting Around

AIR

Domestic Air Services

There are daily flights to Rodrigues Island by Air Mauritius. The trip takes 1½ hours and costs Rs 5490 per person return (minimum stay five days, maximum stay 30 days) or Rs 6120 (for stays of less than five days). Mauritians are charged half-price.

Air Mauritius also offers helicopter tours and charters from SSR (Sir Seewoosagur Ramgoolam) airport and a number of major hotels. 'Helitours' cost Rs 4800 for a 15 minute flight, with a maximum of four passengers (Rs 1200 per person). Extended tours last 20 minutes and cost Rs 5600 (Rs 1400 per person). The tours take you over craters, waterfalls and mountains in the region of your hotel.

If you have money to burn, you can hire the whole helicopter for around Rs 12,000 per hour. Depending on the helicopter's operational base, repositioning flight time charges may also be required. For information and reservations, contact the Air Mauritius Helicopter section (☎ 6373552; fax 6373424).

BUS

Bus services are generally good – if a bit slow – and can take you just about anywhere. The express buses are faster than the standard buses and only cost a little more.

The buses are single deck Ashok Leylands, Bedfords or Tatas in varying states of disrepair. There are five large bus companies: Corporation Nationale de Transport, Rose Hill Transport, United Bus Service, Triolet Bus Service and Mauritius Bus Transport, along with a score of individual operators.

To offset the bombed-out appearance of many of their vehicles, the private operators give the buses exotic, jet-set names such as 'Eiffel Tower', 'Arizona Express', 'Angel of Paradise', 'Sacred Arrow' and 'British Airways'!

A Swedish traveller made the following observations about bus travel:

Even the buses reflect the ethnic and religious mosaic of the country. In almost all buses, I saw stickers attached that showed all the gods and saints that protected the bus and its passengers, such as Jesus, Buddha, Vishnu, Sir Seewoosagur Ramgoolam, Krishna, Virgin Mary; and Donald Duck, Batman and Rambo.

Mikael Parkvall

No bus service covers the entire island. Rather, there are regional routes and services. The three main regions (north, centre and south) are served from major bus terminuses in Port Louis and Curepipe. If you want to go from Mahébourg to Grand Baie, for example, you must take two buses – from Mahébourg to Port Louis, and then from Port Louis to Grand Baie. Tamarin to Mahébourg involves two changes, one at Baie du Cap and the other at Souillac. The tourist office can supply a booklet, entitled *Mauritius – Information Guide*, which has a neat listing of bus operators, destinations, route numbers and departure points.

There is rarely a long wait for a bus in the main towns. During the busy hours they run every 10 minutes. In more remote areas you may have to wait up to half an hour or more. Buses in urban areas start running at around 5.30 am and stop between 6 and 8 pm; in rural regions buses operate between 6.30 am and 6.30 pm. The only late-night bus service operates until 11 pm between Port Louis and Curepipe and runs via Rose Hill, Quatre Bornes and Vacoas.

A trip shouldn't cost more than around Rs 20 on a standard service or Rs 22 on an express service. Each bus has a conductor who is often indistinguishable from the passengers, until he asks you for money. Keep small change handy, as large notes can sometimes be difficult to change. Keep your tickets, as inspectors often board to check them.

The buses are almost always packed, especially on the main routes, but with all the stops, turnover is quick. If you start the trip standing, you're likely to end up sitting.

The services appear to be fast because of the drivers' Niki Lauda impersonations, but the frequent stops slow things down. By standard service, it takes approximately an hour from Mahébourg to Curepipe, an hour from Curepipe to Port Louis and an hour from Port Louis to Grand Baie. The exceptions are the express services which cost a bit more, but take around half the time.

Be warned that some travellers have faced problems with taking large bags/backpacks on a bus. If it takes up a seat, you will probably have to pay for that extra seat. A few travellers have even been refused entry to a full bus if they have a large bag.

For bus-related information, contact the National Transport Authority (☎ 2121448).

CAR & MOTORCYCLE

Mauritian roads range from an excellent motorway to heavily potholed highways and minor roads. The motorway system runs from SSR airport to Port Louis and continues north.

Elsewhere the state of the highways and minor roads is inconsistent: a marvellous stretch of newly paved minor road will suddenly give way to a heavily patched and potholed major road. The danger comes from the drivers, not the roads. The heavy volume of buses is a hazard too, especially when they pick up speed and pass one another. Fortunately the frequency of townships and stops prevents the bus drivers getting completely carried away. Night driving should be avoided unless you enjoy an assault course of ill-lit oncoming vehicles, unfathomable potholes and weaving pedestrians. It is worth pointing out that the shock absorbers on many vehicles have long since given up the fight with the potholes.

There is not a great deal of scope for visitors to see Mauritius by motorbike, the most enjoyable area for this being around Grand Baie where motorbike/moped rental is available. At present, there are hardly any machines on the island over 70cc, which is a blessing, considering the number of people. The only bikes over 200cc have 'police' written on them.

Road Rules

The speed limit is supposed to be 50km/h in the built-up areas or 80km/h on the open road. Not many people stick to these limits and the island has its fair share of accidents. Motorists seem to think they can save on electricity by not switching on or repairing their headlights and the police are better at people control than traffic control.

Traffic congestion is heavy in Port Louis. There are many pedestrian zebra crossings, but cross with care. Don't expect courtesy or drivers worried about their insurance – you'll get knocked over.

Rental

In 1992, the government agreed to drop import tax on rental cars. The car rental agencies did reduce their charges, but car rental is still not great value. Drivers must be more than 23 years of age (some companies require a minimum age of 18 or 21), have held a driving licence for at least one year and payment must be made in advance. Many travellers say they were never asked to produce an international driver's licence when renting a car. However, all foreigners are technically required to have an international driver's licence if they wish to drive, so it's safest to carry one. If you're stopped by the police, you will have to show it.

Car rental prices differ from company to company. On average, a Reef Cub costs Rs 700 a day (cheaper for longer rentals) with unlimited mileage. On top of that you may be required to pay a deposit of up to Rs 12,000, refundable on the safe return of the vehicle. In addition you pay for petrol (around Rs 14.15 per litre) and about Rs 300 if you decide to have the car delivered or collected.

Top of the range is a Hyundai Accent or Mitsubishi Galant which will cost around Rs 1500 a day plus all the extras. If you're after some serious pampering, you can also hire a chauffeur for about Rs 450 a day.

For moped rental, Grand Baie offers the widest choice. Expect to pay at least Rs 150/300 for a half/full day. A deposit of around Rs 500 is often required.

Private Hire A far cheaper alternative is private car hire – all unofficial, of course. Legally speaking, you simply borrow a friend's car and slip him or her some money for the petrol and for presents for the kids. Of course, this does not include insurance, so it's somewhat of a risk to all parties involved.

There is usually no shortage of 'friends'. Ask small hotel and pension operators to put you in touch with someone. Donations range from around Rs 300 to Rs 600 a day, depending on the state of the car and the disposition of the car owner.

BICYCLE

Although some roads are too busy to make getting around on a bicycle enjoyable, it is really one of the best ways to see Mauritius. It is amazing how much ground you can cover in a day without killing yourself or getting saddle-sore. Around the coast roads, there are few hills. The inland roads are not particularly undulating either. You only really understand the scale until you actually travel around the island and see that you're usually in the next place before you realise you've left the last one. Be cautious whenever cycling on any road, especially the busy main ones. Avoid cycling at night, as most roads are poorly lit and traffic can be erratic.

Rental

The cheapest rental deals start at around Rs 25/100 per hour/day. Rental models are usually mountain bikes. All should have a lock. Check the state of the bike before riding off into the sunset, as some are mighty uncomfortable and look like they are about to keel over and die! To find out where you can hire a bike, ask at your hotel or contact a travel agent (for further information see Getting Around in the Grand Baie section in the North Mauritius chapter).

HITCHING

Hitching is never entirely safe in any country and is not recommended, especially for women. Travellers who make the decision to hitch, should be aware that they are taking a small but potentially serious risk. For those who do decide to hitch, hopefully the below advice will help to make their journey as fast and safe as possible.

Getting a lift in Mauritius is subject to pretty much the same quirks of luck and fate that one experiences hitching anywhere. Travellers are advised not to hitch at night and women shouldn't hitch alone – even several women together shouldn't accept lifts from only men; ascertain that there are women and/or children in the vehicle before climbing in.

BOAT

For advice on sailing around Mauritius, contact Yacht Charters (☎ 2638395; fax 2637814) on Route Royale (Royal Road) in Grand Baie.

You can charter a yacht or join a sailing tour in Grand Baie (for details see Activities in the Mauritius Facts for the Visitor chapter). Other popular sails are to Île Plate (Flat Island), Coin de Mire (Gunner's Quoin) and Baie du Tombeau (Tomb Bay).

To visit other, smaller islands dotted around the coastline, contact a local fisherman and make it worth his while to give up the day's catch. At Mahébourg, for instance, fishermen may take a group out for the day for about Rs 250 to Rs 400 per person, but not for less than around Rs 800 overall.

Some hotels and guesthouses run boat trips to the nearest islands. Île aux Cerfs, however, has a daily ferry service between 9 am and 4 pm, with crossings every 30 minutes. It costs Rs 70 per person return.

There are always the pirogues (small canoes) for getting across rivers and bays. Again, agree on a price before you set off, to avoid confusion later.

The only way of getting to the outer isles of Cargados Carajos is by yacht, unless you know someone high up in the relevant ministry or with the administrators. There are 52 small islands in the group, which lies 370km north-east of Mauritius.

Passenger Ships

The only passenger service is on the MV *Mauritius Pride*, which runs several times each month to Rodrigues Island. For details see Getting There & Away in the Rodrigues & the Outer Islands chapter.

LOCAL TRANSPORT
The Airport

Mauritian taxis have a meter, but they are not always used. You should agree on a price before the driver takes you first to your hotel and then to the cleaners! Refer to the taxi section below for more details and a table of sample fares from the airport. When making your hotel/guesthouse reservation, ask if they do airport transfers – the smaller places often charge a lower rate than the taxis.

A cheap alternative if you are backpacking or carrying little luggage is the public bus service. Ignore efforts by taxi drivers to deny the existence of this service. Express buses travelling between Mahébourg and Port Louis stop at a small bus shelter just outside the entrance gates to the airport terminal once an hour, between 6.30 am and 6.30 pm. When leaving the terminal, walk straight across the car park to the bus stop – a distance of about 500m.

If you want to get a bus from Grand Baie to the airport, you'll have to take a bus to Port Louis and from there get a bus to Mahébourg (which stops at the airport). Overall, a taxi is far quicker and much more convenient – especially if you have several pieces of luggage.

The terminal at SSR airport has a restaurant, bar and some duty-free shops. The major banks have offices open for the arrival and departure of most international flights. With the vast majority of arrivals belonging to organised tour parties or package groups, the tourist board sees no need for an information counter. However, the Mauritius Chamber of Commerce & Industry runs an accommodation service for independent travellers.

There are some pushy porters at the airport who attempt to grab your bags or suitcases even when you do not require their services. A firm, polite refusal is enough to see them off. If you do need their help, make sure you tip them (around Rs 10).

Taxi

The biggest drawback to using Mauritian taxis is the ridiculous shenanigans sometimes required to negotiate a reasonable fare.

You *must* agree on the price before getting into the taxi, and make sure there is no doubt about it. If you arrange a daily rate and itinerary, it helps to get the details down in writing. Ignore sudden requests for extra petrol money en route.

Many guesthouse managers/owners have attempted to mitigate their guest's constant frustration with rip-offs by making price arrangements with local taxi drivers. The quotes given under such arrangements, particularly those from small guesthouses, are often acceptable. Once you've got a feel for the rates, you can venture into independent bargaining.

The fleet of venerable British Morris Minors and Morris Oxfords has been replaced by less appealing Japanese vehicles. Taxis are easily recognised on the road by their white registration plates with black figures; private cars have the opposite colour scheme for their registration plates. At the time of writing, there were plans to make it compulsory for all taxis to have a taxi sign on their roof, which will make it easier for visitors to identify them.

As a general rule, fares quoted by the taxi driver include payment for the return to base. A taxi operator, whose base of operation is at the airport or a hotel, may claim an additional fee of Rs 15 for every bag over 100cm in width or length transported in the cab. Some taxis charge around Rs 25 for a surfboard. To repeat a golden rule: when using a taxi at the airport or elsewhere on Mauritius, fix a price before you ride.

For around Rs 1500 to Rs 2000 you can hire a taxi for a full-day tour of sights around the island (the fare often varies with how much ground you intend to cover). This allows you to tailor your tour to suit your interests and you can cut costs by forming a group – the price should *not* be calculated per person. Make sure the fare includes waiting time. If you want to squeeze a tour of the whole island into one day, keep in mind that this won't leave much time for sightseeing. You're better off splitting the island tour into two days. In terms of language, although most drivers can speak both French and English, just double check before setting off, to ensure you won't face a day-long communication barrier.

Taxis generally charge more at night. If you want the comfort of air-con, expect to pay an extra Rs 100/200 per hour/day. It's also worth remembering that some taxis charge around Rs 1.30 per minute waiting time. It seems minimal, but can certainly add up if you want to stop for lunch or do some sightseeing on foot. Your best bet is to negotiate a fare with the driver which includes waiting time. As a rough bargaining guide, here are some of the fares you can expect to pay for one-way trips (at the time of writing, there were unconfirmed plans to hike taxi rates by around 25%, so keep this in mind):

SSR airport to Mahébourg	Rs 250
SSR airport to Curepipe	Rs 350
SSR airport to Tamarin or Port Louis	Rs 600
SSR airport to Grand Baie	Rs 700
Trou aux Biches to Grand Baie	Rs 100
Trou aux Biches to Port Louis	Rs 300
Trou aux Biches to Curepipe	Rs 500
Centre de Flacq to Port Louis	Rs 600

Share Taxis When individual fares are hard to come by, some cabs will cruise around their area supplementing the bus service.

For quick, short-haul trips, they pick up passengers waiting at the bus stops and charge just a little more than the bus. These are the 'share taxis' or 'taxi trains'. Mind you, if you flag down a share taxi you'll only be swapping a big sardine can for a small one. If you flag down an empty cab, you may have to pay the full fare.

ORGANISED TOURS

The island's main tour operators book most of their customers through overseas travel agencies or through the hotels before the visitors' arrival. If you are pushed for time, but not money, the following tour operators may be worth contacting:

Mauritius Travel & Tourist Bureau
    Corner Royal & Sir William Newton Sts, Port Louis (☎ 2084734/39)
Mauritours
    5 Venkatasananda St, Rose Hill (☎ 4541666 or 4643078)
    10 Sir William Newton St, Port Louis (☎ 2085241)
Mautourco
    Gustave Colin St, Forest Side (☎ 6743695; fax 6743720)
White Sand Tours
    La Chaussée, Port Louis (☎ 2126092)

There are also scores of smaller travel agencies which largely cater for Mauritians going overseas.

MAURITIUS

Port Louis

HIGHLIGHTS

- Stunning views of Port Louis and its environs from Fort Adelaide
- Strolling around the bustling Port Louis market
- Try your luck at the casino or dine out in the impressive new Le Caudan Waterfront complex
- A visit to the Natural History Museum & Mauritius Institute for a taste of the country's history

Some pronounce it 'Por Lwee'; to others it is 'Port Loo-is'. The early Dutch settlers called it Noordt Wester Haven. Port Louis, the burgeoning Mauritian capital, with a population of around 150,000, is a large city in proportion to the size of the island, but relatively small considering the total population of the country. During the day it bustles as a commercial centre – the snarling traffic can be a nightmare at times. Nights are quiet and some might even say dead.

There is a distinct Muslim area around Muammar El Khadafi Square, and a Chinatown around Royal St.

The once varied architecture of the city is being replaced by nondescript concrete structures. The new hot spot in town is the swanky Le Caudan Waterfront complex, which among other things, houses a casino, cinemas, shops and eating joints. The centre of Port Louis, where you'll find most of the businesses and sites of interest, is easily covered on foot.

Orientation

The only disorienting thing about Port Louis is the street names. First, they are a mixture of English and French – even the government maps and literature mix up 'rue' and 'street', 'route' and 'road'. Then there are similar-sounding names. Beware, there are three E Laurent Sts, all in the centre of town! There is Eugène Laurent, Edouard Laurent and Edgar Laurent.

On top of that there are renamed streets, and streets which change name halfway along. For example, Desforges St (or Rue Desforges) has become Sir Seewoosagur Ramgoolam St, which some old maps have as Aldophe de Plevitz St, which is really what is now called Intendance St, which runs into Jules Koenig St, which becomes Sir John Pope Hennessy St...! Still with me?

Others have been changed for political or historical reasons, depending on who has fallen in or out of favour. New Moka St is now President John Kennedy St, but so there are no hard feelings, Muammar El Khadafi Square is on the other side of the city centre.

Sir William Newton St is the main street. The centre point would be Government House, at the top of the Place d'Armes. The three bus stations surround the centre within easy walking distance.

You may not always be able to say exactly where you are, but you can't really get lost. You can walk around Port Louis to see places of interest and do whatever business you have to do. Taxis or buses are not really necessary unless you want to get out to Ste-Croix to see the tomb of Père Laval.

Information

Tourist Office The tourist office, Mauritius Tourism Promotion Authority (☎ 2011703; fax 2125142), is on the ground floor of the Emmanuel Anquetil building on Sir Seewoosagur Ramgoolam St. However it may be shifting to the Air Mauritius Centre (see below for address). It is open Monday to Friday from 9 am to 4 pm and until noon on Saturday.

Air Mauritius (☎ 2087700; fax 2088331) is at the Air Mauritius Centre on President John Kennedy St. Rogers House ('Airline House'), 5 President John Kennedy St, is the headquarters of Air France, Air Madagascar, SAA and Air India. In the same building, there's also an Air Mauritius office and travel agent, Rogers & Co Aviation (☎ 2086801).

Singapore Airlines (☎ 2087695) is at 5 Duke of Edinburgh Ave.

Foreign Consulates Most foreign embassies/consulates are found in Port Louis. Countries with diplomatic representation are listed under Embassies in the Mauritius Facts for the Visitor chapter.

Money There is no shortage of banks in Port Louis centre, but you'll find none in the 'suburbs'. Half of Sir William Newton St seems to be taken up with main offices, with a few sub-branches within walking distance. The main Barclays Bank (☎ 2121816) and the main Mauritius Commercial Bank (☎ 201-2801) are on Queen St and Royal St respectively. The Banque Nationale de Paris Intercontinentale (☎ 2084147) is opposite the main post office.

Post & Communications The main post office (☎ 2082851) in Port Louis is near the harbour, at the bottom of Sir William Newton St. There is a free poste restante service here (counter No 1) which holds letters for around three months. You'll need to show some identification when picking up your mail.

There are also other post offices in the centre of Port Louis, including at the Victoria Square bus station and near the tourist office, in the Emmanuel Anquetil building and opposite the church at the end of Maillard St. They are all open Monday to Friday from 8.15 to 11.15 am and from noon to 4 pm, and on Saturdays from 8.15 to 11.45 am. The last 45 minutes before closing are for stamp sales only.

You can make international calls through the Overseas Telecommunications Service (OTS) at Rogers House, 5 President John Kennedy St. Call ☎ 2081036 for inquiries.

DHL Worldwide Express (☎ 2087711), 14 Monseigneur Gonin St, can arrange air freight around the world. The office is open Monday to Friday from 8.30 am to 4.30 pm and on Saturday from 8.30 am to noon.

American Express The American Express

representative is the Mauritius Travel & Tourist Bureau or MTTB (☎ 2082041; fax 2088607), close to the corner of Sir William Newton and Royal Sts.

Travel Agencies See Organised Tours in the Mauritius Getting Around chapter, for details about tour operators on the island.

Bookshops Port Louis has the best bookshop on the island – Book Court (☎ 2119262; fax 2119263) at Le Caudan Waterfront. It has a well-displayed range of French and English-language books covering a plethora of topics from cooking to economics. There are also a variety of newspapers and magazines; French-language publications include *Le Nouvel Observateur*, *Paris Match* and *Le Point*. English-language publications include *The Times*, *The Sun*, *Daily Mail* and *Sunday Times*.

There are several smaller bookshops in Port Louis including Librairie Bourbon and Librairie Nalanda, both within a few metres of each other on Bourbon St; and Librairie du Trèfle on Royal St. The range of books at these places is not as broad as at Book Court.

Laundry Most hotels in Port Louis either have their own laundry service or can arrange for your clothes to be washed.

Medical Services See Hospitals & Clinics in the Health section of the Mauritius Facts for the Visitor chapter.

Emergency For the police or ambulance, call ☎ 999 and ask to be connected with the required service. Call ☎ 995 for fire.

Dangers & Annoyances Pickpockets, usually operating by expertly slitting pockets or bags, are most prevalent at busy markets and on crowded buses. A recent police crackdown has improved the situation, but you should still exercise caution at all times. A moneybelt, worn under clothing, is a wise idea. Port Louis seems quite dead at night, but locals advise against roaming the streets late in the evening.

MAURITIUS

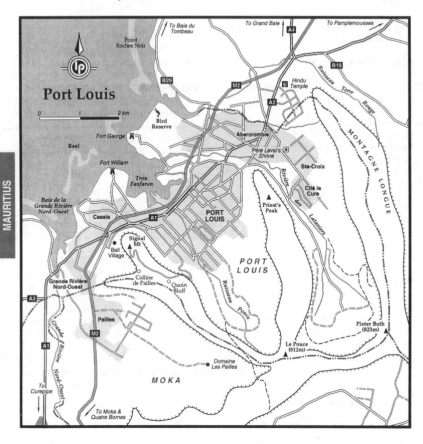

Natural History Museum & Mauritius Institute

Most tourists visit the Museum and Institute, on Chausée St, to see the stuffed replica of the dodo, the 'abnormal member of a group of pigeons', which became extinct between 1681 and 1693. In 1989, the dodo exhibits underwent extensive repairs at the Royal Museum of Scotland in Edinburgh. The most pristine exhibit was returned to this institute in Mauritius three years later.

The dodo is the centrepiece, but there are stuffed representations of other extinct birds such as the Seychelles Dutch pigeon, the Bourbon crested starling, broad-billed and Mascarene parrots and the solitaire. The stuffing extends to specimens of other birds, animals and fish that are still with us.

If you want to read more about Mauritius, there is a library upstairs at the back of the building. Sometimes the Institute, formerly the offices of the French East India Company, plays host to a commercial or artistic exhibition.

The Institute (☎ 2120639) is open on weekdays except Wednesday from 9 am to 4 pm, and on weekends from 9 am to noon. Admission is free.

Mauritius Postal Museum

This little museum, next door to the main post office, houses a collection of Mauritian stamps and assorted philately. Items on display include a range of old stamps, telegraph machines, printing plates and other interesting postal paraphernalia. There are also replicas of the two renowned 'Post Office' stamp which date back to 1847. The museum (☎ 2082851) is open Monday to Friday from 9 am to 4 pm and also on Saturday from 9 to 11.30 am. Admission is free. There's a collection of stamps and souvenirs for sale.

At the time of writing, there were plans to open a Mauritian stamp museum at Le Caudan Waterfront. Call the complex (☎ 2116560) to find out whether this has happened.

Jummah Mosque

Mauritius' main mosque, built in the 1850s, is stuck in the middle of Chinatown! There is a sign just inside the heavy, carved wooden doors on Royal St inviting visitors every day except Thursday and Friday between 10 am and noon. If you wish to visit, do so with respect – see Society & Conduct in the Facts about the Region chapter at the beginning of this book.

Père Laval's Shrine

This is the Lourdes of the Indian Ocean. To get there, take the Père Laval bus from Labourdonnais bus terminal. For Rs 5, it goes directly to the shrine and church at Ste-Croix, via Sir Seewoosagur Ramgoolam St, Plaine Verte and Abercrombie.

The shrine is separate from the church and is open for pilgrims daily from 6 am to 6 pm. Pilgrimage tours arrive mostly from Réunion, but also from South Africa, the UK, France and the Seychelles. You get a strange feeling when you look at the coloured plaster effigy of Père Laval on top of the tomb. Many pilgrims touch the effigy and, in turn, touch their children. Miracle cures are said to have taken place.

To learn more about Père Jacques Laval, visit the shop and permanent exhibition of his robe, mitre, letters and photographs.

Père Laval (1803-64) is said to have converted more than 67,000 people to Christianity during his 23 years in Mauritius.

Opening hours are 8.30 am to 5 pm from Monday to Saturday, and 10 am to 4.30 pm on Sundays. The church is an interesting example of modern architecture and design, with an unusual and effective use of mosaic and stained-glass windows.

Other Churches & Cathedrals

Other notable places of worship are the St Louis Cathedral (1932) at the top of Sir William Newton St, the St James Cathedral (1828) at the top of Poudrière St, and the Holy Sacrament Church (1879) on Menagerie St, Cassis.

Place d'Armes

A statue of Mahé de La Bourdonnais stands near the quayside end of the avenue, which leads up to the colonial Government House. The avenue is lined with half-buried cannons chained together, which are supposed to symbolise peace.

Company Gardens

Beginning near Chaussée St, next to the Mauritius Institute, this was once the vegetable patch of the French East India Company. It is now a meeting place and shady retreat

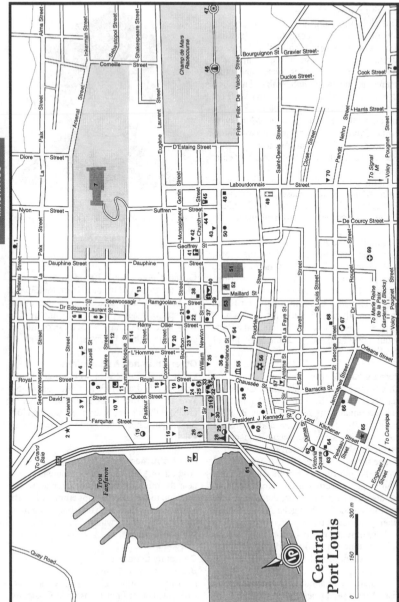

PLACES TO STAY
6 Hotel Le Grand
   Carnot
12 Hotel Moderne
14 Bourbon Tourist
   Hotel
38 City (Ambassador)
   Hotel
48 Rossignol Hotel
61 Labourdonnais
   Waterfront Hotel;
   Le Caudan
   Waterfront
   Complex
64 Tandoori Tourist
   Hotel &
   Restaurant
68 Le Saint Georges
   Hotel

PLACES TO EAT
3 Kwang Chow
4 Lai Min
5 Poisson D'Or
8 Foong Shing
10 Merchant Navy Club
13 Providence 'Hotel'
   Bakery &
   Restaurant
16 Namaste
18 First Restaurant
19 Chez Madeleine
20 Paloma
23 Underground
   Restaurant
30 Cari Poulé;
   Singapore Airlines
32 Snow White
35 La Bonne Marmite &
   Rocking Boat Pub
42 DSL (Deva
   Saraswatee
   Laxmi) Coffee
   House

43 Hotel National
   Restaurant
44 Chez Kayoum
   Snack Bar
54 La Flore
   Mauricienne
57 La Palmeraie
70 Le Patrimoine

OTHER
1 Muammar El
   Khadafi Square
2 Police Station
7 Fort Adelaide
   (The Citadel)
9 L'Amicale Chinese
   Gaming House
11 Jummah Mosque
15 Immigration Square
   Bus Station
17 Market
21 Librairie Nalanda
22 Librairie Bourbon
24 Librairie du Trèfle
25 Mauritius
   Commercial Bank
26 Banque Nationale
   de Paris
   Intercontinentale
27 Main Post Office;
   Mauritius Postal
   Museum
28 Mahé de La
   Bourdonnais
   Statue
29 Labourdonnais
   Bus Terminal
31 Barclays Bank
33 Mauritours
34 MTTB (American
   Express)
36 Government
   House
37 Municipal Theatre

39 Mauritius Tourism
   Promotion
   Authority (Tourist
   Office); Co-op
   Cafeteria
40 Centre Post Office
41 St Louis Cathedral
45 Jolie Madame Bar
46 King Edward VII
   Statue
47 Malartic Tomb
49 St James Cathedral
50 Luna Park Cinema
51 Supreme Court
52 Police Station
53 Town Hall
55 Natural History
   Museum &
   Mauritius Institute
56 Company Gardens
58 Local Handicraft
   Centre
59 Air Mauritius
   Centre
60 Rogers House:
   OTS; US
   Embassy;
   Australian High
   Commission;
   Rogers &
   Co Aviation;
   Air Madagascar;
   Air France; SAA;
   Air India
62 Taxi Stand
63 Victoria Square Bus
   Station
65 Police Station
66 Passport &
   Immigration Office
67 French Embassy
69 Jeetoo (Civil)
   Hospital
71 Chinese Pagoda

for lovers, strollers and statues. The line of statues includes that of the poet Léoville L'Homme.

Fort Adelaide

Fort Adelaide is also called the Citadel because it resembles a Moorish fortress, high on the crown of the hill. It is one of four forts in and around Port Louis that were built by the British. The other three, Fort George, Fort Victoria and Fort William, are in ruins or inaccessible. There is rumoured to be a tunnel linking Fort Adelaide with

Fort George, at the northern entrance to Port Louis harbour.

There are splendid views of Port Louis from Fort Adelaide – you can see how the city is mushrooming. After dark this is apparently a popular retreat for young lovers, who come here for the romantic city view and seclusion. At the time of writing, there were plans to build a restaurant and theatre inside the fort.

Signal Mt

It used to be possible to drive to the top of

Signal Mt, via the Military Rd, for another good view of Port Louis and its surroundings. These days, you can only get up here by foot.

Le Pouce

For details about the hike to this peak, see the boxed story on Hiking & Trekking under Activities in the Mauritius Facts for the Visitor chapter.

Champ de Mars Racecourse

Also known as the Hippodrome, the 'Field of Mars' was a military training ground until the Mauritian Turf Club was founded in 1812. The police and army still use it for the odd manoeuvre during the off-season. The racing season is from around May to late November. There are two monuments – a statue of King Edward VII, by the sculptor Prosper d'Epinay, and the Malartic Tomb, an obelisk to a French governor. The latter was blown down by a cyclone in 1892 and re-erected the following year.

For more details about horse racing see Spectator Sport in the Mauritius Facts for the Visitor chapter.

Chinese Pagoda, Astrologers & Dragons

The Chinese flavour is evident around the capital – one interesting building is the Chinese Pagoda on Volcy Pougnet St. There are several Chinese astrologers around the old centre of Port Louis. Around Rémy Ollier St there are a number of ladies' hairdressers with evocative names like Dragon Rouge, Dragon Royal and Dragon Magique.

Organised Tours

If you're interested in a tour of Port Louis contact Citirama (☎ 2122484; fax 2123348). They conduct a three hour tour which takes in all the main sites around town. It costs Rs 350 per person and advance bookings are essential. They may also be able to tailor-make other tours on request.

Places to Stay

With most tourists heading north to the beach resort area, the choice of places to stay in Port Louis is decidedly limited and quite lacklustre.

Because many of the hotels often appear empty, it is worth negotiating a cheaper rate, especially if you are staying for a few days. Check to see if the price includes a ceiling fan, towels, toilet paper, soap and breakfast. The showers are rarely wonderful in the cheaper places. Instead of a hot spray, you'll often get a cold dribble because the heater at the shower head is invariably broken.

Places to Stay – bottom end

Hotel Le Grand Carnot (☎ 2403054), at 17 Dr Edouard Laurent St, makes an effort to cater to travellers, making it one of the best budget options in town. Singles/doubles with private bath cost Rs 250/350, including breakfast.

Hotel Moderne (☎ 2402382), a small place at 36 Rivière St, is run by the owners of Hotel Le Grand Carnot. It offers ordinary doubles with a communal bathroom for around Rs 250, including breakfast.

Tandoori Tourist Hotel & Restaurant (☎ 2122131), on the corner of Victoria Square bus station and Jemmapes St, is a bargain, although not a 'red hot' one. Owned by Mr Narrainen and managed by his son, Navin, the Tandoori has 17 basic rooms of various sizes, most with an attached bathroom. Singles/doubles are Rs 200/300, but choose carefully as some rooms can cop a bit of traffic noise.

City (Ambassador) Hotel (☎ 2120466; fax 2085340), on Sir Seewoosagur Ramgoolam St, does not rate well among travellers. Worn and weary singles/doubles cost Rs 495/605, including breakfast and air-conditioning.

Bourbon Tourist Hotel (☎ 2404407), at 36 Jummah Mosque St, is OK but has somewhat of an institutional feel to it. Air-con singles/doubles with attached bath go for Rs 500/550, including breakfast.

Rossignol Hotel (☎ 2121983) is out towards the Champ de Mars racecourse. Quite frankly, it's a rather shabby place which attracts few foreigners. If you're still interested, singles/doubles with bath cost Rs 250/350, including breakfast.

Places to Stay – middle

Le Saint Georges Hotel (☎ 2112581; fax 2110885), at 19 St George St, has 60 comfortable rooms with air-con and attached bath for Rs 750/900 a single/double. The most luxurious rooms cost Rs 1250/1400 a single/double. Breakfast is included in all room tariffs. Good meals are available in the restaurant (see Places to Eat). This hotel is becoming increasingly popular with business travellers, so try to book well ahead.

Places to Stay – top end

Labourdonnais Waterfront Hotel (☎ 2024000; fax 2024040), overlooking the harbour, is by far the most exclusive place to stay in Port Louis. Facilities in this grand hotel include two restaurants (see Places to Eat), a relaxing bar, swimming pool, health centre and business centre. They can also arrange deep-sea fishing and island tours. The cheapest singles/doubles will set you back Rs 3150/4400, including breakfast. If you want luxury, go for the presidential suite which costs around Rs 12,700. Lots of business travellers stay here so an advance reservation is wise.

Places to Eat

Port Louis is spiced with small, cheap eating establishments ranging from cosy cafés to ramshackle roadside stalls. There's also a handful of more expensive restaurants serving Indian, Chinese, Créole or European fare. The only drawback is that most places close in the evening, but you can always get a late-night bite at Le Caudan Waterfront (see below for details). Remember that most restaurants whack government tax onto the bill and there are few places open on Sunday.

Co-op Cafeteria, in the Emmanuel Anquetil building, offers very cheap lunches and is popular with nearby office workers. You can get a big plate of fish and chips for around Rs 20. But cafeteria is the word.

Providence 'Hotel' Bakery & Restaurant, on Sir Seewoosagur Ramgoolam St, also attracts office workers in search of cheap snacks.

Poisson D'Or, on Anquetil St, is a simple, but cheap, little Chinese restaurant. A bowl of noodles or fried rice costs around Rs 35.

Foong Shing, on Rémy Ollier St, is another source of tasty and reasonably priced Chinese food.

Namaste, near the corner of Farquhar and Corderie Sts, serves cheap curries and biryanis for between Rs 25 and Rs 40.

Chez Kayoum Snack Bar, on Church St, is nothing fancy, but quite good for a quick bite; snacks cost from Rs 15 to Rs 40.

Merchant Navy Club, at the bottom end of Rivière St near the Immigration Square bus station, is a relaxing private club where you can enjoy a drink and a snack in peaceful surroundings. Temporary membership is open to visiting ship and yacht crews (making this a bit of a blokes hangout), but they also allow access to passing visitors. Snacks are served between 9 am and 10.30 pm. There is a billiard room, table tennis, Space Invaders and a bar. Toasted sandwiches are around Rs 15 and coffee is Rs 12.

Beer costs Rs 16/27 for a small/large bottle, while soft drinks are Rs 8.50. Quite a few travellers have recommended this place.

Chez Madeleine, on Bourbon St, offers cheap eats such as fried rice (Rs 50) and chicken soup (Rs 50).

Hotel National Restaurant, opposite the Luna Park cinema, is in a converted colonial home behind wrought-iron gates. This forlorn place once functioned as a hotel. Today it is in a dismal state of dusty decay. It offers Chinese food for lunch – although it's usually empty.

Le Caudan Waterfront (☎ 2116560), near the harbour, has a range of restaurants offering Indian, Mediterranean, Chinese and western fare. There's also the usual selection of fast food – pizza, pasta, hamburgers and greasy chips. Or you can come here just for a coffee and cake. Most eating places are open daily from around 10.30 am to 11 pm.

DSL (Deva Saraswatee Laxmi) Coffee House (☎ 2120259), Geoffroy St, specialises in south Indian food. It's on the 1st floor and diners can sit inside or outside along the narrow balcony. Main dishes start at around Rs 40 and there are some good vegetarian options.

Paloma (☎ 2085861), on L'Homme St, is a Chinese-European restaurant where main dishes cost between Rs 50 and Rs 100. The restaurant is open daily except Sunday from 10 am to 5 pm.

Snow White (☎ 2083528), on the corner of Sir William Newton and Queen Sts, is more centrally located than the Paloma and is more popular (especially with lunching office workers). Fried rice with prawns costs Rs 70, vegetable noodles are Rs 55. It's open daily except Sunday from 10 am to 3 pm.

First Restaurant (☎ 2120685), not far from Snow White, serves Europeanised Chinese food. It's a pleasant surprise at the top of a seedy staircase and is open daily from 11 am to 2.30 pm and 6 to 9.30 pm. The menu has all the usual Chinese stuff, such as sweet and sour pork (Rs 75) and stir-fried seasonal vegetables (Rs 40). For a real culinary adventure try the chicken feet (Rs 80).

Tandoori Tourist Hotel & Restaurant (☎ 2120031) (see Places to Stay) is popular at lunchtime and offers main courses from between Rs 45 and Rs 100. It's open Monday to Saturday from 8 am to 5 pm.

Underground Restaurant (☎ 2120064), on Bourbon St between L'Homme and Rémy Ollier Sts, serves a variety of dishes for between Rs 40 and Rs 70. The menu is mostly in French, so ask for help if you can't make sense of anything. Items include chicken, chips and salad (Rs 50), fried rice (Rs 35) and prawn curry (Rs 60).

La Flore Mauricienne (☎ 2122200), on Intendance St, near Government House, is a popular place for diplomatic and business lunches. It specialises in French and Créole cuisine, but is only open for lunch on weekdays. Main dishes are upwards of Rs 130.

MAURITIUS

Cari Poulé (☎ 2121295), next to the Singapore Airlines office on Duke of Edinburgh Ave, is probably the best Indian restaurant in town. A mixed vegetable curry costs Rs 110, while meat eaters can tuck into a rogan josh for Rs 150. From Monday to Friday it opens between 11 am and 3 pm. On Saturday, opening hours are extended for dinner from 7 to 11 pm.

Lai Min (☎ 2420042), on Royal St, is known for its Chinese cuisine but according to some travellers, it's overpriced. Set menus for a minimum of two people range from Rs 180 to Rs 320 per person. Individual dishes cost between Rs 70 and Rs 350. Lai Min is open daily from 11.30 am to 2.30 pm and 6.30 to 9.30 pm.

Kwang Chow (☎ 2409735), not far from Lai Min, is a cheaper Chinese alternative.

La Palmeraie (☎ 2122597), at 7 Sir Antelne St, is only open for lunches on weekdays. Expect to pay upwards of Rs 100 for a main course.

La Bonne Marmite (☎ 2122403) and the cosy *Rocking Boat Pub*, on Sir William Newton St, are in an attractive old building, formerly the oldest pharmacy in Mauritius. This somewhat pricey restaurant serves good Indian, Chinese and Créole food. Try the fish steak with Créole sauce, or the king prawns sautéed in a garlic-brandy sauce; each costs Rs 250. The restaurant is only open for lunch and is closed on weekends.

Le Patrimoine (☎ 2086286), on Labourdonnais St, specialises in Indian and Créole food. Main dishes range in price from Rs 50 to Rs 150.

Le Saint Georges Hotel (see Places to Stay) has a little restaurant that serves Créole and Indian cuisine. Main dishes hover around Rs 230 and desserts are about Rs 50. There's a variety of wines on offer; a bottle of South African wine costs between Rs 280 and Rs 400, while a bottle of French Chablis Bourgogne is Rs 900.

L'escale (☎ 2024000), at the Labourdonnais Waterfront Hotel (see Places to Stay), is recommended for a dose of pampering. Main dishes range from Rs 60 to Rs 350. There is a broad menu offering everything from an Australian sirloin steak (Rs 185) to a caesar salad with grilled chicken or fish (Rs 125). Or perhaps you might like to chomp into a giant traditional hot dog (Rs 120). The hotel also has a more upmarket seafood speciality restaurant, *La Rose des Vents*, with goodies such as grilled lobster in a light spring onion and butter sauce (Rs 140) and iced nougat parfait flavoured with honey (Rs 80). Nonresidents are welcome at both restaurants, but should try to book ahead.

Entertainment

Port Louis is certainly not abuzz with activity after dusk – indeed, some would say it is dead. However, the swish new *Le Caudan Waterfront* (☎ 2116560), overlooking the harbour, has pumped life into the capital. Apart from a collection of eating places, there's a flash casino and an impressive, three screen cinema (see below).

Cinemas The best cinema in Mauritius is at Le Caudan Waterfront, near the harbour. This attractive, three screen cinema complex shows the latest releases from around the world (in English and French). There are screenings at 11.30 am and 3, 6 and 9 pm (see newspapers to double check). Tickets cost Rs 80.

Less impressive is the Luna Park cinema, up towards the Champ de Mars racecourse. It predominantly screens French, Hindi and the occasional Tamil film.

Casino If you're feeling lucky, head for Le Caudan Waterfront, which has a glitzy casino offering all the usual games, including blackjack and American roulette, as well as slot machines. Tidy dress is expected so don't turn up in jeans and a T-shirt.

Gaming House *L'Amicale Chinese Gaming House*, near the corner of Anquetil and Royal Sts, is open Monday to Saturday from 7 pm until 2 am and from noon until 2 am on Sunday. It is not plush as far as casinos go, but very plush as far as Chinese gambling joints go.

L'Amicale has had its fair share of celebrities, as seen in the entrance hall. The gaming house doesn't overly welcome ordinary mortal sightseers with open arms, but neither does it shun them. As long as you are suitably dressed and look but don't disturb, they'll tolerate you in an inscrutable way.

It is fascinating to watch the croupiers shuffling, stacking, dealing and tossing big five cent coins onto bets to weigh them down. The games differ from the western versions and basically revolve around dice, dominoes and cards. Following is a brief description of some common Chinese gambling games you may see here.

Fan Tan is an ancient Chinese game practically unknown in the west. The dealer takes an inverted silver cup and plunges it into a pile of porcelain buttons, then moves the cup to one side. After all bets have been placed, the buttons are counted out in groups of four. The aim of the game is to bet on how many will remain after the last set of four has been taken out. You can bet on numbers one, two, three, four, as well as odd or even.

Dai Siu (Cantonese: 'big-small') is a very popular game, also known as *sik po* (dice treasure) or *cu sik* (guessing dice). The game is played with three dice which are placed in a covered glass container, then shaken. You bet that the total of the toss will be 'small' (from three to nine) or 'big' (10 to 18). Unless you bet directly on three of a kind, you lose on combinations where all three dice come up the same: 2-2-2, 3-3-3 etc.

Pai Kao is Chinese dominoes, and similar to mahjong. One player takes the role of banker and the other players individually compare their hands against the banker. In return for providing the gambling facilities, the casino generally deducts a commission from the winnings rather than being directly involved in the game.

Theatre You may be able to catch one of the local productions at the *Municipal Theatre*, behind Government House on Sir William Newton St.

Plays in Créole by local amateur groups usually take place each month. Prices vary according to what's playing – for instance, more renowned performances cost anywhere between Rs 50 to Rs 250. Sometimes entry fees go to charity.

The theatre, in a style similar to that of the London theatres, has changed little since it was built in 1822. It seats about 600 on three levels, has an exquisitely painted dome ceiling with chandeliers and is often used for Hindu weddings. You won't see anything like it now – it takes you right back in time. Usually there is a caretaker at the back entrance who may show you around, take you backstage and put on the house and stage lights.

Bars There are just a sprinkling of watering holes around town. You could try the unpretentious *Jolie Madame Bar* on the corner of Suffren and Church Sts (not recommended for unaccompanied women). For more salubrious surroundings, there's the *Merchant Navy Club* (see Places to Eat). If you're after a real dose of pampering, head for the elegant bar at the *Labourdonnais Waterfront Hotel* (see Places to Stay).

Things to Buy

You can pick up some interesting souvenirs at the city market (see the boxed text below). Alternatively, there are a handful of tourist-oriented shops in town where you can buy knick-knacks for friends back home. For

---

Port Louis Market

While you're in Port Louis try and squeeze in a visit to the vibrant city market, between Farquhar and Queen Sts. It has suffered several fires in its long existence, each time springing back from the ashes livelier than ever. The market has become one of the town's most popular tourist attractions and is certainly worth a look – just for the ambience if nothing else. It's full of sights, sounds and smells and gives you a real taste of local life. It's open Monday to Friday from around 6 am to 5.30 pm and on Saturday from 6 am to noon.

There's a somewhat smelly meat and fish section, as well as a large fruit and vegetable area surrounded by little alleys of craft, souvenir, clothing and aromatic spice stalls. There are some interesting Malagasy handicrafts for sale, such as leather bags, belts and wooden masks. You may come across vendors selling wild and wonderful medicinal plants and herbs – some with alluring aphrodisiac qualities, others which promise to burn unwanted tummy flab!

The hustling in the market can get mighty fierce at times, making it difficult to browse. Watch out for pickpockets – see Dangers & Annoyances earlier in this chapter. Vendors often inflate prices for tourists who seem to have lots of money and little time to spend it, so make sure you bargain hard. If you have no idea about how much something should cost, start by slashing the price by at least 30%, although you may even be able to trim prices by as much as 50%. ■

upmarket shopping there's Le Caudan Waterfront, which has an assortment of trendy clothing, jewellery and handicraft shops – most are open Monday to Friday from 9.30 am to 5.30 pm, on Saturday from 9 am to 7 pm and on Sunday from 9 am to noon. If the prices are too high for you, it's still good for some leisurely window-shopping.

For more information see Things to Buy in the Mauritius Facts for the Visitor chapter. Refer to Ecology & Environment in the Facts about Mauritius chapter for important information about shells, coral and turtle shell products which should not be purchased.

Getting There & Away

Bus There are two major bus stations in Port Louis within easy walking distance of the city centre. Buses for the southern and western routes use the Victoria Square terminus; those for the northern and eastern routes are based at Immigration Square (see the Central Port Louis map for locations).

Buses running the shorter routes to the north of Port Louis, including Baie du Tombeau (Rs 6) and Ste-Croix (Père Laval's tomb) (Rs 6), use the small Labourdonnais bus terminal, just off President John Kennedy St.

Buses on the southern route to Pointe aux Sables leave from Dumas St, the short road which runs into Victoria Square.

Getting Around

The Airport There are no direct airport buses, but express bus services operating between Port Louis and Mahébourg run via the airport. They start running early in the morning, but stop early in the evening. Allow two hours for the journey, just to be safe. The fare is Rs 15.

Expect to pay around Rs 600 for a taxi ride from Port Louis to the airport.

Taxi In Port Louis the cabs have a printed list of tariffs that they are obliged to show you. In practise it may prove hard to fathom the correct charge. See the Mauritius Getting Around chapter for more information on the trials and tribulations of dealing with taxi drivers. You should prepare for a bargaining session by asking an impartial local or your hotel staff for a rough idea of the going rate before taking a taxi. As a rough guide, expect to pay between Rs 30 and Rs 50 for a short hop across town. Keep in mind that taxi fares may have been increased by around 25% by now.

North Mauritius

HIGHLIGHTS

- Indulging in a tantalising array of water activities
- A fascinating stroll around the Sir Seewoosagur Ramgoolam Botanical Gardens in Pamplemousses
- Superb golden beaches of Baie de L'Arsenal, Troux aux Biches, Peréybère and Poudre d'Or
- Grand Baie, a busy tourist town with a cosmopolitan ambience
- Day trip to one of the nearby islands such as Coin de Mire or Île Plate

The northern part of the island is divided into two districts: Pamplemousses in the west and Rivière du Rempart in the east.

The north-west coastline is practically all tourist development, for international visitors and local holiday-makers alike. In contrast, there is scant development on the north-east coast, probably because there are few beaches. In between, stretches a plain of sugar cane fields, which slopes gently down to the sea. There are no mountains.

Grand Baie is the lively holiday centre with a concentration of hotels, guesthouses, apartments, restaurants, shops, and a small but busy beach. Peréybère, a few km to the north, is similar but considerably smaller, quieter and somewhat cheaper.

Moving west around Pointe aux Canonniers, you'll find a 12km stretch of terrific beach on which several luxury hotels have sprung up. There are still some good, clean public beaches, the biggest being Mon Choisy.

When the coast road heads inland to join the Port Louis road, the area becomes quiet and private again. Just 6km north of the capital is the Baie du Tombeau strip of budget hotels and guesthouses. The beaches here are also smaller and dowdier. This is a popular weekend retreat for sports and social clubs.

The main attraction in the interior is the Sir Seewoosagur Ramgoolam Botanical Gardens at Pamplemousses. Elsewhere, there is little of specific fascination, but the area is worth travelling around for its beauty.

BAIE DU TOMBEAU

'Tomb Bay', if you like (though nobody calls it that), was so named because it's a tomb for many ships. Pieter Both, a Dutch East Indies governor, went down with one in 1615. The distinctive mountain peak with the bobble on top, visible behind Port Louis, was named after him. It was predicted that the round boulder would topple off when British rule ended in Mauritius. So much for predictions.

The bay itself is sheltered within high cliffs. Access is possible for swimming, but in recent years there have been reports of serious pollution. An old pier acts as a good high diving point and is popular with local youths. At the mouth of the Rivière du Tombeau, the bay is the site of frequent searches by treasure hunters, convinced that pirates buried loot there. Not a single piece of eight has been found.

Route Royale (Royal Road), the coast road which stretches from Baie du Tombeau village down to Elizabethville, past the Dockers Flats and the New Goodwill rum distillery, is dotted with a number of small hotels and guesthouses. However few travellers choose to stay here, accounting for the diminishing number of hotels and the absence of restaurants. The Trou aux Biches beach crowd doesn't usually stray this far.

Places to Stay

The choice of accommodation in Baie du Tombeau is meagre and unremarkable. Over recent years, quite a few places have closed down due to poor business.

Corotel (☎ 2472355; fax 2472472), overlooking Baie du Tombeau, has singles/doubles with private bath for Rs 550/750, including breakfast. Air-con rooms cost Rs 650/850 a single/double. There's a restaurant; dishes include smoked marlin (Rs 90), sweet and sour prawns (Rs 125) and vegetable curry (Rs 45).

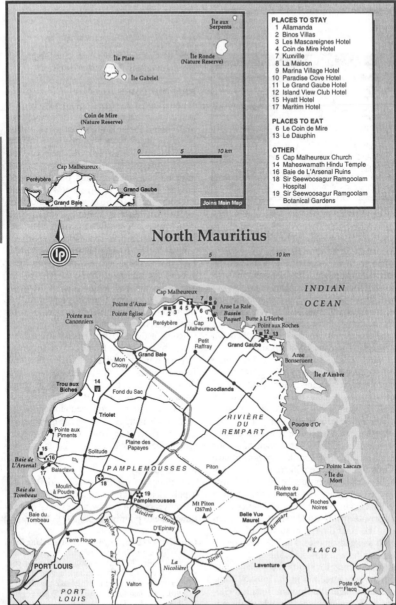

PLACES TO STAY
1 Allamanda
2 Binos Villas
3 Les Mascareignes Hotel
4 Coin de Mire Hotel
7 Kuxville
8 La Maison
9 Marina Village Hotel
10 Paradise Cove Hotel
11 Le Grand Gaube Hotel
12 Island View Club Hotel
15 Hyatt Hotel
17 Maritim Hotel

PLACES TO EAT
6 Le Coin de Mire
13 Le Dauphin

OTHER
5 Cap Malheureux Church
14 Maheswarnath Hindu Temple
16 Baie de L'Arsenal Ruins
18 Sir Seewoosagur Ramgoolam Hospital
19 Sir Seewoosagur Ramgoolam Botanical Gardens

Joins Main Map

North Mauritius

0   5   10 km

Île aux Serpents

Île Plate

Île Ronde (Nature Reserve)

Île Gabriel

Coin de Mire (Nature Reserve)

Cap Malheureux
Peréybère
Grand Gaube
Grand Baie

MAURITIUS

Cap Malheureux

Pointe d'Azur
Pointe Église
Pointe aux Canonniers

7 8 9
1 2 3 4 5 6 10
Anse La Raie
Bassin Paquet
Butte à L'Herbe
Point aux Roches
11 12 13

Peréybère
Cap Malheureux
Petit Raffray
Grand Gaube

INDIAN OCEAN

Anse Bonseruent

Île d'Ambre

Mon Choisy
Grand Baie
Trou aux Biches
14
Fond du Sac
Goodlands

Triolet

RIVIÈRE DU REMPART

Poudre d'Or

Pointe aux Piments
Plaine des Papayes

15
16
Baie de L'Arsenal
17 Balaclava
Solitude
Piton
Pointe Lascars
Île du Mort

18
Moulin à Poudre
PAMPLEMOUSSES

19
Baie du Tombeau
Pamplemousses
Mt Piton (267m)
Rivière du Rempart
Roches Noires

Baie du Tombeau

Rivière Citrons
D'Epinay
Belle Vue Maurel

Terre Rouge

FLACQ

PORT LOUIS

La Nicolière
Valton

Laventure

Poste de Flacq

PORT LOUIS

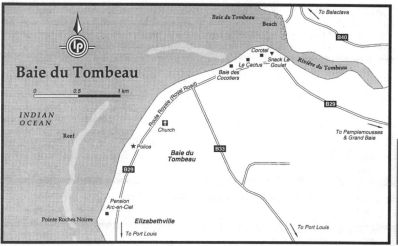

Le Cactus (☎ 2472485), near the Corotel, is smaller and more basic. Simple double rooms with attached bath go for Rs 350 per night.

Baie des Cocotiers (☎ 2472442), Route Royale, is a complex of self-catering bungalows from around Rs 550 per night. At the time of writing, there were rumours that this place may be closing down.

Pension Arc-en-Ciel (☎ 2472592; fax 2472966), towards Pointe Roches Noires, is the first lodging you'll come to after Elizabethville. This pension, run by Alan Tanyan, has singles/doubles for Rs 350/525 or Rs 525/725 with air-con. All rooms have a private bath and breakfast is included in the price; half-board is an extra Rs 150 per person. There's a swimming pool and billiard table.

Places to Eat

There are no independent restaurants in this area, which restricts you to eating at your hotel or venturing to the Grand Baie locality.

Snack Le Goulet (no phone), overlooking Baie du Tombeau from the cliff top, is a ramshackle little place which sells some groceries and a few mundane snacks.

Getting There & Away

Baie du Tombeau is not on the bus route to Grand Baie or Trou aux Biches. Instead, you can take a bus from Labourdonnais bus terminal in Port Louis. The buses turn around just past Snack Le Goulet.

A taxi from Port Louis to Baie du Tombeau costs at least Rs 150 (one way), Rs 300 from Grand Baie to Baie du Tombeau and Rs 200 from Trou aux Biches.

BALACLAVA & BAIE DE L'ARSENAL

The next bay north of Baie du Tombeau is the secluded but gorgeous Baie de L'Arsenal (also known as Baie aux Tortues). There you'll also find Balaclava, once one of the island's 'undiscovered' beauty spots, now rapidly being developed by hotel entrepreneurs. As it is tucked away from the public road in the grounds of the Maritim Hotel (see Places to Stay & Eat, below), it is still secluded. Nonresidents should ask at the security hut at the entrance to the hotel grounds for permission to visit the ruins complex. About 30m beyond the hut, a track on the right leads down to the ruined buildings of the French arsenal, flour mill and lime kiln, covered in vegetation and set among streams and waterfalls. The ensemble of buildings looks like an ancient water temple and garden. From here you can look across to the opposite riverbank, which is marred by the sprawling outlines of a hotel building site.

By the way, the name Balaclava has no connection with the Crimean War. It is thought to be a Créole reference to the 'black lava' which once covered much of Mauritius.

Places to Stay & Eat

Maritim Hotel (☎ 2615600; fax 2615670), overlooking Baie de L'Arsenal, is an upmarket hotel near a great swimming beach. There are huge gardens and an assortment of facilities including tennis courts and a golf course. Singles/doubles cost Rs 2800/4000, including breakfast. A sumptuous suite will set you back Rs 8000 (single or double occupancy). The hotel has two restaurants and a pool bar.

Hyatt Hotel (☎ 2615757; fax 2615709), on the coastline just north of Balaclava, was scheduled to start operating way back in 1993. Nobody seems to know when, or indeed if, it will open. Contact them directly for further details.

Getting There & Away

From the south, Balaclava can be reached on the B41 road from Moulin à Poudre; from the north, there is a road zigzagging inland from Pointe aux Piments to Balaclava. A taxi from Port Louis to Balaclava costs around Rs 250.

TROU AUX BICHES

The name means 'hole of the does'. Trou aux Biches is the sister 'hole' of the Trou aux Cerfs (stags) in Curepipe, only here there is no actual hole to speak of. Instead there are some luxury hotels, guesthouses, a golf course and a fine beach.

Trou aux Biches may be the Sunset Strip of Mauritius but it is still relatively sedate, although it can get busy on weekends. (As yet, there are no wild infestations of tourists here in the Indian Ocean as you'll find in Bali, Majorca or Montego Bay.) There are still some good stretches with beaches not overlooked by hotels. This is a chic area, but you can still find some reasonably priced guesthouses and apartments here.

Things to See

Some of the best public beaches are at Mon Choisy, which can get quite busy on weekends. If you're a sun worshipper, remember to slap on plenty of sunscreen.

At the Aquarium Centre (☎ 2656187), off Route Royale, you can see a variety of marine creatures. At the time of writing there were plans to move the Aquarium Centre from Trou aux Biches to another location (possibly Pointe aux Piments), so make sure you check first. Admission costs Rs 80.

Water/Other Activities

See Activities in the Mauritius Facts for the Visitor chapter.

Weddings & Honeymoons

Mauritius, in common with many other Indian Ocean islands, promotes itself as a romance centre. Trou aux Biches and nearby Grand Baie, in particular, are becoming increasingly popular wedding and honeymoon destinations. The deluxe hotels have been quick to swoop on this lucrative market segment, offering special honeymoon packages and pampering lovestruck couples with flowers, champagne and other dreamy extras. More and more couples are choosing Mauritius to pledge their vows of eternal love and many hotels have staff specially trained to make all nuptial arrangements.

Couples planning to marry on Mauritius must be resident on the island at least three working days before the ceremony. A visit to the relevant ministry in Port Louis is necessary before the wedding day. Mauritian law requires that divorced women must allow a minimum 300 day interval between divorce and a new wedding date, or a pregnancy test taken locally must be negative. It seems divorced men can get rehitched quicker!

Most tour operators can arrange documentation for a nominal charge and provide optional extras such as videos, horse-drawn carriages, tropical cocktails, flower garlands, musical entertainers, cakes and photographers.

The relevant Mauritian authority for wedding technicalities is the Registrar of Civil Status (☎ 2011727), Emmanuel Anquetil building, Port Louis. It's easiest to make arrangements through a hotel or tour operator, rather than hassle over documentation and other preparations yourself. ■

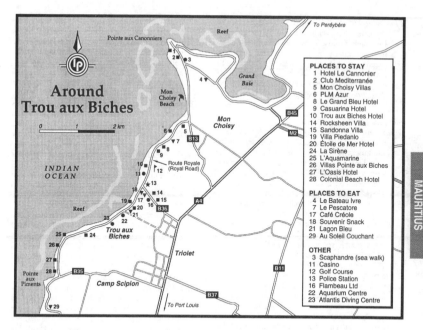

Around Trou aux Biches

PLACES TO STAY
1 Hotel Le Cannonier
2 Club Mediterranée
5 Mon Choisy Villas
6 PLM Azur
8 Le Grand Bleu Hotel
9 Casuarina Hotel
10 Trou aux Biches Hotel
14 Rocksheen Villa
15 Sandonna Villa
19 Villa Piedanlo
20 Étoile de Mer Hotel
24 La Sirène
25 L'Aquamarine
26 Villas Pointe aux Biches
27 L'Oasis Hotel
28 Colonial Beach Hotel

PLACES TO EAT
4 Le Bateau Ivre
7 Le Pescatore
17 Café Créole
18 Souvenir Snack
21 Lagon Bleu
29 Au Soleil Couchant

OTHER
3 Scaphandre (sea walk)
11 Casino
12 Golf Course
13 Police Station
16 Flambeau Ltd
22 Aquarium Centre
23 Atlantis Diving Centre

Organised Tours

See Organised Tours in the Grand Baie section, later in this chapter.

Places to Stay

You're advised to book well in advance at any hotel/guesthouse in Trou aux Biches, as they can fill up in a flash – especially during the high season. On the plus side, most places should slash prices during the low season or for long bookings. Most hotels/guesthouses can arrange excursions and car hire.

Places to Stay – bottom end

Rocksheen Villa (☎/fax 2655043), at 161 Morcellement Jhuboo (not far from the police station), is a homely guesthouse run by a delightful couple – Joy, a Mauritian, and his Scottish wife Sheena. There are just a few rooms which cost Rs 400/500 /600 for a single/double/triple, including breakfast. There's also a pleasant self-catering studio for Rs 500/600 for double/triple occupancy. The rooms are spotlessly clean and all with a private bathroom. Airport transfers can be arranged (with advance notice) for a charge, as well as island tours.

Sandonna Villa (☎ 2657360; fax 2655908), in the same area as Rocksheen Villa, is a smart guesthouse with doubles/triples (all with private bath) for Rs 400/500. This place fronts onto a main road, so request a quiet room. Breakfast is an extra Rs 50 per person and there's a small restaurant where you can have a meal.

L'Oasis Hotel (☎ 2655808; fax 2655207), Route Royale, has singles/doubles for Rs 700/850 and apartments (maximum of four people) for Rs 1400 per night. There's also a restaurant and swimming pool.

L'Aquamarine (☎ 2656923), near L'Oasis Hotel, is signposted by some crudely painted signs at the gate informing you what it is called, not what it is. It has slightly run-down one-bedroom studios for around Rs 385 per night and a two bedroom bungalow with cooking facilities for Rs 565.

La Sirène (☎ 2656026), near L'Aquamarine, is a hotel and restaurant run by Mr Bakaoolah. A single/double costs Rs 350/500, including breakfast; half-board is Rs 500/770.

Souvenir Snack (☎ 2657047) (see Places to Eat) has a few self-catering apartments for Rs 500/600/ 1200 for two/four/eight people. The owners can also organise a half/full day fishing trip for Rs 6000/7500 (maximum of five people). Speak to Mr Callichurn for further details.

MAURITIUS

Flambeau Ltd (☎ 2657894; fax 2616361), not far from the police station, is run by the amicable Lutchmun family. They own several self-catering apartments; a three bedroom apartment (maximum of six people) costs Rs 800 per night and a four bedroom apartment (maximum of 10 people) costs Rs 900 per night. There is a low season discount of around 10%.

Places to Stay – middle

Villas Pointe aux Biches (☎ 2655901; fax 2655904) is on the coastal road between Trou aux Biches and Pointe aux Piments. This is a small complex of bungalows, each containing four self-catering air-con studios. Singles/doubles cost Rs 1000/1500 and breakfast is an extra Rs 150 per person. There's a pool to splash around in.

Étoile de Mer Hotel (☎ 2656178), further north, offers rooms, studios and suites – with breakfast. Some travellers have complained about poor service and lack of cleanliness here. The rates for single/double rooms are Rs 770/1210; Rs 990/1474 for a single/double studio; and Rs 1395/1870 for a single/double suite. Facilities include a pool and restaurant.

Villa Piedanlo (☎ 4264012), diagonally opposite Étoile de Mer Hotel, consists of bungalows which cost around Rs 900 per night.

Casuarina Hotel (☎ 2656178; fax 2656111), Route Royale, has self-catering family villas, as well as air-con rooms. Facilities at this pleasant hotel include a pool, tennis courts, boutique and bar. A self-catering bungalow with two bedrooms and private bath costs Rs 2450 per night; a studio costs Rs 1450 a single/double. Air-con rooms cost Rs 2150/3300 a single/double on half-board. They usually hold a séga evening once a week.

Le Grand Bleu Hotel (☎ 2655812; fax 2655842), near the Casuarina Hotel, has 20 air-con rooms with kitchenette and attached bath. Single/double/triple rooms cost Rs 1000/1200/1250, including breakfast. Lunch or dinner is available for Rs 200 per person.

Mon Choisy Villas (☎ 2655934), near Mon Choisy beach, offers air-con double rooms for Rs 800, including breakfast. Two-room studios are also available for Rs 1200 per night. The service here can be somewhat unenthusiastic.

Colonial Beach Hotel (☎ 2615187; fax 2615247), at Pointe aux Piments, has comfortable single/double rooms with private bath for Rs 1370/1880 on half-board. There's a swimming pool, games room, snorkelling facilities and restaurant.

Places to Stay – top end

Trou aux Biches Hotel (☎ 2656562; fax 2656611), near a nice beach, is an upmarket resort-style hotel set in sprawling grounds (you'll even get a map when you check in!). It's a member of the Beachcomber chain of hotels. Accommodation is in comfortable bungalows: standard singles are between Rs 4400 and Rs 7900; doubles are between Rs 6400 and Rs 9800 (tariffs vary according to the time of year). All rates are on a half-board basis. When making a reservation request a sea-facing bungalow. The resort includes several restaurants, shops, pool, tennis courts, baby-sitting facilities, water activities, casino and golf course. There are also bicycles for hire (Rs 50 per hour). After a tough day on the beach, muscles can be revitalised with a massage (Rs 500 for one hour). This hotel is a popular wedding venue – contact the management if you're interested. The Beachcomber Card, which every guest receives on registration, is valid here – for more details see Accommodation in the Mauritius Facts for the Visitor chapter.

PLM Azur (☎ 2656074; fax 2656749), further north, is another swanky hotel with well-appointed singles/doubles for Rs 3015/4145 on half-board. The price increases to Rs 3370/4625 from 28 December to 5 January. The hotel offers the usual shore and water activities. The tennis courts can be used by nonresidents for Rs 150 per day.

Club Méditerranée (☎ 2638610; fax 2638617), at Pointe aux Canonniers, has bungalows for Rs 2455 per person per night or Rs 16,678 per person for seven nights. It also allows day visitors. For around Rs 650/850 you can have a half/full day at the club with a meal and full run of the facilities and activities. There is tight security at the entrance to ensure nobody slips through without coughing up the cash.

Hotel Le Cannonier (☎ 2637999; fax 2637864), just beyond the Club Méditerranée, is a five star hotel with plenty of land and water activities to indulge in. Prices for singles/doubles/triples are Rs 3050/3920/5110. There are two restaurants, a swimming pool and tennis courts.

Places to Eat

There is a fairly good selection of restaurants catering for most tastes, but those on a shoe-string budget may want to try the cheaper eateries in Grand Baie. Self-caterers have a choice of several small grocery stores in Trou aux Biches, but the supermarkets in Grand Baie are far better stocked.

Souvenir Snack (☎ 2657047), near the police station, is one of the best eating joints for a cheap and cheerful feed. This unpretentious little place attracts a constant stream of hungry travellers from the beach in search of sustenance. It's nothing flash, with just a few tables and chairs, but the servings are generous. Options include fried noodles with chicken (Rs 30), mushroom omelette (Rs 40), chicken and chips (Rs 50) and crab curry (Rs 80). A small bottle of beer is Rs 23. It's open Monday to Saturday from 7 am to 7 pm and Sunday from 7 am to noon. You can eat in or take-away.

Café Créole (☎ 2656228), near Souvenir Snack, offers a range of dishes including pizza Marguerita (Rs 75), octopus salad Mauritian-style (Rs 60) and grilled fish with garlic butter (Rs 90). There's a buffet dinner with live music on Saturday for Rs 300 per person. The restaurant is open daily for breakfast, lunch and dinner.

L'Exotique, at Le Grand Bleu Hotel (see Places to Stay), serves Créole, Indian and European food. Main dishes start at around Rs 120. The restaurant is open daily from noon to 2 pm and 7 to 10 pm.

Lagon Bleu (☎ 2616174), further south, specialises in grilled seafood; crab soup is Rs 75, shrimps in red sauce is Rs 150. Open daily from 10 am to 11 pm.

Au Soleil Couchant (☎ 2616786), south of Pointe aux Piments, offers good Créole and Chinese food at reasonable prices.

La Sirène (see Places to Stay) concentrates on seafood and Indian dishes. Main courses start at around Rs 100; dishes include fish tandoori (Rs 98), seafood pancake (Rs 100) and beef Kashmiri (Rs 98). There's also a set menu for Rs 210 per person. The restaurant is open daily from 11.30 am to 10 pm.

Le Pescatore (☎ 2616337) overlooks the sea and is a stylish and relaxing restaurant with tasty (though pricey) food. Seafood is the speciality and dishes include giant prawns tails with ginger and shallots (Rs 490) and seafood lasagne (Rs 320). Some travellers highly praise the food here, while others say it is overpriced – see for yourself.

Le Bateau Ivre (☎ 2638766) (the Drunken Boat), at Pointe aux Canonniers, has an emphasis on seafood. The roadside location nearer to Grand Baie is not so attractive, but the food is good, if somewhat overpriced. Main dishes are around Rs 340; some unusual options include marinated duck with grilled apples (Rs 380) and red snapper with eggplant caviar (Rs 420). For lobster, be prepared to fork out at least Rs 720! The restaurant is open daily from 7 pm to midnight.

La Caravelle (☎ 2656562), at the Trou aux Biches Hotel (see Places to Stay), offers a special Mauritian buffet dinner on Tuesday for Rs 550 per person (for residents it's included in their room tariff). Nonresidents should book at least one day in advance.

Entertainment

Séga Dances & Discos For information about séga dances and discos in the north, see Entertainment in the Grand Baie section later in this chapter.

It's séga time

The séga is a dance originally performed by slaves trapped in a living hell. They were stripped of their independence but not of their optimism, and the séga became a symbol of hope and freedom, allowing them to temporarily forget their troubles. Today the séga beats proudly in the heart of every Mauritian.

The coastal fishing villages still retain traditional instruments like the *ravane*, a wooden hoop over a stretched piece of goat skin. Most of these original instruments are rapidly disappearing however, being phased out by more modern equipment.

The séga is a rhythmic swaying of the hips to the beat of the ravane. The tune starts slowly and at first the dancing is slow and leisurely. The tempo soon picks up until the dancer is completely engulfed and taken over by the pulsating beat.

The man usually stands in the dancing area with hands on hips waiting for the woman to shuffle towards him. The two then face each other with a waist and shoulder grasp and ... the séga begins.

There are a few rules to dancing the séga, the main one being to let the music and the occasion sweep through your body. When you hear '*En Bas! En Bas!* (Down! Down!)' bend your knees and lower your body gently downwards while swaying your hips.

It's best for women to avoid wearing miniskirts. Colourful full length skirts are preferable. Men are free to wear whatever they please, but the more formal the attire the more difficult the séga becomes. Open-neck shirts are fine.

Let yourself go and enjoy the séga. You will be surprised at how quickly you pick up the infectious rhythm.

Justin Flynn

MAURITIUS

Casino There's a casino at the Trou aux Biches Hotel (see Places to Stay), which is open to nonresidents. The slot machines are open daily from around 9.30 am to midnight, while the games room (American roulette, black jack etc) is open from 10 pm until early morning. Tidy dress is expected; entry is free for foreigners.

Getting There & Around
Bus The bus to Cap Malheureux from the Immigration Square bus station in Port Louis will take you to Trou aux Biches for Rs 13. It's a 30 to 45 minute journey.

Taxi A taxi to Grand Baie costs Rs 100; to Port Louis around Rs 220; to the airport Rs 600; and to Curepipe about Rs 400.

Car In Trou aux Biches, Flambeau Ltd (☎ 2657894; fax 2616361) has hire cars for Rs 850 per day (Rs 750 per day for a minimum of four days). Air-con cars are Rs 950 per day (Rs 800 per day for minimum rentals of four days). They can also arrange motorcycle/bicycle rental (see below) and taxis. Most hotels should also be able to arrange car hire.

See also the Grand Baie Getting Around section for information about car rental.

Motorcycle & Bicycle Flambeau Ltd (☎ 265-7894; fax 2616361) rents out mopeds for Rs 150/300 for a half/full day. They also have bicycles for Rs 25/100 per hour/day. A range of water activities can also be arranged here – just have a chat to the owners. Some hotels may also be able to organise bicycle hire. See the Grand Baie Getting Around section for more details about moped and bicycle hire.

GRAND BAIE
This is the main holiday centre for Mauritians and tourists alike. Grand Baie used to be a tiny fishing village which only came to life on weekends and school holidays. Now it is buzzing and congested, with a cosmopolitan ambience and practically everything in the town catering to tourists. The main street is lined with trendy boutiques selling a mishmash of pricey items from traditional handicrafts to designer swimwear. It's a great place to simply wander at leisure – take care when crossing the road, as cars and motorcycles can zip by at incredible speeds. Some travellers love this place, while others detest the commercialism and crowds.

Grand Baie was called De Bogt Zonder Eyndt (Bay, or Bend, Without End), by the Dutch in the 17th century. Apart from the bay itself, there are few attractions. There's a better chance of mixing with other non-package visitors here than probably anywhere else on the island, as most of the accommodation is self-catering and in single units or small developments. You are not locked out of or into the hotel set.

The main beach is quite close to the main road, so it can get noisy and crowded. A prime diving site in the area is the deep chasm at Whale Rock.

Information
Côte Nord is an attractive bilingual (French/ English) free visitors' guide published monthly and available at most shops and hotels. It has listings of places to stay, shops, restaurants, sports facilities and other services. It also has some articles focusing on areas of touristic interest. Another fairly useful source of information is the *Tourist Directory*, a small telephone book with listings of hotels, restaurants, health centres, shops etc.

The supermarkets sell maps and postcards at cheaper prices than most other shops.

Money The Mauritius Commercial Bank (MCB) has a foreign exchange counter open from Monday to Saturday from 9 am to 6 pm; on Sunday from 9 am to 2 pm. The main MCB is opposite the main beach near the Grand Baie Store. Barclays Bank, further along the main street towards Peréybère on the same side as the MCB, has an exchange counter which is open the same hours as the MCB foreign exchange counter. The Banque Nationale de Paris Intercontinentale (BNPI) is near the Grand Baie Store, on Route Royale. Avoid changing money at hotels, as the rate is often not as good as the banks.

Post & Communications The post office is diagonally opposite the police station, outside the main part of town. It is open Monday to Friday from 8.15 to 11.15 am and noon to 4 pm; on Saturdays from 8.15 to 11.45 am. There's a poste restante facility here – letters are held for a maximum of three months (no charge).

For domestic calls, you can use the phone in the post office. Local and international calls can be made at the public telephones on the main street. Making international calls from hotels is usually more expensive.

Travel Agencies See Organised Tours later in the Grand Baie section for details about excursions offered by travel agencies in the Grand Baie area.

Bookshop Papyrus (☎ 2637070), not far from the post office, is a reasonably well-stocked bookshop which sells a range of local and foreign magazines, newspapers, books and postcards. French-language publications on sale include *Le Monde*, *Le Point*, *France Soir* and *Figaro Journal*. English-language publications include *Time*, *Newsweek*, *Sunday Times*, *International Express* and the *Sunday Telegraph*. For lazy beach reading, there's *Cosmopolitan*, *Marie Claire* and even the Australian *Women's Weekly*. The shop is open daily except Sunday from 9 am to 6 pm.

Medical Services The *Tourist Directory* has a comprehensive listing of contact details for doctors, dentists and pharmacies. *Côte Nord* is another option, or ask for advice from your hotel.

See Health in the Mauritius Facts for the Visitor chapter for hospitals and clinics on the island.

Dangers & Annoyances The boom in tourism in the Grand Baie area has attracted petty thieves and burglars. The crimes are generally small-scale stuff, but you should never leave valuables unattended.

Refer to Dangers & Annoyances in the Mauritius Facts for the Visitor chapter for details about exclusion from beaches.

Ruins

About 2km south-east of Grand Baie, near The Vale village, are the ruins of a sugar mill belonging to the Daruty family. There are some splendid views from here across the cane fields and the pyramids of boulders. Inquire locally if you're interested in having a look around.

Coin de Mire & Île Plate

The two nearest islands off the northern tip of Mauritius, Coin de Mire and Île Plate, make good day trips.

Coin de Mire, 4km off the coast, was so named because it resembles the wedge used to steady the aim of a cannon.

Further out is Île Plate, which has a lighthouse; it is the more popular island, offering easier landing and good snorkelling. There is a small army barracks here, as it is a training ground for the Special Mobile Force.

Many hotels and bungalow/flat owners can arrange boat trips to nearby Île Plate for around Rs 1200 per person, including lunch. Some yacht charter operations may also run day trips (see Activities in the Mauritius Facts for the Visitor chapter).

Île Ronde & Île aux Serpents

Île Ronde (Round Island) and Île aux Serpents (Snake Island) are about 24km from Mauritius. Both are important nature reserves, but are difficult and dangerous to land on because of the sheer cliffs that drop into deep water.

Île aux Serpents, ironically, is round and has no snakes, but it is a renowned bird sanctuary.

Naturalist Gerald Durrell, in his book *Golden Bats & Pink Pigeons*, describes Île Ronde as a 'curious geological formation'. He wrote: 'The whole island was composed of tuff, and this soft stuff had been smoothed and sculpted by the wind and rain into pleats and scallops, so that the whole island was like a gigantic stone crinoline dropped on the surface of the sea with, here and there, standing up like jagged brocade, turrets, arches and flying buttresses carved by the elements'.

Île Ronde covers 151 hectares and scientists

MAURITIUS

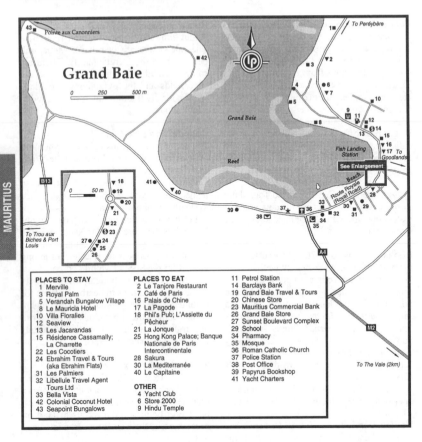

Grand Baie

PLACES TO STAY
1 Merville
3 Royal Palm
5 Verandah Bungalow Village
8 Le Mauricia Hotel
10 Villa Floralies
12 Seaview
13 Les Jacarandas
15 Résidence Cassamally;
   La Charrette
22 Les Cocotiers
24 Ebrahim Travel & Tours
   (aka Ebrahim Flats)
31 Les Palmiers
32 Libellule Travel Agent
   Tours Ltd
33 Bella Vista
42 Colonial Coconut Hotel
43 Seapoint Bungalows

PLACES TO EAT
2 Le Tanjore Restaurant
7 Café de Paris
16 Palais de Chine
17 La Pagode
18 Phil's Pub; L'Assiette du
   Pêcheur
21 La Jonque
25 Hong Kong Palace; Banque
   Nationale de Paris
   Intercontinentale
28 Sakura
30 La Mediterranée
40 Le Capitaine

OTHER
4 Yacht Club
6 Store 2000
9 Hindu Temple

11 Petrol Station
14 Barclays Bank
19 Grand Baie Travel & Tours
20 Chinese Store
23 Mauritius Commercial Bank
26 Grand Baie Store
27 Sunset Boulevard Complex
29 School
34 Pharmacy
35 Mosque
36 Roman Catholic Church
37 Police Station
38 Post Office
39 Papyrus Bookshop
41 Yacht Charters

believe it has the greatest number of endangered species in the world. Many of the plants, such as the Round Island hurricane palm (only a few left on the island) and bottle palm, are unique to the island.

The endemic fauna includes reptiles, such as the keel scale boa and burrowing boa (possibly extinct); three types of skink: Bojer's skink, Bouton's skink and Telfair's skink; and three types of gecko: Round Island gecko, ornate day gecko, and night gecko. Among the seabirds which breed on the island are the wedge-tailed shearwater, the white-tailed tropic bird and the gadfly petrel.

Since 1984, Île Ronde has been managed as a nature reserve by the Mauritian government and MWAF. Although goats and rabbits were introduced here in the 19th century, rats were never able to find their way onto the island. As a result, rare plant species once found on Mauritius, but long since wiped out by rats, have since been discovered on the island. In 1986, the remaining goats and rabbits were eradicated. Scientists and volunteers make regular trips to the island to weed out introduced species, plant endemic species, and conduct surveys of reptiles and birds.

Water Activities

See Activities in the Mauritius Facts for the Visitor chapter.

Organised Tours

Being a tourist hotbed, Grand Baie has lots of travel agencies, most offering a range of tours and other services such as apartment rental, airport transfers etc.

Grand Baie Travel & Tours (GBTT) (☎ 263-8771; fax 2638274), in the centre of town, probably offers the greatest range of day tours. There's a 'Wild Mauritius' tour, which visits La Vanille Crocodile Park, the Mahébourg Naval Museum and stops for lunch at Domaine du Chasseur (Rs 700 per person with lunch). Other options include a tour of Port Louis and Pamplemousses (Rs 300/550 without/with lunch); a trip to Île aux Cerfs (Rs 200, lunch not included); a tour of the south, which visits Curepipe, Trou aux Cerfs, Grand Bassin, Black River Gorges and Chamarel (Rs 450/650 without/with lunch); a visit to Domaine Les Pailles (Rs 1200 with lunch); and an 'Inside Mauritius' tour, which visits Casela Bird Park, Rose Hill and Moka (Rs 750 per person with lunch). For all tours, children are charged around half-price. Similarly priced tours are also available at Mautourco (☎ 2637800; fax 2637888), which has an office at Le Mauricia Hotel (see Places to Stay). Mautourco's head office (☎ 6743695; fax 6743720) is at Forest Side.

Libellule Travel Agent Tours Ltd (☎ 263-6156; fax 2635352) and Ebrahim Travel & Tours (☎ 2637845; fax 2638564), both on Route Royale, offer a variety of tours including of the south for Rs 150 per person and of Île aux Cerfs for Rs 150 per person. If you'd like to shop until you drop, Libellule Travel Agent Tours Ltd has a shopping tour of Port Louis, Rose Hill and Curepipe (Rs 150 per person).

Places to Stay – bottom end

There are no pensions in Grand Baie – you have to move on to Peréybère for one. However, every other building in town seems to be a bungalow or apartment to rent. There

are some excellent deals around, especially if you arrive at a quiet time of the year with three friends in tow. Most apartments are fully furnished and have a shower, kitchen, small gas cooker and fridge. You'll be lucky, though, to get air-con at the lower end of the market. The following are a few of the possibilities (see the map for locations).

Libellule Travel Agent Tours Ltd (☎ 2636156; fax 2635352), on Route Royale, offers apartments from around Rs 350 per day. There are also some bungalows on the beach from Rs 1000 to Rs 3500 per night. The owner, Mr Kalam Azad Joomun, can arrange car/bicycle rental, water activities and excursions (see Activities in the Mauritius Facts for the Visitor chapter).

Ebrahim Travel & Tours (aka Ebrahim Flats) (☎ 2637845; fax 2638564), also on Route Royale, rents flats (maximum of two people) from Rs 250 to Rs 350 per night; Rs 350 to Rs 450 (maximum of four people); and Rs 450 to Rs 600 (maximum of six people). They also organise tours and hire out cars, mopeds and bicycles.

Résidence Cassamally (☎ 2637521), also known as *La Résidence*, has one-bedroom self-catering apartments for Rs 450; two-bedroom versions for Rs 600, and a better, two bedroom air-con flat for Rs 700 per night. The price includes breakfast.

La Charette restaurant (see Places to Eat) has some properties to let. A bedroom with attached bath costs Rs 400 per night or Rs 450 with a kitchenette; a two bedroom flat with a kitchen and lounge is Rs 500. Contact the owners on ☎ 2638727 or inquire at the restaurant.

Other options include *self-catering apartments* run by Mr Mansoor Khodabacus (☎ 2638831), which range from Rs 350 to Rs 1200 per night. Another possibility is *Obelix* (☎/fax 2638727) which rents out similarly priced apartments.

Places to Stay – middle

Apartments or bungalows to let in this range generally have better decor and facilities. Many can be rented through Grand Baie Travel & Tours (GBTT) (☎ 2638771; fax 2638274).

Note that most middle and top-end hotels charge different room rates according to the high/low season (which differs from place to place). Clarify the rate you will be charged when making your reservation.

MAURITIUS

Colonial Coconut Hotel (☎ 2638720; fax 2637116), towards Pointe aux Canonniers, has been adapted and extended using traditional materials and designs from a villa originally built in 1920. The Norwegian crime writer, Jon Michelet, stayed here to write his best-selling thriller, 'Le Coconut'. Prices for single/double/triple rooms on half-board start at Rs 1200/1600/1910 in the low season and rise about 15% in the high season (November to January). On Wednesday evenings, the group 'Trio du Coconut' plays the traditional forms of séga. There's also a restaurant, pool and water activities can be arranged. This place is popular with travellers, so try to book ahead.

Les Palmiers (☎ 2638464; fax 2428711) is centrally located and run by the enthusiastic Robert Chan. There are two-bedroom flats (maximum of four people) for Rs 500 per night; an extra bed costs Rs 50. There are also some studios (maximum of two people) for Rs 350 per night. A continental-style breakfast is available for Rs 50 per person. There is a laundry service and car/bicycle hire can be arranged. This is also a popular place, so book ahead.

Seapoint Bungalows (☎ 2638604; fax 6867380) is at Pointe aux Canonniers. It's a complex of self-catering beach bungalows. The 10 double-storey two-bedroom units on the beach can be occupied by a maximum of five people. The cost per night is from Rs 900/1200 during the low/high season.

Villa Floralies (☎ 2638269; fax 2635379) is a block of units on a back road to Grand Gaube. Singles/doubles are Rs 300/450 per night. Discounts are offered for stays of more than one month.

Les Jacarandas (contact Grand Baie Travel & Tours (GBTT) ☎ 2638771; fax 2638274) is another block of flats. There are self-catering two-bedroom units for around Rs 700 per night. GBTT also rents out more upmarket self-catering flats, *Les Cocotiers* and *Seaview*, for upwards of Rs 900 per night.

Bella Vista (☎ 2638489; fax 2635195), Route Royale, offers single/double rooms for Rs 900/1200, with breakfast. Apartments (maximum of four people) go for Rs 1800 per night. An extra bed costs Rs 330.

Veranda Bungalow Village (☎ 2638015; fax 2637369) is a beautifully laid-out complex near the yacht club. Each of the 35 wood-and-thatch bungalows has a verandah and accommodates two to five people. Tariffs range from Rs 1500 to Rs 3075. One-bedroom studios are also available at Rs 1950 per night. Single/double rooms cost Rs 1120/2200, including breakfast. There is a bar, restaurant, swimming pool and bicycles for hire (Rs 25/100 per hour/day).

Places to Stay – top end

Royal Palm (☎ 2638353; fax 2638455), part of the Beachcomber group, is *the* place to stay if you're seeking pure luxury and have money to burn. Rated as one of the island's top hotels, the cheapest single/double will set you back a cool Rs 7700/11,600, including breakfast. If you're really in the mood to live it up, go for the royal suite – a luscious Rs 62,000! Apart from all the usual topnotch facilities, guests are provided with a Beachcomber Card – for more details see Accommodation in the Mauritius Facts for the Visitor chapter.

Merville (☎ 2638621; fax 2638146), further north, is much more affordable than the Royal Palm but obviously not as breathtaking. Standard singles/doubles are Rs 3725/5830 on half-board. Stylish suites cost Rs 7475/10,106 a single/double. Facilities include a pool, tennis court, restaurant and a range of water activities.

Le Mauricia Hotel (☎ 2637800; fax 2637888), beside the beach, competes in the lower bracket of the top-end range. It belongs to the Beachcomber hotel group and offers comfortable singles/doubles/triples for Rs 2850/4300/5700 on half-board. The most expensive season is from late December to early January when rates rise to Rs 4800/6200/8600, on half-board. Family rooms and suites are also available. There's a large swimming pool, several restaurants, tennis courts and a bounty of water activities. The Beachcomber Card, which every guest receives on registration, is valid here – see Accommodation in the Mauritius Facts for the Visitor chapter. There is a Mautourco office in this hotel (see Organised Tours earlier), which can arrange various land and water excursions.

Places to Eat

You are spoiled with choices in Grand Baie. Although Chinese places still dominate and are generally the least expensive, there is also an increasing number of competing restaurants offering different fare. Food and service standards seem to be erratic in Grand Baie, probably because this is such a busy tourist area.

La Pagode (☎ 2638733), on the main road, has the usual selection of Chinese dishes such as wanton soup (Rs 55) and shrimps chopsuey (Rs 85). Desserts cost around Rs 30.

La Jonque (☎ 2638729) is near La Pagode and offers Chinese-oriented cuisine, including shark fin soup (Rs 85) and squid curry (Rs 95).

Palais de Chine (☎ 2637120), nearby, is also a Chinese speciality restaurant which has similar prices to the above two places.

Hong Kong Palace (☎ 2636308), further along the main road, is yes, you guessed it, another Chinese restaurant. It's above the BNPI and is open daily for lunch and dinner. Grilled chicken with lemon sauce costs Rs 125, fried vegetable rice is Rs 60 and sautéed prawns with cashewnuts costs Rs 175.

La Charette (☎ 2638976), also in the centre of town, offers Indian cuisine as well as a selection of Chinese and European fare. Menu items include chicken masala (Rs 90), beef with oyster sauce (Rs 90), octopus salad (Rs 50) and prawns masala (Rs 210).

Café de Paris (☎ 2638022), further north, has a European menu with main dishes hovering around Rs 160 and desserts for about Rs 90.

La Mediterranée (☎ 2638019) does French and Créole food; seafood curry is Rs 190, beef with Créole sauce is Rs 220. For a splurge, try the grilled lobster with garlic sauce (Rs 600). This restaurant is open daily except Sunday from 11 am to 2.30 pm and 6.30 to 10.30 pm.

Le Capitaine (☎ 2638108) is in a pleasant setting by the sea, but the food gets mixed reports from travellers. It serves European and Indian food with seafood as a speciality; main dishes are around Rs 150. It's open daily from 11 am to 3 pm and 7 to 11 pm.

Sakura (☎ 2635700), on the main road, is a Japanese restaurant which is open daily except Sunday from 6.30 to 10.30 pm. It offers genuine Japanese food, but is a little overpriced; the set sushi dinner costs Rs 330 per person, while the set tempura dinner is cheaper at Rs 250 per person. Some meals are only available with advance reservation, such as shabu-shabu and sukiyaki.

Phil's Pub (☎ 2638589) is also on the main road and serves drinks at the bar from around 11 am to 1 pm and 7 to 11 pm.

L'Assiette du Pêcheur (☎ 2638589), attached to Phil's Pub, is a specialist seafood restaurant with main dishes for around Rs 180 and desserts for about Rs 70. It's open daily for lunch and dinner.

Café de la Plage (☎ 2637041), at the trendy Sunset Boulevard complex, is recommended for a treat. Specialising in seafood and Chinese fare, it charges from Rs 100 to Rs 450 for a main dish. This pleasant restaurant overlooks the sea, making it a great place to daydream as you dine. It's open every day from around 11 am to 11 pm.

Sunset Café (☎ 2639602), also in the Sunset Boulevard complex, has an easy-going ambience and is good for a light lunch or afternoon snack. Overlooking the sea, it has seating indoors and outdoors and is open daily from 8.30 am to 6.30 pm. There's a good range of refreshing juices, such as pineapple, carrot, apple and even beetroot, for Rs 50 a shot. Light munchies include hot dogs (Rs 60), salads (between Rs 80 and Rs 150) and that old favourite, the banana split (Rs 70). Or perhaps you'd just like to sip on a cappuccino (Rs 45) or espresso (Rs 35).

Le Tanjore Restaurant (☎ 2636030), on the road towards Peréybère, cooks up hearty Indian cuisine and is open daily for lunch from noon to 3 pm and dinner from 7 to 11 pm. Menu items include fish tikka (Rs 110), vegetarian kofta curry (Rs 90), daal fry (Rs 70) and lamb masala (Rs 110).

Le Mauricia Hotel (☎ 2637800) (see Places to Stay) offers a buffet dinner daily except Tuesday and Friday. Try the Créole buffet on Wednesday night (Rs 550 per person; included in the room tariff for residents). If you're not staying here, it's a good idea to book ahead.

Grand Baie Store (☎ 2638566) and *Store 2000* (☎ 2638992) are the best places in this area to buy groceries and other essentials. You can even pick up a snorkel, mask and flipper set (Rs 350).

Entertainment

Séga Dances & Discos The Mauritius Tourism Promotion Authority (☎ 2011703; fax 2125142) in Port Louis publishes a newssheet of coming events every two months or so, which includes a programme of dancing and séga nights at most hotels and discos. Events are also covered in *Côte Nord*, a publication described under Information earlier in this section. For details about séga, see Arts in the Facts about Mauritius chapter. Most major hotels lay on at least one séga night per week. Ticket prices to these events vary from place to place, but usually cost between Rs 300 and Rs 600 (including a buffet dinner). Hotels often have other forms of entertainment such as live music and theme evenings.

Apart from the hotels, the main local jive shops and discos in Grand Baie include *Speedy* and *Dream On*. Admission to discos usually costs at least Rs 100.

Casino For those with an urge to gamble, there's a casino at the Trou aux Biches Hotel (see Entertainment in the Trou aux Biches section earlier).

Things to Buy

As a popular holiday destination, Grand Baie has an ever-increasing number of shops aimed specifically at the tourist. You'll find few bargains here however, as most shops seem to have no trouble in selling their stuff at inflated prices. Nonetheless, the shops at Grand Baie are great for a leisurely browse. There are some particularly suave shops at the chic Sunset Boulevard complex, many of which specialise in clothing. If you're after a sexy swimsuit to make heads turn, you'll probably find it here – at a pretty price of course.

Getting There & Away
Bus Buses run through Grand Baie en route from Port Louis to Cap Malheureux for Rs 12. They regularly leave from Immigration Square bus station in Port Louis. The trip goes via Triolet and Trou aux Biches and takes about an hour to Grand Baie.

There are bus services between Grand Baie and Pamplemousses (Rs 10).

Taxi For taxi rides from Grand Baie, expect to pay Rs 100 to Trou aux Biches; Rs 250 to Port Louis; and around Rs 600 to the airport. Taxis usually charge a little more after dark.

Getting Around
Car Some car rental companies in Grand Baie are: Contract Cars (☎ 2638564) which charges from Rs 650 per day; Libellule Travel Agent Tours Ltd (☎ 2636156; fax 2635352) and Ebrahim Travel & Tours (☎ 2637845; fax 2638564) which both charge Rs 600/800 for a minimoke/car per day; and La Colombière (☎ 2637600), Europcar (☎ 263-7948) and Avis (☎ 2637600), which all charge from around Rs 1400 per day.

Find out if the management of your hotel or guesthouse has a special discount agreement with a local company. Whichever company you choose, check all the surcharges before agreeing on a final price. Most should include unlimited mileage, insurance, tax and offer a discount for long rentals. Be sure to have a contact name and telephone number in case of a breakdown. For more details about car rental see the Mauritius Getting Around chapter.

Motorcycle Grand Baie probably has the largest number of moped rental companies on Mauritius, so it's a good place to hire a moped to scoot around the island. Some of the guesthouses and hotels may be able to find you a moped to hire. Rental charges hover around Rs 200 per day with insurance, but you should negotiate a discount if you intend renting for a few days. A deposit of around Rs 500 per moped seems to be standard practice.

One possibility is Coastal Tour (☎ 263-8050; fax 2636161) which rents out mopeds for Rs 200 per day and offers a 10% discount for rentals of more than one week. Ebrahim Travel & Tours (see Car) hires out mopeds for around Rs 175 per day and motorcycles from Rs 250 to Rs 350 per day.

Bicycle Many hotels, guesthouses and travel agents can arrange bicycle hire. Rates vary, but expect to pay between Rs 100 and Rs 150 per day, less if you hire for several days. One possibility is Ebrahim Travel & Tours (see Car), which charges Rs 100 per day.

Bicycle is a great way to get around – but watch out for speeding traffic, especially on the main roads. Before setting off on your merry way, make sure your bike is in good condition. Several travellers have advised against riding at night, as many roads have little or no lighting. For more information about bicycle hire, see the Mauritius Getting Around chapter.

PERÉYBÈRE
Peréybère is a rapidly expanding resort a couple of km north of Grand Baie. It has a good beach and reef, and a range of budget accommodation (mostly self-catering) and eating places. If Grand Baie is too much of a scene for you, Peréybère is a good alternative.

Things to See & Do
Beaches, snorkelling and windsurfing are all excellent off Peréybère. On the main public beach, the persistence of souvenir pedlars and people trying to sell you excursions can sometimes become wearisome.

Snorkelling is best off the 'private' beaches. Turn down the track opposite the Stephan Boutique until you reach Pointe d'Azur. The

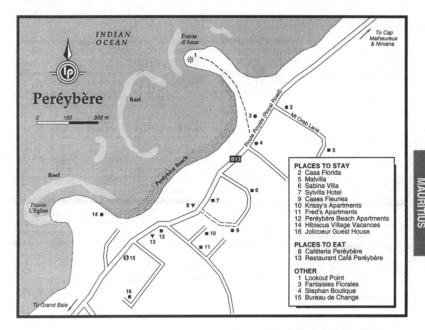

beaches on either side are good bases for snorkelling expeditions. Another relatively secluded beach lies to the south of the Hibiscus Village Vacances. Masks, snorkels and flippers are sold in the supermarkets at Grand Baie (for around Rs 350), but it's not easy to find any for hire.

Places to Stay

Jolicoeur Guest House (☎/fax 2638202), heading out of Peréybère towards Grand Baie, is run by Welsh expatriate Arthur Hooper and his Mauritian wife, Marie. It is a rather ordinary, two storey house with seven rooms, but it is relatively inexpensive and has a fairly easy-going feel to it. Singles/doubles are Rs 330/385, including breakfast. Excursions can be arranged.

Casa Florida (☎ 2637371; fax 2636209), Mt Oreb Lane, is more upmarket. It's a pleasant complex of self-catering studios and two-bedroom apartments. Prices for the studios start at Rs 550/680 for singles/doubles, with breakfast. Apartments cost Rs 920/995/1070 for doubles/triples/quadruples, including breakfast. There are also some single/double rooms for Rs 350/460 or superior

rooms for Rs 980/1280; breakfast is included in the price. Half-board is also available for an extra Rs 150 per person. The restaurant serves dishes such as chicken curry (Rs 80) and prawn cocktail (Rs 80). There's also a swimming pool.

Cases Fleuries (☎ 2638868; fax 2081614), on a back street off the main road, has attractive studio apartments for Rs 1100 per night and two-bedroom bungalows for Rs 990 per night. The studios and bungalows can both accommodate up to four people.

Krissy's Apartments (☎ 2638859), not far from Cases Fleuries, consists of one and two-bedroom, self-catering apartments which are priced at Rs 660 per night.

Fred's Apartments (☎ 2638830; fax 2637531), in the same area as Krissy's Apartments, is a well-kept and relaxing place which is especially popular with German travellers. Fred is German and his brochures and notices are all in German, and the present manager is called Günther. There are 10 studios (maximum of two people) for Rs 850 per night. A two bedroom bungalow (maximum of four people) costs Rs 1050 per night. Breakfast is an additional Rs 90 per person. Discounts are offered for long stayers and car/boat hire can be arranged.

Peréybère Beach Apartments (☎/fax 2638679), Route Royale, has apartments with two bedrooms, a bathroom and a kitchen. The daily rate is Rs 600.

Sylvilla Hotel (☎ 2638590), in the centre of town, has ordinary singles/doubles for Rs 350/500. Try to look at a few rooms first as some are better than others. There's also a restaurant here and the manager can arrange excursions.

Malvilla (☎ 2638939; fax 2638806) is inland on Mt Oreb Lane. The four one-bedroom units cost Rs 450 per night and the two-bedroom units are Rs 720. Breakfast/dinner costs Rs 55/200 per person.

Sabina Villa (☎/fax 2638903), further south, has small apartments for Rs 350/450 a single/double. Accommodation for five people costs Rs 600 per night.

Hibiscus Village Vacances (☎ 2638554; fax 2638553), on the shore heading out of Peréybère towards Grand Baie, is much more upmarket. The beach on its doorstep is quite poor but the public Peréybère beach is close at hand. Single/double rooms are Rs 1360/1660, including breakfast; on half-board they're Rs 1580/2100. The hotel also has a scuba diving centre and restaurant. Special séga nights are usually held here once a week.

At the time of writing, the owners of *Rocksheen Villa* (☎/fax 2655043) in Trou aux Biches were planning to operate several self-catering apartments not far from the beach in Peréybère. The charge for a one bedroom/two bedroom apartment is expected to be around Rs 400/500 per night. Advance bookings are essential.

Places to Eat

Since much of the accommodation in Peréybère is self-catering, you'll have to do your major shopping errands in Grand Baie, for example, at the *Grand Baie Store* or *Store 2000* (see Places to Eat in the Grand Baie section). The Chinese general store *Stephan Boutique* (☎ 2638858), in Peréybère, has a smaller selection. There are also two stores on the Cap Malheureux road, about 1km north of the village.

For a cheap beach munch, try the snack stalls and vans which often set up in front of the beach. A meal of beef or chicken noodles here costs around Rs 20.

Restaurant Café Peréybère (☎ 2638700), in the centre, serves Chinese-oriented dishes such as sweet and sour pork (Rs 65) and shrimps fooyang (Rs 70).

Cafétaria Peréybère (☎ 2638539), near the main beach, has an emphasis on Chinese fare. For something light there's spring rolls (Rs 45), for something exotic there's sweet and sour crab (Rs 170), and for something old-fashioned there's roast chicken and chips (Rs 85).

Nirvana (☎ 2626068), away from the centre, is highly recommended for its Indian food. The interior is pleasant, the staff are friendly and the food is terrific. Items include lamb biryani (Rs 145), murg makhni (boneless tandoori chicken with tomato and cream gravy) (Rs 115), lobster masala (Rs 290) and an assortment of vegatable dishes for around Rs 90. For sweet-tooths, expect to pay about Rs 60 for a dessert – try the gajar halwa, which is made from carrot. The restaurant is open daily except Sunday for lunch and dinner.

Things to Buy

Fantaisies Florales has a small shop and showroom displaying various products featuring dried flowers.

Getting There & Around

Travelling to Peréybère is the same as for Grand Baie (see Grand Baie – Getting There & Away). If you want to hire a car, moped, or bicycle, find out if the management of your hotel or guesthouse has a special discount agreement with a local company. Most of these companies are happy to deliver and collect from your hotel or guesthouse. Alternatively, contact a hire company in nearby Grand Baie (see Getting Around in the Grand Baie section).

CAP MALHEUREUX

Cap Malheureux is a peaceful village with a picturesque church, the Nôtre Dame Auxilia Trice, and a good view of Coin de Mire island. The most northerly tip of Mauritius, it was named the 'Cape of Misfortune' after several ships were wrecked in the area.

Grand Gaube, about 6km east of Cap Malheureux, is a small fishing village with a decent beach.

Places to Stay – Cap Malheureux

Allamanda (☎ 2638110), towards Cap Malheureux, is a block of 12 self-catering apartments about 2km north of Peréybère near Cap Malheureux. They are basic, but inexpensive. The genial owner, Mr Sivayan Peramal, works as a policeman and also operates a taxi service. One-bedroom apartments (maximum of two occupants) cost Rs 200 per night and two-bedroom apartments (maximum of four occupants) are Rs 300 per night. You can get a reasonable load of laundry done for about Rs 100.

Binos Villas (☎ 2627027), near Allamanda, offers two-bedroom flats for around Rs 400 per night.

Les Mascareignes Hotel (☎ 2637373; fax 2637372) is approximately 2km west of Cap Malheureux. At the time of writing it was under renovation, but it should be open by now. Single/double rooms are expected to cost in the vicinity of Rs 550/750.

Coin de Mire Hotel (☎ 2627302; fax 2627305), near Les Mascareignes Hotel, has comfortable studios (maximum of two people) for Rs 1315 and single/double/triple rooms for Rs 1325/1860/2385 on half-board (from February to November; prices are higher in December and January). There's a pool, restaurant, water activities, and bicycles for hire (Rs 40/125 per hour/day).

La Maison (☎ 2638974; fax 2637009), near the beach at Cap Malheureux, is a super-luxury residence for guests with exclusive tastes and fat wallets. Beautifully appointed apartments cost a whopping Rs 12,500/15,000 per night in the low/high season! Decadent extras include a pool, fine restaurant and hire of a limousine and a yacht, complete with attendants.

Kuxville (☎ 2627913; fax 2627407), about 1.5km east of Cap Malheureux village, is an old favourite, especially with German tourists. The bungalows, apartments or studios, with two to four beds each, have individual names such as 'Fritz', 'Olaf' and 'Elke'. Rates are given in Deutschmarks and must be paid in such or other foreign currency. They range from Rs 1442 (DM 120) per double for a night in studio 'Stephan', to Rs 1923 (DM 160) for the two bedroom 'Fritz' bungalow. The price includes a maid/cook. There is a small beach in front of the complex. Diving, fishing and sightseeing tours can be organised.

Marina Village Hotel (☎ 2627651; fax 2627650) is just east of Kuxville, at Anse La Raie. It consists of two-storey blocks with self-catering bungalows (maximum of six people). Prices start at Rs 1330 for ground floor units and rise to Rs 1600 for units on the 1st floor. Breakfast/dinner is an additional Rs 150/200 per person. Facilities include a pool, tennis court and restaurant.

Paradise Cove Hotel (☎ 2627983; fax 2627736), at Anse La Raie, is part of Le Meridien group and is a fabulous choice (if you can afford it). Suitably luxurious single/double rooms go for Rs 5450/8200, while opulent suites cost Rs 6450/9200. The rates include half-board. There are two restaurants, a swimming pool, tennis courts and a multitude of water activities.

Le Coin de Mire (☎ 2628070), opposite the church in Cap Malheureux, has a few apartments above the restaurant (see Places to Eat) for Rs 550/650 a double/triple. More upmarket apartments are also available for Rs 2500 per night. Breakfast is an extra Rs 75 per person.

Places to Stay – Grand Gaube

Island View Club Hotel (☎ 2839544; fax 2839233), in Grand Gaube, has single/double rooms for Rs 880/1650 on a half-board basis and a swimming pool for guests.

Le Grand Gaube Hotel (☎ 2839350; fax 2839420) is an upmarket hotel with comfortable single/double/triple rooms are Rs 2300/4600/5800 on half-board. More expensive suites are also available and there's a pool and restaurant. The service can be variable here.

Places to Eat

Le Coin de Mire (☎ 2628070), in Cap Malheureux, specialises in Créole and Chinese food. It's open daily from 9.30 am to 10 pm and charges around Rs 80 for a main course. Fish stew costs Rs 80, fried noodles with vegies is Rs 40 and a cheese omelette is Rs 35. The owners also rent out a few apartments (see Places to Stay).

Le Dauphin (☎ 2838199), in Grand Gaube, is more upmarket and serves a hotchpotch of cuisines including Mauritian, Chinese, Middle Eastern, Italian and Créole. Expect to fork out around Rs 200 for a main dish. The restaurant is open daily except Monday from 10.30 am to 3 pm and 7 to 10 pm.

Getting There & Around

There are frequent buses running between Cap Malheureux or Grand Gaube and Port Louis (from the Immigration Square bus station) for Rs 11. A taxi to Port Louis will cost at least Rs 450; Rs 750 to the airport.

GOODLANDS

Goodlands is a large town but isn't a place to stay. It's worth calling in to the large Historic Marine model boat-building factory at the St Antoine Industrial Estate (on the road to

MAURITIUS

Poudre d'Or). It's open Monday to Friday from 8 am to 5 pm and on Saturdays from 8 am to noon. (See Things to Buy in the Mauritius Facts for the Visitor chapter).

There is also an impressive Hindu temple in Goodlands and several large colonial and Créole houses.

There are beaches around Poudre d'Or and about 10km down the coast at Roches Noires. Roches Noires (Black Rocks) is so named because of the black lava rocks which fringe the shore.

POUDRE D'OR

Whether the name, which means 'gold powder', refers to the sandy beaches or the treasure said to be buried near the church, we don't know, but this is the sort of place that is rich in history and character, if not in tourist developments.

St Géran Monument

It was off Poudre d'Or in 1744 that the famous *St Géran* was wrecked in a storm and sank, with many lives lost. The disaster inspired the love story *Paul et Virginie*, by Bernardin de St Pierre, later in the 18th century.

The *St Géran* was carrying machinery from France for the first sugar refinery on the island. A French diving expedition excavated the wreck in 1966 and the results of the expedition are on display at the Naval Museum in Mahébourg. A small, disappointing monument was erected on the shore near Poudre d'Or in 1944.

Islands

Île d'Ambre and Île Bernache are within easy striking distance of Poudre d'Or, only 30 minutes by boat. Some local fishermen may be able to organise trips to the uninhabited islands for around Rs 500 – just ask around.

Sunken Treasure

There are no signs and nothing in the tourist literature or any of the histories about the sunken treasure. Generally, either few people know about it or it was given up as a lost

cause years ago, but the evidence is there, on the surface at least.

If you take a line about 200m due north from the steeple of Ste Philomène Church, you come to a deep hole at the river's edge. It is surrounded by reeds, often submerged and only accessible by pirogue. But the hole is there, it is deep, and is said to lead to a tunnel, perhaps connecting with another under the church or at the shore.

Somewhere inside is a treasure trove, possibly that of the infamous French pirate Olivier Levasseur, who was known as 'La Buse' (The Buzzard). La Buse's treasure has been the object of a long and controversial search at Bel Ombre in the Seychelles (see the Seychelles chapters). One theory is that people are looking in the wrong place, and that Poudre d'Or would be a better bet. See Roy Norvill's *Treasure Seekers' Treasury* for more about treasure-seeking.

About 10 years ago, a French team of treasure-hunting divers unofficially and unsuccessfully tried to excavate the hole. They found only a few coins.

Place to Eat

Coin du Nord, a little café next to the river on the road to Rivière du Rempart, serves basic meals. It's open daily from around 2 to 7 pm.

Getting There & Away

If you're coming from Port Louis (Immigration Square station) there is a regular bus service to Rivière du Rempart (Rs 12), or to Goodlands (Rs 12) and Grand Gaube, via Pamplemousses (Rs 14). Buses to Poudre d'Or are Rs 12.

PAMPLEMOUSSES

It is believed that the village of Pamplemousses, which means 'grapefruit', was named after the citrus plant, introduced into Mauritius from Java by the Dutch.

The Sir Seewoosagur Ramgoolam Botanical Gardens at Pamplemousses (also referred to as the Royal Botanic Gardens) were started by Governor Mahé de La Bourdonnais in 1735, as a vegetable garden for his Mon Plaisir Château. They were transformed by

French horticulturalist Pierre Poivre in 1768. He imported plants from around the world in a bid to market spices. The gardens were neglected between 1810 and 1849, until a British horticulturalist, James Duncan, took over. He spruced things up and introduced the variety of palms seen today.

Pamplemousses provided a testing site for new sugar cane varieties and, in 1866 when a malaria epidemic hit Mauritius, the botanical gardens acted as a nursery for the eucalyptus trees used to dry out marshes, the breeding sites of the mosquitoes.

Cyclones have periodically decimated the gardens.

Sir Seewoosagur Ramgoolam Botanical Gardens

The gardens are hardly one of the wonders of the world, but they are a fascinating feature of Mauritius. If you are not botanically minded, you probably will be after a visit. If you are so minded, you won't want to leave. The gates (all the way from Crystal Palace in London) are open each day from 8.30 am to 5.30 pm and entry is free.

The best time to see the gardens is between December and April. It's a big place, so you'll need time and a decent map, such as the one in this book.

You can hire a guide in the gardens – expect to pay around Rs 50 per person. Make sure you negotiate a fee and the duration of your tour *before* you start. If you are happy with their guiding, you may like to tip them something extra, it's really up to you.

There are few flowers in the gardens; it is not a horticultural display. Having said that, one of the main features is the giant Victoria regia water lily, native to the Amazon region. The flowers at the centre of the huge trays open white one day and close red the next. Other star attractions include the 'decorative' golden bamboo and the vast variety of palms, which come in all shapes and sizes. Some of the more prominent are the talipot palms, which flower once after 40 to 60 years and then die, the stubby bottle palms, and the tall royal palms lining Poivre Ave, as well as the raffia, sugar, toddy, fever, fan and even sex palms.

Savour the smells – ginger, cinnamon, nutmeg, camphor, lemon, eucalyptus, sandalwood and others. Your guide (if you have one) will know which ones to sniff. It's like walking through a department store trying on all the perfumes or aftershaves! Standing beside the more conventional mahogany, ebony and fig trees, you'll see the marmalade box tree, the chewing-gum tree, the fish poison tree and the sausage tree. There is a 200-year-old Buddha tree and, for Christians, the cross tree, with leaves shaped like a cross.

The gardens also play the roles of wildlife sanctuary, cemetery and art gallery. Sir Seewoosagur Ramgoolam, the first prime minister of Mauritius after independence, was cremated on a concrete block outside the château. His ashes were scattered on the Ganges. An enclosure with Java deer is near a pen of giant Aldabra tortoises. There is an old one with a noticeably chipped shell, damaged when a tourist threw a rock at it to make it move. He was fined Rs 500 and a fence was built around the pen.

You can't get away from Paul and Virginie,

Pierre Poivre transformed the Sir Seewoosagur Ramgoolam Botanical Gardens in 1768 by importing plants from overseas.

MAURITIUS

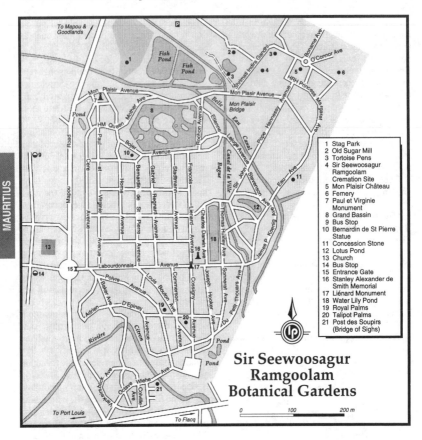

1 Stag Park
2 Old Sugar Mill
3 Tortoise Pens
4 Sir Seewoosagur
   Ramgoolam
   Cremation Site
5 Mon Plaisir Château
6 Fernery
7 Paul et Virginie
   Monument
8 Grand Bassin
9 Bus Stop
10 Bernardin de St Pierre
   Statue
11 Concession Stone
12 Lotus Pond
13 Church
14 Bus Stop
15 Entrance Gate
16 Stanley Alexander de
   Smith Memorial
17 Liénard Monument
18 Water Lily Pond
19 Royal Palms
20 Talipot Palms
21 Post des Soupirs
   (Bridge of Sighs)

Sir Seewoosagur Ramgoolam Botanical Gardens

the lovers immortalised in Bernardin de St Pierre's novel. The stone on the avenue named after them was supposed to be the tomb of the fictional characters but it is in fact only the base of an old statue to the goddess Flora.

The Mon Plaisir Château is now used for administration only and not open to the public. It is not the original palace; the 'old sugar mill' is also a reconstruction.

Getting There & Away

Pamplemousses is 11km north-east of Port Louis. To get there, take the Grand Gaube, Rivière du Rempart, Roches Noires or Centre de Flacq buses from Immigration Square bus station in Port Louis. There are also some direct buses from Peréybère and Grand Baie. From Trou aux Biches and Grand Baie, you can also go up to Grand Gaube and change, or down to Port Louis and change.

Central Mauritius

HIGHLIGHTS

- A walk around the rim of the Trou aux Cerfs crater in Curepipe which boasts incredible views around the island
- Rambling through the beautiful Black River Gorges National Park
- A refreshing dip in the cool and picturesque Tamarind Falls
- The environs of Moka town with its bubbling brooks, waterfalls, towering mountains and valleys

The central plateau of the island is split between the Plaines Wilhems district in the south and west and the Moka district in the north and east. Plaines Wilhems is the main residential area of Mauritius, with a conglomeration of towns practically linked to each other from Port Louis down to Curepipe.

The Moka mountain range fringes the area to the north; the Black River range to the west. Quartier Militaire is at the centre of the Moka district and is, perhaps as the name suggests, the bleakest area on the island. South of Curepipe, around Mare aux Vacoas, the countryside is more appealing. The climate is cooler and less humid on the plateau and the way of life more European.

With the exception of Curepipe, there is little of interest for visitors in the towns, although there are some beautiful areas on the other side of the motorway, around Moka village.

CUREPIPE

Curepipe and its environs owe their size and prominence to the malaria epidemic of 1867, which caused thousands of people to flee infested Port Louis for the healthier hill country.

It probably takes its name from a town in the south-west of France. For those who will not accept dull explanations, it could have been named by French soldiers who used the place as a rest and smoke stop where they could 'cure' (clean) their pipes on the way to or from the Quartier Militaire.

Curepipe has the flavour of an English market town. The Franco-Mauritians stay mostly in the suburbs around Curepipe, particularly Floreal, and come into Curepipe – by car, of course – to shop. A lot of the other locals come in by bus or walk under the shade of umbrellas. Umbrellas are a safe either-way bet any day, because it also rains frequently in Curepipe.

Curepipe is now the centre of the tea and the model-ship building industries and the town is worth visiting if only to see the contrast with Port Louis. It also offers better shopping than the capital and is peaceful by comparison.

Orientation

The street-naming confusion is not as big a problem here as in Port Louis. The main confusion may arise over Route Royale (Royal Road), the main drag from Port Louis, which runs through the centre of town, leading out south, towards Mahébourg. It is also labelled Plaines Wilhems St on some maps and Port Louis Rd on others.

The wide road running past the bus station, by the way, is not an attempt at a motorway. There used to be two roads with a railway line between them until the Mauritian railways were closed in 1964.

Information

Money Most of the banks are on the Mahébourg Main Rd. The two main banks, the Mauritius Commercial Bank (MCB) and Barclays Bank, are opposite each other at the western end of Châteauneuf St. Further along the main road, towards Mahébourg, is the Banque Nationale de Paris Intercontinentale and the State Commercial Bank, and towards Port Louis is the Hong Kong & Shanghai Bank.

MAURITIUS

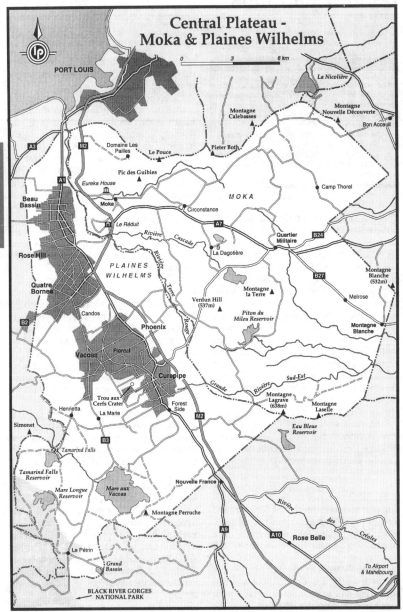

Central Plateau –
Moka & Plaines Wilhelms

0   3   6 km

PORT LOUIS

La Nicolière

Montagne
Calebasses

Montagne
Nouvelle Découverte

Bon Acceuil

A3

M2

Domaine Les
Pailles

Le Pouce

Pieter Both

A1

Pic des Guibies

Eureka House

Moka

M O K A

Camp Thorel

Beau
Bassin

Le Réduit

Circonstance

A7

Quartier
Militaire

B24

Rose Hill

Rivière   *Cascade*

La Dagotière

B27

Montagne
Blanche
(532m)

Quatre
Bornes

*PLAINES
WILHELMS*

Rivière   Terre

Montagne
la Terre

Melrose

B2

Candos

Verdun Hill
(537m)

*Piton du
Mileu Reservoir*

Montagne
Blanche

Phoenix

Rivière   Rouge

Vacoas

Floreal

Curepipe

Grande   *Rivière*   *Sud-Est*

Trou aux
Cerfs Crater

Forest
Side

Montagne
Lagrave
(638m)

Montagne
Laselle

Henrietta

La Marie

M2

*Eau Bleue
Reservoir*

Simonet

B3

Tamarind Falls

*Tamarind Falls
Reservoir*

*Mare Longue
Reservoir*

*Mare aux
Vacoas*

Nouvelle France

Rivière

des

Montagne Perruche

Créoles

A9

A10   Rose Belle

Le Pétrin

*Grand
Bassin*

To Airport
& Mahébourg

BLACK RIVER GORGES
NATIONAL PARK

Wood vs Concrete

A huge, noisy machine grinds and groans its way around a Mauritian construction site, hoisting large slabs of concrete into the air. Bit by bit the pieces fall into place and become a dwelling sadly lacking in character and originality.

This scene is becoming all too familiar in Mauritius. Many locals feel that their island is slowly being stripped of its beauty. A beauty that is evaporated each time a building with a distinct Créole architectural flavour is demolished to make way for modern development.

While the sun and beach attract most tourists to Mauritius, the stunning array of Créole architecture can be just as alluring.

Villa Surprise in Curepipe

Some houses in Mauritius flaunt the conventions of traditional architecture. The verandah, turrets, balustrades, auvents and the decorative ironwork are all features of traditional Mauritian architecture.

But Mauritius suffered a concrete epidemic in the 1960s which destroyed many beautiful houses that were perfectly habitable. They were replaced by constructions deficient in character and considered more practical by urban planners.

For more than a century the old houses resisted the ravages of cyclones and their sloping roofs kept out the heaviest rains and the strongest winds. While mother nature has been kept at bay, modernisation it seems is more stubborn.

The battle between wood and concrete is gaining momentum. Time will tell if the fine old wooden Créole houses will escape the fate of the dodo, or become architectually extinct, replaced by a sea of brick and concrete.

Justin Flynn

Post The main post office (☎ 6763085) is behind the bus station and is open from 8.15 am to 4 pm on weekdays; on Saturdays from 8.15 to 11.45 am. Poste restante is also here (free service).

Bookshops Allot Bookshop and Librairie du Trèfle, both in the Cosmos Arcade, have a reasonably good selection of books and magazines in French and English. Another source of books on Mauritius is Editions de L'Océan Indien (EOI) (☎ 6749065) which has an outlet in Curepipe.

Trou aux Cerfs

Possibly the main attraction of Curepipe for tourists, apart from the shopping, is the Trou aux Cerfs crater. It's been extinct for a long time and the crater floor is now heavily wooded, but the crater affords lovely views around the island. A tarred road leads gently up to and around the rim. There are benches for rest and reflection, and a radar station for keeping an electronic eye on cyclone activity.

Municipal Centre

Grouped together on Elizabeth Ave are the Hôtel de Ville (town hall), Carnegie Library, pond and gardens. The colonial-style town hall, built in 1902, has recently been restored. In the gardens is a bronze statue of the famous fictitious lovers Paul and Virginie, by Mauritian sculptor Prosper d'Epinay. The

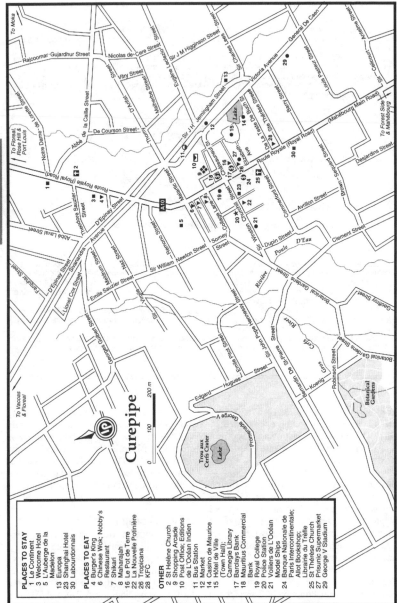

Curepipe

0   100   200 m

PLACES TO STAY
1 Le Continent
3 Welcome Hotel
5 L'Auberge de la
   Madelon
13 Europa
23 Shanghai Hotel
30 Labourdonnais

PLACES TO EAT
4 Burger's King
6 Chinese Wok; Nobby's
   Restaurant
7 Shikari
8 Maharajah
16 Le Pot de Terre
22 La Nouvelle Potinière
26 Tropicana
28 KFC

OTHER
2 St Hélène Church
9 Shopping Arcade
10 Post Office; Editions
   de L'Océan Indien
11 Bus Station
12 Market
14 Kasino de Maurice
15 Hôtel de Ville
   (Town Hall);
   Carnegie Library
17 Barclays Bank
18 Mauritius Commercial
   Bank
19 Royal College
20 Police Station
21 Voiliers de L'Océan
   Model Ships
24 Banque Nationale de
   Paris Intercontinentale;
   Allot Bookshop;
   Librairie du Trèfle
25 St Thérèse Church
27 Prisunic Supermarket
29 George V Stadium

statue is to Curepipe and Mauritius what the Little Mermaid is to Copenhagen and Denmark. There are also statues of the French astronomer Abbé la Caille and poet Paul Jean Toulet.

Botanical Gardens
The gardens are nowhere near as large or impressive as those of Pamplemousses, but they are well kept and informal, with little nature trails leading off from the main paths. There are no guides, on paper or on foot. It's a popular spot for picnics and lovers' trysts. The gardens are open daily from 8 am to 5 pm and entry is free.

Market
The fruit and vegetable market, under the cover of the bus station, is open from early morning until 6 pm from Monday to Saturday and only until noon on Sunday.

On Saturdays and Wednesdays there is a large market in the suburb of Forest Side. It's open from around 6 am to 6 pm.

Places to Stay
Accommodation is rather dreary in Curepipe, probably because most tourists opt to come here on a day trip, rather than stay. In fact over recent years, quite a few hotels have closed down because of poor business.

Places to Stay – bottom end
Welcome Hotel (☎ 6747292), on Route Royale, is one of the best budget options and is run by a friendly family. Tidy singles/doubles with common bath are Rs 250/350, or Rs 300/400 with private bath. All rates include breakfast; other meals are available with prior notice.

L'Auberge de la Madelon (☎ 6761520; fax 6762550), at 10 Sir John Pope Hennessy St, is another good choice. Comfortable singles/ doubles with private bath cost Rs 365/385, including breakfast. All rooms have a fridge and TV. At the time of writing, a restaurant was being planned.

Le Continent (☎ 6766793) is a large pension de famille at 184 Route Royale. If you're strapped for cash it's ideal, with ordinary single/double rooms for around Rs 190/220. All rooms have a private bath.

Labourdonnais (☎ 6761634) is past St Thérèse Church, at 270 Route Royale (Mahébourg Main Rd). The doubles are overpriced at Rs 440, including breakfast.

Europa (☎ 6766000; fax 6765084) is a soulless edifice east of the lake and is often used for conferences. Lacking any shred of character, it offers rooms (all doubles) for Rs 250 per night. No meals are available.

Places to Stay – middle
Shanghai Hotel (☎ 6761965; fax 6744267), in the town centre, has decent singles/doubles for Rs 440/550, including breakfast. You can get a meal in the Golden Lion restaurant which is connected with the hotel.

Mandarin (☎ 6965031; fax 6866858), north of Curepipe in Floreal, has 90 comfortable rooms, all with attached bath. Singles/doubles/triples are Rs 495/715/880, including breakfast. There's also a restaurant.

Places to Eat
At the bus station there are various eating stalls which serve good chicken or beef biryani. *Prisunic* also has a variety of supermarket foods and take-away snacks.

Where the Mahébourg Main Rd kinks and becomes Route Royale and heads towards Port Louis, there is a bunch of small, cheap restaurants. Popular fast-food joints include *KFC* and *Burger's King* (Burger King's brother?!).

Nobby's Restaurant (☎ 6761318), on Route Royale, offers good European and Créole cuisine in dimly lit surroundings. Spaghetti bolognaise costs Rs 125, seafood kebab is Rs 225. It's open daily, except Thursday night and Sunday, for lunch and dinner.

Le Pot de Terre (☎ 6762204), facing the Prisunic supermarket, is an unpretentious little place which is great for a cup of coffee and snack or a light meal. Sandwiches cost Rs 12, while a more filling feed such as steak with chips and salad is Rs 65. Cakes are between Rs 5 and Rs 10. It's open from 7.30 am to 7 pm.

Tropicana (☎ 6763286), opposite Barclays Bank, is a lacklustre Chinese restaurant with fare such as fried noodles (Rs 60) and fish with ginger (Rs 80). It's open daily except Sunday from 11 am to 2.30 pm and 6 to 9 pm.

La Nouvelle Potinière (☎ 6762648), near the Shanghai Hotel on Sir Winston Churchill St, is a popular European restaurant. It's open from noon to 2.30 pm and 7 to 10 pm (closed on Sunday).

MAURITIUS

Main dishes are upwards of Rs 150 and desserts are around Rs 50. The menu is entirely in French, so ask for help if you can't make sense of anything.

Maharajah (☎ 6761826) is in the centre of town and specialises in Indian food. The ambience is rather humdrum and the food is a bit overpriced. Chicken curry costs Rs 155, a vegetarian thali is Rs 120. It's open daily except Sunday from 10 am to 2.30 pm and 6.30 to 10.30 pm.

Shikari (☎ 6764505), also in the centre, is a pleasant Indian restaurant which is open daily except Sunday for lunch and dinner. Chicken tandoori is Rs 90, chicken with prawns is Rs 125.

Chinese Wok (☎ 6761548) has the usual Chinese fare including pork with vegetables (Rs 80), prawns with cashewnuts (Rs 110) and fried noodles (Rs 80). For something special, there's sweet and sour lobster (Rs 350). Apart from Sunday, this restaurant is open for lunch and dinner.

Entertainment
The *Casino de Maurice* is open weekdays from 8 pm until the wee hours of the morning and from 2 pm on Sundays. Tidy dress is expected.

Things to Buy
Shopping hours in Curepipe are longer than in Port Louis. Shops are open from 9 am to 6 pm every day except Thursday, when they close at around 1 pm. Most shops are closed on Sunday.

There are several model-ship building workshops in the Curepipe suburb of Forest Side. A visit to at least one is worthwhile. For more details about shopping in Curepipe, see Things to Buy in the Mauritius Facts for the Visitor chapter.

Getting There & Around
Curepipe is well linked by bus to Port Louis, Mahébourg, Tamarin, Centre de Flacq, Moka and surrounding towns such as Quatre Bornes. Most of the sights, such as the Trou aux Cerfs crater and the botanical gardens, are easy walks. Expect to pay around Rs 300 for a taxi ride from Curepipe to the airport.

There is little or no opportunity to rent motorbikes or bicycles in the town, unless you do so privately.

AROUND CUREPIPE
The region to the south-west of Curepipe is a natural parkland and mini lake district, pleasant for drives and walks.

The largest lake on the island is the reservoir Mare aux Vacoas, flanked on the east, 3km away, by Mare Longue and Tamarind Falls, accessible from the Tamarin road.

Near Henrietta, en route from Vacoas to Mare aux Vacoas, is a stone cairn, a monument to the English navigator Matthew Flinders. He arrived in Mauritius from Australia on the leaky ship *Cumberland* in 1803, on his way back to Britain and his wife. The poor bloke didn't know France and Britain were at war and he was imprisoned for more than six years. He died, aged 40, a few years after his return to England. For an interesting read on the subject, take a look at *In the Grips of the Eagle: Matthew Flinders at Île de France (1803-1810)* by Madeleine Ly-Tio-Fane.

Tamarind Falls
These falls are awkward to reach, but it's worth the effort for a beautiful, deep, cool bathe at the bottom of the series of seven falls. You can see them from the Vacoas side, if you follow the signs from Henrietta.

From Curepipe or Quatre Bornes, take a bus to Henrietta, then walk to Tamarind Falls. For details about hiking to Tamarind Falls from the south, see the boxed text Hiking & Trekking, under Activities in the Mauritius Facts for the Visitor chapter.

If you're coming from Tamarin, turn right about 3km north of Tamarin, at the roundabout to Magenta and Yemen. A tarred, bumpy road through cane fields leads to the Magenta and Tamarind Falls turn-off. Continue past all the 'Private Estate', 'Permit Needed' and 'Prohibited Entry' signs, down towards the power station. Leave your car or bike and walk along the river up to the falls. The path is quite heavily overgrown and you must cross to the other side and boulder-hop the last 300m along the river bed to reach the top, but you will be richly rewarded.

Plaine Champagne & Black River Gorges National Park
The beautiful highland area south-west of Curepipe, traversed by Mauritius' only mountain road, is like no other part of the island. The route climbs out of Curepipe and after

MAURITIUS

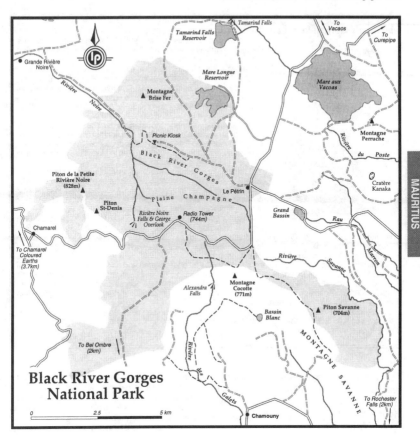

Black River Gorges National Park

0   2.5   5 km

about 6km reaches the dam wall of the large reservoir, Mare aux Vacoas. Surrounded by casuarina and coniferous trees, it more resembles a North American scene than one from the tropical Indian Ocean! Four km south along the road is the forestry station of Le Pétrin, which is the jumping-off point for several hikes into the Macchabée Reserve, now the Black River Gorges National Park.

At Le Pétrin, one road heads east 2km to Grand Bassin – the sacred lake of the Hindus – while the main route climbs up onto Plaine Champagne, the rainiest part of Mauritius and the largest natural area on the island. The

road's high point at 744m is marked by a radio tower. About 3km beyond it is the Rivière Noire overlook, affording a spectacular view of waterfalls and Piton de la Petite Rivière Noire (828m), the highest point on Mauritius. In another 10km, the road drops to the coast at Grande Case Noyale.

The best time to visit is during the flowering season between September and January. Look for the rare tambalacoque or dodo tree, the black ebony trees and the exotic birds that perch in them. You may also run into a band of monkeys, deer or wild pigs (see Flora & Fauna in the Facts about Mauritius chapter).

Mahatma Gandhi Institute

More than half of Mauritius' population is Indian and the Mahatma Gandhi Institute was set up in 1970 to preserve and promote Indian heritage. The campus itself is relatively featureless, but its museum houses important Indian historical records.

The Mahatma Gandhi Institute's **Folk Museum of Indian Immigration** was opened in 1991 and has archives and artefacts connected with Indian immigration to Mauritius. There are around 2000 volumes of Indian immigration archives dating from 1842 to 1910, as well as a fascinating register listing various historic details of Indian immigration from 1868 onwards. These records include immigration certificates, marriage certificates, immigrants' photos, work contracts and lists of arrivals and returned immigrants. If you had any Indian ancestors who migrated to Mauritius, this is perhaps the best place to trace your roots.

There's just a small collection of artefacts on display, including jewellery worn by early Indian immigrants, old kitchen utensils, traditional musical instruments, books, and even the original cooking vessels used to prepare food for new Indian immigrants landing at Apravasi Ghat in Port Louis.

The museum is open Monday to Friday from 9.30 am to 3.30 pm and on Saturday from 9 am to noon. Admission is free. Before visiting, it's a good idea to ring ahead, as a guide (free) may be arranged to take you around the museum. At the time of writing, there were rumours that the museum may be shifting (possibly to Apravasi Ghat), so make sure you check ahead.

Apart from a secondary school and short courses for both children and adults, the Mahatma Gandhi Institute offers a range of longer diploma courses including Indian music and dance, fine arts, Indian languages and Indian philosophy. There are plans to also introduce degree courses. The institute has produced some interesting Indian music cassettes which are specifically linked to Mauritian Indian culture – such as *Bhojpuri Wedding Songs of Mauritius*.

The institute (☎ 4332166; fax 4332235) is located in Moka and you'll have no trouble finding it – there's a special exit from the motorway. It's open Monday to Friday from 9 am to 4.30 pm (see museum opening hours, above). ■

For further information about visiting these areas, see National Parks in the Facts About Mauritius chapter, and the boxed text, Hiking & Trekking, in the Mauritius Facts for the Visitor chapter.

Grand Bassin

This crater lake is a renowned pilgrimage site. Each year in February/March, most of the island's Hindus come here for Maha Shivaratri celebrations on a pilgrimage to pay homage to Lord Shiva who links the holy water of Grand Bassin to that of the Ganges:

According to legend, Shiva and his wife Parvati were circling the earth on a contraption made from flowers when they spied the dazzling beauty of an island and its encircling emerald sea. Shiva, who was carrying the Ganges River on his head to protect the world from floods, decided to land. After a bumpy descent, a couple of drops of water sprayed from his head and landed in a crater to form a natural lake. The Ganges expressed unhappiness about its water being left on an uninhabited island, but Shiva soothingly replied that dwellers from the banks of the Ganges would return one day to settle on the island and perform an annual pilgrimage, during which the water would be scooped out of the lake and presented as an offering.

For more information on Maha Shivaratri, see the boxed text under Public Holidays & Special Events in the Mauritius Facts for the Visitor chapter.

MOKA TOWN & AROUND

Bubbling brooks, waterfalls, valleys, towering mountains and some wonderful real estate make the area around the town of Moka pleasant and picturesque.

Only 12km south of Port Louis, Moka is also the centre of academia, with the University of Mauritius and the Mahatma Gandhi Institute.

Le Réduit

This is *the* house in Mauritius – the governor's residence, now used by the military. Unfortunately, the house is open to the public only two days a year, in March and October.

Le Réduit, which means 'refuge', was built in 1778 by the French governor Barthélémy David, who succeeded Mahé de La Bourdonnais. It was from here, in 1874, that the English governor's wife, Lady Gomm, sent out invitations to her ball with the famous Mauritian Blue stamps, misprinted with 'Post Office' instead of 'Post Paid'. The few remaining stamps are now worth a fortune.

You can still walk around the gardens, sometimes under armed, although polite, escort. The grounds are open Monday to Friday from 9.30 am to noon.

There is a 1km, forest-lined drive from the main gate and guard post down to the big colonial mansion. The countryside around Le Réduit estate is marvellous, particularly at the driveway entrance, where you look down from the roadside into the lush valley of the Rivière Cascade.

The two ravines which border Le Réduit so dramatically are to be dammed below their confluence – so enjoy the view before it sinks out of sight some time before the year 2000.

Across the road is an old chapel and overgrown cemetery, where a few former governors have been laid to rest. Along the road is a village overlooking a little bridge and waterfall.

To get to Le Réduit, take the St Pierre bus from Port Louis, Curepipe or Rose Hill and get off at the University of Mauritius. The gate to Le Réduit is only a few hundred metres away. If you're driving or cycling, follow the Port Louis-Curepipe motorway and turn west at the roundabout to the university.

Eureka House

Eureka stands about 4km from Le Réduit, on the other side of the Port Louis-Curepipe motorway, just off the road to Moka.

This country house, lying under Montagne Ory, was restored and opened to the public in 1986 as a museum. It was built in the 1830s and purchased in 1856 by Eugène Leclézio, the first Mauritian Master of the Supreme Court. Like Le Réduit, and any of the properties around this area, it has terrific views across the river valley.

Entry to Eureka House costs Rs 100 per person. It is open from 9.30 am to 5 pm every day except Sunday. A guided tour around and inside the house is free and optional. There is a music room, a Chinese room and a French East India Company room. Whether the rooms were always used as such or have just been created as showrooms for collections of Chinese and Indian household goods, is unclear. The top floor occasionally displays paintings by local artists. On the ground floor, note the colonial shower contraption. Lining the interior walls are some fine antique maps of Asia and Africa.

You should take time to amble round the

Eureka House was built in the 1830s and restored and opened to the public as a museum in 1986.

gardens and enjoy the views across the gorge.

The courtyard behind the house is surrounded by stone cottages which were once the staff quarters and kitchen.

To get to Eureka, take the same St Pierre bus as for Le Réduit, but get off at Moka. To get to Eureka from Moka, take the Port Louis road, across the Barclay Bridge, past the Moka Eye Hospital, and then follow the road leading up to Le Pouce mountain.

Domaine Les Pailles

Opened in 1991, Domaine Les Pailles (☎ 2124225; fax 2124226) is an elaborate cultural and heritage centre which cost close to US$10 million to complete. The facilities available here include rides in horse-drawn carriages and a train; a working replica of a traditional ox-driven sugar mill; a rum distillery producing the estate's own brew; a spice garden; a natural spring and a children's play area.

A small cottage, Le Lodge, has been built high in the surrounding hill, which can be visited only with a minimum of eight people. Access is provided by the same ex-British Army Land Rovers which are used to run visitors around on mini-safaris to observe the local fauna and flora.

The Domaine has its own riding centre, Les Ecuries du Domaine, with about 42 horses available for dressage and jumping; and for riding in the foothills. Welsh ponies are provided for children to ride.

The centre also has a handful of restaurants. *Le Fouquets* is a luxury restaurant (closed on Sunday) which caters to businessfolk or visitors with plenty of money to spend on their tastebuds. Main dishes are around Rs 240. *La Cannelle Rouge* is a less formal restaurant which offers a range of quick meals, from pancakes to curries. Main dishes are around Rs 160. It's open from 10 am to 5 pm daily except Sunday. *Dolce Vita* specialises in Italian cuisine; pizzas are around Rs 110. It's open daily for lunch from noon to 4 pm and for dinner only on Wednesday, Friday and Saturday. For excellent Indian food, there's *Indra* which is open

daily except Sunday for lunch and dinner; expect to pay around Rs 160 for a main dish.

Jazz fans may be interested in *Le Jazz Club des Ecuries du Domaine* (☎ 2081998), which was closed at the time of writing but is planned to reopen. It's best to ring ahead to check. There's also a casino which is open daily.

Admission to the Domaine costs Rs 60 for adults and Rs 40 for children under 12 years old. A two hour jeep mountain tour costs Rs 380/200 for adults/children. Set lunch menus cost Rs 350/220 plus tax for adults/children. A ride in a horse-drawn carriage costs Rs 70 per person, while a short train tour costs Rs 50/35 for adults/children. Mini-golf costs Rs 25 per person.

To get to the Domaine, take any bus running between Port Louis and Curepipe, and ask to get off at Domaine Les Pailles (it's clearly signposted). From the road it takes less than half an hour on foot to the reception centre. Alternatively, you can take a 10 minute taxi ride from Port Louis or Moka.

The Moka Range

The Moka range contains a number of moderate challenges for the energetic – namely Le Pouce, Junction Peak, Pic des Guibies and Snail Rock. All are relatively easy ascents. The road to Le Pouce is signposted off the Port Louis-Moka road near the turnoff to Eureka. Le Pouce and Snail Rock can be included on a cross-country trek from Moka to Port Louis. For more details get Robert VR Marsh's *Mountains of Mauritius* (see Books in the Mauritius Facts for the Visitor chapter). For more information about treks, see the boxed text Hiking & Trekking, in the Mauritius Facts for the Visitor chapter.

Places to Stay

There are a number of hotels and boarding houses in between Port Louis and Curepipe. Most of them are pretty unremarkable.

Places to Stay – Quatre Bornes

Gold Crest Hotel (☎ 4545945; fax 4549599), on St Jean Rd, is the most upmarket place to stay. Well-appointed singles/doubles cost Rs 1170/1535, including half-board. A suite costs Rs 1440/1740 for a single/double. The hotel also has a smart bar and restaurant.

Le Gavnor Hotel (☎ 4548039; fax 4546742) is nearby on the same street and offers rooms (single or double occupancy) from Rs 350 per night. The service can be a bit brash here.

El Monaco (☎ 4252608; fax 4251072), on St Jean Rd, is more expensive but a far better choice. Singles/ doubles/triples go for Rs 495/605/715 including breakfast. There's also a restaurant.

The Riverview (☎ 4644957; fax 4660630), on Route Royale (Royal Rd) in the Belle Rose district, has single/double rooms at Rs 450/500, including breakfast.

Garden House (☎/fax 4649882), on the corner of Ollier Ave and Stanley Ave, is set in a spacious garden. Singles/doubles cost around Rs 600/750.

Le Gibier (☎ 4246072), at 2 Stanley Ave, offers single/double rooms with a communal bathroom for Rs 300/350, including breakfast.

Victoria (☎ 4245811), a pension de famille across from the bus park at 1 Ave Victoria, is good if you're on a shoestring budget. It has eight basic rooms with shared bath for Rs 150/300 a single/double, including breakfast.

Auberge de Quatre Bornes (☎ 4242163), Trianon Ave, Morcellement St Jean, has just a few ordinary rooms for Rs 175/350 a single/double, including breakfast.

Places to Stay – Rose Hill

International (☎ 4641793) has unexciting rooms with private bath for Rs 350 (single or double occupancy).

Auberge de Rose Hill (☎ 4641793), at 275 Route Royale (Royal Rd), has single/double/triple rooms with private bath for around Rs 250/275/ 325, including breakfast.

Pension de Famille Naheed (☎ 4646495), at 37 Boundary Rd, is good if you're strapped for cash. Basic single/double rooms go for just Rs 150/250, including breakfast.

Places to Stay – Moka

Joensu's Guest House (☎/fax 4334680), at Telfair roundabout, has singles/doubles/triples/quadruples with private bath for Rs 300/450/550/650, including breakfast. Half-board is also available. The owners can arrange island tours and airport transfers (with advance notice).

Places to Stay – Coromandel

About 7km south of Port Louis, on the climb up to Beau Bassin and Rose Hill, is Coromandel, an industrial area with several garment factories.

Sunray Hotel (☎ 2334777) is a rather characterless place with singles/doubles for Rs 270/300.

Places to Eat

Café Dragon Vert (☎ 4244564), in La Louise, Quatre Bornes, is a Chinese speciality place with reasonably priced dishes.

Chopsticks (☎ 4247459), on St Jean Rd, Quatre Bornes, and *Mandarin* (☎ 6964551), on Route Royale (Royal Rd), Vacoas, also have an emphasis on Chinese fare.

Entertainment

For nightlife you could try *Melody's* (☎ 464-4097), a disco at Commercial Centre in Rose Hill.

MAURITIUS

The East Coast

HIGHLIGHTS

- Boat trip to Île aux Cerfs for water activities, sunbathing and fine cuisine
- Taking it easy on the casuarina-fringed beach at Belle Mare
- Tour the huge FUEL sugar mill (June to November)
- Trou d'Eau Douce, a quirky village with a sea pool fed by a freshwater underground stream

The east coast of Mauritius was settled early in the 17th century by the Dutch, who cleared the ebony forests and introduced sugar cane.

The east coast district of Flacq is quieter than the Trou aux Biches or Flic en Flac areas on the west coast. Beaches are the major attraction and, as usual, big hotels have picked the prime stretches, but there is still enough sand and sea left to go around, particularly along Belle Mare beach and around Île aux Cerfs. The only trouble is the paucity of budget accommodation: it is difficult to find a moderately priced place to stay on a chance visit.

Inland, farmers place more emphasis on crop alternatives to sugar cane than anywhere else in Mauritius.

ÎLE AUX CERFS

There are no stags (*cerfs*) remaining on this small island which now belongs to Le Touessrok Sun Hotel and attracts large numbers of holiday-makers on the east coast.

The ferry runs several times each hour between 9 am and 4 pm and costs Rs 70 per person return, although this is expected to increase. Le Touessrok Sun Hotel residents travel for free – well, the room rates at the hotel aren't exactly peanuts. What you get when you step off the ferry is a sheltered, crowded beach and lagoon for water sports or sunbathing, restaurants and several souvenir stalls. You can walk only around the seaward half of the island, that is, clockwise from the landing site. That takes about half an hour and there are several isolated coves and bathing spots along the way. It doesn't take long to get away from the masses, but watch out for purple sea urchins. The west side of the island is impassable because of thick vegetation, and the water there is muddy anyway.

On the island is a boatshed where you can hire water skis, pedalos, sailboards, surfcats, Laser dinghies and canoes. Two-hour boat trips are offered to the Grande Rivière Sud-Est waterfall; and there's also a tour around Île aux Cerfs.

If you want to see stags, on the mainland there is a private stag park on the road between Le St Géran Sun and Belle Mare Plage hotels. There is no admittance, but you can watch the deer wading through the misty marshes in the early morning.

There are a number of private tour operators who also run trips to Île aux Cerfs and other areas. One possibility is Bateau Vicky (☎ 4192902) which offers a variety of tours, including a return trip to Île aux Cerfs (Rs 70 per person); a one hour glass-bottom boat tour and trip to Île aux Cerfs (Rs 250 per person); and a trip to Île aux Cerfs including a barbeque fish and salad lunch, dessert, soft drinks and beer (Rs 450 per person). The owners of Chez Tino (☎ 4192769) (see Places to Eat – Trou d'Eau Douce & Île aux Cerfs) can also arrange a return boat trip to Île aux Cerfs for Rs 70 per person; Rs 450 including a barbeque lunch.

BELLE MARE

This is a long, luscious, casuarina-fringed public beach. You can see it all from atop a reconstructed lime kiln, converted into a lookout tower. On the other side of the road stand the ruins of a sugar mill. There are more substantial sugar mill ruins behind Belle Mare village.

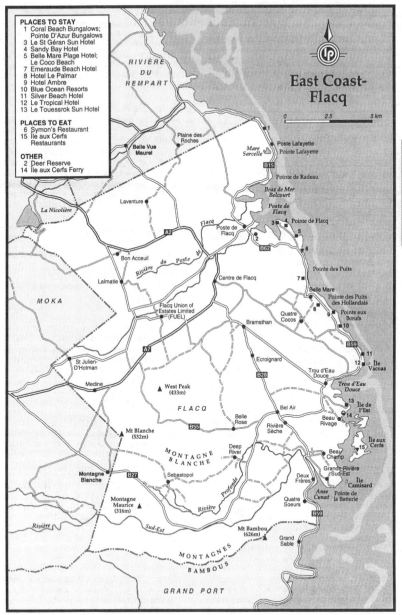

PLACES TO STAY
1 Coral Beach Bungalows;
  Pointe D'Azur Bungalows
3 Le St Géran Sun Hotel
4 Sandy Bay Hotel
5 Belle Mare Plage Hotel;
  Le Coco Beach
7 Emeraude Beach Hotel
8 Hotel Le Palmar
9 Hotel Ambre
10 Blue Ocean Resorts
11 Silver Beach Hotel
12 Le Tropical Hotel
13 Le Touessrok Sun Hotel

PLACES TO EAT
6 Symon's Restaurant
15 Île aux Cerfs
   Restaurants

OTHER
2 Deer Reserve
14 Île aux Cerfs Ferry

East Coast-
Flacq

0   2.5   5 km

MAURITIUS

Young Farmers Training College

Situated on the road from Belle Mare to Trou d'Eau Douce, the college is experimenting with alternatives to sugar cane.

TROU D'EAU DOUCE

The village takes its name, 'hole of sweet water', from a sea pool fed by a freshwater underground stream. Trou d'Eau Douce has lots of character, and steep lanes leading down to the harbour.

CENTRE DE FLACQ & ENVIRONS

The only town on the east coast is Centre de Flacq. It's a pleasant, if busy, market town that does not really cater for visitors.

Hindu Temple

There is an attractive temple on a small island linked by a causeway to Poste de Flacq. It is a beautiful sight seen from Le St Géran Sun Hotel across the bay. The temple is open daily from sunrise to sunset. Visitors are welcome but should behave with respect (see Society & Conduct in the Facts about the Region chapter at the beginning of this book).

Flacq Union of Estates Limited (FUEL)

This sugar mill, a few km west of Centre de Flacq, is the largest on the island, and it's even reputed to be one of the largest in the world! There are usually tours from June to late November, the time when cane is harvested. These tours are held daily, except Sunday, in the afternoon. There is no admission charge, but the guide will appreciate a tip.

PLACES TO STAY
Poste Lafayette

Pointe D'Azur Bungalows (☎/fax 4105026) has self-catering bungalows (maximum of six people) for Rs 700 per night. Breakfast is an extra Rs 100 per person (no other meals are available).

Coral Beach Bungalows (☎/fax 4105039) has six self-catering studios with a private bathroom for Rs 500 per person. Breakfast costs an extra Rs 70. The studios are designed for two, but an additional bed can be provided for an extra Rs 125. This pleasant complex is in a great position right on the beach. It also has a swimming pool,

bicycles, some water activities and the helpful owners can arrange excursions. There's also a small restaurant (residents only) which is open for breakfast and dinner. If you want lunch, you can get sandwiches or rolls for around Rs 50. Dishes on the dinner menu include lamb curry (Rs 165), grilled fish (Rs 175) and chicken in coconut milk (Rs 160).

Belle Mare & Pointe de Flacq

Le Surcouf Village Hotel (☎ 4151800; fax 4151860), on the coastal road, Belle Mare, has single/double rooms for Rs 1386/2244 on a half-board basis. There's a restaurant and pool for residents.

Sandy Bay Hotel (☎ 4132055; fax 4132054) is a rather kitsch place on the Pointe de Flacq. Single/double rooms cost Rs 950/1240 on half-board. It has a restaurant, swimming pool and even a bunch of slot machines for gamblers.

Emeraude Beach Hotel (☎ 4151107/8; fax 4151109), on Route Royale (Royal Rd), Belle Mare, offers single/double rooms for Rs 1155/1430 including breakfast, or Rs 1375/1840 on half-board. It also has a restaurant and swimming pool. You have to cross the road to get to the beach.

Hotel Le Palmar (☎ 4151041; fax 4151043), on the coastal road, Belle Mare, has rooms and studios. Prices for single/double rooms are Rs 1375/1990, on half-board. Facilities include a pool, bar and restaurant.

Hotel Ambre (☎ 4151544; fax 4151595), at Baie de Palmar, Belle Mare, has over 200 rooms and 20 suites. The rates vary throughout the year according to busy and quiet periods, so clarify this when making your reservation. For instance, from August to November a single/double/triple costs Rs 1060/5320/6330, on half-board. Facilities are good – there's a pool, tennis court, mini-golf and three restaurants.

Le St Géran Sun Hotel (☎ 4151825; fax 4151985), perched on the peninsula of the Belle Mare beach, is the flagship of the South African Sun International group. It's owned by Sol Krezner, who also owns the Sun City in the 'homeland' of Bophuthatswana, South Africa. Along with the usual leisure facilities, Le St Géran has a casino (for residents only) and golf course (which non-residents can use, if the hotel is not full, for a staggering Rs 1000 per person). The swimming pool has been tripled in size and enhanced with trees to form small islets for private dining. The Suncard, which every guest receives on registration, is valid here – for more details see Accommodation in the Mauritius Facts for the Visitor chapter. The 163 rooms are available on half-board basis only. Prices for a standard single/double are Rs 6480/9520 per night, but rates vary according to the season, so check when booking.

The beach gets muddy on the bay side, but there is a superb view across the bay to the Hindu temple at Poste de Flacq. Decadent touches include three fine restaurants, a pool, sauna and tennis court. For those who want to lash out on a massage, be prepared to say goodbye to around Rs 750 per hour.

Belle Mare Plage Hotel (☎ 4151515; fax 4151993) is about 1km south along the beach. Standard single/double rooms are Rs 4600/7800 on a half-board basis. Swanky deluxe suites cost Rs 8300/14,600. Like Le St Géran Sun Hotel, it has recently spent millions of rupees sprucing up its image with extensive renovations. Golf enthusiasts will be interested in the 18 hole golf course (for residents use only). Although this hotel is certainly luxurious, the service can be a little sluggish at times.

Le Coco Beach (☎ 4151010; fax 4151888), near the Belle Mare Plage Hotel, is a wildly colourful place which evokes somewhat of a carnival ambience. Some will love the candy-coloured decor, while others will find it ridiculously overdone. Comfortable singles/doubles go for Rs 2930/4280. The hotel is part of the Sun International chain. The Suncard, which every guest receives on registration, is valid here – for more details see Accommodation in the Mauritius Facts for the Visitor chapter.

Blue Ocean Resorts (☎ 2123243; fax 2087882), at Palmar beach, Belle Mare, has self-catering bungalows (maximum of two people) for around Rs 500/900 during the low season (May to September)/high season (October to April).

Trou d'Eau Douce

Silver Beach Hotel (☎ 4192600; fax 4192604), on Route Royale, offers singles/doubles for Rs 2000/2600 on half-board. There's a swimming pool and restaurant, however this place is somehow lacking in character.

Résidence Valmarin (☎ 4151196; fax 2638274) has just four deluxe apartments, each with two bedrooms, for Rs 1000 per person. There's also a pool.

Chez Tino (☎ 4192769) (see Places to Eat) can organise accommodation in a three-bedroom bungalow at Trou d'Eau Douce for around Rs 400 per night.

Le Tropical Hotel (☎ 4192300; fax 4192302), at La Pelouse, has 48 rooms at Rs 2250/3040 for a single/double, on half-board. The price includes a return boat trip to Île aux Cerfs. There's also a pool here.

Le Touessrok Sun Hotel (☎ 4192451; fax 4192025), overlooking the sea, is one of the most intriguing structures in Mauritius. It was designed by a Mauritian architect and built in 1978 around an islet and small lagoon, on the tip of a peninsula. To give each room a good view, the blocks were built around the islet on various levels and connected to the main hotel building by a covered bridge. Le Touessrok, named after a town in Brittany, is owned by the Sun International group, which spent some 400 million rupees on renovations in 1993. A standard single/double room on half-board costs around Rs 7160/10,460 (prices vary according to high/low season, so ask when making your reservation). Since the beach is small and poor, guests have free use of a ferry to shuttle across to Île aux Cerfs, the hotel's own island hideaway, for swimming, sunbathing and water sports; or they can use the hotel pool. Other facilities include four restaurants, shops and tennis courts. The Suncard, which every guest receives on registration, is valid here – for more details see Accommodation in the Mauritius Facts for the Visitor chapter.

PLACES TO EAT
Trou d'Eau Douce & Île aux Cerfs

Chez Tino, on Route Royale, Trou d'Eau Douce, is a nice little place with reasonably priced food. Items include tuna salad (Rs 75), chicken Créole (Rs 80), shrimp curry (Rs 150) and fried noodles with chicken (Rs 50). There's also a take-away service. It's open daily from 11 am to 3 pm and 7 to 10 pm.

Reflets de L'Est, across the road from Chez Tino, serves cheap eats and is open daily from 4 pm to around midnight.

Restaurant Sept, at Sept Croisées, Trou d'Eau Douce, specialises in Indian cuisine and seafood dishes. Expect to pay upwards of Rs 75 for a main dish. The restaurant is open daily for lunch and dinner.

Le Tropical Hotel has a restaurant serving Créole, Chinese and European cuisine. Main dishes start from about Rs 150, while gala dinners/buffets cost Rs 325/375. Nonresidents should book in advance.

Paul et Virginie Restaurant, on the beach, and **La Chaumière**, on the hillside, are the two restaurants at Île aux Cerfs. A meal at each costs around Rs 350. These restaurants are open daily for lunch.

Belle Mare & Centre de Flacq

If you're into self-catering, Centre de Flacq has a big open market on Sunday from early morning until 6 pm. There are also fish landing stations at Trou d'Eau Douce and Belle Mare.

Belle Mare Plage Hotel (see Places to Stay) has a Créole and European restaurant with steep prices. Main dishes start at around Rs 300 and set menus are available for Rs 700 per person. It's open daily from 12.30 to 3 pm and 7.30 to 9.30 pm.

MAURITIUS

Emeraude Beach Hotel (see Places to Stay) has a more affordable pizzeria, where pizzas (cooked in wood-fired ovens) cost around Rs 170. The restaurant is open daily for lunch and dinner.

Chez Manuel, in the hill village of St Julien (near the FUEL), specialises in Chinese food. Main dishes are around Rs 90, crispy sliced beef is Rs 80, fried noodles are Rs 30 and prawns in garlic butter are Rs 180. It is open daily except Sunday from 11 am to 3 pm and 6 to 9.30 pm.

Symon's Restaurant, at Pointe de Flacq, offers Chinese, Créole and European food. Main dishes start at around Rs 65; for a treat, try the pan-fried steak Créole-style (Rs 115). It's a clean, airy place open daily from 11.30 am to 10 pm.

GETTING THERE & AWAY

The bus from Port Louis (Immigration Square bus station) to Centre de Flacq costs Rs 12 and is a wild rollercoaster ride. Centre de Flacq is also linked by bus to Rose Hill (via the Quartier Militaire), to Curepipe, to Mahébourg (via Grand Sable on the coast), and to Grand Gaube in the north (via Rivière du Rempart and Poste Lafayette).

GETTING AROUND

Bus

A bus between Centre de Flacq and Belle Mare/Trou d'Eau Douce costs Rs 10.

Taxi

Taxis leave from Centre de Flacq and charge around Rs 100 to go to Le St Géran Sun or Belle Mare Plage hotels.

The West Coast

HIGHLIGHTS

- Spectacular waterfall and unusual coloured earths of Chamarel
- Laid-back Tamarin, the surfing centre of Mauritius
- A variety of feathery and furry creatures at Casela Bird Park
- Superb deep-sea fishing at Grande Rivière Noire

The Rivière Noire district has many attractions. The south-west coast is the centre for big-game fishing and, to a lesser extent, diving and surfing. It also boasts good, long beaches and the island's best nature reserve, the Macchabée Forest and Rivière Noire gorges.

In the north, most of the coastal plain is comprised of cane fields but in the south, where the Port Louis road hits the coast at Tamarin, the plateau drops steeply towards the sea. Along the way are a couple of detours to the contrasting beach resorts of Pointe aux Sables and Flic en Flac.

POINTE AUX SABLES

If there were a red-light area in Mauritius, Pointe aux Sables would be it. But the impression it gives is more a dirty orange. Although there are beaches and a few hotels, it is a long way from being a Pattaya Beach (Thailand).

Pointe aux Sables is almost a mirror image of Baie du Tombeau on the north side of Port Louis, but its image is duller. Baie du Tombeau is seen as a class below Trou aux Biches and Grand Baie. Well, Pointe aux Sables is a class below that. It's not that bad, but few travellers choose to stay here. Locals advise against walking around the streets at night.

There aren't many things to see around Pointe aux Sables. The beach at the point is popular on weekends and looks much better for swimming or relaxing than the public beach near Pointe aux Sables village.

Places to Stay

Accommodation options are grim in this area. Most places are quite seedy and mainly attract young local lovers in search of some privacy.

Villa Anna (☎ 2344573) is the first place you come to on the road from Port Louis. It's supposed to be a pension de famille, but is actually a few spartan and overpriced bungalows, without cooking facilities, costing Rs 350 per night. A larger bungalow costs Rs 400.

Sun & Sea (☎ 2345273), further along the main road, is more salubrious but still far from cheery. Rooms (doubles only) with attached bath are Rs 350 per night. At the time of writing, there were plans to open a restaurant here.

Places to Eat

There were once a few restaurants in this area, but these days you're limited to the shop/snack bar near the beach at the point itself, where the coast road from Port Louis does a right turn and heads inland again. It has little to offer though. If the Sun & Sea hotel does open a restaurant, this will probably be the best bet.

Getting There & Away

Buses for Pointe aux Sables leave from Dumas St, next to the Victoria Square bus station in Port Louis. The journey takes you through interesting districts of the capital, with such features as the 1866 Vagrant Depot. The trip between Port Louis and Pointe aux Sables costs around Rs 10/150 by bus/taxi.

FLIC EN FLAC

The name Flic en Flac is thought to come from the old Dutch name, 'Fried Landt Flaak', or 'Free and Flat Land'. On older maps this was spelt as Fri-lan-Flac, subsequently adapted by the French into Flic en Flac. The

MAURITIUS

MAURITIUS

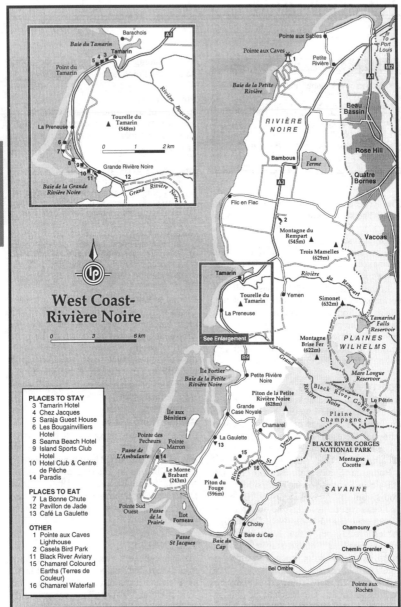

West Coast-
Rivière Noire

0   3   6 km

PLACES TO STAY
3 Tamarin Hotel
4 Chez Jacques
5 Saraja Guest House
6 Les Bougainvilliers
   Hotel
8 Seama Beach Hotel
9 Island Sports Club
   Hotel
10 Hotel Club & Centre
   de Pêche
14 Paradis

PLACES TO EAT
7 La Bonne Chute
12 Pavillon de Jade
13 Café La Gaulette

OTHER
1 Pointe aux Caves
   Lighthouse
2 Casela Bird Park
11 Black River Aviary
15 Chamarel Coloured
   Earths (Terres de
   Couleur)
16 Chamarel Waterfall

Dutch word 'flaak' is the same as in 'Boere Vlakte' (Farmer's Plain) or 'Groote Vlakte' (Great Plain), and is the origin of the name Flacq, which is very common on Mauritius. Finally, to round off this musing on place names, a modern-day French slang interpretation of Flic en Flac would be 'policeman in strife'!

Flic en Flac, off the Port Louis-Tamarin road, lies at the bottom of a 3km straight road running through cane fields. It is not as cute and carefree as its name suggests. Rather, it is an increasingly busy holiday village that lies and relies on a great stretch of beach, and caters for the middle range in the market rather than the budget level, which prefers Tamarin. There are lots of apartment blocks (a real eyesore) springing up in this area to cater to the increasing influx of tourists.

Casela Bird Park

This bird park, between Tamarin and the turn-off down to Flic en Flac, is well landscaped and has good views across the Rivière du Rempart valley. As well as parrot, pheasant and rare pink pigeon, there are leopard, tiger, lemur, monkey and deer. One of the giant tortoises is 150 years old. The park is open every day from 9 am to 5 pm and the entrance fee is Rs 100/75 on weekdays/weekends.

Trois Cavernes

Unlike Casela Bird Park, this is not a tourist spot. In the cane fields, just south of the turn-off to Flic en Flac, are three caves – tunnels formed in the lava. A local character, Dr du Casse, used to throw parties in one of the caves. Now he is buried there.

Mountain Climbing

Behind Casela Bird Park stands Mauritius' 'Pocket Matterhorn', the Montagne du Rempart. You can drive up to the base and park at Tamarin Pumping Station, just off the beginning of the road to Magenta. The climb is steep and difficult by Mauritian standards, although it should only take three hours up and two hours down.

Trois Mamelles, east of Montagne du Rempart, has three peaks to scale. The approach is better from Quatre Bornes than from Tamarin. Take the road from La Louise to Bassin. From there you need permission to go through cane fields and begin the climb. Refer to Robert Marsh's climber's guide *Mountains of Mauritius* (see Books in the Mauritius Facts for the Visitor chapter).

Diving Sites

The Cathedral cave, off Flic en Flac, is a favourite dive at a depth of 27m. Ask at your hotel for further details about diving in the area. Hotels in this area which have a diving centre include Villas Caroline and La Pirogue Sun Hotel.

Places to Stay

Flic en Flac is well off for accommodation, with several bungalows to let as back-ups for some upmarket guesthouses and hotels. The luxury hotels are grouped at Wolmar, a small settlement lining the beach, about 2km south of Flic en Flac.

Places to Stay – Flic en Flac

Easy World Apartments (☎ 4538557; fax 4645233), on the main road, provides self-catering apartments for between Rs 400 and Rs 600, including breakfast. In December and January, prices increase by around Rs 100.

C & A Bungalows (☎ 4257575), just off the main road, has self-catering studios which are similarly priced to Easy World Apartments.

White Orchid (☎ 4538430; fax 4538128), in the centre of Flic en Flac village, is run by Linda Appadoo. There are several self-catering bungalows and apartments which start at around Rs 350 per person per night.

Little Acorn (☎/fax 4538431), run by Mrs Mary Moutia, consists of six self-catering apartments (maximum of two people) and bungalows (maximum of four people) which each cost Rs 700 per night. A studio (maximum of two people) is Rs 400.

Golden Reef (☎ 4538841) has apartments for Rs 600 and bungalows for Rs 1000 per night. There's a pool and tennis court.

Flic en Flac Hotel (☎ 4538537; fax 4538374) is further inland and has doubles for Rs 900, including breakfast. They offer a discount for long stayers.

Manisa (☎ 4538558; fax 4538562), further south, has 40 rooms and five suites. There's also a swimming

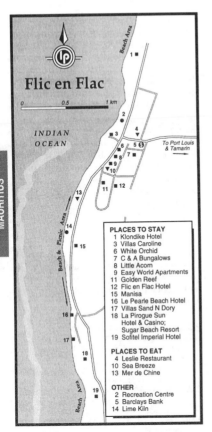

Flic en Flac

INDIAN
OCEAN

To Port Louis
& Tamarin

PLACES TO STAY
1 Klondike Hotel
3 Villas Caroline
6 White Orchid
7 C & A Bungalows
8 Little Acorn
9 Easy World Apartments
11 Golden Reef
12 Flic en Flac Hotel
15 Manisa
16 Le Pearle Beach Hotel
17 Villas Sand N Dory
18 La Pirogue Sun
   Hotel & Casino;
   Sugar Beach Resort
19 Sofitel Imperial Hotel

PLACES TO EAT
4 Leslie Restaurant
10 Sea Breeze
13 Mer de Chine

OTHER
2 Recreation Centre
5 Barclays Bank
14 Lime Kiln

Villas Caroline (☎ 4538411; fax 4538144), once an inexpensive option, has grown in reputation, size and, alas, price over the years. Right on the beach, it is known for good food and a good diving school. The group of six villas has been expanded by a 32 room complex. There are single/double rooms with air-con for Rs 1800/2460, on half-board. Fully equipped self-catering bungalows with air-con cost Rs 2400 for one to four people. Facilities include a pool, water activities, bar and restaurant.

Places to Stay – Wolmar

Le Pearle Beach Hotel (☎ 4538428; fax 4538405), on the beach, offers air-con single/double/triple rooms at Rs 1600/2500/3150 on a half-board basis. There's a swimming pool, billiard room, water activities and pleasant restaurant.

Villas Sand N Dory (☎ 4538420; fax 2085385), further south, has self-catering apartments and rooms. One-bedroom apartments cost Rs 1185/2580 for single/double occupancy; two-bedroom apartments cost Rs 1040/1510/1830 for occupancy by two/three/four persons, including breakfast. Single/double rooms cost Rs 1040/1720, including breakfast. Dinner is a steep Rs 300 extra per person.

Sofitel Imperial Hotel (☎ 4538700; fax 4538320), also south of town, has single/double rooms for Rs 3900/6250, including breakfast. Also available are deluxe and presidential suites which cost an awesome Rs 15,900 and Rs 17,000 respectively. Facilities include tennis courts and a golf course. Some of the staff here can be somewhat snooty and brash, which detracts from this otherwise impressive hotel.

La Pirogue Sun Hotel & Casino (☎ 4538441; fax 4538449) is the most luxurious place to stay and belongs to the Sun International group. A pirogue is a dugout canoe, but the term is also loosely applied to small local fishing boats. The main building of the hotel has a white, concrete roof shaped like the sail on such a vessel. Standard single/double rooms cost Rs 3820/5760 on half-board. Superior single/double rooms on half-board cost Rs 5180/7640. The Suncard, which every guest receives on registration, is valid here – for more details see Accommodation in the Mauritius Facts for the Visitor chapter. The hotel casino is open to nonresidents for Rs 150 per person. There's a swimming pool, tennis court and several fine restaurants.

Sugar Beach Resort (☎ 5438441; fax 5438449), not far from La Pirogue Sun Hotel & Casino, is another Sun International hotel. Attractive single/double rooms cost Rs 4600/7000, however prices are expected to rise. There's a pool, tennis court, health centre, restaurants and water activities. This is a

pool and restaurant. Single/double rooms cost Rs 1300/1600 and suites cost Rs 1800. All these prices are on half-board basis. The staff can be a little indifferent here according to some travellers.

Klondike Hotel (☎ 4538333; fax 4538337) is tucked away on the northern edge of town. It's a small 'village' composed of self-catering bungalows and studios. Rates for the studios are Rs 1600/2260 for single/double occupancy. Rates for accommodation in one-bedroom bungalows (maximum of four people) and two-bedroom bungalows (maximum of six people) are Rs 1495/1675. The groovy swimming pool forms an ingenious optical illusion which seems to merge the pool and the sea. There's also a tennis court and water activities.

MAURITIUS

beautiful hotel, although the service is not as slick as it should be for a place of this standard. The Suncard, which every guest receives on registration, is valid here – for more details refer to Accommodation in the Mauritius Facts for the Visitor chapter.

Places to Eat

Sea Breeze (☎ 4538413), in the centre, is very popular with locals and tourists who come for the tasty Chinese cuisine. Main dishes range from Rs 60 to Rs 475. The Chinese fondue costs Rs 300 per person and is recommended by travellers. Special à la carte options include prawns in rice wine (Rs 120), grilled lobster (Rs 300) and Peking duck (Rs 450). The restaurant is open daily except Tuesday from 11.30 am to 2.30 pm and 6 to 10 pm.

Leslie Restaurant is on the roadside just before the road hits the seashore and Flic en Flac. The food is OK but nothing to write home about.

Mer de Chine is down at the start of the beach and serves rather unexciting Chinese, Créole and European food. It is open daily from 11 am to 3 pm and 6 to 10 pm. Main courses start at around Rs 65.

Villas Caroline (see Places to Stay) has a good restaurant which is open to nonresidents, but prices are a little high. There's a Mauritian buffet on Wednesday night (Rs 385 per person) and a European buffet on Saturday night (Rs 440 per person). The restaurant is open daily from noon to 2.30 pm and 7.30 to 10 pm.

Klondike Hotel (see Places to Stay) has a daily buffet dinner (accompanied by live music on Monday, Wednesday and Friday) for Rs 275 per person. On Saturday there's a special barbeque buffet and séga show for Rs 320 per person. Nonresidents are advised to book ahead, especially on Saturday night.

Manisa (see Places to Stay) has a restaurant which offers a buffet on Friday and Saturday nights for Rs 250 per person. It's usually comprised of Mauritian or Indian food.

Le Pearle Beach Hotel (see Places to Stay) is recommended for a special meal. If you really want to get into the holiday mood, try the buffet breakfast for Rs 150 per person. There are also buffet dinners (Rs 350 per person) accompanied by live music: Tuesday (Chinese), Thursday (Créole) and Friday (seafood). On Saturday there's a séga show and barbeque buffet dinner for Rs 375 per person.

Getting There & Away

There is a bus from Port Louis to Flic en Flac usually every hour (Rs 14). A taxi from Port Louis to Flic en Flac will cost you around Rs 250 (one way).

Getting Around

Most of the hotels and guesthouses should be able to arrange bicycle hire – expect to pay around Rs 160 per day.

TAMARIN

This is the surfing centre of Mauritius, although you can go for weeks without seeing a surfer. The character of the place is more laid-back than Flic en Flac and rougher around the edges. It has a good beach and is well situated for most of the other sights. The village is encircled by salt evaporation ponds.

See Activities in the Mauritius Facts for the Visitor chapter for details about the best surf spots in the area.

Shellorama Museum

On the road from Tamarin to Grande Rivière Noire at La Preneuse, the Shellorama Museum boasts the biggest private collection of shells in the Indian Ocean. If you are considering buying shells, please read the Ecology & Environment conservation note in the Facts about Mauritius chapter. The museum is open Monday to Friday from 9 am to 5 pm and on Saturday from 9 am to 1 pm. Entry is free.

Tamarin Bay Beach

This is a small public beach with good views across the river estuary to Montagne du Rempart.

Places to Stay

Chez Jacques (☎ 6836445) is on the main road down to the beach. It's nothing fancy but it's cheap, with flats for Rs 350 for the top floor, Rs 275 for the middle floor and Rs 200 for the ground floor. It can be very friendly within the small complex of apartments or too close for comfort, depending on who you have for neighbours. Travellers have reported varied luck with reductions for stays over a week. There are bicycles and surfboards for hire (Rs 100 each per day).

Saraja Guest House (☎ 6836168), on Anthurium Ave, is run by the Cooshna family. It's basic but good if you're on a tight budget. There are two double rooms with common bath for Rs 125, as well as six apartments for Rs 250 a double.

MAURITIUS

Tamarin Hotel (☎ 6836581; fax 6836927) is right on the beach, but is not marvellous value for money. Single/double rooms are Rs 650/825 including breakfast; an extra bed is Rs 180. There's a swimming pool and restaurant.

Places to Eat

There's not much of a choice in Tamarin itself, apart from the *Tamarin Hotel* and a few snack stalls. If you're self-catering, there are several Chinese-run stores in the area.

La Bonne Chute (see Places to Stay & Eat in Grande Rivière Noire for details) is about 3km away, on the road to Grande Rivière Noire.

Getting There & Around

The Quatre Bornes-Baie du Cap bus service covers Tamarin and Grande Rivière Noire. You have to change at Baie du Cap for Souillac and Mahébourg, and at Quatre Bornes for Curepipe and Port Louis. For the fastest route to Port Louis, take the Quatre Bornes bus to Bambous and then catch the Port Louis bus there. The fare on any leg is around Rs 12.

A taxi from the airport to Tamarin costs about Rs 600; from Tamarin to Quatre Bornes it's Rs 300; to Port Louis it's Rs 400 and to Curepipe it's Rs 500.

Bicycles are available for hire at Chez Jacques (see Places to Stay) for Rs 100 per day. Local boats can be hired for deep-sea fishing, snorkelling or cruising – make sure you know exactly what you're getting before paying. Ask your hotel to recommend a reliable operator.

GRANDE RIVIÈRE NOIRE & LE MORNE

If Tamarin is surf city, Grande Rivière Noire is the main centre for deep-sea fishing. The surrounding district is picturesque and has a low population density, making it a pleasant retreat.

Le Morne is the sheer rock mountain standing at the neck of the tap-shaped peninsula at the south-west corner of the island.

Martello Tower

Situated at La Preneuse, this ancient lookout station stands with its cannons aimed at the sea. La Preneuse got its name from a French ship involved in a naval battle between the English and French in this area during the late 18th century. This famous battle was first recorded in *Voyages, Aventures et Combats* by Louis Garnenay. The battle has more recently been made into a novel, *Le Vingt Floréal Au Matin*, by Marcelle Lagesse.

Chamarel

The spectacular waterfall and unusual 'coloured earths' of Chamarel are not actually in the village of Chamarel, but nearly 4km further south. They attract hordes of tourists each year. The 100m waterfall (the highest in Mauritius) is halfway down an estate road and can be appreciated from several good vantage points. It is difficult to walk down to the base of the cascade.

Further down the road is the area with seven differently coloured layers of earth, which are intriguing but not mind-blowing. It is believed that the colour bands are the result of the uneven cooling of molten rock. A curious quality of the coloured earth is that when it is mixed together in a tube, after several days, each colour separates again. You can buy various trinkets with a test-tube creation of the various colours at the entrance gate.

Chamarel is today the name of the village here and its environs. It was named after Charles de Chazal de Chamarel, who owned an estate here in the late 18th century. It was here that Charles de Chazal entertained Matthew Flinders during his 'on parole' captivity on Mauritius during the Napoleonic Wars. You can read more about Flinders' time on Mauritius in Madeleine Ly-Tio-Fane's book *In the Grips of the Eagle*.

To get to both these attractions, take the steep corkscrew road inland, at Grande Case Noyale, 5km north of Le Morne. From here it's almost 4km to the village of Chamarel. Keep to the right as you pass through the village and continue for 2km until you come to a gate and a stall, the entrance to the estate road to the coloured earth and the waterfall. It's here that you pay an admission charge of Rs 15 per person. The waterfall is about 1km down this road and the coloured earth is about 1km further.

At the time of writing, there were plans to build an early 18th century French colonial-style house not far from the Chamarel waterfall, which will be called **La Maison de Paul et Virginie**. This house will exhibit an interesting and extensive collection of prints and paintings related to Bernardin de St Pierre's romantic novel *Paul et Virginie*.

Places to Eat There are a few good eating options in and around Chamarel.

Le Chamarel Restaurant (☎ 6836421) has lovely views from the hill on which it is situated. Although a little expensive, the food and ambience are good. Another restaurant in this area is *Varangue sur Morne*.

La Cascade is scheduled to open in 1998 and will boast breathtaking views of the Chamarel waterfall. The menu will have an emphasis on local cuisine made from fresh farm products.

Getting There & Away There are infrequent buses from Baie du Cap to Chamarel or you can take the Baie du Cap bus from La Preneuse, get off at Grand Case Noyale, and walk uphill about 7km to the coloured earth. From Quatre Bornes there's a bus service departing daily for Chamarel (Rs 15).

If you are travelling by car or taxi, you can also get here via the scenic road which crosses Plaine Champagne.

All the major tour operators run excursions to Chamarel, usually including it with Grand Bassin and Trou aux Cerfs in Curepipe.

Cécile Waterfall
Just after the Grand Bassin crossroads, on the way to Plaine Champagne and Chamarel, there is a viewing area overlooking Cécile Waterfall and the Savanne mountain range.

Le Morne Peninsula
Formerly the site of the Dinarobin Hotel, the peninsula has been completely taken over by a hotel which effectively restricts access by charging an admission fee of around Rs 200 to nonresidents. The sandy coastline contin-

ues, uninterrupted, for 4km around the hammerhead, after the Paradis hotel's beach.

Le Morne Brabant
Reminiscent of the Rock of Gibraltar, Le Morne Brabant is very imposing. The cliffs are said to be unscaleable, but, in the early 19th century, escaped slaves managed to hide out on top. The story says that the slaves, ignorant of the fact that slavery had been abolished, panicked when they saw a troop of soldiers making their way up the cliffs one day. Believing they were to be recaptured, the slaves flung themselves from the cliff tops. Thus the name: Le Morne, the 'mournful one'.

As you descend the road from Chamarel to the coast, the mountain to the north-west actually looks more mournful. The profile resembles an old lady's face with a bulbous nose and a beady eye.

Deep-Sea Fishing & Diving
At the Hotel Club & Centre de Pêche in Grande Rivière Noire, a fishing boat can be hired for a minimum of six hours at a minimum price of Rs 7000. The Paradis hotel offers similarly priced boats. Also at Grande Rivière Noire is the private Bonanza angling club.

There are diving centres at the Island Sports Club and Paradis hotels.

For less expensive fishing and diving options, have a chat with Francisco at Les Bougainvilliers Hotel (see Places to Stay & Eat below).

For more information about water activities see Activities in the Mauritius Facts for the Visitor chapter.

Places to Stay & Eat
You can't camp on the beach at Le Morne, but if you carry on south-east for 8km to Baie du Cap you'll find a good site. This is one of the more peaceful beaches on the island.

Places to Stay & Eat – La Preneuse & Grande Rivière Noire
To find out about individual bungalows to let along the La Preneuse road, call ☎ 6964389.

MAURITIUS

Les Bougainvilliers Hotel (☎ 6836525; fax 6836332) is directly behind the telecommunications tower at La Preneuse. Chris Poulos, the interesting septuagenarian owner, runs this down-to-earth house on the beach. There are five double rooms for Rs 660, including breakfast. The only other meal available is lunch. The friendly and helpful manager, Francisco, can organise good deals for car hire (from Rs 600 per day), fishing trips (Rs 5000 per day per boat; maximum of four people) and island excursions.

La Bonne Chute (☎ 6836552) is in an awkward position beside the Caltex petrol station on the main road. The speciality is seafood; lobster soup is Rs 125, steamed fresh crab is Rs 295. It's open daily except Sunday from noon to 3 pm and 7 to 10 pm.

Seama Beach Hotel (☎ 6836031) is opposite the public beach at La Preneuse. It offers mid-range accommodation and meals in its own *La Paille-en-Queue Restaurant*.

Hotel Club & Centre de Pêche (☎ 6836522; fax 6836318) has accommodation with prices determined by the deep-sea angling season from November to March. Singles/doubles during the high season are Rs 1820/2700 and Rs 1620/2300 during the low season, on a half-board basis. There is a daily Rs 400 supplement per person from 23 December to 2 January. Rates for hiring a boat to go deep-sea fishing start at around Rs 8000 for a full day (nine hours) or Rs 7000 for a half-day (six hours). Not surprisingly, the hotel's restaurant specialises in seafood. Main dishes are around Rs 225; special dishes include oysters and seafood gratin. It's open daily from noon to 2 pm and 7.30 to 10 pm.

Island Sports Club Hotel (☎ 6835353; fax 6836547), next door to the Hotel Club & Centre de Pêche, has singles/doubles for Rs 1960/2920 on half-board. The hotel has a pool, gymnasium, diving and can arrange deep-sea fishing trips and excursions.

Pavillon de Jade, just south of Grande Rivière Noire, is a Chinese restaurant offering meals (including take-away) at reasonable prices. It's open daily except Monday from 11 am to 4 pm and 6 to 11 pm.

Places to Stay & Eat – Le Morne

Paradis (☎ 4505050; fax 4505140), about 12km south of Grande Rivière Noire, at Le Morne, belongs to the Beachcomber group. Suitably luxurious single/double rooms cost Rs 4800/7000 on a half-board basis. There are also some self-catering bungalows for Rs 4500 per night (maximum of five people). Guests can enjoy the usual water sports, games and activities – there's an 18 hole golf course (Rs 200/1000 for residents/nonresidents), diving centre, horse-riding school and deep-sea fishing centre, all of which you pay for. The Beachcomber Card, which every guest receives on registration, is valid here – for more details see Accommodation in the Mauritius Facts for the Visitor chapter. Nonresidents are charged an 'admission fee' of Rs 200, but this is graciously deducted from the bill if you dine at the hotel.

Café La Gaulette is about 3km before you reach the turn-off for the Paradis hotel, in the village of La Gaulette. It once offered inexpensive food, but the prices have been creeping up over the years. A Chinese or Créole main dish will set you back around Rs 200.

South Mauritius

The southern region of Mauritius comprises the districts of Savanne and Grand Port, centred around the towns of Souillac and Mahébourg. The area differs little from the rest of the island, with mountains, forests, rivers, beaches, historic sites and plenty of sugar cane plantations. Its main attraction is the lack of tourism development.

MAHÉBOURG

Mahébourg, named after the famous French governor Mahé de La Bourdonnais but pronounced 'may burg', was once a busy port. Now it's a run-down commercial centre with a small fishing fleet.

But the town is a lot friendlier, has more character and is more relaxed than the tourist spiels would have you believe. It is also the nearest centre to the airport and visitors may find themselves spending the first or last few days there. The bay is a picturesque backdrop for the town, with the sea changing from one intense colour to another at great speed.

Naval Museum

The château housing the museum is on the outskirts of Mahébourg on the Curepipe road. It used to belong to the De Robillard family and played an important part in the island's history.

It was here in 1810 that the injured commanders of the French and English fleets were taken for treatment after the Battle of Grand Port. The story of the French naval victory is displayed in the museum, along with salvaged items from the British frigate *Magicienne*, which sank in the battle. Dives on the wreck in 1933 retrieved cannons, grapeshot and bottles.

A more famous wreck is that of the *St Géran*, sunk on 17 August 1744, off the north-east coast of Mauritius. The disaster inspired the love story *Paul et Virginie*, written shortly afterwards by Bernardin de St Pierre. Two maidens, who refused to undress and thus give themselves a chance of swimming to shore, went down with the ship. Bernardin de St Pierre was moved by this chaste sacrifice. The ship's bell was salvaged by French divers in 1966 and is on display at the museum.

A more recent sea disaster was the sinking of the British steamer *Trevessa*. She went down on 4 June 1923 in the middle of the Indian Ocean, 2576km from Mauritius, on her way from Fremantle, Western Australia. Sixteen men survived at sea for 25 days in an open lifeboat which landed at Bel Ombre, near Le Morne, in the south-west of Mauritius. Exhibited at the museum is the last biscuit ration, a razor and the cigarette-tin lid used to measure out the water rations. The survival is commemorated each year on Seafarers' Day (29 June), the day the lifeboat reached Mauritius.

The museum also contains a copy of a painting of Robert Surcouf, the 'King of the Corsairs', his pistol and the sword of one of his captives, Captain Rivington of the English ship *Kent*. The *Kent* was taken by Surcouf's *Confiance* on 7 October 1800 in the Bay of Bengal.

Other exhibits include lithographs of the lovers Paul and Virginie; the furniture of Mahé de La Bourdonnais; early Dutch and Portuguese maps of Mauritius (one based on a visit by Abel Tasman in 1642); paintings of Prince Maurice of Orange (after whom the island is named), Pieter Both (the Dutch East

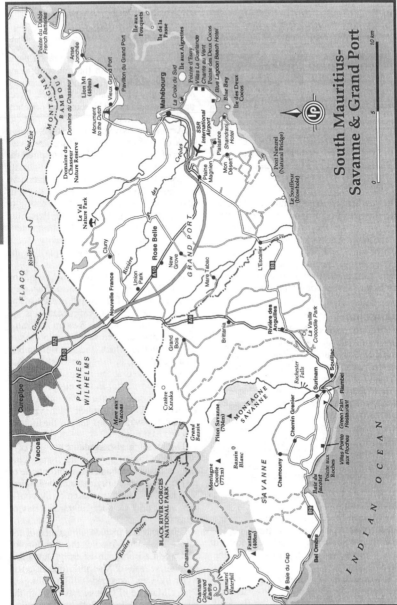

MAURITIUS

South Mauritius–
Savanne & Grand Port

Indies governor who drowned during a cyclone in 1615), Pierre Poivre (the botanist and creator of the Pamplemousses botanical gardens); and the death mask of poet-journalist Paul Jean Toulet (1867-1920).

The museum (☎ 6319329), set at the end of a tree-lined drive and surrounded by pleasant river walks, is open daily except Tuesday from 9 am to 5 pm. Admission is free.

Assembly of God Church

This is not a significant building or religious group; there are probably several similar congregations throughout the island. A visit to one when there is a service in progress adds a bit of local colour and warmth to an otherwise ponderous round of 'sightseeing'. The church is near Rue des Flamands, on Rue de Maurice.

Île aux Aigrettes

This island was established as a nature reserve in 1985. Many of the plant species found on the island's 25 hectares are very rare remnants of the coastal forests of Mauritius. As part of a MWAF project, approximately half of the island has been cleared of introduced species and native plants are being replanted. The ecosystem is also being restored with the eradication of rats and shrews, which are imported pests that cause damage to rare plant species and prevent the reintroduction of endemic reptiles, such as snakes (burrowing boa), skinks (Telfair's) and geckos (Gunther's).

The island serves as a convenient quarantine station for pink pigeons and Mauritius kestrels sent from overseas breeding schemes for eventual release in the wild. Guests at the nearby La Croix du Sud hotel on the mainland have become used to the sight of kestrels popping over from the island for a visit.

For details on Mauritius' wildlife see Flora & Fauna in the Facts about Mauritius chapter.

Beaches

Blue Bay is the official public beach closest to Mahébourg. This attractive beach can get quite busy on weekends. Good 'private'

beaches stretch back to Mahébourg, past Pointe des Deux Cocos to Pointe D'Esny.

Organised Tours

Most hotels and guesthouses can organise boat trips to Île aux Cerfs (described in the East Coast chapter) and other islands closer to Mahébourg. Their minimum return rates for the day are usually between Rs 500 to Rs 600 per person.

Should you charter a boat from Mahébourg, there are French fort ruins on Île de la Passe off Vieux Grand Port, a governor's summer residence on Île des Deux Cocos off Blue Bay and the nature reserve on Île aux Aigrettes, described above.

Places to Stay – Mahébourg

Mahébourg caters well for independent travellers. Most travellers come from Réunion and stay in the several cheap boarding houses lining the beach front. The standards of these pensions de famille vary from year to year, depending on which has been the latest to do renovations or change managers.

Pension St Tropez (☎ 6319646), near the Blue Bay road, is run by Ashok Beejadhur. It's cheap but the cleanliness is variable. The house is right on the water's edge and has five rooms with a communal bathroom for Rs 200/250 a single/double, including breakfast. One-bedroom and two-bedroom bungalows are also available for Rs 300/500 respectively.

Aquarelle (☎ 6319479) is next door to the Pension St Tropez and is much better value. Rates are Rs 250/370 including breakfast, for single/double rooms with common bath; Rs 420 for a one bedroom bungalow, including breakfast. Rooms 1 and 2 are recommended for their views across the bay.

Pension Nôtre Dame (☎ 6319582) is next to the church at the top of Rue du Souffleur. This residence, part of the convent, is run by nuns and has simple but tidy singles/doubles with communal bath for Rs 200/350 without breakfast, or Rs 270/480 with breakfast. If the doors are locked when you get here, just ring the doorbell.

Hôtel Les Aigrettes (☎/fax 6319094), on Rue du Chaland, has 19 airy apartments and is not a bad choice. Prices start at Rs 450/650 for a single/double, including breakfast. There are also double rooms with a TV for Rs 700. Long-stay discounts can be negotiated. There's a restaurant for residents only; the set dinner costs Rs 180 per person.

PLACES TO STAY
14 Hôtel Les Aigrettes
16 Aquarelle
17 Pension St Tropez
18 Pension Nôtre Dame; Church

PLACES TO EAT
1 Restaurant Monte Carlo
12 Recréation Café
15 Le Vacancier

OTHER
2 Express Buses to Port Louis
3 Bus Station
4 Market
5 Odéon Cinema
6 Barclays Bank
7 Police Station
8 Post Office
9 Mauritius Commercial Bank
10 Hong Kong & Shanghai Bank
11 Petrol Stations
13 J.H. Arnulphy Car Hire
19 Hospital

Mahébourg

0   100   200 m

To Airport,
Naval Museum
& Port Louis

To Blue Bay

Kohinoor (☎ 6318608), Royal Rd, is a pension de famille which has been recommended by several travellers. It has double rooms for around Rs 220 per night and offers reasonably priced meals. The owner, Mr Bassaruth, is a friendly character who takes an interest in his guests. If you do end up staying here, let us know how it was!

Places to Stay – Around Mahébourg

La Croix du Sud (☎ 6319505; fax 6319603) is on the Mahébourg-Blue Bay road, at Pointe Jérôme. It's an upmarket bungalow resort with a lush garden landscape at its centre. Room rates vary according to the busy and quiet months. During the quiet season singles/doubles/triples cost Rs 1650/2100/2650, including breakfast; in the high season

(November, January, March and April) they're Rs 1850/2500/3050, with breakfast. Half-board is available for an extra Rs 250 per person. The hotel has two swimming pools, a fitness centre, tennis court (open to nonresidents for Rs 125 per hour), as well as a range of water activities, including free glass-bottom boat excursions. Bikes can be hired for Rs 50/150 per hour/day. Trips can be arranged to Île aux Cerfs and Île aux Aigrettes. There is a séga night each Friday. The hotel's restaurant, *Les Aigrettes*, offers special dinner buffet menus (see Places to Eat for details). On the hotel beach you may be approached by pedlars selling trinkets made from corals, shells etc. Please do not buy these items since this only hastens the destruction of the marine environment – see Ecology & Environment in the Facts about Mauritius chapter.

Chantemer (☎ 6319688; fax 4643964) is a homely residence right on the beach, owned by a charming couple. Beautifully appointed and spotlessly clean doubles with private bathroom cost Rs 1300, including breakfast. If you can afford it go for a delightful suite which costs around Rs 1600, with breakfast. Prices vary according to the high/low season, so ask when making your reservation. The owners can organise water activities, including scuba diving, windsurfing and fishing. This place is popular with travellers, so it's a good idea to book ahead.

Villas Le Guerlande (☎ 6319882; fax 6319225) is another fine choice in this area. It's a small complex of self-catering bungalows in a pleasant garden setting. A two bedroom bungalow with kitchen, terrace and sea view costs Rs 1540/1650/1870 for double/triple/quadruple occupancy – single occupancy costs the same as double. Breakfast is included in this price. There are also cheaper rooms for Rs 880/1210 a single/double. Evening meals are available for Rs 350 per person. Windsurfers can be hired for Rs 250 per hour.

Chante au Vent (☎/fax 6319614) is less impressive than the above two places, but is still nice. This pension de famille is on the beach, about 4km from Mahébourg. Rooms (doubles only) with bath start at Rs 770, including breakfast. The best room costs Rs 880 per night.

Blue Lagoon Beach Hotel (☎ 6319529; fax 6319045), some 6km south of Mahébourg at Blue Bay, is a recently renovated hotel with a fine beach. It is particularly popular with Réunionnais and South African visitors. Single/double rooms cost Rs 1200/1700, including breakfast; Rs 1380/2050 on half-board. During the high season, prices rise by around 10%. Facilities include a small pool, tennis court, bar and restaurant (see Places to Eat). Water activities are also available.

Shandrani Hotel (☎ 6374301; fax 6374313), not far from SSR airport, is a fine place set in its own spacious grounds. It's actually on the other side of Blue Bay from the Blue Lagoon Beach Hotel. This hotel offers terrific rooms at equally terrific prices. Singles/doubles/triples start at Rs 5100/7600/9550, on half-board. Opulent suites range from Rs 10,700 to Rs 17,500, on a half-board basis. The Shandrani has all the sport and leisure activities of other luxury beach hotels, including diving, game fishing and horse riding. There's also a swimming pool, tennis court and three restaurants. Located very close to the airport, it discourages nonresidents by charging a Rs 150 entry fee. The hotel is a member of the Beachcomber group. The Beachcomber Card, which every guest receives on registration, is valid here – for more details see Accommodation in the Mauritius Facts for the Visitor chapter.

Places to Eat

Aquarelle (see Places to Stay) has a very good restaurant and is one of the best places to get a hearty home-made feed. It serves French and Créole cuisine with most main dishes starting at around Rs 120; smoked salmon salad is Rs 150, spaghetti bolognaise is Rs 100 and desserts are about Rs 35.

Le Vacancier, near the Aquarelle, is a tiny place with a very limited menu. It's best suited for a light bite on the run. There's crab soup (Rs 60), fish with ginger (Rs 110) and other similar fare which you can eat here or take-away. It's open daily from 10.30 am to 10.30 pm.

Restaurant Monte Carlo, on Rue de la Passe, serves European, Créole, Indian and Chinese food. It's a pleasant place and quite reasonably priced; Créole-style fish salad is Rs 100, chicken curry with prawns is Rs 150 and a small bottle of beer is Rs 22.

Recréation Café, on Rue de Labourdonnais, offers a selection of cheap snacks.

Les Aigrettes, at La Croix du Sud (see Places to Stay), offers special dinner buffet menus four times a week: Tuesday (Chinese); Wednesday (international); Thursday (Indian); and Saturday (gastronomy). Each buffet costs Rs 325 (plus 10% tax) per person. Nonresidents must book in advance.

Blue Lagoon Beach Hotel (see Places to Stay) has a restaurant serving a buffet dinner each night for Rs 330 per person. If you're not staying here advance bookings are recommended.

Entertainment

Mahébourg differs little from Curepipe or Port Louis for nightlife. A good night out requires a 6km trip out to the *Blue Lagoon Beach Hotel* in Blue Bay, or even further afield to the plusher *Shandrani Hotel*, near the airport.

There is one cinema, the *Odéon*, not far from the bus station.

Getting There & Away

Bus The quickest way to get to Port Louis and continue, for example, from there to Grand Baie, is to take the express service which leaves quite regularly during the day. It costs a bit more, but takes around half the time of the standard services which can take up to two hours to reach Port Louis.

On a much less frequent basis, buses run in the other direction from Mahébourg to Centre de Flacq (Rs 20), via Vieux Grand Port and Grand Sable, and to Souillac (Rs 12), via Rivière des Anguilles.

MAURITIUS

Taxi A taxi from SSR international airport to Mahébourg costs around Rs 250. For tips on dealing with taxi drivers on arrival, see Taxi in the Mauritius Getting Around chapter.

Getting Around

Car & Motorcycle JH Arnulphy Car Hire (☎ 6318346; fax 6319991) is open daily from 8.30 to 11.30 am and 12.30 to 4 pm. Prices for a small car start at about Rs 940 for one day with unlimited mileage. If you hire for at least four days, it costs Rs 875 per day. You will also have to pay a deposit or collision damage waiver of Rs 10,000 insurance and tax. Delivery or collection at the airport costs an additional Rs 60.

It is sometimes possible to hire a moped at the Nôtre Dame store opposite the Pension Nôtre Dame. Expect to pay around Rs 250 per day.

Bicycle Bicycles are available for hire from JH Arnulphy Car Hire (see Car & Motorcycle above) and some local pensions or hotels for around Rs 75 per day. Blue Bay is a leisurely excursion by bicycle.

AROUND MAHÉBOURG
Domaine du Chasseur

If you feel like a break from beach life, a visit to this large estate on the south-east coast is highly recommended. Domaine du Chasseur (☎ 6345097; fax 6345261) covers some 900 hectares of forested slopes. Visitors have a choice of activities, including hiking, birdwatching, and accompanied mini-safaris.

The forest contains many different species of trees, such as ebony, cinnamon, eucalyptus and traveller's palm. Various types of wildlife roam here: Javanese deer, boar, monkey, and many endemic species of bird, including a pair of Mauritian kestrels – one of the world's rarest birds of prey. You can watch the kestrels being fed white mice daily at around 3 pm. Hikers are charged Rs 200 for admission and provided with a sketch map of the estate and a guided tour in French or English. There is no compulsion to take the guided tour. Guests staying at the bunga-

lows or eating at the restaurant are excused from the admission charge.

There are about 28km of rough tracks available for hiking, with the most popular route being a one hour return climb to the helicopter landing pad and excellent viewpoint.

Accommodation is provided on the hillside in bungalows – a great spot if you fancy a splurge away from the beach. Rates for single/double occupancy are around Rs 1350/1950.

The restaurant is along the hillside in the form of individual tables protected by thatched pagodas and linked by walkways. It's an original idea with fine views and the cuisine is worth a splurge. Gourmets will appreciate the wine cellar and fine old spirits. Expect to pay at least Rs 400 per person for a three course meal plus a couple of beers.

Getting There Domaine du Chasseur is at Anse Jonchée, close to the village of Vieux Grand Port. From the main road, it's a 3km drive (or walk), passing through flat cane fields then climbing steeply along an increasingly rough track, to the restaurant and bungalows and the trailhead for hikes into the forest. If you phone ahead, it is usually possible to arrange to be picked up at the main road where there are frequent bus connections between Mahébourg and Centre de Flacq (Rs 22). From Mahébourg it's about 20 minutes by taxi – expect to pay around Rs 200 one way.

Vieux Grand Port

About 7km north of Mahébourg, Vieux Grand Port has great historical significance for Mauritians, but unfortunately few historical remains for visitors.

The Dutch made Vieux Grand Port their base and called it Fort Frederick Henrik. About 4km from Mahébourg, on the banks of a river, is a monument commemorating the first landing by Dutch sailors, which took place on 9 September 1598 under the command of Wybrand Van Warwick. The monument was erected in 1948 by the Mauritius Historical Society.

OLIVIER CIRENDINI

OLIVIER CIRENDINI

PAUL PIAIA

Mauritius
Top: A green blanket of Victoria Regia water lillies at Sir Seewoosagur Ramgoolam Botanical Gardens, Pamplemousses, Mauritius.
Bottom left: Peppers are used to tickle the taste buds in a variety of Créole and Indian dishes.
Bottom right: Picturesque Coin de Mire island from Ilot Gabriel, off the north coast of Mauritius.

ROBERT STRAUSS

JULIAN SMITH

PAUL PIAIA

Mauritius
The emphasis on outdoor life is strong in Mauritius – from sailing a yacht on Blue Bay near Mahébourg to enjoying the sun or taking in the scenery at Chamarel Falls, central Mauritius.

Beside the new church on the roadside at the northern end of Vieux Grand Port are the ruins of a Dutch settlement, although many believe they are French ruins.

Unfortunately the Salle d'Armes, once an attractive little maze between the coral rocks beside the sea, has been turned into a quarry. There's nothing left now, just a pile of rubble where there was once said to be an old duelling ground with a great 'buccaneer' atmosphere.

Vieux Grand Port was also the site of the only French naval victory to be inscribed on the Arc de Triomphe in Paris. The relics of the 1810 battle with the English are on display at the Naval Museum in Mahébourg.

The area is historically important for the sugar industry. The Ferney sugar estate, 5km from Mahébourg, is one of the oldest in Mauritius. Nearby is a monument commemorating the introduction of sugar cane by the Dutch in 1639.

Pointe du Diable

'Devil's Point', 8km north of Vieux Grand Port, was once the site of a French coastal battery. The cannons remain.

Lion Mt

Overlooking Vieux Grand Port is Lion Mt, so named because it resembles a crouching lion. There are two routes up – one via the road opposite the church in the town and through the cemetery; and the other via the police station. Both lead through sugar cane fields on the footslopes. It's worth asking someone in the village to direct you to the path, as it can be a little difficult to find. The climb is relatively easy although steep, but can be dangerous because it becomes slippery when wet.

Le Val Nature Park

The road into Le Val is at Union Park village, about halfway on the Mahébourg-Curepipe road. Cluny village, the gateway to Le Val Nature Park in the valley of the Rivière des Créoles, is about 7km down the road.

Many of the amazing anthurium flowers are grown at Le Val in shade houses. There are also water fields full of watercress, which complements many Créole meals, and attempts at prawn farming. Other facilities include a small aquarium and a deer park. Le Val is open Monday to Friday from 9 am to 5 pm. Admission costs Rs 20.

There is a bus service from Curepipe to Rose Belle, via Cluny (Rs 10).

Le Souffleur

The reef which nearly surrounds Mauritius has a major break in it on the south-east coast. Instead of beach and calm lagoon, the sea rushes up against lava rocks and cliffs, carving out a variety of stacks and other coastline sculptures, the best known of which is Le Souffleur (blowhole). It doesn't blow like a whale every day because it depends on the sea conditions. In fact, erosion is rapidly diminishing its grandeur, but even when Le Souffleur is dormant, there is still a knee-trembling power rumbling away below.

If you walk for about 20 minutes along the cliffs east from Le Souffleur, you'll come to a spectacular natural bridge formed when the roof of a sea cave collapsed.

To get there, take the Plaine Magnien-Souillac road (or bus from Mahébourg to Souillac). About 6km from Plaine Magnien, as you enter the village of L'Escalier, is the entry to the Savanne sugar mill. Follow the signs for some 4km to Le Souffleur, through the mill grounds and the cane fields. The blowhole is at the end of the biggest promontory, joined to the shore and car park by landfill. Cars and bicycles can go all the way down. You can visit Le Souffleur Monday to Friday from 8 am to 6 pm and on Saturday from 7 am to noon. Entry is free.

SOUILLAC

Named after the Vicomte de Souillac, the island's French governor from 1779 to 1787, Souillac, like Mahébourg, is of little interest in itself. It is not particularly welcoming or helpful to visitors, probably because it is not used to getting them. Souillac seems a place that Mauritians like to visit. Gris Gris and Robert Edward Hart's house are popular school outings.

MAURITIUS

Robert Edward Hart Museum

Robert Edward Hart (1891-1954) was a renowned Mauritian poet, appreciated by the French and English alike. He wrote in French and translations of his poetry are hard to find. He lived out the last 13 years of his life at Le Nef, a coral beach cottage about 500m east along the shore from the Souillac bus park. It was taken over by the Mauritius Institute and opened to the public in 1967. The bedroom and kitchen have been maintained.

On display are copies and originals of Hart's letters, plays, speeches and poetry, as well as his spectacles, pith helmet and fiddle. One speech, on love and marriage, was delivered at the Curepipe Hotel in November 1914, for the benefit of English and French war victims. The museum (☎ 6256101) is open from 9 am to 4 pm every day except Sunday. Entry is free.

Gris Gris

Continue along the road past Le Nef and the Robert Edward Hart Museum and you come to a grassy cliff top, which affords a view of the black rocky coastline where the reef is broken, and a path down to Gris Gris beach. It is a popular spot for shell collecting but a wooden sign warns of the dangers of swimming here. 'Gris Gris' is said to mean 'sorcery' or 'black magic'.

La Roche qui Pleure

'The rock that cries' is a little further east along the coast from Gris Gris and resembles a crying man. In fact it looks like the profile of Robert Edward Hart. Two pictures in the Robert Edward Hart Museum show the comparison in case you can't find the actual rock.

Telfair Gardens

More like a small municipal park than actual gardens, the Telfair Gardens are hardly an outstanding sight. But they are conveniently opposite the bus park in Souillac, on the road to the Robert Edward Hart Museum and Gris Gris. The gardens were named after Sir Charles Telfair, secretary to the first English governor, sugar baron and superintendent of Sir Seewoosagur Ramgoolam Botanical Gardens. You get a good view across the bay from Telfair to the graveyard at Cemetery Point, where Hart is buried.

There is a concrete slab informing you that swimming is hazardous because of dangerous currents off the rocks at the foot of the park.

Rochester Falls

A 5km walk from Souillac, past the Terracine sugar mill and through the cane fields along a well-marked route, brings you to this gushing little number. The falls are not so much high as wide, a sort of pocket-sized Niagara. A car can just about make it along the potholed cane field tracks; this is something a new taxi won't risk, but an old one might for around Rs 300 return from Souillac.

La Vanille Crocodile Park

This small zoo and 'handbag factory' is 2km south of the hill town of Rivière des Anguilles on the road to Britannia. Nile crocodile were imported here from Madagascar in 1985 and have been joined by giant tortoise, monkey, deer, bat, giant land crab, lizard and other wildlife. It's a pleasant spot to ramble through thick, steamy forest and enjoy the local fauna and flora. The park is open daily from 9.30 am to 5 pm. Admission costs Rs 60/30 for an adult/child during the week and Rs 50/25 on weekends.

Beaches

Reef-protected beaches at Riambel and further west at Pointe aux Roches provide good swimming. Wild and windswept Gris Gris is far too dangerous.

Baie du Cap

In spite of a great variety in coastal scenery, including some marvellous stretches of casuarina-lined beaches at La Prairie, west of the bay, this area has not been developed. Years ago surfers discovered the good waves around Macondé Point, on the other side of the bay.

Baie du Jacotet

It is said there is a buried treasure on Îlot Sancho, a stone's throw from the shore – under the old cannon perhaps? There is also a good surfing spot nearby. And by Bel Ombre stands a monument to the survivors of the *Trevessa*, at the place where the lifeboat landed after 25 days at sea (see Naval Museum in the Mahébourg section).

Places to Stay

Villas Pointe aux Roches (☎ 6256111; fax 6256110) is about 4km west of Souillac, past Riambel on the coast road. The villas are 27 rather ugly-looking white boxes set among palm trees facing a lovely beach. The bar is a great place to watch the surf thundering onto the rocks. Single/double rooms cost Rs 800/1320 including breakfast; Rs 1045/1600 on half-board. Facilities include a pool, mini-golf and restaurant (see Places to Eat). There are bikes (Rs 100 per day) and a catamaran tour to Île aux Cerfs (Rs 1250 per person including lunch and transfer).

Places to Eat

Choices in Souillac are slim. There is a local café next to the bus park which serves cheap fast food.

Le Batelage is a pleasant restaurant not far from Rochester Falls, which specialises in seafood. Try the squid with Créole sauce (Rs 145) or the tiger prawns in green pepper sauce (Rs 230). For sweet-tooths, dessert possibilities include melba peach (Rs 60) and banana caramel (Rs 50). The restaurant is open daily for lunch and dinner.

Green Palm Restaurant, on the coastal road, is not nearly as impressive as Le Batelage. It serves Indian, Chinese and European cuisine; Créole-style fish costs Rs 250, fried chicken with vegetables is Rs 100, milkshakes cost Rs 35 and a small bottle of beer is Rs 25.

Villas Pointe aux Roches (see Places to Stay) offers a buffet dinner every Wednesday and Saturday night, sometimes accompanied by a séga show. It costs around Rs 350 per person. Nonresidents are welcome but should try to book ahead.

Getting There & Around

Souillac and Rivière des Anguilles are on the Baie du Cap-Mahébourg bus route. There are also regular buses to and from Curepipe, via Rivière des Anguilles (Rs 10).

There is a bus service running direct between Curepipe, Souillac and Pointe aux Roches about three times a day. A taxi from Souillac to Villas Pointe aux Roches costs around Rs 150.

MAURITIUS

Rodrigues & the Outer Islands

HIGHLIGHTS

- Guided tour of the caves at Caverne Patate
- Scuba-diving off Pointe Coton, Pointe Roche Noire and Pointe Palmiste
- Hiking around Mt Limon and Mt Malartic
- A boat trip to nearby islands such as Île Cocos, Île aux Sables, Île aux Crabes and Île Hermitage

RODRIGUES ISLAND

Rodrigues is a volcanic island, 18km long and 8km wide, which lies 560km to the north-east of Mauritius. It's surrounded by a coral reef and is similar to Mauritius in vegetation, mountains, beaches and climate.

Compared to Mauritius, Rodrigues is more vulnerable during the November to May cyclone season. The most recent major cyclone, Bella, raged past the island in January 1991, when wind speeds in excess of 200km/h were recorded. The island has been hit with several smaller cyclones since then. The wettest months are February and March.

The population grew rapidly early in this century, but has now stabilised at about 37,000. One of the island's major problems is the strain that such a relatively large population puts on land resources. In contrast to Mauritius, the people are more African than Indian in origin and most are Roman Catholics. Many liberated slaves settled on Rodrigues.

The economic mainstays for the islanders are fishing, subsistence agriculture, handicrafts, an infant tourism industry, and subsidised imports from Mauritius.

For the time being Rodrigues remains unspoiled, but it is receiving increasing attention from Mauritian tour operators keen to promote something different. Compared to Mauritius, Rodrigues is much less hectic and has far less tourist hype. Perhaps that's why the people seem more relaxed and willing to chat to visitors. Rodrigues does not have the tropical lushness of Mauritius, but has a rugged beauty which grows on you.

It's not a bad idea to take with you supplies of any special items, such as prescription medicines or films. The extra cost of transport is reflected in the prices of goods imported from Mauritius.

History

The Portuguese had the honour of discovering Rodrigues (for Europe) and naming it after one of their intrepid seamen, but it was the Dutch who first set foot on the island, albeit very briefly, in September 1601.

The Frenchman, François Leguat, and a small band of Huguenot companions sailed away from religious persecution in France and arrived here in 1691. Leguat enjoyed his paradisiacal existence on the island, but the lack of female company was an impediment to perfection. The island's fauna and flora was a source of wonder and comestibles – survival rather than conservation was top priority in those days. Leguat's journal, entitled *Voyage et Aventure de François Leguat en Deux Îles Désertes des Indes Orientales*, provides a vivid account of the group's two year stay, and was a publishing success in Europe.

Subsequent visitors to Rodrigues set about ruthlessly removing the island's thousands of giant tortoise which were a prized source of nourishment. Rodrigues also had a big flightless bird, the solitaire, which went the same way as the dodo and just as quickly.

The French returned early in the 18th century for another attempt at colonisation, but had abandoned Rodrigues by the end of the century. In 1809, the British landed on the island and used it as a provisional base from which to attack and capture Mauritius.

Until it gained independence with Mauritius in 1968, Rodrigues had an uneventful history. There is now a Ministry of Rodrigues in the Mauritian government which appoints

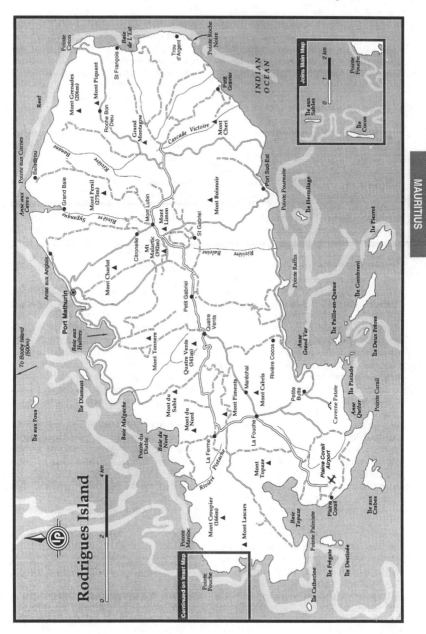

MAURITIUS

Rodrigues Island

an Island Secretary to look after the island's affairs. There are two political parties on Rodrigues: Organisation du Peuple Rodriguais (OPR), the dominant party, led by Serge Clair, and Mouvement Rodriguais, headed by Voulmally Nicola.

Flora & Fauna

Since the island's colonisation in the 17th century, its thick forest cover has been destroyed by felling and intensive grazing. The secondary growth with which this has been replaced consists mostly of introduced plant species. Of the 38 or so remaining species of plants native to Rodrigues, all but two are considered endangered, vulnerable, or rare. Species of which continued existence depend on one or two specimens in the wild include café marron, bois pipe, mandrinette and bois pasner.

The Mauritian government is acting to protect vegetation plots of critical importance, such as Grande Montagne, Pigeon, Cascades, Mourouk, St Louis and Anse Quitor. These plots are fenced off from animal depredation and carefully weeded to remove the much faster growing introduced species. Rare species are propagated in government nurseries on Rodrigues and then planted in these plots where they have a better chance of survival and regeneration.

It is hoped that these areas will act as refuges for the island's rare endemic fauna, such as the Rodrigues warbler, Rodrigues fody and Rodrigues fruit bat. The warbler population has made a shaky recovery from virtual extinction in the 1960s to an estimated 50 birds in the early 1990s. The Rodrigues fody population has also increased from very low numbers in the 1960s to approximately 400 birds in 1991. The Rodrigues fruit bat spends the day in communal roosts, usually in old mango trees, and becomes active at night when it searches for fruits, flowers and leaves. A common haunt for the bats is the valley about 4km south of Port Mathurin, towards Mont Lubin.

Colonies of seabirds, including fairy tern and noddy, nest on Île Cocos and Île aux Sables off the north-west coast.

Information

Tourist Office At the time of writing there was no tourist office on the island, but it is rumoured that one will eventually be established in Port Mathurin. The locals are happy to help tourists and are a great source of information about the island.

For information about maps of Rodrigues, see Maps in the Mauritius Facts for the Visitor chapter. For books about Rodrigues see Books in the Mauritius Facts for the Visitor chapter.

Money Barclays Bank (☎ 8311553), Indian Ocean International Bank (☎ 8311591), State Bank (☎ 8311642) and Mauritius Commercial Bank (☎ 8311833) all have offices in Port Mathurin. Opening hours are from 9.15 am to 3.15 pm Monday to Friday; and from 9.15 to 11.15 am on Saturday. You can change money at all banks.

Post The main post office (☎ 8312098) is on Rue Mann in Port Mathurin. Opening hours are Monday to Friday from 8.15 to 11.15 am and from noon to 4 pm; and from 8.15 to 11.45 am on Saturday. There are also small post offices at La Ferme and Mont Lubin.

The DHL Worldwide Express representative on Rodrigues is Mauritours (see under Organised Tours, later in this chapter). DHL can arrange air freight around the world.

Telephone All Rodrigues numbers consist of seven digits. To call Rodrigues from Mauritius, dial ☎ 00095 followed by the Rodrigues number. To call Rodrigues from abroad, dial the international access code followed by the Mauritius country code (230) and the Rodrigues number. To call Mauritius from Rodrigues, simply dial the full Mauritius number.

The Overseas Telecommunications Services (OTS) (☎ 8311816) office on Mont Vénus is open weekdays from 7.30 am to 3.30 pm and on weekends from 8 am to noon.

Dangers & Annoyances Drinking-water is generally neither chlorinated nor filtrated. Bottled water is available from shops and most hotels/pensions; a 1L bottle costs around Rs 8 but hotels and restaurants usually charge more.

Port Mathurin

As the administrative, commercial and industrial hub of the island, Port Mathurin is a natural base for visitors. An adjacent section of town, known as Camp du Roi, is being developed as an administrative, commercial and industrial complex. There's a court house, fire station, police station and offices for banks, trading companies and social services.

Things to See & Do

Beaches Pointe Coton, on the east coast, has the best beach on the island. There are other nice beaches at St François, Trou d'Argent and Petit Gravier.

Caves At Caverne Patate, in the south-west corner of the island, are some interesting caves with impressive stalagmite and stalactite formations.

The requisite permit is issued at the Administration Office (☎ 8311504) on Rue Jenner, Port Mathurin. There are guided tours daily at 9 am, 10.30 am, 1 pm and 2.30 pm. The permit charge is Rs 50 (for one to 10 people) and you should arrive at the cave entrance on the day and time specified on your permit. Wear strong shoes and take a jacket or pullover.

To get to the caves, take the road to Petite Butte. The cave warden's hut is down a small track, close to the Centre Communal. You can take the bus to La Fouche and ask the driver to let you off at the right spot.

Most hotels/pensions and tour operators can arrange cave tours.

Hiking As the island is relatively small, it's perfect for simply rambling around at your own leisure. The island is hilly and hiking is good around Mt Limon and Mt Malartic, the highest points at more than 390m above sea level. The best coastal hiking is from Port Mathurin, around the east end of the island, to Port Sud-Est.

There's a long hike along the coastal road from La Ferme to Port Mathurin via Baie aux Huîtres.

Diving There are several good scuba-diving locations around Rodrigues, but unfortunately there is no diving school or public-use compressor on the island, and you need a boat. The best dives are off Pointe Coton and Pointe Roche Noire, on the east coast, and off Pointe Palmiste, on the west. Baladirou, at Pointe aux Cornes, is also popular for diving.

Cotton Bay Hotel has a diving centre which is also open to nonresidents – see Places to Stay for more details. Henri Tours (see Organised Tours) can organise cheaper diving trips; a one hour dive costs Rs 450 per person.

Horse Riding Cotton Bay Hotel offers horse riding – see Places to Stay for details.

Offshore Islands

There are many small islands dotted around Rodrigues. The four islands most commonly visited are Île Cocos, Île aux Sables, Île aux Crabes and Île Hermitage.

The permits required to visit Île Cocos, barely 1km in length, and its even smaller neighbour, Île aux Sables, can be obtained from the Administration Office (☎ 8311504) on Rue Jenner, Port Mathurin. Each permit is valid for a maximum of 12 people, costs Rs 200 and includes the return boat fare. Henri Tours and Mauritours can also arrange trips – see Organised Tours.

Both islands are nature reserves populated by several species of birds, such as the noddy, fairy tern and frigate bird. The excursion (four hour round trip) usually includes a lunch stop – freshly caught fish grilled on Île Cocos. Check if the excursion price includes lunch. The full walk around Île Cocos takes about 45 minutes, and there are two guards who can provide directions or information about the fauna and flora.

No permits are required to visit Île aux Crabes and Île Hermitage. Île aux Crabes is about 20 minutes by boat from Pointe Corail,

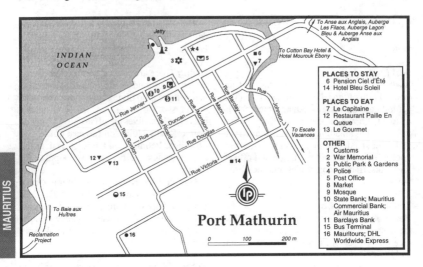

MAURITIUS

Port Mathurin

To Anse aux Anglais, Auberge Les Filaos, Auberge Lagon Bleu & Auberge Anse aux Anglais

To Cotton Bay Hotel & Hotel Mourouk Ebony

To Escale Vacances

To Baie aux Huîtres

INDIAN OCEAN

Jetty

Rue Jenner
Rue Ricard
Rue Gordon
Rue Duncan
Rue Morrison
Rue Mann
Rue Barclay
Rue Johnson
Rue Douglas
Rue Victoria

Reclamation Project

0   100   200 m

PLACES TO STAY
6 Pension Ciel d'Été
14 Hotel Bleu Soleil

PLACES TO EAT
7 Le Capitaine
12 Restaurant Paille En Queue
13 Le Gourmet

OTHER
1 Customs
2 War Memorial
3 Public Park & Gardens
4 Police
5 Post Office
8 Market
9 Mosque
10 State Bank; Mauritius Commercial Bank; Air Mauritius
11 Barclays Bank
15 Bus Terminal
16 Mauritours; DHL Worldwide Express

but don't expect much in the way of crabs – the island is being used for a sheep-farming project!

Île Hermitage, a tiny island renowned for its beauty (and possibly hidden treasure), is accessible by boat from Port Sud-Est (about 25 minutes) or Petite Butte (about 90 minutes).

It's also possible to hire local boats at Rivière Cocos for trips to Île Gombrani or Île Paille-en-Queue.

Organised Tours
Henri Tours (☎ 8311823; fax 8311726), on Rue Mann, Port Mathurin, is a down-to-earth place which offers a variety of tours. This small company is run by Henri Meunier, an affable guy who will happily explain the tours on offer. Snorkelling trips and excursions to nearby islands, such as Île Cocos, can also be arranged; a one day visit to Île Cocos, including lunch and snorkelling gear, costs Rs 400 per person. A tour of Rodrigues is Rs 200 per person; Rs 350 with lunch. The office is open Monday to Friday from 8 am to 4 pm and on Saturday from 8 am to noon.

The more business-like, but still friendly and helpful Mauritours (☎ 8312710; fax

8312713), at the Max Center, Camp du Roi, can also organise a number of tours. Options include a full-day 4WD tour of the island for Rs 1800 (maximum of four people); a day tour to Île Cocos including a barbeque lunch and soft drinks for Rs 550 per person; a half-day excursion to Caverne Patate for Rs 275 per person; and a half-day tour of Port Mathurin for Rs 140 per person. The office is open Monday to Friday from 8 am to 4 pm and on Saturday from 8 am to noon. It is also the DHL Worldwide Express representative on Rodrigues.

Most of the hotels and guesthouses can also arrange tours and transport for guests.

Places to Stay
Camping If you have a tent, you can camp just about anywhere on the island. Don't forget to bring along a torch.

Pensions de Famille There is a good selection of pensions de famille in and around Port Mathurin.

Auberge Les Filaos (☎ 8311644; fax 8312026) is at Anse aux Anglais, 2km east of Port Mathurin, and is a popular choice. There are 18 comfortable rooms, 11 with private bath (and private balcony) and seven with common bath. Singles/doubles with common bath are Rs 300/450, while singles/doubles with private bath go for Rs 500/600; both include breakfast. Half-board costs an additional Rs 100 per person. They do airport transfers for Rs 100 per person (one way) with advance notice. The owner's amicable son, Jean-Marc Begue, can arrange various tours: a full-day 4WD tour of the island (maximum of five people) costs Rs 350 per person, including lunch; a half/full day fishing trip is Rs 800/1400 (maximum of three people); and a day trip to Île Cocos costs Rs 450 per person, including lunch. Nonresidents can also go on these tours but must book ahead.

Auberge Anse aux Anglais (☎ 8312179; fax 8311973), right next door to the Auberge Les Filaos, is also good but more expensive. Singles/doubles with private bath cost Rs 700/1000 on a half-board basis only. Airport transfers cost a hefty Rs 200 per person (one way). Island tours and fishing trips can be organised and there are bicycles for hire (Rs 150 per day).

Auberge Lagon Bleu (☎ 8311823; fax 8311726), in the same area, is owned by Henri (of Henri Tours) and has just a few rooms which are basic but cheap. Rooms with attached bath are Rs 200/400/500 for single/double/triple occupancy, including breakfast. On a half-board basis they cost Rs 300/550/750.

Pension Ciel d'Été (☎ 8311587; fax 8312004), on Rue Jenner in Port Mathurin, has 12 rooms. Singles/doubles are Rs 350/600, including breakfast; Rs 500/900 on half-board.

Hotels If you fancy a touch of style, then there are a handful hotels around the island to choose from.

Escale Vacances (☎ 8312555; fax 8312075), in Port Mathurin, is a delightful, 23 room hotel that's excellent value for money. Squeaky-clean singles/doubles without air-con cost Rs 350/600, including breakfast; Rs 900/1500 on half-board. Singles/doubles with air-con cost Rs 450/700, including breakfast; Rs 1040/1700 on half-board. The rooms are tastefully furnished and all have an attached bath. There's also a swimming pool and a good restaurant (see Places to Eat).

Hotel Beau Soleil (☎ 8311673; fax 8311916), on Rue Victoria, has 28 rooms, all with private bath. Standard singles/doubles cost Rs 500/800, including breakfast; Rs 600/1000 on half-board. Superior rooms go for Rs 600/900 with breakfast, or Rs 750/1200 on half-board. The service here can be a tad lacklustre and the rooms are OK but not crash hot.

Hotel Mourouk Ebony (☎ 8313350; fax 8313355) is in an isolated position in the Port Sud-Est area. Accommodation is in comfortable bungalows (each with a shocking-red roof) which cost Rs 1675/2950 a single/double; all rooms are on half-board. There's a small pool, bar and restaurant. Island tours and water activities are available including windsurfing (around Rs 320 per hour). They also rent out bicycles (for a pretty price).

Cotton Bay Hotel (☎ 8313000; fax 8313003), at Pointe Coton, is the most luxurious hotel on the island, beside an excellent beach. Standard single/double rooms cost Rs 2650/4100; superior single/double rooms cost Rs 2830/4460; and deluxe single/double rooms cost Rs 3830/6440. All these prices include half-board. There's a good swimming pool to splash in, games room, tennis court and restaurant. If you fancy a trot around the island, horse riding is available for Rs 400 per hour. There's also the Scuba Diving Centre which charges Rs 700 per person for one dive, Rs 3300 per person for five dives and Rs 6300 per person for 10 dives. Nonresidents can also make use of this facility – ring ahead to make an appointment.

Places to Eat

Apart from the hotels/pensions, there is just a sprinkling of restaurants on Rodrigues. Most specialise in seafood and are closed on Sunday.

Le Capitaine (☎ 8311581) is a seafood speciality place in Port Mathurin, which is open Monday to Saturday from 10 am to 10 pm. They also whip up some Chinese and Créole dishes. Items include vegetarian chopsuey (Rs 45), octopus curry with rice and salad (Rs 75), and desserts for around Rs 25.

Lagon Bleu Restaurant (☎ 8311823), on Rue Mann, also specialises in seafood and is open only for lunch on weekdays from 10 am to 4 pm. Main dishes in this unpretentious little place range from Rs 50 to Rs 250. For a splurge, try the curry lobster with rice and salad (Rs 250).

Le Gourmet (☎ 8311571), on Rue Duncan, offers a selection of Chinese and seafood dishes; fish curry is Rs 50, vegetable fried rice is Rs 45. The restaurant is open Monday to Saturday from 9.30 am to 3 pm and 6 to 9 pm.

Restaurant Paille En Queue (☎ 8312315) is opposite Le Gourmet and has a broad menu with fare such as pork curry (Rs 30) and lobster salad (Rs 150). It focuses on seafood and is open Monday to Saturday from 10 am to 10 pm.

Escale Vacances (see Places to Stay) has a pleasant restaurant and is recommended for a minor splurge. Main dishes cost between Rs 90 and Rs 150. It's open daily from 11.30 am to 2.30 pm and 7.30 to 9.30 pm. Nonresidents are welcome – advance bookings are appreciated.

Entertainment

Traditional Dance & Music The islanders are known for their versions of old colonial ballroom and country dances such as the scottische, waltz and mazurka. The Créoles know them as the *kotis*, *laval* and *mazok*. They also have a more African version of the séga, known as *séga tambour*. The accordion is the main instrument played on the island. Popular local groups are Les Camarons, Racine, and Mighty Guys.

Nightlife on Rodrigues is virtually non-existent – part of the island's appeal to many travellers. To find out about the possibility of any forthcoming events, it's best to ask the locals.

Things to Buy

Handicrafts, especially baskets and hats made from all sorts of materials, are available at shops in Port Mathurin and also at a small shop in the departure area of the airport. In the island's markets you can pick up all sorts of things including handicrafts, spices, jams, local honey and dried octopus. The main market of the week in Port Mathurin is held on Saturday from around 6 to 11 am – it predominantly sells vegetables.

Getting There & Away

Air Air Mauritius operates daily flights to Rodrigues which take 1½ hours one way. The return fare is Rs 5510 (ticket valid for a minimum stay of five days; maximum stay of one month); or Rs 6120 (for stays of less than five days). Mauritian residents travel half-price.

There is a luggage limit of 15kg per person. Each excess kilo costs Rs 9, but you may get away without having to pay extra if you are just a little over. When checking in at the Mauritius airport, you may be asked how much you weigh – don't worry, you won't have to go through the indignity of being weighed like a sack of potatoes – an approximation is fine! In case you're wondering, no, you don't have to pay departure tax for flights between Mauritius and Rodrigues.

The main Air Mauritius office on Rodrigues is in the ADS building in Port Math-urin (☎ 8311632; fax 8311959). It's open Monday to Friday from 8 am to 3.30 pm and on Saturday from 8 am to noon. There is also a representative (☎ 8311301; fax 8311321) at the Plaine Corail airport; it is open to coincide with all flight arrivals. It's a good idea to reconfirm your return ticket here when you arrive.

Boat The MV *Mauritius Pride* does the trip from Mauritius to Rodrigues several times every month. The one-way trip takes about 27 hours, depending on sea conditions. The following prices reflect the 50% surcharge for non-Mauritians. A return fare costs Rs 1350/2700 one way/return (seats), or Rs 2100/4200 one way/return (cabins). Meals are included in the price. This boat is popular with locals, so try to book well ahead.

For further information contact Mauritius Shipping Corporation Ltd (☎ 2412550; fax 2425245), Nova building, 1 Military Rd, Port Louis. On Rodrigues, contact Islands' Service Ltd (☎ 8311555; fax 8312089) in Port Mathurin.

Yacht Due to prevailing winds, Rodrigues is difficult to reach by yacht from Mauritius. The trip takes up to a week, but the journey back is much easier and quicker.

Getting Around

The Airport Flights arrive at Plaine Corail airfield in Rodrigues. The 'Supercopter' bus service to Port Mathurin operates only for flight arrivals and departures and takes about 35 minutes. The price for a one-way ticket is Rs 100. Tour operators and most hotels/pensions can also do airport transfers (for a charge) with advance notice.

Bus & Camionette There are now several private bus lines which operate standard buses and camionettes (small pick-up trucks) from the bus station *(gare routière)* in Port Mathurin. When travelling on a camionette, you may have to pay extra for your backpack.

At present there are bus routes from Port Mathurin to Baie aux Huîtres (Rs 7), La

Ferme via Mont Lubin (Rs 11), Pointe Coton (Rs 11) and Grand Baie (Rs 10). Schedules are somewhat irregular.

Car Rental Ask your hotel/pension manager about car hire or contact Mauritours (☎ 831-2710; fax 8312713), which offers jeep hire for around Rs 1350 per day (Rs 1250 per day if you rent for at least three days). For something cheaper, Henri Tours (☎ 8311823; fax 8311726) charges around Rs 1000 per day for car rental. Make sure you get a contact telephone number in case of a breakdown.

The road system on Rodrigues is being improved and expanded. There are now numerous asphalted roads, but 4WD vehicles or jeeps are still essential for negotiating the unpaved tracks through the steep terrain.

Motorcycle For reasonable prices contact Patrico (☎ 8312044), who charges Rs 300/400 for a moped/motorbike per day. He offers discounts for long rentals. Alternatively, contact Mauritours (☎ 8312710; fax 831-2713), which rents out mopeds for Rs 400 per day. Some hotels/pensions may also be able to arrange moped hire.

Walking Walking is really the best way to see this rugged island and meet its friendly

people. Rodrigues is reasonably small, so no place should be more than a few hours walk away – it's a great way to exercise, take in the fresh air and explore this glorious island.

OUTER ISLANDS

Four other islands or island groups in the Indian Ocean are claimed by Mauritius.

Cargados Carajos (St Brandon)

This 22 island atoll, 370km north-east of Mauritius is, like the Maldives, a diving paradise. Unfortunately it is currently not open to tourists. Fishermen ply the waters and camp on Albatross (in the north) and Coco (in the south), and maintain a base at Raphael (in the central part), but there is no permanent settlement.

Agalega

There are more than 300 people involved in the copra industry on this 70 sq km island, 1100km north of Mauritius, en route to the Seychelles. For further information, contact the Outer Islands Development Corporation (☎ 2422275 or 2402072) in Port Louis.

Tromelin

This island is claimed by both Mauritius and France. Rather than let the dispute upset

MAURITIUS

Octopus & Squid

It scarcely seems credible that *cephalopods*, the tentacled octopus and squid, should be related to oysters, clams, cowries and cone shells, yet all are molluscs. The eight-tentacled octopus usually shelters in a cavity or cave in the coral, coming out to grab unwary fish or crustaceans which it kills with an often venomous bite from its beak-like jaws.

Squid are rather like a longer, streamlined version of an octopus. Like an octopus they move by a form of jet propulsion, squirting out the water which is taken over their gills. They can move at remarkable speed and catch their prey, usually small fish and crustaceans, by shooting out two long tentacles. Like octopus they are also masters of disguise, able to change their colour by squeezing or flattening out cells which contain coloured material.

Cuttlefish are like a larger squid and along with speed and the ability to change colour they are also able to perform a type of animal smokescreen trick. When threatened they turn a dark colour then shoot out a blob of dark ink which takes a cuttlefish-like shape. The real cuttlefish then rapidly turns a lighter colour and shoots away, leaving the predator to grab at its ghost! The familiar cuttlebone found washed up on beaches is a cuttlefish's internal skeleton. It is made up of thin layers and by filling the space between layers with gas the cuttlefish uses it as a flotation device.

Octopus and squid have evolved from earlier *cephalopods* which had shells. The chambered nautilus is the best known and most spectacular survivor of these creatures. The large brown and white nautilus shell is divided into chambers and the tentacled creature can vary its buoyancy by changing the amount of gas and liquid in individual chambers. ∎

relations, both have agreed not to pursue a claim in any way, so no-one lives there.

Chagos Archipelago

The Chagos Archipelago was formerly administered from Mauritius. Then, a few years before independence in 1968, the British annexed the island under the British Indian Ocean Territory and leased the main island, Diego García, to the USA as a military base for its Rapid Deployment Force. The Chagos islanders were moved to Mauritius and given financial compensation for the upheaval. For more details see Population & People in the Facts about Mauritius chapter.

Réunion

Facts about Réunion

RÉUNION

Official Name: Réunion
Area: 2510 sq km
Population: 675,700
Population Growth Rate: 1.7%
Capital: St-Denis
Head of State: Governed as an overseas department of France
Official Language: French
Main Religion: Catholicism
Currency: French franc
Exchange Rate: FF5.68 = US$1
Per Capita GNP: US$8000
Inflation: 2%
Time: UTC +4

Highlights

- Breathtaking and varied scenery, from austere mountains to intriguing amphitheatres
- Superb trekking options including three extraordinary cirques, the active Piton de la Fournaise volcano and Piton des Neiges – Réunion's highest peak
- The colourful cultural melting pot *à la réunionnais* of Créoles, Europeans, Indians and Chinese
- A delicious diversity of food, from traditional Créole curries to *haute cuisine française*

Réunion is so sheer and lush, it looks as if it has risen dripping wet from the deep blue sea. This enchanting island, a mere speck on the map, is sometimes compared to Hawaii. Both share breathtaking landscapes, volcanic activity and a pleasant not-too-stifling climate, but the similarities stop there.

Réunion is completely and distinctly French – a French overseas *département* with mostly proud ties to its European heart: the baguette is a national institution, instant coffee is considered an abomination and English-speaking visitors incommunicado without at least a few words of French. The French flavour interweaves a mélange of cultures, and the island's charm emanates from its flamboyant melting pot *à la réunionnais*. Home to Créoles, Europeans, Indians and a sprinkling of Chinese people, Réunion has a personality all of its own.

A well-kept secret, few people outside *la métropole* (mainland France, that is) know of Réunion and even fewer know of its spectacular natural and scenic wonders. The island's dearth of world-class beaches probably has a lot to do with its avoiding an international tourism invasion, but whatever Réunion lacks at sea level, it more than makes up for in its wildly dramatic mountain country. In fact, Réunion's curvaceous countryside leaves Mauritius looking flat and rather humdrum by comparison!

The forbidding mountains, verdant gorges and awesome amphitheatres offer a veritable potpourri of trekking possibilities. Tourism authorities have recognised that Réunion is a trekker's paradise, and provide well for the walker and backpacker by maintaining tracks and mountain huts. If you loved Nepal or New Zealand you'll also love Réunion, which provides similar quality hiking and trekking but with an exotic tropical twist.

You can also live in style, as the Réunionnais enjoy most of the luxuries of metropolitan France. Unfortunately, this means prices can tower with the peaks, so a respectable budget is requisite. It would be financial suicide to arrive in Réunion on a shoestring – real 'wing and a prayer' stuff – and you may risk being repatriated as *un misérable*!

Réunion has a useful tourist service which helps travellers plan trips, and the advance effort is well worth it. Although not the cheapest destination to visit, it is possible to experience much of Réunion's appeal on a medium-range budget – if you know about cheaper alternatives and book ahead. Work out an itinerary first, make your bookings and simply let the options unfold.

HISTORY

The island of Réunion has a history similar to that of Mauritius and was visited, but not settled, by early Malay, Arab and European mariners. The archipelago, comprised of Mauritius, Rodrigues and Réunion, was christened the Mascarenes by Portuguese navigator Pedro de Mascarenhas, following its European discovery in 1512. Some historians maintain that Réunion had first been named Santa Apolónia after the day in 1507 on which it was sighted by Tristan da Cunha's fleet returning from India. After these initial sightings, the island moved through a succession of names given by the Dutch, English and French explorers who claimed to be the first to spot it.

1600 to 1800

In 1642 the French took the initiative of settling the island, which at the time was called Mascarin, when La Compagnie des Indes Orientales (the French East India Company) sent its ship, the *St-Louis*. No-one actually settled on Réunion until four years later, when the French governor of Fort Dauphin in southern Madagascar banished a dozen mutineers to the island. The mutineers landed at what is now St-Paul and lived in a cave for three years. In fact, this Grotte des Premiers Français still exists and is open to visitors.

On the basis of enthusiastic reports from the mutineers, in 1649 the island was officially claimed by the King of France and renamed Île Bourbon.

However appealing it seemed, there was no great rush to populate and develop the island and, from around 1685, Indian Ocean pirates began using Île Bourbon as a trading base. The 260 settlers benefited from these illicit dealings until the French government and the French East India Company clamped down on them and took control at the beginning of the 18th century.

Until 1715, the French East India Company was content to provide only for its own needs and those of passing ships, but then coffee was introduced, and between 1715 and 1730 it became the island's main cash crop. The island's economy changed dramatically. As coffee required intensive labour, African slaves were introduced despite French East India Company rules forbidding the use of slave labour. During this period, grains, spices and cotton were also brought in as cash crops.

Like Mauritius, Réunion came of age under the governorship of the remarkable Mahé de La Bourdonnais who served from 1735 to 1746. However, La Bourdonnais treated Île de France (Mauritius) as the favoured of the sibling islands and Île Bourbon was left in a Cinderella role.

As a result of poor management and the rivalry between France and Britain during the 18th century, as well as the collapse of the French East India Company, the government of the island passed directly to the French crown in 1764. After the French Revolution, it came under the jurisdiction of the Colonial Assembly. It was at this time that the island's name was changed to La Réunion (which means 'joining' or 'meeting') but for reasons known only to the Colonial Assembly. Certainly the slaves were not officially meeting with anyone; nor did the name find favour with slave owners, who a short time later decided to rename it Île Bonaparte after you-know-who.

In the late 18th century, there were a number of slave revolts and those who managed to escape made their way to the interior. They organised themselves into villages run by democratically elected chiefs and fought to preserve their independence from colonial authorities.

RÉUNION

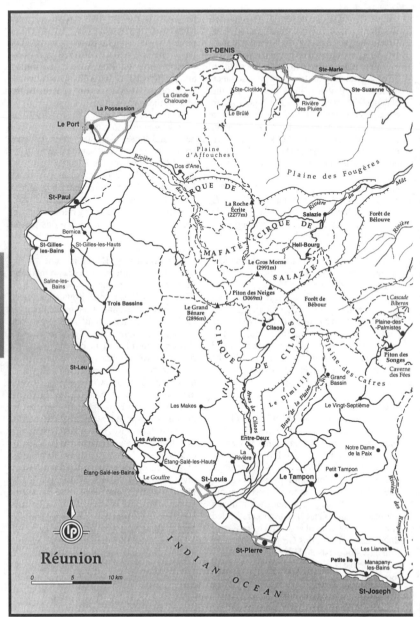

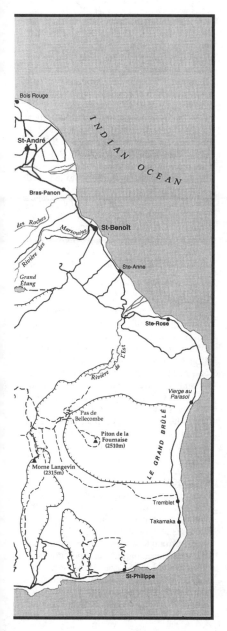

While the Mascarenes remained French colonies, Réunion had the function of providing the islands with food products while Mauritius made the profits by exporting sugar cane.

1800 Onwards

The heretofore productive coffee plantations were destroyed by cyclones very early in the 19th century, and in 1810, during the Napoleonic Wars, Bonaparte lost the island to the *habits rouges* (redcoats). On 9 July, Britain took possession of Réunion but five years later, under the Treaty of Paris, the spoil was returned to the French as Île Bourbon. The British, however, retained their grip on Rodrigues, Mauritius and the Seychelles.

Under British rule, sugar cane was introduced to Réunion and quickly supplanted food production as the primary crop. It resulted in the dispossession of many small farmers who were forced to sell out to those with capital to invest in the new monoculture. The supplanted farmers migrated to the interior to find land and carry on with their agricultural activities. During this period, the Desbassyns brothers rose to success as the island's foremost sugar barons. The vanilla industry, introduced in 1819, also grew rapidly.

In 1848, the Second Republic was proclaimed in France, slavery was abolished, and Île Bourbon again became La Réunion. At the time, the island had a population of over 100,000, mostly freed slaves. Like Mauritius, Réunion immediately experienced a labour crisis and like the British in Mauritius, the French 'solved' the problem by importing contract labourers from India, most of them Hindus, to work the sugar cane. In 1865, around 75,000 immigrants arrived on the island and they remain largely distinct from the Muslim Indians who arrived in the early years of the 20th century.

The golden age of trade and development in Réunion lasted until 1870, with the country flourishing on the trade route between Europe, India and the Far East. However, competition from Cuba and the European sugar beet industry, combined with the opening of the

Suez Canal (which short-circuited the journey around the Cape of Good Hope), resulted in an economic slump; shipping decreased, the sugar industry declined and land and capital was further concentrated in the hands of a small French elite. Some small planters brightened their prospects by turning to geranium oil.

After WWI, in which 14,000 Réunionnais served, the sugar industry regained a bit of momentum but it again suffered badly through the blockade of the island during WWII.

In 1936, a left-wing political group, the Comité d'Action Démocratique et Sociale, was founded on a platform of integration with France, but after the island eventually became a Département Français d'Outre-Mer (DOM) in 1946, they changed their minds, hoping instead for self-government (with continuing infusions of capital assistance from France). The conservatives who initially opposed integration with France for fear of losing their privileges as colonists also did an about-face when they realised that the alternative to French integration would probably be a corrupt and chaotic independence.

Despite all the second thoughts, the island now falls under the jurisdiction of the French Minister for DOM-TOM. There have been feeble independence movements from time to time but, unlike those in France's Pacific territories, they have never amounted to anything. Even the Communist Party on the island seeks autonomy rather than independence and until recently, Réunion seemed satisfied to remain totally French.

In February 1991, however, anti-government riots in St-Denis left 10 people dead, and a reactionary visit by the French prime minister Michel Rocard in mid-March drew jeers from the crowds. By 1993, things appeared to have calmed down but there were still undercurrents of discontent.

As a French department, Réunion suffers from some of the ills affecting metropolitan France; the unemployment rate is extremely high, particularly affecting young people (39% of the population is under 20); recently, various financial and political scandals have shaken Réunion.

A few important facts have marked the current events of the island during the last two years. In 1996, the SMIC (minimum wage) was brought to the same level as the one in metropolitan France (the Revenu Minimum d'Insertion, or minimum welfare payment, however remains 20% lower than the one in mainland France) and in 1997 state-employed people began a strike. They protested against a bill aiming at reducing the financial benefits (from 53% to 3%) of future state-employed people in Réunion. The movement was supported by Paul Vergès, the Communist leader of the island and Margie Sudre, the former Secrétaire d'État à la francophonie (junior minister of French-speaking communities) and the spouse of Camille Sudre, manager of *Télé Free-DOM*, whose transmitters were seized in 1991, provoking a wave of violence. This bill was still being discussed at the time of writing.

GEOGRAPHY

The island of Réunion lies about 800km east of Madagascar and roughly 220km southwest of Mauritius. Just in case anyone was in doubt about its origins, its active volcano, Piton de la Fournaise, erupted in 1986, spewing lava into the sea and adding another few square metres to the island. In September 1992, it erupted again, but this time the lava stream stopped well short of the coast. The island is 2510 sq km in area with a circumference of 207km, a bit larger than Mauritius, but with around half the population.

GEOLOGY

There are two major mountain zones on Réunion; the older covers two-thirds of the island's western half. The highest peak is Piton des Neiges at 3069m, an alpine-class peak. Surrounding it are the three immense and splendid amphitheatres: the cirques of Cilaos, Mafate and Salazie. These long, wide, deep hollows are sheer-walled canyons filled with convoluted peaks and valleys, the eroded remnants of the ancient volcanic shield which surrounded Piton des Neiges.

Volcano Glossary
The following list of geological terms commonly used in discussions about volcanoes may be useful during a visit to Piton de la Fournaise:

aa – Hawaiian term for sharp, rough and chunky lava from gaseous and explosive magma
basalt – a dark coloured rock material that forms from cooled lava
bombs – chunks of volcanic ejecta greater than 64mm that are cooled and rounded in mid-flight
caldera – the often immense depression formed by the collapse of a volcanic cone into its magma chamber
cinder slag – the mass of rough fragments of rock derived from volcanic lava
cirque – semicircular, amphitheatre-like hollow resembling a glacial cirque (deep, steep-walled hollow)
dyke – a vertical intrusion of igneous material often up through cracks in horizontal rock layers
fissure – a break or fracture in the earth's crust where vulcanism may occur
graben – a valley formed by spreading and subsidence of surface material
hornitos – a small mound of spatter built on a lava flow (usually pahoehoe) by gradual accumulation of ejected lava clots
laccolith – a mushroom-shaped dome of igneous material that has flowed upward through rock layers and then spread out horizontally, often causing hills to appear on the surface
lava – flowing molten rock, the name for magma after it has been ejected from a volcano
lava cave or **lava tube** – a tunnel or cavern caused by the withdrawal of a lava stream flowing beneath an already solidified surface
magma – molten rock before it reaches the surface and becomes lava
magma chamber – a reservoir of magma from which volcanic materials are derived
obsidian – dark coloured volcanic glass
pahoehoe – Hawaiian term for ropy, smooth-flowing lava
pillow lava – lava formed in underwater or subglacial eruptions causing it to solidify immediately and form pillow-like bulbs
plug – material that has solidified in volcanic vents and is revealed by erosion
pseudocraters – small craters formed by steam explosions when molten material flows into a body of water
pumice – solidified lava froth. Pumice is so light and porous it will float on water.
rhyolite – light-coloured acid lava often solidified into beautifully variegated rock
scoria – porous and glassy black or red volcanic gravel formed in fountain-like eruptions
shield volcano – flattish cones of oozing pahoehoe lava. Réunion's Piton de la Fournaise is a shield volcano.
sill – a finger or vein of molten material that squeezes between existing rock layers and solidifies
tephra – a collective term for all types of materials ejected from a volcano and transported through the air

RÉUNION

The smaller mountain zone lies in the south-east and is still evolving, with several extinct volcanoes and one that is still very much alive, the Piton de la Fournaise. This rumbling peak still pops its cork relatively frequently in spectacular fashion, and between eruptions quietly steams and hisses away. No-one lives in the shadow of the volcano, where lava flowing down to the shore has left a remarkable jumbled slope of cooled black volcanic rock. It's undoubtedly the island's most popular and intriguing attraction.

Between these two major mountainous zones are the high plains and the valley plains, and all the central uplands are ringed by a coastal plain of varying width. Numer-ous rivers wind their way down from the Piton des Neiges range, down through the cirques, cutting deeply into the coastal plains.

CLIMATE

Réunion not only cops it from the volcano now and again, it also gets a lashing from cyclones. A major recent one was Cyclone Clotilde, which crashed into the island on Black Friday (13 February 1987 – a memorable Friday the 13th), causing millions of dollars of damage to crops, roads and buildings. There was another nasty cyclone in 1992.

Because of the high mountains, the island's climate varies more than that of Mauritius.

However, it still experiences only two distinct seasons: the hot, rainy (cyclonic!) summer from October to March and the cool, dry winter from April to September. The windward east coast is considerably wetter than the dry, brown west coast, but the wettest region is the heights above the east coast – the Takamaka region, the Plaine-des-Palmistes and the northern and eastern slopes of Piton de la Fournaise.

Temperatures on the coast average 21°C during winter and 28°C during summer. In the mountains, they drop to a 12°C winter average and an 18°C summer average. The south-east trade winds blow all year round and can make tramping around the volcano or up the Piton des Neiges uncomfortably cold in winter.

Mist and clouds surround the higher peaks and plains much of the time. They lift, drop and swirl spasmodically during the day. The best time for viewing the landscape is at first light, before the clouds begin to build and the sun sets everything steaming.

FLORA & FAUNA
Flora
Parts of Réunion are like a grand botanical garden. Between the coast and the alpine peaks one finds palms, screw pines (also known as pandanus or *vacoas*), casuarinas (*filaos*), vanilla, spices, other tropical fruit and vegetable crops, rainforest and alpine

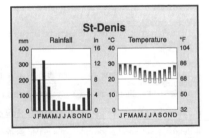

flora. More than half the cultivable land area of Réunion is planted in sugar cane, on slopes up to about 800m above sea level.

Away from cultivated areas, especially on the east coast, the vegetation is lush and thick. Unlike the natural forests of Mauritius, which were done over by the defoliating Dutch, many of the forest species and environments of Réunion have survived to the present day. You won't find any of the large and grand rainforest trees which were once present; perhaps the best remaining example of the natural vegetation cover is found in the Forêt de Bélouve east of the Cirque de Salazie.

At the other extreme, the lava fields around the volcano exhibit a barren, moon-like face of the island. Here the various stages of vegetation growth, from a bare new lava base, are evident. The first plant to appear on lava is one the French call *branle*

Storm Alert
Réunion's anti-cyclone measures are based on three levels of alert:

* The first, known as a *vigilance cyclonique* (cyclone watch), goes into effect whenever a cyclone is detected. It requires people to make sure they have enough supplies (food, batteries, candles, water etc), the cancellation of all trekking and boating, and attention to radio communications regarding the storm's path.
* The *alerte orange* (orange alert) denotes an important threat in the next 24 hour period. Schools and day nurseries are closed, but businesses remain open. As a preventive measure, the population is urged to bring indoors any objects or animals that might be carried away and to protect all doors and windows. And, of course, to listen to the radio.
* The *alerte rouge* (red alert) is announced when danger is imminent. It includes a ban on driving, and the population is advised to obey the instructions broadcast by radio. Use of the telephone is also restricted.

Both water and electrical services are shut down during cyclones. Animals drowned by flood waters can contaminate the water supply, and tap water must be treated after the storm has passed. It is also dangerous to touch the electrical wires brought down by the storm, and to cross flooded gullies. ■

vert. Its leaves contain a combustible oil. Much later in the growth cycle come tamarind and other acacia trees.

There is a large and active forestry division, the Office National des Forêts (ONF), which is more concerned with preserving than chopping the forests. Afforestation has concentrated primarily on Japanese cryptomerias, tamarinds, coloured woods, casuarinas and cabbage palms.

Like any tropical island, Réunion has a wealth of flowering species – orchids, hibiscus, bougainvillea – and flowering trees or bushes, such as the flamboyant, frangipani, jacaranda, grevillea, acacia and mimosa.

Fauna
Birds Since the arrival of humans, the flora on Réunion has fared much better than the wildlife. Like Mauritius, Réunion had dodos and giant tortoises which quickly disappeared. Another extinct wonder was the crested bourbon bird; if you want to see what it looked like, have a look at the model in the Musée d'Histoire Naturelle in St-Denis.

The rarest bird on the island now is the *merle blanc* or cuckoo shrike (Coracina newtoni). The Créoles call it *tuit tuit*, for obvious reasons. Probably the best chance of seeing it is on the Plaine des Chicots, directly south of the capital, St-Denis, near the foot of La Roche Écrite. It is exclusive to the island, but there is a closely related species on Mauritius. Bulbuls, which resemble blackbirds and are locally known as *merles*, are more common.

The *vierge* or Mascarene paradise flycatcher is a pretty little bird with a violet head, a small crest and a long, flowing red tail. Créoles believe the bird has seen the Virgin Mary. Other unique birds native to the highlands include the *tec-tec* or Réunion stonechat – the Créole name is onomatopoeic – and the *papangue* or Réunion harrier, a protected hawk-like bird which begins life as a little brown bird and turns black and white as it grows older. Falcons and swallows are also seen.

Mynahs, introduced at the end of the 18th century to keep the grasshoppers under

The tenrec is a small hedgehog-like animal introduced from Madagascar.

control, are common, as are the small, red cardinal-like birds known as *fodies*. The best known sea bird is the white *paille-en-queue* (Phaeton lepturus) or white-tailed tropicbird, which sports two long tail plumes. Other sea birds include the shearwaters and visiting albatross. Common game birds include moorhens (which may be observed around the ponds near St-Paul, Bois Rouge and Gol) and introduced quails, francolins and partridges.

Birdwatchers may want to hunt up a copy of the field guide *Oiseaux de la Réunion.* The text is in French and there are accurate colour illustrations of all species present on the island, identified by their Latin, English, French and Réunionnais names.

Other Animals During the rainy season, many of Réunion's roads are paved in squashed frogs! There are also tenrecs, introduced from Madagascar, which resemble hedgehogs. They are few in number and don't seem to find the roads as much of a challenge as their British counterparts.

There are a few other land creatures – some lonely deer (introduced for hunters), hare (also introduced) and a few chameleons *(endormi)* – but you'd be very lucky to spot any of them. On the bright side, there are no poisonous or toothy nasties of any description.

Insects & Spiders The mosquitoes that plague Réunion's rainy season can be tenacious. Oddly enough, they seem to be at their

RÉUNION

worst in St-Denis. The higher into the hills you go, the less evident the whining little bloodsuckers become.

The most interesting creepy crawlers are not spiders, but the giant millipedes – some as long as a human foot – which loll around beneath rocks in more humid areas.

Fish Réunion, without beach fronts and reef lagoons, lacks optimum diving and snorkelling, but both activities are well catered for around St-Gilles-les-Bains.

The rivers contain rainbow trout (introduced) and a sort of small fry called *bichiques* – delicious when cooked in a Créole curry.

Sea Cucumbers
The sea cucumber, or bêche-de-mer, is another variety of echinoderm. They are typically cucumber-like in shape but with a soft, leathery feel. There are a variety of types including *Holothuria*, *Stichopus* and *Thelonota*. You can see them scattered across shallow reef flats where they feed either on plankton or by filtering sand. Their mouth is at one end, their anus at the other and some varieties will, when alarmed, expel long sticky threads from their anus as a defence mechanism. Sea cucumbers are quite harmless. ∎

Endangered Species
Although land turtles were numerous on Réunion when the island was first settled, the first colonists and their animals made short work of them. Due to the hunting of sea turtles for their meat and for their shell, which is used in jewellery and other ornaments, their numbers are decreasing dramatically throughout the Indian Ocean region and worldwide. Sea turtles are farmed in Réunion (see St-Leu in the Around the Coast chapter).

GOVERNMENT & POLITICS
In 1946 Réunion became a Département Français d'Outre-Mer (DOM) (overseas French department). It became, and remains, party to the French economy. Other DOMs are Guadeloupe, Martinique and French

Guiana. The Indian Ocean island of Mayotte, one of the Comoros Islands, has quasi-departmental status. France also has three Territoires d'Outre-Mer (TOMs) (overseas territories), which are New Caledonia, Wallis & Futuna and French Polynesia. You may see or hear the expression DOM-TOM (the acronym of Départements d'Outre-Mer & Territoires d'Outre-Mer). In 1986, France was admitted to the IOC (Indian Ocean Commission) because of its sovereignty over Réunion (and Mayotte).

Government affairs in Réunion are the responsibility of the French Minister for DOM-TOM. The département is administered by a prefect and an elected council, and is represented in the French National Assembly by five deputies, and in the French Senate by three councillors.

ECONOMY
Réunion imports about 66% of what it needs from *la métropole* (France). In turn, France imports around 71% of Réunion's products. The island's imports are increasing at a much faster rate than its exports, and the inflation rate on the island is higher than in the métropole.

France spends an estimated 10% of its social security budget on the 1.2% of the population living in the DOM-TOMs. The official unemployment rate of Réunion is a staggering 37%.

Agriculture
The basis of the island's economy is agriculture, which, in turn, is based on the sugar cane that covers 65% of the arable land and accounts for around 80% of the agricultural revenue. Sugar has a guaranteed market and fixed prices within the European Union (EU). From the molasses, rum and cane spirit are produced, but these are not widely available outside France. There are several sugar factories which offer tours to visitors during the cutting season around July.

Réunion is the one of the world's largest producers of geranium oil, but don't expect to see acres of beautiful flowers as in the Netherlands. The oil, used as a fixative in

---

Vetiver, Geranium & Vanilla

Native to southern Africa, the geranium was introduced into Réunion in the 19th century. Vetiver was brought in from India. Both sweet-smelling plants have long been among the island's main sources of revenue and are grown as crops. Geranium oil is extracted in small stills operated by the descendants of the earliest colonial settlers, known as the *petits blancs des hauts*, who migrated to the cirques when the coastal areas were taken over by wealthy planters. Production of these high-altitude plants has fallen drastically since the 1960s. Some people say it's due to conflicting policies, some of which are aimed at promoting and others at limiting the production of essential oils. Other people prefer to blame the difficulties involved in cultivating the plants. Whatever the reasons, the end product continues to be of exceptional quality, and Réunion furnishes basic perfume oils to the greatest Parisian houses. Photo-journalist Sébastião Salgado has done a documentary on the subject.

Equally valued by connoisseurs is the bourbon vanilla from the Indian Ocean. It was in Réunion, in 1861, that a slave known as Albius discovered a method of artificial fertilisation of this member of the orchid family, which twines its stalk around the trunks of trees. Renowned for its rich aroma, and for being very expensive, Réunion's vanilla production has fallen to less than 1% of the world's supply. Madagascar and the Comoros are still vying with the newcomers: China, Mexico, Uganda, and especially Indonesia, which has taken over from Madagascar's place as principal world supplier. ■

---

perfumes, is drawn from the leaves of the plants. It is still a cottage industry, concentrated mainly around Le Maïdo and Le Tampon, and most producers use a crude, but effective, home-made still to extract oil.

Oil from vetiver (an Asian grass) roots is also produced, though on a much smaller scale (around 15 tonnes annually), in the foothills near St-Pierre and St-Joseph. There were also once large plantations of ylang-ylang, a bush whose yellow flowers yield an overpowering essence, but this industry died out during the 1970s. (Madagascar and the Comoros still produce substantial quantities of ylang-ylang.)

The cultivation of vanilla, which is concentrated on the east coast between Ste-Suzanne and St-Philippe, has been a limited but stable earner since the last century. Tobacco has recently made a comeback and popular spice crops include black pepper, cloves and cinnamon. Maize, potatoes, lentils, beans, garlic, onions and such warm weather fruits as lychees, mandarins, oranges, bananas, lemons, papayas and mangoes are also produced in significant amounts.

Livestock-wise, pig-breeding satisfies local consumption and poultry farms keep the populace in eggs and the ubiquitous *cari poulet* (chicken curry).

With few good harbours, the fishing industry is small and restricted; however, Réunion oversees fish factories on the sub-Antarctic French islands of St-Paul and Amsterdam more than 3000km to the south-east.

Tourism

One of the biggest drawbacks to the development of Réunion as an international tourism destination (and revenue earner) is the tropical paradise image of nearby Mauritius, which is cheaper and has much better beaches. Réunion mainly attracts visitors from France, followed by Mauritians. In 1995 there were 304,000 visitors to Réunion, of which 249,100 were from France, 9300 were from other parts of Europe, 27,700 from Mauritius, 10,300 from Madagascar and 7600 from the rest of the world. It is expected that by the turn of the century, there will be close to 500,000 visitors to Réunion annually.

POPULATION & PEOPLE

Réunion has a larger land area than Mauritius, but its estimated population of 675,700 is about half that of its neighbour. Réunion's population density is 269.2 people per sq km.

Because the birthrate has been quite high for the past 25 years, the population is weighted in favour of youth, with 39% of the population under 20 years of age. The population is expected to grow to 700,000 by the turn of the century.

Réunion has the same population mix of

Europeans, Indians, Chinese and Créoles as Mauritius, but in different proportions. The Indians *(malabars)* comprise about 20% of the population and the Chinese 3%. The Muslim community *(z'arabes)* constitutes about 1%. The Créoles are the largest ethnic group, comprising around 40% of the population. After the Créoles, Europeans (ie French) make up the largest group. They are involved in the island's administration and business, generally come from France and are called *z'oreilles* (the ears) by the Créoles, who may be straining to hear what's being said about them in the local *patois*.

ARTS

One of the great pleasures of visiting Réunion is experiencing Créole-flavoured French culture, or French-flavoured Créole culture. For news of cultural activities on the island contact the Office Départemental de la Culture (☎ 41 11 41; fax 41 55 71), in St-Denis. It publishes a free monthly newsletter, *Trajectoires*, available at tourist and travel offices, giving details of forthcoming theatre, jazz and classical music performances, exhibitions, conferences etc, some of which have youth and student rates.

Dance

It is interesting to see how the *séga* (traditional dance) differs here from the Mauritian, Seychellois and Malagasy versions. There are more variations in Réunion because the slaves adopted and adapted the dances of the white settlers, particularly the quadrille, to their own African rhythms. The séga is now danced by everyone in the manner of a shuffling rock step.

The more traditional slaves' dance in Réunion is called the *maloya*, a slower, more reflective rhythm, similar to the New Orleans blues. A séga or maloya performance is often accompanied by melancholy ballads or *romances*. Séga and maloya music, as well as other Créole sounds, are available on cassette for around FF80.

Instruments used by the band range from traditional home-made percussion pieces, such as the hide-covered *houleur* drum and the maraca-like *caïambe*, to the accordion and modern band instruments.

Music

Réunion mixes the African rhythms of reggae, séga and maloya with the best of French, British and American rock and folk music. As for Créole-flavoured modern sounds, the Réunionnais leave that to their tropical cousins in Martinique and Guadeloupe (these are also popular listening in Réunion). Compagnie Créole (a Caribbean group from Réunion), now based in Paris, has won a greater middle-of-the-road success. A local favourite is rastaman Michel Fock, known professionally as Ti-Fock, who adds a synthesised touch to traditional maloya and séga rhythms.

It's all catchy stuff, and you'll hear it in bars, discos and vehicles throughout the Indian Ocean. A good selection of séga, maloya and jazz recordings is available at Megatop (☎ 41 00 41) at the corner of Rue Alexis de Villeneuve and Rue Jean Chatel in St-Denis.

St-Louis is a relatively quiet, dull town for visitors, but it boasts several good folk groups such as Pangar, Lèv la Têt and Jeunesse Komèla. At St-Gilles-les-Bains, several hotels and restaurants offer folk soirées with music and dancing.

Architecture

The distinctive 18th century Créole architecture of Réunion is evident in both the *grandes villas créoles* (homes of wealthy planters and other *colons)* and the *tit' cases créoles*, the homes of the common folk.

The style which is marked primarily by the lovely *varangues* (immense open verandahs) fringed with delicate, lace-like *lambrequins* or *dentelles* (rows of carved wooden cutout borders above roofs, windows and overhangs) is at risk of being undermined by modern European square block architecture. The cost and the effort involved in designing, creating and maintaining the traditional look is generally no longer considered cost effective. However, there is now an organised government entity, the Conseil Départemental d'Architecture, which strives to preserve the remaining examples.

Theatre

The island has several excellent professional theatre groups. Théâtre Vollard (☎ 21 25 26) is the most established. The group works out of the 300 seat theatre at 23 Rue Léopold Rambaud in St-Denis. Other professional troupes include Théâtre Talipot and the Théâtre Dallon.

Of the companies, Vollard is the most conventional and Talipot the more progressive and experimental. Both base the classic or avant-garde forms of western theatre on Créole traditions. Their island tours usually cover the main theatres: Théâtre Fourçade, Théâtre Vollard, the Salle François Truffaut and Théâtre de Champ-Fleuri, all in St-Denis; the Théâtre Luc Donat in Le Tampon; and the Théâtre de Plein Air amphitheatre outside St-Gilles-les-Bains. Sometimes the groups take productions overseas to Madagascar, Mauritius and Mayotte.

Painting, Etching & Woodwork

If there is a distinctive Créole sculpture or painting style in the Indian Ocean, it's easy to miss. The tone favoured by local artists seems to be European. It doesn't always work but it can be interesting: it's either too bright and gaudy, too ordered and dull, or too much like Gauguin!

There are at least 15 professional artists living and working in Réunion. Among them is Philippe Turpin of Cilaos who etches onto copper and then rolls the prints off the inky plates. But the effect, like the technique, has little to do with Créole tradition. Instead, he captures the wonder of Réunion in a fantastical, almost medieval way; his renditions of the cirques resemble illustrations of fairy kingdoms. His prices are fantastic too, but the work is worth the money if you have it. Turpin's studio in the mountain spa village of Cilaos is open to the public.

The work of other artists and artisans can be seen at several places around the island, including Galerie Artisanale (☎ 29 56 66) at the Continent complex in St-Denis, the Bou-

tique Artisanale de L'Association Lacaze (☎ 21 55 47) at Place Sarda Garriga in St-Denis, and at Galerie Vincent (☎ 27 32 73) between Le Tampon and St-Pierre.

Woodworking, including 'East India Company' furniture and miniature replicas of Créole architecture homes, is on display and sale at the Centre Artisanal du Bois (☎ 39 06 12) in La Rivière, St-Louis.

If you'd like to see a bit of transplanted European art, visit the Musée Léon Dierx on Rue de Paris in St-Denis.

SOCIETY & CONDUCT

Réunion has a number of mosques and temples and visitors should dress and behave appropriately – see Society & Conduct in the Facts about the Region chapter at the beginning of this book.

RELIGION
Catholicism

The Catholic faith dominates the island's religious character. It is visible in the shrines along every highway and byway, in caves and at cliff tops (many of these were constructed for family members killed in accidents on those sites), and in the many saint's days and holidays. St-Denis shuts down on Sunday, when half the city goes to *the* beach – Boucan Canot!

Other Religions

Hindus and Muslims follow their respective religions freely and most large towns have both a mosque and a temple. Traditional Hindu rites such as *pandialé* or *teemeedee*, which includes fire-walking, and *cavadee*, which includes the practice of piercing one's cheeks with silver needles, often take place. For further information on these rites, see Public Holidays & Special Events in the Mauritius Facts for the Visitor chapter. Interestingly, a great deal of syncretism with Catholicism has evolved over the years, and vice versa. In fact, many of the Malabar-Réunionnais participate in Catholic rites and rituals as well as those of the Indian community.

Apart from celebration of Chinese New

RÉUNION

St-Expédit

Oddly enough, one popular saint in Réunion is St-Expédit, whose origin is attributed to a box of *un*attributed religious relics and icons shipped from Rome to a new chapel in Paris. Legend has it that the nuns who received the box saw the Italian word *espedito* (expedited) on the box and guess what? The new chapel was christened La Chapelle de St-Expédit!

The idea was brought to Réunion in 1931 when a local woman erected a statue to the 'saint' in l'Église de la Déliverance as a *remerciement* (thanks offering) for answering her prayer to return to Réunion. Another version has it that Réunion had requested that the Vatican send the relics of a powerful saint who could be used as the island's patron, and the box bore the word *expédit*. Either way, it's bizarre.

Over the years, the saint's following was somehow twisted into a rather sinister voodoo cult. Shrines to St-Expédit, which are normally covered in brilliant red paint representing blood, abound around the southern end of the island and are used primarily for wishing ill on others. Beheaded statues are normally the result of either unanswered petitions or the fears of paranoid potential victims. ■

Year, the Sino-Réunionnais community is not very conspicuous in its traditional or religious practices.

LANGUAGE

French is the official language, but Créole is the most widely spoken. Few people speak English. (For some useful French words, see Language in the Facts about the Region chapter, at the beginning of this book.)

Réunion Créole is even beyond understanding by most French people. A word which means one thing in French can mean something completely different in Créole. And where a word does have the same meaning, Créoles usually pronounce it differently.

The Créoles have quite a number of *bons mots* and charming idioms, which are often the result of Hindi, Arab and Malagasy influences or misinterpretations of the original French word. *Bonbon la fesse* (bum toffee) is a suppository, *conserves* (preserves) are sunglasses, *bazaar* is the market and *coeur d'amant* (lover's heart) is a cardamom seed. *Coco* is your head, *caze* is a house, *marmaille* is a child, *baba* is a baby, *band* means family, *le fait noir* means night, and, if the stars are out, *mi aime jou* means 'I love you'.

Two basic rules of Créole speech are not to pronounce 'r', or to do so lightly, and to turn the soft 'j' or 'ch' sounds of French into 'z' or 's', as in *manzay* for *manger* (to eat), *zamais* for *jamais* (never), and *sontay* for *chanter* (to sing).

There are French-Créole dictionaries for sale in Réunion, but currently none for English-speakers.

Facts for the Visitor

PLANNING
When to Go

Climate should be your first consideration if you want to experience Réunion at its best. Unless you have webbed feet, there's no point in setting out to explore the cirques on foot if all you can expect weather-wise is swirling mist, pouring rain and slippery slide walking tracks. The only time to seriously consider trekking through Réunion's spectacular mountain country is during the dry season from April to September. For more specific information, see Climate in the Facts about Réunion chapter.

The downside of climate-related trip planning is that everyone else has the same idea. You're strongly advised to book well in advance, especially during the peak tourist times. April, May and the French school holidays from late July to early September are the busiest times to visit, and in August you risk being left high and dry without accommodation unless you book in advance. This is also high trekking season and the gîtes de montagne (mountain cabins or lodges) are packed out, so if you dare brave the crowds, you may want to pack a tent. Even nonwalkers will have problems, having to battle it out at the beach resorts or manoeuvre through the heavy traffic.

The Christmas/New Year holidays also attract crowds which fill hotels and pensions. However, the northern winter holidays fall in the middle of Réunion's hot rainy season so there isn't much of a demand on gîtes de montagne. It's also worth keeping in mind that October and November can sometimes get unexpectedly busy.

The quietest times are during cyclone-prone February and March. The seasons normally change in April and that isn't too bad for a visit but for maximum spatial and climatic enjoyment, May and June are probably the best months of all.

One traveller, however, recommends visiting between late September and mid-October:

The climate was beautiful – the coast had warm days with bright sun every morning and usually a bit of cloud cover in the afternoon and the occasional windy day. In the evenings you could eat outside (in long trousers rather than shorts, though). Up in the mountains, the mornings were sunny and if you climbed above the clouds the afternoons were, too. (Climbing the volcano we got bad sunburn on the few square inches of skin we forgot to smear with sun cream.) It was perfect hiking weather. Evenings were pleasantly cool and there were no mozzies!

Furthermore, flights were cheap; hotels weren't all full and some had reduced off-season rates; it was dry but most of the waterfalls were still doing their stuff; and the coast wasn't swamped with tourists. The only drawback is that some places may be closed – it's best to ring restaurants to make sure they're open, especially if you must travel some way to get there.

Maps

Syndicats d'Initiative distribute several maps of the island, including the fairly good *Excursion Carte Touristique*. You can also pick up town plans from the appropriate Syndicats d'Initiative.

Most island maps include at least some of the hiking trails and gîtes de montagne. For all purposes, the IGN (Institut Géographique National) 512 map of the island, available for FF58, is currently the best and most detailed. Although it's fairly accurate, one potentially dangerous oversight is the casual placing of the gîtes. For the most part they are marked in the vicinity of where they should be rather than the exact location. When you are trying to find a gîte at the end of a long walk, sweaty, sore and starving, and you take a wrong turn in the track, the IGN map will only be saved from the fire by its other attributes.

The best hiking maps are the TOP25 1:25,000 series produced by IGN. They cover the island in six sheets, using good relief shading and showing vegetation cover. Contour lines are at 10m intervals. These maps replace the old Carte Topographique 1:25,000 series which took nine sheets to cover the island and four sheets for the cirques; with the new series, you need to purchase only two sheets (4402RT and 4405RT) for most cirque hiking. Piton de la Fournaise is now covered in one sheet (4406RT) as opposed to two previously. The maps cost FF70 per sheet.

What to Bring

For details, see What to Bring in the Regional Facts for the Visitor chapter at the beginning of this book.

HIGHLIGHTS
Trekking

The volcano and the high rugged cirques of Cilaos, Salazie and Mafate are superb. No visitor to the island should miss them even if it means visiting one of the villages (Cilaos, Hell-Bourg or Salazie) or driving to one of the lookout points. Climb the volcano and peer into the daunting Cratère Dolmieu or trek through the jumbled peaks and valleys of the Cirque de Mafate.

Beaches

The best beaches are all on the west coast. The main tourist beaches include those at St-Gilles-les-Bains, Saline-les-Bains, Hermitage-les-Bains and Étang-Salé-les-Bains. *The* beach as far as locals are concerned is Boucan Canot.

TOURIST OFFICES
Local Tourist Offices

To compensate for its high costs, Réunion has very good tourist information resources and with the funding of the French government behind them, services are generally as good as you may expect.

For sources of trekking information, see the Trekking in Réunion chapter. Ordinary tourist queries should be taken to the main Syndicat d'Initiative (☎ 41 83 00; fax 21 37 76) in St-Denis at 48 Rue Ste-Marie. It has efficient staff, a couple of whom speak English, and they also operate a useful information and welcome counter at Roland Garros airport to meet international flights. They'll

offer plenty of advice and information and provide myriad maps, brochures and advertising.

Addresses of Syndicats d'Initiative and tourist offices around the island are:

Syndicat d'Initiative de St-Denis, 48 Rue Ste-Marie, 97400 St-Denis (☎ 41 83 00; fax 21 37 76)
Office Municipal du Tourisme de St-André, 68 Centre Commercial de St-André, 97440 St-André (☎ 46 91 63; fax 46 52 16)
Syndicat d'Initiative de Salazie, Rue Georges Pompidou, 97433 Salazie (☎ 47 50 14; fax 47 60 06)
Syndicat d'Initiative de Bras-Panon, Route Nationale, 97412 Bras-Panon (☎ 51 50 62)
Syndicat d'Initiative de St-Benoît (Centre d'Affaires Agora), 21 Route Nationale, 97470 St-Benoît (☎ 50 21 29; fax 50 88 49)
Pays d'Accueil des Hautes Plaines, 213 Route Nationale 3, Bourg-Murat, 97418 Plaine-des-Cafres (☎ 59 08 92)
Office Municipal du Tourisme de St-Philippe, Place de la Mairie, Rue Leconte-Delisle, 97442 St-Philippe (☎ 37 10 43; fax 37 10 97)
Syndicat d'Initiative de St-Pierre, 17 Boulevard Hubert-Delisle, 97410 St-Pierre (☎ 25 02 36)
Syndicat d'Initiative de Cilaos, 2 Rue Mac Auliffe, 97413 Cilaos (☎ 31 78 03; fax 31 70 30)
Syndicat d'Initiative de l'Entre-Deux, 9 Rue Fortuné Hoareau, 97414 Entre-Deux (☎ 39 69 60; fax 39 57 70)
Syndicat d'Initiative de l'Étang-Salé, 74 Rue Octave Bénard, 97427 Étang-Salé-les-Bains (☎ 26 67 32; fax 26 67 92)
Syndicat d'Initiative de l'Ouest, Galerie Amandine, 97434 St-Gilles-les-Bains (☎ 24 57 47; fax 24 34 40)
Syndicat d'Initiative de La Possession, 25 Rue Sarda Garriga, 97419 La Possession (☎ 22 26 66; fax 22 25 17)

The Comité du Tourisme de la Réunion publishes a monthly magazine called *RUN* which outlines current happenings of interest to tourists and contains articles about various aspects of the island. In addition, twice annually, they publish *RUN – le guide*, a useful directory of hotels, restaurants, discos, travel agencies and other addresses of tourist interest.

These publications are available at Syndicats d'Initiative and at many hotels around the island. If you want to obtain a copy before you arrive in Réunion, contact the

Comité du Tourisme de la Réunion (☎ 21 00 41; fax 20 25 93) at Place du 20 Décembre 1848 in St-Denis, or the office in France (see the list below in the Tourist Offices Abroad section).

For information on accommodation in rural gîtes, contact the Relais Départemental des Gîtes de France (☎ 90 78 90; fax 41 84 29) at 10 Place Sarda Garriga in St-Denis. In France, contact Maison des Gîtes de France (☎ 01 49 70 75 75; fax 01 49 70 75 76), 59 Rue Saint-Lazare, 75439 Paris.

Tourist Offices Abroad

For advance information on Réunion, you could contact the Comité du Tourisme de la Réunion, 90 Rue de la Boétie, 75008 Paris (☎ 01 40 75 02 79; fax 01 40 75 02 73). Another possibility is the Conseil Général de la Réunion, 78 Rue de la Chapelle, 75018 Paris (☎ 01 40 38 66 70), although it mainly supplies business-related information.

France's tourism representatives abroad include:

Australia
   25 Bligh St, Sydney, NSW 2000 (☎ (02) 9231 5244; fax 9221 8682)
Canada
   30 St Patrick St, Suite 700, Toronto, Ontario M5T 3A3 (☎ (416) 593 4723)
Ireland
   35 Lower Abbey St, Dublin 1 (☎ (01) 703 4046)
South Africa
   Oxford Manor, 196 Oxford Rd (1st floor) (PO Box 41022, Craighall 2024), Illovo (☎ (011) 880 8062; fax 880 7772)
Switzerland
   2 Rue de Thalberg, 1201 Geneva (☎ (022) 732 8610; fax 731 5873)
UK
   178 Picadilly, London W1V 0AL (☎ (0171) 493 5174; fax 493 6594)
USA
   444 Madison Ave (16th floor), New York, NY 10022 (☎ (212) 838 7800; fax 838 78 55)

VISAS & DOCUMENTS
Visas

The visa requirements for entry to Réunion are the same as for France. Citizens of the USA, Canada, New Zealand, the European Union (EU) and a handful of other countries may enter Réunion for up to three months without a visa, but Australians and others must have a visa.

Visa applications should be made to the French embassy or consulate nearest your home address.

Visa Extensions It is difficult to get a tourist visa extension except in the case of emergencies (eg medical problems). For visa extension queries, contact the Service de l'États Civile et des Étrangers at La Préfecture (☎ 40 75 80) in St-Denis.

Those who don't need a visa and wish to stay for longer than three months need to apply for a *carte de séjour* (residence permit). Again, contact the Service de l'États Civile et des Étrangers.

Documents

Onward Ticket All visitors should have an onward ticket (or they could be asked to leave money to cover the cost of one). You may also be asked by immigration authorities to supply the name of your intended accommodation in Réunion.

Travel Insurance EU nationals will enjoy to a certain extent the benefits of reciprocal agreements between member countries. Other nationals are advised to carry medical/travel insurance. For more details, see the Regional Facts for the Visitor chapter at the beginning of this book.

EMBASSIES
French Embassies & Consulates Abroad

Australia
   6 Perth Ave, Yarralumla, Canberra, ACT 2600 (☎ (06) 216 0100; fax 216 0127)
Belgium
   14 Place de Louvain, 1000 Brussels (☎ (02) 229 8500; fax 229 8510)
Canada
   42 Sussex Drive, Ottowa, Ontario K1M 2C9 (☎ (613) 789 1795; fax 789 0279)
Germany
   Kurfürstendamm 211, D-10719, Berlin (☎ (030) 885 90243; fax 882 5295)

RÉUNION

Japan
11-44 4-chome, Minami Azabu, Minato-ku, Tokyo 106 (☎ (03) 5420 8800; fax 5420 8922)
Mauritius
14 St George St, Port Louis (☎ (230) 208 4103)
New Zealand
Robert Jones House, 1-3 Willeston St, Wellington (☎ (04) 472 0200; fax 472 5887)
South Africa
1009 Main Tower, Cape Town Center, Heerengracht, 8001, Cape Town (☎ (021) 212 050; fax 261 096)
UK
58 Knightsbridge, London SW1X 7JT (☎ (0171) 201 1000)
USA
4104 Reservoir Rd NW, Washington DC 20007 (☎ (202) 944 6000; fax 944 6166)

Other countries with French embassies/consulates include Hong Kong, India, Ireland, Israel, Italy, Luxembourg, Madagascar, Morocco, Netherlands, Seychelles, Singapore, Spain and Switzerland.

Foreign Consulates in Réunion

Since Réunion isn't an independent country, only a few countries have diplomatic representation, including:

Belgium
33 Rue Félix-Guyon, BP 785, 97476 St-Denis (☎ 90 20 89 or 21 79 72; fax 90 20 88)
Germany
110 Rue Général de Gaulle, 97400 St-Denis (☎/fax 41 84 78)
India
266 Rue Maréchal Leclerc, 97400 St-Denis (☎ 41 75 47; fax 21 01 70)
Madagascar
77 Rue Juliette Dodu, 97400 St-Denis (☎ 21 66 00; fax 21 10 08)
South Africa
83 Rue Jules Verne, BP 8, 97821 Le Port (☎ 42 61 18; fax 42 16 12)
UK
94B Ave Leconte Delisle, 97490 Ste-Clotilde (☎ 29 14 91; fax 29 39 91)

CUSTOMS

Airline passengers may bring duty-free goods into Réunion: 200 cigarettes or 50 cigars or 250g of tobacco; 1L of spirits or 2L of wine; one quarter litre of eau de toilette.

If you are bringing in currency upwards of FF50,000, it must be declared at customs.

The importation of plants or plant material is prohibited unless first cleared by Réunion officials. For further details, call the Réunion Plant Protection Agency (☎ 48 61 45).

For information on any customs issues, contact Réunion's customs services (☎ 90 81 00; fax 41 09 81) at 7 Ave de la Victoire in St-Denis.

The export of sea turtle products such as shells and decorative turtle items is banned by international wildlife trade controls and the items may be confiscated in the country they are imported into. This applies even if the public information indicates that the turtles are captive bred.

MONEY
Costs

For information on costs in Réunion, see Costs in the Regional Facts for the Visitor chapter, at the beginning of this book.

Currency

The French franc (abbreviated in this book by the letters 'FF') is the unit of currency and the more francs you have, the happier you'll feel about staying in Réunion. They can certainly disappear in a flash if you are not prepared!

One franc is divided into 100 centimes. French coins come in denominations of 5, 10, 20 and 50 centimes and 1, 2, 5, 10 and 20FF. Banknotes are issued in denominations of 20, 50, 100, 200 and 500FF.

Currency Exchange

At the time of going to press, the exchange rates of the French franc were as follows:

Australia	A$1	=	FF4.39
Britain	UK£	=	FF9.45
Canada	C$1	=	FF4.15
Germany	DM1	=	FF3.38
Japan	¥100	=	FF5.00
New Zealand	NZ$1	=	FF3.98
Singapore	S$1	=	FF4.06
USA	US$1	=	FF5.68

RÉUNION

Changing Money

The main banks in Réunion are Banque de la Réunion (BR), Crédit Agricole (CA), Banque Française Commerciale (BFC) and Banque Nationale de Paris Intercontinentale (BNPI). There's technically no problem changing major foreign currencies in Réunion – all banks offer exchange facilities – but low official exchange rates and punitive commissions on changing foreign currency travellers cheques make it sensible to carry French francs – or at least French franc travellers cheques – for your stay in Réunion.

Be warned that the money-exchange counter at Roland Garros airport is only open Monday to Friday from 10 am to 1.30 pm and 3 to 6.30 pm and on Saturday from 8.30 to 11.30 am. If you're arriving at an odd hour, be sure to have some French francs.

The American Express agency in Réunion is Bourbon Voyages (☎ 94 76 94; fax 41 72 85) at 14 Rue Rontaunay in St-Denis however they don't change money or travellers cheques.

Most major credit cards are widely accepted in Réunion. International Visa and MasterCard charge cards may be used in some bank cash dispensers.

Travellers have reported some difficulty with Eurocheques – especially at hotels and restaurants. It's safest to have a credit card for back-up, as most places seem to prefer this mode of payment.

Tipping & Bargaining

Many restaurants include service charges in their prices and surprisingly don't encourage additional tipping, but those which advertise *service non compris* on their menus do expect something. Also surprisingly, neither do taxi drivers seem to expect tips. Naturally, *un pourboire* would be accepted, but with prices so high anyway, few people seem inclined to increase the agony of it all.

Few shops in Réunion are open to bargaining. However, some markets, such as the Grand Marché in St-Denis and the St-Paul market, are certainly open to some friendly haggling. Hotels have fixed tariffs, but it's definitely worthwhile asking for a discount in the low season. Similarly, if you will be staying for more than a week, you may also be given a better deal.

POST & COMMUNICATIONS

Post

Post offices (known as *La Poste* or PTTs) are open Monday to Friday from 8 am to 6 pm, and on Saturdays from 8 am to noon. Many close for lunch between noon and 2 pm; those that do remain open through the lunch hour can get extremely crowded.

Since French post offices normally offer a vast array of services – from banking to gas and telephone bill collection – queues can be long and slow. Fortunately, there's normally a special desk or window for those poor souls who only require a couple of postcard stamps.

The main post office is in St-Denis, on the corner of Rue Maréchal Leclerc and Rue Juliette Dodu. Poste restante is also here.

There's also a post office at the Roland Garros airport which is open Monday to Friday from 9.30 am to 12.30 pm and 1.30 to 4.30 pm; on Saturday from 8 to 11 am.

Sending Mail

Air-mail letters under 20g to anywhere within France (including DOM-TOM) cost FF3. To anywhere else in the EU they also cost FF3. To the rest of the world, they're around FF4.

For packages, SAL (Surface Air-Lifted) is available at a considerable discount over regular air-mail and it's quite reliable.

Receiving Mail

Poste restante is at the main post office in St-Denis on the corner of Rue Juliette Dodu and Rue Maréchal Leclerc. To avoid confusion, post should be addressed according to French tradition – with the *nom de famille* (surname or family name) first, followed by the *prénom* (first name). If you want things to run even more smoothly, tell potential correspondents to put your surname in capital letters. Poste restante charges a couple of francs tax per letter collected; if you're expecting a bag of mail, get an address!

RÉUNION

Telephone

The Réunion telephone and telex system is efficient. There are about 500 public telephones scattered around the island and you can directly dial international numbers on them. However, very few coin phones remain in Réunion; most public telephones accept only *télécartes* (telephone cards). Telephone cards with 50 or 120 impulses are available at post offices and shops for FF35 and FF85 respectively.

Local calls cost FF1. Calls to France are FF4.50 per minute. Calls to Australia are FF11.90 per minute, and FF7.86 per minute to Belgium or the UK. Calls to Canada or the USA cost FF8.64 per minute, and FF14.03 per minute to India. Charges usually increase during peak times.

To phone Réunion from abroad, dial the international access code followed by the Réunion code (262) and the number desired.

BOOKS

There is a fine selection of French-language books in Réunion, predominantly in St-Denis. If you plan to do a lot of reading in English, you'd better bring along some paperbacks. The best chance of finding English-language reading material is at the major bookshops in St-Denis (see Bookshops in the St-Denis chapter).

The central library is beside the bus station in St-Denis. It's open from Monday to Friday, but the books are for reference only. The departmental borrowing library is at the corner of Rue Roland Garros and Rue Jean Chatel.

Remember that a bookshop is *une librairie*. The word for a library is *une bibliothèque*.

Travel Guides

If you want the best guidebook in English (and practically the only guidebook in English), you're looking at it! In English, the only locally available guide is the translation of Albert Trotet's locally published booklet, *Tourist Guide to Réunion Island*. If you're especially interested in architecture, it's worth the investment. However, there are few English copies still available and you

may have to resort to the French version, *Guide Touristique de la Réunion*.

The only other English-language option is the *Visitor's Guide to Mauritius, Rodrigues & Réunion* by Katerina & Eric Roberts but it's rather short on practical travel information and Réunion only gets 25 pages.

There are several standard French guides: the colourful *La Réunion Aujourd'hui* by Hureau & Bruyère; the detailed *Le Guide Pratique* by Serge Hoarau; the very general *à la Réunion, à l'Île Maurice, aux Seychelles*; and the oddly organised *Îles de l'Ocean Indien: Réunion, Maurice, Les Seychelles* by Jean-Pierre Jardel. In addition, there's another expanded tourist brochure sort of book entitled *Evasions Réunion*, edited by Agostina Calderon. The photos are nice and it includes a large map.

Bonjour Réunion, part of the French *Bonjour* series, is a very good source of basic background material on the island and is full of fine colour photos. It purports to be a travel guide *pour voyageurs curieux*, but the very limited practical information is next to useless.

Of several German-language guides available, the best seems to be the *Richtig Reisen – Réunion* by Dirk & Henriette Althoff.

For books about trekking see Books in the Trekking in Réunion chapter.

Fiction

The market for historical romances seems to have been cornered by one Daniel Vauxelaire, whose books are in French. In *Blue Africa*, however, Colin Simpson refers to one called *Island of Fire* by fellow-Australian writer Helga Mayne. Set among slaves and Napoleonic officers, it sounds like a variation on *Mandingo*.

General

If you're looking for a French treatise on the island, the best choice is Catherine Lavaux's *La Réunion: Du Battant des Lames au Sommet des Montagnes*. In the paperback *Que Sais-Je* series, there's a general interest history book on Réunion by André Scherer.

Sous le signe de la tortue, voyages anciens

OLIVIER CIRENDINI

SARINA SINGH

Réunion
Top: A source of nourishment in St-Gilles-les-Bains, Réunion for generations.
Bottom: Colourful, vibrant and open for business – the seafront St-Paul market, Réunion.

OLIVIER CIRENDINI

OLIVIER CIRENDINI

ROBERT WILLOX

Réunion
Top: Traditional Créole grocery stores like this in Le Bélier, Réunion are a welcome sight for hungry self-catering trekkers.
Bottom left: A modest example of Réunion's distinctive 18th century Créole architecture.
Bottom right: Stunning La Ravine St-Gilles in Réunion features majestic waterfalls and rock pools.

à l'île Bourbon (1611-1725) is an interesting book which contains old texts gathered by Albert Lougnon, which outline the first journeys made by boat to Réunion.

Taking the emphasis off the French text, with good colour plates of the island, are the books by Folco, Salvat & Robert: *La Réunion* has photos from ground level, and *La Réunion – Vue du Ciel* contains magnificent aerial shots. For a cheaper, colourful alternative and an accompanying English translation of the text, there's *L'Île de la Réunion* by Claude Huc.

For pre-trip reading, you can look out for *Blue Africa* by Australian Colin Simpson, writing about his organised tour through Africa. It has a chapter on Réunion.

Réunion is a fascinating place for the magically minded. Créole beliefs and potions have spawned a number of books on voodoo-style sorcery. For the serious student there is a four book set entitled *Vertus et Secrets des Plantes Médicinales des Tropiques et de la Réunion* by Dr Robert Zamore & Ary Ebroin. You will have to conjure up a couple of thousand francs for it though!

The treasure hunter extraordinaire of the island is a character called Bibique. He has written a book called *Sur la Piste des Frères de la Côte*, which is about the Indian Ocean pirates and their booty.

The bible of Créole cookery is *Les Délices de la Cuisine Créole*. It costs around FF3000 for the six volume set, but it's the *crème de la crème* of cookbooks. Some of the table d'hôte owners have copies. You can also pick up some considerably cheaper (but far less impressive) cookbooks.

NEWSPAPERS & MAGAZINES

There are three daily morning papers published in St-Denis and sold around the island.

There are two popular daily newspapers: the conservative *Le Journal de l'Île de la Réunion (JIR)* and the more liberal *Le Quotidien*. Each costs FF5 and carries sections on local, métropole, Indian Ocean and world news. They're both good for features and great for up-to-date information and views on the Comoros, Madagascar and Mauritius. The *JIR* also has a large Sunday edition. Free classified advertising is available in *Le Quotidien* on Friday and the *JIR* on Tuesday and Wednesday. Every Wednesday, Le Quotidien has a page of news in English.

The communist daily, *Témoignages* (FF5), presents all these items as well, but from a different perspective.

You can pick up some English-language newspapers at a few places, including the airport and several of the major bookshops in St-Denis. But by far the best range of newspapers and magazines (in English, French and several other languages) is at Le Tabac du Rallye in St-Denis (for further details see Bookshops in the St-Denis chapter).

There are four weekly magazines which carry the week's radio and television programme lists, as well as some general interest articles. These are: *Télé 7*, *Télé Mag*, *Visu* and *Star Télé*.

A magazine of interest to visitors is the bi-monthly *Plein Sud* which is published in Réunion but focuses on history, oddities, culture and (especially) leisure activities throughout the Indian Ocean region.

RADIO & TV

There are two government (RFO) radio stations and scores of 'free' stations such as Radio Free-DOM, Radio Arc-en-Ciel and Radio Dominique; these cover the island and satisfy a range of creeds and tastes.

Television viewers have the choice of two government (RFO) channels as well as an independent station. Most of the programming on the RFOs is produced and shown in the métropole first.

PHOTOGRAPHY

There's plenty of scope for sensational photography on Réunion. The volcano may not perform on cue, but several photographers have caught it in the act and have colour shots of the eruption on display or for sale.

Stocks of film are plentiful and fresh, but more expensive than in Europe. A 36 exposure colour print film costs around FF58;

processing is also expensive at FF4 per print and an additional FF18 per roll.

For further information on photography in this part of the world, see Photography in the Regional Facts for the Visitor chapter at the beginning of this book.

TIME

Réunion is four hours ahead of GMT (Greenwich Mean Time) and UTC (Universal Time Coordinated), making it three hours ahead of France, Switzerland, Belgium, Italy and Germany in the winter and two hours ahead in the summer. It is four hours ahead of London in the winter and three hours ahead in summer. It's two hours ahead of Johannesburg year-round, and in the winter, nine hours ahead of New York and Toronto, 12 hours ahead of San Francisco and Vancouver and four hours behind Perth, Australia.

ELECTRICITY

The electric current in Réunion is 220V AC at 50 Hz. Outlets take continental two-pin plugs, so British and non-European visitors should use an adaptor for electric appliances.

LAUNDRY

All of the top-end hotels, most of the mid-range hotels and some of the budget hotels and guesthouses offer a laundry service. To cut costs, bundle together your clothes and head for a self-service laundry or dry-cleaner – these are mainly found in the larger towns.

WEIGHTS & MEASURES

Réunion uses the metric system. For a conversion chart, see the inside back cover of this book.

HEALTH

For general travel health information, see Health in the Regional Facts for the Visitor chapter at the beginning of this book.

Vaccinations

Vaccination certificates for cholera and yellow fever are only required of travellers arriving from an infected area.

Water

Tap water is safe to drink everywhere on the island. Mineral water is widely available.

Health Precautions

Although there are mosquitoes on the island, there is no malaria. However, authorities ask that visitors 'take some form of antimalarial treatment before they fall ill' if they're coming from Madagascar or another area where malaria is endemic. For further details see Health in the Regional Facts for the Visitor chapter.

The greatest health threat in Réunion will probably be spraining, blistering, twisting or breaking something while hiking. If the worst does happen, the best medical care is at hand. Réunion has a large health service, more than 1000 doctors, 200 pharmacies and the best equipment and emergency services in the Indian Ocean.

DANGERS & ANNOYANCES
Emergency Phone Numbers

For hazardous situations the emergency number for police is ☎ 17. The ambulance is on ☎ 15 and the fire brigade is on ☎ 18.

Stolen Travellers Cheques

For information on what to do if your travellers cheques are stolen/lost, see Dangers & Annoyances in the Regional Facts for the Visitor chapter, at the beginning of this book.

LEGAL MATTERS

See Legal Matters in the Regional Facts for the Visitor chapter.

BUSINESS HOURS

Lunches are long, relaxed affairs in Réunion; shops and businesses are generally open daily (except Sunday) from around 9 am to noon and 2.30 to 6 pm. Some shops are closed on Monday mornings. On Sunday, the streets are almost eerily silent.

The main banks – Banque de la Réunion (BR), Crédit Agricole (CA), Banque Nationale de Paris Intercontinentale (BNPI) and Banque Française Commerciale (BFC) – are open Monday to Friday from 8 am to 4 pm, all with branches in most major towns. The foreign-exchange counter at Roland Garros airport is open Monday to Friday from 10 am to 1.30 pm and 3 to 6.30 pm and on Saturday from 8.30 to 11.30 am.

PUBLIC HOLIDAYS & SPECIAL EVENTS

Most offices, shops and museums in Réunion are closed on *jours fériés* (public holidays), which are as follows:

New Year's Day – 1 January
Easter Monday – late March or April
Labour Day – 1 May
Victory Day 1945 – 8 May
Ascension Day – 19 May
Bastille Day (National Day) – 14 July
Assumption Day – 15 August
All Saints' Day – 1 November
Armistice Day 1918 – 11 November
Abolition of Slavery Day – 20 December
Christmas Day – 25 December

Major festivals in Réunion involve exhibitions with sales, competitions, sports events, music, dancing and various other activities. For exact details contact any of the Syndicats d'Initiative (Tourist Offices) or the *mairie* (town hall) in the respective towns. The Indian community is principally made up of Tamil Hindus and they hold some amazing rites, including cavadees and fire-walking ceremonies. The Hindu temple in St-André is the most popular location for these events. Again, the Syndicats d'Initiative should have details.

Towns and villages across the island take turns at celebrating over a week or weekend; the excuse is to honour their primary product, which can be anything from chou chou to sugar cane. One British couple attended several of these festivals and made the following assessment:

Don't expect a lot of local colour at most of these events. You'll hear more amplified rap, reggae and rock than any indigenous music. There's usually a beauty contest in which the girls are white, or made up to look as pale as possible, and the feted produce is most apparent in its relative absence!

Ginette & Peter Scott

Festivals in Réunion include:

Fête du Miel Vert (honey)
    Le Tampon, one week in mid-January
Fête du Vacoa (rope made from the screw pine fronds)
    St-Benoît, April
Fête du Chou Chou
    Hell-Bourg, first weekend in May
Fête de la Vanille (vanilla)
    Bras-Panon, 10 days in mid-May
Fête des Goyaviers (guava trees)
    Plaine-des-Palmistes, a weekend in June
Fête de la Canne (sugar cane)
    Ste-Rose, end of July
Fête de St-Paul
    St-Paul, two weeks in July
Foire du Bois (wood)
    La Rivière, St-Louis, 10 days at the beginning of August
Fête du Safran (saffron)
    St-Joseph, 10 days in August
Exposition des Fleurs (flower show)
    Le Tampon, end of September or beginning of October
Fête de la Rose (roses)
    St-Benoît, five days in November
Fête des Lentilles (lentils)
    Cilaos, a weekend in November
Fête des Mangoustans (mangosteens)
    St-Benoît, November
Foire de St-Pierre
    St-Pierre, 10 days at the beginning of December
Fête des Letchis (lychees)
    St-Denis, one week in mid-December
Fête de l'Ail (garlic)
    Petite-Île, a weekend in December

ACTIVITIES

In true French style, the recreational emphasis in Réunion is on sweat, adventure, pushing beyond conventional limits and all that. Whether or not anyone actually breaks new ground, however, seems to be immaterial as long as some suffering is involved! There are established clubs for just about every sort of activity you can imagine: flying, parachuting, sailboarding, hang-gliding, canyoning, equitation, mountain biking, diving, deep-sea fishing, sailing, water-skiing and numerous competitive sports. Water activities are clustered around the waterfront at St-Gilles-les-Bains (and are emerging in neighbouring communities), the holiday and leisure centre of Réunion.

What's On inquiries should be directed to the Syndicats d'Initiative or the Office

RÉUNION

Départemental de la Culture (☎ 41 11 41; fax 41 55 71) in St-Denis. The local press should also have details on events. Another good source of information is the *RUN* magazine, available free from Syndicats d'Initiative and many hotels around the island (see Tourist Offices earlier in this chapter).

Trekking

For information on trekking, see the Trekking in Réunion chapter.

Deep-Sea Fishing

Experts reckon the prime time for deep-sea fishing in Réunion is from around November to April. A boat with crew costs roughly FF1800/2600 per half/full day (maximum of around six people). This usually includes soft drinks and a light lunch. If you intend spending several days fishing, you should negotiate a discount. Some operators may offer individual rates of between FF450 to FF600 per person for a half-day or FF800 to FF900 for a full day.

Contact any of the major tour operators or the fishing charters in and around St-Gilles-les-Bains: Marlin Club de la Réunion (☎ 24 56 78; fax 44 72 56), Réunion Fishing Club (☎ 24 34 74; fax 24 39 46), Centre de Pêche Europa (☎ 43 43 85), Sinbad (☎ 33 01 74), Blue Marlin (☎ 22 54 47), Jolly Jumper II (☎ 44 72 56), Magnum (☎ 88 48 26), Maeva (☎ 33 71 48), Cronos (☎ 43 33 57), Stepholie (☎ 24 51 51), Pêche au Gros (☎ 42 34 77 day or ☎ 23 71 58 evening), Alpha (☎ 24 02 02) and Octopus II (☎/fax 24 40 06).

Diving

Diving specialists are concentrated around St-Gilles-les-Bains. Most places generally charge around FF150 per person for a 20 minute dive, FF180 per person for a 40 minute dive, or FF750 per person for five dives. (For more information on diving in the Indian Ocean, see Activities in the Regional Facts for the Visitor chapter at the beginning of the book.) Contact one of the below organisations if you're interested in diving in Réunion:

Au Gloria Maris, M Flores, St-Gilles-les-Bains (☎ 24 41 42)
Bleu Marine, Port de Plaisance, St-Gilles-les-Bains (☎ 24 22 00; fax 24 30 04)
Bourbon Marine, St-Gilles-les-Bains (☎ 24 45 05)
Corail Club de Plongée, Zone Portuaire, St-Gilles-les-Bains (☎ 24 37 25; fax 24 46 38)
Comité Régional des Etudes et Sports Sous-Marins, Président Masanneli, Maison Régionale des Sports, St-Denis (☎ 20 09 79)
Club de Plongée du Grand Bleu, St-Gilles-les-Bains, Zone Portuaire (☎ 24 33 94)
Club de Plongée et Exploration GEO, Enceinte Portuaire de St-Gilles, St-Gilles-les-Bains (☎ 24 56 03; fax 24 33 50)
Korrigan Centre de Plongée, Route des Colimaçons, St-Leu (☎ 34 77 47; fax 44 20 13)
Manta Plongée, Plage des Brisants, St-Gilles-les-Bains (☎/fax 24 37 10)
Plongée Sous-Marine, 121 Chemin de la Piscine, St-Paul (☎/fax 44 27 74)

Surfing

There are several surfing clubs and schools, but the only surf spots are around St-Gilles-les-Bains. One good location is at Ravine des Colimaçons, not far from Le Corail Turtle Farm near St-Leu. Roches Noires beach at St-Gilles-les-Bains itself is also a popular surf spot. If you're keen to ride the waves but could do with a few pointers, contact one of the following organisations. Private lessons for beginners cost around FF135 per hour; group classes are considerably cheaper.

Shark Alert

If you plan on riding the waves or doing some snorkelling, diving, swimming or other water activity, it's wise to stick to professional recommendations on where to do it. Sharks can pose a real problem and, sadly, there have been a number of fatal shark attacks in the past. Surfers should be aware that sharks can sometimes mistake surfboards for large fish (a potential feed) and may thus be attacked.

Although the west coast is not supposed to be as dangerous as the east coast, don't assume that it's a 'shark-free zone' – there have been some attacks reported here too. Late afternoons are said to be the most risky time of day, especially offshore of the mouths of rivers and streams. So before you plunge into the drink, be sure to seek some local advice. ■

Aloha Surf Club, Patrick Flores, Boucan-Canot (☎ 24 12 58)

Boucan Surf Club Jardin des Vagues (☎ 34 79 88)

École de Body Board et Surf des Roches Noires, 4 bis Lot des Charmilles, St-Gilles-les-Bains (☎/fax 24 63 28)

Sud Surf Club, 16 Rue R-Payet, 97427 Étang-Salé-les-Bains (☎ 25 34 28)

Canyoning

For adventure seekers, there's the exhilaration of canyoning, challenging you to abseil down rugged gorges and cliffs into water holes or lagoons below. Canyoning (with a guide) usually costs around FF250/400 per person for a half/full day.

Kalanoro, Bras-Panon (☎ 51 71 10; fax 51 72 94) or bookings through Maison de la Montagne, 10 Place Sarda Garriga, St-Denis (☎ 90 78 78; fax 41 84 29)

Maham, Cascade des Demoiselles, Hell-Bourg (☎/fax 47 82 82) or inquire at Maison de la Montagne, 10 Place Sarda Garriga, St-Denis (☎ 90 78 78; fax 41 84 29)

Réunion Sensations, c/o Maison de la Montagne, 10 Place Sarda Garriga, St-Denis (☎ 90 78 78; fax 41 84 29) or 2 Rue Mac Auliffe, Cilaos (☎ 31 71 71; fax 31 80 54)

Ric A Ric, 94 Route Desbassyns, Le Guillaume (☎ 32 44 20; fax 32 44 85)

Canoeing, Kayaking, Sailboarding & Water-Skiing

Contact any of the following for information and prices of canoeing, kayaking, sailboarding and water-skiing.

Blue Cat, 2 Rue des Brisants, Zone Portuaire, St-Gilles-les-Bains (☎ 24 32 04)

Club Nautique de Bourbon, 2 Rue des Brisants, 97434 St-Gilles-les-Bains (☎ 24 40 93)

Club Nautique Bénedict, Rue Bouvet, St-Benoît (☎ 50 55 30)

Ski Nautique Club de St-Paul, 1 Rue de la Croix, l'Étang, St-Paul (☎ 45 42 87)

Société Nautique de St-Paul, 78 Route de la Baie, St-Paul (☎ 22 56 46)

Société Nautique de St-Pierre, BP 123, St-Pierre (☎ 25 04 03)

Paragliding, Hang-Gliding, Abseiling & Rock Climbing

The following organisations may be of help if you're interested in paragliding, hang-gliding, abseiling or rock climbing.

Aventures Ocean Indien, Souris-Blanche, Trois-Bassins (☎ 24 13 42)

Azurtech, Grande Ravine, La Souris Chaude, Saline-les-Bains (☎ 85 04 00; fax 33 91 36)

Compagnie des Guides de la Réunion, Maison de la Montagne, 2 Rue Mac Auliffe, Cilaos (☎ 31 71 71; fax 31 80 54)

Parapente Réunion, 4 CD 12 des Colimaçons, St-Leu (☎ 24 87 84; fax 24 87 15)

Centre École de Parachutisme de la Réunion, St-Pierre (☎ 25 54 41)

Mountain Biking

Recently, Réunion has seen an explosion of interest in the *vélo tout terrain* (VTT) or mountain bike. The usual charge seems to be around FF80/110 for a half/full day. For further details (including where bikes can be rented), see Bicycle in the Réunion Getting Around chapter.

Golf

There are three golf courses on the island. They charge between FF120 and FF190 on weekdays and from FF180 to FF250 on weekends.

Golf Club du Bassin Bleu, St-Gilles-les-Hauts (☎ 55 53 58)

Golf Club du Colorado, Zone de Loisirs du Colorado, La Montagne, St-Denis (☎ 23 79 50)

Golf Club de Bourbon, Étang-Salé-les-Bains (☎ 26 33 39)

Horse Riding

If the idea of exploring the countryside on horseback appeals to you, contact one of the below organisations. Most places charge between FF90 to FF140 per hour or FF250/500 for a half/full day.

Centre Équestre Acti-Merens, 49 Chemin Notre Dame de la Paix, Petite Ferme, Le Tampon (☎ 59 18 84)

Centre Équestre de Grand-Étang, Route de la Plaine-des-Palmistes, Plaines-des-Palmistes (☎ 50 90 03)

Centre d'Équitation du Colorado, 17 Chemin des Mimosas, La Montagne, St-Denis (☎ 23 62 51)

Club Hippique de l'Hermitage, 203 Rue Général de Gaulle, St-Gilles-les-Bains (☎ 24 47 73)

Crinière Réunion, Chemin Lautret, St-Gilles-les-Bains (☎ 55 54 29)

RÉUNION

La Diligence, Vingt-Huitième, Bourg-Murat, Plaine-des-Cafres (☎ 59 10 10)

Ranch Kikouyou, BP 19 Grand-Fond, Entre-Deux (☎ 39 60 62)

4WD Excursions

For a day tour by 4WD expect to pay approximately FF500 to FF550 per person. Tailor-made tours are possible – contact one of the below operators for details.

Indi Aventure, 14 Rue des Lanternes, St-Gilles-les-Bains (☎ 24 23 87)

Thierry Nativel, Grand Fond, Entre-Deux (☎ 39 50 87)

Tours

There are a few sugar factories which offer tours to visitors – inquire at any Syndicat d'Initiative. There's a two hour tour of St-Denis, which visits the main tourist attractions (see Organised Tours in the St-Denis chapter).

WORK

EU citizens have the right to live and work in Réunion for up to three months. For longer, you need an employer to fill out forms or provide a guarantee of means for at least one year. This will enable you to apply at Immigration for a *carte de séjour* which will allow you to remain for five to 10 years.

The going rate for private English lessons by a native English-speaker is around FF100 per hour. If you have a telephone, you can advertise your services free in *Le Quotidien* on Friday and the *Journal de l'Île de la Réunion* on Tuesday and Wednesday.

For formal English-related employment, you could try the Chambre de Commerce et de l'Industrie. Alternatively, you may be able to find work at the Université de la Réunion as a *repetiteur* (tutor) (apply to the Faculté d'Anglais at the university) or as a *maître auxiliare* (substitute teacher) (apply at the Rectorat in St-Denis).

ACCOMMODATION

Advance preparation in choosing and booking accommodation is a very good idea because of the high cost and equally high demand, especially during French holidays:

late July to early September. You won't be able to see, let alone appreciate, the beauty of the island if a chunk of your time is taken up in search of a place to stay. That doesn't mean there isn't a range of accommodation, but things do fill up and some places are permanently packed out.

Camping

Camping is possible either in the wild or at several organised camping and caravan sites. It is the cheapest official accommodation alternative and fees range from around FF15 to FF60 per day.

There are community camping and caravan sites at Hermitage-les-Bains (☎ 24 42 35, open August and late December to early February only), Cilaos (☎ 31 77 41, open year-round), St-Leu (☎ 34 80 03, open August only), Colorado (☎ 23 74 12, year-round), Grande Anse (☎ 56 81 03, school holidays only) and Rivière des Roches (☎ 51 58 59, year-round). Also in Cilaos, there's a forestry camp site which may be used free of charge with permission from the Office National des Forêts, Rue du Père Boiteau, Cilaos (☎ 31 71 40). These public camp sites aren't particularly well policed, and robbery and vandalism are real problems, especially at Hermitage-les-Bains. Campers at any of the official sites are required to clear out at the announcement of a cyclone warning.

Another option is the Camping à la Ferme (an organisation of privately owned French camp sites) of Mme Lucette Ahrel (☎ 51 36 26) at 37 Rue Pignolet, Chemin de la Petite Plaine in Plaine-des-Palmistes. She charges FF10 per day for the site and an extra FF10 per person per day.

If you're heading for the cirques in August, you may want to carry a tent and forego the urban life in the gîtes. There are also emergency shelters along some of the main trekking paths, but they provide only a roof. Remember to avoid pitching your tent under large trees, as falling branches are a danger.

Youth Hostels

Réunion has three *auberges de jeunesse* (youth hostels) – at Bernica (☎ 22 89 75),

Entre-Deux (☎ 39 59 20) and Hell-Bourg (☎ 47 82 65). They're operated by the Fédération Réunionnaise des Auberges de Jeunesse, which is an affiliate of the French Youth Hostels League (Ligue Française pour les Auberges de la Jeunesse).

Officially, the hostels are only open to Hostelling International (HI) card holders. Others may be required to purchase a French Youth Hostel association membership or an international guest card for about FF100 (available at most youth hostels).

For lodging, guests over 18 years of age pay FF70 per night and an additional FF10 for breakfast. Evening meals are available for FF45 per person. Further inquiries and reservations can be made through the Féderation des Auberges de Jeunesse (☎ 41 15 34) in St-Denis.

VVF Holiday Villages

The four VVFs (Villages Vacances Familles) which, like the rural gîtes, are a French holiday institution, are relatively quiet, low-key and nothing like a Butlins camp. In order to stay, you need to first join the VVF organisation, which costs around FF100 per family.

There are VVFs at St-Leu (☎ 34 81 43; fax 34 78 43), St-Gilles-les-Bains (☎ 24 29 39; fax 24 41 02), Cilaos (☎ 31 71 39; fax 31 80 85) and La Saline (☎ 24 60 10; fax 24 66 33).

Chambres d'Hôte

These small and personal bed and breakfast (B&B) establishments are normally convenient to places of interest to tourists. There are numerous chambres d'hôte on the island and they provide a pleasant introduction to Créole life. All are family-run, but some treat guests more like a member of the family than others. B&B rates are from around FF150 for a double room. Hearty traditional meals cost about FF80 per person and must be reserved in advance. You can reserve a room by telephoning the proprietor directly. Some can also be booked through the Relais Départemental des Gîtes de France (see Gîtes Ruraux later in this section).

Pensions de Famille

Pensions de famille are the only budget alternative to hotels in St-Denis, where there are no chambres d'hôte. There are few vacancies for visitors because so many rooms are taken on a long-term basis by students, foreigners looking for work and contract tradespeople. The pensions are mainly in the capital and there are a few scattered around the island. They vary from the shoddy dosshouse to well-run guesthouses, and rates range from around FF120 to FF200 per night for a double room, including breakfast. Evening meals cost at least FF50 per person.

Gîtes de Montagne

Gîtes de montagne are basic mountain cabins or lodges, operated by the government through Maison de la Montagne. It is possible to organise a walking holiday using the gîtes de montagne only, as there are 11 distributed around the interior of the island. Cirque de Mafate, inaccessible by road, has five of them: at Îlet à Bourse, La Nouvelle, Roche Plate, Grand Place and Marla. La Roche Écrite is another one en route between St-Denis and the Cirque de Salazie. Bélouve and Piton des Neiges gîtes are between Salazie and Cilaos cirques, and Volcan is accessible by road, en route to the volcano at Pas de Bellecombe. Basse Vallée is in the south-eastern part of the island.

The gîtes in Réunion are generally in better condition than their counterparts in metropolitan France and, thanks to recently installed solar panels, they have electricity. Not all, however, get as cushy as providing warm showers. The most basic is at Piton des Neiges, which currently has no hot water or showers. There are plans to improve facilities here however.

The gîtes must be booked and paid for in advance and reservations are not refundable, unless a cyclone or a cyclone alert prevents your arrival. A night in each without food costs around FF70 per person and must be booked through Maison de la Montagne: the main office (☎ 90 78 78; fax 41 84 29) is at 10 Place Sarda Garriga, 97400 St-Denis. The Cilaos office (☎ 31 71 71; fax 31 80 54) is at

2 Rue Mac Auliffe, 97413. It's highly recommended to book well in advance, especially during the busy tourist season (see When to Go earlier in this chapter).

When making a booking for a gîte de montagne, make sure you ask about meal arrangements. In many cases, you have to arrange this with the gîte caretaker independently *after* you've booked and paid for your accommodation. If your French isn't crash hot, politely request someone at Maison de la Montagne to make the meal arrangements for you. Keep in mind that not all gîtes provide meals, so you might have to take your own supplies. Again, ask while you make your booking to avoid confusion later. Breakfasts are also available in all gîtes (except Piton des Neiges) for around FF25 per person but they usually consist only of biscuits, preserves and coffee, and aren't worth the money. Several provide a better breakfast for FF35. Dinner ranges from FF65 to FF85 per person.

Sleeping arrangements are mostly bunk beds in rooms sleeping two to 39 people. There are two blankets and a mattress cover per bed. The blankets are often dusty, so bring a sleep-sheet or sleeping bag. It's not a bad idea to also bring along toilet paper and a torch. It can get quite chilly at night, so warm clothing will be in order. Cooking is done mostly by a wood-fired stove, but some kitchens are so filthy you probably won't bother.

For more information about gîtes and trekking-related information, see the Trekking in Réunion chapter.

On arrival and departure you must 'book' in and out with the manager who will collect your booking ticket. In theory, you're not meant to occupy a gîte before 3 pm or remain past 10 am. The telephone numbers of individual gîtes are:

Basse Vallée	☎ 37 00 75
Bélouve	☎ 41 21 23
Grand Place	☎ 43 85 42
Îlet à Bourse	☎ 43 43 93
Marla	☎ 43 78 31
La Nouvelle	☎ 43 61 77
Piton des Neiges	☎ 51 15 26
Roche Écrite	☎ 43 99 84
Roche Plate	☎ 59 13 94
Volcan 1 & 2	☎ 21 28 96
Volcan 3	☎ 21 28 96

Gîtes d'Étape

The privately owned gîtes d'étape, five of which – two at Aurère, two at La Nouvelle and one at Grand-Place-les-Hauts – are in roadless areas of the Cirque de Mafate, function much the same as the gîtes de montagne. They charge about the same but they generally aren't as tidy or well kept. Accommodation is in dormitories, and some of them offer common cooking facilities. At some, the host may prepare meals with advance notice.

Gîtes Ruraux

Gîtes ruraux (also known as Gîtes de France) are private houses and lodges which families and groups can rent for self-catering holidays. There are over 80 gîtes ruraux in Réunion, mainly in the southern half of the island and around Plaine-des-Palmistes and Plaine-des-Cafres. There are none in St-Denis (the nearest is at Le Brûlé) or on the coast, but several are within striking distance – mainly in the St-Paul and St-Leu areas.

There is a wide selection of gîtes ruraux, with facilities for lodging up to 12 people. Most have fridges and hot water, and bed sheets are available in some cases. If there are vacancies, some gîtes will allow overnight guests, but they're normally only let by the week or weekend. Costs vary from around FF1200 to FF2700 per week and FF500 to FF1800 for a weekend (note that not all offer just weekend bookings). A security bond equivalent to one week's rent is required in advance.

You may book the gîtes by phoning the proprietors directly or contacting the Relais Départemental des Gîtes de France (☎ 90 78 90; fax 41 84 29), 10 Place Sarda Garriga, 97400 St-Denis. They publish a handy booklet entitled *Vacances en Gîtes de France* containing photos and full details on each gîte. In France, for information on Réunion's gîtes ruraux, contact Maison des Gîtes de France (☎ 01 49 70 75 75; fax 01 49 70 75 76), 59 Rue Saint-Lazare, 75439 Paris.

Hotels

Réunion isn't flush with hotels so getting a room can often be difficult. Primarily, they're found in St-Denis and around the beach resorts of the west coast, especially St-Gilles-les-Bains. Most hotels on the island are either in the three, two or one star category, and lots are unclassed. There is only a sprinkling of four-star hotels.

Many of the mid-range hotels attract businesspeople and can get booked out quite quickly. It's wise to make reservations well in advance, so your choices are not limited. If you will be staying for more than one week, it's worth asking for a discount when making your booking. Keep a lookout for special deals offered by hotels, particularly during the low season.

FOOD
Local Food

As in France proper, much time and effort in Réunion is devoted to growing, preparing and enjoying food. What's more, the Réunionnais have an array of culinary traditions to choose from: French, Indian, Chinese and Créole, and many recipes contain elements of several cuisines.

Just as in la métropole, the Réunionnais begin the day with a *petit déjeuner* (breakfast) usually consisting of a bread roll and croissant accompanied by butter and jam. This is washed down with at least one cup of coffee and perhaps a glass of juice. Lunch is the main meal of the day for many people and the restaurants sure do fill up fast at lunchtime.

Most imaginable fruits and vegetables, as well as a few unknown in Europe and elsewhere, are available. Among the latter, two stand out – the *tomate d'arbuste*, the sweet tree tomato New Zealanders call tamarillo, and the pear-shaped, green vegetable called *chou chou*, which was introduced from Brazil; in Australia it's called a choko and in Europe, a crystophène.

Other common ingredients in Créole dishes are some sort of *graines*, which may be red or white beans (*haricots*), lentils (*lentilles*) or peas (*petits pois*), invariably served as a creamy side dish along with *rougail* (spicy hot tomato and vegetable chutney) and *brèdes*, digestive greens which resemble spinach.

Réunion is not a vegetarian's paradise. In the highlands, chicken (*poulet*) and meat (primarily beef, goat or pork) are central to practically every dish. On the coast, there is the additional choice of fish or crustaceans.

More often than not, the meat or fish available is cooked in a mild Indian curry and served on a rice base; specialities include octopus curry (*cari poulpe*), jackfruit curry (*cari p'tit jacques*) and smoked pork curry (*cari boucané*). Heart of palm and vanilla figure in many recipes. Arabic influences are evident in the addition of cloves, cinnamon and nutmeg in some recipes, while the Swahili contribution is coconut cream. The Chinese have contributed ginger.

If you want to spice up the meal, there is often a bowl of *piments* (chillies). Beware, you need only a smidgen of this stuff. A teaspoonful may cauterise your insides!

Good home cooking wouldn't be the same without the cakes. They're not the fancy fruit, cream and pastry delicacies of the

RÉUNION

Sea Urchins

The spiny sea urchins are another member of the *echinoderm* group which includes starfish and sea cucumbers. With a ball-like body covered in spines it is the sea urchin which gives the group its name, Greek for spiny (*echino*) and skin (*derm*). The spines can vary considerably from the short blunt spines of the slate-pencil urchin to the long, sharp black spines of *Diadema* urchins. These spines will easily penetrate skin if the urchin is stepped on or handled and once broken off they are very hard to remove and can cause infection.

When an urchin dies the spines fall off and the circular 'sea egg' which remains makes a fine if fragile ornament. It's easy to see the five armed, star pattern on the casing which shows the urchin's relation to starfish. The sea urchin's mouth at the bottom is a complex structure known as Aristotle's lantern and with this the urchin grazes as it crawls across the sea bottom. Despite the formidable protection of its spines, urchins hide away during daylight and come out to feed at night. Spines or not, some triggerfish will still eat sea urchins. ∎

pâtisserie, but sweet and heavy puddings made out of sweet potatoes, chou chou, cassava or rice.

Tables d'Hôte

Most chambres d'hôte are *tables d'hôte* as well, but many establishments have only table d'hôte. These places dish up three to four-course treats accompanied by wine, punch or rum for around FF80 per person. The Créole cuisine you'll find in the tables d'hôte (the cheapest places to eat) is rich and filling, though it rarely gets too daring; these set meals normally contain meat (vegetarians be warned) and about 80% of the time you'll wind up with cari poulet. If you like variety, you'll occasionally have to splash out on a restaurant.

There are quite a few tables d'hôte in the Cirque de Salazie, the Plaine-des-Cafres and the Plaine-des-Palmistes. Some cater for clubs and other large parties. To reserve, just telephone or get the tourist office to book for you.

Eating Out

There is a dearth of budget eating houses in Réunion and unless you can subsist on snacks (tiny samosas and meatballs are sold on the streets for around FF2 each), you won't find much for less than FF25. There are a few Chinese-Créole restaurants or cafés where a reasonably filling meal costs between FF30 and FF60. Thereafter, set-menu lunches offered by most restaurants for between FF55 and FF90 are the best value. Many restaurants take Sunday, Monday or Tuesday as a day off. It's a good idea to ring ahead to check that the restaurant you intend dining at will be open.

Vegetarian

Vegetarians are not particularly well catered for in Réunion, however most restaurants do have at least one pure vegetarian item on their menu, often in the form of an elaborate salad. A word of caution – make sure you ask exactly what is in the salad before you order, as many include meat or seafood of some kind. Créole restaurants are one of the best options for vegetarians, as they usually have

a range of hearty veg specialities, such as lentils or vegetable curries.

For versatility, your best bet is to stay in self-catering accommodation, which will allow you to whip up your favourite dishes when you tire of the limited vegetarian options at the restaurants. You can get fruits and vegetables at most supermarkets. For greater variety and better prices, head for a fruit and vegetable market – such as the Petit Marché in St-Denis or the St-Paul market. Traveller Stephen Clarke gives some advice for vegetarians:

A tip for vegetarians is to stick to starters. In most restaurants serving French food, they'll have salads; for example, mixed salads or *crudités* (although they may contain tuna so you'll have to ask). In the mountains, you might be lucky enough to get *chèvre chaud*, local goat's milk cheese on toast with a bed of green salad. In Créole restaurants they'll have *gratin de chou chou* or *salade de palmiste*, and they'll always be happy to serve up rice with rougaille and *graines* (either beans or lentils).

Self-Catering

When camping, trekking from gîte to gîte or renting a bungalow, the cheapest places to get provisions are the supermarkets and department stores such as Score and Prisunic. Here, you'll find the same cheap and nasty pre-packaged and instant food items you probably carry on outdoor trips at home. For fruit and vegetables, the markets are better value.

Local cheeses are available at some supermarkets and from the smaller grocers in the highland areas. The fresh goat's cheeses are very good and baguettes are available everywhere, as are pre-made baguette sandwiches. One Créole variation is the *sandwich aux achards de légumes*, a sort of pickled vegetable sandwich. Then there are the small snacks and titbits which are available in shops and street stalls all around the island. Small chicken, fish or beef samosas cost from FF2 to FF4 each. Or you can try *bon bon piments*, spicy meat fritters, and *bouchons*, Chinese-style meat dumplings which cost around FF4 and are served with soy or pepper sauce.

DRINKS
Nonalcoholic Drinks
Coffee & Tea Expect to pay around FF6 for a small cup of black coffee. If you want it with milk *(café au lait)*, it goes for FF8. A large cup of coffee costs FF10/12 without/ with milk. Tea, which is not as popular as coffee, is similarly priced. Many restaurants and hotels charge more.

Alcoholic Drinks
Fruit Brews The variety of home-made rums and punches available in Réunion is astounding. The cheapest seems to be a blend of cheap *charette* rum, sugar and fruit juice. It's quite rough, and discriminating palates will want to move a bit upmarket.

A lot better is *punch créole*, a mixture of rum, fruit juice, cane syrup and a blend of herbs and berries. Every table or chambre d'hôte landlady prides herself on her brew. Choose from a mixed-fruit and mixed-spice *rhum arrangé* or a single-fruit brew of banana, vanilla, lychee (rhum rose) or pineapple. You'll normally have the opportunity to taste several. Commercially produced varieties are available in most stores and in bars or restaurants. Isautier of St-Pierre and Chatel of Ste-Clotilde are the main distillers.

Wine True to French tradition, most meals are accompanied by wine. The full French selection is available from about FF20 a bottle for Vin Royal (a no-frills table wine) to several hundred francs for a reputed label. There are also Italian and Spanish table wines for around FF30. South African wines range from FF26 to FF250 a bottle. The spa resort of Cilaos has its own concoction, more like a sherry than a wine.

Beer The local brew is Bière Bourbon (affectionately known as Dodo); not a bad drop at all at FF8 to FF10 (ridiculously more in many restaurants and bars). There is also a range of imported beers which includes such surprises as Heineken Malt from the Netherlands and Tennants Stout from Scotland. A 150ml bottle of imported beer costs between FF10 and FF15 over the counter and as much as FF40 in some bars and restaurants.

ENTERTAINMENT
Cinemas
There are cinemas in most population centres around the island and films are screened in Réunion shortly after their release in metropolitan France. Tickets cost FF45. If you're after an English-language film, don't hold your breath – they are few and far between!

Other Options
For night owls, there are bars, discos and

RÉUNION

Rhum arrangé
If you want to make your own alcoholic fruit brew try this recipe.

Macerate in a litre of Charrette rum:

* One vanilla bean split lengthwise to release its aroma.
* One sprig of faham (this perfumed orchid is available from the island's markets, especially at the market in St-Paul).
* A pinch of ginger.
* The peel of half an orange.
* Two heaped teaspoons of brown sugar or some honey.

You can also add a few plums, some raisins and a couple of cloves.
Let stand for approximately two months prior to serving. The mixture will have taken on a deep amber colour.
There are countless other recipes. ∎

casinos dotted around the island – see Entertainment sections under individual towns for further information. For details about theatre, see Arts in the Facts about Réunion chapter.

SPECTATOR SPORT

The affluent European lifestyle leads to many sporting as well as cultural distractions. There is nothing particularly Réunionnais about the main Créole pastimes on the island: soccer, volleyball and handball are all popular, judging by the extent given to the local leagues in the press. *Pétanque* or *boules*, a game in which metal balls are thrown to land as near as possible to a target ball, is another favourite. Boxing, cycling, martial arts, athletics, hockey and even rugby are also popular. The surrounding Indian Ocean countries provide competition on an international basis.

For detailed information on what's on, contact the Syndicat d'Initiative in St-Denis, or call the organisations listed in the Activities section earlier in this chapter.

THINGS TO BUY

The Syndicats d'Initiative market a selection of local handicrafts. Otherwise, as with agricultural products, each town and surrounding region is known for a special craft. This regional variation was re-established during WWII when supplies were blocked and the islanders had to make their own clothes, furniture and utensils as well as grow their own food. Times were hard, but the crafts taken up are now paying dividends.

The tourist and craft shops also sell a variety of art prints, lithographs and poster reproductions ranging in price from FF50 to FF180.

There's also a granny's cupboard full of concoctions made from the various fruits, spices and herbs available. They can be bought in their natural state of preservation, or as jams, compotes, pâtés, sweets, rums, punches and liqueurs. A 1L bottle of dark or white rum is about FF35, Rhum Vieux is

FF60 for a 700ml bottle and Planter's Punch is around FF30 for 700ml.

Several shops, particularly in St-Gilles-les-Bains, specialise in fashionable tropical wear, beachwear and accessories at inflated prices. Mind you, you'll see very few good T-shirt designs in Réunion and T-shirts are quite expensive, often upwards of FF60.

If you come across shops selling any sea turtle products such as shells and decorative turtle items, you should not purchase them as they are banned by international wildlife trade controls. At the time of writing it was legal to produce turtle products in Réunion, although this law may change, however these items may be confiscated in the country they are imported into and this applies even if the public information indicates that the turtles are captive bred.

Some other less localised crafts include wicker and bamboo work, hat-making and stone-carving. The following is a rundown of some villages and their specialities:

Cilaos
> The nuns in Cilaos have been doing embroidery since the beginning of the century, when a doctor's daughter, Angèle MacAuliffe, introduced the craft. There are now around 120 embroiderers and an embroidery school at Cilaos. The needlework includes everything from table mats to huge tablecloths at prices ranging from FF60 to FF4500. For the widest selection, visit the Maison de la Broderie (☎ 31 77 48; fax 31 80 54). Vetiver grass, the roots of which produce an essence used in perfumes, is woven into smaller items such as purses, hats and corn-dolly-style mascots. Cilaos also makes its own distinctive sweet wine for around FF35 per bottle.

Entre-Deux
> North-west of Le Tampon is Entre-Deux, which is known for slippers and *babouches* (scarves), woven out of *chocas* fibre.

St-Philippe & St-André
> In the St-Philippe and St-André areas, the fronds of the screw pine (pandanus) are made into mats, baskets and handbags of all sizes, including the traditional *tante* lunchbox. St-André also produces colourful patchwork quilts and mats known as *tapis mendiants* (beggars' mats), which cost between FF1500 and FF3300. Quilt bags are available for around FF140.

Étang-Salé-les-Hauts
  Artisans here turn out cane chairs made of lilac and casuarina wood.
Ste-Suzanne
  This small seaside town is known for its bamboo work, primarily baskets and fanciful bird cages.
La Rivière, St-Louis
  Tamarind, olive and camphor wood is made into period furniture like that original y introduced by the French East India Company. For a good selection, visit the Centre Artisanal du Bois (☎ 39 06 12).
La Possession
  Créole rag dolls hail from this otherwise unremarkable town west of St-Denis. Prices range from around FF100 to FF230.

RÉUNION

Getting There & Away

AIR

There are flights between Réunion and Mauritius, the Seychelles, Comoros, Mayotte, Madagascar (Antananarivo or Tamatave), South Africa (Johannesburg or Durban), Kenya (Nairobi) and, of course, metropolitan France. For many other international destinations, you'll have to get a connecting flight from Mauritius.

Airline Offices

Most of the airline offices are in St-Denis and some have branches in towns around the island. Offices of international airlines represented in Réunion include:

Air Austral
    4 Rue de Nice, 97473 St-Denis (☎ 90 90 90; fax 90 90 91)
Air France
    7 Ave de la Victoire, 97477 St-Denis (☎ 40 38 38; fax 40 38 40)
    7 Rue Archambaud, St-Pierre (☎ 25 06 06; fax 35 19 06)
Air Liberté
    83 Rue Labourdonnais, 97400 St-Denis (☎ 94 72 00; fax 41 68 00)
Air Madagascar
    2 Rue Victor Mac Auliffe, 97461 St-Denis (☎ 21 05 21; fax 21 10 08)
Air Mauritius
    Angle de Rue Alexis de Villeneuve and Rue Charles Gounod, 97400 St-Denis (☎ 94 83 83; fax 20 08 77)
Air Outre Mer (AOM)
    7 Rue Jean Chatel, 97479 St-Denis (☎ 94 77 77; fax 20 07 16)
    11 Rue François de Mahy, 97410 St-Pierre (☎ 96 17 00; fax 25 44 88)
Nouvelles Frontières
    92 Rue Alexis de Villeneuve, 97400 St-Denis (☎ 21 54 54; fax 20 26 37)

France

Fares between France and Réunion vary according to low/high season. Generally, it's more expensive to travel from July to mid-September and at around Christmas time. Many airlines flying between metropolitan France and Réunion offer discounts for students and travellers over 60 years of age. Shop around for the lowest fares and keep your eyes open for special deals/packages which pop up from time to time.

Air France operates nine to 12 flights weekly between the métropole and Réunion and the trip takes about 12 hours. The airline has flights between St-Denis and Lyon, Bordeaux, Toulouse and Marseille. Air France splits the year into light blue and dark blue rating periods. The light blue period is the cheapest (FF3890 return) and includes most of March, May, June and October. Dark blue is the peak period, also the most expensive (FF6090 return), and falls during the French holidays in July-August and December-January. For further details, contact Air France (☎ 01 802 802 802), 119 Ave des Champs-Élysées, 75008 Paris.

Air France now has a great deal of competition on this route. Air Outre Mer (AOM) has seven flights weekly from France. Low-season return fares begin at FF3718 and during the high season they're FF7290. For reservations call ☎ 01 49 79 12 34 in Paris. Another good option is Air Liberté, which also operates several weekly flights between France and Réunion. For further details call central reservations (☎ 01 49 79 09 09) in Paris.

Any of these airlines may be contacted through the tour operator Nouvelles Frontières (☎ 01 41 41 58 58; fax 01 40 65 99 36), 87 Blvd de Grenelle, 75015 Paris; in Réunion they're at 92 Rue Alexis de Villeneuve, 97400 St-Denis (☎ 21 54 54; fax 20 26 37). Nouvelles Frontières offers very competitive fares between France and Réunion.

Other companies worth checking for low fares to Réunion include Nouvelle Liberté (☎ 01 40 41 91 91), 38 Rue du Sentier, 75002 Paris; Fuaj (Fédération Unie des Auberges de Jeunesse) (☎ 01 48 04 70 40), 9 Rue Brantôme, 75003 Paris, and Voyageurs dans les Îles (☎ 01 42 86 16 39), 55 Rue Sainte-Anne, 75002 Paris.

Africa & Indian Ocean Countries

Another option for reaching Réunion is via Mauritius; Air Mauritius and Air France have several flights daily between the two islands. See the Mauritius Getting There & Away chapter for details.

A return excursion fare (valid for one month) between Mauritius and Réunion costs approximately FF1200 (Mauritian Rs 2635 if you're coming the other way). The flight takes around 40 minutes and is popular with visitors from Réunion in search of a cheap holiday on Mauritius. This might explain why the same return excursion fare purchased in Réunion is so much more expensive.

Average return fares to other destinations include: Antananarivo, Madagascar (FF2545); Tamatave, Madagascar (FF2545); Seychelles (FF3221); Moroni, Comoros (FF3850); Mayotte (FF2700); Johannesburg, South Africa (FF4480); Durban, South Africa (FF3030); and Nairobi, Kenya (FF4080).

In many respects, particularly if you'd like a stop in the Seychelles, it's worth considering 'interlining', ie flying from A to Z with as many stopovers as you want going one direction, rather than buying individual tickets. And always do it through a knowledgeable travel agent and not the airlines. That way, the fare may be calculated on a mileage basis rather than the sum of your journey's parts.

Arriving in Réunion

Customs and immigration procedures on arrival in Réunion are pretty much the same as in France. Roland Garros airport (formerly called Gillot airport) is a spacious, modern and well-designed complex, about 11km east of St-Denis. It has a bank, post office, tourist information counter, restaurant and café, shops, car hire desks and luggage lockers (which costs FF20 per piece per day). You can change money at the bank on Monday to Friday from 10 am to 1.30 pm and 3 to 6.30 pm and from 8.30 to 11.30 am on Saturday (closed Sunday). The helpful tourist information counter is staffed, usually from around 11 am to 8 pm, in order to meet

flights from France. The post office is open Monday to Friday from 9.30 am to 12.30 pm and 1.30 to 4.30 pm and on Saturday from 8 to 11 am. For airline arrival/departure information, call ☎ 28 16 16.

When you arrive at Roland Garros airport, you'll have to pay a deposit of FF10 for a baggage trolley, so have the change on hand. Once you've finished with the trolley, return it to the trolley line-up just outside the door of the terminal; when you plug in the little key to attach it to the other trolleys, your FF10 will pop out. Don't be intimidated by people demanding to return the trolley for you!

SEA

The water transport situation is much the same in Réunion as in Mauritius. There is now little chance, with the 'no passengers' policy, of a berth on a ship of the Compagnie Générale Maritime. Besides that, cruise liners mostly give Réunion a miss in favour of the Seychelles or Mauritius. The main shipping companies are based in Le Port.

The MV *Mauritius Pride* sails several times each month between the Mauritian capital, Port Louis, and Le Port in Réunion. The return fare starts at FF800/950 in the low/high season and the trip takes around 12 hours. Note that during the summer (cyclonic) season between October and March, trips may be cancelled. For further information and a contact address, see the Mauritius Getting There & Away chapter.

Yacht

There are a number of long-distance yacht charters. Ylang-Ylang (☎ 24 41 18), 48 Rue Général de Gaulle in St-Gilles-les-Bains, runs return cruises to Mauritius lasting seven, 12 and 14 days. These are mainly for divers, and your chances of booking a one-way berth back to Réunion are remote.

You may be able to find out about potential charters at Le Forbhan restaurant at the docks in Le Port, which often has information about passenger sailing possibilities. It's also worth asking at any tourist office, as

RÉUNION

well as having a look in the local newspapers.

LEAVING RÉUNION

The airport duty-free shop is well stocked; a 1L bottle of blended whisky costs around FF75. There's currently no departure tax, however there are rumours that one may be introduced – if it is, hopefully it will arrive after you depart!

Getting Around

AIR

Domestic Air Services

When you're walking around the volcano or the cirques it can resemble a scene from *Apocalypse Now*; the sky buzzes with noisy squadrons of helicopters on sightseeing forays. Helicopter tours are very popular with visitors and are a sensational way of taking in the awesome landscape. They're certainly not cheap, but most travellers rate it as a highlight of their visit to Réunion.

Several companies are cashing in on the appeal of Réunion seen from above. The tours usually depart from Roland Garros airport or St-Gilles-les-Bains airstrip. Helilagon (☎ 55 55 55; fax 22 86 78) is at L'Eperon just outside St-Gilles-les-Bains. A 35 minute tour of all three cirques costs FF1080/980 in the high/low season. For something cheaper, the helicopter drops you at the Cirque de Mafate to explore at your leisure and picks you up at the end of the day for FF380 per person. To visit two cirques by helicopter and have a stop at the Cirque de Mafate will cost FF850/750 in the high/low season.

Heli Réunion (☎ 93 11 11; fax 29 51 70) offers similar tours. For example, a 35 minute tour of the three cirques costs FF1080/980 in the high/low season. A 25 minute tour only over the cirques of Salazie and Mafate costs FF850/750 in the high/low season. Air Réunion International (☎ 93 11 11; fax 29 51 70) offers helicopter and light aircraft tours of the island. The price starts at around FF750 per person for a 25 minute overview of Cirque de Salazie and the Cirque de Mafate, and climbs to FF1180 for a 50 minute sweep over all three cirques and the volcano.

These aerial sightseeing trips are extremely popular and almost any travel agency on the island will make arrangements for you. It will be a bit less expensive if you can make up a party of five for a light plane trip, although planes don't really have the sightseeing flexibility you'll get with a helicopter. You could also inquire at the Aéro Club de Roland Garros (☎ 52 31 69) for possibly cheaper deals.

Another option is to thoroughly expose yourself to the elements in an ultra-light aircraft. Air Evasion (☎ 25 19 72; fax 25 93 34) charges FF680 per person for a 40 minute buzz over the three cirques. Their other possibilities include a 30 minute tour of the volcano (FF500 per person) and a 20 minute tour of Cilaos (FF250 per person).

BUS

The Réunion bus service 'Cars Jaunes' (Yellow Coaches), comprised of a number of formerly private lines, covers most parts of the island with several main routes. There are a few variations on these routes – for example, some buses cover only part of a particular route – so make sure you inquire before making firm plans. For bus information call: St-Denis (☎ 41 51 10); St-Pierre (☎ 35 67 28); St-André (☎ 46 80 00); St-Paul (☎ 22 54 38); St-Benoît (☎ 50 10 69); St-Joseph (☎ 56 03 90).

St-Denis to St-Pierre
This bus travels via Le Port, St-Paul, St-Gilles-les-Bains, St-Leu and St-Louis. South of St-Gilles-les-Bains, there is an option of two routes: *par les bas* (the low road) and *par les hauts* (the high road). The former is much quicker but the latter is useful if you want to reach La Possession, Rivière des Galets or Trois-Bassins. Buses leave approximately every half hour from either end.

St-Denis to St-Benoît
This bus travels via Rivière des Pluies, Ste-Marie, Ste-Suzanne, St-André and Bras-Panon. Get off at the terminal in St-André to catch a bus to Salazie, Hell-Bourg or Grand Îlet.

St-Pierre to St-Benoît
The coastal bus travels via Grand Bois, Petite Île, St-Joseph, Vincendo, St-Philippe, Tremblet, Ste-Rose and Ste-Anne. Alternatively, you can take the high road via Le Tampon, Plaine-des-Cafres and Plaine-des-Palmistes.

St-André to Salazie
There are around four buses daily between St-André and Salazie/Hell-Bourg; two of these continue from Hell-Bourg on to Îlet à Vidot. There is another bus which runs twice daily between St-André and Grand Îlet/Le Bélier.

St-Pierre or St-Louis to the Cirque de Cilaos
This route runs via La Rivière, Petit Serré, Pavillon, Peter Both and Palmiste Rouge. There are about eight buses each way on weekdays and Saturdays and less on Sunday (the Sunday routes don't include St-Pierre and only go as far as St-Louis). One or two of these continues to Îlet à Cordes, useful for reaching the Col du Taïbit trailhead, and quite a few connect Cilaos with the village of Bras Sec.

Fares work out at around FF0.50 per km and the last buses generally run between 7 and 8 pm. Timetables are available from the Syndicat d'Initiative or the *gare routière* (main bus station) in St-Denis.

Public buses in Réunion are luxurious Mercedes, Renault or Volvo touring coaches, complete with stereo radio and cassette players. Although there's a conductor, there is no bell to stop the bus; when approaching your stop you must yell *devant!* (ahead!) or clap your hands! Sometimes the radio is so loud that you also have to shout or whistle.

CAR

The road system on the island is excellent and it's well signposted. Route Nationale 1, the main road around the island, approaches motorway standards in parts.

La Corniche, built in 1963 along the sheer cliff face between St-Denis and La Possession, is said to be one of the world's most expensive stretches of road. As the road follows the old railway line through tunnels, it passes a network of artificial caves and shelters used for seismic tests.

Heading into the mountains via the cirque roads – especially the route into Cilaos – is a magnificent experience. The superbly engineered roads snake through hairpin bends, up steep slopes and along sheer drops, surrounded all the while by glorious – and distracting – scenery. Adding to the challenge are those local motorists who enjoy asserting their confidence on the road: small Peugeots, Renaults and Citröens either zoom past at dizzying speeds or intimidate cautious drivers into clearing out of the way. Anyone who's driven in France will have some idea; try to keep a cool head.

Road Rules

As with the rest of France, Réunion keeps to the right. To drive in Réunion, you must have either a valid French or international driver's licence.

Rental

In French, 'car hire' is *location de voitures* and, as you may imagine, there are quite a few firms specialising in providing wheels for visitors. Most companies stipulate that the driver must be at least 21 to 23 years of age, have held a driving licence for at least a year, have a passport or other piece of identity and hire the vehicle for at least one or two days. If your personal auto insurance isn't valid in Réunion, you'll also need to purchase CDW (collision damage waiver) insurance. Even with the insurance, you may be personally responsible for around FF4000 accidental damage to the vehicle; read the small print carefully.

With the main firms, prices and regulations don't vary much. If you don't have a credit card, you'll usually have to pay a cash deposit of anywhere between FF1000 and FF5000. In some cases, the total hire cost is payable in advance.

Expect to pay upwards of around FF200 per day for car hire (all taxes included and unlimited km). If you intend hiring a car for at least a couple of days, ask for a discount. Rental charges are often also subject to 9% value added tax. If you're receiving or dropping the vehicle at anywhere but the main rental office, there'll probably be delivery/collection charges as well. In addition, the hirer pays for petrol, which costs around FF6 per litre.

The good news is that there are some less expensive options. In most towns, there are smaller car-hire agencies (sometimes attached to a local garage) which charge about 20% less than the major firms. However, be warned that some of the cheaper places may give you an old rattletrap and ask for a hefty deposit. Another way of saving precious francs is to keep your eyes open for any special car-hire deals that pop up from time to time, especially during the low season.

Some major and minor car rental firms around Réunion include:

Au Bas Prix
    35 Rue Suffren, 97460 St-Paul (☎ 22 69 89; fax 22 54 27)
Avis Cotrans Cadjee
    17 Boulevard du Chaudron, 97490 Ste-Clotilde (☎ 48 84 84; fax 29 51 51)
ADA
    9 Boulevard Doret, 97400 St-Denis (☎ 21 59 01; fax 41 89 40)
Budget
    2 Rue Pierre Auber, 97490 Ste-Clotilde (☎ 28 92 00; fax 28 93 00)
Citer Foucque
    69 Boulevard du Chaudron, 97490 Ste-Clotilde (☎ 48 87 87; fax 48 87 99)
Europcar/Inter Rent
    1 Boulevard Doret, 97400 St-Denis (☎ 21 81 01)
    Coralia Novotel, Les Filaos, 97434 St-Gilles-les-Bains (☎ 24 51 15)
Euro Location
    91 Rue d'Après, 97400 St-Denis (☎ 20 06 11; fax 21 38 17)
Europcar
    Gillot La Ferme, 97438 Ste-Marie (☎ 93 14 15; fax 93 14 14)
Euro Rent
    Ave de Lattre de Tassigny, 97490 Ste-Clotilde (☎ 28 85 85; fax 28 86 00)
ERL
    14 Rue Léopold Rambaud, 97490 Ste-Clotilde (☎ 21 66 81)
    Rue Général de Gaulle, 97434 St-Gilles-les-Bains (☎ 24 02 25; fax 24 06 02)
GIS
    180 Rue Général de Gaulle, 97434 St-Gilles-les-Bains (☎ 24 09 73; fax 24 55 20)
    79 Chaussée Royale 97460 St-Paul (☎ 45 24 84; fax 45 48 99)
Hertz Locamac
    82 Rue de la République, 97400 St-Denis (☎ 21 06 14; fax 41 39 42)
ITC Tropicar
    12 Rue Mahatma Gandhi, 97419 La Possession (☎ 43 07 03; fax 42 15 74)
Location St-Gilles
    216 Rue Général de Gaulle, 97434 St-Gilles-les-Bains (☎ 24 08 18; fax 24 05 63)

MOTORCYCLE

Although mopeds, Vespa scooters and motorcycles will be useful for getting around in a small area, those who would use them as a means of long-distance transport will largely share the concerns of cyclists: the amount and speed of traffic, and the steep and winding nature of mountain roads. Although both the coastal and highland roads are in good condition, beginner bikers should think twice – and have a good insurance policy – before attempting them. There are not many places that rent out motorcycles; St-Gilles-les-Bains probably has the most possibilities – ask at any tourist office.

BICYCLE

Due to the traffic, the haste of most motorists and the steep and precarious nature of the mountain roads, those considering cycling as a form of transport in Réunion should be prepared for some hair-raising and potentially dangerous situations.

The coastal roads are too busy for casual cycling and the cirque roads are too steep, but the back roads and rugged terrain of the interior are ideally suited to mountain bikes.

Rental

In recent years, there has been a growing interest in the *vélo tout terrain* (VTT) or mountain bike, and several stations VTT have sprung up to provide information, hire bikes and organise backcountry tours. Most places charge around FF80/110 for a half/full day, but you may be able to get a better deal, especially if you intend to hire a bike for more than one day. If you're interested, ask at any tourist office or contact one of the following:

Cilaos Fun, Place de l'Église, 97413 Cilaos (☎ 31 76 99)
Loca VTT, 129 Rue Général de Gaulle, St-Gilles-les-Bains (☎ 24 44 64)
Location Bicyclettes, St-Gilles-les-Bains (☎ 85 92 09)
Parc du Maïdo, Route du Maïdo, La Petite France (☎ 22 96 00; fax 32 52 00)
Rando Bike, 100 Route du Volcan, Plaine-des-Cafres (☎ 59 15 88)
Vélos des Cimes, Rue des Trois-Mares, Cilaos (☎ 31 75 11)
VTT Evasion, 64 Rue Leconte Delisle, St-Philippe (☎ 37 10 43)
VTT Découverte, Place Julius-Bénard, St-Gilles-les-Bains (☎ 24 55 56; fax 24 51 79)

RÉUNION

HITCHING

Hitching is never entirely safe in any country and is not recommended, especially for women. Travellers who make the decision to hitch should be aware that they are taking a small but potentially serious risk. For those who do decide to hitch, hopefully the below advice will help to make their journeys as fast and safe as possible.

Getting a lift in Réunion is subject to pretty much the same quirks of luck and fate that one experiences hitching anywhere. Your chances may be better if you're away from the tourist beats, where curious local people will help you. If you're tramping around the cirques in the rain, you'll probably be passed by carloads of other less sympathetic tourists. Hitching on the main roads can be more difficult, primarily because vehicles travel so fast, it's difficult (and dangerous) to stop in a hurry.

The standard advice not to hitch at night applies in Réunion, too. Furthermore, women shouldn't hitch alone and even several women together shouldn't accept lifts from only men; ascertain there are women and/ or children in the vehicle before climbing in.

BOAT
Yacht

Yacht and catamaran charter companies run cruises around the island and further afield, mainly for diving and fishing expeditions. For further information, see Sea in the Réunion Getting There & Away chapter and Activities in the Réunion Facts for the Visitor chapter.

Motorboat

If you prefer to hire a boat and buzz around on your own, small motorboats are available for around FF1500 for a half day or FF7000 per week (it's worth bargaining to try and knock down the price a little). Larger boats rigged for deep-sea fishing may be hired for around FF2600 to FF3000 per day. Contact Abysses (☎ 41 22 90; fax 21 65 59) at the Port de Plaisance de la Pointe des Galets in Le Port. Also see Activities in the Réunion Facts for the Visitor chapter.

LOCAL TRANSPORT
The Airport

A taxi between St-Denis and Roland Garros airport costs FF100 by day and FF150 after dark. The airport is about 11km east of St-Denis.

A special airport bus travels frequently through the day between Roland Garros airport and gare routière (St-Denis); it costs FF25 per person. For details, ask at the tourist information counter at the airport. To catch the regular public bus into St-Denis, walk straight across the airport car park and under the motorway flyover, then continue along the road leading up the hill. The bus stop is several hundred metres away on the right. The bus to catch is coming from St-Benoît (or Ste-Marie).

Taxi

Taxis operate in the towns on the normal hire-on-demand basis. In country areas, where there are no buses, they operate on a scheduled *taxi-collectif* timetable.

Regular taxi fares start with FF28 on the meter and an FF10 surcharge at night. To give you an idea of prices (during the day), it costs FF250 from St-Denis to Boucan Canot beach; FF100 from St-Denis to Roland Garros airport; and at least FF800 from St-Denis to Cilaos.

It's also possible to hire a taxi and driver for a day tour around the island. You'll pay around FF1000 for the day – it's best to share with other people, so you can split the cost. It's definitely worth negotiating a fare, especially if you intend hiring a taxi for at least half a day. Book in advance through one of the island tour operators (see Organised Tours below), through a Syndicat d'Initiative, or direct with taxi drivers. If you have friends in Réunion, ask them if they know of a good (and reasonably priced) taxi driver.

There are usually taxi stands in most of the major towns including St-Denis, St-Pierre, Le Tampon, St-Benoît, St-Leu, Salazie, St-Paul and St-André.

Taxi-collectifs are usually Peugeot station wagons, seating up to eight people, which run from the main towns out to the surrounding villages. The timetables should be posted at the taxi stands. Alternatively, ask local shopkeepers, or chambre and table d'hôte owners. The taxi-collectifs generally circulate from around 7 am to 6 pm (although there's a later one between Cilaos and St-Louis) and they cost about the same as buses.

ORGANISED TOURS

If you're visiting on a brief stopover (such as a day tour from Mauritius) or if you prefer to leave the organisation to someone else, you may want to approach the private tour agencies. Their offerings range from bus-based sightseeing tours to more adventurous and offbeat options. Travellers have complained that some of the cheaper tour operators don't provide a very good service. It may be worthwhile paying a little more in the end to avoid disappointment – remember to always ask what is included before you pay.

To give you some idea of costs, Bourbon Voyages (see below for address) offers a bus tour (from 7.30 am to 5 pm) of one of the cirques for FF380 per person, including lunch. A 4WD day tour to the volcano costs FF630 per person, including lunch. They can also arrange other things, including helicopter tours, fishing trips and scuba diving excursions. If you're after an English-speaking guide, it may be possible with advance notice.

Souprayenmestry (☎ 44 81 69; fax 44 91 62) offers various bus day tours. Some of these include: a tour to Salazie on Tuesday; to Maïdo on Wednesday; to the volcano on Friday, and to Cilaos on Saturday. Each tour costs FF98/50 for adults/children. Some of Réunion's tour operators include:

Agora Voyages
192 Rue Général de Gaulle, 97434 St-Gilles-les-Bains (☎ 33 08 08; fax 33 08 09)
Atlas Voyages
104 Rue Général de Gaulle, 97434 St-Gilles-les-Bains (☎ 24 35 00; fax 24 38 00)
Bourbon Voyages
14 Rue Rontaunay, 97463 St-Denis (☎ 94 76 94; fax 41 72 85). Bourbon Voyages is the American Express affiliate and has offices in St-Benoît (☎ 50 25 25), St-Pierre (☎ 25 03 18), St-Louis (☎ 26 11 36), St-Leu (☎ 34 78 78), St-Joseph (☎ 56 24 77) and Le Tampon (☎ 27 27 10).
Comète Voyages Réunion
Angle de la (corner of) Rue Jules Auber and Rue Moulin à Vent, 97400 St-Denis (☎ 21 31 00; fax 41 37 71)
Euro-Voyages Réunion
20 Rue de l'Est, 97400 St-Denis (☎ 21 89 00; fax 41 30 00)
L'Orion Voyages
22 Résidence Bénédicte, 97434 St-Gilles-les-Bains (☎ 24 64 24)
Nouvelles Frontières
92 Rue Alexis de Villeneuve, 97400 St-Denis (☎ 21 54 54; fax 20 26 37)
Objectif
Chemin Summer, 97434 St-Gilles-les-Bains (☎ 33 08 33; fax 24 26 80)
Papangue Tours
5 Rue de Nice, 97400 St-Denis (☎ 41 61 92; fax 41 61 96)
Réucir Voyages
45 Rue Juliette Dodu, 97400 St-Denis (☎ 41 55 66; fax 21 02 51)
Ségatours
35 Rue Ste-Anne, 97400 St-Denis (☎ 20 37 30)
Tropic Voyages
15 Ave de la Victoire, 97400 St-Denis (☎ 21 03 54; fax 21 54 44)
Voyages Mutualistes et Coopératifs
14 Boulevard Doret, 97400 St-Denis (☎ 94 77 17; fax 94 77 21)
VVF Voyages
L'Hermitage, 97434 St-Gilles-les-Bains (☎ 24 39 78; fax 24 00 17)

RÉUNION

St-Denis

HIGHLIGHTS

- The architectural splendour of Créole mansions
- A stroll down Le Barachois, the seafront park lined with cannons and cafés
- The interesting Musée Léon Dierx art gallery
- The hill districts of La Montagne and Le Brûlé, offering majestic views and great jumping-off points to some terrific treks

St-Denis (pronounced 'san-de-NEE') is an attractive, lively and expensive capital city. Even visitors with a healthy supply of cash may feel a bit alien unless they have local friends to introduce them around the café set or some other clique. Perhaps that's why most tourists don't remain longer than it takes to book gîtes de montagne and arrive or depart from the island.

St-Denis is known to some as the Paris of the Indian Ocean but unlike Paris, you won't find loads of down-at-heel student travellers struggling to survive on a slim budget. In their place are legions of hopeful workers from Madagascar, Mauritius, the African mainland and the EU – some legal and some not – searching for lucrative employment in the Indian Ocean's extension of the developed world.

History

St-Denis was founded in 1668 by the governor Regnault. Its name was taken from the Rivière St-Denis, on whose banks it was built (the river was named for a ship which ran aground there in 1667). In 1738, the capital was shifted to St-Denis from St-Paul by the governor Mahé de La Bourdonnais. Numerous attempts at constructing a harbour near Le Barachois were foiled by a succession of cyclones.

Today, the population of this buzzing capital city and its suburbs is about 130,000, of whom around 50,000 live in the centre.

The traffic in town can sometimes be a veritable nightmare – especially from around 7.45 to 9 am and 4 to 6 pm, when cars clog the roads and traffic moves at a snail's pace – avoid the roads at these times if you want to keep your sanity!

Orientation

The main shopping area is strung along Rue Maréchal Leclerc and several blocks north of it. Where Rue Maréchal Leclerc turns the corner at Rue Charles Gounod and heads eastward out of town, the shops head downmarket; here one finds small shops and stalls selling relatively inexpensive clothing and other goods.

The chic area of town is Le Barachois, St-Denis' promenade venue, which lies at the western end of the waterfront. Here are the upmarket bars and sidewalk cafés as well as the Hôtel Le Saint-Denis, one of the town's ritziest places to stay.

Information

Tourist Offices Tourist queries should be taken to the tourist office known as the Syndicat d'Initiative de St-Denis (☎ 41 83 00; fax 21 37 76), 48 Rue Sainte-Marie. However it may be shifting to Maison de la Montagne (see below), so check first. Several of the staff speak English and they can provide plenty of information, maps and brochures. There's a public phone here as well as toilets. The office is open Monday to Friday from 8.30 am to 1 pm and 2 to 5.30 pm and on Saturday from 9 am to noon and 2 to 5 pm.

If you're looking for information on any forthcoming events, make inquiries at the Syndicat d'Initiative or call the Office Départemental de la Culture (☎ 41 11 41; fax 41 55 71). For trekking information and bookings, go to Maison de la Montagne (☎ 90 78 78; fax 41 84 29) at 10 Place Sarda Garriga (near Le Barachois). You can plan your itinerary using the large model of the island in their office. For further information about trekking and gîtes de montagne, see the Trekking in Réunion chapter and Accommodation in the Réunion Facts for the Visitor chapter.

Foreign Consulates Since Réunion is not an independent country, St-Denis lacks the usual complement of embassies and consulates befitting a capital city. Countries with diplomatic representation are listed under Embassies in the Réunion Facts for the Visitor chapter.

Money The main banks (all located in the city centre) are Banque de la Réunion (BR), Crédit Agricole (CA), Banque Nationale de Paris Intercontinentale (BNPI) and Banque Française Commerciale (BFC) and all will change money. They're open Monday to Friday from 9 am to 4 pm. The money-exchange counter at Roland Garros airport is open Monday to Friday from 10 am to 1.30 pm and 3 to 6.30 pm; on Saturday from 8.30 to 11.30 am (closed Sunday).

The American Express agency is Bourbon Voyages (☎ 94 76 94; fax 41 72 85) at 14 Rue Rontaunay but they don't change money or travellers cheques.

Post & Communications The main post office is on the corner of Rue Maréchal Leclerc and Rue Juliette Dodu and is open Monday to Friday from 7.30 am to 6 pm, and on Saturday from 8 am to noon. Poste restante is also at the main post office.

There's also a post office at Roland Garros airport which is open Monday to Friday from 9.30 am to 12.30 pm and 1.30 to 4.30 pm and on Saturday from 8 to 11 am.

There are a few coin phones in St-Denis. Télécartes with 50 (FF37) or 120 (FF87) impulses can be purchased at post offices and at a number of shops.

Travel Agencies For details on tour operators, see Organised Tours in the Réunion Getting Around chapter.

Bookshops The attractive Librairie Papeterie Gerard (☎ 20 08 15; fax 21 34 51) is on Rue de la Compagnie. It has an excellent range of well-displayed titles (almost entirely in French), but few newspapers or magazines. It's open Monday to Saturday from 8.30 am to noon and 2 to 6.30 pm.

L'entrepôt (☎ 21 90 99; fax 20 18 69), opposite the Ritz cinema on Rue Juliette Dodu, has a good selection of predominantly French-language books. There is also a range of French and English-language newspapers and magazines. The shop is open Monday to Friday from 9 am to 6.30 pm; on Saturday from 9 am to 12.30 pm and 2.30 to 6.30 pm.

The less impressive Librairie de la Réunion (☎ 21 01 58), on Ave de la Victoire, has an assortment of French-language books. It supplies the university across the street, so it also carries a few English-language titles. This place is open Monday to Saturday from 8.30 am to 6 pm. There are also some bookshops on Rue Juliette Dodu.

Le Tabac du Rallye (☎ 20 34 66), a busy newsagent next to Le Rallye, has the best stock of French and English-language newspapers/magazines in town. It's open daily from around 6 am to 11 pm. Apart from a plethora of French newspapers and magazines, it also has the widest selection of English publications in Réunion, including: *The Sun* (FF12), *The Daily Telegraph* (FF19), *The Mirror* (FF13.50), *The Independent* (FF19), *The Observer* (FF29.50), *The European* (FF30), *Financial Times* (FF26.50), *Time Magazine* (FF36) and *Newsweek* (FF36). It also stocks some Chinese, Italian and German publications.

Laundry There's a dry-cleaning service and automatic laundrette, Pressing Arc-en-ciel (☎ 29 43 94), at the Continent shopping complex (between St-Denis and Roland Garros airport). The machines cost FF30 to wash up to 7kg and FF2 per five minutes to dry. Washing powder costs FF2 per load. There's also a dry-cleaning service here; they charge FF45 to dry-clean trousers.

The more centrally located Pressing Blanchisserie (☎ 21 87 48), on Rue Juliette Dodu, charge FF15 for washing and drying

RÉUNION

1kg of clothes (self-service), or FF40 if you want them to do it for you. To get a shirt dry-cleaned will cost you FF25; trousers are FF35.

Créole Houses & Interesting Buildings

There is a variety of impressive Créole mansions in St-Denis; the larger ones are mainly strung out along Rue de Paris between Rue Pasteur and Rue Roland Garros. They include the family home of former French prime minister under Giscard d'Estaing, Raymond Barre, which is near the corner of Rue de Paris and Rue Maréchal Leclerc.

Smaller places are just as charming, and since the grounds are generally more compact, you'll get a better look at the characteristic verandahs and intricate lambrequins (ornamental window and door borders). The best advice is to wander and see what you discover. Good places to begin include along Rue Alexis de Villeneuve between Rue Juliette Dodu and Rue Jean Chatel; along Rue Juliette Dodu just south of Rue Alexis de Villeneuve; along Juliette Dodu just south of Rue Monseigneur de Beaumont; and along Rue Roland Garros between Rue Juliette Dodu and Rue Jean Chatel.

Also of interest are the Monument aux Morts, the tall victory monument; the hôtel de ville (town hall), considered by many to be the city's most beautiful building; the Cathédrale de St-Denis, built between 1829 and 1832; the university, opposite the cathedral (built in 1759), which also served as a religious school, a barracks and a hospital; and the Préfecture which was begun in 1735 by Governor Dumas, and served as the Compagnie des Indes headquarters. In front of the building is a statue of the former governor, Mahé de La Bourdonnais.

Musée Léon Dierx

More an art gallery than a museum, the Musée Léon Dierx (☎ 20 24 82) is housed in the former bishops' palace, constructed in 1845, and situated on Rue de Paris, near Rue Sainte-Marie. Most of the paintings, by both French and Réunionnais artists, date from the turn of the last century. The collection was donated by art dealer Ambroise Vollard and includes a lithograph by Renoir, a bronze by Picasso and works by Chagall, Cézanne, Delacroix, Degas and Gauguin. The museum is named after the Réunionnais poet and painter Léon Dierx (1858-1912). It's open daily, except Monday, from 9 am to noon and 1 to 5 pm. Admission is free.

Jardin de l'Etat & Musée d'Histoire Naturelle

The Jardin de l'Etat was originally established beside the river by the French East India Company in 1764. In 1773, after several floods, it was relocated and named the Jardin du Roi. For many years it served as a repository for the plants and crops destined for distribution to local planters. In 1834, the Palais Législatif was constructed and 20 years later, Mayor Gustave Manes installed in it the Musée d'Histoire Naturelle (Natural History Museum), and renamed the garden Jardin Colonial. The name wasn't changed to Jardin de l'Etat until Réunion became a full French département.

The gardens are quiet and well kept, featuring numerous perfume plants, tropical oddities from around the world and lots of orchids. You may also want to take a look at the monuments to the botanist Pierre Poivre, who was based on Mauritius (Île de France) and to agronomist Joseph Hubert from St-Benoît, who brought many useful agricultural specimens – including cloves, mangosteen, lychees, jamalac and breadfruit – to Réunion.

While the Musée d'Histoire Naturelle (☎ 20 02 19) isn't spectacular, it does contain stuffed specimens of the island's former fauna, including dugongs, giant tortoises, the crested bourbon bird and even a rare coelacanthe caught off the Comoros islands. The museum is open Monday to Saturday from 10 am to 5 pm. Entry costs FF10 for adults and FF5 for children.

Le Barachois

This seafront park, lined by cannons facing out to sea, is the main promenade venue in St-Denis. The park has *boules* matches, cafés and a monument to the French aviator Roland Garros, the first pilot to cross the Mediterranean and the inventor who worked out a way of timing machine-gun fire so it could be directed through a turning propeller. In 1988, Réunion commemorated the centenary of Garros' birth in St-Denis.

Nearby is Place Sarda Garriga, with its pleasant park. It was named after the governor who abolished slavery in Réunion on 20 December 1848.

Hindu Temple

The small but wildly colourful Hindu temple stands out among the shops east of the centre along Rue Maréchal Leclerc, opposite Rue de Montreuil. If you wish to visit, do so with respect (see Society & Conduct in the Facts about the Region chapter at the beginning of the book). Remember to remove your shoes and any leather items. Photography is not allowed.

Grande Mosquée

The Grande Mosquée (Masjid Noor-E-Islam) is near the corner of Rue Maréchal Leclerc and Rue Jules Auber. It is open daily from 9 am to noon and 2 to 4 pm. This is a place of worship so if you wish to visit, dress and behave with respect (see Society & Conduct in the Facts about the Region chapter). Shoes have to be taken off and photography is not permitted.

Grand Marché

The Grand Marché on Rue Maréchal Leclerc is the main handicraft market in St-Denis, although it's not as atmospheric as the market in Port Louis (Mauritius). There's a mishmash of items for sale including Malagasy wooden handicrafts, spices, baskets, embroidery, T-shirts, furniture and a jumble of knick-knacks. The prices are rather inflated, so it's certainly worth trying to bargain them down. The market is open daily from around 8.30 am to 5.30 pm. There are usually a larger number of stalls during the tourist season. The **Petit Marché**, about 2km east of the Grand Marché, predominantly sells fruit and vegetables.

La Montagne & Le Brûlé

These hill districts behind St-Denis offer great views over the town and are starting points for treks to Plaine d'Affouches, La Roche Écrite and even over the mountains into the Cirque de Salazie. Access to these areas is by taxi or bus up the steep, winding roads; to reach Le Brûlé at 800m, take bus 23/23A from the gare routière. For La Montagne, take bus Nos 21 or 22.

From Le Brûlé, there are some pleasant walks along the Route Forestière de la Roche Écrite. One of the nicest is to the waterfall, Cascade Maniquet, about 4km from the village.

Another possibility is Bassin du Diable, a wild and isolated valley accessible from upper Bellepierre, the first village downhill from Le Brûlé. The track turns off to the right (headed uphill) at a small reservoir. The valley lies about 4.5km along this track, which traverses the slopes above the eastern side of the Rivière St-Denis.

La Roche Écrite

Like the higher Piton des Neiges, this 2277m peak is often obscured in clouds. Although it isn't technically *in* the Cirque de Mafate, it does offer a spectacular view of the lower cirque. Dawn is the best time to see it. There is a choice of four routes to reach the peak:

- Along RF1 from Le Brûlé village above St-Denis to the GÉte de la Plaine des Chicots (La Roche Écrite) (three hours), then to Caverne des Soldats, through huge slabs of lava and limestone, and the summit (1½ hours).
- From Le Quinzième hamlet on the La Montagne road by footpath (at least four hours) or GR R2 *variante* from the kiosk overlooking the upper Rivière St-Denis to the Plaine d'Affouches (two hours) and on to join the Le Brûlé route at the GÉte de la Plaine des Chicots (La Roche Écrite) (two hours). From there, it's at least 1½ hours to the summit.
- From Grand Îlet along the road to Mare à Martin. The path winds precariously up the side of the mountain, making it a steep and difficult climb that is only for the fit. Allow at least two hours for the ascent.
- From Dos d'Ane east along the Cirque rim to the GÉte de la Plaine des Chicots (La Roche Écrite) (about three hours) to meet up with the previously described routes.

RÉUNION

REUNION

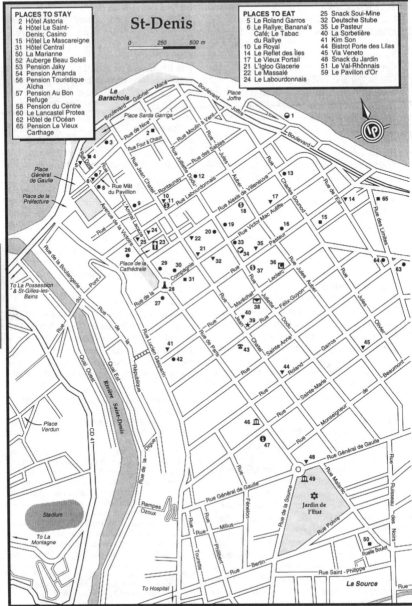

PLACES TO STAY
2   Hôtel Astoria
4   Hôtel Le Saint-
    Denis; Casino
15 Hôtel Le Mascareigne
31 Hôtel Central
50 La Marianne
52 Auberge Beau Soleil
53 Pension Jaky
54 Pension Amanda
56 Pension Touristique
    Aïcha
57 Pension Au Bon
    Refuge
58 Pension du Centre
60 Le Lancastel Protea
62 Hôtel de l'Océan
65 Pension Le Vieux
    Carthage

PLACES TO EAT
5   Le Roland Garros
6   Le Rallye; Banana's
    Café; Le Tabac
    du Rallye
10 Le Royal
14 Le Reflet des Îles
17 Le Vieux Portail
21 L'Igloo Glacerie
22 Le Massalé
24 Le Labourdonnais
25 Snack Soui-Mine
32 Deutsche Stube
35 Le Pasteur
40 La Sorbetière
41 Kim Son
44 Bistrot Porte des Lilas
45 Via Veneto
48 Snack du Jardin
51 Le Val-Rhônnais
59 Le Pavillon d'Or

St-Denis

0   250   500 m

OTHER		29	Librairie de la Réunion
1	Gare Routière	30	Librairie Papeterie Gerard
	(Main Bus Terminal)	33	Air Madagascar
3	Maison de la Montagne	34	Madagascar Consulate
7	Air Austral	36	Grande Mosquée
8	Air France	37	Banque Nationale de Paris
9	Bourbon Voyages		Intercontinentale
	(American Express)	38	La Poste (Post Office)
11	Banque de la Réunion	39	Police
12	Pressing Blanchisserie	42	Grand Marché
13	Air Mauritius	43	France Telecom
16	Plaza Cinema		(Telephone Office)
18	Banque Française	46	Musée Léon Dierx
	Commerciale	47	Syndicat d'Initiative
19	Ritz Cinema		(Tourist Office)
20	L'entrepôt	49	Jardin de l'Etat;
23	Cathédrale de St-Denis		Musée d'Histoire Naturelle
26	University	55	Église St-Jacques
27	Hôtel de Ville	61	Hindu Temple
	(Town Hall)	63	Petit Marché
28	Monument aux Morts	64	Prisunic

Organised Tours

There's a city tour from 9 to 11 am every Tuesday and Thursday which takes in all the main sights. It costs FF50 per person and should be booked at least one day in advance at the Syndicat d'Initiative (see Information earlier in this chapter). The Syndicat d'Initiative can also arrange other excursions such as helicopter tours.

For more details about tours, see Organised Tours in the Réunion Getting Around chapter.

Places to Stay

There is high local demand throughout the year for accommodation (especially budget) in St-Denis, so advance booking is highly recommended. Most establishments require at least partial advance payment. There are no chambres d'hôte in St-Denis and there are few rooms available for less than FF150 (double occupancy). The pensions are probably the cheapest option, but the cleanliness, facilities and service can be dodgy in some. Also, the standards can literally change overnight – it's probably best to check out a few places before deciding where to stay.

Places to Stay – bottom end

Pensions de Famille There is no shortage of cheap pensions in St-Denis.

Pension Au Bon Refuge (☎ 20 19 86; fax 20 12 68), at 13 Rue Saint-Jacques, is nothing fancy but tries to cater for travellers. There are individual rooms, some mere cubby-holes, as well as some communal rooms (the communal showers and toilets could do with a good scrubbing). It costs FF130/150 for a single/double and FF75 per person for a bed in a communal room. Breakfast costs FF15 and the set dinner is FF55 per person. The owners can arrange tours to various places around the island.

Pension Touristique Aïcha (☎ 20 37 02), at 24 Rue St-Jacques, opposite Pension Au Bon Refuge, is a nicer option. It charges FF125/150 a single/ double and FF20 per person for breakfast. Satiating Indian meals cost FF70.

Pension du Centre (☎ 41 73 02; fax 94 17 33), 272 Rue Maréchal Leclerc, is more like a hostel or unclassed hotel, hidden at the end of an alley between Rue Voltaire and a paved laneway. It's primarily an option for long-term contract workers and is a bit grubby but the owner, M Nassor, is a friendly character. Rooms with communal toilet start at FF120.

Pension Jaky (no phone), at 148 Rue Général de Gaulle, is a seedy joint that offers very basic facilities. Mainly catering to itinerant and contract workers, it's around FF50 for a dorm bed, but you might have to get them to change the sheets. At the time of writing there were rumours that this place may be closing down.

Pension Roger (☎ 41 24 38), at 22 Rue Mazagran (a couple of blocks east of the Jardin de l'Etat), charges FF55 per person in dormitory rooms. The service here can be rather sloppy at times.

Pension Butor (☎ 21 26 90), east of town at 6 Rue du Butor, costs around FF65 for a dorm bed, but this place is not highly praised by travellers. As with much of the bottom-end accommodation in St-Denis, most of the guests are long-term workers from Madagascar and Mauritius.

Pension Amanda (☎ 21 57 18), at 20 Rue Amédée Bédier (behind the Église St-Jacques), is a far more salubrious choice. Good singles/doubles go for FF130/170. Cooking facilities are available for self-caterers.

Pension Le Vieux Carthage (☎ 20 24 18), at 13 Rue des Limites, is popular with travellers and not a bad choice. There's a small restaurant out the front where you'll get a plat du jour for around FF40. Room rates are FF160/200 a single/double. Breakfast costs FF25 extra per person.

Auberge Beau Soleil (☎ 21 67 10; fax 21 62 11), at 93 Rue d'Après, south of Rue Général de Gaulle, offers singles/doubles for FF150/200. Evening meals cost an additional FF50 per person and breakfast is FF20. They also have dorm beds for FF100 per person, including breakfast.

Pension Le Palmier (☎ 41 55 55), at 16 Rue Saint Bernard, charges FF150 for a double, including breakfast.

Villa Les Bougainvilliers (☎ 29 12 96; fax 29 63 77), in the foothills east of town at 12 Ave Desbassyns in Ste-Clotilde, charges FF150/180 for a single/double. They also have studios from FF220 per night.

Pension Les Anthuriums (☎ 28 19 44), also in Ste-Clotilde at 26 Allée de l'Ancienne Poste, charges FF120/200 a single/double, breakfast included, with a minimum stay of three nights.

Le Home Fleuri de Cendrillon (☎ 23 63 28) is up in La Montagne. The minimum stay in this family home is three nights and single/double rooms with bath cost FF120/200 (breakfast is FF20 per person). They may offer discounts for long stays, especially in the low season.

Gîtes The gîtes detailed below are located in St-Denis' surrounding peaks.

Mme Sylvaine Robert (☎ 23 00 15), at 105 Route des Azelées up in Le Brûlé, is a good point of departure for walking trips to the Plaine d'Affouches and La Roche Écrite. A self-contained unit holds two guests and rents for FF1176 per week. Bookings may be made direct, or through the Relais Départemental des Gîtes de France (☎ 90 78 90; fax 41 84 29) at 10 Place Sarda Garriga in St-Denis.

Mme Jacqueline Lepée (☎ 23 02 32) also has a gîte in the mountain area, at 17 Chemin Cimetière in Le Brûlé. It costs FF550 for the weekend or FF1100 for the week (maximum of two people). Bookings for this gîte can also be made direct, or through the Relais Départemental des Gîtes de France (☎ 90 78 90; fax 41 84 29).

Zone de Loisirs du Colorado (☎ 23 74 12), or Colorado Leisure Area, has some tiny *cabanes* (cabins) renting for around FF40 per night. They're extremely basic but are an option if everything else is booked out. It lies within a half-hour walk of La Montagne village.

Gîte de Montagne All gîtes de montagne must be booked through the Maison de la Montagne in St-Denis or Cilaos (see Accommodation in the Réunion Facts for the Visitor chapter).

Gîte de la Plaine des Chicots (La Roche Écrite) (☎ 43 99 84) is high above St-Denis near the base of La Roche Écrite. The only access is by foot (for information, see La Roche Écrite earlier in this section). A bunk costs FF70 per person and breakfast/dinner is FF30/85.

Places to Stay – middle

Hôtel Le Mascareigne (☎ 21 15 28; fax 21 24 19), 3 Rue Lafférière, is one of the cheapest hotels in town. Basic singles/doubles with private bath cost FF230/260, or FF180/210 without bath; breakfast is included in the price. Try to take a look at a few rooms first, as some are better than others.

La Marianne (☎ 21 80 80; fax 21 85 00), near the Jardin de l'Etat at 5 Ruelle Boulot, is a popular, two star hotel with air-con rooms priced at FF250/300/360 a single/double/triple, including breakfast. The rooms are comfortable and the staff are friendly, making this place a splendid choice.

Hôtel Central (☎ 21 18 08; fax 21 64 33) is a two star hotel centrally located at 37 Rue de la Compagnie. Single/double/triple rooms with breakfast start at FF315/349/475; an extra bed is FF70.

Hôtel Astoria (☎ 20 05 58; fax 40 26 30), at 16 Rue Juliette Dodu, has 16 rooms; they charge FF220/300 a single/double. Breakfast costs FF30 per person.

Hôtel de l'Océan (☎ 41 43 08; fax 21 76 59), 10 Boulevard de l'Océan (near Rue Maréchal Leclerc towards the sea), is a 41 room hotel which is rather lacking in character. Singles/doubles cost FF250/300. Breakfast is an extra FF20 per person.

Le Lancastel Protea (☎ 94 70 70; fax 20 12 05) is a huge, 135 room place near the sea on Boulevard Lancastel. It's not great value for money – the rooms are dreary, the beds are hard and the service is lacklustre. If you're still interested, rooms (single/double occupancy) start at FF249 per night.

Les Jardins de Bourbon (☎ 40 72 40; fax 30 32 28) is a large residential-style two star hotel at Rampes de St-François. Studios (all with a kitchenette) cost FF300/2100/5500/4900/3500 for one night/one week/one month/two months/three months or longer. Rates are for single or double occupancy.

Places to Stay – top end

Hôtel Le Saint-Denis (☎ 21 80 20; fax 21 97 41), 2 Rue Doret at Le Barachois, is one of Réunion's most upmarket hotels. This four star place is centrally located, and has a swimming pool, bar and several restaurants. It is also very close to the casino. Air-con singles/doubles cost FF760/820. If you're in the mood to live it up, go for a suite which will set you back a cool FF1100.

Hôtel Mercure Créolia (☎ 94 26 26; fax 94 27 27), at 14 Rue du Stade in Montgaillard, is perched on the side of a hill and commands sensational views over the town. Although this four star hotel is not as central as the Hôtel Le Saint-Denis, it is a touch more impressive. Facilities include a large swimming pool, sauna, tennis court, bar and restaurant. Air-con doubles range from FF470 to FF850. Alternatively, they have a package which entitles you to a superior room, breakfast and hire car, for FF760 per day.

Places to Eat

Thanks to the French passion for *la gastronomie*, there's a restaurant or café around virtually every corner in St-Denis. New places keep springing up – ask locals for their recommendations. Lunch is somewhat of a sacred institution for the Réunionnais and this is especially evident in St-Denis. Most restaurants/cafés fill up between noon and 2 pm and during this time getting a table can be difficult.

At lunchtime, you should be able to get a reasonable *plat du jour* or *menu du jour* (set meal) for between FF40 and FF80, but to experience haute cuisine in Réunion, you'll have to bid *adieu* to a pile of francs.

You may also want to check the 'Restaurants' classified page in the daily newspapers for menus and special offers. Most cafés, bars and restaurants have a menu and price list on display, which saves embarrassing questions like *Combien?* Those pensions which serve meals are often a cheap option. Also reasonably cheap, are the small snack bars dotted around Place Sarda Garriga at Le Barachois, which sell fast eats for people on the run.

Snack Soui-Mine, near the corner of Rue Labourdonnais and Ave de la Victoire, is good value for weekday lunches. It is very popular with office workers and there can be queues at 12.30 pm, but they soon disappear. The set menu costs around FF35.

La Récreation (☎ 21 50 69), on Ave de la Victoire opposite the university, also gets busy at lunchtime. There are salads for FF35, while main dishes cost around FF45. It's open daily, except Sunday, from 7 am to 10 pm.

Snack du Jardin (☎ 21 76 57), opposite the Jardin de l'Etat, is a small and unpretentious Sino-Créole fast-food joint which is open Monday to Saturday from 6 am to 8 pm and only until lunch on Sunday. A big portion of sauté mine (fried noodles) is FF35, chop suey is FF30 and riz cantonnais (fried rice) costs FF25. There's also refreshing ice cream for FF7.

L'Igloo Glacerie (☎ 21 34 69), at 67 Rue Jean Chatel, is *the* place to indulge in a tantalising array of wild and wonderful ice cream creations (listed in a 20 page menu!). Their passionfruit ice cream is positively divine. Other tempting treats include strawberry sundae (FF44) and peach milkshake (FF33). There is also a variety of snacks; a toasted sandwich costs around FF42 – you might have to ask to see the snack menu.

La Sorbetière (☎ 21 19 06), on Rue Jean Chatel, is another super place for ice cream and they also whip up a range of snacks.

Le Royal (☎ 20 05 48), at 143 Rue Jean Chatel, is a good meeting place and is open daily except Sunday. It offers French and Créole food and is particularly popular at lunchtime with a three course set menu for around FF75.

Le Massalé is a little eat-in or takeaway place near the corner of Rue Alexis de Villeneuve and Rue Jean Chatel which serves authentic Indian snacks and sweets. There is a mouthwatering array of samosas – fish, crab, chicken – for around FF2.50 each. Balfi Amande, a traditional Indian sweet flavoured with almond, costs FF7.

RÉUNION

Le Vieux Carai (☎ 28 45 78), east of town at 74 Ave Leconte Delisle in Ste-Clotilde, serves good Créole and Chinese meals. It's open daily except Monday evening and Sunday.

Le Roland Garros (☎ 41 44 37), near Le Barachois, is a quiet and sophisticated place, which specialises in French and Créole cuisine. Dishes include octopus stew (FF86), ravioli (FF66) and grilled duck fillet (FF103). It offers terrace seating where you can put away a few Bourbons, read tasteful novels and just observe the passing scene. (Those in search of reading material will find magazines and newspapers at the nearby Le Tabac du Rallye.)

Le Pavillon d'Or (☎ 21 49 86), at 224 Rue Maréchal Leclerc, offers tasty, but slightly expensive, Chinese food. It's open daily, except Sunday, for lunch and dinner.

Deutsche Stube (☎ 21 14 26), at 34 Rue de la Compagnie, has a range of French and Créole cuisine. It's open every day except Sunday.

Kim Son (☎ 21 75 00) is a small Vietnamese restaurant at 13 Rue Maréchal Leclerc. It's upper midrange pricewise, but is wonderful for a little splurge. Try nems if you're after delicious Vietnamese spring rolls with mint and fish sauce. It's closed on Sunday.

Via Veneto (☎ 21 92 71) is a reasonably priced Italian restaurant at the corner of Rue Sainte-Marie and Rue Jules Auber. They are closed on Monday evening and on Sunday.

Le Reflet des Îles (☎ 21 73 82), at 27 Rue de l'Est near the corner of Rue Pasteur, is heartily recommended for Créole cuisine. It's open for lunch and dinner daily except Sunday and main dishes are around FF80. For a treat, try the lobster curry (FF130), followed by mango mousse (FF25). This is one of the few places in St-Denis that has a menu in English – but you'll probably have to ask for it.

Le Vieux Portail (☎ 41 09 42), 43 Rue Victor Mac Auliffe, offers terrific Créole food and grillades (grills). Main courses go for between FF50 and FF170. Desserts are from FF25 to FF45; try the assortment of Créole cakes for FF28. It's closed on Monday.

Le Pasteur (☎ 21 92 05), at 49 Rue Pasteur, serves tasty cuisine indienne (Indian cuisine). It's open daily for lunch and dinner.

Les Délices de L'Orient (☎ 41 44 20), at 59 Rue Juliette Dodu, is another speciality restaurant – this time in cuisine chinoise (Chinese cuisine). It's closed on Sunday.

Le Labourdonnais (☎ 21 44 26), at 14 Rue L'Amiral Lacaze, is one of the town's top French restaurants ... with top prices to match. It's great for a super special meal and is open daily, except Saturday lunch and Sunday. It's not a bad idea to book ahead.

Chez Piat (☎ 21 45 76), at 60 Rue Pasteur, is also pricey but does good French food. It's open daily, except Saturday lunch, Monday evening and all day Sunday.

Bistrot Porte des Lilas (☎ 41 45 55), at 173 Rue Jean Chatel, is another upmarket restaurant specialising in cuisine métro (French cuisine).

Le Val-Rhônnais (☎ 41 41 70), at 44 Rue Monthyon, is a homely little place which serves excellent 'Rhône Valley' cuisine. Main dishes are about FF90. They also do heavenly desserts for around FF35. It's open daily, except Saturday night and Sunday, from 11.30 am to 10 pm.

Le Kaloupilé (☎ 94 26 26), at the Hôtel Mercure Créolia (see Places to Stay), offers Créole and French main courses for around FF130 and desserts for FF35. There's a poolside seafood buffet dinner every Tuesday and a barbeque buffet dinner every Thursday; each costs FF180 per person (drinks cost extra). Nonresidents are welcome, but are advised to book ahead.

L'Oasis (☎ 21 80 20), at the Hôtel Le Saint-Denis (see Places to Stay), offers good eats in pleasant surroundings daily from 6.30 am to midnight. Main courses range from FF60 to FF145, or if you just crave something sweet, desserts are around FF40.

Continent, a large shopping complex between St-Denis and Roland Garros airport, has an array of shops including a very well-stocked supermarket. To give self-caterers some idea about prices, a small jar of coffee is FF13.95, cornflakes cost FF19.30, a loaf of bread is FF15 and a 1.5L bottle of coke is FF9.20. You can also buy alcohol here; a 12 pack of Bourbon beer is FF41.50, a can of Heineken beer is FF7.95 and South African wines range from FF26 to FF250 a bottle. This complex also has some popular eating places; salads cost around FF50, hamburgers are FF20, pizzas are around FF55 and a cappuccino is FF15.

Entertainment

For information about cultural activities call the Office Départemental de la Culture (☎ 41 11 41; fax 41 55 71) in St-Denis. It publishes a free monthly newsletter, *Trajectoires*, available at tourist and travel offices, giving details of forthcoming theatre, jazz and classical music performances, exhibitions, cinema and conferences, some of which have youth and student rates. Another good source of information is the *RUN* magazine, available free from the Syndicat d'Initiative and most hotels. It's also worth checking out the newspapers to see if anything special is happening in town.

Cinemas St-Denis has two main cinemas, the *Ritz* on Rue Juliette Dodu and the *Plaza* on Rue Pasteur. The Plaza sometimes (once in a blue moon) shows English-language films with subtitles. Tickets cost around FF45.

Casino The casino (☎ 41 33 33), near the Hôtel Le Saint-Denis, is open daily from 11 to 2 am. Admission is free but entry to the gambling section (American roulette, black jack etc) costs FF65 per person and is open from 10 pm. Everyone is expected to dress in smart casual (no T-shirts, shorts, sneakers etc) and you should have some identification with you.

Discos Little of Paris has rubbed off on St-Denis as far as nightlife goes but there are a few discos and clubs. Like anywhere else, places go in and out of fashion, so it's best to ask locals what the flavour of the month is. Be warned that drinks at most nightclubs are ridiculously expensive.

Banana's Café (☎ 20 31 32), near Le Rallye, is *the* place to be seen. This funky nightclub is full of cool people wearing cool clothes, saying cool things and drinking cool drinks. It's open every night except Monday; most people roll in after 10 pm.

Le First (☎ 41 68 25), at 8 Ave de la Victoire, is another disco, but is far less in vogue. It's closed on Sunday and Monday.

Le Club (☎ 30 42 72), on Boulevard de la Providence, is open Friday and Saturday night only.

Le Gin-Get (☎ 41 65 65), on Rue André-Malraux, is open every night except Sunday and Monday.

Le Shaker (☎ 20 39 69), at 20 Rue de Nice, usually runs piano jazz sessions with the house ensemble and various guest performers. It's open daily, except Sunday, from 6.30 pm.

Theatre There are frequent theatrical festivals and spectacles, normally with two or three plays per performance. Details of what's on can be found in the daily newspapers, or call the Office Départemental de la Culture.

Pubs The capital has a number of good watering holes, which are great for a cold beer and the opportunity to mingle with the locals.

Le Rallye (☎ 21 34 27), at the bottom of Ave de la Victoire, near Le Barachois, is a down-to-earth bar/café which is a popular hangout with the younger crowd. It's open every day from early morning until around midnight.

La Distillerie (☎ 21 80 20), the bar at the Hôtel Le Saint-Denis, often has live music performances – ring ahead to find out. *Le Guétali* (☎ 94 26 26) is another hotel bar, this time at the Hôtel Mercure Créolia. *Le Pub Alexander* (☎ 21 19 32), at 108 Rue Pasteur, is open nightly except Sunday.

Getting There & Away

The gare routière complex, near Place Joffre, contains both the city and long-distance bus terminals. See Bus in the Réunion Getting Around chapter for details on buses to and from St-Denis.

Getting Around

The Airport Taxis between St-Denis and Roland Garros airport cost FF100 by day and at night, the price shoots up to FF150.

There is a daily airport bus which frequently travels throughout the day between the airport and St-Denis (FF25 per person). In St-Denis, passengers are only picked-up/dropped at the gare routière.

To get the regular bus into St-Denis, you need to cross the airport car park, walk under the motorway flyover and follow the road uphill. It's about 300m from there to the bus stop. The bus you're looking for is St-Benoît to St-Denis and it will cost around FF6 into town. To reach the airport, take any St-Benoît bus from the gare routière or along Rue Maréchal Leclerc.

Bus St-Denis is relatively small and getting around the centre on foot is a breeze, but there is nevertheless a good city bus service. It goes just about everywhere in town. The city is divided into two zones – 1 (FF7.50) and all zones (FF12.50). Weekly passes for

RÉUNION

zone 1/all zones cost FF53/80; monthly passes cost FF179/252. Reduced fares are offered to students and children. Hang onto your ticket after boarding, as random checks are common.

Bus stops are well marked; work out the bus routes by trial and error or rely on locals to help sort you out. Alternatively, you can get a free booklet, *Plan du réseau Saint-Denis Bus* or *Le Guide Saint-Denis Bus*, which provides bus timetables and routes. These are available from the gare routière or the Syndicat d'Initiative.

Taxi Taxis around town are generally expensive and you won't get by paying about FF30 for even a hop of a couple of blocks. A trip across town will set you back at least FF60. If you intend hiring a taxi for at least a day, negotiate a discount.

RÉUNION

Around the Coast

There are surprising differences in atmosphere between the 15 or so main communities around the coast of Réunion. Some are quiet and insulated, others seem industrious and still others turn a vivacious and outgoing face on the world. For example, most people find St-Pierre lively and pleasant, but St-Benoît uninteresting. St-Philippe is a much nicer place than St-Joseph, and Ste-Suzanne is preferable to Ste-Marie. Keep in mind, however, that these are personal opinions and you may find the opposite to be true – and that even the most agreeable of towns will appear dead and dull on Saturday afternoon and Sunday.

For short-term visitors, the holiday and accommodation centre stretches from Boucan Canot just north of St-Gilles-les-Bains south to Étang-Salé-les-Bains. This area contains all of Réunion's paltry 30km of beaches. The south-eastern end of the island, however, is the emptiest, most remote and least developed region. It lies under the shadow of the volcano and in the path of lava flows.

While the west coast is lined with *filaos* (casuarina trees), the east coast is fringed by *vacoas* (screw pines). The fibre from its fronds is made into rope and you may see strands of it left to dry on the roadside.

The East Coast

STE-MARIE

After leaving St-Denis towards the east and before reaching Roland Garros airport and Ste-Marie, the coastal highway crosses the wide boulder-strewn beds of the Rivière des Pluies. Much of the time the riverbed is deceptively dry and one wonders if all that space between the banks is justified. During the cyclone season, however, a furious torrent of water rages down and often disrupts the commute into and out of St-Denis.

At Rivière des Pluies village is the locally

famous **shrine** of La Vierge Noire (the Black Virgin). Several legends are attributed to the shrine; one states that the olive wood virgin saved an escaped slave by allowing a bougainvillea to grow on the rock where he'd taken refuge, hiding him from his pursuers.

Places to Stay & Eat

Most travellers visit Ste-Marie on a day trip from St-Denis, accounting for the handful of restaurants but lack of places to stay.

Le Capricorne (☎ 48 81 70), at Roland Garros airport, is open daily for lunch and dinner. Although overpriced, their French and Créole food is not bad.

La Belle Étoile (☎ 53 40 78), a Chinese and French restaurant at Ravine des Chèvres-les-Bas, is open daily, except Wednesday and Sunday nights, for lunch and dinner. Expect to pay around FF70 for a meal.

Le Balzac (☎ 53 26 00), in La Mare, has a good choice of Chinese, Créole and French food.

Le Piton Fougère (☎ 53 88 04), 272 Route des Fleurs, offers traditional home-made Créole food at reasonable prices. You should book ahead.

STE-SUZANNE

Ste-Suzanne, one of the prettiest towns on the Réunion coast, was the site of the first population on the island; in 1646, 12 mutineers exiled by Governor Pronis from Fort Dauphin in Madagascar settled for three years at the site of present-day Quartier Français. The area is now a main sugar-producing centre, which will be obvious as you approach

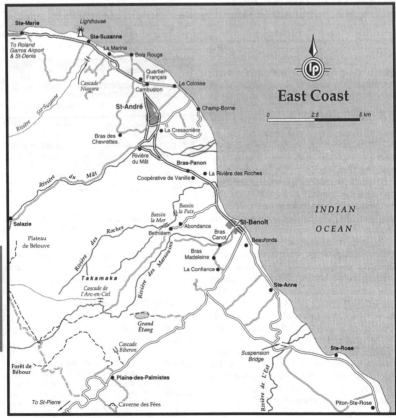

from any direction. The most imposing and beautiful structure at Ste-Suzanne is the classic lighthouse perched on the rocks near the western end of town.

Cascade Niagara

Just beyond the church on the highway south towards St-André is a track signposted to Cascade Niagara, a 30m waterfall on the Rivière Ste-Suzanne. From turning off the main road, go about 2km then bear right at the next two road junctions to wind up at the waterfall and attendant tropical pool. At the weekends, it's a popular picnic site.

Le Domaine du Grand Hazier

Garden fans will especially enjoy a visit to this 18th century sugar planter's residence, an official French historical monument, whose two hectare garden is planted with a variety of tropical flowers and fruit trees. It's open daily for guided tours by reservation only – call ☎ 52 32 81. A tour costs FF35 per person.

Places to Stay & Eat

Like Ste-Marie, few travellers stay in Ste-Suzanne. However, there are a couple of chambres d'hôte here, as well as some restaurants.

Mme Caladama (☎ 46 11 43), in Quartier Français, has a chambre d'hôte which offers doubles for FF140, including breakfast.

M Payet (☎ 46 10 78) has a gîte in Quartier Français and charges FF1905 per week (maximum of six people). It costs FF925 for the weekend.

Le Bocage (☎ 52 21 54), Chemin Bocage, has Chinese and French food on its menu and is open daily, except Monday, until 2.30 pm for lunch and until 10 pm for dinner.

Le Niagara (☎ 52 25 80), 79 Ave Pierre-Mendes-France, specialises in grillades et cuisine créole (grills and Créole cuisine).

ST-ANDRÉ

This town of over 30,000 people contains one of the largest Indian communities in Réunion thanks to a policy of importing cheap labour to work in the sugar cane fields after slavery was abolished in 1848. Today, St-André has two Tamoul (Tamil) temples, one known as Le Colosse near the coast north-east of town. The other, the Kali Temple with its monumental gateway, the Gopuram, is right in the centre on Ave de l'Île de France. The latter is open to visitors (shoes must be removed before entering).

In the church square and bus park, the cemetery and the town hall, there are large *ficus nitida* trees; these are known as *élastiques* by the Créoles, due to the elastic, rubber-like gum in their bark. Also, take a look at the Maison Valliamé, a classic Créole mansion on the main street.

Information

Tourist Office The local Syndicat d'Initiative is known as the Office Municipal de Tourisme de St-André (☎ 46 91 63; fax 46 52 16). It's found at 68 Centre Commercial de St-André, not far from the bus terminal. The office is open Tuesday to Friday from 8.30 am to noon and 1.30 to 5.30 pm. On Saturday it's open from 8.30 am to noon and 1 to 4.30 pm.

La Maison de la Vanille (Vanilla House)

At Rue de la Gare in the centre, this old Créole mansion is open to the public Tuesday to Sunday from 9 am to noon (last visit at 11.30 am) and 2 to 6 pm (last visit at 5.30 pm). It's set amid lawns, gardens and vanilla planta-

tions and visitors can learn the elaborate process of hand pollination necessary to coax the vanilla orchid to produce those gloriously aromatic beans we know and love. Admission costs FF25 per person (entry is free for children under 13). Guided tours are available with advance request – call ☎ 46 00 14.

Champ-Borne

If you are staying awhile in St-André, a trip to Champ-Borne on the coast is worthwhile. This place has borne the brunt of several cyclones and storms; in 1962, a tidal wave caused by Cyclone Jenny swept over the area and destroyed the local church. The remains still stand. Two shipwrecks dating to the turn of the last century lie just offshore.

Sugar Refinery

North of town at Bois Rouge, also on the coast, is a sugar refinery. Guided tours may be arranged through the Syndicat d'Initiative in St-Denis or the refinery itself (☎ 41 36 94).

Special Events

Tamil fire-walking ceremonies are normally held around January, while the Cavadee festival usually takes place in January/February. Contact the Syndicat d'Initiative for specific dates.

Places to Stay

Pluies d'Or (☎ 46 18 16), at 3 Allée des Sapoties in La Cressonnière, is a friendly pension de famille. Single/double rooms cost FF125/200, including breakfast.

Georges de Palmas (☎ 46 00 07) has a chambre d'hôte at Bras des Chevrettes. Singles/doubles are FF110/140.

Mme Gaston Cadet (☎ 46 56 37) has a chambre d'hôte on Rue du Stade. She also charges FF110/140 for a single/double.

Hôtel Île de France (☎ 58 18 50; fax 50 18 55), on Rue de Stade, has doubles for FF220. Breakfast is an additional FF30 per person.

Places to Eat

Le Ficus Nitida (☎ 46 01 41), at 2 Pont Minot, gets its name from the élastique tree. The cuisine at this restaurant stretches from French to Italian to Créole. The bill stretches from around FF60 to FF120 per person. You can eat here every day except on Monday and Tuesday evenings.

Le Beau Rivage (☎ 46 08 66), in Champ-Borne, at the Place de la Mairie (Town Hall Square), has Chinese, French and Créole dishes to choose from. It's open daily except on Sunday evenings and Mondays.

La Coupole (☎ 46 94 77), in the centre, is recommended for its fine Créole and French food. They also prepare some Chinese dishes. This place is open every day except Sunday and Tuesday nights.

Pluies d'Or (see Places to Stay) has a small restaurant which specialises in home-cooked Créole cuisine.

Le Saint-André (☎ 46 74 31), on Rue de la Gare, offers a hotchpotch of French, Chinese and Créole fare. It's closed every Sunday.

Le Restaurant Law-Shun (☎ 46 04 08) is on Ave de Bourbon and is a Chinese speciality place. There's a good range to choose from and the prices are not too high. It's open daily (except Sunday) for lunch and dinner.

Getting There & Away
All the buses between St-Denis and St-Benoît pass through St-André. If you're travelling to the Cirque de Salazie from St-Denis by bus, you will have to change buses at St-André. The drive up the valley of the Rivière du Mât to the cirque is astounding.

BRAS-PANON
Bras-Panon, with a population of around 8500, is Réunion's vanilla capital, so most visitors are interested in the government-run Coopérative de Vanille which was begun in 1968. Vanilla was first introduced in Réunion (the orchid is a native of Mexico) in 1819. However, lacking the Mexican insect responsible for pollination of the orchid (which in turn causes the fertilisation of the plant and the production of vanilla beans), it's necessary to pollinate by hand. The process was discovered in 1861 by Créole slave Edmond Albius and it's still in use today.

Information
Tourist Office The Coopérative de Vanille (see below) on Route Nationale also houses the Syndicat d'Initiative, or Office de Tourisme de Bras-Panon (☎/fax 51 50 62), which, among other things, can provide details about nice walks in the area. The office is open Monday to Friday from 8 am to noon and 1.15 to 5 pm.

Coopérative de Vanille
If you want to learn all there is to know about Réunion's famous *vanille Bourbon* and vanilla production in general, watch a video film of the vanilla production process and pick up a few samples. The factory and sales and exhibition shops are open Monday to Friday from 8 to 11.30 am and 1.30 to 4.30 pm; on Saturday from 9 to 11.30 am and 1.30 to 4.30 pm. Entry costs FF20 per person. For further information call ☎ 51 70 12.

Rivière des Roches & Cascade de la Paix
A pleasant walk follows along the Rivière des Roches to the waterfalls at Bassin de la Paix. If you want to have a go, head south on the main road past the Rivière des Roches and turn right at the first opportunity. Then turn right again and follow the road up the valley. After 4.5km, you'll reach a house from which a rough track descends to the lovely 10m-high falls.

Places to Stay
Gîte de Bethléem (no phone) is up on the hills about equidistant from Bras-Panon and St-Benoît. It accommodates up to 20 people and costs FF50 per person per day. Bookings should be made through the Syndicat d'Initiative in Bras-Panon (☎/fax 51 50 62).

Municipal camp site (☎ 51 58 59), near the river at Rivière des Roches village, is another cheap accommodation option. It's open year-round.

Places to Eat
Le Bec Fin (☎ 51 52 24), on the main road, offers scrumptious Créole and Chinese alternatives. It's open daily except Sunday evening and Wednesday.

Regal Exotique (☎ 51 60 84), on Chemin Lamartine in Rivière des Roches, is a Créole speciality restaurant.

Chez Nicolas (☎ 51 62 19), on Chemin Crépu, also serves Créole cuisine.

ST-BENOÎT
St-Benoît is another agricultural and fishing centre. It specialises in rice, spices, lychees, coffee, maize and sugar and also in the sprat-like delicacy *bichiques* (small fry of various species). These are caught at the mouth of the Rivière des Marsouins, which runs through the decidedly uninteresting centre of town.

Information

Tourist Office The Syndicat d'Initiative de St-Benoît (☎ 50 21 29; fax 50 88 49) is on 21 Route Nationale in the centre. The staff are helpful and there's a heap of free brochures as well as postcards and souvenirs for sale. It's open Monday to Friday from 9 am to noon and 2 to 5 pm; on Saturday from 9 am to noon.

L'Habitation du Cratère

Orchid afficionados won't want to miss this orchid cultivation centre which claims to have 30,000 plants, representing 1600 different species. It's located on Route Départemental 54 about 7km from St-Benoît. Visits must be arranged through the Syndicat d'Initiative in town.

La Confiance

About 6km from St-Benoît along the road towards Plaine-des-Palmistes is the village of La Confiance. It's the site of Le Domaine de la Confiance (☎ 50 90 72), a grand 18th century Créole mansion. It's considered a protected historical monument and is attended by a garden of lush tropical vegetation and a ruined sugar mill. It's open daily and entry is free. The owner, Mlle Nicole Carrère, runs a table d'hôte daily except Sunday, which is open to garden visitors by reservation only.

Catherine Lavaux says in her celebrated book on the island: 'If you have only one day to tour the island, go very early in the morning to the volcano then return to wait for your plane at La Confiance. You will have two unforgettable impressions and the desire to return'.

Grand Étang

Twelve km from St-Benoît along the road towards Plaine-des-Palmistes, before the L'Echo lookout point, is the turning onto a 6km road/track to Grand Étang, the 'big pond'. This mysterious-looking lake lies at the bottom of a vertical ridge separating it from the Rivière des Marsouins valley. It's an awesome spot.

Takamaka

The 15km drive (or walk, if you're very energetic) up the Rivière des Marsouins to Takamaka ends in glorious views of the Cascade de l'Arc-en-Ciel waterfall and an immense (for Réunion, anyway) hydroelectric complex. From the end of the road, there's a track that carries on to the Forêt de Bébour and eventually to Piton des Neiges and the three cirques.

Places to Stay

Hôtel Armony (☎ 50 18 38; fax 50 86 60), at La Marine, has a swimming pool and well-appointed singles/doubles for FF300/350. Breakfast is FF50 per person.

Hôtel Le Bouvet (☎ 50 14 96) is a small, unclassified hotel near the sea at 75 Route Nationale. Rooms (single or double occupancy) cost FF200; breakfast is an extra FF20 per person.

Hôtel Grand Étang (☎ 50 93 24), on Route des Plaines, towards Plaine-des-Palmistes, offers homely accommodation in the countryside. Doubles/triples cost FF250/350. There's also a restaurant (see Places to Eat).

Mme Marguerite Derand (☎ 50 90 76) has a chambre d'hôte near the school on Route de Cambourg, at 20 Chemin de Ceinture. She charges FF150 for a single or double room.

Places to Eat

Le Café de Chine (☎ 50 12 47), at the Place du Marché, obviously serves Chinese cuisine. It's closed on Thursday.

Le Lotus (☎ 50 21 92), on Ave Jean-Jaures, is another Chinese restaurant which is open daily for lunch and dinner, except on Sunday and Monday nights. They do good noodle dishes.

Hôtel Grand Étang (☎ 50 93 24), Route des Plaines, is reasonably good value and offers a range of Créole, Chinese and French food. It's closed every Monday.

Le Saint-Benoît (☎ 50 27 11), on Rue Mont-Fleury, does tasty Créole fare as well as French cuisine. Apart from Sunday, you can come here every day until 2.30 pm for lunch and until 10 pm for dinner.

Hôtel Le Bouvet (☎ 50 14 96) (see Places to Stay) has a restaurant which specialises in Créole and French cuisine. Nonresidents should book in advance.

Hôtel Armony (☎ 50 18 38) (see Places to Stay) has a more upmarket restaurant which also offers French and Créole dishes.

Getting There & Away

From St-Benoît, there's a scenic road that cuts across to St-Pierre and St-Louis, via the

RÉUNION

Plaine-des-Palmistes and Le Tampon. Alternatively, you can continue south along the scenic coastal road through Ste-Anne, Ste-Rose, St-Philippe and St-Joseph to reach St-Pierre. This is the way to go if you want to see Le Grand Brûlé, the eerie landscape created by lava from Piton de la Fournaise on its route to the sea.

There are several buses daily to St-Pierre via the high road and about four buses via the coastal road. Buses to and from St-Denis leave approximately every 15 minutes.

STE-ANNE
The village of Ste-Anne, about 8km south along the coast road from St-Benoît, is noted for its unusual church. Its cornerstone was laid in 1857 but the ornamental baroque-style stonework inside and out was intricately carved under the direction of one man, Father Daubemberger from Alsace, beginning in the 1920s. The style, ornately covered in fruits and flowers, is reminiscent of the renowned Mestizo architecture of the Andes in South America. 'Père Daubem' died in 1948; he was laid to rest inside the church itself.

STE-ROSE
The small fishing community of Ste-Rose has its harbour at the inlet of La Marine, where there's a monument (a lava pyramid in fact) to the young English commander Corbett, defeated and killed in an 1809 battle against the French commander, Bouvet.

Between Ste-Anne and Ste-Rose is a lovely old Pont d'Anglais suspension bridge over the Rivière de l'Est, now bypassed by the main highway. It's open to pedestrians, however, and there are nice picnic spots at the southern end. It's claimed it was the longest suspension bridge in the world at the time of its construction in 1894.

Notre Dame de la Lave
There's another famous church, Notre Dame de la Lave, at Piton Ste-Rose, 4.5km south of town. The lava flow from a 1977 eruption went through the village, split when it came to the church and reformed again on the other side. Many see the escape as a miracle of divine intervention. Just as miraculously, there was no loss of life during the eruption. A wooden log 'washed up' by the lava and found at the door of the church is now a memorial beside it. The road cuts through the solidified lava flow.

L'Anse des Cascades
About 3km south of Piton Ste-Rose, turn off towards the sea from the main road to reach L'Anse des Cascades. In this little fishing port, the water from the hills drops dramatically into the sea. It's worth a look, especially after it rains.

La Vierge au Parasol
From Bois Blanc, the road continues south along the coast, then climbs and drops into the 6km-wide volcanic ravine known as Le Grand Brûlé. Just inside the ravine, beside the road, is the shrine, La Vierge au Parasol. Yes, the Virgin Mary is holding a parasol. The brolly is not for protection against the sun or rain. It was set up by a Bois-Blanc planter at the turn of the century in the hope of protecting his vanilla beans from volcanic hellfire and brimstone.

Look out also in this area for the red shrines dedicated to St-Expédit (see boxed text in the Facts about Réunion chapter for more information).

Places to Stay & Eat
Mme Adam de Villiers (☎ 47 21 33), on the main road, has a small chambre d'hôte; single or double occupancy costs FF190. Dinner is an extra FF80 per person.

Rose Des Laves (☎ 47 38 77), on Chemin du Petit Brûlé, offers double rooms for FF120, or bungalows for FF200.

L'Anse des Cascades (☎ 47 20 42), at Piton Ste-Rose, is a small Créole restaurant which is open for lunch only (closed on Wednesdays). It may open in the evening if there's sufficient demand, so phone in advance if you're interested.

Les Deux Pitons (☎ 47 23 16), also in Piton-Ste-Rose, is open daily for lunch and dinner and serves Chinese, Créole and French cuisine.

Bel Air (☎ 47 22 50), Piton-Ste-Rose, specialises in Créole fare. It's closed on Mondays.

Entertainment
If you feel like grooving, Ste-Rose has a disco, *Roz d'Zil* (☎ 47 36 06), at the hamlet of Ravine Glissante about 1.5km south of town. It's open every Saturday.

Getting There & Away
There are around 10 buses daily between St-Benoît and Ste-Rose.

The South Coast

THE SOUTH-EAST CORNER
Along the route from Ste-Rose to St-Philippe, the Route Nationale crosses the deserted Le Grand Brûlé, the immense ravine formed by the main lava flow from the volcano, and the steep slopes of Les Grandes Pentes, the conduits for lava flows ancient and modern.

The last flow which reached the sea down this route was in 1976. In March 1986, the lava took a more southerly route and crossed the main road between Pointe du Tremblet and Pointe de la Table at Takamaka and Tremblet villages. This eruption added over 30 hectares to the island's area, but more than 450 people had to be evacuated and several homes were lost. In the 1992 eruptions, the lava slowed and cooled halfway down the slope and never threatened the road.

As one rounds the south-eastern corner from Le Grand Brûlé, the rugged lava coastline opens up a bit and the coastal plain widens, accommodating agricultural activities as well as the village of St-Philippe and, further along, the town of St-Joseph. There are a couple of viable beaches in the area which provide relatively uncrowded alternatives to the popular west coast beaches.

Information
Tourist Office At the Office de Tourisme de St-Philippe (☎ 37 10 43; fax 37 10 97), Place de la Mairie, Rue Leconte-Delisle, you can pick up information on the entire south-eastern coast of the island. It's open daily from 9 am to 5 pm.

Interpretive Centre & Les Sentinelles
On the roadside near the southern end of the Grand Brûlé, there's an interpretive centre with pictures and descriptions of what's going on there.

Just north of the interpretive centre is a turning inland marked 'Symboise pour Volcan et Oiseaux'. Follow this road about 1km to the parking lot, from which it's a 100m walk to the edge of the 1976 lava flow and a garden of bizarre sculptures known as Les Sentinelles. They were created by the Réunionnais sculptor Monsieur Mayo.

Volcano Climb
After the road makes its dramatic exit from the ravine near Tremblet, there's a GR R2 trailhead from which the extremely energetic can climb to the summit of the volcano, Piton de la Fournaise. It's a steep, rugged and normally wet walk and is considered one of Réunion's most challenging, so don't take it lightly. Traveller Frederic Belton of the USA writes, 'For any real masochistic trekkers looking for tough walks, I will heartily recommend the route up the volcano from le Tremblet via Nez Coupé du Tremblet...'

Plan on two to three days to reach the gîte at Pas de Bellecombe. An alternative route takes off from the village of Takamaka (not to be confused with the Takamaka region further north) and joins the Tremblet route at the Abri du Tremblet bivouac gîte. For more information on visiting the volcano, see Piton de la Fournaise in the Trekking in Réunion chapter.

Les Puits
Along the coast on either side of the village of St-Philippe is a series of four mysterious *puits* (wells), artificially dug into the lava rock; three of them are named after the French, English and Arabs, and the fourth is called Puits du Tremblet. The purpose of the wells and who created them is unknown. Some far-fetched theories even attribute them to the Egyptians!

A traveller writes:

Puits du Tremblet is accessible from the road via a short walking track just south of Le Grand Brûlé. The

RÉUNION

most interesting of the wells are the Puits des Anglais at Le-Baril, 4km west of St-Philippe, and the Puits Arabes, 5km in the opposite direction. The road to the sea at Basse Vallée takes you to Le Cap Méchant and the Puits des Français, providing a good view of the sea crashing against the black lava cliffs and rocks.

Notre Dame de la Paix

Near St-Philippe and on the other side of the road, is another curiosity – a cave in the rock face by the road which contains an altar and several rows of pews. This church cavern is called Notre Dame de la Paix.

Forest Walks

There are several forest walks *(sentiers forestières)*, zigging and zagging into the hills from Mare Longue, Le Baril, Basse Vallée and Langevin; the last two lead to tracks which eventually wind up at the Plaine des Sables and the volcano.

The Langevin track ascends the Rivière Langevin to meet up with the volcano road on the Plaine des Sables, passing lots of waterfalls and inviting pools along the way. It's a manageable 10km walk upstream to the waterfall, Cascade de la Grande Ravine, and the trout-laden waters of Grand Galet (you can also get there in a vehicle).

The Basse Vallée track ascends the hopefully named Vallée Heureuse (Lucky Valley) to connect with the Tremblet/Takamaka routes of the GR R2 from the east coast. See Places to Stay in this section for information about the Basse Vallée Gîte de Montagne.

The track from Mare Longue is especially interesting; known as a Sentier Botanique (Botanical Path), it features a variety of rare plants. There's also **Le Jardin des Parfums et des Épices** (the Fragrance and Spice Garden), a formal three hectare garden, planted with perfume-yielding plants, fruit trees and spices. This garden is open daily, except Tuesday, but you must book at least one day in advance if you wish to visit. It costs FF30/15 for adults/children. Visits (including a guided tour) may be arranged through the Office de Tourisme de St-Philippe (☎ 37 10 43; fax 37 10 97) on Rue

Leconte-Delisle (open daily from 9 am to 5 pm).

Places to Stay

The village of Le Baril is the base normally used by visitors. This is owing partly to its superb location above a stunning black lava coast and partly to the fact that there's no other place to stay in the area.

Hôtel Le Baril (☎ 37 01 04; fax 37 07 62), on the Route Nationale, is a small, two star hotel and restaurant set above the rocky shoreline among pandanus trees. They charge FF280/330 for a single/double. The hotel has a swimming pool and restaurant.

Basse Vallée Gîte de Montagne (☎ 37 00 75) is about 8km above the hamlet of Basse Vallée, along the Route Forestière de Basse Vallée or the GR R2 variante. The charge is FF70 per person per night; breakfast/dinner is an extra FF25/80. Bookings must be made through Maison de la Montagne in St-Denis or Cilaos (see Accommodation in the Réunion Facts for the Visitor chapter).

Places to Eat

Hôtel Le Baril (☎ 37 01 04) (see Places to Stay) has a good, if somewhat pricey, restaurant specialising in Chinese and Créole food. It's open daily from 11.30 am to around 10 pm.

Le Cap Méchant (☎ 37 00 61) at the cape of the same name in Basse Vallée offers tasty Créole cuisine, as well as Chinese alternatives. It's open daily for lunch and dinner.

L'Étoile de Mer (☎ 37 04 60) is also at Basse Vallée and also serves Créole and Chinese specialities. It's open daily from noon to 10.30 pm.

La Canot (☎ 37 00 36) offers Créole, French and Chinese fare; it's open daily from 9.30 am to 6 pm and for dinner with advance booking.

Le Pinpin (☎ 37 04 19), in Basse Vallée, offers an assortment of cheap munchies.

Getting There & Away

St-Philippe lies on the coastal bus route between St-Benoît and St-Pierre; there are around four buses daily in either direction.

ST-JOSEPH

St-Joseph, at the mouth of the magnificent valley of the Rivière des Remparts, is a rather dull town. The area (especially the nearby village of Vincendo) is known primarily for its production of baskets and bags from the fronds of the vacoa.

East of St-Joseph, it's possible to swim at the black-sand beach of La Marine de Vincendo, the old port for the village of the same name. The fishing community has since moved along to Langevin's harbour. The shady avenue leading to the coast is lined with vacoas.

Rivière des Remparts
The best view over the Rivière des Remparts valley is from the head of the valley at Nez de Boeuf, more than 30km north of St-Joseph on the road to the volcano. Other good views are available from lookout points near Notre Dame de la Paix village, accessible only via the town of Le Tampon.

From St-Joseph, there's a walking track which gently ascends the river valley for an incredible 30km, then arduously scales the valley headwall to meet the volcano road at Nez de Boeuf. It's probably better, and much more easily done, in the opposite direction as a means of returning from the volcano to the coast. Along the route at Roche Plate hamlet, there's a remote table d'hôte operated by Mme Begue (☎ 59 13 94).

By vehicle (or bus from St-Joseph), it's also possible to ascend for 22km along the eastern rim of the valley, through plantations of tea and geraniums to the village of Grand Coude. Along the route there are several scenic lookouts over the Rivière des Remparts.

Manapany-les-Bains
The main attraction in this area is Manapany-les-Bains, with a safe natural swimming pool between the rocks and Le Manapany, one of Réunion's most acclaimed restaurants (see Places to Eat).

Just west of the village is the spectacular Ravine Manapany. Here the road crosses a dramatic gorge and there's a steep pedestrian track leading down to the river mouth. Still further west, seaward from the village of Petite Île, is the attractive white-sand beach at Grande Anse. This was once a favourite bathing spot but there are now large placards

announcing that swimming is forbidden. However, if you're desperate to get wet, there is a protected bathing pool. Within sight is Petite-Île, Réunion's only offshore island, which serves as a sea bird nesting site.

Le Goyave to Petite Île
This circuit trip along some wildly twisting roads through the gentle and fertile heights from Le Goyave, through Les Lianes and Manapany-les-Hauts to Petite Île, will introduce you to sugar cane, vetiver, garlic and geraniums, among other produce. There are also superb views up towards the higher heights and down towards the sea far below. It's best in a private vehicle, naturally, but there are small short-haul buses from the *gare routière* (bus station) in St-Joseph which do the route.

Places to Stay
M Jean-Paul Grondin (☎ 56 51 66), on Boulevard de l'Ocean at Manapany-les-Bains, has three gîtes accommodating from three to eight people each. Per week it costs FF1300/1500/1900 for three/five/eight people.

Jean-Pierre Chan-Shit-Sang (☎ 56 14 44), over 20km inland at Grand Coude, operates a gîte and chambre d'hôte. For the former, he charges FF1100/1693 per weekend/week. The latter costs FF150 per person; meals are an extra FF90.

Mme Turpin (☎ 37 27 03) has a rather remote chambre d'hôte at La Crête, about 8km inland from Vincendo. Single/double accommodation costs FF100/140 and meals are FF75 extra.

Camp site (☎ 56 81 03), at Grande Anse, provides picnic tables, toilets and washing up areas.

Places to Eat
Le Manapany (☎ 56 55 58), in Manapany-les-Bains, is rated by many as one of the finest restaurants in Réunion and bills itself as a specialist in cuisine réunionnaise évolutive. Apart from its splendid location overlooking the sea, it's noted for special seafood dishes, and a good selection of house rums and punches. Meal prices range from around FF130 to FF220. It is open daily except Sunday night and Monday.

Le Tajine (☎ 37 32 51), in Vincendo, specialises in North African cuisine. It's open daily except Sunday and Wednesday nights.

Les Hirondelles (☎ 56 17 88), Rue Raphaël Babet, is a Chinese and Créole restaurant which is open daily except Monday.

RÉUNION

L'Orient Express (☎ 56 28 38), on the same street as Les Hirondelles, also serves Chinese and Créole fare and is open daily.

Chez Donald (☎ 34 41 28), in the same area as L'Orient Express, offers a similar menu and is closed on Sunday night.

Pizzeria La Gondole (☎ 56 16 12), on Rue Raphaël Babet, is great for pasta or pizza; it's closed every Tuesday.

Mme Gilette Técher (☎ 37 40 06) offers table d'hôte for FF80 up in the hills at Jacques Payet hamlet. Take the turn-off several hundred metres east of Bras-Panon village.

Getting There & Away

St-Joseph lies on the coastal bus route between St-Pierre and St-Benoît.

ST-PIERRE

More than 55,000 people make St-Pierre Réunion's third largest *commune* after St-Denis and St-Paul. Although St-Pierre has a pleasantly lively atmosphere, there's not really a great deal to see in or around the town.

Information

Tourist Office The Syndicat d'Initiative, known as the Office de Tourisme de St-Pierre (☎ 25 02 36), is at 17 Boulevard Hubert-Delisle. It isn't as helpful as most other tourist offices, but they do have tourist literature and can answer most queries. The office is open Monday to Friday from 8.30 am to noon and 2.30 to 5.45 pm; on Saturday from 10 am to noon and 3 to 4.45 pm.

Money The Banque de la Réunion is at 18 Rue des Bons Enfants and the Banque Nationale de Paris Intercontinentale is just opposite. They're open from 8 am to 4 pm during the week.

Post & Communications The main post office at 108 Rue des Bons Enfants is open weekdays from 7.30 am to 5 pm and on Saturdays from 8 to 11 am.

Interesting Buildings

There aren't many sights in the centre of town, but if you're near the hôtel de ville (town hall), it doesn't take five minutes to pop inside and have a look at this 200 year old building which was restored in 1975. The counter clerk should let you in and upstairs anytime between 9 am and 5 pm Monday to Friday.

On Rue des Bons Enfants is the Médiathèque (☎ 35 13 24), a cultural centre with exhibits.

There is also a mosque in the centre, on Rue François de Mahy, and a Hindu temple at La Ravine Blanche at the western end of town. Both are open to visitors; if you wish to visit do so with respect (see Society & Conduct in the Facts about the Region chapter at the beginning of this book).

Grave of Le Sitarane

In the cemetery at the western end of Boulevard Hubert-Delisle is the grave of the African bandit/sorcerer Le Sitarane, marked by a black cross. It represents a shadowy side of Réunion. At the turn of the last century, Le Sitarane and his men raided and robbed numerous homes in the St-Pierre and Le Tampon areas, killing the occupants and using their remains for purposes of black magic.

Eventually, the gang was surprised while raiding a house. They were caught, identified by objects they'd dropped while fleeing and sentenced to death by hanging. Today, the grave is apparently used for rites and offerings by people hoping to bring misfortune upon others.

Cockfighting

Although few foreigners will feel compelled to attend the occasional matches at 184 Rue du Four à Chaux, it's interesting to know that cockfighting is still a fairly popular gambling attraction among some Réunionnais. For further information on this rather barbaric pastime, ask at the Syndicat d'Initiative.

Market

The market, adjacent to the gare routière, is open Monday to Saturday from 7 am to 6 pm, and 7 am to noon on Sundays and holidays. Although mainly a fruit and vegetable

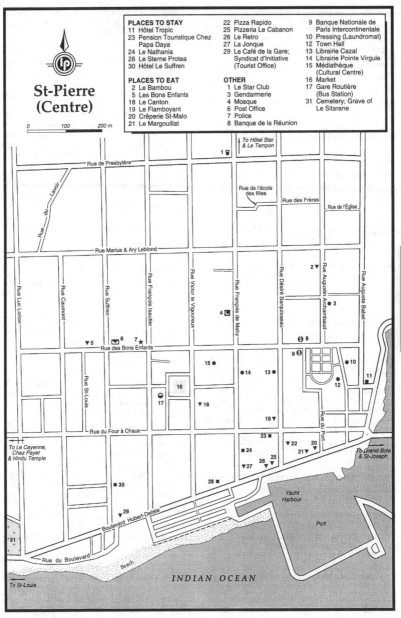

St-Pierre (Centre)

0   100   200 m

RÉUNION

PLACES TO STAY
11 Hôtel Tropic
23 Pension Touristique Chez
    Papa Daya
24 Le Nathania
28 Le Sterne Protea
30 Hôtel Le Suffren

PLACES TO EAT
2 Le Bambou
5 Les Bons Enfants
18 Le Canton
19 Le Flamboyant
20 Crêperie St-Malo
21 Le Margouillat

22 Pizza Rapido
25 Pizzeria Le Cabanon
26 Le Retro
27 La Jonque
29 Le Café de la Gare;
    Syndicat d'Initiative
    (Tourist Office)

OTHER
1 Le Star Club
3 Gendarmerie
4 Mosque
6 Post Office
7 Police
8 Banque de la Réunion

9 Banque Nationale de
    Paris Intercontinentale
10 Pressing (Laundromat)
12 Town Hall
13 Librairie Cazal
14 Librairie Pointe Virgule
15 Médiathèque
    (Cultural Centre)
16 Market
17 Gare Routière
    (Bus Station)
31 Cemetery; Grave of
    Le Sitarane

market, there are also some souvenirs and handicrafts for sale. One of the best times to go is on Saturday morning, when there are usually more handicraft stalls set up.

Beach

St-Pierre also has a clean municipal beach protected by a reef and a jetty, making the town a favourite lair for yachties. Unfortunately, it's subject to strong winds and sunbathers are liable to get a real sandblasting.

Places to Stay

Chambres d'Hôte There are several chambres d'hôte in the area, but none are right in town.

M Lebon (☎ 49 73 78) is at 11 Chemin Maurice Técher in Ravine-des-Cabris about 7km from St-Pierre. Rooms cost FF150 a single or double, including breakfast.

Mme Mireille-Rita Malet (☎ 25 61 90) is at 52 Allée des Aubépines in Bassin-Plat, just 3km from town. She charges FF150/170 for a single/double, including breakfast.

Pensions de Famille The following pensions de famille are good value.

Pension Touristique Chez Papa Daya (☎ 25 64 87 day, 25 11 34 evening), at 27 Rue du Four à Chaux, is a cheap and cheerful option. It's not far from the beach and rooms (singles/doubles) range from FF150 to FF200. There's also a kitchen for self-catering and a lounge.

Mme Fontaine Luline (☎ 25 50 07) has a pension de famille at 46 Rue Rodier. She charges FF100 per person per night and FF1900 for monthly rentals. Breakfast is an extra FF25 per person.

Hotels St-Pierre has several hotel options that cater for a range of budgets.

Hôtel Tropic (☎ 25 90 70; fax 35 10 32), at 2 Rue Auguste Babet, has 15 air-con double rooms costing from FF170 to FF220 per night. Breakfast is an extra FF20 per person.

Le Sterne Protea (☎ 25 70 00; fax 35 01 41), on Boulevard Hubert-Delisle, is a three star hotel overlooking the sea. The least expensive single/double rooms cost FF450/550; breakfast is an extra FF58 per person. There's a good pool here to splash around in.

Le Nathania (☎ 25 04 57; fax 35 27 05), also rated as three star, is a small place not far from the beach, at 12 Rue François de Mahy. Singles/doubles go for FF300/400; breakfast is an extra FF50 per person.

Hôtel Le Suffren (☎ 35 19 10; fax 25 99 43), 14 Rue Suffren, is also just a short distance from the seafront with 18 rooms costing FF360/400 a single/double. Breakfast costs an additional FF55 per person.

Demotel Résidence de Tourisme (☎ 31 11 60; fax 31 17 51), east of town on Allée des Lataniers in Grand-Bois, has comfortable bungalows from FF420 (single/double occupancy). They offer a discount if you stay for at least one week. There's a pool for guests.

Hôtel Star (☎ 27 20 69), out of town at 88 Condé Ravine des Cabris (on the Ligne des 400 route to Le Tampon), has doubles ranging from FF200 to FF300. Breakfast is an additional FF35 per person.

Places to Eat

For some reason, St-Pierre is one of the gastronomic centres of Réunion; there's a restaurant on nearly every corner and a few in between so you'll have no shortage of choices.

There are several beach snack places and a wide selection of restaurants along Boulevard Hubert-Delisle offering a slightly snooty sidewalk café ambience.

La Jonque (☎ 25 57 78), near the corner of Boulevard Hubert-Delisle and Rue François de Mahy, specialises in Chinese and Indian cuisine. It's closed only on Tuesday night.

Pizzeria Le Cabanon (☎ 25 71 46), on Boulevard Hubert-Delisle, is good if you're craving a pizza. They also do some French dishes. It's closed on Monday. Nearby is *Pizza Rapido* (☎ 25 96 95) which also does pizzas.

Le Canton (☎ 25 08 04), at 16 Rue Victor le Vigoureux, serves mainly Chinese food, as well as a dash of Créole fare. They have huge lunch specials for around FF30 to FF50. It's open daily (except Sunday and Tuesday nights and on Monday), for lunch and dinner.

Les Bons Enfants (☎ 25 08 27) is naturally on Rue des Bons Enfants, and has inexpensive cuisine chinoise. It's closed on Sunday, otherwise open until 2 pm for lunch and 9.30 pm for dinner.

Le Retro (☎ 25 33 06), on Boulevard Hubert-Delisle, is recommended for its Créole and French preparations. It's open daily until 3 pm for lunch and until 10.30 pm for dinner.

Le Café de la Gare (☎ 35 24 44), just behind the Syndicat d'Initiative, is a pleasant place for a relatively inexpensive meal and is open every day. You can get pizzas from FF35 to FF65, salads from FF45 to FF78 and a cold beer for FF12. There's also a more expensive menu; main dishes range from FF70 to FF150.

Le Margouillat (☎ 25 05 60), on Boulevard Hubert-Delisle, is a popular French restaurant that's open every day except Wednesday and Sunday.

Crêperie St-Malo (☎ 25 75 25), at the bottom of Rue du Port, specialises in cuisine bretonne (Breton cuisine). They offer delectable crêpes from FF35.

Le Flamboyant (☎ 35 02 15), on Rue Désiré Barquisseau, cooks up delicious (and expensive) French specialities. It is open daily, except Monday, for lunch and dinner.

Le Bambou (☎ 25 58 66) – no, it's not Chinese – at 15 Rue Augustin Archambaud offers cuisine métro. It's closed every Sunday and Monday.

Le Goutali (☎ 25 04 78), at 2 Rue Marius & Ary Leblond, cooks up sizzling hot grills as well as Créole food.

Le Cayenne (☎ 25 39 26), west of the centre on Rue de Cayenne, serves good, but not crash hot, Chinese and Créole food. It is open every day except on Sunday night.

Chez Payet (☎ 25 23 65), also west of town on Rue Mahatma Gandhi, specialises purely in Créole cuisine; it's closed every Sunday.

Le Nathania (☎ 25 04 57) (see Places to Stay) has a restaurant which serves a bit of everything – French, Créole and Chinese creations. It's open daily; nonresidents should try to book ahead.

Le Sterne Protea (☎ 25 70 00) (see Places to Stay) is recommended for a dose of pampering. Their restaurant does tremendous Créole and French food and is open every day. Again, it's wise for nonresidents to book in advance.

Entertainment

St-Pierre has a number of discos for night owls. *Le Star Club* (☎ 35 05 00), on Rue de Presbytère at the upper end of town, is open on Friday and Saturday nights. There's also *Le Chapiteau* (☎ 31 00 81), *Le Pop's Dancing* (☎ 49 59 67), *Le Refuge* (☎ 49 56 32), *La Plage* (☎ 35 20 90) and *Le Prestige* (☎ 49 52 60).

For a drink you could try the popular *Aquarum* (☎ 35 25 02), Front de Mer, which is open from 7 pm to around midnight. Other pubs in St-Pierre include *Le Malone's* (☎ 25 81 41), *Pub Le 32* (☎ 25 40 16) and *Le Bato Fou* (☎ 25 65 61).

Getting There & Away

Buses to and from St-Denis run frequently every day along the western side of the island via St-Louis and St-Paul, so you shouldn't have to wait too long for transport. They also run several times a day to St-Benoît across the centre of the island via Plaine-des-Palmistes; and four times via the south-eastern coast road through St-Joseph and Ste-Anne.

The West Coast

ST-LOUIS

You have to go to St-Louis to get the bus to Cilaos but there's really no other reason to visit. The gare routière is isolated on the southern side of town near a couple of snack bars and the church, which is the oldest on the island, dating to 1733.

If you do find yourself stuck for a day or two, there's a scenic 15km drive up to the hill village of Les Makes, and a further twisting 10km drive or walk up the Route Forestière 14 to La Fenêtre, (the Window). There, clouds permitting, you'll have a grand view into the Cirque de Cilaos. There's also a 2km trip to the coastal lagoon Étang du Gol at Bel Air, where you'll find a pleasant picnic site.

About 1.5km west of St-Louis, at Le Camp du Gol, is an old sugar refinery, Sucrerie du Gol. Behind it stands a château dating to the end of the 18th century.

Places to Stay

Accommodation is very limited in St-Louis as few travellers stay overnight here. Bookings for all of these can be made through the Relais Départemental des Gîtes de France (☎ 90 78 90; fax 41 84 29) in St-Denis.

M Jean-Luc d'Eurveilher (☎ 37 82 77) is in Les Makes, 14km inland from the main town. This chambre d'hôte costs FF130/200 a single/double, including breakfast.

Jean Vitry has a gîte in Les Makes which can accommodate up to five people for FF1740 per week.

M Fontaine also has a gîte in Les Makes which is FF2020/1010 per week/weekend. It can accommodate a maximum of six people.

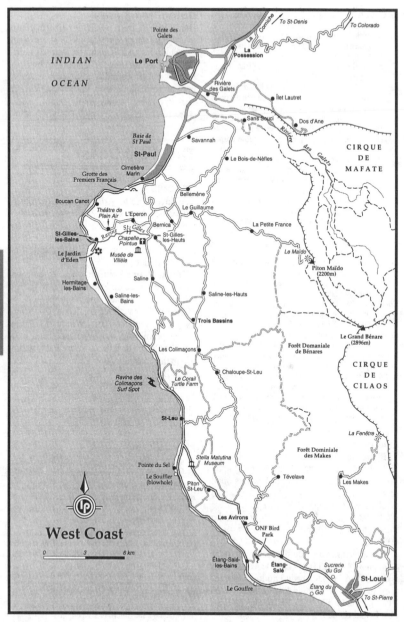

RÉUNION

West Coast

0   3   6 km

Places to Eat

St-Louis has just a handful of restaurants and most seem to focus on Chinese and Créole food.

Restaurant Les Bons Amis (☎ 26 10 19), on the Route Nationale, offers a selection of Chinese and Créole cuisine.

Chez Michel (☎ 26 11 13), on Rue Lambert, also specialises in Chinese and Créole fare. This restaurant is open daily except Sunday.

Le Samourai (☎ 26 75 52), on Rue Verte, has a fairly good range of French, Créole and Chinese dishes. It's closed on Sunday evening, but open every other day for lunch and dinner.

La Butte Fougères (☎ 37 83 56), 8 Rue Voltaire, serves good Créole and French food and is open every day except Sunday night and on Monday.

La Place (☎ 26 02 52), on Rue de la Plage, has the usual selection of Chinese and Créole fare and is only open on weekdays from 9 am to around 3 pm.

ÉTANG-SALÉ-LES-BAINS

If you're coming from the south, Étang-Salé-les-Bains is the beginning of the holiday coast, though the area remains very much an agricultural community. On weekends, the black-sand beach is much quieter than the coast further north around St-Gilles-les-Bains. Étang-Salé-les-Bains itself is sheltered by a coral reef which, with extreme caution, is accessible on foot at low tide (shoes are essential to avoid serious cuts on the coral).

Information

Tourist Office The Syndicat d'Initiative, known as the Office de Tourisme de l'Étang-Salé (☎ 26 67 32; fax 26 67 92), is housed in the old train station on Rue Octave Bénard. They have information on the entire stretch of coast between St-Louis and St-Leu. The office is open Monday to Friday from 8.30 am to noon and 2.30 to 6 pm; on Saturday from 9.30 am to noon and 2.30 to 6 pm and on Sunday from 9.30 am to noon.

Le Gouffre

Just off Route Nationale 1, 2km south of Étang-Salé-les-Bains, is Le Gouffre, an abyss in the basalt cliffs where the waves dramatically roar in and foam up, sending plumes of spray into the air. Don't venture too close.

Office National des Forêts Bird Park

On the road from Étang-Salé-les-Bains to Étang-Salé-les-Hauts, just where it forks to the left to go to Les Avirons, is a two hectare bird park operated by the Office National des Forêts. This route is beautifully crimson when all the flamboyant trees are in bloom.

Places to Stay

Despite its tendency to consider itself part of the holiday coast, Étang-Salé-les-Bains has limited accommodation (admittedly, some people like it that way!).

Mme Savigny (☎ 26 31 09), 3 Sentier des Prunes, in Ravine Sheunon, has a chambre d'hôte which costs FF150 for a double, including breakfast and FF80 per person for table d'hôte.

Caro Beach Village (☎ 91 79 79; fax 24 34 46), on Rue Octave Bénard, has comfortable singles/doubles for FF295/395. Bungalows (maximum of four people) go for FF570 per night. Breakfast is an extra FF55 per person.

Places to Eat

There are just a sprinkling of restaurants in Étang-Salé-les-Bains and none stand out.

La Louisiane (☎ 26 63 92) is on the main road and serves Créole and French cuisine. It's closed on Sunday night and all day Tuesday.

L'Été Indien (☎ 26 67 33), also on the main road, is open daily, except Monday, from 11 am to around 11.30 pm. You can get reasonably priced Créole and French food as well as snacks.

LES AVIRONS

Les Avirons (the Oars) is a pretty hill town with commanding views and a reputation, along with Étang-Salé-les-Hauts, for turning out artisans specialising in woodcrafts and replicas of French East India Company furniture. They also make distinctive cane chairs known as *de Gol* (no, that's not the Créole name of the former French president!). Their predecessors were said to have originally made the oars for all the island's boats, hence the name of the town. However, one traveller suggests the name is derived from the Malagasy word for a high place with a view.

The excursion into the mountains or cirques from Les Avirons is by way of Tévelave and, 11km up the mountain, by way of Route Forestière 6.

Places to Stay

The chambres d'hôte are all up in the heights – in this case, they're all in Tévelave, 11km north of Les Avirons.

Mme François Turpin (☎ 38 30 67) charges FF120/160 for a single/double at her chambre d'hôte.

Mme Marie-Anne Tipary (☎ 38 00 71) has a similarly priced chambre d'hôte to that of Mme Turpin.

Mme Darty (☎ 54 01 94), at Le Plate (near Tévelave), has a small chambre d'hôte with singles/doubles for FF125/200, including breakfast. An evening meal costs FF75 per person.

M Jerry Vitry (☎ 38 30 55), in Tévelave, has a gîte with accommodation for FF60 per person per night.

Mme Augustin Cadet (☎ 38 01 34), at Chemin Fond Maurice, Les Avirons, has accommodation for four people and charges around FF1250 per week.

Auberge Les Fougères (☎ 38 32 96; fax 38 30 26), on Route des Merles, Le Tévelave, offers pleasant accommodation with a homely ambience. Singles/doubles go for FF200/270; breakfast is an extra FF30 per person.

ST-LEU

The name St-Leu was derived from the original name 'Boucan-de-Laleu' which appeared on an early map of the island at this site. Historically, the place has had its share of problems; a violent slave rebellion in 1811 and devastating cyclones in 1932 and 1989. It was, however, the one town on Réunion which was spared the ravages of the cholera epidemic which decimated St-Denis and St-Louis in 1859. In 1978, the people of the nearby village of Stella were unemployed en masse when the sugar refinery ceased operations. Area inhabitants are now more occupied with fishing than farming.

Beach

A few km north of St-Leu the beach changes from black sand to white sand. Swimming is safe and there's a reef for protection. At the mouth of the Ravine des Colimaçons, north of town, there's a break in the reef which serves as a prime surf spot, considered one of the best in the Indian Ocean. For further details on surfing, see Activities in the Réunion Facts for the Visitor chapter.

Notre Dame de la Salette

You may want to seek out the chapel of Notre Dame de la Salette, built in the Virgin Mary's honour in 1859 as a plea for protection against the cholera epidemic sweeping the island. It must have worked because St-Leu's populace was spared. Every year on 19 September, thousands of people make a pilgrimage to the chapel.

Conservatoire Botanique National de Mascarin

This garden, on the old property of Chateauvieux at Les Colimaçons, is open Tuesday to Sunday from 9 am to 5 pm. There are guided tours at 10 and 11 am and at 2.30 and 3.30 pm. Advance bookings are necessary for groups of more than 10 people. Admission is FF25/10 for adults/children. For further inquiries call ☎ 24 92 27.

Le Corail Turtle Farm

Le Corail Turtle Farm (☎ 34 81 10), at Pointe des Châteaux, is 2km north of St-Leu on Route Nationale 1. Entry costs FF30 for adults and FF20 for children. It's open daily from 9 am to 6 pm.

There is a chance you could feel sorry for the turtles as they swim around in circles, confined to their small tanks. The enterprise includes between 18,000 and 26,000 turtles, covering three generations, and produces up to 7000 individuals each year (well, actually, the turtles themselves do the producing). The original stock was brought to Réunion from the French islands of Tromelin and Europa, the former located between Mauritius and the Seychelles and the latter in the Mozambique Channel between Africa and southern Madagascar.

The farm also has an exhibition of the breeding process and the ritual and symbolic significance of the turtle. Finally, it tells about the contributions of turtle farming to the causes of conservation, the economy and human health.

There are several items and knick-knacks for sale in the shop, however North Americans and Australasians are not permitted to import turtle products. We strongly urge you not to buy anything made of turtle shell or coral as it contributes to the problem by providing incentives for the collectors (also see Things to Buy in the Réunion Facts for the Visitor chapter).

Stella Matutina

This quirky museum (☎ 34 16 24) at the village of Stella, 4km south of St-Leu on the inland route towards Les Avirons (known as l'Allée des Flamboyants), tells the agricultural and industrial history of Réunion. It's dedicated primarily to the sugar industry, but does provide insight into the history of the island, and has exhibits on other products known and loved by the Réunionnais: vanilla, orchids, geraniums and vetiver. It's open Tuesday to Sunday from 9.30 am to 5.30 pm. Admission is FF30/15 for adults/children. Guided tours are available – it's best to book ahead.

Hôtel de Ville

The stone hôtel de ville on the main road, an old store built by the French East India Company, is worth a look.

Le Souffler

Located on the main road between St-Leu and Étang-Salé-les-Bains is Le Souffler (blowhole), a rocky crevice along the seafront which spurts up a tower of water as the waves crash against it. If the sea is calm, the effect is obviously not as spectacular.

Places to Stay

Camping There is a camp site near the shore in St-Leu which charges around FF3 per sq metre per day for tent or caravan space plus FF15 for electricity. The site is well lit and has a shower and toilet block. Bookings may be made through the Service du Garde Champêtre (☎ 34 80 03) at the town hall. It's

open only in August. Some travellers have reported that the site isn't safe; don't leave anything in your tent.

Village Vacances Famille There is only one VVF in St-Leu.

Le Laleu (☎ 34 81 43; fax 34 78 43) is the VVF holiday village in St-Leu. Prices range from FF220 per night for one or two people on weekdays and FF400 on weekends.

Chambres d'Hôte The following chambres d'hôte are located within 10km of St-Leu.

Mme Aliette René (☎ 54 80 81), CD13, Bras Mouton, (at Colimaçons-les-Hauts, in the hills 10km north of St-Leu), has clean guest bedrooms for FF150/200 a single/double, including breakfast.
Mme Julia Maillot (☎ 54 82 92), at 4 Chemin des Hortensias in Chaloupe-St-Leu, on the high road between St-Leu and Trois-Bassins, runs a chambre and table d'hôte. She charges FF100/130 a single/double, including breakfast. Dinner costs FF80 per person.
M Ivrin Cadet (☎ 54 85 00), at 20 Chemin Payet Emmanuel, also in Chaloupe-St-Leu, has a chambre d'hôte for FF150 per night. He also owns a gîte (see below).

Gîtes There are numerous gîtes de France in the St-Leu area, the majority in the vicinity of Piton-St-Leu, 11km south of town. You can book the following gîtes direct or through the Relais Départemental des Gîtes de France (☎ 90 78 90; fax 41 84 29) in St-Denis.

Mme Crescence (☎ 34 41 75) is the nearest to town, with a cosy little place in Étang. She charges FF1400 per week or FF700 for the weekend.
M Henri René (☎ 54 80 81), in Bras Mouton, is another nice option. To get there, turn inland just north of Le Corail Turtle Farm and wind your way 10km or so up the hill (there's currently no public transport heading this way). He charges FF1250/340 for a week/weekend (maximum of two people), or FF1750/670 per week/weekend (maximum of four people).
M Ivrin Cadet (☎ 54 85 00), at 20 Chemin Payet Emmanuel in Chaloupe-St-Leu, has a gîte with accommodation for up to six people. He charges FF1008 for the weekend or FF1680 for one week.

Hotels St-Leu has several worthwhile hotel options.

Apolonia (☎ 34 62 62; fax 34 61 61) is a 127 room hotel near the sea, on Boulevard Bonnier. Because of its size the personal touch has been lost, but the rooms are comfortable enough. Singles/doubles/ triples will set you back FF405/550/708 with breakfast, or FF525/790/1068 on a half-board basis. Facilities include a swimming pool, health centre and restaurant.

Iloha Village Hotel (☎ 34 89 89; fax 34 89 90), Pointe des Châteaux, is a delightful, three star hotel with sea views. There's a fine restaurant, tennis courts and a swimming pool. Well-appointed single/ double rooms cost FF340/380; double/triple bun- galows are FF450/535 and bungalows for four/ five/six people cost FF620/705/790. Breakfast costs FF55; half/full board is an extra FF175/275 per person. This is a fabulous place to catch up on some serious relaxation.

Battants des Lames (☎ 34 80 18), on Rue de Général Lambert, offers accommodation in bungalows which cost around FF490 per day. A discount is available if you stay for at least one week.

Places to Eat

Le Palais d'Asie (☎ 34 80 41), at 5 Rue de l'Etang, offers good and reasonably priced Chinese meals. It's closed on Tuesday.

La Varangue (☎ 34 78 45), near the shore at 36 Rue du Lagon, has the usual Créole menu.

Le Souffleur (☎ 26 61 13), on Route Nationale 1, is recommended for its tasty Créole fare. It's closed on Monday and Sunday.

Iloha Village Hotel (☎ 34 89 89) (see Places to Stay) has a pleasant restaurant offering an array of dishes. It is open seven days a week; it's a good idea for nonresidents to book ahead.

Apolonia (☎ 34 62 62) (see Places to Stay) has a restaurant which attempts to have a go at every- thing – there's Créole, Indian, Chinese and French items on the menu. Some travellers rave about the food, while others do not – judge for yourself.

ST-GILLES-LES-BAINS

The beach scene may not be what Réunion is all about but at times, you have to wonder. On weekends and during holiday periods, St-Gilles-les-Bains becomes ridiculously overcrowded. It's pretty much like Brighton, Bondi or Santa Monica on a hot, sunny Sunday with packed restaurants, cramped beaches and all-day traffic snarls which seem particularly constipated if you're coming

from the St-Denis side. The excitement centres on the 20km stretch of lagoon and white coral sand beach stretching from Boucan Canot to La Souris Chaude (the hot mouse?!). On either side of this area, the sand is of the black volcanic variety.

In the 1800s, the small fishing village of St-Gilles-les-Bains belonged to the estate of the Desbassyns family. After the road from St-Paul arrived in 1863, however, it was discovered by holiday-makers and has been growing more popular ever since.

Information

Tourist Office Tourist information is avail- able from the Syndicat d'Initiative known as the Office de Tourisme de l'Ouest (☎ 24 57 47; fax 24 34 40), in the Galerie Amandine in the centre of St-Gilles-les-Bains. This is one of the most helpful offices on the island and there are loads of glossy brochures, booklets and souvenirs. The office is open on Monday from 2 to 6 pm; Tuesday to Friday from 8.30 am to 12.30 pm and 1 to 6 pm; Saturday from 9 am to 5 pm; and on Sunday from 9 am to noon. Phew!

Bookshops For newspapers and magazines, go to Maison de la Presse on Rue Général de Gaulle. You'll also find bookshops in the arcades near the Syndicat d'Initiative and behind the Score supermarket.

Théâtre de Plein Air

On the road between upper and lower St- Gilles, the modern Théâtre de Plein Air (Open-Air Theatre) (☎ 24 47 71) is often used for concerts and plays. The hills rise behind the audience, and the town and sea act as a backdrop.

La Ravine St-Gilles

About 1km inland from the Théâtre de Plein Air, on the road to St-Gilles-les-Hauts, is a parking area and a path down to an old irrigation and water supply system. The area encompasses a stunning series of waterfalls and pools which are, from top to bottom: Bassin Malheur, Bassin des Aigrettes and Bassin du Cormoran.

RÉUNION

Beaching it up in Réunion

Roches Noires, a popular surfing spot, is St-Gilles-les-Bains' main beach area and the French sometimes refer to it as *Le St-Tropez de la Réunion*. It's rather touristy but is nevertheless a nice place to sit in the sun and laze the day away.

Further south, between St-Gilles-les-Bains and Saline-les-Bains, around Hermitage-les-Bains, the reef is well out from the shore, thus creating stony shallows and calm seas. Watch out for sea cucumbers and sea anemones. This long casuarina-lined stretch of beach, ploughed and scraped regularly, is good for snorkelling and sunbathing.

North of St-Gilles-les-Bains and 7km south of St-Paul is Boucan Canot, the best beach on the island and the favourite of the Réunionnais. The sea is more animated here than around the sheltered lagoons south of Pointe des Aigrettes, and you can even body-surf when the waves are right. For those who prefer docile water, there's a seawater swimming pool.

Good surfing in the area is found at Boucan Canot and Roches Noires beaches (St-Leu further south is said to be Réunion's best). Unfortunately, sharks can be a real problem for surfers and other water enthusiasts along this coast and although it's not as dangerous as the east coast of the island, there have been some nasty incidents. Heed local advice! See the boxed text on sharks under Activities in the Réunion Facts for the Visitor chapter. ■

Bassin du Cormoran, the most accessible, is reached along the lower path which cuts away from the irrigation canal about 10m from the car park. When the water level is right, the falls are excellent for swimming and provide an alternative to the beach on hot days. On weekends, the area is packed with picnickers. The rather stagnant pool in the Bassin des Aigrettes is reached by a slightly precarious 800m walk along irrigation channels and through two slippery tunnels.

Musée de Villèle

Near St-Gilles-les-Hauts is the Musée de Villèle (☎ 55 64 10). Built in 1787, this colonial mansion became the home of the wealthy and very powerful Mme Panon-Desbassyns (the name originated because the family's turf surrounded the Bassins above St-Gilles-les-Bains). She was a coffee and sugar baron who, among other things, held 300 slaves. Legend has it that she was a cruel mistress and that her tormented screams can still be heard from the hellish fires whenever the volcano is erupting. She died in 1846 and her body lies in the Chapelle Pointue, which is visible on the left as you cross the Ravine St-Gilles on the road towards Saline-les-Bains.

A bit further, on the other side of the road, is Mme Panon-Desbassyns' house and the ruins of the sugar mill. Guided tours are available, in French, from the caretakers who conduct a lightning tour unlocking and locking doors as you proceed. Exhibits include a clock presented to the Desbassyns by Napoleon; a set of china from Mauritius featuring *Paul et Virginie*, the love story by Bernardin de St Pierre (see Mauritius section); a commemoration of the Réunion-born aviator Roland Garros (1888-1915); an English cannonball (a memento of British rule!); a collection of French East India Company furniture and china; and a Gobelin tapestry depicting Christ.

The well-preserved mansion is open daily, except Tuesday, from 9.30 am to noon and 2 to 5 pm. Admission costs FF10 per person.

Village Artisanal de L'Eperon

At L'Eperon, near St-Gilles-les-Hauts, is a picturesque old grist mill, L'Usine de L'Eperon. It's now occupied by the Village Artisanal de L'Eperon run by M Le Gall (☎ 22 73 01). The shop is open Monday to Saturday from 8.30 am to noon and 1.30 to 6 pm. There's also an interesting Hindu temple nearby.

The only public transport to L'Eperon is the infrequent short-haul bus which travels between Grand Fond and Trois Bassins, passing through L'Eperon.

Le Maïdo

One of the most superb views of the Cirque de Mafate is available at Le Maïdo viewpoint

RÉUNION

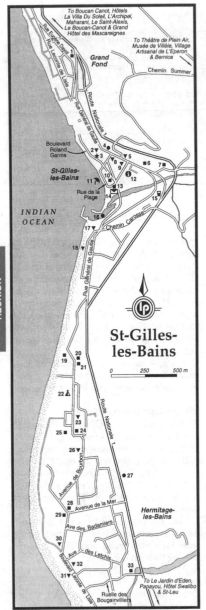

PLACES TO STAY
1   Les Emeraudes
6   L'Abri-Côtier
7   Hôtel Les Aigrettes
10 Le Plaza Créole
13 Caro Beach Hotel
19 Le Récif
20 Hôtel Les Créoles
21 Les Brisants Résidence
    de Tourisme
22 Camping Municipal
24 Alamanda Hotel; Casino
25 VVF St-Gilles
28 Hôtel Blue Beach
29 Hôtel Coralia Novotel
33 Le Bougainvillier

PLACES TO EAT
2   Le Cesario
5   Le Piccolo; Le Bourbon
8   La Canne à Sucre
9   Chez Loulou
17 Le St-Gilles
18 Alpha
23 L'Auberge du Bonheur;
    Moulin du Tango
26 Score Supermarket
30 Les Trois Roches
    (Chez Go)
31 La Bobine
32 L'Esquinade

OTHER
3   Police
4   Maison de la Presse
11 Roches Noires Beach
12 Syndicat d'Initiative
    (Tourist Office)
14 Post Office
15 Dancing des Roches Noires
16 Yacht Harbour
27 Réunion Air Service

at 2204m above sea level. The name comes from a Malagasy word meaning 'burnt land', probably due to its vulnerability to fire on the dry western slopes of the island. It's a long road up the mountain from Le Guillaume in the heights above St-Gilles-les-Bains, winding through forests and past picnic sites galore.

From Le Maïdo, one can see the island's highest points: Le Gros Morne (2991m), Piton des Neiges (3069m) and Le Grand Bénare (2896m). You'll need to get an early start if you want to see anything, however. The clouds normally obscure the view by 10 am. There's a tough walk along the cirque rim to the summit of Le Grand Bénare. Allow at least six hours for the return trip and always be prepared for dramatic changes in the weather.

It's also possible to travel on foot into the Cirque de Mafate from Le Maïdo. A spectacular trip is from the lookout along the western wall of the cirque, high above the Rivière des Galets, to the hamlet of Sans Souci near Le Port. Although the route begins with a steep descent, it's a relatively easy trip because there's very little climbing involved. The problem is that there are no gîtes along the route; to make a two day trip of it without camping will involve an extremely difficult side trip across the gorge of the Rivière des Galets to reach the gîte at Grand Place. For other options, see the Trekking in Réunion chapter.

Le Jardin d'Eden

If you haven't guessed, the name of this self-proclaimed *jardin ethno-botanique* (ethno-botanical garden) means 'The Garden of Eden'. As silly as that may sound, it's a worthwhile visit with sections dedicated to such interesting concepts as the sacred plants of the Hindus, medicinal plants, edible tropical plants, spices, aphrodisiac plants, cactus, aquatic plants and simply 'blue flowers'.

Le Jardin d'Eden (☎ 33 83 16) is open Tuesday to Saturday from 9.30 am to 12.30 pm and 2.30 to 6 pm, and on Sundays from 10 am to 6 pm. Admission is FF30/15 for adults/children.

La Petite France

The village of La Petite France on the road to Piton Maïdo is the best place to visit geranium farms and watch the distillation of the oil used in perfumes. The property of M Lougnon is open to visitors; for further information, check with the Syndicat d'Initiative in St-Gilles-les-Bains.

Water Activities

Being a tourist hot spot, there are a bundle of water activities offered in and around St-Gilles-les-Bains. Most agencies offering 'nauti' activities – surfing, deep-sea fishing, sailboarding, boat charters, diving, snorkelling etc – are based around the harbour south of the river mouth in St-Gilles-les-Bains. See Activities in the Réunion Facts for the Visitor chapter for more information about water activities.

Visiobul (☎ 85 23 46) offers a popular tour in an extraordinary boat with an underwater glass compartment, allowing you to get a close look at undersea life. It costs FF75/45 for adults/children.

Places to Stay

There's plenty of accommodation in the area, but almost everything is booked out during holiday periods and on weekends. Unless you like risks, don't arrive without a reservation.

Camping Robbery is rife at this popular site so don't leave anything in your tent.

Camping Municipal (☎ 24 42 35), at Hermitage-les-Bains, is in a good location beside the beach but isn't as tidy or organised as it could be. Sites cost FF60 per day for a 25 sq metre patch and use of the facilities. Additional charges include FF6 per day for water and FF10 per day for electricity, FF1 per person per day tax and FF8 per day for vehicle parking. It's open in August and from 23 December to 6 February. Long-term stays cost FF1000 per month. On the camp site noticeboard, you'll often find 'For Sale' notices for tents, most asking from around FF1200 to F3000.

If the official site is full and you don't have anything to lose, have a look along the shore between Boucan Canot beach and the turnoff to St-Gilles-les-Hauts. There are a couple of unofficial camp sites lost among the casuarina trees with no attached 'Camping Interdit' (Camping Prohibited) signs. Fresh water is available from a roadside pump.

Youth Hostel The area has one youth hostel – in Bernica.

Youth Hostel (Auberge de Jeunesse) (☎ 22 89 75), at Bernica in the hills behind St-Gilles-les-Bains, charges HI members FF70 for dormitory accommodation plus FF10 for breakfast. Evening meals cost FF45.

RÉUNION

Village Vacances Famille VVF annual membership costs FF100 per family.

VVF St-Gilles (☎ 24 29 39; fax 24 41 02), at St-Gilles-les-Bains, is open to VVF affiliates only. There are two and three-room bungalows starting at FF250 per night on weekdays and FF380 per night on weekends. Some travellers say that it has a rather indifferent atmosphere and isn't as nice as the one in St-Leu.

Chambres d'Hôte There are three nearby chambres d'hôte worth seeking out.

Mme Grondin (☎ 22 74 15) runs a homely establishment at Bernica, 5km uphill from St-Gilles-les-Hauts. She charges FF175 for a single/double, including breakfast.
Mme Céline Maillot (☎ 55 69 83) offers a chambre d'hôte at Coin des Artistes, L'Eperon, on the road between St-Gilles-les-Bains and St-Gilles-les-Hauts. Singles/doubles are FF160/200, including breakfast. Meals cost a steep FF100 per person.
Mme Thérèse Ramincoupin (☎ 55 69 13) has a chambre d'hôte on Chemin Bosse in Bernica. She charges FF150 for single/double occupancy, with breakfast.

Far up the mountainside at La Petite France above Le Guillaume, on the road to Le Maïdo, are two chambres d'hôte:

M Lougnon (☎ 32 44 26) has several rooms in a quiet setting for FF250 a single/double, including breakfast.
Mme Magdeleine (☎ 32 53 50) also has a couple of rooms for FF80/160 a single/double, including breakfast. Meals cost FF75 extra.

Pensions de Famille There are three pensions de famille in the St-Gilles-les-Bains area.

Le Bougainvillier (☎/fax 33 82 48) is on Ruelle des Bougainvilliers, a quiet back street about five minutes walk from the beach at Hermitage-les-Bains. Rooms cost FF230 for single or double occupancy and extra beds are FF60 each. Breakfast costs FF30 per person.
Auberge Cadet des Îles (☎ 24 63 73), at 55 Rue Lacaussade, has double rooms for FF225. Breakfast costs FF25 and evening meals are FF80.
Les Cytises (☎ 24 41 55; fax 24 03 63) is at 44 Rue Eugène Dayot in Grand Fond. A self-catering bungalow accommodating three people costs FF300 per day or FF6600 per month.

Bungalows & Holiday Flats The three places listed below are all easy to find.

Les Bungalows (☎ 24 46 06), at 27 Ave des Badamiers, has fully equipped units from FF280 a double.
Le Récif (☎ 24 50 51; fax 24 38 85), at Ave de Bourbon, charges FF385/500 for single/double rooms. There are also bungalows for FF620 (maximum four people) or FF890 (maximum six people). Facilities include a pool and restaurant.
Les Brisants Résidence de Tourisme (☎ 24 50 51; fax 24 38 85), on Ave de Bourbon, offers fully equipped apartments for FF515 (maximum of four people) or FF710 (maximum of six people).

At 76 Rue Lacaussade there is a private air-conditioned home (☎ 24 69 92) which accommodates four people and costs FF450 per day. Call for further details.

Gîtes With tourism on the rise in the St-Gilles-les-Bains area, there is expected to be an increase in private gîtes. If you're interested in this type of accommodation, it's best to contact the Relais Départemental des Gîtes de France (☎ 90 78 90; fax 41 84 29), 10 Place Sarda Garriga in St-Denis, or ask at the Syndicat d'Initiative in St-Gilles-les-Bains itself. One possibility is:

M Lougnon (☎ 32 44 26), who charges FF2295 per week. It's a good base for walks to Le Maïdo and Le Grand Bénare.

Hotels – bottom end There is a good range of budget accommodation in the St-Gilles-les-Bains area.

Le Dory Flane (☎ 33 82 41), at 21 Ave de la Mer, is a popular budget option. For single/double rooms, they charge FF140/180. Air-con studio flats cost FF250.
Hôtel La Villa Du Soleil (☎ 24 38 69; fax 24 39 09), 54 Route de Boucan Canot, is a family-run hotel and great value for money. Run by two friendly brothers, Philippe and Patrick Payet, it has eight well-kept rooms for FF240/280 a single/double. Breakfast costs FF20 per person. There's also a small swimming pool.
Le Plaza Créole (☎ 24 42 84), at Roches Noires beach, is a restaurant and brasserie with some chalet-style rooms out the back. Rooms range from FF260 to FF360 per night.

L'Abri-Côtier (☎ 24 44 64; fax 24 50 71), at 129 Rue Général de Gaulle, has six rooms for FF180 (single/double occupancy).

Hôtel Les Palmes (☎ 24 47 12; fax 24 30 62) is also on Rue Général de Gaulle. Accommodation is in bungalows which go for FF260/350/390 a single/double/triple. Breakfast costs an extra FF30.

Hotels – middle There's a good selection of mid-range hotels to choose from ranging from FF330 to FF540 a single.

Caro Beach Hotel (☎ 24 42 49; fax 24 34 46), at Roches Noires beach, is a three star hotel charging FF450/580 for a single/double. Breakfast is an additional FF55. They also have apartments (maximum four people) for FF780 per night. There's a swimming pool here.

Hôtel Blue Beach (☎ 24 50 25; fax 24 36 22) is a three star place on Ave de la Mer in Hermitage-les-Bains. Comfortable rooms are FF450/580 a single/double; breakfast is FF60. This hotel also has a pool and the restaurant serves French and Créole fare.

Hôtel Swalibo (☎ 24 10 97; fax 24 64 29) is south of St-Gilles-les-Bains in Saline-les-Bains. Single/double rooms in this three star hotel cost FF420/495. There's also a pool.

Hôtel L'Archipel (☎ 24 05 34; fax 24 47 24) is north of Grand Fond just a couple of hundred metres along the road towards L'Eperon. Singles/doubles in this attractive three star place are FF455/560 and breakfast is an extra FF60. There's a nice pool and restaurant here.

Hôtel Les Aigrettes (☎ 33 05 05; fax 24 30 50), a three star hotel on Chemin Bottard in St-Gilles-les-Bains, charges FF530/670 a single/double, including breakfast. They also have a swimming pool.

Le Boucan-Canot (☎ 24 41 20; fax 24 02 77) is another three star hotel near Boucan Canot beach. It charges FF540/580 for nice singles/doubles; breakfast is an extra FF60 per person. There's a pool, and a restaurant which specialises in Créole and French cuisine.

Hôtel Les Créoles (☎ 33 09 09; fax 33 09 19), on Ave de Bourbon, has a three star rating. Clean single/double rooms go for FF440/570 and guests have use of the pool.

Alamanda Hotel (☎ 24 51 00; fax 24 02 42) is a two star place on Ave de Bourbon. There are 57 rooms for FF330/440 a single/double and yes, there's also a pool here.

Les Emeraudes (☎ 24 20 20; fax 24 07 06) is on Rue Eugène Dayot, Grand Fond. It's about a 10 minute walk from Roches Noires beach. Rooms cost around FF400; lower rates are available for longer stays.

Hotels – top end There are four top of the range hotels around St-Gilles-les-Bains worth checking out.

Hôtel Maharani (☎ 33 06 06; fax 24 32 97), 28 Route de Boucan Canot, offers plush accommodation with a distinct Indian flavour. It's filled with beautiful furniture and fittings from the subcontinent and has an authentic Indian restaurant (see Places to Eat). Singles/doubles go for FF875/1080, but if you can afford it go for one of the swish deluxe rooms which cost FF1190/1430. Facilities include a swimming pool, jacuzzi and two restaurants.

Le Saint-Alexis (☎ 24 42 04; fax 24 00 13), 44 Route de Boucan Canot, is one of the most upmarket hotels in Réunion and is recommended for those with an appetite for luxury. This swanky hotel sits right on the beach, and although comfortable, the standard rooms are a little lacking in character. Doubles (all rooms with a jacuzzi) start from around FF1000. If you want some serious pampering, the best suite will lighten your wallet by a cool FF1900. Decadent touches include a swimming pool and two restaurants.

Hôtel Coralia Novotel (☎ 24 44 44; fax 24 01 67), in Hermitage-les-Bains, is a three star hotel with rather overpriced singles/doubles from FF650/780. Breakfast is FF70 per person. Like most top-end hotels, there's a pool to splash in, as well as a tennis court and a good restaurant.

Grand Hôtel des Mascareignes (☎ 24 36 24; fax 24 37 24), at Boucan Canot, is a 156 room hotel which charges FF760/820 for a standard single/double. The very luxurious 'senior suite' is a whopping FF2000. There are all the usual extras, including a tennis court, swimming pool, snack bar and restaurant.

Places to Eat
St-Gilles-les-Bains is well endowed with eating places, with new restaurants constantly coming onto the scene. There are plenty of relatively cheap snack stalls around the beach areas, which are perfect for a light bite. There are also roadside stands along Route Nationale 1 selling roast chickens for around FF40, but get there early to ensure freshness. Most other restaurants, however good or mediocre in appearance or reputation, have set menus from about FF60 to FF80.

La Bobine (☎ 33 83 41), at Hermitage-les-Bains, is good for a quick beach munch. They serve great grilled fish for around FF40 and are open seven days a week.

RÉUNION

L'Esquinade (☎ 33 83 14) is another swift-serve beach restaurant at Hermitage-les-Bains; it specialises in Créole and French food and is also open every day.

Les Trois Roches (Chez Go) (☎ 33 82 61), nearby, is recommended for its Créole meals which cost around FF75. It's closed Monday nights and all day Tuesday.

L'Auberge du Bonheur (☎ 24 09 97), in Hermitage-les-Bains, offers slightly expensive Chinese-oriented cuisine. It's closed on Monday.

Le Plaza Créole (☎ 24 42 84), attached to the hotel of the same name on Roches Noires beach, has terrific Créole specialities (mainly seafood). The restaurant is open every day from 10 am to 11 pm.

Chez Loulou (☎ 24 46 36), on Rue Général de Gaulle, has tasty Créole food. It's closed on Sunday night, but is otherwise open for lunch and dinner.

Le Bourbon (☎ 24 48 01), also on Rue Général de Gaulle, has French and Créole meals from around FF50; it's closed on Wednesday.

Le Piccolo (☎ 24 51 51), nearby, is recommended for Italian food. They also do some French dishes. It's open daily, except Thursday, for lunch and dinner.

La Canne à Sucre (☎ 24 02 56), in the same area, is recommended for its Créole and French food. It's closed on Monday.

Le Cesario (☎ 24 49 15), 22 Rue Général de Gaulle, is the place to go if you're craving cuisine italienne (Italian cuisine). It's open daily for lunch and dinner.

Le St-Gilles (☎ 24 43 12), at the harbour in St-Gilles-les-Bains, seems to be a favourite with business-people; it offers French dishes for around FF80. It's closed on Monday, but open all other days until 2.30 pm for lunch and until 10.30 pm for dinner.

Alpha (☎ 24 02 02), nearby, is a seafood speciality restaurant which is open daily, except Monday, from 10 am to 11 pm.

Le Tandjore (☎ 33 06 06), at the Hôtel Maharani (see Places to Stay), is an elegant Indian restaurant overlooking the sea, although the haute gastronomie indienne gets mixed reports. Nonresidents are welcome, but it's a good idea to book ahead. Main dishes are around FF140. Every Friday night there's a buffet accompanied by live Indian music/dancing; it costs FF220 per person (drinks not included).

Hôtel Blue Beach (☎ 24 50 25) (see Places to Stay) has a restaurant serving Créole and French dishes, often accompanied by some sort of live entertainment on Friday evening. French and Créole fare is also offered in the restaurant at the *Hôtel Les Créoles* (☎ 33 09 09).

Papayou (☎ 24 65 38), at Salines-les-Bains, has a range of French and Créole specialities. It's closed on Monday evening and all day Tuesday.

Palais de L'Orient (☎ 24 68 90), on Route Nationale 1, offers reasonably priced Chinese food. The restaurant is open daily, except Tuesday, for lunch and dinner.

Entertainment

As one would imagine, St-Gilles-les-Bains is relatively flush with nightlife. Apart from a casino, there are discos, pubs and some music programmes. For details about what's currently happening in town, ask locals or at the Syndicat d'Initiative.

Casino There's a casino (☎ 24 47 00) on Ave de Bourbon which is open on weekdays from 11 am to 2 am and on weekends from 11 am to 4 am. The gambling tables (blackjack, American Roulette etc) open at 10 pm and entry costs FF65.

Discos The St-Gilles-les-Bains area has a greater density of discos than anywhere else on the island. It's best to ask the locals which place is the flavour of the month, as places seem to go in and out of fashion.

Le Swing (☎ 24 45 98), at Grand Fond near the turn-off to St-Gilles-les-Hauts and the Théâtre de Plein Air, is open only on Friday, Saturday and holidays. *Le Privé* (☎ 24 16 62), on Rue Général de Gaulle, is another possibility, but isn't anything crash hot. It's open every night except Tuesday.

At Hermitage-les-Bains is *Moulin du Tango* (☎ 24 53 90), which operates on Wednesday, Friday and Saturday from 10 pm until the wee hours of the morning.

Dancing des Roches Noires (☎ 24 44 15), on Rue Générale de Gaulle, is open only on Saturday from 10 pm to dawn. Other options include *Le Palladium* (☎ 33 84 84), *Le Pussy Cat* (☎ 24 05 11), *Ailleurs* (☎ 22 93 01) and *Le Vandome* (☎ 24 55 02).

Music There are several hotels that conduct their own music performances (usually accompanying a buffet dinner). It's worth double checking the below places, as the opening hours may have changed since the time of writing.

Hôtel Coralia Novotel (☎ 24 44 44) has a

buffet fish barbecue on Monday night, accompanied by live music (FF160 per person). On Wednesday, there's a Créole evening with Créole singers (FF175 per person) and on Saturday, it's a buffet beef barbecue to the strains of the hotel music ensemble (FF165 per person).

Le Récif (☎ 24 50 51) offers a Créole buffet dinner every Tuesday (FF170 per person) and has jazz performances on Thursday nights. *Hôtel Les Aigrettes* (☎ 33 05 05) stages folk music programmes on Tuesday and Saturday nights.

Pubs Some of the better known pubs in St-Gilles-les-Bains include: *La Canne à Sucre* (☎ 24 02 56), *La Rhumerie* (☎ 24 55 99), *Chez Nous* (☎ 24 08 08), *Le Piccolo* (☎ 24 51 51), *Le Sombrero* (☎ 33 03 85) and *Le Pub la Case* (☎ 24 48 64).

Getting There & Away
St-Gilles-les-Bains lies on the St-Denis to St-Pierre line and buses leave approximately every half hour between 8 am and 6 pm in either direction; the bus stops are along the Route Nationale in both Hermitage-les-Bains and St-Gilles-les-Bains. The trip to St-Denis takes at least an hour and costs FF18.60.

Getting Around
For details about car and bicycle hire in the St-Gilles-les-Bains area, see the Réunion Getting Around chapter.

St-Gilles-les-Bains is also a popular take-off spot for helicopter tours around the island. For details, see Air in the Réunion Getting Around chapter.

ST-PAUL
Pleasantly attractive and worthwhile for a few hours of exploration, St-Paul is often bypassed by those scurrying towards the surf and white sand further south. As the original capital of Réunion, it bears a tropical and colonial air, with historical buildings along the seaside promenade, lined with cannons and shaded by straggly coconut trees. Most people find the black-sand beach pleasant to

look at but on closer inspection, the noise reveals its primary purpose for the locals.

In addition to the main attractions described later in this section, there are a couple of minor sights. The town hall, built in 1767, is an old French East India Company building. There's also an interesting Hindu temple along Rue St-Louis, dedicated to Lord Shiva.

Information
Money The Banque Français Commerciale is found on Rue du Commerce and the Crédit Agricole is on Chaussée Royale. They're both open weekdays from 8 am to 4 pm.

Post & Communications The post office is at 38 Rue Rhin et Danube and is open weekdays from 7.30 am to 6 pm and Saturdays from 8 am to noon.

Cimetière Marin
The only St-Paul site that could be considered a real attraction is the bright and well-kept cemetery near the southern end of town, a great place to wander and recall the island's tumultuous, renegade and mercantile past. It contains the plots and remains of Réunion's writers, rogues and respectable gentry. 'Celebrity graves' are well signposted and include those of the poet Leconte de Lisle (1818-94), complete with an epitaph extracted from one of his works, and Eugène Dayot, who lived from 1810 to 1852.

And then there's the grave of Eraste Feuillet (1801-30) who died because he took a sense of remorse too far. Feuillet, a young sea captain, awoke one morning in a hotel and, forgetting he was on dry land, tossed an empty toilet-water bottle out of the window. Unfortunately, it struck an unwitting passer-by who became miffed and challenged Feuillet to a duel. Fortunately, the irate adversary's pistol jammed, but unfortunately, Feuillet had a sense of honour and offered his own weapon as a replacement. And the bugger accepted it! Feuillet's epitaph reads simply 'Victime de sa générosité' (victim of his generosity).

The cemetery's greatest attraction, however, is the final resting place of the pirate Olivier Levasseur, 'La Buse' (the Buzzard),

RÉUNION

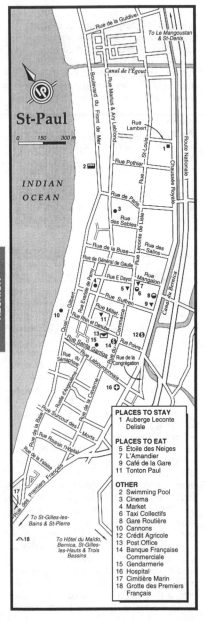

St-Paul

INDIAN
OCEAN

RÉUNION

PLACES TO STAY
1 Auberge Leconte
  Delisle

PLACES TO EAT
5 Étoile des Neiges
7 L'Amandier
9 Café de la Gare
11 Tonton Paul

OTHER
2 Swimming Pool
3 Cinema
4 Market
6 Taxi Collectifs
8 Gare Routière
10 Cannons
12 Crédit Agricole
13 Post Office
14 Banque Française
   Commerciale
15 Gendarmerie
16 Hospital
17 Cimitière Marin
18 Grotte des Premiers
   Français

who came to the Indian Ocean in 1720 in search of easy prey, after the Caribbean and Atlantic trade routes became too well policed. After stealing a fortune in treasure from the Portuguese vessel *La Vierge du Cap*, La Buse based himself on the east coast of Madagascar. He was the last Indian Ocean pirate to be apprehended. He was captured, taken to St-Paul and hanged on 7 July 1730. There are people still searching for his treasure in Mauritius, the Seychelles and Réunion.

La Buse still has disciples. On his grave, marked by the pirates' trademark skull and crossbones, stand recently placed *remerciement* (thank you) plaques and on some nights, secret admirers place cigarettes, glasses of rum, fruit and other offerings on the grave; many attribute them to a religious cult. Ironically, the epitaph of the gravestone beside the pirate's reads 'Here lies an honest man', just in case anyone should think the neighbourhood was the wrong side of the burial ground!

Grotte des Premiers Français
Across the highway from the Cimetière Marin is a small park in a cave-studded cliff face. The largest cave is said to have sheltered the mutineers from Madagascar who arrived in Réunion in 1646, the first Frenchmen to settle on the island. On one side is the shrine of Notre Dame des Lourdes, which at times becomes waterlogged, and on the other is a cold waterfall suitable for bathing if you don't mind spectators or sharing it with the local lads.

Chemin de la Tour des Roches & Ravine du Bernica
These two pleasant walks up the slopes directly behind St-Paul are signposted on the Route Nationale 1 just inland from the centre of town. On the paved Tour des Roches path are the remains of an old mill, heaps of coconut and banana trees and a nice view over the town. The dirt track up the Ravine du Bernica where, according to legend, La Buse deposited one of his treasures, follows the course of a clear stream up a lovely and quiet gorge.

Market

Held on the seafront, this colourful market is a popular attraction in St-Paul and predominantly sells fruit and vegetables. You may also come across cages of live chickens and sad-looking rabbits. There are a handful of handicraft stalls selling mainly Malagasy items (although not nearly as big a range as at the Grand Marché in St-Denis). Items include embroidery work, carved wooden pieces and T-shirts. Don't forget to bargain! The ambience is laid-back, making it an interesting place to explore at leisure. It's only open on Friday from around 7 am to 7 pm and on Saturday from 8 am to noon. It's best to go after 9 am, by when most stalls are set up.

Places to Stay

For a wider choice of accommodation, you'll have to head south to Boucan Canot or St-Gilles-les-Bains. Most travellers visit St-Paul on a day trip, which explains the limited accommodation.

Auberge Leconte Delisle (☎ 45 43 92), at 8 Rue Lambert at the north end of town, has rooms (single/double occupancy) for FF180. There are also studios for FF250 a double.

Hôtel du Maïdo (☎ 32 52 52; fax 32 52 00), out of town on Route du Maïdo (towards La Petite France), offers comfortable rooms costing FF270/350 a single/double. Rated as a two star hotel, facilities include a games room and restaurant.

Places to Eat

St-Paul has some good restaurant options but on weekends nearly everything is dead. For cheap eats, you could try *L'Amandier* or *Café de la Gare* which are both near the gare routière.

Tonton Paul (☎ 22 56 05), on Rue Millet, serves Chinese lunches every day except Sunday.

Étoile des Neiges (☎ 22 54 48), a Chinese and Créole restaurant on Rue Leconte de Lisle, has meals starting at around FF40. It's closed on Sunday.

Hôtel du Maïdo (☎ 32 52 52) (see Places to Stay) has a good, though slightly pricey restaurant, which serves French and Créole cuisine seven days a week. Nonresidents should book ahead.

Auberge Leconte Delisle (☎ 45 43 92) (see Places to Stay) specialises in cuisine créole et métro. The restaurant is open daily except Sunday evening and on Monday.

Le Loup (☎ 45 60 13), at Rue Marius & Ary Leblond, serves an assortment of grilled delights at reasonable prices. It's closed on Sunday and Monday.

Le Mangoustan (☎ 44 22 22), way up the Rivière des Galets at Rue des Rosiers in La Plaine, proudly claims that its speciality is nouvelle cuisine créole. You can dine here every day except Sunday.

Getting There & Away

St-Paul lies on the St-Denis to St-Pierre bus route and there are departures more or less half hourly from the gare routière in either town.

LE PORT & LA POSSESSION

As they head west out of St-Denis, vehicles are crowded onto the cliff-hugging stretch of coastal motorway known as La Corniche. After 14km, the highway issues onto open ground at the industrial centre of La Possession, really little more than a suburb of Réunion's main port area, which is known appropriately as Le Port. It was here that Governor Pronis took possession of the island in the name of the French king in 1640. There is little of interest in either place, but the highlands above them are another matter.

Midway between St-Denis and La Possession is the village of La Grande Chaloupe, which has a small **railway museum**. There are a handful of restored locomotives and other historical railway items on display. For further information, ask at the tourist office in St-Denis or La Possession.

Information

Tourist Office For tourist information, go to the Office de Tourisme de La Possession (☎ 22 26 66; fax 22 25 17) at 25 Rue Sarda Garriga in La Possession. It's open Monday to Saturday from 8.30 am to noon and 1.30 to 5 pm.

Dos d'Ane

Dos d'Ane village is an alternative starting or finishing point for treks to the Plaine d'Affouches and La Roche Écrite, as well as into the Cirque de Mafate via the Rivière des

RÉUNION

The Coastal Highway
The first 13km stretch of the highway west of St-Denis is a frequent subject of conversation in Réunion. This beautiful four lane road, which links the island's capital, port and beaches, has to be partially closed down for more than 50 days a year. And for good reason: virtually stolen from the ocean and constructed along the base of cliffs that are often more than 120m high, it is frequently bombarded by boulders that break off the cliff face and land in the midst of traffic. The danger is not to be taken lightly, since it causes at least one fatal accident a year, and it has resulted in many protective measures. One of the most recent steps taken has involved the installation of some anti-submarine netting left over from WWII and discovered in a storage depot, which mountaineers have stretched over the rock face. Nevertheless, traffic control remains the best protection. As a result, the two inside lanes of the highway are shut down when the rain gauge rises above 15mm, and safety patrols inspect this section of road every two hours.
At the same time, engineers are constantly seeking solutions to reduce the risk even further ... and to keep traffic moving smoothly. ∎

Galets route. An easy day walk from Dos d'Ane will get you to the gîte de montagne at Grand Place, while a magnificent but more challenging route will take you up the beautiful Bras des Merles to Aurère.

Unfortunately, there's no public transport to Dos d'Ane, so those without a vehicle will have to take a taxi from the small town of Rivière des Galets, which lies along the St-Denis to St-Pierre bus route.

Places to Stay

Auberge de Marie-Claire (☎ 32 00 04), at 2 Allée Vivien, Dos d'Ane, charges FF220 for a double room.

Le Galet Rond (☎ 32 01 56; fax 32 04 07), Rue Roland Jamin, has double rooms with/without bath for FF240/220. There's a large, somewhat characterless restaurant; the Créole set menu is FF90 per person.

M Axel Nativel (☎ 32 01 47), at Dos d'Ane, operates a basic gîte d'étape. A bed costs FF65 and meals are available at the table d'hôte (see Places to Eat). It's a good option for trekkers setting to and from the Cirque de Mafate.

Places to Eat

La Terrasse du Vietnam (☎ 22 15 44), Route de la Montagne in La Possession, offers tasty home-cooked Vietnamese dishes for around FF70; the set menu costs FF150. It's open daily from noon to 2.30 pm and 7.30 to 10 pm.

Haï Phong (☎ 22 39 80), at 32 Rue Raymond Mondon in La Possession, is another very good Vietnamese restaurant. Main dishes are between FF45 and FF80. It's open Monday to Friday from 11.30 am to 2 pm and 7.30 to 10 pm; only open for dinner on Saturday (closed Sunday).

Lions de Lyon (☎ 22 21 41), at 10 Rue Camp Magliore in La Possession, offers impressive cuisine gastronomique de Lyon at equally impressive prices. This place is ideal for a major splurge; expect to pay around FF230 for a meal. It's closed on Sundays.

Le Poteau Vert (☎ 32 01 47), the table d'hôte of M Axel Nativel in Dos d'Ane village, is recommended by anyone who's ever eaten there. Not only is it in a superb setting, it's also a welcome option for trekkers entering or leaving the Cirque de Mafate. Meals cost FF70 per person.

Le Moulin (☎ 22 18 18), at 19 Rue Sarda Garriga in La Possession, is a small, unpretentious snack bar which is open daily from 6 am to 7.30 pm. It offers cheap eats such as sandwiches (FF20), hot dogs (FF12), cakes (FF7.50) and ice creams (FF5 to FF10). It's also good for a quick breakfast.

Le Boeuf (☎ 22 15 15), above Le Moulin, specialises in pizzas and French food. Pizzas cost from FF30 to FF58. Other main dishes cost between FF60 and FF80. It's open daily, except Sunday, from noon to 2.30 pm and 6 to 10.30 pm.

La Grenouille (☎ 43 29 28) is at 38 Rue de St-Paul in Le Port. This is a French, Créole and Italian restaurant with main dishes from about FF45. It's open daily, except Sunday, from 7 am (for breakfast) to around 5 pm.

The Interior

HIGHLIGHTS

- A fantastic range of day walks, taking in the waterfalls and flora and fauna
- A dip in the *Sources Thermales* (hot springs) in Cilaos to relieve those aching muscles
- The towering Cascade du Voile de la Mariée falls near Salazie
- Exploring the intriguing cirques of Cilaos, Salazie and Mafate
- A visit to Îlet à Bourse, an attractive village with a garden-like setting and great views

Réunion's interior is a tremendous tramping ground, an exotic and mountainous terrain that manages to provide outdoor thrills without being too dangerous or overly challenging. With beachcombing limited on the island, the mountain and cirque country provides room to roam and as an additional bonus, the scenery is as breathtaking as the sometimes humid tropical climate.

Undoubtedly the best way to explore this country is on foot. There are hundreds of walks that would take another book to cover in any worthwhile detail, but some of the most popular options are covered in the Trekking in Réunion chapter.

The Cirques

Like the leaves of a three-leaf clover, the cirques of Cilaos, Salazie and Mafate dominate the heart of the island. Although they superficially resemble volcanic craters, they are actually the product of the same erosional forces that sharpened the peak of the Matterhorn in Switzerland. The massif was originally one immense volcanic dome known as a shield volcano. After volcanic activity ceased, aeons of erosion scoured out amphitheatres on three sides of the summit, Piton des Neiges, and sculpted the ridge and valley landscape visible today.

It's worth travelling the roads into these amazing amphitheatres for the trip alone. If you go by bus or taxi, the ride can be hairraising; the roads edge along cliffs and gorges, corkscrew up and around mountain sides and hairpin bends, and pass through tunnels and over viaducts. At a contortion called Le Boucle on the trip into Cilaos, the road even makes a complete loop over itself.

Here, the cloud and mist formations provide wonderful special effects, and during (and just after) the rainy season, the world is green, lush and dripping. The Cilaos and Salazie cirques seem to be enchanted kingdoms and the Cirque de Mafate is wild, secluded and bizarre.

CILAOS & THE CIRQUE DE CILAOS

The quaint town of Cilaos developed as a spa resort at the end of the 19th century when the thermal baths were constructed. The name, pronounced 'see-LA-oos', is thought to be derived from the Malagasy word *tsy laosana*, a place from which one never returns. Most of the village's inhabitants are descended from settlers who came from Brittany and Normandy in the 1700s.

The area is known for the production of lentils, local embroidery and sweet red and white wines reminiscent of sherry and tawny port, respectively.

Information

Tourist Office The Syndicat d'Initiative, known as the Office de Tourisme de Cilaos (☎ 31 78 03; fax 31 70 30), at 2 Rue Mac Auliffe, is very helpful and well stocked with brochures, interesting souvenirs and some terrific postcards. It's open Monday to Saturday from 8.30 am to noon and 1 to 6 pm, and Sunday from 9 am to 1 pm. This is also the Cilaos headquarters for Maison de la Montagne (☎ 31 71 71; fax 31 80 54), which will book gîtes de montagne and provide trekking information.

RÉUNION

Money There aren't any banks in Cilaos so make sure you have enough francs with you.

Sources Thermales

Although they were probably known for some time by escaped slaves hiding out in the cirque, the *sources thermales* (thermal springs) of Cilaos were brought to the attention of the outside world in 1815 by a goat hunter from St-Louis, M Paulin Técher. The first track into the cirque was constructed in 1842 and the springs formed the basis of Cilaos' existence as a colonial health resort and hill retreat from the sticky coast. The water gushing from the spring is hot and the active ingredient seems to be bicarbonate of soda with traces of magnesium, iron, calcium, sulphur and a weak radioactivity. It's said to cure rheumatism, among other bone and muscular ailments.

The first thermal station was opened to the public in 1896, but the source was ruined in a cyclone in 1948 and not revived until 1971. Over the years, the baths and walls became heavily stained and the station was closed in mid-1987 and turned into a museum. A new complex, using the same source, was opened just uphill from the Hôtel des Thermes. It has a bigger pool, plush private cubicles, a sauna, gymnasium, café and reception area. It's open Monday to Saturday from 8 am to noon and 2 to 5 pm, and Sunday from 8 am to 2 pm.

A jacuzzi at the Établissement Thermal Irénée Accot (☎ 31 72 27; fax 31 76 57) costs FF110 per person for 20 minutes, while a sauna of the same duration is FF80 per person. For a dose of pampering, try the relaxing two hour sauna and seaweed treatment (accompanied by soothing music) for FF305 per person. There's also an assortment of other tempting options to choose from.

All this (most of this, anyway) is magic for relaxing after a long hike when your feet are sore and your muscles stiff. If you don't want or need a bath, you can always visit the spring itself. Of the massages, however, one traveller has written:

Be warned; don't expect a Créole beauty to give you a massage as a friend of mine did. He was most disappointed when he discovered that the massage he booked at the thermal station was to be performed by a machine!!

Gillian Chambers

Maison de la Broderie (Embroidery House)

Although the designs and procedures came originally from Brittany, Cilaos' embroidery tradition began at the turn of the 20th century when Dr Jean-Marie Mac Auliffe arrived to practise thermal medicine. His daughter Angèle took up embroidery as a pastime, learning her technique from books and from the sisters who taught the young village girls how to embroider handkerchiefs. Angèle soon organised a small needlework club, which led to an embroidery workshop of 20 ladies and the distinctive Cilaos style evolved. Angèle died in 1908, aged 31, during a measles epidemic in St-Denis.

In 1953, however, the sisters of Notre-Dame-des-Neiges opened a workshop and school which continues to operate. There are now more than 120 professional embroiders at work in Cilaos. The Maison de la Broderie (☎ 31 77 48; fax 31 80 54) on Rue des Écoles, built under the direction of mayor Irénée Accot in 1984, provides a venue for both teachers and students. Here, they embroider children's clothes, baptism dresses, serviettes, place settings and table cloths for sale and exhibition. The centre is open to the public Monday to Saturday from 9 am to noon and 2 to 5 pm, and on Sunday from 9 am to noon. Admission (including a guided tour) costs FF5 per person.

Philippe Turpin's Studio

The signposted studio (☎ 31 73 64) of Cilaos-born artist and former primary school teacher, Philippe Turpin, is on Rue Vinceslas Rivière just uphill from Rue des Écoles. Entry is free. It's a good idea to call in advance, to make sure Philippe is there. The etchings from copper engravings of Cilaos and other landscapes on Réunion capture the feel of the island perhaps better than the oil-based forms normally used for tropical scenes. Other prints depict fantasy scenes, magical forests and people, star signs and Gothic romances. Prices for his creations start at around FF100. The Syndicat d'Initiative also has a collection of his work for sale.

Walks

There are some excellent short walks or day walks from Cilaos. Some of the better walks are suggested below but for different routes or more detailed and longer treks from Cilaos, see the Trekking in Réunion chapter.

Cascade de Bras Rouge This day walk begins by following the road behind the Maison de la Montagne; turn downhill between the hotel Le P'tit Randonneur and the hostel Le Sentier. From the end of the road, there's a track which descends to the old thermal station where you'll find the start of the track which traverses the slopes above the Bras des Étangs. After about two hours, you'll arrive at the waterfall Cascade de Bras Rouge.

From the waterfall, the route continues up the side of the cirque to the Îlet à Cordes road and from there up to the Col du Taïbit and into the Cirque de Mafate.

Bras Sec The road to Bras Sec village (just east of Cilaos) passes through a lovely forest of Japanese cryptomerias. Hikers, however, can take the short cut across the Ravine du Bras de Benjoin. Begin by following the road north from the lake, Mare à Joncs, then taking the right fork at the hospital. After a couple of hundred metres straight on, the road will turn into the unpaved track which descends into the Ravine du Bras de Benjoin, then climbs into the village of Bras Sec. Allow about two hours for this walk.

From the southern end of Bras Sec village, it's possible to continue along the Sentier des Calumets to the village of Palmiste Rouge (at least four hours). The track leaves from the village and climbs to the foot of Bonnet de Prêtre, the 'priest's bonnet'. Here, take the left fork, the Sentier Forestier which traverses the walls of Les Calumets and

emerges at Palmiste Rouge. From the village, it's possible to return the way you came, or walk out to the main St-Louis-to-Cilaos road (2km) and catch a bus back to Cilaos.

Buses run frequently between Cilaos and Bras Sec every day except on Sunday, when there are only a couple running in either direction.

Roche Merveilleuse The signposted path off the road behind the Hôtel des Thermes ascends to Roche Merveilleuse (just north of Cilaos) in the Forêt du Grand Matarum. The walk takes at least two hours each way; be sure to follow the right fork at the Plateau des Chênes (yes, there are oak trees!) or you'll wind up en route to the Col du Taïbit. It's also possible to drive to Roche Merveilleuse along Route Forestière 11.

La Chapelle A pleasant and slightly challenging day hike is to La Chapelle (just west of Cilaos). It begins near the village of Bras des Étangs and quickly descends into the Ravine Henri Dijoux. After about 3km, the track climbs 200m up and over a crest before plunging into the Ravine de Bras Rouge and following it upstream to the cave of La Chapelle. An alternative route is via the Cascade de Bras Rouge (described earlier in this section), which lies only 500m upstream from La Chapelle.

La Chapelle has been featured in a David Attenborough TV nature film because from the end of October through to November, the martins raise their young without nests; the parents – and then their young – simply hang onto the ceiling of the cave. If you go there during the breeding season, please don't disturb the birds!

Peter & Ginette Scott

Coteau de Kervéguen Those with a great deal of energy may want to consider the day walk to the Coteau de Kervéguen which separates the Cirque de Cilaos from the Forêt de Bébour. It begins from the picnic kiosk along the road to Bras Sec, and climbs nearly 1000m to the crest. Plan on at least seven hours for the return trip from the picnic

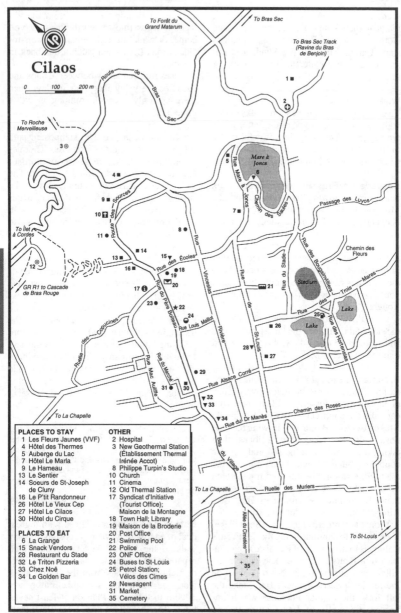

Cilaos

0   100   200 m

To Forêt du
Grand Matarum

To Bras Sec

To Bras Sec Track
(Ravine du Bras
de Benjoin)

To Roche
Merveilleuse

To Îlet
à Cordes

Route des Sources

Route de Bras Sec

Mare à
Joncs

Rue Mare à Joncs

Chemin des Salazes

Passage des Luyos

Chemin des
Fleurs

Rue des Écoles

Rue Vinoslias

Rue du Père Boiteau

Rue des Bougainvilliers

Stadium

Trois Mares

Rue des Hortensias

Lake

Lake

Rue de

Rue du Stade

Rue St-Louis

GR R1 to Cascade
de Bras Rouge

Ruelle des Capucines

Rue Louis Maillot

Rue Rivière

Rue Alsace Corré

Rue Mac Auliffe

Rue du Marché

To La Chapelle

Chemin des Roses

Rue du Dr Manès

Bras du Village

To La Chapelle

Ruelle des Muriers

Allée du Cimetière

To St-Louis

RÉUNION

PLACES TO STAY
1   Les Fleurs Jaunes (VVF)
4   Hôtel des Thermes
5   Auberge du Lac
7   Hôtel Le Marla
9   Le Hameau
13 Le Sentier
14 Soeurs de St-Joseph
    de Cluny
16 Le P'tit Randonneur
26 Hôtel Le Vieux Cep
27 Hôtel Le Cilaos
30 Hôtel du Cirque

PLACES TO EAT
6   La Grange
15 Snack Vendors
28 Restaurant du Stade
32 Le Triton Pizzeria
33 Chez Noë
34 Le Golden Bar

OTHER
2   Hospital
3   New Geothermal Station
    (Établissement Thermal
    Irénée Accot)
8   Philippe Turpin's Studio
10 Church
11 Cinema
12 Old Thermal Station
17 Syndicat d'Initiative
    (Tourist Office);
    Maison de la Montagne
18 Town Hall; Library
19 Maison de la Broderie
20 Post Office
21 Swimming Pool
22 Police
23 ONF Office
24 Buses to St-Louis
25 Petrol Station;
    Vélos des Cimes
29 Newsagent
31 Market
35 Cemetery

kiosk, longer from Cilaos. This is also an alternative route to use for the gîte de montagne and the climb to the summit of Piton des Neiges; from the crest, turn left and follow the track 3km to the gîte.

If you have a few days and would like a real challenge, it's possible to continue to Entre-Deux. From the summit, follow the track about another 1km, and take a right turn. This track leads to the 2350m Sommet de l'Entre-Deux. Then for about 5km it follows a knife-edge crest between the steep slopes of Les Calumets inside the Cirque de Cilaos and the spectacular Le Dimitile, which slopes dramatically down to Les Hautes Plaines, before descending Le Dimitile into Entre-Deux. Alternatively, from the Coteau de Kervéguen, you can continue straight along to the Plaine-des-Cafres or the Col de Bébour.

Col du Taïbit The Col du Taïbit is the trekkers' Cilaos gateway to the Cirque de Mafate, and there are several ways of getting there. The easiest is to take a bus along the Îlet à Cordes road to the trailhead, which is about 6km from Cilaos village. Alternatively, you can trek from Cilaos to Marla via the Col du Taïbit in six hours. See the Tour des Cirques section in the Trekking in Réunion chapter for details.

Piton des Neiges There are several ways to explore Piton des Neiges, the highest point in Réunion at 3069m.

You can hike from Cilaos or Hell-Bourg or base yourself at the Gîte de la Caverne Dufour (Piton des Neiges). For full details see the Tour des Cirques section in the Trekking in Réunion chapter.

Places to Stay

Cilaos is well endowed with accommodation options, but it can become crowded during the tourist season – for peace of mind, you're advised to book ahead.

Camping There are two camping grounds around Cilaos.

Camping de Cilaos and *Gîte d'Étape Eucalyptus* (☎ 31 77 41), in Matarum, is a good option, with 120 sites and two small gîtes. The site and buildings are clean, and there are showers and toilets as well as a bar and restaurant where three-course meals cost FF60 to FF80. You'll pay FF40 per night for a 20 sq metre tent site, and gîte beds cost FF40 per person without sheets.

Camp site (☎ 31 71 40) belongs to the Office National des Forêts. Use it free of charge with authorisation from the office on Rue du Père Boiteau.

Hostels There are a number of hostel options, some offering meals.

Le Hameau (☎ 31 70 94), just downhill from the Hôtel des Thermes, in the old seminary at 5 Chemin Séminaire, is the rather quirky unofficial youth hostel. Rooms are available on a full-board basis only and go for FF185/310 for a single/double.

Soeurs de St-Joseph de Cluny (☎ 31 71 22), also known as *Notre Dame des Neiges* (Our Lady of the Snows), is an ex-boarding school for girls located at 80 Rue du Père Boiteau. It has accommodation for 40 people in partitioned dormitories, with kitchen facilities available. It's rarely crowded and dormitory beds cost FF50 per person plus FF10 for linen, if necessary.

Le Sentier (☎ 31 71 54), nearby, is another hostel which is actually more like a budget hotel. It costs FF60 per person but claustrophobes should note that most of the rooms and windows are tiny. Meals are available and range from FF60 to FF80.

Auberge du Lac (☎ 31 76 30) is at 13 Rue Mare à Joncs, just north of Mare à Joncs, Cilaos' largest lake. There are just a few rooms; singles or doubles cost FF170; breakfast is an extra FF30 per person.

Village Vacance Famille (VVF) Remember that if you are a nonmember of the VVF it will cost you a FF100 per family annual joining fee.

Les Fleurs Jaunes (☎ 31 71 39; fax 31 80 85), the VVF, is to the north of town behind the hospital. Rooms (all on a full-board basis) range from FF200 to FF240. There are also bungalows for FF260. They accept only members of the VVF.

Chambres d'Hôte Due to high demand, there are numerous chambres d'hôte in Cilaos. Most include breakfast in their room tariff.

RÉUNION

Mme Gardebien (☎ 31 72 15) operates a chambre d'hôte at 50 Rue St-Louis and although it seems less intimate than some others, it's not unfriendly. Rooms cost FF120/160 a single/double and meals are FF80.

M Luc Payet (☎ 31 77 79) is in a good location at 1 Ruelle des Artisans just west of the town centre. Rooms cost FF200 whether they're occupied by one or two people. Meals are an extra FF80.

M Christian Dijoux (☎ 25 56 64) has a place in Bras Sec itself, at 40 Chemin Saül. Rooms go for FF170 a single/double. Meals cost FF80.

M Dijoux (☎ 25 56 45) is on the same street and charges FF60 per person; FF80 for a meal.

Mme Hélèe Payet (☎ 35 18 13) is another chambre d'hôte way out in Îlet à Cordes at the western edge of the cirque. She charges FF120/160 a single/double. Meals cost FF80.

Dan tan Lontan (☎ 25 69 80) is 18km from Cilaos in Îlet Haute, an oddly named village considering it's at the very bottom of the cirque! The house is an hour's walk uphill from La Maison Forestière at Le Pavillon. The beds cost FF70 and meals are FF85.

Mme Aurélien Nassibou (☎ 31 71 77) is not far from the camp site on the road towards Bras Sec. She charges FF150 for a single/double.

Mme Hoareau (☎ 31 72 09), at Rue des Chênes up in Matarum, charges FF80/120 a single/double.

Mme Marie-Jeanne Begue (☎ 25 57 08), at Chemin Chryptomérias in Bras Sec, has rooms for FF125 a single or double.

Mme Flavie (☎ 31 71 23), at 8 Chemin Matarum, just outside Cilaos, charges FF120/160 for a single/ double. Meals are an additional FF80.

Gîtes There are four gîtes worth investigating.

Gîte de la Caverne Dufour (Piton des Neiges) (☎ 51 15 26), at Caverne Dufour along the trekking route to Piton des Neiges, costs FF60 per person. Meals must be booked in advance and cost FF60 extra. Although not the best equipped gîte, it is still popular, so book as far in advance as possible through Maison de la Montagne in St-Denis or Cilaos (see Accommodation in the Réunion Facts for the Visitor chapter).

Le Grand Bénare (☎ 31 78 29) is conveniently located in town at 2 Rue Vinceslas Rivière. A bed costs FF70 per night; meals are an additional FF80 per person.

Gîte du Cap Noir (☎ 31 70 52), about 2km from town on the main road towards St-Louis, has the capacity to hold up to 14 people. It rents out for FF2240 per week or FF1792 for a weekend. If there are only 12 guests, the weekend rate drops to FF1570; for a maximum of six people the weekend rate is FF1120.

Mme Aurélien Nassibou (☎ 31 71 77), who also has a chambre d'hôte, owns two gîtes, one for independent travellers and the other for groups. They cost around FF75 per person per night.

Hotels There are several hotel options which cater for most budgets.

Hôtel Le Marla (☎ 31 72 33; fax 31 72 98), not far from the lake, on Rue Mare à Joncs, is very popular with budget travellers. Double rooms with shared shower cost FF140, while singles or doubles with attached bath are FF160. Breakfast is FF20 per person and set-menu meals are FF80.

Le P'tit Randonneur (☎ 31 79 55), at 65 Rue du Père Boiteau, is another relatively cheap choice. Single/ double rooms cost FF150/200. Breakfast is FF20.

Hôtel du Cirque (☎ 31 70 68; fax 31 80 46), at 27 Rue du Père Boiteau, is conveniently located in the centre of town, but gets mixed reports from travellers. Rooms cost FF240/320 a single/double including breakfast. Meals in the restaurant are between FF60 and FF90.

Hôtel Le Vieux Cep (☎ 31 71 89; fax 31 77 68) is at 2 Rue des Trois Mares and has comfortable single/ double rooms (including breakfast) for FF340/ 385.

Hôtel Le Cilaos (☎ 31 71 50), at 44 Rue de St-Louis, has unexciting singles/doubles for FF250/300. Breakfast is FF25 per person.

Hôtel des Thermes (☎ 31 89 00; fax 31 74 73), 8 Route des Sources, is the most upmarket hotel in Cilaos. Room rates are FF430/490 a single/double including breakfast. Built in 1936, the Hôtel des Thermes is worth a visit in itself.

Places to Eat

For cheap munchies, there are usually some mobile snack stalls on Rue des Écoles. Samosas cost around FF2 and sandwich rolls are FF20.

Le Golden Bar (☎ 31 70 52), at the southern end of Rue du Père Boiteau, has a selection of snacks and Créole dishes.

Chez Noë (☎ 31 79 93), at 41 Rue du Père Boiteau, has an emphasis on Créole cuisine. It's closed on Monday.

Le Triton Pizzeria (☎ 31 79 41), next door, serves a range of Italian and Créole dishes. It's open every day except Tuesday and some Monday nights.

Le Moulin A Café (☎ 31 80 80), at 68 Rue du Père Boiteau, is a pleasant little place which charges from FF35 to FF70 for a main course. It's also good for a hot cappuccino (FF15), chocolate milkshake (FF15) or an ice cream (FF25). It is closed on Friday.

Restaurant du Stade (☎ 31 75 09), on Rue de St-Louis, is ideal for hearty home-cooked meals. It's run by the very jolly Mme Gillette, who serves large (she's used to cooking for her 11 children!) and appetising Créole meals for around FF60.

La Grange (☎ 31 70 38) is located in a picturesque setting near the lake and charges around FF50 to FF80 for a main dish (French or Créole food).

Most of the hotels also have restaurants (see Places to Stay for locations).

Le Sentier serves French/Créole food; prices range from FF70 to FF160.

Hôtel Le Marla has a good restaurant with a choice of several set menus daily, usually consisting of soup or starter, salad, main course and dessert for FF60. The focus is on Créole but there are occasionally other cuisines. On cool days, there's often a log fire to keep you toasty.

Hôtel du Cirque has a broad menu with Créole, Chinese and French specialities. It's open every day for lunch and dinner.

Hôtel des Thermes has a top-class restaurant with top-class prices. Specialising in Créole and French fare, the food is certainly good, but not exceptional. It's best to book ahead if you're not staying at the hotel.

Hôtel Le Vieux Cep is more affordable and offers terrific Créole and French food; it's open daily.

Le P'tit Randonneur specialises in Créole fare.

Auberge du Lac is another Créole speciality place. If you're not staying here, it's a good idea to book ahead.

Entertainment

If you want to catch a movie, there's a small *cinema* opposite the church, which is only open on Saturday night (although more often during the tourist season).

There used to be a disco in Cilaos, but it apparently closed down after being the centre of one too many late-night brawls!

If you fancy a bit of a paddle, there's a *pool* just off Rue de St-Louis which is open to the public only on Wednesday from 8.30 am to noon and 1.30 to 4 pm. Admission costs FF8.

Things to Buy

Cilaos is noted for its lentils and home-made sweet wine. You'll get lentils with most meals, particularly at the chambres and tables d'hôte, and probably a sip of the wine too.

There are several places in Cilaos and Bras Sec which have signs saying they sell Vin de Cilaos. It's also available at the Syndicat d'Initiative for FF35 in an officially labelled bottle but on the roadside, it's available in liquor bottles for about FF20.

Cilaos is also a good place to stock up on groceries for trekking trips through the cirques.

Getting There & Away

Cilaos is 112km from St-Denis by road and 37km from the nearest coastal town, St-Louis. The road into the Cirque de Cilaos begins at St-Louis and twists and contorts its way steeply into the lofty cirque floor. Le Pavillon, where a road bridge crosses the Bras de Cilaos, marks the spot from which early visitors to the cirque either had to be carried on a palanquin or had to begin walking.

To get to Cilaos from St-Denis, take a bus towards St-Pierre and change buses at St-Louis. From St-Louis, there are around eight buses daily on weekdays and Saturday, and four on Sunday (the Sunday routes run only between St-Louis and Cilaos and don't include St-Pierre). One or two of these services continue on to Îlet à Cordes, useful for reaching the Col du Taïbit trailhead, and quite a few connect Cilaos with the village of Bras Sec. The fare from St-Louis to Cilaos, Îlet à Cordes or Bras Sec is FF31.

There are also taxi-collectifs running twice daily between Cilaos and St-Louis for FF30, leaving Cilaos early in the morning and late at night. Inquire at the Syndicat d'Initiative for exact times and pick-up points.

Getting Around

Mountain bikes can be hired from Vélos des Cimes (☎ 31 75 11), Rue des Trois Mares, which charges FF50/100 for a half/full day. For more information about mountain bikes, see Bicycle in the Réunion Getting Around chapter.

HELL-BOURG & THE CIRQUE DE SALAZIE

The Cirque de Salazie, the wettest of the three cirques, is busier and more varied than

RÉUNION

Cilaos, and although it's a bit 'flatter' (although 'flat' is not the first word that will spring to mind when you see it!), the scenery and approach are nearly as awesome. The name is thought to derive from the Malagasy word *salazane*, which means 'sentry stakes'.

The community of Salazie sits at the eastern entrance to the cirque, while Hell-Bourg occupies a beautiful setting 9km further up the slopes. Named after former governor Admiral de Hell rather than the state of the town, it served as a thermal resort until its springs dried up. Visitors can still see the ruins of the old baths and the Hôtel des Salazes which once accommodated the thermal crowd. Hell-Bourg is also one of the best places to see Créole architecture.

Grand Îlet is a perfect introduction to rural Réunion and home to several pleasant and rustic chambres and tables d'hôte. Still further up is Le Bélier, the Cirque de Salazie's main gateway to the Cirque de Mafate.

Information
Tourist Office The Syndicat d'Initiative de Salazie (☎ 47 50 14; fax 47 60 06) occupies a small office opposite the *mairie* (town hall) in Salazie. It is open Monday to Saturday from 9 am to 3 pm, and Sunday from 9 to 11 am. It has the usual stock of glossy brochures and leaflets.

Cascade du Voile de la Mariée
A couple of km from Salazie on the road towards Hell-Bourg, below the turn-off to Grand Îlet, is the Cascade du Voile de la Mariée (Bridal Veil Falls). These towering falls drop in several stages from the often cloud-obscured heights into the ravine at the roadside.

Mare à Poule d'Eau
On the road from Salazie to Hell-Bourg, at the top of the corkscrew section, is the village of Mare à Poule d'Eau with its superb viewpoint. If you want to see the Mare à Poule d'Eau (Water Chicken Pond) itself, take the road on the right (if you're coming from Salazie) beside the village school. This leads to a track which eventually follows a

stream course for about 100m before reaching the pond. It's a favourite angling spot for locals but, because of nasty algae, it's not suitable for swimming. During the rainy season, the mosquitoes can be overwhelming.

Anciens Thermes
The old spa at Hell-Bourg is found in the ravine near the western end of town, and it's a nice short walk from the centre. Head downhill from the Hôtel Le Relais des Cimes along the main street. Where the street begins climbing to the gendarmerie, bear right and follow the track down to the river, where you'll see the blue-tiled ruins of the old baths. There's not much left now, but it's a quiet and leafy spot. Cross the clunky steel bridge and climb the hill and you'll connect with the Îlet à Vidot road.

Jardin de la Villa des Chataigniers
This late-19th century flower and palm garden at 5 Rue Amiral Lacaze in Hell-Bourg is planted densely around a series of walls, walkways, kiosks, terraces and fountains. You'll find a variety of tropical flowering plants including camellias, orchids, anthuriums, asters, nasturtiums etc. You can arrange a visit by phoning the owner, M Jean-François Folio (☎ 47 80 98). Admission is FF20 per person.

Élevage de Truites
Near Hell-Bourg is the trout farm Élevage de Truites, also known as the Parc Piscicole d'Hell-Bourg. It was established in 1940 and is now operated by M Paul Irigoyen. Entry is FF7 per person unless you're fishing, in which case entry is free but self-caught trout cost FF70 per kg. Even habitually unlucky or impatient anglers will be able to score a catch here. The farm is open daily from 9 am to 6 pm.

Les Sources Pétrifiantes
These iron-rich hot springs, discovered in 1916 by an illegal hunter, are popular with day hikers from Hell-Bourg. At least many day hikers start out for the springs; quite a few are intimidated by the narrow tracks

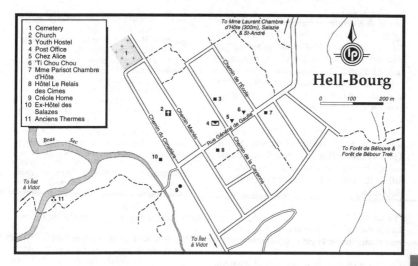

1 Cemetery
2 Church
3 Youth Hostel
4 Post Office
5 Chez Alice
6 'Ti Chou Chou
7 Mme Parisot Chambre
  d'Hôte
8 Hôtel Le Relais
  des Cimes
9 Créole Home
10 Ex-Hôtel des
  Salazes
11 Anciens Thermes

Hell-Bourg

along precipitous slopes and turn back short of the destination.

Begin by following the variation on the Col de Fourche route (see Col de Fourche below). After 2km on this track, turn left on the track across the Ravine Goyave. It then climbs up and over the ridge before descending to the springs. There are waterfalls both upstream and downstream from the site.

Piton d'Enchaing

The 1352m-high summit of this prominent flat-topped peak, in the heart of the Cirque de Salazie, is a popular day-hiking destination from Hell-Bourg. The peak was named after an escaped slave who took refuge on its summit, from which he was able to survey the entire Cirque de Salazie and report to other fugitives on the presence of pursuers and bounty hunters.

It's a rather steep and difficult walk which concludes with a precipitous gain of 500m of elevation, so bring energy snacks and allow plenty of time for rests; at least five hours return from Hell-Bourg (see Fourth day: Marla to Hell-Bourg, in the Tour des Cirques section of the Trekking in Réunion chapter).

Piton des Neiges

This highly popular trek may be started in either Cilaos (see Cilaos earlier in this chapter) or Hell-Bourg. Most people choose to stay overnight at the Gîte de la Caverne Dufour (Piton des Neiges) and then make the early-morning trek to the summit from there. For information see Second day: Gîte de la Caverne Dufour (Piton des Neiges) to the summit of Piton des Neiges and to Cilaos, in the Trekking in Réunion chapter.

There's normally no point in being at the summit after the clouds close in at around 8.30 am.

Col de Fourche

The Col de Fourche is a popular entrance into the Cirque de Mafate. Although most people opt for the shorter and easier route via Le Bélier (from which there's a motorable road approaching within a few hundred metres of the Col), the main GR R1 route is from Hell-Bourg. You can reach the trailhead by bus from Hell-Bourg, or walk via a shortcut from the gendarmerie in Hell-Bourg, down past the old thermal baths and back up to the road. The track leaves from the end of the Îlet à Vidot road. There's also a variation which turns left a couple of hundred metres before the end of the road – this is the track to use for Les Sources Pétrifiantes – meeting up with the main track at a relatively level spot called Le Grand Sable.

From Le Grand Sable, two hours from the trailhead, the route climbs steadily for about 5km up to Col de Fourche.

For information, see Fourth day: Marla to Col des Bœufs, in the Four Days in Mafate section in the Trekking in Réunion chapter. The section explains how to get from Marla to Hell-Bourg via the Col de Fourche. Just follow the instructions in reverse starting at Hell-Bourg.

Places to Stay
Youth Hostel This hostel is very popular all year round and it's best to book ahead.

Youth Hostel (Auberge de Jeunesse) (☎ 47 82 65) is in a majestic old colonial home, Maison Morange, at Chemin de la Cayenne in Hell-Bourg. Beds cost FF70 per person for card-carrying HI members. The kitchen is open to guests who wish to cook their own meals. Alternatively, evening meals are available for FF60 and breakfast for FF15. There are hot showers and laundry facilities, including a washing machine which will be a welcome sight for trekkers just in from the muddy trail. In the high season, the hostel is very popular with trekkers and in the off season, it frequently fills with work camp visitors. If it's full, you may be able to pitch a tent outside for around FF30.

Chambres d'Hôte
For inexpensive accommodation, Grand Îlet, with a handful of chambres d'hôte, is better than Hell-Bourg. It's also a good jumping-off point for treks into the Cirque de Mafate.

Mme Jeanine Grondin (☎ 47 70 66) has some rooms on Rue de l'Église right in Grand Îlet. She charges FF100/130 a single/double.
Mme Jeanne Marie Grondin (☎ 47 70 51) charges FF100/150 for a single/double room.
Mme Christine Boyer (☎ 47 70 87) charges FF100/120 for a single/double. It's a bit difficult to find: get off the bus near the church and walk up the hill signposted to La Nouvelle. Pass the pharmacy and keep going uphill until you reach a restaurant near the top of the hill. Here you turn left down a track and the chambre d'hôte will be on your left near the bottom of the track.

M Christian Maillot (☎ 47 71 39) is further into the hills, beyond Grand Îlet towards the Cirque de Mafate at Le Bélier. His quirky chambre d'hôte is similarly priced to that of Mme Boyer. To get there, take the bus to Le Bélier and walk downhill along the road for several hundred metres. Turn right along the first track and follow it until you see the chambre d'hôte on the right. For trekkers, this is a better option than Grand Îlet because it's an hour's walking nearer Bord à Martin and Col de Fourche.
Mme Madeleine Parisot (☎ 47 83 48), in Hell-Bourg, is a friendly chambre d'hôte, with double rooms for FF120; breakfast is an extra FF10 and dinner (which should be booked in advance) is FF80.
Mme Madeleine Laurent (☎ 47 80 60) is located a bit further from town, 900m from Hell-Bourg towards Mare à Poule d'Eau. She charges FF100/150 a single/double.

Gîtes There are two gîtes in the area.

Bélouve Gîte de Montagne (☎ 41 21 23) is about two hours walking above Hell-Bourg and costs FF70 per person. Breakfast is an additional FF25 and dinner is FF80. Bookings should be made through Maison de la Montagne in St-Denis or Cilaos (see Accommodation in the Réunion Facts for the Visitor chapter).
M Jean-Pierre Robert (☎ 47 90 14) is a gîte de France at Mare à Martin, 4km by road above Grand Îlet. He charges FF60 per night per person.

Hotels There is only one hotel worth considering and, although well kept, the service can sometimes be a little indifferent.

Hôtel Le Relais des Cimes (☎ 47 81 58; fax 47 82 11), on Rue Général de Gaulle in Hell-Bourg, has comfortable singles/doubles for FF300/380, including breakfast.

Places to Eat
While Cilaos is known for its lentils, the name Hell-Bourg is locally synonymous with chou chou, a green, pear-shaped vegetable (known in Europe as *crystophène*) imported from Brazil in 1834.

'Ti Chou Chou (☎ 47 80 93), on Rue Général de Gaulle, is a simple little restaurant with a varied Créole menu. Plats du jour cost around FF60.
Chez Alice (☎ 47 86 24), not far away, cooks up a Créole storm. Alice serves up hearty plats du jour, including generous salads, main dishes and desserts, for around FF70. It's popular, especially at lunchtime, but is closed on Mondays.

Chez Cocotier (☎ 47 84 01), on Rue Général de Gaulle, has tasty Créole eats at affordable prices.

Hôtel Le Relais des Cimes (☎ 47 81 58), in Hell-Bourg, has a restaurant which serves Créole and French specialities for FF60 to FF120. It's open every day for lunch and dinner.

Hong Kong Saigon (☎ 47 58 34), at Mare à Poule d'Eau, serves reasonably priced Vietnamese food. It's open every day for lunch and dinner.

Restaurant Le Voile de la Mariée (☎ 47 53 54) lies on the road towards Hell-Bourg near the Grand Îlet turn-off. The view is great and the food is not bad at all – they do French and Créole lunches. Main dishes are around FF80. It's closed on Monday.

Restaurant Le P'tit Bambou (☎ 47 51 51), in Salazie, has good main dishes (Créole and French) for around FF65. Desserts are from FF18. It's closed on Wednesday.

Getting There & Away

The road alongside the gorge of the Rivière du Mât from St-André to Salazie winds past superb waterfall displays and, in places, swinging bridges cross the chasm to small farms clinging to the slopes. Just above the village of Salazie, the road forks; the left fork goes to Hell-Bourg and Îlet à Vidot and the right leads to Grand Îlet, Mare à Martin and Le Bélier. There are around six buses a day in either direction between St-André and Salazie, four of which continue on to Hell-Bourg (two of these continue on to Îlet à Vidot) and two that go to Grand Îlet and Le Bélier. The fare to Salazie is FF9.30, Hell-Bourg FF9.30, Grand Îlet FF15.50 and Le Bélier FF18.60.

THE CIRQUE DE MAFATE

Despite its remoteness, the Cirque de Mafate is populated and there are several villages large enough to support shops and other minor enterprises. Not much happens in these generally grotty and sleepy little places but they do provide reminders of civilisation dropped onto an otherwise formidable landscape.

For information on trekking in the Cirque de Mafate, see the Four Days in Mafate section in the Trekking in Réunion chapter.

Remember, for all gîte de montagne bookings, you must make advance reservations at Maison de la Montagne (see Accommodation in the Réunion Facts for the Visitor chapter).

Marla

This very quirky little settlement at 1540m is the highest community in Réunion. Although there were once 40 households in the area, most of the houses have been abandoned and only a handful of families remains.

Marla Gîte de Montagne (☎ 43 78 31) has beds for FF70 per person; breakfast/dinner costs FF25/70 extra.

M Hoareau (☎ 43 78 31) owns a private gîte and charges FF50 per person. Breakfast is an additional FF25 and dinner is FF70.

La Nouvelle

The 'capital' of Mafate, La Nouvelle is the cirque's largest village and supply depot. The popular gîte de montagne here will accommodate up to 42 people. If the action at the gîte de montagne is too much for you, there are several private gîtes in La Nouvelle.

La Nouvelle Gîte de Montagne (☎ 43 61 77) offers beds for FF80 per person. Breakfast is FF35 and dinner is FF85.

Sylvain Bègue (☎ 43 82 77) has beds for FF60 per person.

César Manrique (☎ 43 43 16) offers singles or doubles for FF130.

Alain Bègue (☎ 43 43 10) has accommodation for FF90 per person, including breakfast. Meals cost FF65 extra.

J Cuvelier (☎ 43 49 63) charges FF60 per person; breakfast is an extra FF25 and dinner is FF70.

Îlet à Bourse

This pleasant village is probably the tidiest in the Cirque de Mafate and its gîte sits in a lovely garden-like setting with an awesome view down the cirque. It's a convenient first night stop if you're coming over Bord à Martin from Le Bélier. It's also within a couple of hours walking from either Aurère or Grand Place.

Îlet à Bourse Gîte de Montagne (☎ 43 43 93) offers beds for FF70 per person, while breakfast/dinner is an extra FF25/65.

Aurère

Undoubtedly the grottiest of the Mafate communities, Aurère is nevertheless beautifully positioned, perched Machu Picchu-like

RÉUNION

above the precipitous canyon of the Bras Bémale and beneath the Piton Cabris.

Less than 1km downhill on the northern side of the Aurère eyrie is a magnificent lookout over the convoluted Bras des Merles – it's particularly beautiful at sunset. To get there, follow the track marked Sentier Botanique, then turn left at the sign pointing to Bras des Merles. From there, it's about 350m to the lookout.

M Georget Boyer (☎ 43 28 37) has a private gîte with beds for FF60. Evening meals are FF60 per person.

Grand Place
This two level village lies above the rushing Rivière des Galets near the cirque's main outlet. The gîte is in the lower section, known as Cayenne. The village shop lies 15 to 20 minutes walk uphill in Grand-Place-les-Hauts.

Grand Place Gîte de Montagne (☎ 43 85 42) can accommodate up to 16 people. It charges FF70 per person and FF15/65 for breakfast/dinner.

Roche Plate
The community of Roche Plate sits on sloping ground near the western rim of the Cirque de Mafate. Most people who visit Roche Plate are doing the popular four day route through upper Mafate from Col de Fourche via the La Nouvelle and Roche Plate gîtes to Marla, and on over the Col du Taïbit to Cilaos.

Roche Plate Gîte de Montagne (☎ 59 13 94) has beds for FF70 per person. Breakfast is an additional FF25 and dinner is FF65.

Les Hautes Plaines

Réunion's only cross-island route passes through the Plaine-des-Palmistes and the Plaine-des-Cafres, collectively known as Les Hautes Plaines, the high plains. These relatively large open areas actually form the saddle which separates the massif, comprised of the three cirques, from the volcano,

Piton de la Fournaise. Because there's a road which approaches within a few km of the summit, nearly all visitors to the volcano arrive from this side. The plains also serve as starting points for trekking excursions into Cirque de Salazie and Cirque de Cilaos.

Because the plains provide a cool retreat for the lowlanders during particularly hot and humid weather, the highway and beauty spots are well attended during weekends and holidays.

PLAINE-DES-PALMISTES
There were once large numbers of palm trees on the Plaine-des-Palmistes (hence the name) but due to heavy historical consumption of heart-of-palm salad, they've all but disappeared and are now protected. The community is divided into two villages. The main settlement and centre of action is Le Premier, literally 'the first' village for those coming from St-Benoît. Le Premier is often referred to simply as Plaine-des-Palmistes.

Cascade Biberon
The waterfall Cascade Biberon, a great place for a cool swim, lies at the northern edge of the Plaine-des-Palmistes, an easy 2km walk (if the weather is not too wet) from Le Premier. Follow the road north near the north-eastern end of the village and then the first track on the left. It crosses a few streams, but when it reaches the normally dry, boulder-strewn bed of the Ravine Sèche, the path disappears. You must join it upstream where the electricity wires cross to the opposite bank.

Forêt de Bébour
The Forêt de Bébour is a busy weekend picnic and leisure area. Although the Col de Bébour is normally the limit of activity from the southern access, the Route Forestière 2 continues on to the Bélouve gîte above Hell-Bourg, paralleled by a series of walking tracks. For a description of the entire route, see Forêt de Bélouve & Forêt de Bébour Trek in the Trekking in Réunion chapter.

Piton des Songes
On the summit of Piton des Songes is a cross,

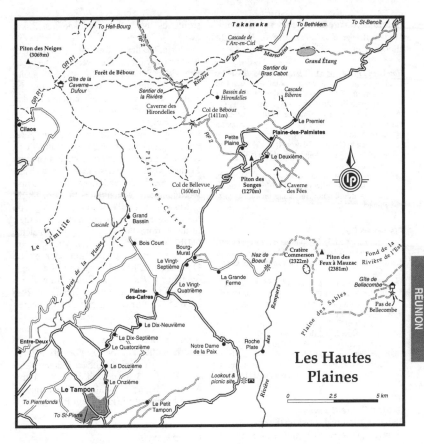

Les Hautes Plaines

shrine and small reservoir pond. From the peak, it's possible to see across the plain and down to St-Benoît and the sea. Access to the summit is from Bras des Calumets at the top of the winding road leading up from Le Deuxième village.

Places to Stay

Camping This private camp site is in a popular rural area and lies near the end of the Forêt de Bélouve and Forêt de Bébour track from Hell-Bourg (see Trekking in Réunion chapter for details of that trek).

Mme Lucette Ahrel (☎ 51 36 26), at 37 Rue Pignolet, Chemin de la Petite Plaine, Plaine-des-Palmistes, has a private camp site. She charges FF10 per day for the site and an additional FF10 per person per day.

Gîtes There is one gîte option, nearby in Le Deuxième.

Mme Paulette Plante (☎ 51 33 45) is at Rue Eugène Rochetaing, north of the cross-island road in Le Deuxième. She rents a basic, four person gîte d'étape for FF80 per night per person. She also runs a table d'hôte; meals cost FF65.

Hotels If you prefer more upmarket accommodation, there is a handful of hotels to choose from.

Hôtel des Plaines (☎ 51 31 97; fax 51 45 70), in Le Deuxième, is a three star hotel with standard rooms for FF280/360 a single/double. Breakfast is an extra FF40 per person. Some travellers say the service can sometimes be a little slapdash.

Les Azalées (☎ 51 34 24; fax 28 17 97) is a nice option on the Route Nationale in Le Premier, 300m from the track to Cascade Biberon. It has 36 rooms for FF245 a single or double; breakfast is FF35 per person.

Les Hirondelles (☎ 51 43 99), on Rue Jean Thévenin at Petite Plaine, offers a set of fairly basic bungalows. A double unit, including breakfast, costs FF240.

Places to Eat

Les Platanes (☎ 51 31 69), on Rue de la République, is a good Créole, Chinese and French restaurant, which is open for lunch and dinner daily except Monday.

Le Gadiamb (☎ 51 46 80), *Chez David* (☎ 51 41 20) and *La Tanguiere* (☎ 51 32 83) are all on Rue de la République and offer Créole creations.

Hôtel des Plaines (☎ 51 31 97), in Le Deuxième, has a French and Créole restaurant which is open daily for lunch and dinner, but meals are somewhat expensive at FF75 to FF200.

Coeur de Palmier (☎ 51 43 71), on Rue Pignolet in Petite Plaine, has a choice of Indian, Chinese and Créole dishes. Advance bookings are essential.

Getting There & Away

Plaine-des-Palmistes lies on the cross-island highway between St-Benoît and St-Pierre. For bus information, see Getting There & Away under Le Tampon & Plaine-des-Cafres, following.

LE TAMPON & PLAINE-DES-CAFRES

The Plaine-des-Cafres, once a refuge for runaway slaves from the coast, serves as a convenient gateway for visiting the volcano but is also pleasantly scenic in its own right. This area of dispersed population and gentle farmland is hemmed in between the two great massifs of the island, the cirques and Piton de la Fournaise, and provides a dramatic contrast to the thick forests on the slopes above and the barren lava desert that surrounds the hulking volcano just 30km away.

The Plaine-des-Cafres is hazily delimited; it's normally defined as everything between Bras-de-la-Plaine (at the foot of Le Dimitile) to the Rivière des Remparts, from Le Tampon to the crest of the winding road that descends towards Plaine-des-Palmistes.

The metropolis of the Plaine-des-Cafres, Le Tampon loudly proclaims itself the geranium capital of the world but in reality, it's a relatively uninteresting way-station en route to more worthwhile destinations. The absorbent name is derived from the Malagasy word *tampony*, which refers to a small hill.

Most of the Plaine-des-Cafres villages on the cross-island road are named for their distance from the sea. Thus, Le Onzième (11th), just north of Le Tampon, is 11km from the sea, followed 1km later by Le Douzième (12th) and so on up to Le Vingt-Septième (27th), where Route Forestière 5 turns off to the volcano. Le Trentième, 2km beyond the turn-off, is the last numbered village before Plaine-des-Palmistes.

Information

Tourist Office For tourist information, go to the Pays d'Accueil des Hautes Plaines (☎ 59 08 92), at 213 Route Nationale 3, Bourg-Murat, Plaines-des-Cafres. The office is open Monday to Friday from 8.30 am to 6 pm.

Grand Bassin

Opposite the church in Le Vingt-Troisième (23rd) village (also known simply as Plaine-des-Cafres), turn north and continue 5km to Bois Court. Just before the lookout point at the end of the road, turn left on Rue Roland Hoareau. After 100m, you'll see the beginning of the track which descends about 2km to Grand Bassin, known as *la vallée perdue* (the lost valley).

This picturesque basin in the gorge is formed by the confluence of the Bras Sec, the Bras de Suzanne and the Bras des Roches Noires. It's a quiet community with a lovely waterfall and a handful of gîtes. From here, there's a 10km walking track (some travellers have reported difficulty in finding this track, so ask locals for help) which descends the Bras-de-la-Plaine all the way to Entre-Deux.

La Maison du Volcan (Volcano House)

If you wish to know more about the behaviour of volcanoes in general and Piton de la Fournaise in particular, visit La Maison du Volcan (☎ 59 00 26) on the cross-island road, on the Le Tampon side of Le Vingt-Septième. Here, scientists keep as close a watch as possible on the volcano's moods, and are prepared to issue warnings to the local populace in case of an impending violent eruption. It's open Tuesday to Sunday from 9.30 am to 5.30 pm (last entry at 4.45 pm) and admission is FF30/15 for adults/children.

Notre Dame de la Paix

Three km beyond Notre Dame de la Paix village (coming from Le Vingt-Quatrième), where the road skirts the Rivière des Remparts, is a picnic and barbecue area and a lookout point. If you happen to be there in late afternoon when the sun is low and the valley is filled with cloud, try standing on the fence for a super special effect: your shadow projected onto the cloud by the sun behind will be encircled by a rainbow ring. Without the clouds, the expanse of the valley below is just as inspiring.

Places to Stay

Chambres d'Hôte It seems that half the chambres d'hôte in Réunion are on the Plaine-des-Cafres so there's no shortage of inexpensive accommodation.

M Roger Payet (☎ 57 04 71), 163 Route du Petit Tampon, at Le Petit Tampon, 5km up a twisting road from Le Tampon, has a chambre d'hôte. It costs FF100/120 a single/double.
Mme Lucot Payet (☎ 27 83 15), at 74 Route du Petit Tampon, charges FF110/130 a single/double.
Mme Huguette Mangue (☎ 27 36 85), at 64 Chemin Jamerosas in Le Tampon itself, has singles/doubles for FF130/150, including breakfast.
Mme Hélène Defaud (☎ 27 40 63), in the upper suburb of Trois Mares near Le Tampon, at 32 Impasse Georges Brassens, charges FF160 for a double room.

Mme Jeanine Mondon (☎ 27 45 57) is another option, at 58 Chemin Zazo Dassy in Le Tampon. She charges FF150/180 for singles/doubles. For table d'hôte, you'll pay FF80.
Mme Louise Magnan (☎ 27 56 91) is at Chemin Henri Cabeau, Bois Court (moving up the valley to upper Plaine-des-Cafres). A room is FF120/150 for single/double occupancy. Meals cost FF80.
Jean-Louis Lacouture (☎ 59 04 91), on the Route Nationale, has singles/doubles for FF150/180. For a meal, you'll have to pay a steep FF100 per person.
Mme Anne Rivière (☎ 27 59 78), in Le Vingt-Deuxième, lets four rooms in her home for FF150/180 a single/double. Meals are FF90.
M Sylvio & Mme Thérèse Mussard (☎ 27 57 59), on Chemin Notre Dame de la Paix, 6km from Le Vingt-Troisième, have a relaxing farmhouse with two guest bedrooms. They charge FF100/150 for a single/double and FF80 for a meal.
Mme Tenon (☎ 59 10 41), further up the road, beside the gendarmerie, at Le Vingt-Quatrième, has rooms for FF100/150 a single/double, with breakfast. Table d'hôte meals are FF80.
Mme Chantal Guesdon (☎ 27 59 25), located in Grande Ferme, about 7km from Le Vingt-Septième, is a popular choice. Doubles cost FF200 and meals are FF80 per person. This is a particularly convenient meeting point if you're hoping to hitch up to the volcano.

Gîtes There's also a wealth of gîte options around Le Tampon.

M Hubert Frédéric Lauret (☎ 57 60 35) offers accommodation in a rustic, chalet-style gîte on Chemin de Notre Dame de la Paix, just a few km from the Rivière des Remparts lookout. He charges FF2352/1176 for the week/weekend (maximum of eight people). There's also a gîte that accommodates five people which costs FF1790/895 per week/weekend.
M Jean-Claude Coutant (☎ 59 03 16) has a gîte along the road to the volcano, 3.5km from Bourg-Murat. He charges FF170 per person, including breakfast.
Marius & Jocelyne Boyer (☎ 57 46 00) own a pleasant gîte at Pont d'Yves (about 8km from Le Tampon). They charge FF1500 per week (maximum of six people).
Mme Jeanne-Marie Nativel (☎ 27 51 91) has a dormitory gîte with beds for FF70, with breakfast. Meals are FF70.
Mme Marie Josée Sery (☎ 59 10 34) offers four dormitories with beds for FF70 per person, including breakfast. Meals are an additional FF65.

RÉUNION

Mme Sery-Picard (☎ 27 51 02) has dorm beds for FF70 per person, including breakfast. Dinner is an extra FF80.

There are several gîtes with table d'hôte in Grand Bassin, a scenic spot in the Gorges de Bras de la Plaine.

Hotels The area's reasonably priced hotels provide a good alternative to the gîtes and chambres d'hôte.

Hôtel Outre-Mer (☎ 57 30 30; fax 57 29 29), at 8 Rue Bourbon in Le Tampon, has 35 rooms for FF250 (single/double occupancy). Breakfast is an extra FF50 per person.

Le Château Enchanté (☎ 27 07 90), near the intersection known as Six-Cent, has doubles for FF150 in their older section, while in the renovated section they go for FF200. Breakfast is FF25. There's a small swimming pool for guests.

Hôtel Les Orchidées (☎ 27 11 15; fax 27 77 03) is at the bottom of Rue Jules Ferry. It's reasonable value at FF225 for a single/double (breakfast is FF25).

Auberge La Fermette (☎ 27 50 08; fax 27 53 78), at Chemin Bois Court (upper Plaine-des-Cafres), costs FF220 for a single or double. Breakfast is FF20 per person.

Hôtel L'Allemand (☎ 27 51 27; fax 59 12 70), at Le Vingt-Troisième, offers singles/doubles/triples for FF150/190/240. Breakfast is FF25 extra.

Les Géraniums (☎ 59 11 06; fax 59 21 83), Le Vingt-Quatrième, has tidy singles/doubles for FF300/340; breakfast is an additional FF40.

Auberge du Volcan (☎ 27 50 91; fax 59 17 21) is 4km further along the Route Nationale at Bourg-Murat. It's a popular little place which has a cosy log-fire and woodsmoke atmosphere. Rooms cost FF160 a single or double and breakfast is FF20 per person.

Hôtel La Diligence (☎ 59 10 10; fax 59 11 81) is towards Plaine-des-Palmistes at Le Vingt-Huitième. It has accommodation in rather worn and weary two and three bed bungalows for FF295 and FF350 respectively; breakfast is FF32 per person.

Hôtel Adret (☎ 59 00 85) is on Route du Volcan and offers singles/doubles for FF200/260. Breakfast/dinner costs FF25/85 per person.

Places to Eat

Chez Cocotier (☎ 59 08 30), at La Ravine Blanche near Le Vingt-Troisième, is open every day, except Sunday night and Monday. It's speciality is French and Créole cuisine.

Chez Bruno (☎ 57 16 31), on Rue du Tampon, has a selection of French and Créole dishes to choose from. It's closed on Sunday, but open every other day for lunch and dinner.

La Fournaise (☎ 27 19 87), on Rue Marius & Ary Leblond, the main road through Le Tampon, goes for authentic French cooking with plats du jour for FF70.

Le Croque Au Sel (☎ 57 22 60), 11 Impasse Millerand, has great cuisine métro and is open daily except Sunday. Traveller Robert Garnett praises their imaginative desserts: 'I had something called a Colonel, which was lemon sorbet and vodka – with a lot of vodka (they even provided a straw!).'

La Tonkinoise (☎ 27 09 14), on Rue Marius & Ary Leblond, is a Vietnamese restaurant with generous plats du jour for around FF75. It's closed on Monday.

Le Panda (☎ 27 34 65), also on Rue Marius & Ary Leblond, offers Chinese and Créole food. It's closed on Sunday and Monday.

Les Délices de Chine (☎ 57 50 93), Rue Hubert Delisle, specialises in Chinese cuisine.

Pizza Dona (☎ 27 30 44), at 460 Rue Hubert Delisle, offers French food at reasonable prices.

Some of the hotels also have restaurants (see Places to Stay for location).

Hôtel Les Orchidées has a good dining room serving French and Créole fare. It's open daily except Sunday evening and Monday.

Hôtel La Diligence offers Créole and French cuisine at its restaurant. It's open every day for lunch and dinner.

Les Géraniums also specialises in Créole and French fare. It's open daily from 11.30 am to 10.30 pm. Nonresidents should book ahead.

Auberge du Volcan is recommended for its Créole preparations. The restaurant is open daily except Sunday evening and Monday.

Entertainment

The *Théâtre Luc Donat* (☎ 27 24 36), on Rue de l'Église in Le Tampon, stages many of the musical and theatrical productions which play in St-Denis. Le Tampon also has a *cinema* on Rue Hubert Delisle (mainly French-language films).

Getting There & Away

There are about three buses a day each way between St-Benoît and St-Pierre via Le Tampon, Plaine-des-Cafres and Plaine-des-Palmistes. The Plaine-des-Palmistes to Plaine-des-Cafres (Vingt-Troisième) fare is FF13.50; from Le Tampon to Plaine-des-Cafres, FF7.50; and from Le Tampon to

St-Pierre, FF8. Taxi-collectifs operate between Le Tampon and surrounding villages, costing from around FF8 to FF12 per trip.

ENTRE-DEUX

This community got its strange name, 'between two', because it lies between two rivers – the Bras de Cilaos and the Bras-de-la-Plaine, which together form the Rivière St-Étienne. This is a fruit and tobacco-growing enclave which is pleasant enough in itself, but for tourists it's used primarily as a staging point for the tough trek up the slopes of Le Dimitile to a super view over the Cirque de Cilaos. Start by taking the Jean Lauret path from Entre-Deux. If you leave at dawn, the ascent and descent of Le Dimitile (1837m) can be done in a single day; plan on at least 16 hours.

Information

Tourist Office The Office de Tourisme de l'Entre-Deux (☎ 39 69 60; fax 39 57 70) is at 9 Rue Fortuné Hoareau. It's open Tuesday to Friday from 8 am to 3 pm and from 8 to 11 am on the weekend.

Places to Stay & Eat

Youth Hostel (Auberge de Jeunesse) (☎ 39 59 20) is along the main road into town. It charges the standard FF70 per person (for HI members). Evening meals cost FF50 and breakfast is FF15 per person.

Mme Jacqueline Corré (☎ 39 53 43) has a chambre d'hôte at Grand Fond Intérieur. Rooms cost FF75 per person, including breakfast. Dinner is FF80.

Mme Noé Fontaine (☎ 39 51 21) runs a chambre d'hôte at 18 Chemin Pifarelli. She charges FF175/280 for a single/double, including breakfast and dinner.

If you're not a superhuman trekker or you think this is cutting things too closely for a single day, there are several gîtes at Le Dimitile:

M Beldan (☎ 39 50 46) charges FF65 per person and FF80 for a meal.

M Payet (☎ 39 66 42) offers a room, breakfast and meal for FF170 per person.

M Bardil (☎ 39 60 84) is similarly priced to M Payet's gîte.

Getting There & Away

There are minor bus lines operating between Entre-Deux and the gares routière in St-Pierre and St-Louis. There's also a bus to and from Le Tampon.

RÉUNION

Trekking in Réunion

HIGHLIGHTS

- Climbing the live volcano and exploring the two major craters
- Trekking to the summit of Piton des Neiges at dawn and catching breathtaking views of the island through the early morning mist
- Hiking from the heights of the volcano to the rolling waves along the coast
- Spending the night in one of the gîtes dotted throughout the cirques

Instead of serene lagoons, postcards from Réunion usually depict remote villages, sharp mountain crests or fluffy clouds floating among the peaks. They show the sky of the Indian Ocean vast above inaccessible cirques, the Piton des Neiges mountain which rarely sees the rain turn into snow, Piton de la Fournaise that still vents its rage from time to time, and the crystal-clear music of waterfalls hurtling down a mountainside.

Once you have left the narrow coastal region, this volcanic island's highest point rises more than 3000m above the sea and can be seen for what it is: the progeny of a mountain. Created in a volcano's fiery youth, the island now offers itself to the trekker.

One of the pleasures of hiking in Réunion is the opportunity to visit sites that are inaccessible except on foot or by helicopter, to encounter the inhabitants of Réunion who have chosen to live in the cirques, or to discover the rich plant life of this tropical island. In short, hiking affords the opportunity of seeing a different Réunion.

Thanks to the Office National des Forêts (ONF), the former Île Bourbon can boast of nearly a thousand km of hiking trails. These are generally very well signposted, particularly the ones maintained by the Grande Randonnée (GR) and their off-shoots (the GR R1 does a tour of Piton des Neiges; the GR R2 crosses the island). There are many other trails, often made by the island's inhab-

itants through daily use, and they too are open to walkers. They present varying degrees of difficulty. Some are very close to being climbing trails; others are simply a reasonable hike or walk and are accessible to all. As a general rule, the island's temperature and terrain make the simple act of walking quite arduous. Even hikers who have broken in their boots in the Alps or Nepal have been surprised. Indeed, many paths seem to avoid level ground on purpose: they descend into a gully, shoot off up the flank of a hill etc. The trails described in this chapter, however, are within the capabilities of anyone in good physical condition and sufficiently motivated. Some itineraries are even suitable for children.

The routes described have been selected from among the most popular. There are dozens of others and countless variations. Owing to the differences in altitude of the terrain, hikers will find distances on the map and km indications to be, in general, extremely deceptive. Therefore 'average' hiking times have been included, taking only brief pauses into account.

Lastly, you will also find a few itineraries for walks in the island's uplands and along the coast.

INFORMATION

The Maison de la Montagne is the main, if not the sole, source of information on hiking and mountain accommodation. It can provide guides and organise tours for *randonneurs* (walkers). It is located near Le Barachois in St-Denis at 10 Place Sarda Garriga (☎ 90 78 78; fax 41 84 29). The office is open Monday to Thursday from 9 am to 5.30 pm, Friday from 9 am to 4.30 pm and Saturday from 9 am to 4 pm. The huge relief map on the wall gives an excellent idea of the vagaries of Réunion's terrain, and provides information regarding the condition of trails. The Maison de la Montagne manages some of the gîtes scattered about

What's in a Name?

The history of Réunion's cirques is haunted with the most dreadful element of Mascarene history: slavery. The island's gullies, îlets (or villages), and mountain peaks are impregnated with the memory of that era's history, written in letters of blood, and many of the important sites in the cirques owe their names to former 'marrons', the term (from the Spanish cimarron) once used to describe runaway slaves. Mafate, Cimendef, Dimitile and Enchaing were among those slaves. The latter runaway, with his female companion, is said to have remained in hiding for over 20 years on the peak named after him. The landscape also bears reminders of slave hunters like Bronchard and Mussard. As for the Îlet-à-Malheur (Misfortune), its name recalls a bloody incident that occurred there in 1829 during a hunt for runaway slaves.

The Malagasy origin of many names is also no accident. The population of the large neighbour island paid a heavy tribute to the slave trade and, in addition to other rich resources, contributed much of the manpower for the ships of the fine gentlemen the French Crown had sent out to the Indian Ocean.

In those days, Réunion was known as Île Bourbon. 'We need blacks to till the soil,' wrote in 1671 a man named Dubois, who had set sail on a ship of the French East India Company to cruise the Indian Ocean around the Mascarenes. 'The blacks can be acquired in Madagascar, and especially in the provinces of Antongil and Galemboulle and their environs. There, one can find black slaves who can be purchased from their masters at low cost in return for the small amount of goods we provide.'

An island paradise lying on the trade route of the large sailing ships, uninhabited Île Bourbon, although rich in fruits, turtles and birdlife and favoured with air 'so healthy ... and salubrious that the sick who go ashore there regain their health as soon as they breathe it in,' was nonetheless short of exportable wealth. Thus, spice trees, coffee plants and sugar cane were brought into the 'large wild island' by sea, and imported with those products was the manpower needed to plant and cultivate them. From the 1750s, the majority of the island's population was made up of slaves. Many of the men who toiled on the low-lying plantations raised their eyes to the impenetrable heights of the cirques in prayer. Braving the savagely punitive search parties, many such slaves chose to become runaways. Those dreamers of freedom were the earliest inhabitants of Île Bourbon's uplands, where they founded their villages.

With the abolition of slavery in 1848 such cheap labour was replaced with the importation of other 'servants': Chinese from Canton, Indians from Malabar or Gujarat. ■

the island (see the Food & Accommodation section in this chapter), and you can also get information on other types of open-air activities, such as rafting and canoeing.

Maison de la Montagne also has an office in Cilaos (☎ 31 71 71; fax 31 80 54), at 2 Rue Mac Auliffe, thus saving an obligatory trip to St-Denis. The office is open Monday to Saturday from 8.30 am to 12.30 pm and from 1.30 to 5.30 pm. It is also open on some holidays and on Sunday from 9 am to 1 pm.

What to Bring

Good shoes are essential for hiking the trails of Réunion, which are of gravel and stone and often very steep (in both directions) with muddy or slippery terrain. Hiking shoes with good ankle support are better than sneakers.

A canteen (2L is often not an undue amount for a day's hiking) is a must, and you should also have a rain poncho and a warm garment (a wool pullover or jersey). When night falls in the island's higher points, the temperature is often cool and sometimes downright cold.

Add a good sun cream, some kind of headgear to protect your head from the intense sun, insect repellent and a flashlight, and you're ready to go.

Sleeping bags are optional unless you plan to camp in the open, since the gîtes provide sheets and blankets. However, don't expect them to be changed on a daily basis, and if you are especially hung up on cleanliness, bring along a sheet.

You will be able to buy most last-minute supplies at a sporting goods store. There is one on Rue Jean-Chatel in St-Denis and another in the shopping centre of the Continent centre on the road to the airport.

Maps

The island's 2510 sq km are covered by the six 1:25,000 scale maps published by the

Institut Géographique National. Map 4402 RT, St-Denis, Cirques de Mafate et de Salazie, is one of the most useful for hikers, since it also covers the northern part of the Cirque de Cilaos. These maps indicate trails and gîtes. They are sold all over the island, including at the Maison de la Montagne.

The overall map of Réunion with a 1:100,000 scale is not precise enough to be of much help to hikers.

Money

You can't change or withdraw money in the remote îlets (villages) in the cirques. Meals and beds in private gîtes must be paid for in cash.

BOOKS

There are several books in French, most of them published locally.

Cirque de Mafate, Découverte et Randonnée, which is published by the ONF, details 26 hikes in that cirque. This small, high-quality guide also describes the fauna, flora and population of Mafate's îlets and includes a 1:25,000 scale map.

Topoguide, *L'île de la Réunion,* sets forth the itineraries of the island's two Grande Randonnée trails, the GR R1, which circles Piton des Neiges, and the GR R2, known as the 'Grande Traversée'. Using IGN maps of a scale of 1:25,000, its data is very precise. It also describes eight one-day hikes of varying degrees of difficulty and devotes several pages to facts about the island.

Sentiers Marmailles is designed more for the peaceful stroller than for the athletic hiker. Its 120 pages describe 46 outings – most taking less than two hours – and the points of departure are accessible by car. They are all suitable for children (the title translates as Paths for Kids) and cover nearly the whole island. It's available at the Maison de la Montagne.

Like the preceding, *50 Itinéraires de Promenades Pédestres à la Réunion* (50 Walking Tours in Réunion) is published by the ONF. It is especially concise, and the itineraries range from a simple stroll lasting a couple of hours to more athletic hikes.

There are maps, and symbols are used to rate the difficulty of each route.

Lastly, a book on the island's flora will help you put a name to the species you will encounter on your hikes. There are a large number of these available in the island's bookshops.

FOOD & ACCOMMODATION

While trekking you will encounter two main types of lodging. Hotels and chambres d'hôte exist in towns that are accessible by road: Hell-Bourg, Cilaos etc. They are described in the pages devoted to each town. In the more remote îlets, you may be staying at gîtes de montagne, which offer dormitory beds but don't always have electricity. Solar showers are not always hot, depending on the weather. However, in recent years considerable effort has been made to improve comfort and, with a few exceptions, facilities are quite adequate. Sheets and blankets are provided.

There are two types of gîtes: those run by the Maison de la Montagne and those that are privately owned. The flood of hikers visiting Réunion has inspired many people to open facilities in the mountains, with varying degrees of success. Another result of this increased interest is that the gîtes are completely booked several weeks in advance, and it is important to make reservations as early as possible. Weekends and vacation periods are the most popular times, and the Gîte du Volcan (Bellecombe) and Gîte de la Caverne Dufour (Piton des Neiges) (booked through the Maison de la Montagne) fill very quickly.

Beds in Maison de la Montagne gîtes must be reserved through the Maison de la Montagne, either in St-Denis or in Cilaos (see Information for addresses). Some visitor centres can also make reservations, such as the Office de Tourisme de l'Ouest (☎ 24 57 47; fax 24 34 40), situated in the Galerie Amandine in St-Gilles-les-Bains (see the St-Gilles-les-Bains section in the Around the Coast chapter for more details). Whether you reserve by telephone or not, you must visit the office in person to pay, for which you will

Trekking in Réunion

The word Réunion conjures images of rocky mountain peaks, a live volcano, humid tropical heat and lush vegetation. In short, Réunion's geological history has made it a haven for the serious and occasional trekker. Whether climbing to the top of Piton de la Fournaise, tramping across solidified lava flows, hiking through the mountain highlands or exploring the coast, Réunion simply cannot and will not disappoint.

Box: The towering Cascade du Voile de la Mariée falls, near Salazie.

Left: The Cirque de Salazie features some breathtaking views, especially the Col du Taïbit which dominates the horizon.

OLIVIER CIRENDINI

OLIVIER CIRENDINI

*Above Right: La Roche
Écrite, smothered in a blanket of white cloud.*

*Right: The unique volcanic
landscape of Piton de la
Fournaise.*

OLIVIER CIRENDINI

OLIVIER CIRENDINI

Above Left: Clouds often roll in and obscure the view from Roche Plate.

Left: Lava formation turns Trois Roches into a lunar landscape.

Broader forecasts, updated twice a day, are also available on ☎ 08 36 68 00 00. Storm-watch bulletins are available on ☎ 08 36 65 10 10. All these services are in French.

GUIDED TREKS
In terms of safety it isn't necessary to hire a qualified mountain guide to hike the majority of the island's trails – unless, of course, you are alone or a novice, or if you want to take a particularly challenging route. That being said, professional assistance is one way to enrich your knowledge of the moun-tains, villages and flora you encounter on your hike.

There are several organisations offering guided treks; they can be contacted through the Maison de la Montagne. Since their main interest is in assembling groups of hikers, they offer fixed itineraries. Maham (☎/fax 47 82 82) offers a Monday to Wednesday trek from Salazie to Hell-Bourg, via Marla, Trois Roches and La Nouvelle. The following days take you to Bélouve, Piton des Neiges and the volcano. It is possible to sign up for the day or days you want, and the cost is FF900 for two days, FF1900 for four days

RÉUNION

Various Itineraries

One Day:
• Col des Bœufs/La Nouvelle/Col des Bœufs
• Cilaos/Col du Taïbit/Cilaos; approximately a five hour hike, if you begin at the trail from Îlet to Cordes, thereby avoiding the preliminary 2½ hour hike from Cilaos.
• Hell-Bourg/Le Grand Sable/Hell-Bourg; a side trip to Trou Blanc is possible if it doesn't rain – the trail includes fording a number of gullies.

Two Days:
• Col des Bœufs/La Nouvelle/Col des Bœufs; overnight at La Nouvelle
• Col des Bœufs/Marla/Col des Bœufs; overnight at Marla
• Col des Bœufs/Marla/Cilaos; overnight at Marla
• Hell-Bourg/Piton des Neiges/Cilaos; overnight at the Caverne Dufour gîte.
• La Roche Écrite; overnight at the Plaine des Chicots gîte.

Three Days:
• Col des Bœufs/La Nouvelle/Marla/Col des Bœufs; overnight at La Nouvelle and Marla
• Col des Bœufs/La Nouvelle/Marla/Cilaos; overnight at La Nouvelle and Marla

Four Days:
• Col des Bœufs/La Nouvelle/Roche Plate/Marla/Cilaos; overnight at La Nouvelle, Roche-Plate and Marla

Five Days:
• Tour of the cirques, with an overnight on the last leg at either Bélier or at the bivouac at Le Grand Sable.

Six Days:
• Hell-Bourg/Piton des Neiges/Cilaos/Marla/Roche Plate/La Nouvelle/Hell-Bourg; overnight at the Caverne Dufour gîte and at Cilaos, Marla, Roche Plate and La Nouvelle. (On the last leg, it is best to proceed via the Col de Fourche rather than towards the Col des Bœufs when leaving the Plaine des Tamarins.)

Seven Days:
• Same itinerary as the above, with an overnight on the last leg at either Bélier or the bivouac at Le Grand Sable.

and FF3300 for the entire week. The price includes the services of a qualified mountain guide, transportation, gîte reservations and most meals. A minimum of six people is required.

You should also inquire about other groups like Altitudes Australes or Rando Run, as well as those of the Bureau des Accompagnateurs, which are varied and among the least expensive.

If the itineraries or dates do not fit in with your plans, you can also contact independent qualified guides. Their telephone numbers appear in the *RUN* magazine, published and regularly updated by the Comité du Tourisme de la Réunion (CTR). It is available at the Maison de la Montagne and at the offices of the CTR just behind the statue of Roland Garros at Le Barachois in St-Denis.

At a cost of FF750/800 per day, the services of a guide are affordable if you are in a group (12 persons or under). Of course, it is more expensive if you're alone, but it may be possible to negotiate a reduced price. At the price mentioned (which does not include gîtes, meals or transport) you will be able to select whatever itinerary you want. You can also inquire at the guide office at the Maison de la Montagne.

Organisations which can suggest routes and possibly offer guided treks include the following:

Maison de la Montagne, 10 Place Sarda Garriga, 97400 St-Denis (☎ 90 78 78; fax 41 84 29)
Maison de la Montagne, 2 Rue Mac Auliffe, 97413 Cilaos (☎ 31 71 71; fax 31 80 54)
Écologie Réunion, 1 Lotissement Payet, Gillot, Ste-Marie (☎ 29 21 38)
Les Randonneurs du Week-end, Le Tampon (☎ 27 00 04)
SREPEN, 4 Rue Jacob, St-Denis (☎ 20 30 30)

FOUR DAYS IN MAFATE

Surrounded by ramparts, crisscrossed with gullies, and studded with narrow ridges, Mafate is the wildest and most remote of Réunion's cirques. Only the Rivière des Galets, on its meandering course towards the coast, has managed to carve a path to it. To the delight of some and the disappointment

of others, the Haut Mafate *route forestière* (forest track), begun in the mid-1970s, stops before it reaches the Col des Bœufs. As of today, therefore, the cirque has no road suitable for motor vehicles, and (unless you take to the air) Mafate's îlets of La Nouvelle, Roche Plate, Marla, Îlet à Bourse, Îlet à Malheur, Grand Place, Aurère and Les Orangers are accessible only on foot.

The cirque's inaccessibility probably explains why the runaway Mafate sought haven in a cleft in its ramparts. A black slave, a chieftain and sorcerer, he gave the cirque its name and was killed in 1751 by François Mussard, a hunter of runaway slaves whose name is now remembered only because it has been given to a dank, dark cave near Piton des Neiges.

Mafate is accessible by four paths: from Cilaos via the Col du Taïbit (2082m); along the banks of the Rivière des Galets (Dos d'Ane or Sans Souci); via the Col des Bœufs or Col de Fourche (1942m); or, finally, via Piton Maïdo. The last option is the most challenging: the Piton rises to 2027m above the îlet of Roche Plate (1110m), and the sun and the gradient combine to make the steep descent of the rampart very difficult. The simplest access is via the Col des Bœufs.

In the Cirque de Mafate, there are gîtes de montagne at Îlet à Bourse, Grand Place (Cayenne), Roche Plate, La Nouvelle and Marla. In addition, there are some gîtes d'étape in La Nouvelle which may be of use to trekkers. Most routes are well signposted, but you should carry a good map.

There are many ways to visit the cirque. The following itinerary is merely one of many. It has the advantage of making a loop after leaving Le Bélier, reaching Mafate by the easiest route, including La Nouvelle – the largest îlet in the cirque – and of going as far as the foot of the Col du Taïbit and Piton Maïdo; it also allows you to spend time at Trois Roches.

However, there are other itineraries, particularly in Bas Mafate, which include Cayenne, Aurère or even Grand Place. Information is available at the Maison de la Montagne.

RÉUNION

Note Remember that accommodation must be booked through the Maison de la Montagne in St-Denis or Cilaos (see Information earlier).

First day: Le Bélier to La Nouvelle
(Walking time: about two hours)

The trail begins just above Petit Col, at the beginning of the Haut Mafate route forestière, a few km outside Le Bélier. A bus runs between Salazie and Le Bélier from Monday to Saturday, departing the *mairie* (town hall) in Salazie at 6.20 and 8 am, noon and 3 and 4.45 pm, and the trip, which costs FF16.60, takes 45 minutes. For the return trip, departure times are 4.45, 7 and 11.15 am and 1.45 and 4 pm. Three alternatives are possible from Le Bélier. If you have a car, you can leave it in the Petit Col car park during your trek. Unfortunately, some cars are broken into. Your second choice is to walk up to Le Bélier taking the route forestière. That means you'll walk for about two hours. The third alternative is to contact Titine Nourry (☎ 47 71 84), who owns a grocery at Le Bélier, below the forest track. She also provides car park service for FF50 a night, and she can drive you as far as Petit Col; the cost is FF100 if you are alone, FF150 for two to four people, and FF200 for five to six. For an additional FF50, she will pick you up at the end of your trek. It's expensive, but the 20 minute ascent to Petit Col by car spares you the two hours of fairly monotonous hiking on the route forestière.

This short first day's hike enables you to acquire your walking legs. It is fairly easy and well within the capabilities of children.

From the Petit Col car park, it only takes 15 minutes to reach the Col des Bœufs, from where you can see the village of Marla, which is at the foot of the Col du Taïbit. Indicating GR R1, which seems to plunge down into the bowels of the earth, the ONF signposts give the distance to La Nouvelle as 4.5km. You now begin a 30 minute descent. The trail, which can be slippery when it rains, leads to the Plaine des Tamarins, which is at an altitude of 1750m. The mountain tamarind tree, native to Réunion, has leaves that

change with age from an acacia-like growth of paired leaves on a central stalk to a more classic, elongated shape, and is used for its wood. The shingled roofs commonly seen in the cirques are made of it. Tamarinds also provide a breeding ground for a yellowish lichen called *barbes de capucin* (monk's beard), which looks as though it has been caught on the branches following the passage of some ghostly forest creature. The effect is even odder when wisps of mist are hanging from tree to tree, and it is enhanced by the way the tamarind trunks have often been contorted by the wind.

Crossing the plain on the wooden blocks that have been laid out through the furze to keep you from sinking into the marshy ground, you will encounter a few peaceful cattle grazing at the side of the trail. This leg of the hike ends when the meagre dwellings of the îlet of Roche Plate can be seen in the distance. An easy stroll soon brings you to the village of La Nouvelle (1420m altitude).

La Nouvelle's economy was once based on cattle-raising, but today its principal resource is tourism. Lunchtime visitors descend from the skies in helicopters, and for a community of only 130 inhabitants there are a large number of gîtes, a bakery and even a telephone booth. For some purists, La Nouvelle is no longer the peaceful haven it once was. Nevertheless, it's still very pleasant and quiet, and its facilities for food and lodging are the best in Mafate.

You will first discover two small abandoned buildings that were formerly the gîte of the Maison de la Montagne. The privately owned *Gîte privé Cuvelier Joseph* (☎ 43 49 63) is 200m further along on the right down a narrow trail signposted 'Gardien du Gîte'. This is a good choice: the small wooden four person dormitories are clean and pleasant, and the showers are hot. A bed costs FF60, a hearty meal FF70, punch included, and breakfast is FF25.

Further down from the former Maison de la Montagne gîte you will pass a *bakery* – the bread is excellent – and the Maison Forestière and arrive at the Épicerie Bègue Lucey. The wooden façade of the *Gîte de France Bègue Sylvio* (☎ 43 43 10) is just beyond. This gîte is a pleasant one, and, in addition to four or eight person dormitories, it also has one double room. Bed and breakfast cost FF90 and a meal is FF60.

A few hundred metres further along brings you to the telephone booth (a revolutionary novelty!) and to a cluster of buildings that house a grocery, a restaurant and the *gîte de montagne* (☎ 43 61 77). At FF80 for a bed (FF60 for children under 12), FF35 for breakfast and FF85 for a meal, it is not the most inexpensive. However, the cooking is widely appreciated and the breakfast is one of the most satisfying in the cirque.

Still further on, the *Épicerie Bègue Alain* (grocery), recognisable by its timber frame, is the best stocked in the village.

From La Nouvelle, the trail to Marla and Trois Roches (through Plaine aux Sables – not to be confused with Plaine des Sables, near Piton de la Fournaise) starts next to the Bègue Lucey grocery. Don't put too much faith in the km indications on the first signposts, which are contradicted only a few metres further along! As for the trail leading to Grand Place, Cayenne and Roche Plate via Le Bronchard, signposts showing the way can be found facing the chapel, next to the telephone booth, which can be identified by the tamarind-shingled roof with eaves that extend to ground level.

Second day: La Nouvelle to Roche Plate via Le Bronchard
(Walking time: about five hours)
The trail, which is signposted in either white and red or all white, traverses cultivated fields and begins with a gentle descent to the bottom of the cirque. After passing a roadside cross, some 15 minutes after setting out, you will see the îlet of Roche Plate in the distance and an intersection leading to the right towards Îlet Cimendal. Your route leads straight ahead towards the bed of the Rivière des Galets, at which you will arrive after two hours of often-steep descent. This is an ideal place to rest.

Leaving the path along the riverbank to

A telephone booth at La Nouvelle
Communication is so much easier now, just ask the people of La Nouvelle. Since the end of 1995 the îlet has been equipped with the very latest in telephone booths. Since this village, located in the heart of the mountains, has no electricity, the telephone is operated by a radio transmitter powered by solar panels.

Unique in the Indian Ocean, this telephone booth is testimony to the determination of La Nouvelle's inhabitants to establish contact with the rest of the island and the world beyond. With ONF assistance, they also had a hand in the construction of the booth itself, which is built of tamarind and cryptomeria wood. Operated by telephone card (available in the La Nouvelle groceries), it is a boon to hikers, as it comes in handy reserving a gîte or a meal. You can even receive calls. The number is ☎ 43 15 35. ■

RÉUNION

Grand Place, Cayenne and the small Îlet de Mafate, you next ford the river and begin the climb to Le Bronchard. The trail will now bend and curve its way up for an hour and a quarter. This section is made even more arduous because it is nearly always open to the scalding sun that seems to take no pity on mere mortals.

The ground will not begin to level out until you reach the white cross that overlooks the large flat Le Bronchard (1261m). You then begin a gentle descent towards Roche Plate, past filaos, fields of grain and an occasional hut. The trail forks several times, but you keep going straight ahead. The first, after a 15 minute hike, points to Îlet à Cordes to the right and precedes the crossroads that leads to a chapel. Next, just after crossing a little bridge, you will come to the path to La

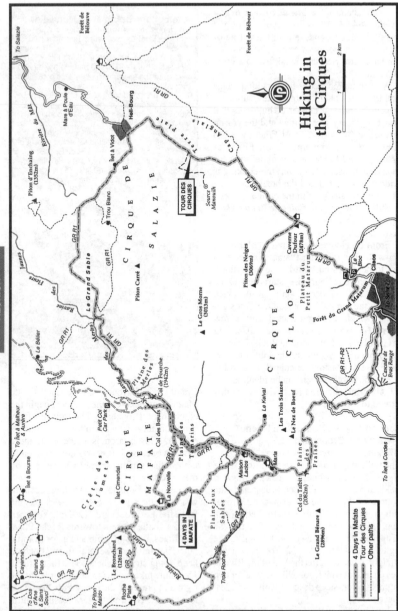

4 Days in Mafate

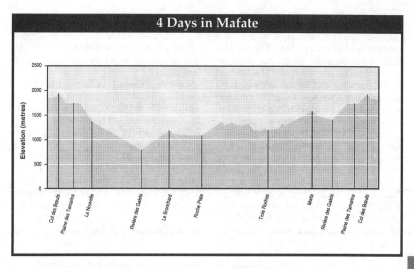

Nouvelle via Trois Roches. A few more minutes walk will bring you to Roche Platé, directly below the majestic Piton Maïdo, which towers some 1000m higher.

The first building you reach is the school. The green-shuttered windows of the *gîte de montagne* (☎ 59 13 94) some 50m further on look out over a fine view. The gîte has a kitchen where you can cook meals and the showers have hot water. The *Gîte privé de mademoiselle Thiburce* (☎ 43 60 01) is a bit further as you continue down the path. Although built of wood and sheet metal, unlike the former's 'hard' construction, it is just as comfortable – aside from having no kitchen – and costs FF5 less.

The food is the same in both establishments. The Thiburce family runs both of them and all the guests share the same menu at a dining hall located about 50m beyond the private gîte. Breakfast costs FF25 and dinner is FF70. The meals vary in quality according to the number being fed, and the traditional rum drink is not always available.

The village *grocery* (perhaps not entirely deserving of the name) is between the two gîtes. It sells fresh drinks, cookies and a variety of fairly expensive tinned goods.

Third day: Roche Plate to Marla via Trois Roches
(Walking time: about five hours)
Briefly retracing the foregoing itinerary, this day begins on the trail to Marla, signposted in white, to the right after the school. Your endurance will be tested from the beginning with a 45 minute ascent, happily rewarded by a panoramic view at the top. Allow your eyes to move from peak to peak, right to left; you can see Le Grand Bénare, Col du Taïbit (its outlines resemble that of a giant horn), Le Gros Morne and Col de Fourche. The trail then begins a descent to the bottom of a gully and rises again to a small plateau. From there, you can hear the refreshing sound of the river below, while ahead the backdrop formed by Col du Taïbit and the Salazes can be seen through the chokas (agaves). Once you have crossed the plateau and made a 15 minute climb up a twisting path, you will come to a few filao trees. These mark the beginning of a rapid descent down the sides of a second gully. After a three hour trek and one final turn of the path you will arrive at Trois-Roches.

This site is certainly one of the cirque's most interesting and unusual. The basalt slab that forms part of the bed of the Rivière des

Galets has been polished by the waters that flow over it before cascading down into what seems to be a bottomless abyss. The shadows of the filaos surround the site and the water turns the rocks into a mixture of white and brown, making this an ideal place for a lengthy pause. Needless to say, it is dangerous to venture too close to the edge, especially since the rocks are very slippery.

Once you have left this tranquil paradise, the trail will be mostly cinder slag (see Volcano Glossary boxed text in the Facts about Réunion chapter). In a few minutes it will cross the path to La Nouvelle and the Plaine aux Sables and head straight to Marla along the bank of the river. After you have hiked for about 20 minutes, the path will veer off to the left and begin a steep ascent up the bank. This sudden change in level of landscape is a reminder of the volcanic origin of the cirques; however, it lasts less than 15 minutes. Next, you cross a dried-out gully and climb up to a small plateau. Another 15 minutes is needed for this steep rocky climb, which ends when you come within sight of some trees; one last change of altitude, and 20 minutes later you will be in Marla.

At an altitude of 1620m, this attractive îlet is the highest of the Mafate cirque. Its name is said to be derived from a Malagasy term meaning 'many people', the village once having been one of the cirque's most populous. Its huts, above which the Col du Taïbit appears to be keeping watch, now shelter only a few dozen people. One of the first places you will come to is the *Gîte privé Hoareau Expédit* (☎ 43 78 31). The tin-roofed shelter is fairly basic and the shower not always hot, but at FF50 per bed, it is certainly affordable. A better choice is the *gîte de montagne* (☎ 43 78 31), which is a bit further on to the left. More solidly constructed, its location is good, the shower is hot and there is a kitchen where you can prepare food. A dormitory bed is FF70 (FF50 for children under 12) and dinner, which is a common meal shared with the people staying at the Gîte privé Hoareau Expédit (they are managed by the same family), costs FF70. Breakfast is FF25 at either gîte.

Marla's *épicerie/bar* is located just below. It is fairly well stocked, prices are reasonable compared to those elsewhere in the cirque, and the small glass of rhum arrangé is excellent at FF10.

Lastly, you have the *Gîte privé Girauday* (☎ 43 83 13), which is located about 100m further on from the grocery. It is very basic. Meals are served in the house with the rooftop which can be seen looming above the fields some 200m further along. They cost FF70. Breakfast costs FF24 and a bed is FF50.

After you reach Marla, you can elect to end your hike by crossing the Col du Taïbit to Cilaos. If so, use – in reverse – the itinerary described for the third day of the tour of the cirques (see Third day: Cilaos to Marla via the Col du Taïbit in the Tour des Cirques section following).

Fourth day: Marla to Col des Bœufs
(Walking time: about 2½ hours)

The trail to Col des Bœufs and Col de Fourche, Kelval and La Nouvelle is on the left before you come to Marla's grocery (the right-hand trail leads to Col du Taïbit). It is signposted in white/red and soon passes a pretty little chapel. Fifteen minutes more will bring you to Maison Laclos, named after its former occupants. This is the oldest dwelling in the cirque; it was abandoned in the aftermath of Hurricane Hyacinthe and can be used as a shelter or as a bivouac site. From there, the left-hand trail leads to La Nouvelle while the trail on the right leads to Kelval.

Taking the former, after hiking for a few minutes you leave the trail leading to Kelval – which bravely climbs the gully on the right – and arrive at a new crossroads to La Nouvelle, to the left. Your signposted path, in yellow/red or yellow/white, continues straight on and will bring you to the Plaine des Tamarins after the easy traversal of a few gullies. Once on the plain, around an hour and a half after departure, you will see on your left a trail signposted white/red coming from La Nouvelle. From here on, your itinerary is the same as that of the first day of this hike, with the sole difference being you will climb towards Col des Bœufs.

Another option is to return to La Nouvelle via Maison Laclos. In that case, you would go to the left and descend the side of the gully created by the winding Rivière des Galets, which you reach after a 15 minute hike. The path then straightens out, makes a junction on the right with a path marked 'Marla par passerelle', and then continues to ascend through the filaos until it reaches a white cross. From here on, the going is easier and the trail continues until it meets the trail to Plaine aux Sables. You will reach La Nouvelle, indicated on the right, after a final climb followed, of course, by a corresponding descent.

If this short day's hike leaves you unsatisfied, you are free to finish it off by climbing to the Plateau du Kelval (1768m). The beauty and peace of this site is definately worth the 1½ hour round-trip detour from Maison Laclos. Roughly signposted in white, the trail begins with a sharp climb along the bed of the gully shortly after the branch-off towards the cols. Fortunately, the filaos create welcome shade, and you will reach the plateau in around half an hour. There, the trail becomes a bit difficult to follow, and you must stay on the left side of the plateau in order to reach the lake at Kelval with its gorse. A few cattle browse alongside this peaceful sheet of water, which reflects the surrounding peaks. This is one of the best places from which to view the Trois Salazes peaks, which rise to the left of the Col du Taïbit. From this vantage point the origin of their name becomes obvious: the root word 'salaze', of Malagasy origin, means 'stakes', like the spits stuck in the ground at either side of a campfire for roasting meat.

TOUR DES CIRQUES

Trekking in the cirques is particularly challenging, owing to the changes in altitude. More than 3500m each way, this classic trek includes the three cirques and Piton des Neiges. It makes a four day loop, starting at Hell-Bourg, and includes the prior itinerary to Marla in the Mafate cirque. Thus, by combining the two treks, it is possible to make either a five, six or seven day hike.

First day: Hell-Bourg to Gîte de la Caverne Dufour (Piton des Neiges)
(Walking time: about 5½ hours)
From the centre of Hell-Bourg you will find the beginning of the trail by following the signposts to a trout farm. The road rises several hundred metres past a military barracks and a forest house until you arrive at a stadium which, although certainly in keeping with sporting-club standards, seems a bit grandiose for the area.

If you are driving and plan to leave your car at Hell-Bourg during the trek, avoid parking it in this somewhat remote area. You should select a more visible location, preferably in town.

The trail, which is signposted yellow/red, begins alongside the stadium and ascends through a wooded area. After 20 minutes or so, an ONF panel indicating Terre Plate and the Manouilh springs will tell you that you're going in the right direction. After an hour's hike, during which you will occasionally be able to see Hell-Bourg down below, you arrive at a small stand before coming to a crossroads with a forest path. The trail now proceeds through a grove of cryptomeria (a species of cedar-like tree native to Réunion), and about two hours after setting out you will come to a fork indicating the Manouilh springs to the right. Continuing straight ahead, you cross a small stream flowing peacefully between beautiful masses of Bolivian fuschias and then begin a fairly arduous climb to the left. After two hours, this will bring you to the large white cross on Cap Anglais where a crossroads shows Bélouve to the left (this is part of another itinerary by which you can visit the Caverne Dufour from Hell-Bourg via the Gîte de Bélouve; it is somewhat less arduous but takes longer). Following the sign pointing right to Piton des Neiges, the trail rapidly joins the GR R1, which is signposted in white/red (sometimes only white). It now climbs less steeply through a kind of heath (known as branles or brandes), grey-blue or grey-green plants of the heather family that are common in uncultivated areas. You now have a short 1½ hour hike to reach the ***Gîte de la Caverne Dufour (Piton***

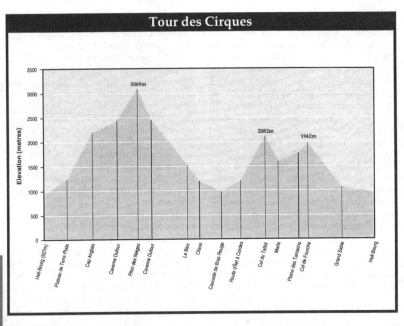

Tour des Cirques

des Neiges) (☎ 51 15 26). This gîte, operated by the Maison de la Montagne, may be fairly basic, but that makes little difference: the hospitality of the managers and the outstanding site, at the foot of Piton des Neiges, will certainly outweigh any relative discomfort. It can accommodate 39 people in dormitories. Water is in short supply and in fact there is no hot water; there are no showers and the toilets are outside. On the other hand, the managers serve an excellent single-dish meal for FF60. Coffee and tea (the only available breakfasts) cost FF7 and beer is FF15. Don't judge this gîte de montagne's spartan aspects too harshly: it is situated at an altitude of 2500m and the food, as well as the bottled fuel to cook it, must be carried up by manpower.

As with all Maison de la Montagne gîtes, you should reserve and pay in advance at either St-Denis or Cilaos (FF60/45 for adults/children under 12). You should also bring some warm clothing, since the nights are cold at this altitude.

You can also reach the Gîte de la Caverne Dufour (and then Piton des Neiges) from Cilaos. Just hike the following section in reverse.

Second day: Gîte de la Caverne Dufour (Piton des Neiges) to the summit of Piton des Neiges and to Cilaos
(Walking time: about six hours)
Many choose (and quite rightly) to leave the gîte before dawn to make the 600m climb to the island's highest point. It takes 1½ hours, but the effort is eased by the fact that packs can be left at the gîte and you can return via the same trail to retrieve them. The path begins directly opposite the gîte. The posts are easily recognisable in white on the rock face, making it easy to follow in the dark. You should however bring a flashlight if you start out before dawn. The trail rises gently over slag and through the heath in a landscape that becomes increasingly rocky the higher you climb.

RÉUNION

The last half hour of the ascent is the most arduous, when the path – the surface is rough slag that makes for slippery footing – is sharply cambered. The landscape, which is now completely stony and volcanic, is very similar to the red, black and ochre region around the island's active volcano, the Piton de la Fournaise.

Now frozen in its 30,000 years of inactivity, the only clues to the Piton des Neiges' volcanic origins are its desolate basalt foothills. Indeed, the active life of this immense volcano, which can be considered the true progenitor of the island of Réunion, took place more than 450,000 years ago, when floods of thick lava poured from the peak. With its collapse, the crater created the cirques of Salazie, Mafate and Cilaos, as well as a fourth, the Cirque des Marsouins, subsequently filled in to become the present-day Bébour plateau.

The view over Cilaos, on the left as you climb, is only a foretaste of the panorama awaiting you at the summit although, unfortunately, clouds frequently pose a problem. If the sky is clear you can see over the entire island. The cirques are spread out beneath you and in the distance looms the dome of Piton de la Fournaise.

Once back at the gîte, you take the white/red signposted GR R1, leaving the Cirque de Salazie and heading to Cilaos. The actual descent begins after you pass an intersection indicating the Plaine-des-Cafres to the left. The trail to Cilaos and Le Bloc (where the GR R1 joins up with the road just before Cilaos) is to the right. You should count on approximately three hours for the 1000m descent to Le Bloc. The trail consists of sharp, hairpin turns and of steps shaped out of the rock and is very hard on the knees. (It will seem even harder should you happen to meet the gîte caretaker climbing in his slippers, a bottle of gas slung over his shoulder, calm, cool and relaxed.)

The km markings painted at the edges of the trail will help you gauge your progress. You will pass PK4 within an hour after departure and a good half hour more will find you at PK3. Not long after, a sign will confirm that you have only one more hour before reaching Le Bloc and the road. First, you will cross the Plateau du Petit Matarum, where there is a sheet-metal shelter and water. The trail then becomes level for a while before redescending to Cilaos, with increasingly abundant tree cover, and there is a small cement belvedere from which you can look out over a broad panorama. Forty minutes more, and you are at Le Bloc. From there, you can get to Cilaos by bus or you can descend the last few km on foot along a scenic road bordered by Japanese cryptomeria and the native *bois de couleur* of the Forêt du Grand Matarum. This is part of the Cilaos biological reservation, which was established to protect the plant life of the Piton des Neiges ramparts.

Known for its mineral water, Cilaos has a thermal bath that can do wonders for a hiker's sore muscles. The jacuzzi, in particular, will help you soak out the muscular aches and pains created by hours of hiking.

See Cilaos in The Interior chapter for information on places to stay and eat.

Third day: Cilaos to Marla via the Col du Taïbit

(Walking time: about six hours)

This third day's hike will take you to the Cirque de Mafate. It begins opposite the hotel-restaurant Le P'tit Randonneur, where a Conseil Général signpost points the way to the Col du Taïbit. The wide path – known as the Bearers' Path – is scantily signposted at the beginning, but it is virtually impossible to make a mistake: it descends in a series of hairpin turns and reaches a footbridge after about 15 minutes, at the level of the old thermal station. The GR R1, indicated by an ONF signpost, begins about 12m further on. Posted in white/red, it descends among huge chokas, or century plants, with long, straight, thick leaves that resemble certain cacti. With age, this plant (its leaves were once used in rope-making) produces a single, light-coloured stalk that can grow to several metres. (At the Roche Plate/Rivière des Remparts gîte they serve excellent salads made of the blue choka, a less-common species that is also known as the 'Vera Cruz' agave.)

RÉUNION

As you continue, you will be able to see the spire of the church in Cilaos for some time if you turn around to look. Soon, you will be able to see the gully down below, which you should be able to reach in about an hour. (This itinerary, if you go back up the bed of the gully, will take you to the Cascade de Bras Rouge. From Cilaos, this makes an agreeable two hour round-trip hike. See Cascade de Bras Rouge in the Cilaos & the Cirque de Cilaos section of The Interior chapter).

Just after it fords the Bras Rouge gully the trail makes a sharp ascent and, after a 45 minute hike, it rises and descends again before rejoining the GR R1 from the right. It is then only a short stretch to arrive at and ford a stream with an ONF signpost. Ten more minutes, and you arrive at the Îlet à Cordes road.

This is an ideal spot for a break, because you are now at the halfway mark and the ascent to the pass is just beginning. (It is also possible to get to this point by hitching from Cilaos and thus halving the time for this hike.)

Signs on the other side of the road indicate the pass as 2½ hours away and Marla 20 minutes further. In fact, two hours are usually sufficient for reaching the pass and it is better to count on 40 minutes for the descent to Marla. The first 15 minutes of climbing is by far the most difficult. The gradient becomes easier after that, and the trail enters a wooded area; in 45 minutes you will reach a signpost indicating a 1½ hour hike to the pass. Now, the trail becomes even easier as you cross the Plaine des Fraises and then begins to rise one final time: in 20 minutes you will reach a small shrine that marks your arrival at the pass and your first view of Mafate. The name 'Taïbit' is derived from a Malagasy word that means 'rabbit droppings', probably because of its shape.

The descent to Marla, which you will soon see below, is via a series of tight hairpin turns and takes approximately 40 minutes. The trail is very steep and slippery when it rains.

For information on places to stay and eat in Marla, see the Roche Plate to Marla via Trois Roches section earlier in this chapter.

Fourth day: Marla to Hell-Bourg
(Walking time: about seven hours)

This final day of hiking is a fairly long one, but the trail is all downhill after you cross the Col de Fourche. It includes fording several gullies, which calls for a brief explanatory note. The water level in Réunion's gullies rises quickly when it rains. It often takes only an hour for the streams to reach maximum capacity, since these gullies are often the only outlets for the vast quantities of water that collect in the hilly upland basins. In fact, you may be surprised at the width of the Rivière des Galets when it reaches the coast across from the town of Le Port. Its vast stony bed, several hundred metres across and traversed by huge bridges, may appear to have a scale far in excess of the needs of the peaceful little stream that usually trickles along it. Such is not always the case: at times of heavy rain, its size can swell to equal that of a river like the Seine.

The gullies of Merles and Fleurs Jaunes, which must be crossed on this trek, are far from daunting. The pleasant leg from Marla to Hell-Bourg poses no problems in dry weather. On the other hand, you shouldn't trek it when it is raining or if there has been a lot of rain.

From Marla, take the marked path below the Maison de la Montagne gîte, in front of the grocery. This takes you quickly to Maison Laclos, where you go to the right towards the Col des Bœufs, Col de Fourche and Hell-Bourg. Less than 15 minutes hiking then brings you to an intersection where you continue straight ahead towards the Plaine des Tamarins. From there, the itinerary follows a variant of the GR R1, signposted in yellow/red or yellow/white, and ends, after fording two small gullies, with a half-hour climb. The first tamarind trees, through which the trail will meander as it gently rises, now come into view, indicating the plain you will reach some 1½ hours after setting out. Another crossroads points to La Nouvelle on the left and the Col de Bœufs and Col de Fourche on the right. In this direction, the trail is again posted with the white/red signs of the GR R1, and another crossroads, barely a half hour after the first, indicates that the Col de Fourche is a half hour to the right.

Once the pass has been crossed, you begin a steep descent. In less than 15 minutes the trail brings you to a fork to Le Bélier (straight ahead, where you can elect to break your trek by spending the night) and, to the right, Le Grand Sable and Hell-Bourg. The Marla to Hell-Bourg route lies in this direction, winding through an open area of young tree growth before coming to another fork, with Le Bélier to the left. Continuing towards Hell-Bourg, the trail now begins to meander from one side of the gully to the other. You will ford the stream five times during your 1½ hour hike after the pass. A wooden bridge enables you to cross a sixth time before climbing for a few minutes to a lookout point above a waterfall. A final crossroads to Le Bélier (at which you will again go right towards Hell-Bourg), brings you to one last crossing of the gully, and then you begin to follow the edge of a peaceful forest of cryptomeria, about 2½ hours after crossing the Fourche pass. Your next landmark is the junction to Trou Blanc, which forks to the right among the trees (this track, signposted in yellow/red, allows for a great, one day hike to and from Hell-Bourg, but is often not useable when it rains). You have now arrived at Le Grand Sable, where you can bivouac if you like.

Your trail, following the white/red GR signposting, continues straight ahead until it comes to a wider road, from which it goes off to the right through the grass. It then makes a gentle descent, and after 30 minutes or so it crosses an intersection that leads to the Piton d'Enchaing on the left (for information on Piton d'Enchaing see the Hell-Bourg & the Cirque de Salazie section in The Interior chapter). A wood-and-metal suspension bridge takes you across the gully, after which you have less than 15 minutes climb to the forest track, which you take to the right. The GR R1 then meets a tarred road that leads to Hell-Bourg.

It is possible to shorten the distance by rejoining the footpath a little before Hell-Bourg. It goes off on the left towards the old

thermal baths through fields of flowers and crosses a metal footbridge that could have been a toy for King Kong!

LE BÉLIER TO CILAOS (Circuit des Trois Cirques)

Walking from Le Bélier begins with scaling the forestry road to Bord à Martin. Pass the helipad (there's a minor route into Mafate via the Augustave track which turns off just to the right of the helipad). The next turning, which is to the left, leads to La Nouvelle via Col de Fourche, and those without a vehicle should follow this short cut to the Col de Fourche. Those with a vehicle may continue on to either Col des Bœufs or turn left at the fork about 3.5km beyond Bord à Martin; the end of the road lies about 600m from Col de Fourche.

To head for lower Mafate (Îlet à Bourse or Aurère), continue past the first La Nouvelle track near Bord à Martin. After a couple of hundred metres, turn right on the track marked Aurère. This route follows the Sentier Scout and includes a very pleasant descent of the Grand Rein ridge. At times it approaches knife-edge sharpness!

Travellers have reported that due to frequent break-ins and theft, it is unwise to leave vehicles at any of the trailheads above Le Bélier.

Via Upper Mafate

This is the more popular option since it requires the least change in altitude. The easiest access is by vehicle along the Route Forestière du Haut Mafate to the Col des Bœufs, beneath the spectacular Crête des Calumets. From there, the track trends downhill all the way to La Nouvelle. Here you have the option of adding one or two days to the route by circling through Roche Plate, which includes a tough slog into and out of the canyon carved by the Rivière des Galets. Overnights along the longer route would be at Le Bélier, La Nouvelle, Roche Plate and Marla. Alternatively, you can follow the easy route through Marla and over the Col du Taïbit to Cilaos.

RÉUNION

Via Lower Mafate

There are several loop options through lower Mafate. Good first-night options from Le Bélier are Îlet à Bourse or Aurère.

On the approach to Aurère from the south (Îlet à Malheur), trekkers cross the breathtaking gorge of the Bras Bémale on a small footbridge. Alternatively, you can take the steep and difficult shortcut; turn right at the sign marked Bémale just north of Îlet à Malheur. It's not recommended if you're carrying a pack.

If you opt to stay at Îlet à Bourse, it's either an easy second day to Aurère or directly west around Piton Carré to Grand Place. If you have a bit more energy, follow the spectacular loop through Aurère, down to Rivière des Galets and on to Grand Place. From Grand Place, there's a tiring detour around a landslide and a gruelling climb up to La Nouvelle. On the last day, it's a relatively easy walk out to Cilaos via Marla.

For a real challenge, from Grand Place head back downstream and turn left on the steep track leading down Rivière des Galets. From there, the route ascends almost vertically to Îlet des Lataniers, and on to Îlet des Orangers, before levelling out and continuing to Roche Plate. (This route is all the more interesting because Roche Plate is plainly visible from the gîte de montagne in Grand Place.) From Roche Plate, you can continue directly to either La Nouvelle or Marla on one of the upper Mafate routes.

FORÊT DE BÉLOUVE & FORÊT DE BÉBOUR TREK

This is at least a full-day walk – about 20km – mostly along tracks (the Sentier des Tamarins and Sentier des Mares et des Bois de Couleurs) paralleling the unsealed Route Forestière 2. The IGN 1:25,000 maps to carry (the TOP25 series) are 4402RT (St-Denis) and 4405RT (St-Pierre) – see Maps in the Réunion Facts for the Visitor chapter. Along the route, hikers will see examples of some of Réunion's most interesting forest habitats, including guava, cryptomeria, tamarinds, various orchids, vines and tree ferns, and native bois de couleur.

The 4.8km climb from the eastern end of Hell-Bourg on the GR R1 takes about two hours. It's steep but the going is good with concrete steps in places and a wonderful view over the Cirque de Salazie.

At the summit (1480m) is the Bélouve Gîte de Montagne (see under Places to Stay in the Hell-Bourg & the Cirque de Salazie section of The Interior chapter for more details), an especially useful accommodation option if you're coming from the opposite direction (bookings must be made through Maison de la Montagne in Cilaos or St-Denis; see Information at the beginning of this chapter). With ONF clearance, it's possible to drive a vehicle to this point from Plaine-des-Palmistes.

At Bélouve gîte, the GR R1 heads southwest along the ridge of Cap Anglais towards Piton des Neiges and the Cirque de Cilaos, but for the forest, follow the Route Forestière 2 southward. It forks in several places, but if you follow your map, there shouldn't be any problems. There are also various other signposted tangents. For thorough exploration of the Forêt de Bélouve, you'll need a couple of nights at the gîte. From here, the very adventurous can strike off eastward along the track that traverses the utterly wild and uninhabited Plaine des Lianes and eventually descends to connect with minor roads above Bras-Panon.

At the Ravine Misère picnic area, the road is blocked by a locked ONF gate. There's also a parking area where trekkers coming from Plaine-des-Palmistes leave their cars.

The picnic area itself offers tables and barbecue pits with wooden rain shelters. From this point, there's a 2.5km nature walk. Heading south, the route forestière is paralleled by the 2.8km Sentier des Mares et des Bois de Couleur.

When you reach the lip of the Rivière des Marsouins gorge, you can continue along the RF2 or follow the shortcut path, the Sentier de la Rivière, which entails a steep 100m descent to the bottom of the gorge. At the river, it's possible to sidetrack 100m upstream to a waterfall with a deep pool that's safe for swimming or 300m downstream to Caverne des Hirondelles (where the RF2 crosses the Rivière des Marsouins). Here you'll find a picnic site and quite an impressive waterfall.

Otherwise, the Sentier de la Rivière continues up the southern side of the gorge to rejoin the RF2. Thereafter, the route descends through coniferous forest with several picnic sites and, as would be expected, there's increased traffic, especially on weekends. You can avoid the crowds by cutting off the RF2 at the Plateau de Duvernay picnic site and following the spectacular 10km Sentier du Bras Cabot track down to Plaine-des-Palmistes. If you prefer to stick with RF2, there's a nice swimming spot at Rivière du Bras Sec about 3km from the junction with the cross-island road.

For further information on the Plaine-des-Palmistes area, see the Les Hautes Plaines section in The Interior chapter.

FROM THE VOLCANO TO THE COAST VIA BASSE VALLÉE

'From shore to mountain top...' was the motto employed by the French East India Company to describe the concessions it was prepared to grant the new settlers of Île Bourbon. Read in reverse, it aptly describes the trails that lead from the scorched summit of Piton de la Fournaise down to the sea.

There are three trails by which you can reach the sea from the volcano's gîte at Bellecombe. The western trail crosses the Plaine des Sables, climbs back up the caldera to the foot of the Chapel Ste-Thérèse and then slithers back down the bed of the Rivière des Remparts in the shadow of Piton Textor. This first trail takes you to the Gîte de Roche Plate-Rivière des Remparts (not to be confused with the Îlet de Roche Plate in the Mafate cirque), which is renowned for its picturesque setting and hospitality (especially the cooking). The descent of the river continues the following day, reaching the coast at St-Joseph. Unfortunately, this attractive trail down the gully is not practicable year-round.

The second trail descends to the east. It presents a greater physical challenge and, with the exception of the mountain refuge at

Tremblet, there is no gîte to break the trek. From the Gîte du Volcan (Bellecombe), this trail follows the Bellecombe rampart to Nez Coupé du Tremblet, where it bifurcates, one fork taking you to the Pointe du Tremblet and the other to Takamaka.

The third trail, which is described in more detail below, is the most classic. It begins like the one just described, but diverges from it at the Plateau de Foc Foc, descending to the Gîte de Basse Vallée and then reaching the coast near Le Cap Méchant.

Here too, it's best to get an early start. Many people opt to sleep at the Gîte du Volcan (Bellecombe) and spend a day touring the craters (see the Tour des Cratères section later in this chapter) prior to setting out the next day along the path traced out by the lava flows to the ocean.

Camping is strictly prohibited in a large area surrounding the volcano.

First day: Gîte du Volcan (Bellecombe) to Gîte de Basse Vallée
(Walking time: about 6½ hours)
From the lunar landscape of Piton de la Fournaise to the cryptomeria trees of the Gîte de Basse Vallée, this day's hike is, among other things, a marvellous illustration of the diversity of the island's landscapes. The heather-like plants of the arid areas give way to mountain tamarind trees, then to medium-altitude hygrophilic vegetation, and finally to bois de couleur and guava trees.

The trek starts with a half-hour hike down the trail that starts across from the gîte. On it, you come to the road, where you leave the craters to your left and begin the descent to the Plaine des Sables. The trail is signposted and indicates a three hour trek (it's actually six hours) to the Gîte de Basse Vallée. The trail soon goes off to the left and it cuts across a rocky landscape of ochre and grey lava, matte and ashy, touched with grey-green patches of heather. Blazed with white or red markings, the path is easy over level ground, but there is little shade.

Approximately an hour and a half after leaving the gîte you will come to a superb lookout point with a view of the caldera and

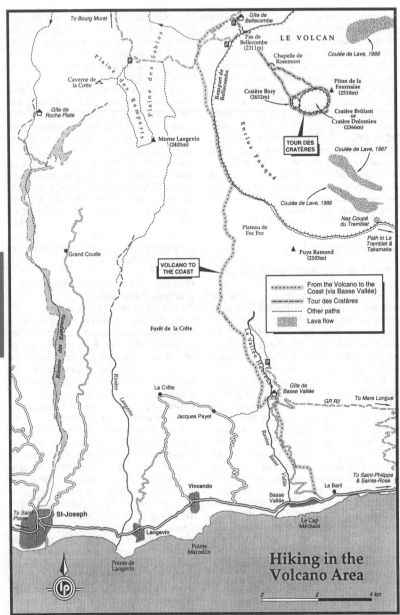

To Bourg Murat

Gîte de
Bellecombe

LE VOLCAN

Pas de
Bellecombe
(2311m)

Chapelle de
Rosemont

Coulée de Lave, 1988

Caverne de
la Cotte

Plaine des Sables

Plaine des Remparts

Rempart de
Bellecombe

Cratère Bory
(2632m)

Piton de la
Fournaise
(2510m)

Gîte de
Roche Plate

Cratère Brûlant
or
Cratère Dolomieu
(2366m)

Morne Langevin
(2403m)

Enclos Fouqué

TOUR DES
CRATÈRES

Coulée de Lave, 1987

Coulée de Lave, 1988

Nez Coupé
du Tremblet

Plateau de
Foc Foc

Path to Le
Tremblet &
Takamaka

Grand Coude

Puys Ramond
(2103m)

VOLCANO TO
THE COAST

From the Volcano to the
Coast (via Basse Vallée)

Tour des Cratères

Other paths

Lava flow

Forêt de la Crête

Rivière des Remparts

Rivière Langevin

La Vallée Heureuse

La Crête

Gîte de
Basse Vallée

GR R2

To Mare Longue

Jacques Payet

Ravine Basse Vallée

Vincendo

Le Baril

To Saint-Philippe
& Sainte-Rose

To Saint
Pierre

St-Joseph

Basse
Vallée

Langevin

Le Cap
Méchant

Pointe
Marcellin

Hiking in the
Volcano Area

Pointe de
Langevin

0   2   4 km

RÉUNION

the flank of the crater. Blackened by lava flows, it is the visible portion of a volcanic cone that has risen 6000m from the ocean floor. Following the rampart, the trail goes on for another half hour through the slag until you come to a fork. Your route is to the right, towards the tiny village of Jacques Payet et de Basse-Valet, which the signpost, in a further burst of optimism, announces as a 2½ hour trek. Leaving the edge of the ramparts, you begin a gentle descent to the Plateau de Foc Foc on an ashy trail punctuated with dried roots bleached by the sun and the wind. The end of the plateau, which should take about an hour to cross, signals the appearance of tamarind trees. You now start on the descent to the sea through an increasingly flourishing landscape in which the diversity of species increases as you lose altitude. Grass begins to replace the rock surface beneath your feet; there are tree-like ferns and calumets, a bamboo endemic to Réunion. Still losing altitude, you will cross a small gully on an old tamarind trunk before passing, on the right, a fork leading to the Jacques Payet forest track. The trail now becomes fairly wide and brings you to a small container that could serve as a shelter if need be. Two and a half hours after leaving the Plateau de Foc Foc you will come to a wooden railing. From here, the path leads through guava trees, which line the heights of La Vallée Heureuse and overlook the gîte, and the going is quicker. The trail continues until you reach a sign indicating the steep descent to the gîte, which is still some 40 minutes away.

Crossing an attractive wood, the trail reaches a gully (be on your guard when it rains) and then continues with a brief climb by which, with the help of a few wooden stairs, you arrive at the forest of cryptomeria in which the gîte is located.

Comfortable and new, the *Gîte de Basse Vallée* (☎ 37 00 75) has a fireplace, a kitchen and good plumbing. Dormitory beds, which must be reserved and paid for in advance at the Maison de la Montagne, are FF70. Breakfast costs FF25, and the fulfilling meal costs FF80, rhum arrangé included.

Second day: Gîte de Basse Vallée to the Coast
(Walking time: about two hours)
There is an 8km-long road suitable for motor vehicles from the gîte to the coast. By the footpath, you can shave 2km from that distance. Since both routes constantly cross each other, you can opt to make this short leg of the journey either by road or on foot. In either case, it is nearly impossible to lose your way.

The forest track descends to the ocean – which seems very near – in hairpin turns, passing through forests and fields of sugar cane, bibasse and mock-pepper.

As for the footpath, for most of its length it traverses a dense forest and then ends with a long straight leg on which you can see the vanilla plants lazily wrapping their slender tendrils around the filao trees. This area is very hospitable to this difficult type of orchid, which likes moderate shade, not too much sun and just the right amount of humidity.

Both routes join up shortly before reaching a forest hut and end at the road a few metres from the bus stop marked 'Case Basse Vallée' on Line I. You can also try hitching to St-Pierre, where a shared taxi to St-Denis will cost FF50, while the bus costs FF42.

LA ROCHE ÉCRITE
(Walking time: about 6½ hours – one or two days)
This hike is undoubtedly one of the most beautiful, and is ideal for those in Réunion for a brief time. In fact, it can be done in one long day, return included. However, you will have a better chance of enjoying clear skies if you sleep at the Gîte de la Plaine des Chicots (La Roche Écrite) so that you can take in the view in the early morning hours. The ascent (more than 1000m between Mamode Camp and Le Brûlé) is gradual and makes this trek accessible to children, providing that you allow two days.

The route is easy to follow but you might like to get hold of the 4402 RT map St-Denis, cirques de Mafate et de Salazie (see Maps earlier in this chapter). It mentions trails and gîtes along the way.

RÉUNION

About 15km, as the crow flies, south of St-Denis, La Roche Écrite is located at the tip of a 2277m-high rampart that overlooks the cirques of Mafate and Salazie. In clear weather the view over the cirques and the island's two highest peaks, Piton des Neiges (3069m) and Gros Morne (3013m) is stunning.

You can begin the trek from St-Denis (at La Providence, just south of St-Denis), but you should take the road between Le Brûlé and Mamode Camp. Many people choose to proceed directly to Mamode Camp, 5.5km above Le Brûlé, which has car parking. The D 42, which you can join at the top of the Rue de Paris near the Jardin de l'État, takes you to the village of Le Brûlé (altitude 800m) via a number of hairpin curves that will give you beautiful views over the capital. Bus Nos 2 and 23 depart for Le Brûlé from the *gare routière* (bus station) on weekends.

The footpath, which is signposted from Mamode Camp, begins with a gentle climb through the cryptomeria, which can be recognised by long trunks reminiscent of certain conifers, before you reach medium-altitude hygrophilic vegetation. From there, the trail will take you through an especially well-preserved area rich in fruits and wildflowers, lichens and mosses. Arborescent ferns open their broad fronds, along with the calumet, a species of grass related to the bamboo. A 1¼ hour hike will bring you to a fork leading to Bois de Nèfles, on the left, which you will pass to continue into a forest of bois de couleur, which gradually gives way to lofty tamarind trees. After about two hours of trekking the *Gîte de la Plaine des Chicots (La Roche Écrite)* (☎ 43 99 84) comes into view. This attractive gîte, operated by the Maison de la Montagne, consists of three small stone buildings with tamarind shingles. It is fairly comfortable, with kitchen, fireplace and hot shower. A bed in the dormitories, which are in the attic storey, costs FF70. Breakfast is FF30 and dinner FF85, including the rhum arrangé, mixed by the custodian. You could make this pleasant spot your goal after a four hour round-trip hike and it's a perfect place for a picnic. It is possible to camp out on the plain.

A few metres beyond the gîte a footpath to the right leads to the Plaine d'Affouches and Dos d'Ane. Your climb to La Roche Écrite continues straight ahead. From here, the footpath is marked in white. The landscape, a vast, gently rising plateau, soon becomes more arid and mineral. Following the marks on the ground you will soon arrive at a fork to La Mare aux Cerfs. This tiny body of water is one of the only places on the island where you might have a chance, very early in the morning, to see some of Réunion's few Java deer.

After the gîte it's a 40 minute hike to the second fork to La Mare aux Cerfs. Twenty minutes further and the steep path down to Salazie (Grand Îlet) forks off to the left. La Roche Écrite is straight ahead, a few hundred metres after the white-painted mark on the ground reading 'PK 9'. It takes an hour and a half from the Gîte de la Plaine des Chicots (La Roche Écrite) to this point.

The view over the cirques and the mountains is stunning and you might be lucky enough to catch a glimpse of a sea of clouds wrapped around the hills.

The return downhill is faster. Going by way of La Mare aux Cerfs is no detour.

STE-ROSE – LA MARINE INLET
(Walking time: one hour)

Far from the steep slopes of the cirques, this short, refreshing stroll will give you a chance to discover coastal plant life at a site that is ideal for picnicking with children. To get to the inlet at Ste-Rose by car (coming from the west), you must follow the sign at the first roundabout as you come into town.

The walk begins at the bar-restaurant and follows the shore to the south. It unfolds in the shade of vacoa or pandanus trees, which seem to be raised on root pylons. The long leaves of the trees are used in basket weaving. Bamboo trees, chokas and filaos also grow on this part of the coast, where the green vegetation contrasts sharply with the black volcanic rocks created by the lava that once flowed down to meet the sea. Following this jagged coastline, against which the pounding ocean sends up clouds of spray, you will

The Cross-Country for Crazies

Crossing a tropical island on foot is a lifelong dream for some people. But some of the contestants in the *Grand Raid* or the *Passe Montagne* need only a few hours and a good pair of trainers to conquer this island.

In 1996 there were more than a thousand participants in the Grand Raid, the larger of these two mountain races, which have existed since 1989. Although it has been dubbed 'The Walk in the Clouds', the 'Grande Traversée' or 'The Race of the Full Moon', some prefer to call it the 'Cross-Country for Crazies'. It is held annually in October or November, and its course changes each year. In broad terms, it starts at Camp Méchant, climbs to the volcano, crosses part of the Plaine des Sables and takes in Piton Textor before descending to the Plaine des Cafres and heading towards Cilaos. The contestants then climb the Col du Taïbit to Mafate, from which they exit via the Col de Fourche. Finally, they pass Le Grand Sable and Grand Îlet and go back up to La Roche Écrite before returning to the coast at La Grande Chaloupe. The winner of the first race – a native of Réunion, as were all of the first eight winners – took 16 hours to cover 125km and 7000m of actual altitude change. The best time for the race is 14 hours 33 minutes.

For its part, the Passe Montagne has been held in May for the past five years. Its course differs from the Grand Raid, but the goal is the same: to cross the island. The starter's pistol is fired at Langevin Point, from where the participants – there were nearly 600 contestants in 1997 – head for Le Barachois at St-Denis, via Grand Galet, Piton Textor, the Col de Bébour, Hell-Bourg, Le Bélier, Aurère, Dos d'Ane and Colorado. The best time for the race is 14 hours 33 minutes.

Anyone can enter and the maximum time allowed is from 55 to 60 hours for either race. You can contact the organisers of the Grand Raid at BP 426, 97468 St-Denis Cedex (☎ 20 32 00; fax 94 19 20). The Passe Montagne is run by Les Randonneurs de la Réunion, BP 372, 97467 St-Denis Cedex (fax 21 97 94).

Far from the crowds and the stopwatch, the Course of the Crazies' cross-country is also a fantastic hike. It follows the route of the GR R2 and eight to 10 days would not be unreasonable to complete it. Starting from the north, the first day takes you to the Gîte de la Plaine des Chicots and the La Roche Écrite itinerary, continuing on to Dos d'Ane. From there, you proceed to Roche Plate the following day and then take in Marla, Cilaos and Caverne Dufour on the third, fourth and fifth days (see Tour des Cirques in the Trekking in Réunion chapter for a description of these treks). On the sixth day, you proceed to Bourg Murat and spend the night at the Gîte du Volcan (Bellecombe). To complete the hike you proceed to the coast by following the Basse Vallée itinerary.

Information about this itinerary, which can be subject to many variations, can be obtained from the Maison de la Montagne. It is also described in Topo-guide *L'île de la Réunion* (see Books in this chapter). ∎

RÉUNION

arrive in around half an hour at the Cayenne refreshment stall. On the way, with a little luck, you may be able to admire one of the countless chameleons that watch over the area, seemingly frozen for eternity.

From Cayenne, you can rejoin the very picturesque Anse des Cascades – another pleasant place for a walk – in approximately four hours. To do this, you must go back a few km along the road and then return to the shore when you reach the 1977 lava flow, following the small square signs for the VTT. Do not venture onto the rocks along the shore just after Cayenne: they're slippery and dangerous.

BASSIN LA PAIX & BASSIN LA MER
(Walking time: two hours)

These two attractive pools fed by high water-falls are one of the charms of the heights above Rivière des Roches, on the east coast not far from Bras-Panon. You will see the direction to Bassin la Paix signposted shortly after you enter the village.

The narrow road twists along for 4km through fields of sugar cane to a car park. The waterfall of Bassin la Paix can be heard roaring below on the right. Two little wooden bridges and a long cement stairway enable you to reach clear waters in a few minutes.

Less visited, Bassin la Mer demands a little more effort. Getting there will take about 45 minutes. It's best to wear trainers, since the path can be slippery or muddy and it ends in a steep descent through rocks and roots. Indicated by an ONF signpost, it first takes you through fields of sugar cane, which quickly give way to thicker vegetation. After viewing the falls lower down, the path enters a small wood where it veers to the right. This fork is not well marked. You've passed it if you come to a little, broken-down metal bridge.

You then arrive at the top of a flight of cement stairs, at the bottom of which you should turn left. A fairly steep descent will bring you to the clear waters of the pool, a tempting spot for a swim.

TOUR DES CRATÈRES

Piton de la Fournaise is a bubbling, smouldering volcano and is probably Réunion's most renowned feature. It is relatively safe and straightforward to visit. Although the volcano occupies a single massif, there are actually two major craters – Dolomieu (or Brûlant), the largest, and Bory, inactive since 1791 – and a host of smaller barnacle-like craters strewn across the slopes of the mountain. Several of these peripheral craters have erupted over the past few years, thankfully providing more spectacle than tragedy. A recent eruption was from the small crater called Zoé, on the mountain's south-eastern flank, in late 1992.

Potential hikers should be aware that temperatures and climatic conditions swing wildly at times, and despite the popularity of this walk, it's still a good haul to the top. Although it may seem harmless enough on a crisp sunny morning, this is a potentially hazardous region. Warm windproof and waterproof clothing are essential. Furthermore, carry plenty of water (the cold wind can cause rapid dehydration!) as well as a few energy snacks.

When crossing the crater floor, under no circumstances wander off the marked path. The clouds and fog can roll in instantaneously, and without reference points the landscape of the crater floor looks indistinguishable. In recent years, there have been several disappearances resulting in fatalities. If you're concerned, carry the IGN 1:25,000 series map 4406RT *Piton de la Fournaise* and perhaps even a compass.

For the best view (potentially, anyway) and most agreeable weather conditions, start as early as possible. The trip begins with a 600m walk from the gîte to the Pas de Belle-combe car park and volcano information post, which is at an altitude of 2353m. The return walk from the gîte to (and around) the summit is approximately 13km and takes five hours under optimum conditions.

Begin the walk by turning left at the information post and following the track along the rim. After several hundred metres, the track turns right and begins its steep descent of the sheer wall to the floor of the immense U-shaped outer crater, known as l'Enclos Foucqué.

At this point, the route is marked by a dashed white line across the lava, reminiscent of a super highway. En route are pustule-like lava domes and bizarre, sculpted lava formations. After several hundred metres, you'll arrive at a small scoria cone, Formica Léo, which can be explored on foot. Two km beyond it is the bizarre lava formation known as Chapelle de Rosemont. At this point, the route splits. The right fork climbs steeply and directly to the 2632m-high, 200m-wide Cratère Bory. The left fork takes a more gradual route up to La Soufrière, the northern wall of the gaping 900m-wide Cratère Dolomieu.

Once at the top, you can decide whether to do the circuit around both craters or just traverse the track along the northern rims connecting the Bory and La Soufrière routes. While walking along the rim, beware of large fissures, holes and, most of all, overhangs. Stay on the marked track and heed the signs.

Although many people opt to stay down at Plaine-des-Cafres, there'll be a much better chance of seeing the volcano with the early light afforded by staying at the gîte here.

Gîte du Volcan (Bellecombe) (☎ 21 28 96) has about 30 beds for FF70 per person. Breakfast is FF25 and dinner is FF85. This is an extremely popular gîte so book through Maison de la Montagne in Cilaos or St-Denis as far in advance as possible.

If you're staying a couple of days at the gîte and are looking for an act to follow the volcano, hike from the gîte down the road into the Fond de la Rivière de l'Est. After about 2km, the road becomes a track and turns east, following the Ravine Savane Cimetière. After 7km, the track ends with a breathtaking view into the gaping amphitheatre, Rond des Cascades, where the Rivière de l'Est begins its journey to the sea.

Getting There & Away

For those with a vehicle, getting to the volcano couldn't be easier because there's an all-weather road which winds and climbs from Bourg-Murat in Le Vingt-Septième all the way to Pas de Bellecombe on the crater's outer rim, just a couple of hours walking from the summit.

It's also possible to trek up the volcano from the south, up the lava flows from St-Philippe or Tremblet, but this is an extremely arduous route made even more difficult by near constant precipitation. Even in the dry season, there's a good chance of some rain. For more information, see The South-East Corner in the Around the Coast chapter.

Most hikers prefer to approach by the much easier route from the west. If you're walking up from Bourg-Murat the gîte should be the objective of the first day's effort. Leave the summit slog until early the next morning when there'll be a better chance of good weather and views.

The route up from the Plaine-des-Cafres passes the panoramic lookout point at Nez de Boeuf, which gives you a view down the deep valley of the Rivière des Remparts 1200m below. It also passes the sinister black hole of an extinct volcano, Cratère Commerson.

About 2km downhill from Cratère Commerson is Sentier Josemont, a marvellous two hour, 6.5km tramp directly to the Gîte du Volcan (Bellecombe) and a far more interesting route than the road. Near the start of the trek is a memorial to the forest ranger Josemont Lauret, who died here from exposure one night in October 1887, a 'victim of his own courage and devotion to his companions'.

The path moves away from the road and into the giant Caverne des Lataniers, where it then proceeds gently down a cliff edge (experiment with the echoes!). At its foot lies the broad expanse of the moon-like Plaine des Sables. The track across this strange terrain is clearly marked by dobs of paint every few metres. At the end of the plain it's an easy climb up to the Gîte du Volcan (Bellecombe).

RÉUNION

Seychelles

Facts about the Seychelles

The Seychelles have some of the most beautiful islands in the Indian Ocean, which undoubtedly rate as among the finest in the world. This is the glorious, lush, idyllic paradise we see in glossy holiday brochures and in seductive adverts for Bounty chocolate bars. In fact, what you see on paper or TV is a half-truth: the real thing is much more stunning, so 'Treasure every moment' as the Seychelles slogan advises.

What appears to be a comfortable, quiet, contented way of life also has, in this case, an intriguing and often dangerous political background. Since President France Albert René grabbed power in 1977 from the elected leader of the formerly independent British colony, there have been periods of turbulence.

Until fairly recently, the Seychelles harboured a hotbed of spies as well as tourists. The setting, the plot and the characters could have graced the pages of a Graham Greene, Frederick Forsyth or Ian Fleming novel. The CIA, KGB and MI5 flitted through the islands during the Cold War era, mixing with communist troops from North Korea and Tanzania, Russian advisers, US military personnel from a satellite tracking station, mercenaries, private detectives, exiled rebels, diplomats and the Mafia. The political rhythms have currently reverted to a more relaxed mode and tourists rarely sense anything untoward.

To exploit its greatest asset (the beauty of the islands) the Seychelles government has deliberately endeavoured to promote savvy tourism. By upping prices and curbing the influx of visitors, the pressures of tourism on the islands' infrastructure have been curtailed, and the ecological wealth of the Seychelles has been recognised as a powerful tourist magnet worthy of protection and preservation.

Most travellers to the Seychelles just spend a day or two on the main island, Mahé, then make a beeline for the more easy going and exotic islands of Praslin or La Digue. For those who really want to play jetsetter there are a handful of smaller, more secluded island hideaways (described in individual chapters). And for those who wish to escape from the chaos and craziness of modern living, US$18 million will buy your very own island paradise to chill out on! Prospective buyers can read more under D'Arros Island in the Outer Islands chapter.

Apart from tremendous beaches and incredible snorkelling and diving opportunities, the Seychelles also boasts ecological highlights – another reason to visit and risk falling in love with these breathtaking islands.

HISTORY

Until the 17th century the Seychelles were uninhabited. There may have been a camp or two of shipwrecked Arab sailors in the

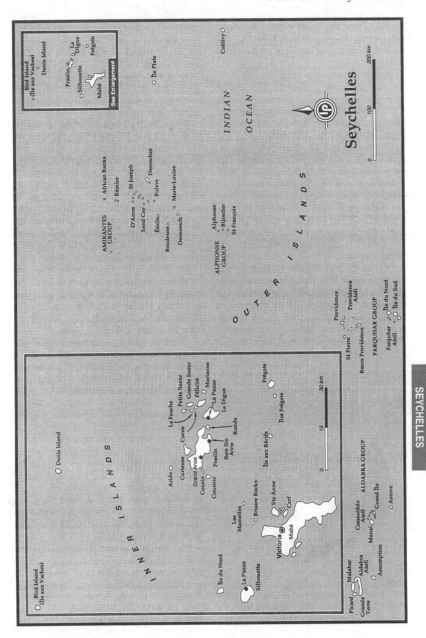

Seychelles

course of the early centuries; they were possibly responsible for the ancient tombs found on Silhouette Island, but whoever built them didn't last long.

Portuguese explorers were the first Europeans to discover the islands. The first recorded landing was left to a British East India Company ship in 1609. The skipper reported that the islands were an ideal spot for replenishing supplies and energy.

The pirates and privateers who had just moved shop from the Caribbean came to the same conclusion and, during lulls in their maraudings, set up temporary bases on the islands. Frégate Island is believed to have been one such base. The name of pirate Olivier 'La Buse' Levasseur still crops up in the continual search for his treasure around Bel Ombre on Mahé (see boxed text in the Mahé chapter).

In 1742, the great Mahé de La Bourdonnais, the governor of Mauritius (then known as Île de France), sent Lazare Picault to check out the islands. Picault named the main island after his governor (and the bay where he landed after himself) and laid the way for the French to claim possession of the islands 12 years later. They were named Séchelles in

The Seychelles was named in honour of Jean Moreau de Sachelles who was finance minister to Louis XV, in 1754.

honour of the finance minister to Louis XV, Jean Moreau de Sachelles.

The first batch of the French and their slaves arrived on Ste Anne Island in 1770. After a few false starts, the settlers began growing spices, cassava, sugar cane, coffee, sweet potatoes and maize, and began exploiting the large colonies of giant tortoise.

When the British started taking an interest in the islands at the end of the 18th century, Queau de Quinssy had been installed as governor. Instead of risking life and limb to fend off British attacks, de Quinssy lowered the French flag and surrendered to the British frigates. When the aggressors sailed on, he raised the flag again. De Quinssy was to capitulate about a dozen times before the Seychelles became a British dependency of Mauritius, after the Napoleonic Wars and the Treaty of Paris in 1814.

De Quinssy, the 'Great Capitulator', was allowed to remain in charge until 1827. He changed his name to De Quincy in deference to his new masters and lived out his days in the Seychelles. His tomb is at Government House in Victoria, Mahé.

The British did little to develop the islands except increase the number of slaves. When slavery was abolished in 1835, the slaves were released. French remained the main language and French culture too was dominant.

The islands were also used by the British as a five-star jail and retreat for political prisoners and exiles, most of whom had a great time there. They included banished tribal kings, sultans and independence leaders who were chipping away at the British Empire. Among them was Archbishop Makarios of Cyprus, who was housed in the governor's lodge at Sans Souci (on Mahé) in 1956. Later, the Southern Maldivian rebel Abdullah Afif Didi was also imprisoned on the island.

The British also thought of reducing the exclusivity of the jail and turning it into a concentration camp for Boer prisoners of war or Irish republican rebels, but this never happened.

In 1903 the Seychelles became a crown colony administered from London. The country went into the political and economic doldrums until 1964, when political parties were formed. France Albert René, a young lawyer, founded the Seychelles People's United Party (SPUP). His colleague in law, James Mancham, led the new Seychelles Democratic Party (SDP).

1965 Onwards

In 1965, an Australian journalist wrote: 'Hardly anything happens in the Seychelles. People show virtually no interest in politics ... the clocks chime twice for those who were not awake the first time'.

The next 20 years resulted in a complete and stunning transformation of the sleepy, forgotten islands, with events that would wake up the world.

Mancham's SDP, made up of the islands' business people and planters, won the elections in 1966 and 1970. René's SPUP fought on a socialist and independence ticket. In June 1975 a coalition of the two parties gave the appearance of unity in the lead up to independence from the UK, which was granted a year later. Sir James Mancham became the first president and René the prime minister.

The flamboyant Sir Jim – poet, playboy and grandson of a Chinese immigrant – placed all his eggs in one basket: tourism. He jetsetted around the world with a beautiful socialite on each arm, putting the Seychelles on the map.

The rich and famous poured in for holidays or to stay and party, party, party. Adnan Khashoggi and other Arab millionaires bought large tracts of land on the islands. Film stars and celebrities went there to enhance their romantic, sexy images. *Goodbye Emmanuelle* was filmed on La Digue.

But in the opinion of René and the SPUP, the wealth was not being spread evenly or fairly and the country was no more than a rich person's playground. René said that poor Créoles were little better off than slaves.

So on 5 June 1977, barely a year after Independence, René and a team of Tanzanian-trained rebels carried out an almost bloodless coup while Mancham was in London attending a conference of Commonwealth leaders. As Mancham said at the time: 'It was no heroic deed to take over the Seychelles. Twenty-five people with sticks could seize control.' Tanzanian and North Korean soldiers were brought in by René to make sure that any opposition would need more than that to take over the country.

An attempt to do so came in November 1981, when a band of mercenaries, led by ex-Congo 'dog of war' Colonel Mike Hoare, bungled a chance to invade the country. The group posed as a South African rugby club on an annual binge, but a customs officer discovered weapons in one of the suitcases. Two people died in a shoot-out at the airport before the mercenaries beat a hasty retreat by hijacking an Air India plane back to South Africa. Five mercenaries, the advance guard, were rounded up, tried and sentenced to death. They were later released and deported. In 1992 the South African government paid the Seychelles government eight million rupees as compensation for the coup.

René had already deported many of the members and supporters of the outlawed SDP party. Opposed to René's one-party, socialist state, these *grands blancs* (rich whites) set up 'resistance movements' in the UK, South Africa and Australia.

The country fell into disarray as the tourist trade dried to a trickle. In 1982 there was a mutiny of NCOs (non-commissioned officers) in the Seychelles army, and a coup plot by Seychelles expatriates was discovered taking place in a London hotel room. Bombings and murders on the islands continued into 1983 as part of a campaign of civil disruption.

In December 1984 thorough intelligence gathering by the Seychelles government foiled another coup plot in the early stages of planning in South Africa. A year later, Gerard Hoareau, the immigration chief under Mancham and leader of the Seychelles resistance movement in the UK, was machine-gunned to death by persons unknown outside his London home. In 1986 there was another attempted coup by majors from within the Seychelles army.

SEYCHELLES

During the early 1990s, René started to rethink his adherence to one-party rule and in December 1991 he surprised his opponents by legalising opposition parties within a multiparty system. Quite possibly, this move might have been prompted by hints from European countries that continued aid would be linked to democratic developments.

Multiparty elections to a 23-member commission were held in July 1992, under the watchful eye of Commonwealth observers. René and his party, the Seychelles People's Progressive Front (SPPF), won 58.4% of the votes. Mancham, who had returned to the Seychelles with a hefty SAS security team, fielded 33.7% for his Democratic Party (DP) and contested the results as rigged and unfair.

In November 1992, the draft constitution prepared by the commission was thrown out after a referendum failed to achieve the required 60% of votes in favour. The opposition, most notably Mancham's Democratic Party, campaigned successfully against proposed linkage between presidential election results and the allocation of national assembly seats. In 1993, a modified multiparty politics constitution was implemented. Elections held in July 1993 resulted in René retaining and still holding power.

GEOGRAPHY & GEOLOGY

The Seychelles lies about 1600km off the coast of East Africa, its nearest neighbour. There are roughly 115 islands, with a combined area of only 455 sq km, situated between the equator and the 10th parallel south.

The central islands are granite, the main three being Mahé, Praslin and La Digue. The outlying islands are coral atolls. The granite islands, which do not share the volcanic nature of Réunion and Mauritius, appear to be peaks of a huge submerged plateau which was left behind by India when the continental plates shifted about 65 million years ago. The highest point in the islands is Morne Seychellois (905m) on Mahé.

CLIMATE

The great news here is that the islands lie outside the cyclone zone, which makes them a safer bet than Mauritius or Réunion for visits during the November to April period.

The seasons are defined by the beginning and end of the south-east trade winds, which usually blow from May to October. During the rest of the year, the islands experience the north-west monsoon winds which bring the rain, especially in January. The turn around periods between the two winds are the calmest.

The rain generally comes in sudden, heavy bursts. Mahé, the most mountainous island, and lofty Silhouette get the highest rainfall. January is the wettest month by far while July and August are the driest. The temperature is constant throughout the year, between 24°C and 31°C, as is the humidity, at around 80%.

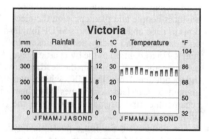

ECOLOGY & ENVIRONMENT

The government has made a deliberate attempt to promote the Seychelles as a savvy tourist destination, thus curtailing the influx of visitors and reducing the strain of tourism on the islands' infrastructure. The government realises that the ecological beauty of the islands (flora, fauna and marine life) is what attracts visitors (and revenue), so protection of these natural assets is crucial. Conservation is a major consideration and development is carefully regulated to protect the natural beauty of the islands. The government even banned visitors to Cocos Island in 1987, in an attempt to protect the damaged coral (for more information, see Cocos Island in the La Digue & Other Inner Islands chapter).

To assist in protecting the Seychelles' magnificent marine life, we strongly urge you not to buy anything made out of turtle shell, nor to buy or take any shells from the beach. Governments are trying to do something about it; please don't contribute to the problems by providing the incentive to continue the practices.

For important information on responsible diving, see the Ecology & Environment section in the Facts about the Region chapter at the beginning of this book.

FLORA & FAUNA

The islands are a haven for wildlife, particularly birds and tropical fish. The government's conservation policies, which include the formation of several marine and nature reserves, seem to work well alongside and within the tourist industry.

Flora

As you would expect from the lush praises heaped on the islands' beauty, the Seychelles are rich in vegetation – but not that rich. Christopher Lee wrote in his book *Political Castaways*:

If there is one criticism to be levelled at the scenery of the Seychelles, it is one of little variation in the colour of its plant life ... Possibly because of the most idyllic reputation of the islands, one expects that a blaze of strong colour will cover the stark granite environment. It doesn't. To the knowing eye there may be a subtle difference in shade, but there is definitely a gap between the often imagined tropical paradise of travel brochures and film locations and the real thing.

He has a point, but only up to a point, for the islands *are* used widely as film and advertisement locations and the travel brochures, if anything, don't do the place justice.

The coconut palm and casuarina are the most common trees on the islands. There are a few banyans (a giant one shades the road at Ma Constance, about 3.5km north of Victoria), screw pines (or *vacoas*), bamboo and tortoise trees (so named because the fruit looks like the tortoises that eat it). Virgin forest now only exists in the higher parts of Mahé and Silhouette, and in the Vallée de Mai on Praslin, one of only three places in

the world where the giant coco de mer palm grows. The other two are Silhouette and Curieuse islands.

Out of about 200 plant species, 80 are endemic. These include the *bois rouge*, which has broad, reddish leaves and red wood, the giant and very rare *bois de fer*, and the *capucin*, named because its seed resembles the hood of a Capuchin monk. The capucin features prominently in the paintings of Marianne North, the English artist who visited the islands in 1883 to paint their plant life. Her work was donated to Kew Botanic Gardens in London and the Seychellois collection is on view in the North Gallery there.

In the high, remote parts of Mahé and Silhouette islands, you may come across the insect-eating pitcher plant, which either clings to adjacent trees or bushes or sprawls along the ground. On the floral front there are plenty of orchids, bougainvilleas, hibiscuses, gardenias and frangipani.

The Botanical Gardens in Victoria are well kept and provide a pleasant and interesting walk. The Vallée de Mai on Praslin is a must (for more information see the Praslin chapter). And for chance discoveries, get yourself away from the beach for a day and head into the hills on Mahé, Silhouette or Praslin.

Fauna

Common mammals and reptiles around the islands are fruit bat or flying fox (*chauves souris*), gecko and skink. Electric wires cause problems for bats: on Mahé you may see their electrocuted cadavers hanging between the wires. There are also some small snakes, but they are not dangerous.

Insect life on the Seychelles is represented by more than 3000 species. Among the more interesting insects are the lumbering rhinoceros beetle whose larvae cause considerable damage by feeding on young shoots of coconut palms; the giant tenebrionid beetle, a bizarre amalgamation of legs and knobbly body, unique to Frégate Island; and the various kinds of wasp, which excel in creating mud pots attached to vegetation, rocks, or walls. Despite an impressive appearance,

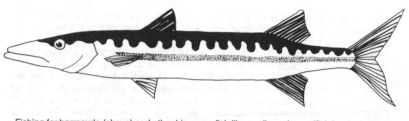

Fishing for barracuda (above) and other big-game fish like marlin and swordfish is a huge attraction in the Seychelles.

the giant millipedes, palm spiders and whip scorpions are not life-threatening, but you can expect a nasty reaction if you handle them.

Birdlife Because of the islands' isolation and the comparatively late arrival of humans, there are many species of birds unique to the Seychelles. Some are plentiful, some are rare and some are now extinct.

Almost every island seems to have one rare species to its name. On Frégate and Aride are the magpie robins (known as *pie chanteuse* in Créole), on Cousin you'll find the bush warbler, La Digue has the paradise flycatcher (or *veuve*) and Praslin has the black parrot. The bare-legged scops owl and the Seychelles kestrel live on Mahé, and Bird Island is home to millions of fairy terns.

In general there are plenty of herons, fodies, sunbirds, lovebirds, egrets, owls, mynahs, sparrows, shearwaters, petrels, plovers, boobies, sooty terns and gulls.

Four of the islands are bird sanctuaries – Bird, Cousin, Aride and Frégate. The Vallée de Mai on Praslin and the Veuve Reserve on La Digue are also protected reserves.

Marine Life Four areas around Mahé and Praslin are designated marine national parks – Port Launay, Baie Ternay, Ste Anne Island and Curieuse. Ste Anne, off Victoria, is well patrolled by the tourist glass-bottom boats. More than 150 species of tropical reef fish have been identified. You have only to snorkel off any reef-protected shore to get an eyeful of beautiful fish and 30 species of coral.

Dolphin and porpoise are common sights in the channels between the islands, and pods occasionally become beached. Whales are rare after excessive hunting around the turn of the century (Victoria was used as an American whaling port). Shark and barracuda are about, but attacks on humans are rare. Now humans get the better of marlin, swordfish and other big-game fish. Historically, people have also posed a threat to green and hawksbill turtle, but, hopefully, that slaughter will be a thing of the past and turtle numbers will increase.

Tortoise The French and English wiped out the giant land tortoise early on from all the islands except Aldabra, where there are still a few thousand left. Several tortoises have been brought to the central islands and now munch their way around pens at hotels and guesthouses. There is a free-roaming colony on Curieuse and perhaps the biggest daddy of all is in the Cousin Island bird reserve (although Bird Island's operators also claim that distinction for Esmeralda!). Giant tortoises, central to the Seychelles coat of arms, are endemic to only two regions in the world. One is the Seychelles, the other is the Galapagos Islands, off Ecuador.

GOVERNMENT & POLITICS
The Seychelles is a republic. The current president, Mr France Albert René, heads a cabinet of around 10 ministers with specific portfolios. In 1993 the constitution was reformed to incorporate multiparty politics and

in July 1993 René won elections held under this revised constitution.

ECONOMY

The Seychelles are very westernised islands with most of the trappings of a western economy. The minimum wage, however, is still around Rs 1600 (US$320) per month.

The islands were, and still are, labelled an idyllic paradise with plenty of fish in the sea and fruit on the trees; a place where traditional work patterns are very different from western ones. With the René government's importation of foreign skills and workers, these patterns are slowly changing.

Tourism

The mainstay of the islands' economy is tourism, as it was before the socialist revolution or coup of 5 June 1977. The coup itself and the subsequent shenanigans had an adverse effect on the holiday industry. The new government made matters worse by trying to reduce the nation's dependency on tourism too quickly and proceeded to build up other less servile enterprises. But it wasn't long before President René realised that the country really couldn't do without tourism. After hiring a series of overseas specialists, the industry is now back in full swing. It employs more than 20% of the workforce and accounts for at least half the country's gross national product. The government continues to invest heavily in tourism development.

In 1986, 66,780 tourists came to the Seychelles. The figure rose to 86,000 in 1989 and increased to 103,000 in 1990, when the income from tourism amounted to Rs 646 million. In 1997 there were around 120,000 visitors to the Seychelles.

Fishing & Agriculture

Fishing and agriculture have also come a long way in the past 10 years or so by making better use of natural resources. The Seychelles' 320km Exclusive Economic Zone, proclaimed in 1977, gave the country control of waters rich in tuna. Victoria is turning into a busy port for foreign trawlers and provides a number of support services. A fishing port has been built along with a tuna processing and canning plant. Fish is the staple diet of the Seychellois, but that is changing with the greater availability and choice in agricultural produce.

The Seychelles Marketing Board (SMB) is responsible for all aspects of the agricultural sector, including production, processing, packaging and distribution of products. It sets and controls prices across the board. Copra (dried coconut kernel) and cinnamon have traditionally been the main agricultural exports but, although production of these has been further developed, the government's first concern is to become self-sufficient in food.

Other industries include the manufacture of paint, detergents, plastics and packaging products, and joint foreign ventures.

POPULATION & PEOPLE

The estimated population of the Seychelles is 73,000. Every shade and hue of skin and hair imaginable exists in the Seychelles, arising out of a mixture of European, African, Indian, Chinese and Arab genes. No creed or colour can be said to dominate since the 1977 coup, when most of the *grands blancs* were dispossessed. Over 60% of the population is under 30 years of age.

The racial harmony of the Seychelles is more likely due to liberal morals than liberal politics. The islands used to have a reputation for being a haven of free love. This was based on the high illegitimacy rate. At one stage during the 1970s, more than 50% of the population was illegitimate. The reasons given were that marriages were expensive and married couples did not stay together long (even though most of the people are Catholic).

During the early days of tourism under James Mancham's promotion, the local promiscuity enhanced an image of a Garden of Eden with all the associated lust, temptation and sin.

That image has been 'cleaned up' by the socialist government and the tourist board now promotes packaged weddings and honeymoons on the islands, leaving any erotic suggestiveness to the famous coco de mer nut.

SEYCHELLES

In the Seychelles the colonial backlash is still somewhat evident, although it's not nearly as strong as it was some years back. With the increase in national pride and identity that developed after Independence and the coup came a more aloof attitude to visitors. But generally, the people are friendly and helpful.

EDUCATION

The education system has developed considerably since René's takeover. Nowadays, between the ages of 3½ and 5½, children can attend a non-compulsory crèche education programme. Primary and secondary level schooling is compulsory up to age 15½. There are several fee-paying schools.

The most significant and controversial aspect of education in the Seychelles has been the National Youth Service (NYS), which was until recently compulsory for school-leavers. During their one-year service, they continued their academic studies and trained in agricultural and industrial work at camps at Port Launay and Cap Ternay. At first, the children were locked away in this communist finishing school for months on end, unable to see their parents, and given over-doses of Marx and Engels courtesy of Cuban, Russian and Angolan teachers. Since the early 1990s, the NYS system is no longer compulsory and has become more practical than political.

The Polytechnic at Mont Fleuri provides a wide range of academic, technical, and vocational courses for students between the ages of 16½ and 20½.

ARTS

There is no indigenous culture in the Seychelles, but aspects of African origin have survived – such as the *séga* and *moutia* dances.

The government has formed the National School of Music and the National Cultural Troupe (NCT) to foster a Créole cultural identity and tradition. It has produced some fine singers, dancers and writers. Créole culture is also preserved and promoted through the Kreol Institute (see boxed text in

the Mahé chapter) and the colourful Festival Kreol (see boxed text below).

Festival Kreol

The vibrant Festival Kreol aims to preserve and promote Créole culture and is worth attending if you're in the vicinity. Held every year around the end of October, this week-long festival is an explosion of Créole cuisine, fashion, art, music and dance. Créole artists from other countries are invited to participate and the festival provides young artists a platform on which to unleash their creative talent. Other events often held during the Festival Kreol include street theatre, forums to discuss Créole literature/linguistics, photographic exhibitions, puppet shows and dance competitions. There are various Créole handicrafts and knick-knacks on sale.

The Festival Kreol has a different venue each year – for any information regarding this festival, contact Michel Marie at the Ministry of Education (☎ 224777; fax 224859), or ask at the tourist office in Victoria (see Information in the Mahé chapter). ■

Dance

The sombre moutia is the typical dance of the Seychelles, with strong African and Malagasy rhythms. The songs are prayers which the slaves turned into work chants, similar to the early black gospel music of the USA. They are accompanied by slow, repetitive dance routines. The moutia is a popular communal dance which normally is danced around a fire and serves as the primary evening entertainment. European influences are evident in the *contredanse*, which has its roots in the court of Louis XIV of France, the Sun King, as well as the *mazok*, which is reminiscent of the French waltz and the *kosez*, a type of quadrille.

The Seychelles version of the séga differs little from that of Mauritius. Séga dance displays are held at most of the large hotels at least one night a week and you may even be lucky enough to stumble onto a more spontaneous celebration.

Music

The Indian, European, Chinese and Arabic backgrounds of the Seychellois people are reflected in their music. The accordion, banjo and violin music, brought to the islands by the early European settlers, has blended with that of the *makalapo*, a stringed instrument with a tin sound box; the *zez*, a monochord sitar; African skin drums; and the *bom*, a bowed instrument.

Patrick Victor is one of the best known musicians on the islands for Créole pop and folk. You can buy his music in most souvenir and music shops. Other popular local stars are David Philoe, Jonise Juliette, Serge Camille, Jones Camille and Hudson Dorothe. Another popular singer, is the late Raymond Lebon.

On a more traditional level are the roving *camtole* bands featuring a fiddle, banjo, accordion and drums. They also accompany contredanses.

Literature

The Kreol Institute on Mahé was set up to research and promote Créole culture, specifically literature. It publishes books in Créole and sells books written by Créole authors. For more information, see the boxed text in the Mahé chapter.

Art

Over the past several decades, more and more artists and craftspeople have settled in the Seychelles and spawned a local industry to cater for the souvenir-hungry tourists (see also Paintings in the Seychelles Facts for the Visitor chapter). If you're keen to do an 'art tour', it's worth getting hold of *Artmap Seychelles*, a free leaflet listing the various artists and their studio addresses. It's produced by the Association for Visual Arts (AVA) (☎ 224777). The tourist office and some hotels have copies.

The best known artist is Michael Adams, whose home and studio (☎ 361006; fax 361200) are at Anse aux Poules Bleues in the south-west of Mahé (for more details, see the Mahé chapter). Adams' work is featured on local calendars and promotional material.

His paintings are incredible and convey the beauty of the Seychelles better than any photograph or film. This is what he says about his work:

I'm basically a jungle person. Every time you look at it, you see a different way of painting it. But the sea is perhaps the main feature of the Seychelles' beauty. The colour is almost edible, but it is hard to capture. It's like trying to remember tastes or a love from a long time ago.

I try and turn objective reality into abstract hieroglyphics, but never leave realism behind. I try to create the same vibrancy you get in 3-D. And because I use water colours, I have to make those colours shout.

Other paintings worth checking out are those by Seychellois artist Christine Harter (☎ 232131; fax 232155) of Praslin and Donald Adelaide (☎ 361370) of Baie Lazare (Mahé). Adelaide's studio is open daily, except Sunday, from 9 am to 6 pm. Gerard Devoud's studio (☎ 361313) is also at Baie Lazare and is open daily from 9 am to 6 pm. If you're on La Digue, pop in and have a look at Barbara Jenson's studio (☎ 234406; fax 376356), and the Zimaz Kreol Art Gallery (☎ 234322), which houses George Camille's creations (for more details see the La Digue & Other Inner Islands chapter).

Italian-born sculptor Antonio Filippin specialises in wood sculpture and has an impressive range of his work on display at the Yellow Gallery (☎ 247658), Beau Vallon, Mahé. The studio is open daily, except Sunday, from 10 am to 5 pm and is worth a look. Antonio is an interesting gentleman and his creations, made from various types of wood, reflect his philosophies on life. Expect to pay upwards of Rs 5000 per piece.

Lorenzo Appiani was responsible for the new sculptures on the roundabouts at either end of 5th June Ave in Victoria. The Freedom Square monument is said to be three wings or birds – Twa Zwazo – representing the continents of Africa, Europe and Asia, each of which has played a part in the development of the Seychelles' people.

Theatre

The Créoles once performed impromptu street theatre known as *sokwe*, but the practice has all but disappeared and theatre arts

SEYCHELLES

aren't yet popular with the Seychellois; public performances these days concentrate on music and dancing. However, the success of the Créole comedy *Bolot Feray* has encouraged greater interest in play writing and theatre performance.

You can purchase tickets to shows by the National Cultural Troupe and visiting companies by calling the National Library (☎ 321333) – ask for Karen Hoareau.

SOCIETY & CONDUCT
Dos & Don'ts

Skimpy beachwear is OK for the hotel pool and beaches, but you may attract lingering gazes and pestering elsewhere. If you want to bathe topless, you're best doing so on secluded beaches, unless you don't mind being ogled.

If you visit a shrine or other holy place, dress and behave with respect – see Society & Conduct in the Facts about the Region chapter at the beginning of this book.

RELIGION

Most Seychellois are Catholic and the majority are avid churchgoers, but there is a widespread belief in the supernatural and in the old magic of spirits known as *gris gris*. Sorcery was outlawed in 1958, but there are a number of *bonhommes* and *bonfemmes di bois*, medicine men and women, practising their cures and curses and concocting potions for love, luck and revenge. These rituals and beliefs resemble those of Caribbean voodoo, but are practised only on a limited scale.

LANGUAGE

English and French are the official languages and both are spoken by most people, although French Créole is the lingua franca. *Kreol seselwa* was 'rehabilitated' and made semi-official in 1981, and is increasingly used in newspapers and literature. There are several novels and poetry collections in Créole for general sale.

For a useful list of French words see under Language in the Facts about the Region chapter at the beginning of this book.

Seychelles Créole is similar to that of Mauritius and Martinique, but differs remarkably from that of Réunion. In the local patois, the soft pronunciation of certain French consonants is hardened and silent syllables are dropped completely. The soft 'j' becomes 'z', for example (see the Mauritius section on Créole for suggested usage). The following phrases may help you venture into Créole:

Good morning/ afternoon.	*Bonzour.*
How are you?	*Comman sava?*
Fine, thanks.	*Mon byen, mersi.*
What's your name?	*Ki mannyer ou appel?*
My name is ...	*Mon appel ...*
Where do you live?	*Koté ou resté?*
I don't understand.	*Mon pas konpran.*
I like it.	*Mon kontan.*
Where is...?	*Ol i...?*
How much is that?	*Kombyen sa?*
I'm thirsty.	*Mon soif.*
Can I have a beer, please?	*Mon kapa ganny en labyer silvouplé?*

Facts for the Visitor

PLANNING
When to Go
The best times to visit really depend on what you like to do. Windsurfing and sailing are best at the start or end of the south-east trade winds (May to October), which can sometimes be up to two months late. The rain can fall in short torrents during the wet season, yet it can be overcast for days during the cooler, drier periods. Some beaches are better during the monsoon season, others during the south-east trade winds. Diving is best in March, April, May, September, October and November. Then there are the busy holiday seasons of December and January and July to August that you must also take into account. Easter can also get busy. Many hotels hike their room rates at these times and you are advised to book well ahead, as it can be tough getting a room.

Maps
There is a dearth of detailed maps on the Seychelles. The tourist offices have a reasonably good map of the major islands – Mahé, Praslin and La Digue; this map also has a small inset of Victoria. It's not very detailed, but is adequate for orientation. Travel agents also stock basic maps for tourists.

What to Bring
Refer to the Planning section of the Regional Facts for the Visitor chapter at the beginning of this book.

HIGHLIGHTS
Of course, the predominant highlight of the Seychelles are the wonderful beaches. Below is a run-down of some recommended beaches and other less obvious attractions.

Beaches
Carana (Mahé – Glacis); Anse Lazio (Praslin); Anse Patates (La Digue); Anse Source d'Argent (La Digue); Anse Cocos (La Digue); Grand Anse & Petite Anse (La Digue); Anse Victorin (Frégate).

Activities
Diving, snorkelling and of course swimming.

Walks
La Reserve and La Brulée (Mahé); Vallée de Mai (Praslin); La Passe to Anse Cocos (La Digue); Frégate Island.

Ecological Interest
Cousin Island; Bird Island; Vallée de Mai (Praslin); Aldabra and Assomption.

TOURIST OFFICES
Local Tourist Offices
The Seychelles Ministry of Tourism (☎ 224030) has its head office at Independence House, PO Box 92, Victoria. It has a public information tourist office full of brochures and assistance nearby (see Information in the Mahé chapter). At the airport, there is an accommodation booking service provided by the National Travel Agency (NTA).

Tourists Offices Abroad
There are Seychelles tourist offices at the following addresses overseas:

Belgium
> 157 Boulevard du Jubilé, 1080 Brussels (☎ (02) 425 6236; fax 426 0629)

France
> 32 Rue de Ponthieu, 75008 Paris (☎ 01 42 89 97 77; fax 01 42 89 97 70)

Germany
> Hoch Strasse 15, D60313 Frankfurt (☎ (069) 292 064; fax 296 230)

India
> Trac Representations, F-12 Connaught Place, New Delhi 110001 (☎ (011) 331 1122; fax 335 0270)

Italy
> Via Giulia 66, 00186 Rome (☎ (039) 6686 9056; fax 6686 8217)

Japan
> Berna Heits, 4-A3 Hiroo 5-4-11, Shibuya, Tokyo 150 (☎ (03) 5449 0461; fax 5449 0462)

Kenya
> 3rd floor, Jubilee Insurance, Exchange building, Nairobi (☎ (0254) 221335; fax 2219787)

UK
> 2nd floor, Eros House, 111 Baker St, London W1M 1FE (☎ (0171) 224 1670; fax 486 1352)

USA
> 82 Second Ave, Suite 900F, New York, NY 10017-4504 (☎ (212) 687 9766; fax 922 9177)

VISAS & DOCUMENTS
Visas
You don't need a visa to enter the Seychelles, just a valid passport, an onward ticket, booked accommodation and sufficient funds for your stay.

Upon arrival by air, you will be given a visitor's visa for up to a month, depending on the departure date printed on your onward ticket.

If you arrive by yacht, you will be issued a visitor's permit for two weeks by the Port Authority. If staying longer, you must apply for an extension. You may be politely approached by a 'security officer' who will further inquire about your visit.

Visa Extensions
If you wish to extend your visa, apply at the Immigration Office (☎ 224030; fax 225035), Independence House, on the corner of Independence and 5th June Aves in Victoria. The office is open Monday to Friday from 8 am to noon and 1 to 4 pm.

Again, you may need proof of sufficient funds and an onward ticket. You will have to fill in a form and leave it, along with your airline ticket and passport. The extension should be processed within a week.

You can extend the visa by up to three months free of charge. Thereafter it is Rs 200 per extension, for a further three months. You can only stay one year on a visitor's visa.

Onward Ticket
If you don't have a ticket on a flight out of the country, you could be asked to deposit money for one with the immigration author-ities. If you haven't booked accommodation, just name any hotel or guesthouse on your disembarkation card and hope it hasn't closed down! If that fails, an immigration officer may escort you to the travel agency counter while you make a booking.

EMBASSIES
Seychelles Embassies & Consulates Abroad
Seychelles has diplomatic representation in the following countries:

Australia
> 23 Marri Crescent, Les Murdie, Perth, WA 6076 (☎ (09) 291 6570; fax 291 9157)

Belgium
> 157 Boulevard du Jubilé, 1080 Brussels (☎ (02) 425 6236; fax 426 0629)

France
> 51 Ave Mozart, 75016, Paris (☎ 01 42 30 57 47; fax 01 42 30 57 40)

UK
> 2nd floor, Eros House, 111 Baker St, London W1M 1FE (☎ (0171) 224 1660; fax 487 5756)

USA
> 82 Second Ave, Suite 900F, New York, NY 10017-4504 (☎ (212) 972 1785; fax 972 1786)

Other countries in which the Seychelles has diplomatic representation include Austria, Canada, Denmark, Finland, Germany, Greece, Hong Kong, India, Indonesia, Israel, Italy, Japan, Jordan, Kenya, Madagascar, Malaysia, Mauritius, Netherlands, Norway, Pakistan, Philippines, Singapore, South Africa, Spain, Sweden, Switzerland and Thailand.

Foreign Embassies & Consulates in the Seychelles
Following are the addresses of the major foreign embassies and consulates in the Seychelles:

France
> Victoria House, Victoria (☎ 224523)

Germany
> PO Box 132, Mont Fleuri (☎ 261222)

Madagascar
> PO Box 68, Plaisance (☎ 344030)

Netherlands
> PO Box 372, Glacis (☎ 261200)

SEYCHELLES

Sweden
New Port (☎ 224710)
UK
PO Box 161, Victoria House, Victoria
(☎ 225225)
USA
PO Box 251, Victoria House, Victoria
(☎ 225256)

Other countries with diplomatic representation include Belgium, China, Cuba, Cyprus, Denmark, Finland, India, Mauritius, Monaco, Norway, the Russian Federation and Switzerland.

CUSTOMS

The international airport is 10km south-east of Victoria. Entry formalities are fairly quick and uncomplicated, although you may be questioned more fully, but politely, at customs. You are permitted to bring in 1L of spirits and 1L of wine; up to 200 cigarettes or 250g of tobacco; 125ml perfume; and 250ml of eau de toilette. Spearguns, along with other weapons and ammunition, are forbidden, as is any food or agricultural produce.

When leaving the Seychelles do not take any shells, corals or preserved fish, turtles etc. The illegal purchase of rare and endangered species directly contributes to their extinction. Tourists who illegally possess or transport these items should also be aware that the items are liable to confiscation on leaving the Seychelles, and to combined fines and confiscation by customs officials in most western countries which have signed agreements on endangered species.

If you are taking home a coco de mer, make sure you have the requisite export certificate.

MONEY
Costs

The Seychelles is not a cheap destination, so don't arrive on a shoestring budget. For more information see the Costs section in the Regional Facts for the Visitor chapter at the beginning of this book.

Currency

The Seychelles unit of currency is the rupee (Rs), which is divided into 100 cents (c). Denominations of notes come in Rs 10, 25, 50 and 100; and coins in Rs 1, 5 and 1c, 5c, 10c and 25c.

The Seychelles rupee (Rs) is tied to an account unit of the International Monetary Fund known as the Special Drawing Right, which also includes the British pound, US dollar, German Deutschmark, French franc and Japanese yen. Although the rates of exchange fluctuate daily, the rupee is generally strong and stable.

Currency Exchange

The rate of exchange is set by the Central Bank of Seychelles. At the time of going to press, the exchange rates were as follows:

Australia	A$1	=	Rs 3.42
Canada	C$1	=	Rs 3.47
Germany	DM1	=	Rs 2.80
France	FF1	=	Rs 0.87
Japan	¥100	=	Rs 0.04
Singapore	S$	=	Rs 3.16
UK	UK£1	=	Rs 7.75
USA	US$1	=	Rs 5

Changing Money

You'll get a better rate for travellers cheques than for cash. The Central Bank issues a list of the rates each day. Make sure you keep the encashment form given to you whenever you change foreign currency – this form must be presented at the airport if you want to change back Seychelles rupees into foreign currency (you may not always get the foreign currency of your choice, however). You can pre-purchase your airport departure tax (Rs 100) at some banks.

No restrictions apply on the amount of rupees you can take into or out of the country. There are few places you can buy or sell Seychelles rupees abroad – not that any visitor would want to. Obviously the best rates of exchange are in the Seychelles.

Victoria, the capital, is well endowed with banks, including the Seychelles Savings Bank (☎ 225251), Banque Française Commerciale (☎ 323096), Bank of Baroda

SEYCHELLES

(☎ 323038), Habib Bank (☎ 224371) and Central Bank (☎ 225200). The main bank is Barclays Bank, which has branches on La Digue (☎ 234148), Praslin (☎ 233344) and around Mahé (Victoria (☎ 224101); Beau Vallon (☎ 247391); airport (☎ 373029). The bigger hotels change money, if you need cash on a Sunday for instance, but their rates do not compare favourably with those of the banks. For banking hours, see Business Hours later in this chapter.

In 1991, as part of a global crackdown, the expansive offices of the Abu Dhabi-based Bank of Credit & Commerce International (BCCI), in the centre of Victoria, were closed following worldwide investigation of one of the biggest bank frauds in history. During its 20-year history of financial mayhem BCCI is estimated to have defrauded over a million investors of many billions of dollars and is reported to have been involved in a dazzling network of organised crime. In 1992 these offices were officially requisitioned.

Credit Cards

Major credit cards (such as Visa and MasterCard) are accepted in most hotels, restaurants and shops, and most banks give cash advances against the cards. Some travellers have reported that not all places accept American Express.

Barclays Bank (☎ 224101; fax 224678) represents Visa and MasterCard; Diners Club is represented by J.K. Parcou (☎ 225303; fax 225193); and American Express is represented by Travel Services Seychelles (TSS) (☎ 322414; fax 321366).

Tipping & Bargaining

Tipping is welcomed but not obligatory. A 10% service charge is added to your bill in hotels and restaurants.

In general, there's a relaxed approach to bargaining. Gentle prompting can sometimes produce discounts for car rental, but the prices marked in shops are seldom negotiable. Markets are more open to a bit of friendly haggling.

POST & COMMUNICATIONS
Postal Rates

Air-mail postcards to all international destinations cost Rs 3. Air-mail letters weighing up to 10g cost Rs 3.50 to Europe or Australia; Rs 4 to the USA or Canada; and Rs 3 to Indian Ocean or African destinations. Aerogrammes cost Rs 2.50.

Sending & Receiving Mail

The mail service is reliable and reasonably quick, and there is a free poste restante service at the main post office in Victoria, located on the corner of Independence Ave and Albert St.

Telephone

The telephone system, run by Cable & Wireless, is one of the world's most modern. Despite protestations from the company, phone bugging is a very open secret in the Seychelles. Originally the bugging was performed by official request, but the tables were turned a few years ago when a stirring conversation between the president and his mistress was recorded and illicitly broadcast on Seychelles radio.

Telephone cards, known as Phonocards, can be purchased at the airport, Cable & Wireless offices, and from shops and post offices on the major islands. Cards are available for Rs 30 (30 units), Rs 60 (60 units) and Rs 100 (120 units).

Local Calls There are public phone boxes all over Mahé, fewer on Praslin.

Local calls cost Rs 0.80 for up to six minutes. Long-distance calls within Mahé, from Victoria to Anse Royale for instance, cost Rs 0.80 for 45 seconds. From Mahé to Praslin or La Digue, calls cost Rs 0.80 for 25 seconds. Calls to the outlying islands of Desroches, Coétivy and Farquhar cost Rs 10 for one minute.

If you wish to contact vessels at sea in the vicinity of the Seychelles, call ☎ 375733. These radio telephone calls are charged at the rate of Rs 2.50 per minute.

International Calls You can make international calls direct using international direct dialling (IDD). The rate per minute for a call to the UK, the USA, Australia, Belgium, Canada, France, Germany, New Zealand and Switzerland is Rs 16.32. The rate per minute for India is Rs 14.94; it's Rs 9.28 to Mauritius; and Rs 19.06 to Sweden. If you are tempted to phone from your hotel room, remember that hotels often add a hefty mark-up to this rate.

Direct operator services, such as USA Direct, UK Direct, and KDD Direct are also available at phone locations with the requisite signs.

Some useful international dialling codes are: Australia 61; Belgium 32; Comoros 269; France 33; Germany 49; India 91; Japan 81; Madagascar 261; Mauritius 230; New Zealand 64; Réunion 262; Seychelles 248; South Africa 27; Switzerland 41; UK 44 and USA 1.

Call ☎ 999 for emergency services and ☎ 151 for the international operator. If you're worried about a freak snowstorm ruining your sunny Seychelles sojourn, the latest weather information is on ☎ 373001!

Fax, Telegraph & Telex

Telegram, telex and telefax services are also available through Cable & Wireless (☎ 322221), on Francis Rachel St, Victoria.

BOOKS
Guidebooks

It is pleasing to be able to say that this guidebook contains the most practical travel information and advice on the Seychelles! Having said that, there is a collection of glossy 'coffee table' books on the Seychelles which make good souvenirs to take back home. Two books which contain more practical information than your average 'coffee table' guidebook are *Visitor's Guide Seychelles* by Sue Heady and *Odyssey Illustrated Guide to Seychelles* by Sarah Carpin. The latter has some great pictures.

History & Politics

There are a couple of interesting books on the Seychelles worth reading before or after you go to the islands for a comparison with the recent past, attitudes and lifestyle of the country. The more picturesque of these is *Forgotten Eden* by Atholl Thomas. It's long out of print, but is still considered to be one of the best books on the country. More politically biased (on the side of the first president, James Mancham) but still quite informative and a good read, is *Political Castaways* by Christopher Lee.

A more recent account is Mancham's own story of his rise and fall in *Paradise Raped*. The book is not available in the Seychelles, but Mancham's locally published collection of poetry *Reflections & Echoes from Seychelles* is still available from the library in Victoria.

France Albert René has his say about the history of the Seychelles United People's Party, the revolution and the necessity of a one-party state in *Seychelles: the New Era*. This follows his collected speeches and writing in *The Torch of Freedom*. The government has also published the *White Book*, which gives full details of the failed mercenary coup attempt by 'Mad Mike' Hoare on 25 November 1981. It's a fascinating account of how to plan a coup or, in this case, how not to plan one. Mad Mike's own version of the bungled coup attempt *The Seychelles Affair* adopts a more novelistic approach. *Seychelles What Next?* by Alain St Ange recounts Seychelles' political history and contains interesting newspaper excerpts, archival photos and personal accounts (Alain St Ange is the son of a formerly prominent Seychelles politician).

For the studious, there is *Men, Women & Money in Seychelles* by Marion & Burton Benedict. Less academic is Guy Lionnet's *Seychelles* in the 'Islands' series.

Leslie Thomas includes a chapter on the Seychelles and Mauritius in his *A World of Islands*. In *The Treasure Seeker's Treasury* by Roy Nevill, the author expounds on the hunt for the treasure of the pirate Olivier 'La Buse' Levasseur at Bel Ombre on Mahé. (Atholl Thomas has more of the story in *Forgotten Eden*, as he talked to the late Reginald Cruise-Wilkins, who spent most of his

SEYCHELLES

life looking for the treasure at Bel Ombre.) In *Island Home* Wendy Weevers-Carter writes about life on Rémire Island in the isolated Amirantes group of atolls. Don't forget Auguste Toussaint's *History of the Indian Ocean* for an overview of the Indian Ocean.

Cookbooks

Sir James Mancham may have fallen out of favour in the Seychelles, but his mum's recipes have not in Eveline Mancham's *La Cuisine Seychelloise*. Traditional Seychelles cuisine is the focus of *Dekouver Marmit*, compiled by the Ministry of Education & Culture.

Flora & Fauna

There are eight books in the series of *Seychelles Nature Handbooks*, which deals with most aspects of nature on the islands – shells, coral reef life, natural history, birds, fish and plant life. Another relevant title is Francis Friedmann's *Flowers & Trees of Seychelles*.

The life and work of artist Marianne North, who visited the Seychelles in 1883 to paint the flora, is set out in *A Vision of Eden*. Another good book that covers the Seychelles' beautiful flora is *The Beautiful Plants of Seychelles* by Adrian & Judith Skerrett. Guy Lionnet is a well-known Seychellois naturalist and historian. About 20 years ago he wrote a small book on the unique coco de mer palm, called *Romance of a Palm*.

Ornithologists will be interested in *The Birds of Seychelles and the Outlying Islands* and *Birds of the Republic of Seychelles*. Also worth a look is Adrian Skerrett's *Beautiful Birds of Seychelles*, and Adrian Skerrett & Ian Bullock's *A Birdwatchers' Guide to Seychelles*.

Aldabra Alone by Tony Beamish looks at life among the giant tortoises, robber crabs, and other incredible natural phenomena during an expedition to the Aldabra group.

American scientist Jeanne Mortimer has produced an educational booklet on the need to protect the tortoise, turtle and terrapin. It's called *Turtles, Tortoises & Terrapins of the Seychelles* and is published by the World Wide Fund for Nature. If nothing else, you'll at least learn the difference between the Ts.

There are still copies of Al Venter's *Underwater Seychelles* available. Dr F D Ommanney writes about the Seychelles and Mauritius in an account of a fisheries expedition entitled *The Shoals of Capricorn*.

Beyond the Reefs by William Travis is, in fact, a reprint in one volume of the author's two works: *Beyond the Reefs* and *Shark for Sale*, first published in 1959 and 1961 respectively. The first work describes Travis' attempts to start a commercial venture diving for shells, and the second details his career move into shark fishing. Travis and his crew have some amazingly close brushes with marine danger in the Seychelles.

Bookshops

There are few good bookshops in the Seychelles. Perhaps the best of the bunch is the small Antigone in the Victoria House arcade, in Victoria. Also in Victoria, but less impressive than Antigone, is the Cosmorama Bookshop. See Bookshops in the Mahé chapter for more information about these bookshops.

Libraries

The National Library (☎ 321333) is housed in a new building on Francis Rachel St, Victoria. It is open Monday to Friday from 8.30 am to 5 pm, and on Saturday from 8.30 am to 4 pm. You can borrow a book by leaving a deposit of Rs 50 and are allowed to take out two books at a time. For more specific research, contact Alain Lucas at the National Archives, located at the National Library. The National Library on La Digue is open Monday to Friday from 10.30 am to 4.30 pm and on Saturday from 9 am to noon. There's also a library on Praslin.

NEWSPAPERS & MAGAZINES

The daily paper is the government-controlled *Nation*. It costs Rs 2 (Rs 7 for a weekend edition); contains stories in English, French and Créole; and carries cinema, TV and radio programmes and adverts.

Antigone bookshop gets the Sunday papers from the UK (usually on Monday). *Time* (Rs 35), *Newsweek* (Rs 19) and other magazines are usually also available.

An independent publication is *Regar* (Rs 6), which is trilingual and published weekly. Other local publications include the political *People* (Rs 3), published bimonthly in three languages by the Seychelles People's Progressive Front (SPPF); and the monthly *L'Echo des Îles* (Rs 5), also trilingual, published by the Roman Catholic Mission. Independent magazine *Seychelles Review* is published monthly (free of charge).

RADIO & TV

The Seychelles Broadcasting Corporation (SBC) provides radio broadcasts on weekdays from 6 am to 1.30 pm and 3 to 10 pm; and on the weekend from 6 am to 10 pm. There is a daily full news bulletin in French at 5 pm, English at 7 pm and Créole at 8 pm.

The Far East Broadcasting Association (FEBA) is a radio station specialising in religious programmes for the Far East, Asia, and some Middle Eastern countries.

SBC provides television broadcasting on Monday to Friday from 5.45 to 10.30 pm; on Saturday from 3 to 11 pm and on Sunday from 2 to 11 pm. Programmes include films from France and Germany, the occasional comedy show from England and nature specials, as well as news bulletins (in Créole at 7 pm, in English at 6 pm and in French at 9 pm). The latest news is supplied to SBC by CNN (Cable News Network International). The upmarket hotels have TV sets in every room and usually run in-house video movies.

PHOTOGRAPHY

As always, it's best to stock up on film from duty-free shops before you arrive. If not, there's a plentiful supply here and several decent developing studios. Photo-Eden (☎ 322457), next to the Pirates Arms in Victoria, and at Mont Fleuri, sells Kodak Gold (36 exposures) for Rs 35 and charges Rs 118 for developing and printing. Slide film is also available and includes Ektachrome 100 for Rs 59. Across the street, Fujicolor (☎ 224966)

boasts a one-hour printing service at Rs 3 per print; it also offers a discount if you have more than five rolls of film developed.

For useful tips, see Photography & Video in the Regional Facts for the Visitor chapter at the beginning of this book.

TIME

Seychelles time is four hours (three hours during the European summer) ahead of Greenwich Mean Time (GMT) and Universal Time Coordinated (UTC), one hour ahead of Madagascar time and two hours ahead of South African time. So when it is noon in the Seychelles it is midnight in San Francisco; 3 am in New York and Toronto; 8 am in London; 6 pm in Sydney; and 8 pm in New Zealand. It is in the same time zone as Mauritius and Réunion.

ELECTRICITY

The current is 240V AC. The plugs in general use are square pins and have three points. You'll probably experience at least one power cut during your stay on the Seychelles – keep a torch/candle handy.

LAUNDRY

Laundry services are widely available at guesthouses and hotels.

WEIGHTS & MEASURES

The metric system is used in the Seychelles, but it's still common to find references to British standards, such as miles, feet and inches. A conversion chart is included on the inside back cover of this book.

HEALTH

After all that talk about the vagaries of the weather, don't throw yourself at the mercy of the sun every chance you get, even if it's probably the only time you'll see it all year. As they say in Australia, 'slip, slop, slap' (slip on a shirt, slop on some sunscreen and slap on a hat) ... or suffer the consequences!

No vaccination certificates are required for entry into the Seychelles. The islands are free of malaria, yellow fever and other nasties. You don't need to take malaria

SEYCHELLES

tablets if you are visiting only the Seychelles, but the mosquitoes are still best avoided, so bring cream, coils and sprays if you react badly to bites.

If you do get ill, you can see a local doctor for a basic consultation fee of around Rs 75. You must pay for prescribed medicines or drugs at the pharmacy. The main outpatient clinic (☎ 388000) is at Mont Fleuri, Victoria (near the Botanical Gardens). The casualty unit at the hospital is open 24 hours. Another option is a private clinic – ask your hotel to recommend one.

Other districts on Mahé have clinics, as do Praslin and La Digue islands. Most clinics are generally open from around 8 am to 4 pm on weekdays. Some private doctors which have been recommended on Mahé are Dr Chetty (☎ 321911), Dr Maurice Albert (☎ 323866) and Dr Jivan (☎ 324008). It's also a good idea to ask your hotel to recommend a good doctor. There is no chemist on Praslin, but the hospital at Baie Ste Anne (☎ 232333) fills prescriptions. There's a small hospital (☎ 234255) on La Digue.

If you have dental problems, one possibility is the Dental Clinic (☎ 225822), Aarti Chambers, Mont Fleuri, Victoria (Mahé). It is open Monday to Friday from 8 am to 4 pm and on Saturday from 8 am to noon (for after hours weekend emergencies, call ☎ 247721 and ask for Georgette). Alternatively, your hotel should be able to recommend a good dentist.

Water
Tap water is safe to drink, although it has more of a 'chlorinated' taste on Mahé than on Praslin.

DANGERS & ANNOYANCES
Break-ins and burglaries are a problem throughout Mahé, so most houses have a guard dog or dogs (which can be a barking nightmare during the wee small hours). Hotel and guesthouse residents are not at a great risk, but long-term visitors should take extra security measures.

Petty theft is very common. Don't take valuables to the beach and *never* leave belongings unattended on the beach – even if you're just going in for a quick dip. Although many beaches may appear deserted when you arrive, it's surprising how quickly someone can materialise from the bushes to casually loiter past. Similarly, nothing of any value should be left in your rental car, especially if it's a Mini Moke (the lock-box at the back is useless and a favourite target for petty thieves).

Most hotels offer safe deposit facilities to their guests. If you place valuables in a hotel safe, remember to get a receipt. It's a good idea to pack your valuables in a small, double-zippered bag which can be padlocked, or use a large envelope with a signed seal which will easily show any tampering. Count money and travellers cheques immediately before and after retrieving them from the safe.

The biggest health hazard, after the sun, are speeding drivers on the roads of Mahé, and to a lesser extent on Praslin. The small number of motor vehicles, ox carts and bicycles on La Digue can hardly be considered lethal. Having said that, there have been a few bicycle collisions on La Digue, so watch it. Be careful when driving or walking on the roads after dark, especially on the busy, twisting hill route between Victoria and Beau Vallon. If the locals are not going too fast, the tourists in their hired Mokes are going too slowly.

The sea is more benign. Here the danger comes only when snorkelling, diving or swimming, from stinging and razor-sharp coral.

Security
As a tourist, you won't generally be hampered by the defence or police forces, unless you give them reason to be suspicious. The army keeps a lower public profile these days. There are a few out-of-bounds areas, such as the NYS camps at Cap Ternay, Port Launay and Ste Anne Island, and the Long Island prison.

LEGAL MATTERS
Refer to Legal Matters in the Regional Facts

for the Visitor chapter at the beginning of this book.

BUSINESS HOURS
Offices and shops keep British rather than French hours, opening at 8.30 am, lunching between noon and 1 pm and closing at 4 pm (government offices) and 5 pm (shops). On Saturdays many shops are open in the morning. Some shops even stay open through lunch and all day on Saturday. In the villages, many shops are open until around 9 pm.

In Victoria, the banks are open Monday to Friday from 8.30 am to 12.30 pm and 2 to 3.30 pm, and on Saturdays from 8.30 to 11.30 am. The branches generally keep shorter hours. At the airport, bank counters are open to meet incoming/departing international flights.

See individual island chapters for details of post office hours.

PUBLIC HOLIDAYS & SPECIAL EVENTS
Public holidays in the Seychelles are as follows:

New Year – 1 & 2 January
Good Friday & Easter – March or April
Labour Day – 1 May
Liberation Day – 5 June
Corpus Christi – 10 June
National Day – 18 June
Independence Day – 29 June
Assumption – 15 August
La Digue Festival – 15 August
All Saints' Day – 1 November
Immaculate Conception – 8 December
Christmas – 25 December

For information about the Festival Kreol (held in late October), see the boxed text in the Facts about the Seychelles chapter.

ACTIVITIES
Water Activities
For visitors the main pursuits are water activities – water-skiing, paragliding, snorkelling, diving and the like. There are plenty of water sports experts around to teach holidaymakers – at a pretty price of course.

At the Berjaya Beau Vallon Bay Beach Resort on Mahé, the Aquatic Sports Centre (☎ 247141) offers paragliding (Rs 150 per person), water-skiing (Rs 100 per 10 minutes), canoeing (Rs 35 per hour), windsurfing (Rs 100 per hour) and snorkelling trips (Rs 150 for three hours). Equipment can be hired and instruction is available for most of these water sports. The centre also provides game fishing expeditions; a full day costs Rs 3000 for the boat (maximum of six people), including soft drinks and lunch. You get a reduction on all of the above prices (except for game fishing) if you're a Berjaya Beau Vallon Bay Beach Resort guest.

On the beach nearby is Leisure 2000, which offers similar activities.

Snorkelling Snorkelling in the Seychelles must be rated as a highlight or 'must do' for any visitor. When snorkelling, remember to wear flippers or canvas shoes to protect your feet, a T-shirt to protect your back and shoulders from sunburn; and never reach into a crevice with your bare hand.

The best spots around Mahé are: the marine national parks at Ste Anne (from a boat) and Port Launay (from the shore); the rocks near Le Northolme Hotel; Anse Soleil in the south-west and Petite Anse just south of it; and Île Souris, just south of Pointe au Sel.

Off Praslin, try around Chauve Souris Island within wading distance of Anse Volbert beach. Alternatively, there's Petite Soeur Island near La Digue, if you can get out there by boat.

Most hotels and diving schools sell or rent snorkelling gear (daily rates are generally between Rs 30 and Rs 50 for a mask, snorkel and fins). If you intend doing a lot of snorkelling, it may be worth bringing your own equipment to cut costs. Spear fishing is strictly forbidden.

On La Digue, La Morena Diving (☎ 234500), near the pier, rents out snorkelling gear (mask, fins, snorkel) for Rs 30 per day. They also provide snorkelling trips for Rs 100 per person. The diving centre at La Digue Island Lodge (☎ 234232; fax 234100) hires out snorkelling sets for Rs 30 per day (deposit of Rs 150 per person). Some other

SEYCHELLES

hotels also rent out snorkelling gear at a similar cost. Also on La Digue, Cool Runner (☎ 234180 or 234175) offers various snorkelling options including a day trip to St Pierre/Curieuse for Rs 425 with a barbeque lunch and soft drinks; and a day trip to Félicité/Grande Soeur Island for Rs 300 with a barbeque lunch and soft drinks. There are also some cheaper options – ask for details.

Diving Diving in the Seychelles, particularly around the outlying islands, is considered world class. Next to the Maldives, the Seychelles offers the best location in the Indian Ocean to take up or pursue diving. The best time for diving is between April and November. During the rest of the year, the sea is rougher and the water cloudier.

A number of hotels have their own diving centre which nonresidents can also use. Because of the popularity of diving, prices are pretty high – so be prepared for a minor assault on your wallet!

See Ecology & Environment in the Facts about the Region chapter at the beginning of this book for important information on responsible diving.

Certificates Certificates are generally issued by the internationally recognised PADI (Professional Association of Diving Instructors) or FAUI (Federation of Australian Underwater Instructors).

Diving Courses An introductory course for a total novice (minimum 12 years of age) lasts a day and includes theory tutorial, a pool training session, and a boat dive on a shallow coral reef with an instructor. The price is around Rs 400, including equipment rental. Subsequent accompanied resort dives cost about Rs 250 each.

For around Rs 2250 you can take the course for an International PADI Open Water Diver Certificate, which requires four days on an intensive course, including five theory tutorials, five pool training sessions and four qualifying dives.

For qualified divers, dives can be arranged for about Rs 230 per dive, depending on whether you rent only cylinder and weights or full equipment. The more dives you take, the bigger the discount.

Also on offer are advanced diver training courses in specialist areas such as night diving, deep diving, natural and compass navigation, and search and recovery diving.

Diving Schools There are several schools offering courses from novice to divemaster. Equipment is available for hire or sometimes even purchase.

The Underwater Centre (☎ 247357; fax 344223), run by British couple David Rowat and Glynis Sanders, is at the Coral Strand Hotel on Mahé and has diving instruction contracts with several of the major hotels. They hire out a mask, snorkel and fin set for Rs 50 per day and offer a variety of dive options. Some of these include PADI certification courses such as the advanced open water diver (Rs 1700) and divemaster (Rs 2500). A PADI introductory scuba course is Rs 500; subsequent accompanied dives are Rs 300. They also have whale shark excursions which cost around Rs 200 per person – have a chat to the owners if you're interested. Marine Divers (☎ 247141 ext 8133; fax 247943) is based at Berjaya Beau Vallon Bay Beach Resort on Mahé and also rents out a snorkelling set for Rs 50 per day. They charge Rs 250 per person for a one-hour dive (residents of the hotel get a 10% discount). Pro-Diving is based at the Plantation Club (☎ 361361; fax 361333), on the west coast of Mahé, and offers basic diving courses for Rs 500 per day and rents diving equipment for Rs 225. The Baobab Pizzeria on Beau Vallon beach runs a school called Le Diable des Mers, (☎ 247104; fax 241776). A dive costs Rs 170/220 with cylinders/full equipment; a night dive is Rs 220/260. There's a discount of 10% for five dives and 15% for 10 dives. A PADI beginners' scuba course is Rs 350 (subsequent accompanied dives are Rs 250). More advanced (and expensive) courses are also available, including an advanced diver course (minimum of two days) for Rs 1500. And if you want the big daddy of dive courses, there's the divemaster course for a mighty Rs 2300.

On Praslin, Diving in Paradise (☎ 232148; fax 232244), Anse Volbert, charges Rs 235 per dive, including equipment and has packages such as five dives for Rs 850 and 10 dives for Rs 1650. They have various courses available, including advanced open water (Rs 1850) and divemaster (Rs 2800). Savuka Diving & Fishing Centre (☎ 233900; fax 233919) arranges diving and fishing trips. It costs Rs 250 per dive – call for further details. There's also an Underwater Centre at the Paradise Sun Hotel (☎ 232255; fax 232019), at the west end of Anse Volbert beach (for details of what they offer, refer to the Underwater Centre in Mahé, earlier in this section).

On La Digue, La Morena Diving (☎ 234500), near the pier, has three-day PADI open water diving courses for Rs 1860; a one day 'Discover scuba diving PADI course' costs Rs 370 and a three day advanced open water course for Rs 1500. One dive (including equipment) costs Rs 175. Discounts are offered if you take at least five dives. You can also hire equipment here, including wetsuits (Rs 20), stabilising vests (Rs 25) and regulators (Rs 25). The diving centre at La Digue Island Lodge (☎ 234232; fax 234100) can arrange diving instruction and expeditions. Diving courses cost from Rs 395 to Rs 1960, while diving trips are Rs 265 per person (one hour) including equipment. The diving centre is open daily from 8.30 am to noon and 1 to 4.30 pm.

Dive Sites The diving schools mentioned in the previous section have a wide choice of favoured dive sites. The schools based on Mahé, for instance, provide clients with a map and annotated list of over 30 sites. The following are just a few sample descriptions taken from the Underwater Centre's list:

Coral Gardens 16m deep, 10 minutes by boat. An immense soft coral area with frequent sand patches. A mixture of soft and hard corals with numerous reef fish. Excellent for photography. Suitable for all divers.

Vista Do Mar Granite Massif 15m deep, 15 minutes by boat. '*The* site for photographers. Amazing walls completely encrusted with blazing soft tree corals and fans of white gorgonias provide a spectacular backdrop for the myriads of iridescent blue damsels and flamboyant anthias, not to mention at least four forms of lion fish.' Suitable for all divers.

Whale Rock A large, submerged granite outcrop, just off shore. Large archways and overhangs make it an excellent site for moray eel, stingray and octopus. Suitable for all divers.

L'Îlot Off the northern tip of Mahé, 25 minutes by boat. A picturesque 'Desert Island' complete with palm trees hosts some remarkable submarine scenery. Sheer walls cut by gulleys, archways and crevices attract large shoals of shade-loving fish. Visited by large pelagic fish, grouper and occasional reef shark. Experienced divers (some current).

Ennerdale Wreck of a British tanker lying at 30m in three sections. Home to shoals of golden snapper and a giant grouper. A long-range dive for experienced divers only.

Shark Bank About 5km off shore. A rock pinnacle and feeding area for many fish, including the large predators. Immense stingrays. A long-range dive for experienced divers only.

Brissare Rocks About 35 minutes by boat. 'An amazing carpet of fire coral' with 'some of the most prolific fish life in the islands'. Among the fish life are shoals of batfish, massive Napoleon wrasse, eagle ray and cruising reef shark. A long-range dive for experienced divers only.

Further afield, 250km to the south-west of Mahé, there is great diving around the Amirantes islands, particularly St Joseph Atoll, Poivre and Desroches. Assomption Island in the Aldabra Group has been described as one of the world's best dive sites.

Windsurfing This is particularly popular on Mahé, and Praslin. If you fancy yourself as a good windsurfer there is a 30km open race from Mahé to Praslin each year.

Surfing There probably are several good spots around the islands, but few people bring their boards to discover them. There are no surfboards for hire and few for loan in the Seychelles.

Sailing The Marine Charter Association (MCA) (☎ 322126; fax 224679), beside the

Yacht Club in Victoria, has several yacht owners among its members who charter cruises around islands near and far. There are also a few 'rogue' operators undercutting the rates. See the Seychelles Getting Around chapter for more details.

Deep-Sea Fishing There is a sponsored National Fishing Competition each year in April. The dates are variable, so check ahead with the MCA.

Minimum half day/full day charter rates start at around Rs 3000. The National Travel Agency (☎ 224900; fax 225111) offers deep-sea fishing from Rs 2000 for a half day including soft drinks; Rs 3000 for a full day including soft drinks and lunch. You may be able to negotiate cheaper prices directly with some of the 30 or so members of the Marine Charter Association (☎ 322126; fax 224679), which is next to the Yacht Club in Victoria. Waterworld (☎/fax 321201) has two boats at the MCA and offers a half-day fishing trip from Rs 2400 including soft drinks and snacks; full day trips cost Rs 3200 with soft drinks and sandwiches. There is a maximum of six people. They also have a shark fishing trip for around Rs 2200.

Mason's Travel has offices on Mahé (☎ 322642; fax 225273), Praslin (☎ 233211; fax 233455) and La Digue (☎ 234227; fax 234266). They charge around Rs 2000/3500 for a half/full day of fishing (maximum of four people), Rs 2500/4000 (maximum of eight people). On Praslin, Diving in Paradise (☎ 232148; fax 232244), Anse Volbert, conducts a half day's game fishing for Rs 500 per person (minimum of five people). Also on Praslin, Hotel Maison des Palmes (☎ 233411; fax 233880) operates game fishing trips from Rs 700/1200 for a half/full day including lunch and soft drinks. Santa Lisa (☎ 233517), at Grand Anse on Praslin, charges Rs 1400 for a half day's fishing including snacks; it's Rs 2200 for a full day including lunch. The affable Edwin Rose (☎ 232298) charges Rs 1400 for half a day and Rs 2400 for a full day including a picnic lunch. The boat takes a maximum of four people.

On La Digue, Michelin (☎ 234043) offers half-day fishing trips (maximum of five people) for Rs 1800 including soft drinks; Rs 2400 for a full day including lunch and soft drinks. Another option is Cool Runner (☎ 234180 or 234175), which offers fishing trips for around Rs 1000. Mason's Travel (☎ 234227; fax 234266), on La Digue, can also arrange fishing trips on request.

Boat Excursions There are loads of boat tours available, giving you the golden opportunity to explore some of the more sequestered islands. Many tours include lunch and snorkelling. For more information see Charters in the Seychelles Getting Around chapter.

Land Activities

The Reef Hotel & Golf Club (☎ 376251; fax 376296), Anse aux Pins, has a golf course which is open to nonresidents for Rs 80/100 for nine/18 holes; it's Rs 80 for club hire and trolley hire is Rs 15/20 for nine/18 holes. Residents of the hotel are charged half price.

Tennis courts are available at most of the major hotels. Many are open to nonresidents for a charge of around Rs 40 per hour, including rackets and balls.

Rock Climbing Because of the inner islands' stark granite nature, there are some fine challenges for rock climbers. A few travellers have made the trip for this purpose alone. The best block and cliff-face climbs are on Praslin and La Digue.

On Praslin, the sites to tackle are en route from Baie Ste Anne over the hill to Anse Marie-Louise, behind Anse Lazio; and at the end of the Anse Kerlan road at Pointe Ste Marie. For cliff climbs on Praslin, go to Anse Possession, just west of La Réserve hotel; Anse Citron on the inland side of the road; and between Anse Gouvernement and Anse Matelot.

Blocks for climbing on La Digue can be found at Anse Caiman, Anse Pierrot, Pointe Source d'Argent, Pointe Belize (between Grand and Petite Anses), Anse Grosse Roche and Anse Patates. There are also good cliff climbs at Pointe Jacques and L'Union, behind the copra factory.

Hiking The Tourism Division of the Ministry of Tourism & Transport has produced a good set of 10 hiking brochures for the Seychelles which describe individual hiking routes, the islands' natural history and points of interest along the way, with informative material on fauna and flora. The brochures are available for Rs 5 each from the tourist office in Victoria (see under Information in the Mahé chapter). Some of the major hikes are described individually in several of the following chapters.

Car parks near some walk sites are targeted by thieves, so don't leave any valuables inside (including the boot) and make sure you lock up. Mokes are an especially easy target.

Several of the major tour operators (Travel Services Seychelles etc) can tailor-make guided walking tours (on request). Speak to them directly for further details.

Organised Walks on Mahé Basil Beaudoin (☎/fax 241790), an experienced guide, organises mountain walks on Mahé. He charges around Rs 300 per person per day and offers trips to Mont Sebert, La Réserve, Les Trois Frères, Congo Rouge, Anse Major, Copolia and Morne Seychellois. Basil heartily recommends the Congo Rouge walk. These walks generally take most of the day, but can be tailor-made to your needs.

WORK
There are many foreigners working in the Seychelles, most of whom are employed on a contract basis by the government or work in the tourist industry.

If you get a job with the government your work permit will be arranged. If you are offered a job by a private company it must apply for a permit on your behalf, with a convincing case for not employing a Seychellois. Direct application for a permit is permitted only if you set up your own business and only after you have received appropriate licences, which are issued if you have a suitable work site, accommodation and qualifications.

For more information about work opportunities, contact your country's Seychelles embassy or consulate.

ACCOMMODATION
The Seychelles tourist industry is heavily controlled by the government. The Seychelles has a range of accommodation options including guesthouses, small hotels, bungalow complexes, luxury hotels and self-catering apartment or chalet villages.

About 75% of accommodation is on Mahé and is registered and regulated by the Seychelles Ministry of Tourism. This is advantageous in that a consistently high and relatively affordable western standard of service and facilities is maintained, but it does cut out the budget end of the market. The Ministry of Tourism does not want any losmens, 'native accommodation', pensions de famille, youth hostels or doss houses. Camping is forbidden everywhere on the islands.

A guesthouse without a licence that takes and charges guests is operating illegally and will be reported by other guesthouse operators. Some owners can't afford to make the necessary renovations to meet Ministry of Tourism standards, and have to let rooms on the sly to 'friends who make a donation'. Others get around the officialdom.

Virtually all the luxury hotels and a couple of the guesthouses charge higher rates for the three peak periods (high season) over Christmas-New Year, Easter and July to August. The majority of hotels impose what they call a 'Christmas supplement' from late December to early January. Make sure you verify the tariff when making your reservation, as many hotels charge different rates at different times of the year.

Accommodation is limited on Praslin and La Digue and you are strongly advised to book well ahead and to confirm your reservation before arrival. If you leave bookings to the last minute, chances are that you will miss out on the best places or on anything altogether.

SEYCHELLES

Prices given in this edition for hotels and guesthouses in the Places to Stay sections are expected to rise by around 5% each year. At the time of writing there were rumours that the government was planning to impose a new tax on hotels – if this has happened, room rates are likely to have jumped a bit more from those given in this book.

FOOD

The Seychelles is the best of all Indian Ocean islands for Créole cuisine. Fish and rice are the staple foods, but for once the rice takes a back seat while more imaginative use is made of fruit, vegetables, herbs and spices. What the chefs do with fish is exceptionally good.

With more than 40 guesthouses trying, encouraged by the tourist authorities, to put on the best in home cooking, the standard and variety of Créole dishes has come out of the closet over the past few years. The Seychelles Hotel & Tourism Training School at Bel Ombre (Mahé) is also playing a part in this renaissance by turning out young chefs for the hotels and restaurants.

The range of fish and seafood available is huge and you'll probably be able to try shark, barracuda, kingfish, octopus, squid, jack fish, red snapper (bourgeois), cordonnier, parrot fish and grouper (vielle) cooked in several different ways. Other Créole dishes standard to the region are the daube, a sweet sauce or stew; rougaille, a tomato-based sauce used with fish, sausages or as a side dish; carri coco, a mild meat or fish curry with coconut cream; fish marinaded in lemon; and brèdes, a local variety of spinach or Chinese cabbage.

Two delicacies served in some restaurants are fruit bat and turtle. However, fruit bat is not widely available, and eating turtle is not advised because of to the endangered status of the green turtle. You can also get the 'millionaire's salad' or heart-of-palm served up at normal prices in some guesthouses. The heart, or the 'apical bud', of the palmiste palm is used, causing the tree to die.

The Créoles are big on soups. The tec-tec soup, which contains small shells, is delicious. On the meat side, pork is becoming

more popular. Chicken fricassee and chicken curry are other favourites.

There is also a wide choice of fruits (and vegetables to a lesser extent), and a fair bit of imagination goes into making desserts. Sweet potatoes, cassava and breadfruit form a big part of the daily Créole diet. Among the more exotic selections are jamalacs, custard apples (coeurs de boeuf), golden apples, corassols, passion fruit and guavas. Bananas come in various kinds – you get the giant St Jacques variety used in cooking or for chips, and the stubby little ones for sweets.

Eating Out

There are about four price levels from which to choose. The cheapest places to eat are the takeaway counters in Victoria where you can fill up for around Rs 25. Then there are a few economy restaurants where you can eat for between Rs 40 and Rs 80.

Some of the guesthouses do good set-menu meals for between Rs 80 and Rs 100. At hotels and higher-class restaurants expect to pay at least Rs 100 for a modest meal.

Choose from Créole, Chinese, Italian and French restaurants and your palate must be subjected to the variety of Créole fish dishes.

The Seychelles Hotel & Tourism Training School at Bel Ombre has a restaurant, but sadly it's not as cheap as you'd expect for the pleasure of letting students experiment on you. Another alternative, if you're staying around Victoria, is to join the Yacht Club for Rs 250 for three months. It has one of the cheapest restaurants on the islands.

Self-Catering

The markets are no longer the colourful affairs of old, but the prices and stocks are a lot more consistent thanks to the control of the Seychelles Marketing Board (SMB). The SMB also runs the main supermarket on Albert St in the centre of Victoria. Ironically, it was the store belonging to ousted president James Mancham's family. There you can buy most imported foodstuffs, household items, wines and spirits. A packet of biscuits costs about Rs 8, long-life milk is Rs 5, a loaf of bread is Rs 6, a packet of pasta is Rs 8, a small box

Underwater Paradise

SHOOT

Beneath the crystal clear waters surrounding the Seychelles lies an underwater paradise waiting to be explored. The Seychelles represents an amazing diving experience. Millions of tropical fish, colourful reef coral, underwater caves and vibrant marine life make these tiny tropical islands a truly remarkable diving location. And with more than 900 species of fish, 100 types of shells and 50 varieties of coral, the Seychelles are also an underwater photographer's dream. Most dive sites are a short 10-20 minute boat ride from the shore.

SEPP SEUFZENECKER

SEPP SEUFZENECKER

Box: A Blackdotted pufferfish.

Above Left: The feather star or crinoid is a member of the echinoderm family which includes starfish and sea cucumbers.

Left: The Hawksbill turtle has suffered a decline in numbers over the years and is still on the endangered species list.

SHOOT

Above Right: A Moorish idol's dorsal fin often extends into a long banner-like streamer.

Right: A soft coral expands its polyps to store sunlight and create energy.

SEPP SEUFZENECKER

of washing powder is Rs 5 and a slice of cake is around Rs 2. You can buy fish down at the fishing port near where the schooner ferries leave for Praslin and La Digue.

It is hard to buy fresh fruit and vegetables on islands other than Mahé because most of the produce is home-grown for household needs only.

DRINKS
Nonalcoholic Drinks
For those who don't trust the water, there is bottled mineral water (Rs 5/8 a small/large bottle).

Seybrew makes soft drinks, such as bitter lemon, fruit cocktail, tonic and ginger ale, under the Seypearl label. For a small bottle of Coca-Cola you'll pay Rs 2.

Alcohol
Beer The local lager beers, Seybrew and EKU, are excellent. They are brewed under German supervision on Mahé. Bottles of Seybrew cost Rs 8.50 in shops, but double or more in hotels and restaurants. EKU costs Rs 9 in shops. The Seychellois also like their Guinness, for Rs 10 per bottle.

Most village stores stock cold beer which you can drink there or takeaway. All bottled drinks include Rs 1 deposit, so your empty bottles are worth taking back.

Wine The cheapest retail wines are South African (around Rs 58 a bottle) and Italian (around Rs 69 a bottle). The Greek plonk is less palatable. The house wine served in restaurants can be mighty rough.

Toddy Toddy, from the coconut palm, is not common because toddy-tappers must have a licence, which is hard to come by.

You've a better chance of finding toddy on Praslin than on Mahé. Look for ladders disappearing up the palm trunks. The toddy is cheap from the source at about Rs 5 per bottle. It ferments quickly and must be drunk shortly after tapping.

Bacca rum, made from cane spirit and

'other things', is the other local hooch, along with Lapuree, which is made from fruit and 'other things'.

ENTERTAINMENT
Cinemas
Movie outlets are limited to the Deepam Cinema (☎ 322585), at the north end of Albert St, in Victoria. The Deepam shows a good selection of English and American films, and seats cost Rs 12 (downstairs) and Rs 14 (balcony). There are sessions on weekdays at 6.45 pm and 8.45 pm and on weekends at 3.15, 6.30 and 8.30 pm – but double check in a newspaper or ring the cinema.

Discos & Nightclubs
The Seychellois bop at the sprinkling of local discos, including the *Lovenut* (☎ 323232) and the *Barrel* (☎ 322136) in Victoria, and the *Katiolo Club* (☎ 375453), just south of the airport. Only Friday and Saturday nights are worth trying. Another hotspot is *Flamboyant* in Victoria.

The main hotels are the focus of the nightlife for tourists. There are discos every other night and most of the large hotels put on séga shows once a week.

Casinos
The Berjaya Beau Vallon Bay Beach Resort (north Mahé) and the Plantation Club (south Mahé) each have a casino (open to nonresidents). On Praslin there's the grandiose Casino Des Îles (see Entertainment in the Praslin chapter for more information).

SPECTATOR SPORT
Soccer, as on all Indian Ocean islands, is the only game which can truly be called a national sport. Within the busy league programme there are occasional international matches against visiting teams at the stadium in Victoria. Réunion is the biggest rival.

Volleyball, basketball and hockey are also very popular. Athletics and boxing are gaining in strength, with the country sending teams to the last three Olympic games.

SEYCHELLES

THINGS TO BUY

Paintings

There are many talented painters and other artists on the Seychelles. For details about some of these artists, see the Art section in the Facts about the Seychelles chapter.

You can purchase the artists' work from their studios, or at Christy's Art Gallery (☎ 321019; fax 322556) on Quincy St in Victoria. It's open on weekdays from 9 am to 5 pm and on Saturday from 9 am to noon. On Praslin, there's Café des Arts (☎ 232170; fax 232155), attached to the hotel of the same name, which has paintings (for sale) by artists such as Christine Harter and Michael Adams (see Arts in the Facts about the Seychelles chapter for more information).

Batik

The best place to buy batik is at the studio of South African-born Ron Gerlach, on the Beau Vallon beach (see Clothes, following).

Pottery

The crockery at the Pirates Arms restaurant in Victoria is made by Seypot, the Seychelles Potters' Cooperative. There are other examples in a display case at the restaurant and the crockery is sold by several shops. For the best prices and selection go to the little pottery workshop itself (☎ 344080), which is at Les Mamelles, opposite the old Isle of Farquhar boat. You can get nice pieces for between Rs 16 and Rs 515. They also have a 'seconds' shelf. Another good place to buy pottery is at Gordon Pottery (☎ 266107), opposite Le Niol Guest House in Victoria. Prices range from Rs 10 to Rs 625.

Clothes

There are a number of shops in Victoria that sell fashionable beachwear and flimsy things with considerably more thought and flair to them than an 'I've been to Seychelles Too' T-shirt. They're also considerably more expensive.

Ron Gerlach's batik studio (☎ 247875), on the beach at Beau Vallon, has nice dresses (Rs 230), shirts (Rs 150), sarongs (Rs 125) and other garments designed by him in silk

or cotton. There are also some T-shirts and cards for sale. The studio is open Monday to Friday from 10 am to 5 pm. Ron Gerlach came from South Africa to the Seychelles almost 30 years ago. You can watch him at work and see the dyed cloth hanging out to dry.

Model Ships

There is only one workshop in the Seychelles compared to the scores on Mauritius, so the prices for a model Victory or Bounty will be a lot dearer here. The factory, La Marine (☎ 371441), is at La Plaine St André, just south of Anse aux Pins. It's open Monday to Friday from 7.30 am to 5 pm and on Saturday from 8 am to 3.30 pm. The models range from Rs 3000 to Rs 30,000. Make sure they are well packed, and check up on all possible freight and duty fees at the other end.

Handicrafts

The Seychelles company for handicrafts development, Compagnie pour Le Développement de L'Artisanat (CODEVAR), has set up a craft village at Anse aux Pins and a shop in Victoria.

Making boxes from local wood and shell is a new craft. Guy César, whose workshop (☎ 322021) is about half a km up Buxton Lane on the north side of Victoria, is an expert. He makes little cigarette and jewel boxes inlaid with mother-of-pearl, and made-to-order backgammon and domino sets. It's best to call ahead before visiting.

Stamps

The stamp tradition of the Seychelles, as in Mauritius, is still healthy, with a variety of new colourful issues released regularly to commemorate everything from the Pope's visit to the coco de mer. There's nothing quite as rare as the Mauritian Blue, but most of the early Seychelles stamps are valuable collector's pieces. There is a special counter for philatelic sales, including first-day covers, at the main post office in Victoria.

Coco de Mer

You can read more about this famous nut of nuts in the Vallée de Mai section of the

Praslin chapter. But in case you don't know much about the nuts and are confronted with an assortment of 'buttocks' on the tourist souvenir stalls in Victoria, here are a few tips about buying.

Perhaps the best place to buy coco de mer nuts is at the Coco de Mer Souvenir Boutique on Praslin. Only the female nuts take the erotic shape most buyers are after. The male nuts are (appropriately) a bit more phallic! They are all in their natural, dirty, husky state from the store and you have to clean and polish them yourselves. They each cost around Rs 1500 to Rs 2000 whether they are big, small, hairy or bald, rotund or oblong.

When you buy here, you are given an export permit, which is a must. This is to save any unscrupulous sale and exploitation of the rare coconut. Your purchase may be confiscated at the airport if you don't have a permit.

Authorised sellers should also issue a receipt. Some nuts are quite heavy in their natural state, so be prepared for baggage problems. The 'processed' souvenir nuts are polished, lacquered and hollowed out and often aren't coco de mer at all. The miniature ones certainly are not.

Spices & Tea
The Home Industries craft shop (☎ 224128) in Victoria sells packets of vanilla (Rs 25 for five sticks), cinnamon (Rs 15 for five sticks), nutmeg and other spices.

Seychelles tea comes in several flavours. You can get it from the lofty tea factory (☎ 378221) and restaurant on the Sans Souci road between Victoria and Port Glaud (see the North Mahé section in the Mahé chapter).

Souvenirs
There is a cluster of souvenir stalls opposite the post office in the centre of Victoria and countless shops dotted around the three main islands. It's a shame to deny the Créole traders a living, but read the Ecology & Environment section about marine products in the Facts about the Seychelles chapter before contemplating going back home with a set of shark dentures, a sprig or two of coral, fish-bone personal adornments and a crustacean work of art that looks better in the sea than on your mantelpiece. As for walking sticks made out of sharks' backbones ... well, there's no accounting for tastes. The palm frond hats-and-mats business has been slow to take off here.

SEYCHELLES

Getting There & Away

AIR

The number of airlines flying to the Seychelles has increased during the 1990s in line with the upturn in tourism.

The regulars are Air France, British Airways, Kenya Airways, Air Seychelles and Aeroflot. In addition, there are chartered flights from Europe during the high season, mainly from Italy.

Australia

Return flights to the Seychelles from Melbourne via Singapore cost around A$1765 in the low season (16 January to 31 March); A$2020 in the high season (16 November to 15 January); and A$1875 during the rest of the year. Another option is to fly to Europe (see Continental Europe, following) or Africa (see Africa, following) and catch a flight from there to the Seychelles. You could also fly direct to Mauritius (with Air Mauritius) and get a flight from there to the Seychelles (see Mauritius & Réunion, following).

The UK

A return ticket from London to the Seychelles on British Airways costs around UK£ 709/866 in the low/high season. On Air Seychelles a return fare from London is around UK£675/825 in the low/high season. With Kenya Airways, a return ticket costs Rs 4580. Aeroflot charges Rs 4800, although you may have to suffer a day or two in

---

Gold Card

As of November 1999 all visitors to the Seychelles must purchase a 'Gold Card'. Costing US$100 it is issued by tour operators or purchased on arrival. The card is valid for life and also entitles the holder to free admission to parks which formerly charged an admission fee. From April 1999 the airport tax doubled in price to a whopping US$40, making the Seychelles an expensive destination in anyone's language.

Moscow and do without an in-flight movie and other frills.

Continental Europe

Most tourists arrive on hotel-flight package holidays from Europe. Air France charges FF5922 for a return ticket between Paris and the Seychelles. The fare varies throughout the year, depending on the busy and quiet seasons. Kenya Airways charges Rs 4521 for a return ticket between France and the Seychelles. Keep your eyes peeled for special discounts which pop up from time to time.

Africa

There are flights from various destinations in Africa, some requiring a connecting flight. A return ticket from Nairobi (Kenya) to the Seychelles with Kenya Airways costs about Rs 2600. Look out for special packages that are often advertised.

Mauritius & Réunion

There are no bargain return flight deals from the Seychelles to Réunion or Mauritius and vice versa. You would be better off taking the Seychelles as a stopover en route from Europe to Mauritius or other countries. A ticket between the Seychelles and Mauritius is around Rs 1650 (ticket valid for five days), or Rs 2300 (ticket valid for one month). For details about flights from Réunion, see the Réunion Getting There & Away chapter.

SEA

Cruise liners regularly call into Victoria, but there are no passenger services directly to the Seychelles. Plenty of yachts visit during the cruising season from April to October.

If you do arrive by yacht, you must wait off Victoria lighthouse, switch to VHF Channel 16 and wait for a customs and health clearance to proceed to the inner harbour. You are given a two-week visa. The authorities will permit pets only if they are kept on board. Any firearms or spearguns must be handed over for safekeeping, to be collected when you leave. Don't make the mistake of trying to bribe officials.

If you want to leave the Seychelles by yacht, there are a few each year looking for crew members. Check the notice board at the Yacht Club in Victoria.

LEAVING THE SEYCHELLES

There is a Rs 100 departure tax on all international flights. This can be paid at the airport or pre-paid at some banks (to save you queuing at the airport). You can change Seychelles rupees back into foreign currency at the airport, but you must present your encashment form (issued whenever you change foreign currency into Seychelles rupees), so hang onto them! You may not always get the foreign currency of your choice, however.

Duty-free goods can be purchased at the airport; a 1L bottle of blended whisky costs around Rs 65 and a bottle of Cointreau is Rs 100. There's a no-frills snack bar in the rather dreary departure lounge; a bottle of Coca-Cola is Rs 5.50 and sandwiches are around Rs 11.

SEYCHELLES

Getting Around

AIR

Domestic Air Services

Air Seychelles (☎ 381300; fax 225933) takes care of all inter-island flights operating out of Seychelles international airport. There are regular flights only to Praslin, Frégate, Desroches, Bird and Denis islands.

Air Seychelles puts on extra flights to meet demand and runs charter flights to D'Arros Island in the Amirantes group.

There are airstrips on the outer islands of Marie-Louise, Coétivy and Île Plate, as well as on Farquhar, Assomption and Cosmolédo atolls. Flights with turbo-prop aircraft are operated by the Islands Development Company (IDC) (☎ 224640).

Check-in time is 30 minutes before departure and the luggage limit is only 10kg (Rs 3 per kilo for excess luggage) – you may be able to stretch the rules if you are connecting with an international flight, but don't bet on it. Fortunately there is a luggage storage facility at the international airport (no charge). Alternatively, if you are returning to a hotel on Mahé, they may be able to store your luggage for you.

Bookings can be made through travel agents or though Air Seychelles. The planes are 20-seat Twin Otters, nine-seat Britten-Norman Islanders and 17-seat Trislander aircraft. The following sections outline routes and return fares.

Mahé to/from Praslin There are frequent flights daily. The one-way trip takes 15 minutes. A ticket costs Rs 343.

Mahé to/from Frégate For details about flights contact the Frégate Island office (☎ 323123; fax 324169) in Victoria. At the time of writing there were no flight schedules, but a return ticket is expected to cost around Rs 415. The one-way trip takes about 15 minutes.

Mahé to/from Desroches There are flights four times a week (Sunday, Monday, Wednesday and Friday). The trip takes one hour. Only excursion packages are available which include return flight and full-board, for Rs 2400/4000 a single/double. For further details and reservations, call the Desroches Island office (☎ 322414; fax 321366) in Victoria.

Mahé to/from Bird Island There are daily departures for this 30-minute flight. Only excursion packages are available for a minimum of one night, including return flight and full-board, for around Rs 990 per person (although this was unconfirmed at the time of writing). For the exact tariff and bookings, contact the Bird Island office (☎ 224925; fax 225074) in Victoria.

Mahé to/from Denis Island Only excursion packages are available for a minimum of two nights, including return flight (flight time 25 minutes) and full-board, for Rs 3080/4440 a single/double. There are flights on Tuesday, Thursday, Sunday and sometimes on Friday. For further information and reservations contact the Denis Island office (☎ 323392; fax 324192) in Victoria.

Helicopter

Helicopter Seychelles (☎ 375400; fax 375277) operates scenic helicopter flights as well as some inter-island transfers. A 15-minute buzz over north or south Mahé costs Rs 315 per person, while a 30-minute trip over all of Mahé is Rs 630 per person. To fly from Mahé to Praslin costs Rs 2950 (maximum of four people). They also fly to other islands including La Digue, Frégate and Denis – ring for details.

BUS

An extensive bus service operates throughout Mahé. A limited service operates on Praslin. The fleet consists of small Italian Iveco buses, which fill up quickly at the terminus in Victoria and are often difficult to board at other stops in town. It is always best to board at the bus station if you can. Some conductors allow standing room, others don't.

The fare is Rs 3 for everywhere on the island. When you want to get off you shout '*Devant!*' Nothing else. 'Stop', 'Whoa' or '*Arrêtez*' don't seem to work. If the driver doesn't hear you, make sure the conductor does. People generally don't stand up until the bus comes to a halt. On Mahé and Praslin the bus stops have signs and there are also markings on the road.

There are 26 routes on Mahé. The main ones are Victoria-Anse aux Pins, Victoria-Beau Vallon and Victoria-Les Mamelles. There's a bus each hour on most routes from early morning until around 7 pm. Timetables and maps of each route are posted at the central bus park in Victoria.

A late night service operates in both directions on the Victoria-Anse aux Pins-Takamaka-Port Glaud-Victoria circuit, and the Victoria-Anse Étoile-Glacis-Beau Vallon-Bel Ombre-Victoria circuit from 8 pm until around midnight.

On Praslin, the basic route is from Anse Boudin to Anse Kerlan (via Anse Volbert, Baie Ste Anne and Grand Anse). Buses run each direction every hour from 6 am to 6.30 pm. Some go via Anse Consolation and others via the Vallée de Mai. As on Mahé, fares are fixed at Rs 3. Unlike those on Mahé, the Praslin buses are rarely full.

CAR & MOTORCYCLE

Most of the road network on Mahé is sealed and in good shape. The worry is not the road surface so much as the bends and the speed at which some drivers take them. On Praslin most of the major roads are surfaced, but on La Digue or the other islands none of them are.

There is no official motorcycle or moped hire in the Seychelles. It is forbidden by the tourist board for safety reasons. When you see the locals whizzing about on the narrow twisting roads, you'll appreciate why.

Road Rules

When driving, do so on the left, the British way, and beware of drivers with fast cars and drowsy brains – especially late on Friday and Saturday nights. The speed limit is supposed to be 65km in Victoria and villages, but few people stick to it. Driving at night you may be startled by running over something that explodes like a pistol shot. Giant African snails, imported by the French, are the cause of the noise.

On Mahé, there are petrol stations in Victoria and other areas, including opposite the airport; at Anse Royale (opposite Kaz Kreol restaurant); Beau Vallon and at Port Glaud.

On Praslin they're only found at Baie Ste Anne and Grand Anse. Petrol costs around Rs 6.5 a litre. As a rough guide for Mini Moke petrol consumption and reasonable mileage, reckon on about 8L and 140km a day.

Rental

Mini Mokes are *the* hire cars in the Seychelles. 'Moking is not a wealth hazard' is the motto of one car hire firm. But at around Rs 350 a day, unfortunately it is.

Many of the Mokes have some sort of mechanical defect. Make sure that basic essentials such as brakes, steering, gears, lights, seatbelts etc actually work – and don't be shy about asking for something to be fixed or to have the car replaced with another one ... which might at least have more acceptable foibles!

Mokes are built for outdoor driving and if you travel in one, you should be prepared to welcome the elements inside. Those little plastic covers that purport to keep the rain out are no match for a thunderous downpour, particularly if a sidewind neatly whips it all through one side of the car and out the other – soaking the occupants en route. During very humid spells, it's really quite refreshing!

You should *never* leave any valuables unattended in your vehicle. Mokes have a useless trunk box (use your own padlock) and anything left inside the vehicle is clearly an easy target for petty theft.

Make certain you have the hire company's out-of-office hours telephone number in case of a breakdown.

SEYCHELLES

There are more than 30 car hire companies, all about the same size and charging roughly the same prices. The government limits each firm to a certain number of vehicles, so none of the companies gets too big.

The standard daily hire rate for a Moke is Rs 350 to Rs 375, including insurance. There is no per km rate. The daily rate is reduced the longer you hire the car. You may be able to get the rate down to Rs 300 per day if you rent for three days or more, and most companies will make offers if you approach them individually. Don't have any qualms about knocking the price down if you intend hiring for a few days. If the rental company refuses to budge, look elsewhere.

After the Moke, Suzuki open jeeps are the most popular vehicles at around Rs 420. Sedan cars are available at Rs 350 or Rs 375 (with air-con), as are chauffeur-driven vehicles for a decadent Rs 700 per day.

One of the oldest hire firms is Victoria Car Hire (☎ 376314; fax 376306), near the Reef Hotel & Golf Club at Anse aux Pins. They charge Rs 350 per day for a Moke including insurance; Rs 300 per day if you rent for at least three days. Jeeps cost Rs 375 per day plus Rs 50 for insurance.

The carelessly named RAM Car Hire (☎ 323443) is known to provide special reductions, particularly if you take a Moke for a week. The office is at English River on the coast road, just north of Victoria. St Louis Car Hire (☎ 266278), at St Louis on the Victoria-Beau Vallon road, charges Rs 300 per day for a Moke, including insurance. Avis (☎ 224511; fax 225193) charges Rs 350 per day for a Moke, including insurance; Rs 330 per day for rentals of at least three days. Hertz (☎ 322447; fax 324111) hires out Mokes for Rs 375 per day, including insurance; Rs 350 per day for rentals of at least three days. Jeeps cost around Rs 400 per day; Rs 380 per day for a minimum rental of three days; Rs 350 per day for one week, or Rs 300 per day for one month. Some of the tour operators can also arrange car hire. The National Travel Agency (NTA) (☎ 224900; fax 225111) charges Rs 350/375 for a Moke/jeep per day, including insurance.

On Praslin, there's Prestige Car Hire (☎ 233226) at Grand Anse. The company has apparently hired cars to people such as Roman Polanski, Richard Chamberlain, Michel Platini and Walter Matthau.

BICYCLE

It's not easy finding bicycles for hire on Mahé, but it's a breeze on Praslin and La Digue. On Mahé you could try contacting Guy Didon at Le Meridien Barbarons (☎ 378253 ext 4019) in Grande Anse. He charges Rs 25/75 per hour/day. For rentals of more than five days, there's a 20% discount. Alternatively, ask your hotel if they are able to arrange bicycle hire. For details about the bicycle hire on Praslin and La Digue, see those individual chapters.

If you are a keen cyclist, don't bring your bike to the Seychelles. One poor tourist had his bike impounded by customs for most of his stay while he waited to get a licence and a bell!

HITCHING

Hitching is never entirely safe in any country, and we don't recommend it. Travellers who decide to hitch should understand that they are taking a small but potentially serious risk. People who choose to hitch will be safer if they travel in pairs and let somebody know where they are planning to go.

WALKING

Because the islands are relatively small and the roads little travelled (away from North Mahé), walking is a pleasurable activity just about anywhere on the Seychelles. There are still lots of wild, hilly and mountainous areas where you can escape the crowds, appreciate the islands' natural scenery and enjoy some of the alternatives to beach-oriented activities.

To facilitate things, local naturalist Katy Beaver, working in conjunction with the Ministry of Tourism and Transport, has come up with a series of hiking guides to interpretive nature trails on Mahé and La Digue. These are available at the tourist office in

Victoria for Rs 5 each, and at several hotel bookshops.

None of the routes is more than a few km, so you won't need to bring cooking or camping equipment, but you should carry energy-rich snacks and more water than you expect to need; you'll sweat buckets climbing in this humidity. Also, carry a sun block and a hat or other head covering as protection from the equatorial sun. If you have a camera or other valuables, place them in a waterproof container to protect them from the frequent tropical downpours which occur throughout the year. Good treaded footwear is also essential since the almost perpetually muddy mountain tracks turn to ski slopes after rain.

From the environmental point of view, keep to the trail as much as possible; carry out all your rubbish; don't pick or damage plants; and don't try to capture or worry wild creatures (although it's difficult to avoid the immense palm spiders which booby trap everything in the forest; you'll constantly be picking sticky silk out of your nose and eyes!).

If you prefer to try a guided walk, get in touch with local mountain guide Basil Beaudoin (☎/fax 241790) who leads hiking and birdwatching trips of varying difficulty into the Mahé backcountry – for details see Hiking (under Activities) in the Seychelles Facts for the Visitor chapter.

BOAT
Inter-Island Ferries

Schooner ferries run regularly between Mahé, Praslin and La Digue. As well as passengers, they carry supplies and mail for the islands. For all other islands you have to charter a boat, take tours or hitch a ride on a government vessel or fishing boat. The schooners are fast and quite comfortable, but you can easily get wet and/or seasick. So take seasickness pills and don't wear your best clothes.

Below are details about inter-island ferries – it's not a bad idea to double check the times (in case they have changed). The ferries are pretty punctual, so don't be late!

Mahé to Praslin There are two schooners sailing Monday to Friday on the Mahé-Praslin route. The trip takes about three hours, depending on sea conditions, and the one-way fare is Rs 50. If you're leaving from Praslin or La Digue, buy your ticket on the boat. There are no booking arrangements – just be there on time (30 minutes before departure is wise).

Cousin (☎ 233343) sails from Praslin to Mahé at 5.30 am on Monday, and at 6 am from Tuesday to Friday. It returns from Mahé at 11 am from Monday to Friday.

La Bellone (☎ 232231) sails from Praslin at 5.30 am on Monday only (although it sometimes also takes passengers on Wednesday and Friday but there is no fixed time). It returns from Mahé at 11 am.

On Praslin, the schooners usually sail to and from the Baie Ste Anne jetty – tides permitting, the Grand Anse jetty may also be used.

In Victoria tickets are available at the ferry pier, north of Independence Ave, at 9 am on the morning you leave. If it's expected to be a busy day, get there early. Also, board early to make sure of a good seat. Check to see if there's a choice of schooners going to Baie Ste Anne or Grand Anse and take the one which is closer to your booked or intended accommodation.

Mahé to La Digue The schooner *La Belle Edma* operates Monday to Friday between Mahé and La Digue. There is no schedule so ring for details on ☎ 234013. The journey takes about 3 hours and the one-way fare is Rs 50. Another possibility is *Assumption*, but there is also no fixed schedule – ring ☎ 234119 for details.

Between May and October this route is notorious for heaving even the most travel-hardened stomachs – the soft option is to fly to Praslin and take the calmer, shorter boat ride from there.

Praslin to La Digue Two schooners, *Silhouette* and *Lady Mary II*, run daily for the 30-minute trip between Praslin and La Digue. The one-way ticket costs Rs 35 per

SEYCHELLES

person; luggage costs Rs 5 per piece. It's a good idea to book ahead – most hotels will do this for you. For details about both schooners, call ☎ 232329.

There are departures from Praslin daily at 7, 9.30 and 10.30 am, and 2.30 and 5 pm. From La Digue, there are departures at 7.30, 10 and 11.30 am, and 3.30 and 5.30 pm. The trip can be a rocky one, sometimes spraying unsuspecting passengers with water – make sure your camera/video is well protected. See if you can spot flying fish skimming over the waves.

Charters

Most tours to islands should include the landing fee – make sure you ask before paying.

The Marine Charter Association (MCA) (☎ 322126; fax 224679), beside the Yacht Club in Victoria, has about 30 members who offer a variety of boats for hire for a variety of purposes and at a variety of high prices. There are schooners, yachts, launches and motor cruisers for cruising, ferrying, fishing and diving. The best months for cruising are April and October. The worst are January, July and August. Most boat owners charge around Rs 3000 per day for the vessel on overnight trips, or around Rs 380 per person for a day trip with a minimum of six people. They should drop the rates during quiet periods.

One of the old salts of the yacht club is an Australian known as Brownie. He has an ocean cruiser called *My Way* which can take up to 40 people on a day trip or 10 people on an overnight trip. For an inner islands trip with eight people he charges around Rs 7000 per day; Rs 10,000 per day for a trip to the Amirantes. A day trip is around Rs 4000. Contact the MCA (☎ 322126; fax 224679) for further details.

On Mahé, VPM Yacht Charter (☎/fax 225676), at the Inter Island Quay in Victoria, offers yacht tours in style. It's best to contact them directly for a rundown of itineraries and costs.

On Praslin, Michel Gardette (☎ 233972; fax 233015) (who owns Villas de Mer on Praslin) is a specialist diving operator and

marine archaeologist who runs Aldabra Cruise Pty Ltd & Aqua Diving Services. Michel has a deep passion for the Seychelles and can arrange trips on his catamaran to the outer islands, Amirantes and Aldabra. Clients can choose to save time by flying to Assomption Island and then sailing and diving in the region before flying back to Mahé. Michel is also a qualified PADI diving instructor and offers a full 13-day sailing trip to Amirantes, Aldabra and the outer islands for Rs 700 per person per day (maximum of eight people), including full-board and two dives per day, but excluding alcoholic drinks. Michel is planning to start return trips to Madagascar and special environmental trips – ask him for details.

Also on Praslin, Diving in Paradise (☎ 232148; fax 232244), Anse Volbert, offers various boat trips including a day trip to La Digue (Rs 100 per person; Rs 300 with one dive); a day trip to Cousin, Curieuse and St Pierre islands (Rs 400 per person; Rs 595 with one dive), including a barbeque lunch; and a day trip to Aride Island (Rs 400 per person; Rs 650 with one dive), including a barbeque lunch – there must be a minimum of 10 people for this trip. They also have speedboat trips for Rs 2000/3400 a half/full day.

For details about other trips, speak to the owner. Also on Praslin, Hotel Maison des Palmes (☎ 233411; fax 233880) offers a good range of boat tours: a half-day trip to Cousin Island including a guided tour (Rs 215 per person); a day trip to Cousin, Curieuse and St Pierre islands, including a picnic lunch, guided tours and snorkelling at St Pierre (Rs 445 per person); a day trip to La Digue, including a picnic lunchbox (Rs 250 per person); a day trip to Aride Island, including guided tour and picnic lunch (Rs 375 per person); and a boat charter (maximum of four people) with crew and lunch from Rs 1000/1800 for a half/full day. The hotel also does glass-bottom boat tours for Rs 100 per person. Nonresidents can go on all tours with advance booking. Santa Lisa (☎ 233517) at Grand Anse on Praslin, offers similarly-priced tours.

There are also some independent boat operators, usually Seychellois, who pick up charters where they can. A number of small boat owners, attached to various hotels, run 'taxi' services to nearby islands such as Silhouette, Cerf, Moyenne and Thérèse islands (from Mahé); and to Curieuse, Cousin, Coco and Félicité (from Praslin and La Digue). Alternatively, you can approach local fishermen at Bel Ombre, Port Glaud, Baie Ste Anne etc and negotiate a price.

One independent Praslin-based boat operator is Edwin Rose (☎ 232298), a cool guy who is a popular choice with travellers. He offers deep-sea fishing trips, as well as boat charters (maximum of four people). A trip to Cousin, Curieuse and St Pierre islands is Rs 400 per person including lunch, and a trip from Praslin to La Digue is Rs 100 per person. Edwin can also tailor-make trips to suit your whims – just have a chat to him.

On La Digue, Michelin (☎ 234043) conducts an array of boat excursions including: a half-day glass-bottom boat trip including snorkelling (Rs 125 per person); a 2½ hour speedboat trip including snorkelling (Rs 200 per person), and a full day speedboat trip to Petite Soeur Island including a barbeque lunch and snorkelling (Rs 350 per person).

A reputable UK yacht charter company is Sunsail which offers various yachting possibilities in the Seychelles. To find out more, contact Sunsail, The Port House, Port Solent, Portsmouth, Hampshire, PO6 4TH, UK (☎ (01705) 222 229; fax 215 125).

Outer Island Services

Schooners take supplies to the outer islands every few months, but they do not take passengers. You may be able to get a berth as a paying or nonpaying crew member. Contact the skippers at the ferry piers at Victoria, Praslin and La Digue.

The Islands Development Corporation (☎ 224640; fax 224467) at New Port, Victoria, also runs a ship to the Aldabra group and other islands en route; it carries government workers and scientists. To go, you need permission from the Ministry of National Development at Independence House, Victoria.

LOCAL TRANSPORT
The Airport

A taxi to Victoria from the airport costs about Rs 60. From Beau Vallon to the airport, expect to pay Rs 85. Large pieces of luggage incur an extra charge of Rs 5. If you arrive during the day and have no mobility problems with your luggage, there is a bus stand about 20m away, directly opposite the airport gates near the petrol station. Buses run about every hour between 6 am and 7.30 pm. The fare to Victoria is Rs 3.

Taxi

Taxi fares on Mahé and Praslin are set by the government. On Mahé you pay Rs 15 for the first km and Rs 5 for each additional km regardless of the number of passengers. There is also a charge of about Rs 11 for each 15 minutes of waiting time and drivers can also charge Rs 5 for each major piece of luggage and for the outward journey to a pick-up point.

Some examples of fares are: Victoria to airport Rs 60; Victoria to Beau Vallon Rs 35; Victoria to Baie Lazare Rs 150; and airport to Grande Anse Rs 95.

Alternatively, you can hire a taxi for a set period and arrange a fee with the driver. If you want to query any fare, get a receipt from the driver and contact the head of the Taxi Operators' Association (☎ 323895), Olivier Maradam St, Victoria.

On Praslin, taxis cost Rs 18 for the first km, and Rs 6 for each additional km. Luggage and waiting charges are the same as on Mahé. Therefore, from the Baie Ste Anne jetty to the Paradise Sun Hotel at Anse Volbert is Rs 51; from the airport to Vallée de Mai is Rs 50; and from Baie Ste Anne jetty to Baie Ste Anne village is Rs 25.

There are only a couple of taxis on La Digue, where the prices are about the same as on Praslin (see Getting Around in the La Digue & Other Inner Islands chapter for more details).

SEYCHELLES

Ox Cart

Only available on La Digue, these are a bit of hype for the tourist image and photo opportunities – see Getting Around in the La Digue & Other Inner Islands chapter for details.

ORGANISED TOURS

Travel Services Seychelles (TSS), Mason's Travel and the National Travel Agency (NTA) run extensive tour programmes involving flights, coaches, boats and accommodation. Most tours include a guide, lunch, entrance fees and transfer to and from your hotel. Some hotels, especially the upmarket ones, run their own tours.

The cheapest and perhaps most popular tours are the glass-bottom boat trips around the Ste Anne Marine National Park off Victoria, which run most days of the week but to a different island each day. A TSS full day excursion with lunch on Cerf or Round Island includes a chance to go swimming and snorkelling and costs Rs 410/245 per adult/child.

If you contact Patrick at the Marine Charter Association (☎ 322126; fax 224679) you can arrange to charter a small boat for almost half the price and with the added advantage of a small group – a minimum of two persons – while the group tours may have as many as 40 passengers on a glass-bottom boat. A half-day trip costs about Rs 125 per person, a full day costs Rs 175 per person, including snorkelling equipment but excluding lunch.

Tour Operators

The main tour operators and travel agents in the Seychelles have their head office in Victoria. A few also have a representative on Praslin and La Digue (see those individual chapters for details):

Bunson Travel Ltd
    Revolution Ave, Victoria (☎ 322682; fax 321322)
Mason's Travel
    Revolution Ave, Victoria (☎ 322642; fax 225273)
National Travel Agency
    Kingsgate House, Victoria (☎ 224900; fax 225111)
Travel Services Seychelles
    Victoria House, Victoria (☎ 322414; fax 321366)

TSS, NTA and Mason's Travel are the largest operators; independent tourists or travellers use them mainly to arrange trips to the smaller islands and snorkelling tours of Ste Anne Marine National Park. Otherwise, these operators are busy with hotel package tourists. Most tour operators offer a discount for children.

Mahé

Mahé was named by the French in honour of the 18th-century governor of Mauritius, Mahé de La Bourdonnais, and is by far the largest of the Seychelles islands. It is home to the country's capital, Victoria (no prizes for guessing who that was named after), and about 88% of the country's 73,000 people. It is 27km long and between 3km and 8km wide, so you can easily drive around it in a day.

A range of granite peaks runs through the centre of the island from north to south. The highest peaks are in the north of the island and include Morne Seychellois (905m), which overlooks Victoria.

About 85% of the country's tourist accommodation and restaurants are on Mahé, so many visitors leave without visiting any of the other quieter, less developed islands, which is a shame.

Not that Mahé is overcrowded. It's top-heavy to the north-east around Victoria, but the further south and west you go the more peaceful it becomes. If you want to get away from everybody, just head into the hills. There are also good beaches and snorkelling points evenly spread around the coast. Beau Vallon is the busiest and one of the largest beaches, although not the best.

Moving south from the centre of Victoria along the coast road, you pass through the suburbs of Le Chantier, Mont Fleuri, Plaisance and Mamelles.

From this route, two main roads head across the mountains to the west coast. The first is the Sans Souci or Forêt Noire road across to Port Glaud, which goes through the districts of Bel Eau, Bel Air and Hermitage before coming to Sans Souci. The second hill road is the La Misère route across to Grande Anse. It begins at Plaisance and goes through the La Louise district of Victoria.

The route north out of Victoria passes through the districts of English River and Union Vale. The steep winding road leading directly west out of the centre of Victoria to Beau Vallon and Bel Ombre goes via the hill district of St Louis. The other hill routes out of town go to Mont Buxton and Belonie.

The international airport is 10km south-east of Victoria.

VICTORIA

About 27,000 people live in Victoria, the only major port in the Seychelles. As it's one of the world's smallest capital cities, you should find it difficult to get lost.

Victoria is the only 'town' in the country; the rest of the settlements are 'villages'. The town centre is marked by the clock tower or *l'horloge*, a replica of the clock tower on London's Vauxhall Bridge, brought to Victoria in 1903 when the Seychelles became a crown colony. The islanders bought it as a memorial to Queen Victoria.

The courthouse and main post office stand solid and untouched since colonial days, although most of the streets emanating from the clock have been rebuilt over the past 20 years, giving the centre a clean and modern look. There are no giant office blocks or other ugly complexes.

Francis Rachel St, named after one of the victims, or 'martyrs', of the 1977 coup, and Albert St (named after Victoria's hubbie rather than President France Albert René) still contain a few old houses and shops, but barely enough to give Victoria any real character.

SEYCHELLES

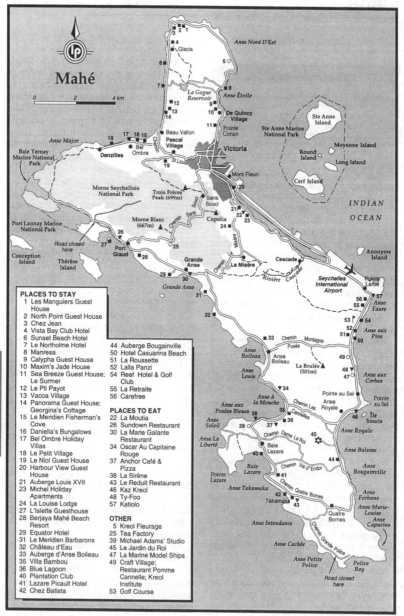

Mahé

0   2   4 km

PLACES TO STAY
1 Les Manguiers Guest House
2 North Point Guest House
3 Chez Jean
4 Vista Bay Club Hotel
5 Sunset Beach Hotel
6 Le Northolme Hotel
7 Manresa
9 Calypha Guest House
10 Maxim's Jade House
11 Sea Breeze Guest House; Le Surmer
12 Le Pti Payot
13 Vacoa Village
14 Panorama Guest House; Georgina's Cottage
15 Le Meridien Fisherman's Cove
16 Daniella's Bungalows
17 Bel Ombre Holiday Villas
18 Le Petit Village
19 Le Niol Guest House
20 Harbour View Guest House
21 Auberge Louis XVII
23 Michel Holiday Apartments
24 La Louise Lodge
27 L'Islette Guesthouse
28 Berjaya Mahé Beach Resort
29 Equator Hotel
31 Le Meridien Barbarons
32 Château d'Eau
33 Auberge d'Anse Boileau
35 Villa Bambou
36 Blue Lagoon
40 Plantation Club
41 Lazare Picault Hotel
42 Chez Batista

44 Auberge Bougainville
50 Hotel Casuarina Beach
51 La Roussette
52 Lalla Panzi
54 Reef Hotel & Golf Club
55 La Retraite
56 Carefree

PLACES TO EAT
22 La Moutia
26 Sundown Restaurant
30 La Marie Galante Restaurant
34 Oscar Au Capitaine Rouge
37 Anchor Café & Pizza
38 La Sirène
43 Le Reduit Restaurant
46 Kaz Kreol
48 Ty-Foo
57 Katiolo

OTHER
5 Kreol Fleurage
25 Tea Factory
39 Michael Adams' Studio
45 Le Jardin du Roi
47 La Marine Model Ships
49 Craft Village; Restaurant Pomme Cannelle; Kreol Institute
53 Golf Course

SEYCHELLES

According to historians and writers, Victoria was never a particularly pleasant place. All of them said it had little character and some called it a shanty slum. So today's Victoria is probably the nicest it's ever been.

Information

Tourist Office The tourist office (☎ 225313; fax 224035), on Independence Ave, has a selection of brochures and general tourist information for visitors. If you're interested in hiking, this is the place to stock up on the guides for individual routes. The office has a good map of Mahé, Praslin and La Digue (free of charge). You can also pick up a copy of *Rendez Vous*, a free booklet with tourist information. The office is open Monday to Friday from 8 am to 5 pm and on Saturday from 9 am to noon.

Foreign Consulates Victoria is home to most of the diplomatic missions – see Embassies in the Seychelles Facts for the Visitor chapter.

Money Victoria is well endowed with banks, including the Seychelles Savings Bank, Barclays Bank, Banque Française Commerciale, Bank of Baroda and Habib Bank. These banks offer money exchange facilities and you can pay your airport departure tax (Rs 100) in advance.

The banks are open Monday to Friday from 8.30 am to 12.30 pm and 2 to 3.30 pm; on Saturday from 8.30 to 11.30 am.

Post & Communications The main post office (☎ 225222), on the corner of Independence Ave and Albert St in Victoria, is open Monday to Friday from 8 am to 4 pm; on Saturdays from 8 am to noon.

The DHL Worldwide Express office (☎ 322802; fax 225367) is at Victoria House, and is open on weekdays from 8 am to noon and 1 to 4 pm; on Saturday from 9 am to noon.

The Cable & Wireless (☎ 322221) office is on Francis Rachel St and is open daily from 8 am to 9 pm for cable, fax, telex and phone services.

Travel Agencies Victoria, being the capital, has the islands' largest concentration of travel agencies. The better known ones are the National Travel Agency (NTA), Mason's Travel and Travel Services Seychelles (TSS). See Organised Tours, later in this chapter, for their contact details and tours on offer.

Airlines The Air Seychelles office (☎ 381300; fax 225933) is in Victoria House, near the clock tower. British Airways (☎ 224910; fax 225596) and Air France (☎ 322414; fax 225048) are both at Kingsgate House on Independence Ave. Aeroflot (☎ 225005; fax 224170) has an office in the Pirates Arms arcade on Independence Ave. Kenya Airways (☎ 322989; fax 324162) is at Cooperative House, Manglier St.

Bookshops The best bookshop in Victoria is Antigone (☎ 225443; fax 224668), in the Victoria House arcade, which is open Monday to Friday from 9 am to 4.30 pm and on Saturday from 9 am to 12.30 pm. It stocks a fairly wide collection of novels and some good books on the Seychelles. There are also souvenirs, postcards, cassettes and CDs for sale. Various newspapers and magazines are available including the *Sunday Mirror* (Rs 10.60), *Sunday Telegraph* (Rs 13.50), *Time* (Rs 35) and *Newsweek* (Rs 19). Cosmorama Bookshop (☎ 322665), on Manglier St, is less impressive and seems to concentrate on educational books. It's open Monday to Friday from 9 am to 4.30 pm and on Saturday from 8.30 am to noon.

Libraries See Libraries in the Seychelles Facts for the Visitor chapter.

Medical Services Victoria has a large hospital (south of the town centre) and a number of good private clinics. See the Health section in the Seychelles Facts for the Visitor chapter for details about medical/dental services on Mahé.

Emergency Call ☎ 999 for emergency services.

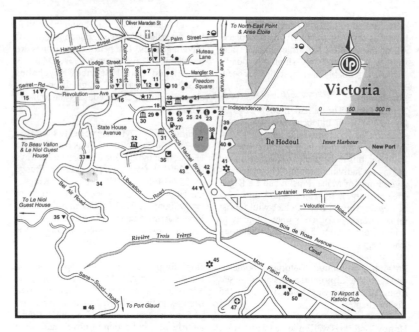

Dangers & Annoyances See Dangers & Annoyances in the Seychelles Facts for the Visitor chapter.

Natural History Museum
The Natural History Museum (☎ 321333) is next to the main post office, right in the heart of town. It is open Monday to Friday from 8.30 am to 4.30 pm and on Saturday from 8.30 am to 12.30 pm. Admission is free.

At the entrance to the museum is the Stone of Possession, laid in 1756 by Corneille Nicolas Morphey to commemorate French possession of the islands. The museum specialises in natural historical items. Inside are some unusual nature exhibits, including bones of the extinct Seychelles crocodile, the giant coconut or robber crabs (see Aldabra Group in the Outer Islands chapter) and some very dried-out grotesque fish; there's also a grossly deformed piglet in a jar – it seems to have a trunk like an elephant. There are shells, butterflies, stuffed birds, crabs,

corals, urchins, turtles, centipedes and scorpions.

Other displays include wreckage of a ship which came to grief off the Amirantes in 1570; an American whaler sunk in 1828; a captured WWI German machine gun and helmet; a voodoo or gris gris display of letters, cards, dominoes, seeds, potions, statues and hair; and an amazing musical contraption called a *bombe*.

National History Museum
This museum (☎ 225253), on State House Ave, has a well displayed collection of historical Seychelles artefacts. It's open on Monday, Tuesday, Thursday and Friday from 8.30 am to 4 pm and on Saturday from 8.30 am to noon. Entry is Rs 10.

Sir Selwyn Clarke Market
Despite what the tourist brochures say, the central market is not the bustling, colourful place it used to be. Produce and prices are

PLACES TO STAY
15 Hilltop Guest House
33 Hotel Bel Air
46 Mountain Rise Hotel
48 Sunrise Guest House
50 Beaufond Lane Guest House

PLACES TO EAT
 6 Delite
12 King Wah
13 Dan's Take Away; Barrel Bar
14 Marie Antoinette
16 Sandy's
24 Tandoor
25 Pirates Arms; Aeroflot
35 Bagatelle
44 Bon Appetit
49 Madame Wang Café & Takeaway

OTHER
 1 Cathedral of the Immaculate
    Conception
 2 Bus Terminal
 3 Schooner Ferries to Praslin & La
    Digue
 4 Cosmorama Bookshop
 5 Deepam Cinema
 7 Sir Selwyn Clarke Market
 8 SMB Supermarket; CODEVAR
 9 Tobruk Club
10 Taxi Stand
11 Mason's Travel; Lovenut
17 Police Station
18 Clock Tower
19 Main Post Office
20 Natural History Museum
21 Kingsgate House; British Airways; Air
    France; National Travel Agency
    (NTA); Seychelles Savings Bank
22 Independence House; Immigration
    Office; Seychelles Ministry of
    Tourism
23 Tourist Office
26 Barclays Bank
27 Petrol Station
28 Crafts Market; Home Industries Craft
    Shop
29 Victoria House; Travel Services
    Seychelles (TSS); Air Seychelles;
    American Consulate; UK & French
    Embassies
30 National History Museum
31 SPUP Museum
32 State House
34 Bel Air Cemetery
36 Mosque
37 Stadium
38 Independence Monument
39 Marine Charter Association (MCA)
40 Yacht Club
41 Jardin des Enfants (Park)
42 National Library
43 Cable & Wireless
45 Botanical Gardens
47 Hospital

controlled by the Seychelles Marketing Board and most people buy from the SMB store. All you'll find in it are bus loads of tourists figuring out how best to spend the hour they've been allotted. The produce also attracts flocks of cattle egrets, known to locals as Madame Paton, which perch on the stalls and pick off unattended morsels.

State House

You can't visit the former British governors' residence, now the offices of the president, unless you have government permission. Inquire at the entrance gate guard post.

Intriguingly, it is said to have been designed by the wife of a governor early this century who, after construction had begun, discovered she had forgotten to put any staircases in the plan!

The 'great capitulator', Le Chevalier Jean Baptiste Queau de Quinssy (or De Quincy), is buried in the grounds. He arrived in 1794 as the French governor and remained in charge through British occupation until he died in 1827.

Botanical Gardens

The gardens (☎ 224644) are next to the hospital, just past Le Chantier roundabout and the Sans Souci road exit, at the south end of town. They are open daily from 6 am to 6 pm and are highly recommended for short and shady walks among a variety of native and introduced trees.

Some trees are identified by discs, most are not. Among those identified are elephant apple trees (from Malaysia), the Rose of Venezuela, pandanus, palmiste palms and coco de mer palms from Praslin.

Within the gardens is a cafeteria, a pen of giant tortoises, an orchid garden and a souvenir shop.

Entry to the gardens is free (however at the time of writing there were rumours that a fee may be introduced). It contains other tropical plants as well as orchids, whose blooms are staggered throughout the year. The best time to visit is between June and August and the worst is during December

SEYCHELLES

and January, when the blossoms are hammered by buckets of rain.

Bel Air Cemetery

You'll find the cemetery at the beginning of the Sans Souci road in Bel Air, not by spotting the gravestones, but by the washing laid out to dry upon them and the surrounding overgrown grass. The cemetery, said to be the first on the islands, is not a standard tourist attraction and has been neglected by authorities.

It is said to contain the grave of a teenage Seychellois giant who was over 3m tall. His memorial stone is the obelisk of the same height. He was gentle and handy for carrying fishing pirogues to and from the water, but the local people feared him and believed he would grow bigger and terrorise the island. He was poisoned in the 1870s, so the story goes. If only there had been a basketball team back then.

The pirate Jean François Hodoul is also said to be buried here among the remains of the family tombs on the higher level of the cemetery. But the stones are so old and worn that no inscriptions are legible.

SPUP Museum

If you are intrigued by the Seychelles' perpetual celebration of 'revolution' and 'liberation', pop into the Seychelles People's United Party (SPUP) headquarters and museum (☎ 224455) on Francis Rachel St. There is an exhibition of photographs covering the history of the party since it was founded by René in 1964. Exhibits include guns and riot shields used to put down early demonstrations and the suitcases (yes, suitcases!) used in the 1977 coup to overthrow President Mancham. The SPUP has now been replaced by the Seychelles People's Progressive Front (SPPF). The museum is open Monday to Friday from 8.30 am to 4.30 pm and on Saturday from 9 am to noon. Admission is free.

Cappucin Friary

The friary, next to the cathedral on the north side of town, was built in 1933 according to a Portuguese design. It is home to several friars. They used to run the mission school across the road.

Cathedral of the Immaculate Conception

This Roman Catholic cathedral next to the friary is more to be heard than seen. It has a clock which chimes twice for every hour and has always done so. It could be a mistake which was never rectified. Or perhaps it was designed that way for the local population: the first chimes woke them up and the repetition told them what time it was. There is also the theory that certain Swiss clocks strike the time twice in order to provide a double check for busy business people.

Monuments

The new 'revolutionary' sculptures are described in the Arts section in the Facts About the Seychelles chapter. As for the old ones, there aren't many left. A statue of Pierre Poivre stands outside the courthouse opposite the post office. Poivre introduced spices to Mauritius and the Seychelles back in the 18th century.

Activities

For details about water activities, such as diving, snorkelling and deep-sea fishing, see under Activities in the Seychelles Facts for the Visitor chapter. For boat charters, see the Seychelles Getting Around chapter.

Organised Tours

The major tour operators (based in Victoria) offer an array of excursions. Several may also be able to arrange walking tours of Mahé (on request). Ask for further details. Tour operators offer fairly similarly-priced excursions and can also organise car hire, boat charters, water activities and general travel arrangements. Some of the tours on offer are described here – keep in mind that prices may have increased by now.

Mason's Travel (☎ 322642; fax 225273), on Revolution Avenue, conducts a full-day bus tour of Mahé at a cost of Rs 220/120 per adult/child including lunch. There's a similarly-priced tour conducted by Travel Services Seychelles (TSS) (☎ 322414; fax 321366), located at Victoria House, not far from the clock tower. TSS also has a 'starlight serenade' cruise which includes a Créole barbeque dinner, music and dance on Round Island (Rs 520/265 per adult/child). If you're pressed for time but not money, TSS runs 'A Tale of Two Islands' tour, which includes a visit to Praslin and La Digue for Rs 830/600 per adult/child (with air transfers); Rs 630/325 (with boat transfers). The price includes lunch and a visit to Vallée de Mai (on Praslin). Alternatively, you can just pop over to La Digue for the day (Rs 755/565 per adult/child by air; Rs 505/265 by boat), including lunch. A day trip to Praslin costs Rs 725/600 for adults/children, including flights, a visit to Vallée de Mai and lunch. Mason's Travel also runs similarly-priced inter-island day tours.

The National Travel Agency (NTA) (☎ 224900; fax 225111), at Kingsgate House on Independence Ave, does a full day 'Mahé Explorer' trip for Rs 225/120 per adult/child including lunch. Their 'Créole Evening' promises to give you a taste of Créole culture, with a séga show and Créole buffet (Rs 310/160 per adult/child). NTA also offers day trips to Praslin and La Digue. A day trip to Praslin and La Digue, for instance, costs Rs 830/600 per adult/child, including flights and lunch.

For excursions to other islands, see the individual islands in each chapter.

Places to Stay

Guesthouses There are several guesthouses in the suburbs, but none in the town centre. Some offer seasonal rates and some take credit cards; most offer laundry services. Be warned that the showers in some of these places render a mere trickle of water.

La Louise Lodge (☎/fax 344349) is a popular place which is a bit of a climb up La Misère hill, some 3km from town. Formerly the Eureka Relais des Îles at La Louise, this homey place is run by Rose Marie and France Adrienne. The rates are Rs 300/500 for a single/double including breakfast, or Rs 350/600 for half-board. Try to get a room

with a good sea view – it may cost an extra Rs 25, but is worth it.

Auberge Louis XVII (☎ 344411; fax 344428), nearby in La Louise, is grander and more expensive. This serene hilltop retreat has sea views, a little pool, bar lounge and delightful restaurant (see Places to Eat). Single/double/triple rooms cost Rs 440/600/850 including breakfast; Rs 525/760/1040 on half-board; Rs 610/900/1185 on full-board. Request one of the bungalows, as these have a private balcony with nice sea views. The Auberge is named after the son of King Louis XVI and Queen Marie-Antoinette of France. Louis XVII was born in 1785 and is reputed to have escaped to the Seychelles during the French Revolution. The royalist governor was sympathetic to his plight and the refugee was able to live in Mahé under the assumed name of Poiret until his death in 1856, when his true identity was revealed.

Mountain Rise Hotel (☎ 225145; fax 225503) is high above Victoria, in the hills of Sans Souci. It is a family mansion with fine views, cool breezes, a small swimming pool, pleasant gardens, organic fruits and its own mountain water. The owners can arrange walks to Trois Frères, excursions to other parts of the island and diving trips. There are six large and well-kept rooms, many furnished with antiques. Rates for a single/double/triple start at Rs 450/650/720 with breakfast; Rs 500/800/1000 on half-board. They usually do a barbeque once a week.

Beaufond Lane Guest House (☎ 322408; fax 224477), down on the coast road in Mont Fleuri district, has three rooms for Rs 275/350 a single/double including breakfast. Meals cost an additional Rs 75. The position near the main road is not the best, but it is close to the centre of town.

Sunrise Guest House (☎ 224560; fax 225290), in the same area, is run by the friendly Chung Faye family and is a popular choice. It has 15 air-con rooms for Rs 325/400 a single/double including breakfast. Rooms with a kitchenette cost an extra Rs 25. Créole and Chinese meals are Rs 75 per person.

Harbour View Guest House (☎ 322473) is on the sea wall, but is unsuitable for swimming. This no-frills guesthouse has basic singles/doubles (some with communal toilet) for Rs 250/350 with breakfast. Meals cost Rs 70.

Hilltop Guest House (☎ 266555) is behind the Marie Antoinette restaurant on Serret Rd, off the road to Beau Vallon. It'll appeal to those who are strapped for cash. A single/double room costs Rs 175/350 including breakfast.

Hotel Bel Air (☎ 224416; fax 224923), behind State House, on the road to Bel Air and Sans Souci, is a relaxing place to stay. It is an old colonial house, built on a rise, and offers seven rooms which are

Rs 430/580/750 a single/double/triple in the high season, and Rs 400/490/640 in the low season. The tariff includes breakfast. Meals cost an additional Rs 90 and the manager, Roland Rassool, can organise fishing trips.

Apartments Those wishing for an alternative to guesthouses may choose to stay in an apartment.

Michel Holiday Apartments (☎ 344540; fax 344566) is between the Seypot pottery and the Seybrew brewery, south of town. There are 16 self-catering flats, but the location leaves a lot to be desired – they're too close to the road and town. A studio for two adults and two children costs around Rs 2500 per week.

Hotels The first hotel in the Seychelles was the Equator, on what is now Francis Rachel St. It closed many years ago and none has replaced it in town.

Places to Eat

Victoria is slightly better off than other areas for restaurants. It is one of the best places on the island for relatively cheap eats.

Pirates Arms (☎ 225001), on Independence Ave, is a popular open-fronted café/restaurant which has been the centre of the island's social activity for many years. A cheeseburger costs Rs 45, a seafood pizza is also Rs 45 and salads cost around Rs 30. It's open Monday to Saturday from 9 am to midnight and on Sunday from 4 to 11 pm.

Tandoor (☎ 225250), also on Independence Ave, is a quieter place which offers Indian cuisine. Dishes include chicken biryani (Rs 45) and tandoori prawn (Rs 60). They are open daily, except Sunday, from 8 am (for breakfast) until 10 pm.

Bon Appetit (☎ 224053), on Francis Rachel St, is a takeaway joint which is only open for lunch from 11.30 am to 2 pm daily except Sunday. The food is cheap; beef curry costs Rs 20 and grilled fish is Rs 16.

Sandy's (☎ 322099), on Revolution Ave, is another bargain takeaway place which is open daily, except Sunday, from 11 am to 2.30 pm and 6 to 9 pm. They whip up things like beef stew (Rs 20), chicken salad (Rs 21) and goat curry (Rs 20).

Dan's Take Away (☎ 323344), opposite Sandy's, is yet another takeaway place where you can get a cheap chow down. Dan offers chicken stew (Rs 17) and beef vegetable (Rs 18) among other things. His doors open daily, except Sunday, from 10.30 am to 9 pm.

Delite (☎ 322173), on Market St, off Albert St, is a tiny place where you can only get banana or vanilla ice cream (Rs 3 per small cone). It's open Monday to Friday from 8 am to 4 pm and on Saturday from 8 am to noon.

King Wah (☎ 323658), on Benezet St, is a small Chinese-speciality restaurant. The place is nothing fancy, but it's good for a cheap and cheerful feed. The family sometimes sits around empty tables chatting or making up takeaway boxes. The main courses cost between Rs 35 and Rs 80; pork fried rice is Rs 30, beef with oyster sauce is Rs 40 and veg chop suey is Rs 30. It's open daily, except Sunday, from 11 am to 1.30 pm and 6 to 9.30 pm.

Madame Wang Café & Takeaway (☎ 324188), on Mont Fleuri Rd, is another Chinese restaurant, but has a more limited menu than King Wah. The prices are reasonable with dishes such as fried rice (Rs 20) and sweet and sour pork (Rs 45). It's open daily, except Sunday, from 9 am to 10 pm.

Marie Antoinette (☎ 266222), on the main Victoria-Beau Vallon hill road, is an atmospheric and popular Créole restaurant. The building, a beautiful old Créole house set in quiet grounds, offers set meals for Rs 95. Try not to book the same night as a tour party, as you may get second-best service. The restaurant is closed on Sundays. Otherwise it is open for lunch between 12.30 and 3 pm and for dinner between 7.30 and 10 pm.

Bagatelle (☎ 224722), on Bel Air road, is *the* place to go for a special dining experience and is rated as one of the finest restaurants in the Seychelles – so fine in fact, that it was given the prestigious 1996 Seychelles restaurant of the year award. The speciality is seafood; crabe au gingembre is Rs 125, salad exotique is Rs 45. Desserts between Rs 30 and Rs 90; crème brulée is Rs 40. To finish off a glorious meal, there's coffee and liqueurs; an Irish coffee is Rs 35. While you're here, make sure you take a look at the towering clump of lush bamboo in the garden, believed to be around 100 years old! The restaurant is open daily, except Monday, from noon to 2 pm for lunch and from 7 to 11 pm for dinner. Advance bookings are wise, especially on Saturday night when diners are serenaded with piano repertoires.

Auberge Louis XVII (☎ 344411) (see Places to Stay) has a charming restaurant which boasts picturesque views of the sea. This place is heartily recommended for a minor splurge and is especially romantic in the evening. It focuses on Créole and international cuisine and is reputed to have the best steaks on the island! Tempting possibilities include seafood lasagne (Rs 65), grilled king prawn Versailles (Rs 110) and homemade ice creams and sorbets (Rs 25). Nonresidents are welcome but should book ahead.

Request a table with a good sea view. It's open daily from noon to 2 pm and 7 to 9.45 pm.

Mountain Rise Hotel (☎ 225145) (see Places to Stay) offers good Créole and international cuisine; a main dish is around Rs 70. Advance bookings are essential.

Clubs There are a couple of alternatives to restaurants or takeaway places.

Yacht Club (☎ 322362), overlooking the harbour, is worth joining if you're going to be spending a lot of time in Victoria. It costs Rs 250 for three months (the fee is waived if you are already a member of an associated yacht club). It's not posh – anyone can join and take advantage of the cheap menu – meals cost around Rs 35. You can also get coffee, tea and snacks.

Tobruk Club (☎ 322475) is a club for ex-servicemen, located on Freedom Square behind Independence Ave. Here you don't have to be a member. Meals cost about Rs 20 and it's open daily from 6 am until late at night. The hall is also rented out to various organisations for discos and dances. Both the hall and club come under the control of the Ministry of Social Services.

Entertainment
Refer to the Entertainment section in the Seychelles Facts for the Visitor chapter.

Things to Buy
See under Things to Buy in the Seychelles Facts for the Visitor chapter.

Getting There & Away
For information on bus routes around Mahé and transport to other islands, see the Seychelles Getting Around chapter.

NORTH MAHÉ
North of an east-west line from the airport to Grande Anse is the more populated and elevated half of the island. South of Victoria, between the town and the airport, the government has reclaimed land from the sea and has started constructing highways. It is also hoping to lease parts of the reclaimed zone to international industry.

Beau Vallon Beach
The Beau Vallon beach is one of the largest and certainly the most popular beach in the Seychelles. The sand is good, clean and relatively free of rocks or coral inshore. The waves can sometimes be large as there is a big break in the reef.

Off the Coral Strand Hotel are two platforms you can swim out to. Nonresidents can mix freely with residents, even to the point of using the beach loungers. The snack and drinks bars of both hotels are handy, and there are several water sports enterprises operating from the beach.

Towards the north end of the beach are restaurants, a supermarket and a couple of shops.

In Beau Vallon village, where the road from Victoria forks to Bel Ombre (west) and Glacis (north-east), there is a petrol station, a Barclays Bank (☎ 247391) (open Monday to Friday from 9 am to 12.30 pm and on Saturdays from 8.30 to 10.45 am), souvenir shops and the police station.

Buses leave regularly from Victoria to Beau Vallon, either the long way around via Glacis or straight over the hill via St Louis. There is also a night bus service between 8 pm and midnight along these routes.

Victoria to Beau Vallon Walk
It's possible to walk between Victoria and Beau Vallon. The route is quite easy, but it passes through an inhabited area and follows the main road part of the way, so you must watch out for traffic which is relatively heavy.

In Victoria, the route begins at the central taxi stand near the clock tower (on the Beau Vallon side it begins at the police station). Follow Revolution Ave west through town. When it turns sharply to the left near the Marie Antoinette restaurant, continue straight ahead along Serret Rd until it ends near the main road about 500m further along.

Turn right and carefully follow the road over the crest of the hill, watching out for traffic. At Le Niol junction, abandon the main road, taking the right fork and continuing down through Pascal Village. After 200m follow the left fork, which soon rejoins the main road. From there it's about 700m to Beau Vallon police station, where you need

SEYCHELLES

to fork right and continue about 500m further to reach Beau Vallon Beach.

Danzilles to Anse Major Walk

This easy and pleasant three hour return walk follows the coastline between the village of Danzilles and Anse Major, west of Beau Vallon, passing some fine examples of glacis rock formations. Most of the walk lies within Morne Seychelloise National Park. Drive or take a bus to Danzilles, then follow the road up the hill; about 100m from the coast, you'll see the trail marker.

The vegetation along the route is typical of the coastal areas of the Seychelles. The ruins at Anse Major are said to have been the property of a wealthy French widow who left her estate to the Catholic mission. The mission established a small agricultural set-tlement at Anse Major, growing cinnamon, vanilla, patchouli and fruit trees. Anse Major has since been taken over by the government. During calm weather the beach is good for swimming and snorkelling. Return to Danzilles by the same route.

Kreol Fleurage

Founded by Mr Hugelmann, a German perfumer who arrived in the Seychelles in 1978, Kreol Fleurage (☎ 241329) is a small centre for the production of natural perfumes. Local plants form the basis for many of these products, which are on sale here for around Rs 135 a bottle (cheaper than at the shops).

There are currently three ladies perfumes for sale: *Ambre Vert* is a spicy perfume made with 32 different plants; *Bambou* focuses on

---

Bel Ombre Treasure Site

This is not a tourist attraction yet, because few tourists know the story behind the site and the government is keeping quiet until it sorts out the maze of claims and counter-claims over the land and exploration rights. But the tale is a fascinating one in the best tradition of pirate adventure.

Olivier Levasseur, known as 'La Buse' (The Buzzard), was one of the last and most infamous of the 18th century pirates hovering around the Indian Ocean in their privateers. He crops up in the histories of Réunion, Mauritius and Madagascar, as does his seizure, along with English pirate John Taylor, of the Portuguese ship *Vierge du Cap*. This prize yielded a fortune in treasure. When La Buse was finally caught and hanged in Réunion in July 1730, he is said to have tossed a piece of paper into the crowd and shouted 'Find my treasure, he who can'.

As La Buse was bound to have called into the Seychelles for rest and recuperation from the raping and pillaging, there was a fair chance his treasure was buried there. In 1941, a retired English guardsman, Reginald Cruise-Wilkins, came to Mahé from Kenya for the sake of his health – he suffered from malaria. Seven years later he began a search at Bel Ombre for La Buse's treasure that was to last until he died some years ago.

A cryptogram which belonged to an old Norwegian whaling skipper, old documents from the archives and strange markings on the shore rocks at Bel Ombre led him, as it had done others, to take up the challenge issued by the pirate. It turned into an obsession for Cruise-Wilkins which cost him thousands of pounds and perhaps his life.

Cruise-Wilkins believed La Buse to be a learned man who had based his treasure-hunt puzzle on Greek mythology and astrology. The markings on the rocks supported this. The pirate, it seems, wanted the seekers to undertake the 12 labours of Hercules. Cruise-Wilkins nearly moved mountains and excavated underground tunnels and steps. But apart from the odd coin, piece of pottery or weapon, he found nothing.

His sons John and Godfrey still live in Bel Ombre and have vowed to carry on where their father left off. The government has now cordoned off the site and put the search on hold until a suitably serious and remunerative solution presents itself. At present there is no move to prolong and exploit the myth, but its tourism value may eventually be realised.

The treasure excavation site is at the first set of rocks heading west along the shore past Le Corsaire. You can see Cruise-Wilkins' retaining walls and the area where the site has been fenced off by the authorities. There are no markings visible on this section, apart from bore holes.

A little 'treasure' has been found elsewhere on the Seychelles islands (see the sections on Ste Anne and Silhouette islands), but there have been no spectacular finds. There seems to be a myth that every pirate buried treasure like a jealous dog or a crazy hermit. Mind you, there couldn't have been a lot to spend it on. ■

a floral aroma and comprises 38 plants; and *Bwanwar*, described by Mr Hugelmann as having an 'exotic' fragrance, is a best seller. It took him two years to create and constitutes 42 different plants! Apart from the Seychelles, these perfumes are also sold in Germany, England and Singapore. Mr Hugelmann was planning a men's line at the time of writing – *Takamaka*, which has taken about two years to create – should be ready by now.

You can visit Kreol Fleurage, located near Anse Étoile, daily from 10 am to 5 pm.

La Gogue Reservoir

La Gogue Reservoir, which could be loosely considered the Seychelles' only mountain lake, is a pleasant wet spot in the centre of Mahé's northernmost peninsula. You can reach it either by the parallel concrete tracks (which are just passable for Mini Mokes) climbing from the east coast near the Manresa (guesthouse), or on foot from near Le Northolme Hotel on the west coast. If you're walking, the latter route is steeper but it passes through less populated areas and is the more enjoyable.

Sauzier Waterfall

Not many people know about this beauty spot near Port Glaud on the west coast. Take a bus to Port Glaud from Victoria. If you have a car, park opposite the small island known as L'Islette and take the track inland alongside the church. Walk straight ahead past the Créole homes for about 10 minutes and when you hear the waterfall, turn left towards it. The cascade is magnificent, the surroundings are peaceful and the water is clean (no washing) and deep enough to swim.

A traveller wrote to say that a lady in one of the Créole homes asks people to sign a book indicating their name, nationality and current hotel address – it seems there have been walking accidents in the area.

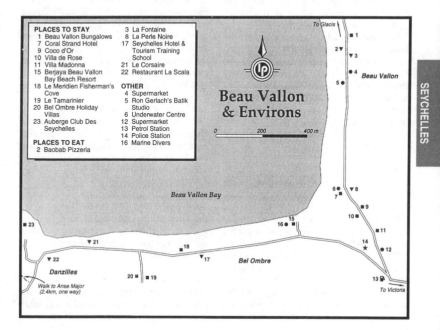

PLACES TO STAY
1 Beau Vallon Bungalows
7 Coral Strand Hotel
9 Coco d'Or
10 Villa de Rose
11 Villa Madonna
15 Berjaya Beau Vallon Bay Beach Resort
18 Le Meridien Fisherman's Cove
19 Le Tamarinier
20 Bel Ombre Holiday Villas
23 Auberge Club Des Seychelles

PLACES TO EAT
2 Baobab Pizzeria

3 La Fontaine
8 La Perle Noire
17 Seychelles Hotel & Tourism Training School
21 Le Corsaire
22 Restaurant La Scala

OTHER
4 Supermarket
5 Ron Gerlach's Batik Studio
6 Underwater Centre
12 Supermarket
13 Petrol Station
14 Police Station
16 Marine Divers

Beau Vallon & Environs

To Glacis

Beau Vallon

Beau Vallon Bay

Bel Ombre

Danzilles

Walk to Anse Major
(2.4km, one way)

To Victoria

SEYCHELLES

Trois Frères Peak Walk

Trois Frères Peak, which forms the mountain backdrop for Victoria, lies in Morne Seychellois National Park. The steep (somewhat challenging) walk to its 699m summit begins at Sans Souci Forest Station on the Forêt Noire route, about 5km from Victoria. Ask the locals to point you in the right direction if necessary. After you pass the FEBA radio station and the Forestry Division offices, look for a right turn 50m before the military checkpoint. Continue along this road for about 250m to the trailhead car park.

Although the climb to the peak is only about 2km each way, it is all steeply uphill from the car park (if you do leave your car here, lock it and don't keep any valuables inside as theft can be a problem) and extremely slippery after rain, so plan on at least two hours up and one hour down. Follow the posts dabbed with yellow paint and the arrows on the rough bits. About 1800m from the car park, the summit track cuts off to the right of the main track and climbs to the peak, which is frequently wrapped in cloud.

The major attractions on the route are the stand of *Nepenthes pervillei* (pitcher plants) atop a rock face about mid-way to the summit, and the potentially incredible view from the peak. Although most people return the way they came, those who would prefer a traverse can tackle the rough track which continues from the summit cutoff for about 5km down to the village of Le Niol, between Beau Vallon and Victoria.

Copolia Walk

Further along the Forêt Noire route is the start of a short and steep but wonderful walk to the summit of the 510m peak, Copolia. Although the walk is just 250m each way, it leads to the most accessible stand of pitcher plants on Mahé.

The walk begins at Val Riche about 6km from Victoria; watch for the signpost on the left side of the road. It is marked by posts dabbed with blue paint and is easy to follow, despite a couple of indistinct forks. The summit of Copolia is a large area of glacis, exposed

granitic rock, and if the weather is clear it's interesting to explore. However, beware of the super-duper dropoff at the end of it!

Port Launay Marine National Park

This is a pretty, sheltered bay with some secluded beaches and good areas for snorkelling. Get a bus to Port Glaud from Victoria and walk or drive the 4km up to Port Launay bay. The road ends at the National Youth Service camp gates before Ternay and you can't go further without permission.

Tea Factory

The tea factory (☎ 378221) and restaurant is on the Sans Souci road between Victoria and Port Glaud, about 4km from the latter in the shadow of Morne Blanc mountain. It is open Monday to Friday from 8 am to 4 pm. If you're feeling a bit peckish, there are snacks such as hot dogs (Rs 15), toasted sandwiches (from Rs 12) and ice cream (Rs 15). There are postcards and souvenirs for sale – a pack of six types of tea (lemon, mint, vanilla, cinnamon, orange and plain) costs Rs 55; one packet of tea is Rs 6. There are also spices for sale; a packet of nine assorted spices costs Rs 40. You can inquire here about visits to the nearby tea plantation itself. There are guided tours from 8.30 am to noon, which cost Rs 10/5 for adults/children.

Tea Factory to Morne Blanc Hike

The imposing white hulk of 667m Morne Blanc and its almost sheer 500m face make a great hiking destination. Although the track is only 600m long, it is quite steep, climbing 250m from start to finish. Unless you're very fit, plan on about an hour for the trip up.

The beginning of the route is signposted 250m up the road from the tea factory, along the Forêt Noire cross-island road, and the trail is marked by intermittent yellow splotches of paint on trees. The return is via the same route.

Rivière Cascade Walk

From Cascade village, near the airport, take the road up past the church until it ends when it crosses the river, and follow a path up the left-hand side of the nearest house for about half a km. Then ask directions along the way. The people are helpful even if you do walk through their gardens (be careful not to trample anything!). The path passes waterfalls and sluices to eventually break away from the river and head for La Misère road.

Places to Stay – Pointe Conan

Sea Breeze Guest House (☎ 241021; fax 241198) is first on the road at Pointe Conan, about 3km north of Victoria. It is a modern complex with six air-conditioned chalets, each with a private terrace for Rs 325/400 a single/double, including breakfast.

Le Surmer (☎ 241811; fax 241527), opposite the Sea Breeze Guest House, is a rather lacklustre place but fairly cheap. Mundane singles/doubles cost Rs 275/350 with breakfast; Rs 375/500 on half-board. Request a sea-facing room. There are also some double rooms with a kitchenette for Rs 250 per night. There's a restaurant open daily for lunch and dinner (nonresidents welcome), which serves Créole and continental cuisine; spaghetti carbonara is Rs 40, octopus curry is Rs 45 and grilled lobster is Rs 175.

Maxim's Jade House (☎ 241489; fax 241409) is further up the coast. This unassuming guesthouse, run by a lovely Chinese couple, has five double rooms with air-con and private bath. Rates for single/double occupancy are Rs 300/350. There's a restaurant where you can get a main dish for around Rs 70.

Places to Stay – Ma Constance

Calypha Guest House (☎/fax 241157), at Ma Constance, 3.5km north of Victoria, is run by Claude and Florienne Brioche. To get there, turn well up the hill at the first opening north of the giant banyan tree, on the main road heading north. The owners manage to keep the price down to Rs 170/275 a single/double. Meals cost Rs 65 per person. Calypha is a modern house with a balcony and good views.

Manresa (☎/fax 241388) is at the other end of Anse Étoile bay at Pointe Cèdre. This guesthouse has five twin bedrooms (all with air-con). All the rooms are named after birds and have balconies; some also have good views across to Ste Anne Island. Rates for a single/double room are Rs 375/500; Rs 400/600 for half-board; Rs 500/700 for full-board. Manresa has a pleasant restaurant called L'Étoile and a bar called La Mer. Although the views are good, the sea here is not great for swimming. You have to get to the west side before the good coves and beaches begin.

Places to Stay – Machabée

North Point Guest House (☎ 241339; fax 241850), at the northern tip of the island, is run by Gilbert Hoareau. This guesthouse has eight rooms and is quite popular with independent travellers. The rates for a single/double room are Rs 300/330 (minimum stay of three days); Rs 330/410 with breakfast.

Les Manguiers Guest House (☎ 241455; fax 241776), nearby, is a house which can be rented for Rs 400 per night (maximum of five people), including breakfast. You'll have some jet-setting neighbours – an Arab sheik has a mansion here and there are some other exclusive properties.

Chez Jean (☎ 241445; fax 225430) is a little further around the point at Machabée village. This guesthouse charges Rs 200/320 for a single/double, or Rs 280/475 on half-board. Mini Moke rental can be arranged for guests at a cost of around Rs 250 per day.

Places to Stay – Glacis

Vista Bay Club Hotel (☎ 261333; fax 261061) is situated on the coast in the Glacis community. Singles/doubles cost around Rs 770/850 with breakfast. The hotel is set away from the shore and has an elevated pedestrian crossing to its thatched restaurant. At the time of writing there were unconfirmed reports that this hotel may be closing down, so make sure you check before rolling up.

Sunset Beach Hotel (☎ 261111; fax 261221) is the next hotel, about 2km south. This is an exclusive holiday village stuck on a rock promontory with a pretty cove beach on one side. Rates for a single/double/triple room in the low season start at Rs 1205/1395/2090 (B&B); and rise to Rs 1385/1755/2630 (half-board). Meals cost Rs 180 per person. If you feel like living the high life, there are also more expensive suites and a luxury villa. There's a pool for residents and a good restaurant (see Places to Eat).

Le Northolme Hotel (☎ 261222; fax 261223), about 1km further down the coast, is the oldest of the current Seychelles hotels. Famous writers such as Ian Fleming and Compton MacKenzie have stayed here and waxed lyrical from their rooms with a view. The trees, rocks, and general windswept feeling might remind Californians of Carmel-by-the-Sea, but the beach isn't outstanding. For those seeking some serious pampering, a blissful one-hour massage costs Rs 200. Single/double rooms go for Rs 1020/1190 with breakfast; Rs 1200/1550 on half-board. Rates vary according to the busy and quiet seasons – verify this when booking.

Places to Stay – Beau Vallon

Le Pti Payot (☎ 261447; fax 261094), at Mare Anglaise, just north of Beau Vallon, is a relaxing place to stay and highly recommended. This pleasant complex of three self-catering chalets perched on a hillside, boasts magical views across Beau Vallon beach. Each chalet has a private balcony with sea views (No 3 has the best views) and can accommodate a maximum of four people. The price per chalet is Rs 500/530 without/with air-con. The amicable manager, Evans Calva, is a former water sports instructor. This place is a favourite among travellers, so be sure to book well ahead to avoid disappointment.

Vacoa Village (☎ 261130; fax 261146) is on the outskirts of Mare Anglaise village. This is a 'Spanish-style self-catering complex' surrounding a pool and gardens. The use of giant boulders and almost troglodyte accommodation is quite pleasant. A one-room studio costs Rs 675/850 for single/double occupancy including breakfast; Rs 825/1150 on half-board and Rs 925/1350 on full-board. Two-room studios are also available.

Panorama Guest House (☎ 247300; fax 247947) is a fairly modern house with 10 rooms, just off Beau Vallon beach. It's managed by the friendly Mary and Bobby Rakic. Singles/doubles with breakfast cost Rs 360/480.

Georgina's Cottage (☎ 247016; fax 247945), just next to the Panorama Guest House, is run by the amicable Patrick and Geraldine Laporte. Their little place exudes a homey atmosphere and is very reasonably priced. Singles/doubles with breakfast cost Rs 195/300 and guests have use of a communal kitchen and washing machine (buy your own washing powder).

Beau Vallon Bungalows (☎ 247382; fax 247955), across from Baobab Pizzeria, offers comfortable single/double/triples for Rs 450/475/575 (B&B); Rs 525/625/800 (half-board). Self-catering bungalows are available for Rs 550/575/675 a single/double/triple with breakfast; Rs 625/725/900 on half-board. A two-bedroom family bungalow is Rs 800 per night, with breakfast.

Coral Strand Hotel (☎ 247036; fax 247517) is well situated near the waterfront, about half a km north of where the road kinks inland to Victoria. This large hotel is a popular hangout with the young crowd in search of beach fun and frolics. It has 103 rooms for Rs 840/920 with breakfast; Rs 1100/1260 on half-board. These daily rates are greatly reduced if you come on a package holiday, as most of the guests seem to do. The hotel is always busy and is a popular gathering spot for expatriate residents, workers and their friends, particularly on weekends. The pool bar is a step off the beach and does good snack lunches as well as more expensive meals. The bar

is open from 10 am to 6 pm. The Underwater Centre diving school is also based at the hotel (see Diving in the Seychelles Facts for the Visitor chapter).

Villa Madonna (☎ 247403), not far from the Coral Strand Hotel, is run by Adeline Port-Louis. It's a quaint place with ordinary singles/doubles for Rs 230/300 including breakfast.

Coco d'Or (☎ 247331; fax 247454), nearby, is much slicker and offers 27 rooms for Rs 455/555 a single/double including breakfast; Rs 525/695 on half-board. A pool was being planned at the time of writing.

Villa de Rose (☎ 247455), in the same area, has two houses that each have rooms for guests. The owner seems eager to please and certainly keeps the place in tip-top condition. Rates for an air-con single/double are Rs 350/500 with breakfast. The rooms are squeaky clean and all have a fridge, tea and coffee making facilities and colour TV. Self-catering apartments are also available for Rs 600 per night (maximum of four people).

Places to Stay – Bel Ombre

Berjaya Beau Vallon Bay Beach Resort (☎ 247141; fax 247943) (try saying that fast five times!) is on Beau Vallon beach, but the main entrance is on the Bel Ombre road. It has 184 rooms and is ·kept busy with package tour groups – the service can be a tad impersonal. Singles/doubles/triples cost Rs 1105/1150/1270 with breakfast and Rs 1270/1480/1765 on half-board. There are also some more opulent suites. Attached to the hotel is a water sports centre, the Marine Divers centre (see Diving in the Seychelles Facts for the Visitor chapter), a casino, tennis courts, car hire desks and shops. Nonresidents can mix freely for coffee, drinks, snacks, meals and occasionally entertainment. The beach is better towards the Coral Strand end. Meals cost around Rs 165 and you can even order from a vegetarian menu (on request).

Le Meridien Fisherman's Cove (☎ 247247; fax 247742), further west, is a splendid choice (if you can afford it). It's certainly a stylish place with all the usual trimmings of a deluxe hotel. The rates for a single/double room are Rs 1495/2150 with breakfast; Rs 1695/2550 for half-board. Rates vary according to the time of year, so double check when making your reservation. Meals cost around Rs 200. If you feel like lashing out, more expensive suites and deluxe rooms are also available. Facilities include tennis courts, a games room and two restaurants

Le Tamarinier (☎ 247611; fax 247711) is on the other side of the road, up a concrete lane called Marie Laure Drive. It's run by France M Hoareau and is a modern guesthouse with singles/doubles for Rs 300/350 (B&B); Rs 380/510 (half-board).

Auberge Club Des Seychelles (☎ 247550; fax 247703) is at Danzilles, and has 40-odd thatched huts scattered about the headland in a leafy garden leading down to the shore. There's an attractive terrace restaurant with a sea view. Rates for single/double/triple rooms are Rs 715/910/1120 with breakfast; Rs 855/1190/1540 on half-board. The management organises a weekly walk to Anse Major with a 'Robinson Crusoe Picnic' and return transport by boat. There is some good snorkelling around this hotel.

Bel Ombre Holiday Villas (☎/fax 247616), in Bel Ombre village, charges Rs 380 per night for a self-catering bungalow (maximum of four people), or Rs 480 (maximum of six people). An extra bed costs Rs 50 per night. There are also some exclusive bungalows (maximum of two people) which go for Rs 420 per night.

Daniella's Bungalows (☎ 247212; fax 247784) offers accommodation in well-kept bungalows. Singles/doubles cost Rs 400/500 with breakfast; Rs 475/650 on half-board.

Le Petit Village (☎ 247474; fax 247771), not far away, is highly recommended and an excellent choice. It has seven delightful units in log cabins, all with a kitchenette, lounge, sundeck, air-con and sea view. A one-bedroom unit (maximum of two people) costs Rs 700 per night, while a two-bedroom unit (maximum of four people) costs Rs 1200 per night. The cost includes daily cleaning. Excursions to nearby islands can be organised, as well as various water activities. Book well ahead, as a place of this calibre fills up in a flash.

Place to Stay – Le Niol

Le Niol Guest House (☎ 266262) is less than 1km up the side road to Le Niol peak from the top of the Victoria-St Louis-Beau Vallon road. At the edge of the Morne Seychelloise National Park forest, it's nothing flash, but may be worth considering if you're going through a cash crisis. There are four very basic rooms for Rs 185/250 a single/double; Rs 200/300 with breakfast. Meals are available for Rs 75 per person.

Place to Stay – Port Glaud

Berjaya Mahé Beach Resort (☎ 378451; fax 378517) is south of Port Glaud, where the road turns away from the coast. This rather unsightly 173-room hotel's multi-storey edifice broke the tradition that all hotels on the islands should be no taller than the height of a palm tree. It is a bit of an eyesore and somewhat lacking in character. Standard singles/doubles cost Rs 955/1000 including breakfast, while the presidential suite costs a

juicy Rs 2220/2290. Half-board is also available for an extra Rs 165 per person. There's a swimming pool, tennis courts and water activities. Island tours can be arranged with advance notice.

Places to Stay – Grande Anse

Equator Hotel (☎ 378228; fax 378244) is just north of Grande Anse bay and village, on a side road. This 60-room hotel is built into the cliff face on various levels and is worth visiting to see the architectural drop to the swimming pool and bar, if nothing else. The rates for single/double rooms are Rs 580/880 on half-board. Rates increase at least 15% during the high season. Facilities here include tennis courts and two restaurants. There is some good swimming and snorkelling to be done between the hotel and Île aux Vaches.

Le Meridien Barbarons (☎ 378253; fax 378484), on the other side of Grande Anse, is a 125-room hotel which is a popular choice. The pool seems to dominate the complex, despite a near perfect beach. Well appointed single/double rooms go for Rs 1330/1930 (B&B); Rs 1690/2290 (half-board). Prices vary throughout the year, so make sure you ask when booking.

Château d'Eau (☎ 378339; fax 378388), further south, on the Barbarons Estate, is a sophisticated guesthouse set in peaceful surroundings. It was under renovation at the time of writing and the tariff was not available, but it's expected to be around Rs 1000 per person per day on half-board! This six-bedroom chateau may suit those in search of a homey yet upmarket atmosphere – it's best to contact them directly to get the exact room rates etc. If you do end up staying here, let us know how it was.

Place to Eat – Glacis

Sunset Beach Hotel (☎ 261111) (see Places to Stay) has a pleasant restaurant with good food. Lunch is an à la carte affair, with dishes such as smoked fish salad (Rs 50), club sandwich (Rs 50) and prawns kebab (Rs 125). Dinner is a set menu (Rs 180 per person). There's a Créole buffet lunch on Sunday (Rs 95 per person) and a Créole buffet dinner on Monday (Rs 180 per person). Nonresidents must make an advance reservation.

Places to Eat – Beau Vallon

Baobab Pizzeria (☎ 247167), which has a sand floor to sink your toes into, is right on the beach and a popular hangout with travellers. The pizzas are properly baked and cost around Rs 35; spaghetti bolognaise is Rs 34. The atmosphere manages to be lively, yet relaxed, and the restaurant is cooled by the sea breezes. Get there before 8 pm to be sure of a seat, especially on weekends. It is open every day from 11.30 am to 3.30 pm and 5.45 to 10.15 pm.

La Fontaine (☎ 247841), across the road, is a more upmarket place which serves Créole food. Options include tuna salad (Rs 30), Créole burger and chips (Rs 40) and lamb curry (Rs 75). Sweettooths can indulge in dessert for around Rs 35. It's open daily from noon to 2 pm and 7 to 10.30 pm.

La Perle Noire (☎ 247046) is opposite the Coral Strand Hotel and is open daily for dinner from 7 pm. The restaurant has a French, Italian and Créole à la carte menu. Pasta dishes cost about Rs 80, chicken curry is Rs 80 and palm heart salad is Rs 50.

Places to Eat – Bel Ombre

Seychelles Hotel & Tourism Training School (☎ 247414; fax 247826) has a restaurant where trainee chefs and waiters can try out their newfound skills on the public. The prices are not as low as you would expect, with a set meal upwards of Rs 90. If you paid less, you'd be prepared to be a guinea pig and taste-test first attempts. But as it is, why not go to a 'qualified' restaurant for the same price? The school restaurant is open Wednesday to Friday from noon to 2 pm and 7.30 to 10.30 pm. It's closed during school holidays.

Le Corsaire (☎ 247171), at Bel Ombre village, is a pleasant restaurant in a large steep-roofed chalet right on the waterside. Dishes include fish lasagne (Rs 60), oxtail stew (Rs 110) and chocolate mousse (Rs 45). For an exotic finale you can sip on a pineapple liqueur (Rs 25). This restaurant is only open for dinner from 7.30 pm. It's closed on Monday.

Restaurant La Scala (☎ 247535) is up the hill towards the Auberge Club Des Seychelles and is run by the Torsi family. It specialises in Italian food and seafood. Goodies on the menu include gnocchi della casa (Rs 45) and tiramisu (Rs 30). It opens for dinner at 7 pm from Monday to Saturday; it's closed on Sundays and all of June. An advance booking is recommended.

Place to Eat – Port Glaud

Sundown Restaurant (☎ 378352) is situated on the water and is good for a laid back meal (only lunch is available). Some dishes on offer are fish curry and rice (Rs 55), tec-tec soup (Rs 25) and spaghetti napolitana (Rs 40). There's even bat curry and rice (Rs 65) – but do the bat population a favour and give this one a miss. The restaurant is open daily, but is sometimes closed on Sunday – ring to check.

Place to Eat – Grande Anse

La Marie Galante Restaurant (☎ 378455) specialises in Créole food. Main dishes are upwards of Rs 70; grilled fish, rice and chutney is Rs 75 and desserts hover around Rs 25. The menu is somewhat limited, but the food is tasty. It's open only for lunch and is closed on Tuesday.

Place to Eat – La Louise

La Moutia (☎ 344433) is about 3km from Victoria, up Les Mamelles hill road. It specialises in Créole cuisine and seafood; main dishes cost around Rs 150. This place is open Monday to Saturday from 11.30 am to 2.30 pm and 7.30 to 11.30 pm. On Sunday it's only open for dinner.

SOUTH MAHÉ

The southern half of Mahé is less mountainous and less populated than the north. 'Moking' tourists can cover the region effortlessly, but there are scores of bays around the coast and it rarely gets crowded.

In the hilly interior, there are some pleasant walks and hikes around Chemin Les Cannelles and Chemin Val d'Endor.

Beaches

Beaches are the main attraction in the south of the island. Starting with Anse Royale, south of Pointe au Sel (also known as Fairyland Point), the beaches along the east coast are smaller, quieter and prettier than most in North Mahé. They're best for relaxing, lagoon swimming and snorkelling, as almost the whole coast is fringed by the reef.

The nicest area for swimming and snorkelling is opposite tiny Île Souris. Although the crowds descend on weekends, it's fairly empty during the week. Continuing south, there are good stretches of beach at Anse Bougainville, Anse Parnel, Anse Forbans (also called Pirates' Bay) and Anse Marie-Louise.

On the west coast, both Anse Boileau and Anse à la Mouche have reef beaches, but are not really suitable for sunbathing or swimming. They are too shallow and too public. The secluded beaches begin at Anse Soleil, but the coast here fronts open sea and that means waves, rips and the need to take additional care when swimming.

There is a rough 2.5km road down to Anse Soleil and Anse Petite Police, which a Mini Moke can just about manage with great risk to the underside. Jeeps are better. The trip is almost impossible in a private sedan. The rewards, however, are worth the effort: there's a palm-fringed beach to laze on and granite boulders to dive or snorkel from (with extreme caution!). You can see some wonderful marine life, including barracuda and small sharks.

At Baie Lazare, the Plantation Club has snaffled the best bit of beach, but there is a fine stretch at Anse Takamaka, where the road heads inland and east.

There is a lovely, wild strip of beach at Anse Intendance at the end of a good secondary road leading down from Quatre Bornes village. Anse Intendance is the wildest beach on Mahé and great for surf watching. Swimming is not allowed because of the violence of the surf and currents.

The road from Quatre Bornes continues a couple of rough km past Anse Cachée and Anse Corail, but is blocked off for security reasons before you come to the aptly named Police Bay. The beach at the end of the public road is wild and beautiful, with high frothing surf, but rogue currents make it unsuitable for bathing.

The bus service from Victoria provides access to most of the island as far south as Takamaka and Quatre Bornes villages; there's even a night service between 8 pm and midnight (see the Seychelles Getting Around section).

La Brulée Walk

At the Cable & Wireless station, near the crest of the Montagne Posée cross-island route between Anse aux Pins and Anse Boileau, is the start of an easy but highly rewarding walk to three spectacular vantage points overlooking the west coast of Mahé.

The track is well marked and easy to follow, first descending through groves of mahogany to cross a stream, and then climbing through dense forest to a small forested plateau area. The routes to the three viewpoints can get a bit confusing so it's wise to

carry the *La Réserve and Brulée* hiking brochure and map, available at the tourist office in Victoria. If you prefer to have a go on your own, the main circular route is marked with green splotches; Viewpoint No 1 has yellow splotches; for Viewpoint No 2 they're red on yellow; and those for Viewpoint No 3 are green on yellow.

Viewpoint No 1 is the best of the three, with a fabulous view over a precipice down to the west coast. Nearer at hand, look for the fruit bat roost down in the valley below. The most remote of the overlooks, Viewpoint No 3, offers the best views of the 501m peak of La Brulée, as well as a glimpse of the east coast, and Viewpoint No 2 offers the most wide-ranging west coast panorama.

Craft Village (Village Artisanal)

The rather contrived craft village (☎ 376100), at Anse aux Pins, is a collection of craft shops grouped around a restored colonial building and restaurant. There are shops selling stuff like silk shirts (around Rs 300), straw hats (around Rs 52), scarves (around Rs 75), ceramic coffee mugs (around Rs 45), shoulder bags (around Rs 225) and paintings and prints (from around Rs 20). There's also a restaurant here called *Restaurant Pomme Cannelle* (☎ 376155), which has dishes such as Créole chicken curry (Rs 68) and seafood cocktail (Rs 42). It's open daily from 10 am to 10 pm. The craft village is open daily from 10 am to 6 pm and entry is free.

Anse Royale

In addition to having a good beach, Anse Royale is home to the new national theatre, where you can see cultural concerts or shows by visiting artists. The Banque Française Commerciale, in the village, exchanges currency; there is also a petrol station.

Le Jardin du Roi

Located in the hills of Anse Royale, Le Jardin du Roi (☎ 371313; fax 371366) is a sprawling and lush garden with lots of aromatic spice plants such as cardamom, cloves, nutmeg, vanilla and cinnamon. There are

Kreol Institute

Near the craft village at Anse aux Pins is the Kreol Institute (or Lenstiti Kreol) (☎ 376351; fax 376286), established to nurture the Seychelles' Créole culture, specifically language and literature. Housed in an old Créole mansion, the institute is primarily a Créole research centre. It also publishes books in Créole, sells books written by Créole authors, gives Créole language lessons and organises social activities throughout the year. The institute strives to promote the Créole language and sometimes runs Créole language educational programs. They have been involved in research into the development of the Créole language. There is a small selection of Créole children's books for sale (Rs 15 to Rs 50) and other Créole books covering a range of topics (Rs 20 to Rs 50). They are also working on an English-Créole dictionary. If you're interested in finding out more about Créole culture, there is a good selection of reference books here (you can't borrow them, but you can get photocopies for Rs 2 per page). There's also a replica of a traditional Créole kitchen on display.

Some people believe the house in which the institute is located is haunted – one story is that on a moonlit night, two lovers strolling by the grand house decided to pop in for a look around. The pearly moon was out, the house was secluded, so naturally the mood became amorous. As the young man leaned over to kiss his sweetheart, he felt someone kissing the back of his neck! Totally freaked out, he swung around to see who it was. Nobody was there, but a chilling ghostly presence caused the startled young lovers to flee from the house, never to return. Other ghostly stories abound.

The Kreol Institute is open Monday to Friday from 8 am to 4 pm. Another vehicle through which Créole culture is promoted is Festival Kreol – see the boxed text in the Facts about the Seychelles chapter. ■

---

pleasant walks through the grounds as well as a small museum. A small crêperie in the compound serves sweet and savoury crêpes; a seafood pancake is Rs 35, a stewed fruit pancake is Rs 30 and home-made ice cream is Rs 25.

The gardens are open daily from 10 am to 5.30 pm. Admission is Rs 20 (free for children under 12 years of age).

Michael Adams' Studio

Michael Adams' studio (☎ 361006; fax 361200), at Anse aux Poules Bleues, should not be missed. The painter's work is explained in more detail under Arts in the Facts about the Seychelles chapter. Adams' wife, Heather, usually looks after visitors. The shop sells original silk-screen work (ranging from Rs 1000 to Rs 7000), B&W lineblocks (ranging from Rs 25 to Rs 125), postcards and calendars. Packing and posting for overseas orders can be arranged. The studio is open Monday to Friday from 9 am to 4 pm and on Saturday from 9 am to noon (it's not a bad idea to ring ahead before you go, to make sure somebody is around).

Chemins Dame Le Roi & Val d'Endor

These are two cross-country lanes leading from Baie Lazare on the west of Mahé through the valley to Anse Bougainville on the east. For the most part, the Chemin Val d'Endor follows the Rivière Bougainville and the Rivière Baie Lazare. Chemin Dame Le Roi runs in a wide loop from Baie Lazare village before joining Chemin Val d'Endor – there's a small pottery just before the junction. Like any other forest walks, these two lanes provide an admirable alternative to lazing around the beach all day.

Places to Stay – East Coast

Carefree (☎ 375237; fax 375654) is the closest guesthouse to the airport, located just past Pointe Larue on Anse Faure. It has four rooms in a nondescript block for Rs 300/350/450 a single/double/triple with breakfast; Rs 380/510/690 on half-board. It's right on the road and next to the sea, although the beach from here down to Pointe au Sel is not too inviting. The Carefree also has a good restaurant; nonresidents are welcome but should try to book ahead. It's open for lunch and dinner; prawn cocktail is Rs 40, grilled lamb chops are Rs 70 and a refreshing coconut sorbet is Rs 20.

La Retraite (☎ 375816) is a guesthouse in Anse aux Pins village, near the school. Run by the affable Hélène Etienne, it has only four rooms and is less houseproud about sand and beach towels lying around the verandah than some of the other overly spic 'n' span guesthouses. Hélène is also a specialist in craftwork. Her room rates are among the island's lowest at Rs 200/260 a single/double including breakfast; Rs 250/400 on half-board.

Lalla Panzi (☎ 376411; fax 375633), at Anse aux Pins, is a small guesthouse run by a German/Seychellois couple. It's also good value for money, with singles/doubles for Rs 220/280 with breakfast. Meals are not provided. The Zulu name was given to the establishment by a previous South African owner.

La Roussette (☎ 376245; fax 376011) is on the other side of the road, at the end of a lane. Single/double/triple rates are Rs 440/575/710 (B&B), or Rs 550/825/1100 (half-board).

Reef Hotel & Golf Club (☎ 376251; fax 376296) is one of the more established hotels on Mahé, with a pool, tennis courts and a golf course opposite (open to nonresidents for Rs 80/100 for nine/18 holes, Rs 80 for club hire, trolley hire for Rs 15/20 for nine/18 holes. Residents of the hotel are charged half price. It tends to cater for budget package tourists. Rates for single/double/triple rooms are Rs 620/680/740 with breakfast; Rs 770/980/1190 on half-board. It has a jetty for boats and fishing, and sailboards for hire, but an unremarkable hotel.

Hotel Casuarina Beach (☎ 376211; fax 376016), further south, is a quiet and relaxing place with a colonial house as an annexe and a swimming pool. Rates for single/double/triple rooms start at Rs 380/580/760 and increase to Rs 510/840/1150 for half-board. The restaurant is open to nonresidents.

Auberge Bougainville (☎ 371788; fax 371808) is the last guesthouse south along the east coast in an isolated position. The service here gets mixed reports from travellers. This place is an old plantation house with seven atmospheric bedrooms upstairs, surrounded by a wooden verandah (rooms in the main house are best). The rooms to the front of the house overlook the sea. Single/double/triple rooms cost Rs 325/415/580 with breakfast; Rs 400/560/720 on half-board. The set menu costs Rs 90. Anse Bougainville and Anse Parnel are nearby for swimming.

Places to Stay – West Coast

Auberge d'Anse Boileau (☎ 376660; fax 376406), at Anse Boileau, is more noted for its restaurant, **Chez Plume**, than its guesthouse. The nine bedrooms, some in thatched units, surround the restaurant and singles/doubles/triples are Rs 300/380/455 including breakfast. Meals are an additional Rs 100 per person. The restaurant is open daily (only for dinner) and main dishes are around Rs 90. Nonresidents should book ahead.

Blue Lagoon (☎ 371197; fax 371565), at Anse à la Mouche, is a small complex of four self-catering bungalows, each with two double bedrooms, a kitchen and a lounge. There are boats available

for diving, as well as deep-sea fishing expeditions. Windsurfing and water-skiing are also provided to get you away from the retirement village surroundings. A bungalow costs Rs 6660 per week for four people; and Rs 590 per week for an extra bed for a child.

Villa Bambou (☎ 371177; fax 371108), next door to the Blue Lagoon, has just three rooms for around Rs 420/590 a single/double including breakfast. Meals are an extra Rs 90. This is a small, homey place.

Lazare Picault Hotel (☎ 361111; fax 361177), on the hillside overlooking the Baie Lazare, provides thatched accommodation for Rs 385/495 a single/double (B&B). You have to cross the road to get to the beach. There's a restaurant; the set dinner is Rs 150, while à la carte dishes are around Rs 80.

Chez Batista (☎ 366300; fax 366509), further south, rents out chalets costing Rs 350/500/785 a single/double/triple with breakfast; Rs 550/850/1050 on half-board. During the peak season (20 December to 15 January) the price creeps up to Rs 450/700/865 with breakfast; Rs 650/1050/1250 on half-board. The owner also runs a cute beachside restaurant (see Places to Eat).

Plantation Club (☎ 361361; fax 361333) is out towards Pointe Lazare, on the north side of the bay. This popular hotel has some 200 rooms and suites, and a casino (open to nonresidents). Comfortable singles/doubles go for Rs 970/1340 with breakfast; Rs 1140/1680 on half-board (from late December to early January prices rise to Rs 1570/1940 with breakfast; Rs 1740/2280 on half-board). There's a pool to splash around in, tennis courts and a diving centre.

Places to Eat – East Coast

Katiolo (☎ 376453), just past the airport at the dip in the road approaching Anse Faure, doubles at night as a disco. It cooks up Créole seafood but the place is, quite frankly, a bit of a barn.

Ty-Foo (☎ 371485), towards Pointe au Sel, is the southern equivalent of the Baobab Pizzeria for popularity and bargain meals. Here you can order Chinese and Créole cuisine such as sweet and sour fish (Rs 30), chicken curry (Rs 35) and lobster with salad (Rs 125). It has a separate bar and some billiard tables. It's open daily from 11 am to 2.30 pm and 6 to 10 pm.

Kaz Kreol (☎ 371680), near Anse Royale village, offers good Créole cuisine. Main dishes are around Rs 70. It's open only for lunch on Tuesday, Wednesday and Thursday (from 12.15 to 3.30 pm), and for lunch and dinner on Friday, Saturday and Sunday. It's closed on Monday.

SEYCHELLES

Places to Eat – West Coast

Anchor Café & Pizza (☎ 371289) is a basic place at Anse à la Mouche, at the southern end. It does cheap snacks such as grilled fish (Rs 24) and salads (Rs 20). It's open daily from 11.30 am to 9.30 pm; on Sunday it closes at 7 pm.

Oscar Au Capitaine Rouge (☎ 371224) is also at Anse à la Mouche, but at the northern end. It serves French cuisine and main dishes cost around Rs 150. It's closed on Wednesday.

La Sirène (☎ 361339) is just before you come to Michael Adams' studio, where the road turns inland. It has the simplest and most basic setting under thatch on the sand, but the Créole food is good. The cost of an average meal is Rs 120 to Rs 150, so there must be overheads somewhere. It's open daily only for lunch.

Chez Batista (☎ 366300), Anse Takamaka, is popular with beach bunnies in search of sustenance. This atmospheric, easy-going little hideaway is in a super position on the beach, with its own sandy floor. You can munch on stuff like grilled chicken with salad and chips (Rs 65), or fish curry with rice and Créole salad (Rs 65), while watching the wild waves. Or perhaps you might like to just sip on an espresso (Rs 12) while doing toe sketches in the sand. They also have a few chalets (see Places to Stay)

Le Reduit Restaurant (☎ 366116), on a small promontory overlooking the southern end of Anse Takamaka, also offers Créole cuisine. Main dishes start at around Rs 65 and it's open daily from 10 am to 11 pm.

STE ANNE MARINE NATIONAL PARK

There are six islands lying within the park a few km off Victoria. All are inhabited, except for Cachée Island, which is a nature reserve, but visitors are permitted to land only on Cerf, Round and Moyenne. Long Island houses a prison, and Île Ste Anne, the site of a National Youth Service camp, is off limits to visitors.

The snorkelling in the park is most impressive and highly recommended. Check out the audible underwater crunch of parrot fish chomping into coral and the inquisitive damsel fish.

Mason's Travel, TSS and NTA travel agencies run glass-bottom boat day trips to each island. NTA (☎ 224900; fax 225111) has a full day 'Starfish Excursion' to Ste Anne Marine National Park for Rs 410/250 per adult/child, including lunch on Cerf or Round Island and snorkelling gear. Only Mason's Travel con-

ducts tours to Moyenne Island (see Moyenne Island, following). For details about hiring your own boat from the Marine Charter Association see the Organised Tours section of the Seychelles Getting Around chapter. There are no ferry services.

Ste Anne Island

Ste Anne Island, the site of the first settlement on the Seychelles back in 1770, recently housed a National Youth Service camp. Visitors are not permitted to land, but there is a good snorkelling site off the southern coastline and an abandoned whaling station nearby.

A chess set belonging to settlers or pirates was found on the island several years ago and there were rumours about buried pirate treasure, but unlike the mysterious hoards at Bel Ombre, somebody is supposed to have surreptitiously swiped the lot about 20 years ago. There's also good snorkelling along the northeast coast.

Moyenne Island

Moyenne is said to be the best of the marine park islands to visit. It is owned by Brendan Grimshaw, a retired journalist, and is open to Mason's Travel tour parties. The Marine Charter Association can sometimes arrange tours to the island providing you give several days notice.

On the island you may be told about buried treasure and ghosts; and shown the ruins of the 'House of Dogs', a home built at the turn of the century by an eccentric Englishwoman as a refuge for stray dogs. There is a marked trail through the Moyenne's nine hectares – taken at a leisurely pace, the hike lasts about 45 minutes. Grimshaw has spent many years regenerating the fauna and flora. You'll come across many species of endemic Seychelles flora, including coco de mer, bwa de fer, the dragon tree and Wright's gardenia. The most noticeable animals are the giant land tortoises, the oldest two being 60-year-old Derek and 50-year-old Julia.

Moyenne also has a couple of excellent snorkelling sites and you can relax afterwards at the *Jolly Roger Bar & Restaurant*

DEANNA SWANEY

SARINA SINGH

Seychelles
Top: The gorgeous beach at Anse Source d'Argent, La Digue – the setting for the film *Crusoe*.
Bottom: Time passes slowly and life is relaxed on La Digue.

SARINA SINGH

SARINA SINGH

SARINA SINGH

Seychelles
Top: Perhaps the finest example of a tropical paradise in the Seychelles is at Anse Lazio, Praslin.
Bottom left: From palm leaf to sunhat, and proud of it too.
Bottom right: Seychellois woman from Mahé.

1 Old Whaling Station
2 Jolly Roger Bar & Restaurant
3 Chez Gaby; National Park
  Visitors' Centre
4 Prison
5 Turtle Beach Bar &
  Restaurant
6 Kapok

Underwater Viewing Areas

To Victoria

STE ANNE MARINE
NATIONAL PARK

Anse
Cabot

Grand
Anse

▲ 250m
Ste Anne

Anse
Manon

Jetty

Ste Anne Channel

▼ 2
Moyenne
Island

▼ 3
Round
Island

Long Island

4

5 ▼
Breakwater

6 ▼

Cerf
Island

108m

Cachée
Island

**Ste Anne Marine
National Park**

0   1   2 km

in a renovated Créole house. Main dishes cost around Rs 75.

Mason's Travel (☎ 322642; fax 225273) operates day tours to Moyenne for Rs 410/245 for an adult/child including lunch.

Round Island

This island, like Curieuse Island near Praslin, was once home to a leper colony. The chapel of the 80-year-old building is now occupied by the kitchen and bar of the *Chez Gaby* restaurant (☎ 322111). If Moyenne is the best island to visit, Round has perhaps the best restaurant – a Créole

culinary highlight for the Seychelles. Chez Gaby is run by the Calais family and is open for lunch daily except Monday and Friday. A meal for two costs around Rs 200.

Only the island ranger lives on Round; the Calais family have to commute daily from Cerf Island.

If you're visiting the restaurant, take a few minutes to follow the tree-shaded circle island track, and don't miss the national park visitors' centre just a few metres from the restaurant.

TSS (☎ 322414; fax 321366) has day trips to Round Island for Rs 410/245 per adult/child including lunch. This includes time for snorkelling and swimming. TSS also has a 'starlight serenade' cruise which visits Round Island in the evening for dinner and dancing (see Organised Tours, earlier in this chapter).

Cerf Island

About 40 people live on Cerf, including Wilbur Smith, the South African novelist, who occasionally visits his holiday home here. The *Turtle Beach Bar & Restaurant* (☎ 225536) offers a Créole buffet barbeque and salad bar lunch daily, except Monday, for Rs 150 per person. Dishes served in the buffet include octopus salad, grilled fish, kebabs, curries, stews and various chutneys. They provide a complimentary boat transfer and advance bookings are essential. There's also *Kapok*, a small restaurant on the same beach.

The island is popular for weekend excursions and you can either go there as part of an organised excursion with a travel agency or hire a boat from the Marine Charter Association. To give you an idea about costs, TSS (☎ 322414; fax 321366) charges Rs 410/245 per adult/child for a day trip to Cerf Island, including lunch.

THÉRÈSE ISLAND

Thérèse is the more interesting of the two islands on the north-west coast of Mahé (the other is known as Conception Island). It is uninhabited now, apart from the residents of an ancient cemetery. From the top of the small hill (160m) you can see across to the huge granite steps on Pointe l'Escalier, the southern head of Port Launay bay. One theory is that the steps were carved out for religious rites by Malay-Polynesians at about the same time they settled the Maldives, but before they reached Madagascar and the Comoros.

The island is privately owned and there is no hotel here. However there is a restaurant, the *Thérèse Island Restaurant* (no phone), which serves a Créole buffet for Rs 185 per person, including the boat transfer. You must book ahead through Mason's Travel

(☎ 322642; fax 225273). Thérèse is also a good snorkelling site, with a large lagoon on its north shore (you have to bring along your own snorkelling gear).

SILHOUETTE ISLAND

Romantics believe that Silhouette received its name because, from Beau Vallon, it appears in silhouette when the sun sets behind its high profile. Historians trace the name to that of a French minister. Watching the sunset from Beau Vallon beach is the pre-dinner thing to do. If the island looks dark and mysterious from Beau Vallon, the impression is confirmed upon landing and visitors have described it as 'eerie' and 'mystical'.

This large granite island, almost 20km from Mahé, rises steeply from around the shore up to three peaks, of which Mt Dauban is the highest (750m). The west side of the island is shielded by a reef that has a small break to allow boats to pass to and from La Passe. The protected waters are good for beach-bumming, swimming and snorkelling. Silhouette is under the control of the Islands Development Company, which is developing livestock and agricultural production on the island.

About 250 people live on the island, formerly the property of the Dauban family. The family mausoleum is at Pointe Ramasse Tout, near the main landing spot at La Passe. A few hundred metres south of Anse Lascars are the remains of what are believed to be Arab tombs, possibly of early shipwrecked seafarers.

Pirate Jean François Hodoul made the island his base – and again, there's gold in 'them thar hills', or so the tourist publicity would have you think. If you want to search, there are caves to explore. If nothing else, they contain stalagmites and stalactites.

Getting into and up to the centre of the island through the dense virgin forest is difficult and provides a good pioneering challenge for visitors.

Swimming Silhouette's best swimming beach is in front of the hotel, but it's a bit

1 Silhouette Island Lodge
2 Planter's House
3 Hospital
4 Copra Press
5 Cemetery
6 Dauban Tomb
7 Cemetery

Silhouette Island

0   1   2 km

shallow at low tide. Other high tide possibilities – although far from ideal – are at Anse Lascars and Anse Patate, both of which have large and chunky fields of coral on the bottom.

Anse La Passe Just south of La Passe village is an antiquated copra press in a shed.

Anse Mondon The route around the northeast end of the island runs from La Passe, north through the hotel grounds, past the odiferous poultry farm and over Belle Vue to Anse Mondon. There, you'll find a small

settlement and some reasonably sheltered snorkelling. Baie Cipaille is also meant to offer snorkelling opportunities. At Anse Mondon, you'll find a pineapple, guava and avocado farm/plantation which was abandoned because of rumours of haunting by phantoms.

Mont Pot à Eau Walk To visit the summit of magnificent 630m Mont Pot à Eau and see its namesake phenomenon, the bizarre carnivorous pitcher plant, will require the better part of a day. Wear light, cool clothing and carry some salty biscuits and lots of water –

you'll sweat a lot and will frequently have to replenish salts and liquids.

From the hotel, head into the village and past the school, where you'll take a very sharp right at the intersection of tracks (there's also a route connecting to this track just south of the bridge near the hotel but it's obscure and passes through peoples' gardens). Follow this track until it begins to lose altitude. There you'll find a concrete spur leading off to the left into a patch of grass. Turn here and follow this track to a T-junction, where you'll turn left again. The track then climbs steadily through patches of coconut trees and rainforest.

At about 200m elevation there's a fork in the track. The left fork will take you over the relatively easy traverse to Grand Barbe on the western shore. For Mont Pot à Eau, take the right fork. The track will continue to climb, crossing the Grande Rivière and passing a stand of coco de mer palms with immense fan-shaped leaves (for further information on the coco de mer, see Vallée de Mai in the Praslin chapter). Be careful not to tread on the monstrous millipedes, slugs and African snails that inhabit the forest floor!

At 400m elevation the track steepens and climbs to a 500m high crest, near which a track branches off to the right. It's reached by passing beneath an immense fallen log. The track climbs gently at first, then enters very thick vegetation where larger trees have fallen, and the resulting sunlight on the forest floor has allowed a profusion of undergrowth. The track disappears at times into dense vegetation; look for the machete blazes on larger trees. At one stage, hikers must balance on a series of slippery logs.

Where the vegetation begins to thin out again, you'll gain a minor summit. From there look around to your right for a faint track leading downhill, across the valley which separates you from Mont Pot à Eau. Once you find the track, it's fairly easy to reach the summit of Mont Pot à Eau; the track loses 50m of altitude, traverses a small saddle and then climbs steeply to the summit.

Once you've reached the summit, with pitcher plants blooming all around, look for

a small boulder on your right. The track on the other side of this boulder leads to the best view down to the hotel and across the southern half of the island. If it's clear, from the opposite side of Mont Pot à Eau's summit you can see the spectacular summit of 750m Mt Dauban.

Guides from the hotel, who work for the Seychelles development corporation, are technically free but you can tip them whatever you feel they're worth. Don't attempt this trip for at least two days after heavy rain; much of the way is over red clay and it can be impossibly slippery, especially on the steep bits.

Grande Barbe The best route to Grande Barbe is the relatively easy southern route over the mountain, which takes about three hours one way from La Passe. For access, see the description under Mont Pot à Eau. From Grande Barbe, a rough track continues north to the foot of Grand Machabée, a rocky outcrop, but since camping is illegal, you'd have to get a very early start in order to get there and back in a single day.

There's no coastal route around the northern part of the island, as is marked on many maps, although you can cross to Anse Mondon via an inland route past Mare aux Cochons.

Place to Stay

Silhouette Island Lodge (☎ 224003; fax 344178) is the only place to stay. It has 12 bungalows and charges Rs 1150/1700 a single/double (full-board) in a standard bungalow (this price increases in the Christmas/New Year period). Some of the bungalows are not beside the sea – be sure you specify your choice. In the restaurant, barred ground doves exasperate the staff and charm guests by ambling over the tables and filching rolls from breakfast tables. In the evening, fruit bats squabble and crash around in the palm trees above. Although the food is good, the bungalows are overpriced in relation to the facilities on offer.

Getting There & Away

You can get to Silhouette Island by helicopter from Mahé for Rs 840 per person (return). arrangements should be made with the Silhouette Island Lodge (see Places to Stay).

Alternatively you can join a tour, arrange a package deal with the hotel, or find your own boat (see the Charters section in the Seychelles Getting Around chapter).

The coral reef makes for tricky access to the island. Once their boat has arrived inside the reef, visitors are ferried to shore in Zodiac dinghies.

Contact a tour operator to find out about trips to Silhouette. The boat leaves Victoria at 9.30 am and returns around 4.30 pm. From Victoria, the trip takes 1½ hours by fast launch and three hours by schooner. The crossing from Beau Vallon to Silhouette takes around 45 minutes by fast launch or two hours by schooner.

To organise your own trip, ask at Marine Charter Association (☎ 322126; fax 224679), or make arrangements with the fishermen. If agreeable, they should take you across for around Rs 90, if time, tide, wind and sea conditions are suitable. Make arrangements around 4 pm the day before you want to go.

SEYCHELLES

Praslin

HIGHLIGHTS

- Anse Lazio beach – glorious white, soft sand and lively waves
- Salazie and Pasquiére Tracks, excellent for walking
- Exploring the nearby islands by boat, especially Cousin Island
- Vallée de Mai, a fascinating prehistoric forest

Praslin, the second largest Seychelles island, is about 35km north-east of Mahé. It is 12km long, and 5km across at its widest point. Lazare Picault, the French navigator, named it Île de Palme (Palm Island) when he stepped ashore in 1744. In 1768, just before the first settlement on Ste Anne Island, a stone of possession was set up at Anse Possession, across from Curieuse on the north of the island. It was renamed in honour of the Duc de Praslin, a French minister of state, who was later guillotined.

The island, like Mahé, has a granite mountain ridge running east-west down the centre. The highest point is Praslin Island Peak (367m), which marks the edge of the island's main attraction, the Vallée de Mai, home of the unique coco de mer palm.

The 5000 inhabitants are scattered around the coast in a series of small settlements. Anse Volbert, Grand Anse and Baie Ste Anne are the main communities. Ferry schooners from Mahé arrive at the latter two.

The pace of life on Praslin is much slower than on Mahé. There is little traffic and no towns. Praslin has a more lush and lazy flavour than Mahé and truly epitomises a tropical paradise. This island is very popular with tourists, and as demand for accommodation often exceeds supply, you'd be wise to book well ahead.

Information

Tourist Office There's a small tourist office (☎ 233346) at the Praslin airport terminal, which provides basic information about the island. It can also help with accommodation bookings. The office is open Monday to Friday from 8 am to 2 pm and 3.15 to 4 pm; on Saturday from 8 am to noon.

Money There are a number of banks where you can change money. Barclays Bank has branches at Baie Ste Anne (☎ 232218) and Grand Anse (☎ 233344). The branch at Baie St Anne is open Monday to Friday from 8.30 am to 2.30 pm and on Saturdays from 8.30 to 11 am. The branch at Grand Anse is open Monday to Friday between 9 am and noon and 1 and 3 pm; on Saturdays from 9 to 11 am. There's a Banque Française Commerciale (☎ 233940) at Grand Anse, which is open Monday to Friday from 8.30 am to 3.30 pm and on Saturday from 9.30 to 11.30 am. Also at Grand Anse is the Seychelles Savings Bank (☎ 233810), which is open Monday to Friday from 8.30 am to 2.30 pm and on Saturday from 9 to 11 am.

You can prepay your airport departure tax of Rs 100 at Barclays Bank in Baie Ste Anne.

Post The main post office (☎ 233212) on Praslin is next to the police station at Grand Anse. It's supposed to be open Monday to Friday from 8 am to noon and 1 to 4 pm, but sometimes closes by 3 pm. Poste restante is here, which holds letters for up to three months (free service).

Travel Agencies The main travel agencies on Praslin are Mason's Travel, National Travel Agency (NTA) and Travel Services Seychelles (TSS). All are centrally located at Grand Anse, and all offer an array of excursions to various islands (see individual islands for details). Mason's Travel (☎ 233211) is open Monday to Friday from 8 am to 5 pm and on Saturday from 8 am to 1 pm. NTA (☎ 233233) is open Monday to Friday from

8 am to 4 pm and on Saturday from 8 am to noon. TSS (☎ 233441) is open Monday to Friday from 8 am to 4 pm and on Saturday from 8 am to noon.

Medical Services See Health in the Seychelles Facts for the Visitor chapter.

Dangers & Annoyances Refer to the Seychelles Facts for the Visitor chapter.

Vallée de Mai

Praslin's Vallée de Mai has the Seychelles' greatest concentration of coco de mer palms – an estimated 4000 (see the Coco de Mer boxed text following). This World Heritage listed valley is a prehistoric forest and home to a number of unique plants.

Other interesting plants in the Vallée de Mai are the wild (red) pineapple, wild coffee and the allspice bush, which produces a sort of variety pack of spices used in Créole cooking.

The palms consist of the palmiste, latanier, splayed traveller's palm and Chinese fans. Their collective fronds provide a designer's or artist's dream: the way the sunlight filters through the forest ceiling and hits the various greens and oranges of the leaves is really something. You can appreciate the wonder of Michael Adams' paintings more after you've been to the Vallée de Mai. Also look out for the Seychelles black parrot which, like the coco de mer, exists only on Praslin.

There are a number of paths you can find yourself without going through the entrance gate, but they are not as beautifully staged as the official ones. You can also see a little waterfall on the road to Grand Anse, just past the car park. A sign says no swimming, bathing or drinking, but you wouldn't want to anyway.

Together with their admission ticket, visitors are given a 'nature trail' guide with notes on most trees and plants. One of them is called the 'dumb cane' because it produces a toxic juice which can cause paralysis of the tongue and throat muscles. It was said to have been used to punish slaves who talked back to their masters. Mme Raville Lesper-

ance, of the Orange Tree Guest House, said it was later used on mothers-in-law!

The Vallée de Mai is open daily from 8 am to 5.30 pm. Entry costs Rs 40 – admission is free for children under 12 years old. There is a small souvenir shop at the entrance gate which sells soft drinks, T-shirts, postcards, books etc.

Vallée de Mai is a unique and rare nature reserve – treat it with the respect that it deserves. Walk only on the marked paths to avoid damaging small plants and animals; do not remove anything from the forest; do not touch the plants or animals – scratching a coco de mer stem can result in infecting the tree; do not drop any rubbish and pick up any litter you may stumble across. The management also requests that visitors do not smoke as fire is a real danger to this forest.

Beaches

The best beach on Praslin (indeed one of the best in the Seychelles) is Anse Lazio, 6.5km from Anse Volbert on the north-west side of the island with glorious white, soft sand, a few rounded granite boulders and a lively line-up of waves. The water is a magical turquoise colour. There's also a more sheltered area with good snorkelling opportunities at the rocky ends of the bay. You should definitely pay a visit to Anse Lazio – the best chance of getting the beach to yourself is in the early morning. It attracts more people in the afternoon and more locals on the weekend. Where the road arrives at the beach, there's a terrific restaurant called Bon Bon Plume (see Places to Eat).

At the time of writing, there were two daily buses which travel direct to Anse Lazio, at 9.20 and 11.40 am. They return at 12.35 and 4.45 pm. Double check these times as they may have changed by now; the bus inquiries number is ☎ 233258. If you want to get to the beach earlier, or stay later, you'll have to hire a taxi (expect to pay around Rs 125 for the one-way trip from Grand Anse). En route, the beaches at Anse Boudin and Anse Takamaka (not to be confused with the beach of the same name on the

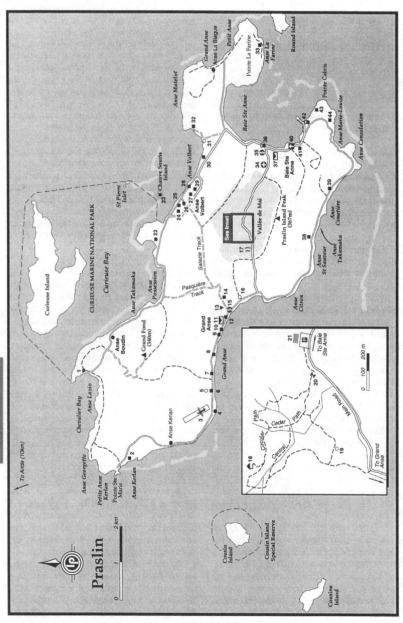

Praslin

SEYCHELLES

south coast of Praslin) are also inviting. Around Anse Lazio is the only bit of Praslin not shielded by a coral reef.

The quality of Anse Lazio is consistent, but not so for other island beaches. For half the year (May to September), the north coast beaches around Anse Volbert are better than those on the south coast around Grand Anse, while the opposite is true from October to April.

The long stretch of beach in front of the Paradise Sun Hotel and Berjaya Praslin Beach Resort at Anse Volbert is good for sunbaking and bumming about. The whole beach, in fact, is called the Côte d'Or (Gold Coast). The lagoon is shallow and a bit like a bath at times. Walk or wade out to Chauve Souris Island and try snorkelling around there.

On the south coast, the reef is much further out and the beaches tend to be less attractive. There are good beaches in the north-west region around Anse Georgette, Petite Anse Kerlan (one of the locations for the film *Castaway* with Oliver Reed) and Anse Kerlan, and to the extreme east at Anse Consolation and Anse Marie-Louise. There is a nice tide pool and small beach at Anse Marie-Louise where the road winds uphill and

inland. Buses from Anse Kerlan village go past Anse Consolation.

Anse Georgette is wilder than Anse Lazio and very remote. To get there from Anse Lazio, walk 2.5km south along an overgrown path which runs parallel to the coast. It's also accessible from the south via the track leading north from Anse Kerlan.

St Pierre Islet

Also good for snorkelling and some sloshing around are the waters around the tiny St Pierre Islet, about 1km seaward from Chauve Souris Island. Boat trips organised by hotels such as the Paradise Sun Hotel and private operators cost around Rs 45 per person.

Grand Fond

The road from Anse Boudin up to 340m Grand Fond hill, the second highest summit on Praslin, can be done by car or Mini Moke, but is nicest on foot. The reward is a fine view across Praslin and the surrounding islands and if you've managed to push a bicycle all the way to the top, you're in store for a great run down. Alternatively, descend along the track which heads south from

PLACES TO STAY					
2	Islanders	27	Berjaya Praslin Beach Resort; Berjaya Pizzeria	4	National Travel Agency (NTA)
6	Villas de Mer			5	Travel Services Seychelles (TSS)
7	Hotel Maison des Palmes	28	Village du Pêcheur	11	Main Post Office; Police Station; Jetty
8	Hotel Marechiaro	29	Laurier Guest House		
9	Indian Ocean Fishing Lodge	30	Acajou	15	Barclays Bank
		32	L'Archipel	16	Mason's Travel
10	Beach Villa Guest House; Coco de Mer Souvenir Boutique	33	Emerald Cove Hotel	17	Waterfall
		38	Villa Flamboyant	18	Shelter
		39	Coco de Mer; Hibiscus	19	Viewing Lodge (collapsed)
12	Cabane des Pêcheurs; Banque Française Commerciale	41	Orange Tree Guest House	20	Entrance Gate
		43	Colibri	21	Vallée de Mai HQ
		44	Château de Feuilles	31	Casino Des Îles; Tante Mimi
14	Britannia			34	Hospital
22	La Réserve	PLACES TO EAT		35	Barclays Bank
23	Chauve Souris Island Lodge	1	Bon Bon Plume	36	Lost Horizon Bar
		13	Steve's Café	37	Post Office; Police Station
24	Paradise Sun Hotel	OTHER		40	Baie Ste Anne Catholic Church
25	Café des Arts	3	Airport Terminal Tourist Office		
26	Duc de Praslin			42	First & Last Bar

SEYCHELLES

Coco de Mer

When General Gordon, of Khartoum, did a reconnaissance of Praslin in 1881 and wandered through the Vallée de Mai, which lies between Baie Ste Anne and Grand Anse, he thought he had discovered the original Garden of Eden. He devised a coat of arms for the then-British colony of the Seychelles in which a coco de mer palm stood on the back of a giant tortoise. Around the palm a snake was entwined, signifying Eden. The republic has retained the coat of arms, but the snake has gone.

The coco de mer, Gordon believed, was the tree of good and evil knowledge used to test Adam and Eve. Its fruit, he wrote, 'externally represents the heart, while the interior represents the thighs and belly, which I consider as the true seat of carnal desires...'

When these amazing nuts originally reached other continents, they were thought to have come from large submarine trees. Hence the name coco de mer (sea coconut). They inspired several different legends and theories when they were washed up on the shores of Indonesia, Sri Lanka, Malaysia, India, the Maldives, Mauritius and other countries. The Indonesians thought the tree might be the home of the mythical

Coco de Mer nut

garuda bird and the Indians attributed healing powers to the nuts. Several of the nuts were made into drinking vessels, decorated in gold and silver, by European rulers and now lie in various museums, including the British Museum.

Because of the female nuts' voluptuous feminine shape, some people believed they had aphrodisiac qualities. The elders of Praslin still hold that they do, if you soak the kernel of the nut overnight and boil it for drinking.

To add to the erotic reputation of the tree, propagation only takes place when the female tree, which bears the nuts, is close to the male tree, which has a long, brown, dangling catkin that resembles a you-know-what. Local folklore is full of stories about people actually seeing or hearing the trees mate, and being cursed for looking! Actually, insects or the wind are responsible for pollinating the trees.

The coco de mer palm grows naturally only on Praslin, Silhouette and Curieuse islands. It is one of about nine varieties of palms and screw pines growing in the Vallée de Mai. The palm only starts to bear fruit after 25 years, and then it takes seven years for a nut to mature. The trees can then live up to 1000 years. Some of the ones in the Vallée de Mai national park are about 30m high and around 800 years old. In the park you'll see many hollow 'bowls' in the ground; these are the sites of dead palms and can last 60 years after the tree has fallen.

There are approximately 4000 palms in the Vallée de Mai. The female palm produces about 20 fruits, of which three to five reach maturity. They each weigh around 20kg, making them the heaviest fruit in the world. The harvesting of the coco de mer nuts is strictly controlled by the government. Some of the younger, green nuts are eaten after they are a year old. The mature ones sell for Rs 1500 and upward.

One of the best places to buy one is at the *Coco de Mer Souvenir Boutique* (☎ 233831), Grand Anse, which is open Monday to Saturday from 9 am to 5 pm. Cut in four, the nuts make good serving bowls. Cut in half, sideways, they can be turned into fruit baskets. See Things to Buy in the Seychelles Facts for the Visitor chapter for further information. ■

Grand Fond and hits the south coast at the Catholic church.

Pointe Cabris

This rocky headland, on the south-east tip of the island, is owned by a wealthy French man. The ruined house overlooking the sea and steps stands testimony to a romantic but rough existence. You get there by taking the track down to the sea immediately before the

Château de Feuilles lodge. However, the owners of the lodge do not encourage visitors strolling round the gardens or stopping en route for picnics.

Walking Routes

There are two long and leisurely forest tracks which traverse the island. The 5km Salazie Track runs from Anse Volbert village to Grand Anse village, and the 3km Pasquière

Track connects Anse Possession on the north coast with Grand Anse on the south coast.

There are also a couple of 'unofficial' walking routes around the perimeter of Vallée de Mai. The most interesting is probably the ascent of 367m Praslin Island Peak, the highest point on the island. The route is a traverse which begins 800m inland from Baie Ste Anne and follows the park boundary to Nouvelle Découverte Estate near Grand Anse.

Near the end of the south coast road at the westernmost point of the island, a track takes off over the hill to the coast at Chevalier Bay, then turns east and continues all the way to Anse Lazio. From Anse Kerlan to Anse Lazio is about 5km and takes less than two hours.

For good views of Round Island and La Digue, follow the road from the northern end of Baie Ste Anne 2km east to the shore at Anse La Blague. Continue on foot east along the shore past Petit Anse, then up the hill and through the village toward Anse La Farine. The path is overgrown to begin with, but it clears near the summit. Local people are happy to help with directions.

Activities

For details about water activities, such as diving, snorkelling and deep-sea fishing, see under Activities in the Seychelles Facts for the Visitor chapter.

Organised Tours

The major tour operators offer similarly priced excursions and can also organise car hire, boat charters, water activities and general travel arrangements. Some of the tours on offer are described below – keep in mind that prices may have gone up by now. For office hours see Travel Agencies, earlier in this chapter.

Mason's Travel (☎ 233211) offers an assortment of tours including a full-day bus tour of Praslin (Rs 225/105 per adult/child including lunch); a half-day tour of Vallée de Mai (Rs 135/60 per adult/child); a full-day tour of Praslin and La Digue (Rs 410/200 per adult/child with lunch). A day tour of La Digue with lunch is Rs 315/200 for adults/children.

Travel Services Seychelles (TSS) (☎ 233441) offers a 'Garden of Eden' 1½-hour tour of Vallée de Mai (Rs 135/60 for adults/children), and a 'Highlights of Praslin' day tour for Rs 225/105 per adult/child. They also conduct a day trip to La Digue including lunch (Rs 315/200 for adults/children). For a tour of Vallée de Mai and La Digue, you'll pay Rs 410/200 per adult/child. They can also arrange walking tours of Praslin (upon request).

Another option is the National Travel Agency (NTA) (☎ 233233) which charges Rs 135/75 for an adult/child for an excursion of Vallée de Mai; Rs 320/160 per adult/child for a day trip to La Digue with lunch; and Rs 420/215 per adult/child for a trip to La Digue and Vallée de Mai, including lunch.

For trips to Cousin, Curieuse and other islands, see the relevant sections later in this chapter.

Places to Stay

Over recent years there has been a steady increase in the number of hotels and guesthouses, to satisfy tourist demand. However, this has not resulted in 'bargain' prices. Praslin is preferred over Mahé by many tourists, so demand for accommodation is high. To avoid disappointment, book your hotel accommodation well in advance (especially during the high season), or risk being left with little choice or missing out altogether.

Places to Stay – bottom end If you're watching your budget then the following places may appeal.

Orange Tree Guest House (☎ 233248), perched on a hilltop above Baie Ste Anne, is reached via a steep and winding track. It is run by Mme Raville Lesperance and has five simple rooms for Rs 200/300 a single/double, including breakfast. No other meals are available. The atmosphere is traditional and homey – Mme Lesperance's English can be challenging! This place is nothing fancy, but good if you're on a shoestring budget.

SEYCHELLES

Colibri (☎/fax 232302) is a tranquil retreat tucked away on Pointe Cabris. Run by Daniella and Robert Maurer – Robert is Swiss and once worked for Swissair – Colibri has nine comfortable rooms overlooking Baie Ste Anne. Standard rooms (doubles only) cost Rs 450 with breakfast; Rs 600 on half-board. For a treat, there are superior rooms for Rs 500 with breakfast; Rs 650 on half-board. Although the Colibri's setting is picturesque, it fronts a rocky coastline.

Cabanes des Pêcheurs (☎/fax 233320) offers five tidy bungalows on the beach. The bungalows are close to the pier in Grand Anse. Rates for single/double/triple occupancy are Rs 350/400/450 including breakfast; Rs 425/550/625 on half-board. Meals are served in the rather kitsch restaurant. The owner, José, is planning to open some upmarket self-catering apartments, which are expected to cost around Rs 800 (double occupancy) with breakfast. Speak to José for more details.

Beach Villa Guest House (☎ 233445), nearby, is run by Mr Auguste Confait. He has nine rooms which cost Rs 275/375/475 for single/double/triple occupancy, including breakfast. Mr Confait can also arrange trips to Curieuse or St Pierre Islet.

Indian Ocean Fishing Lodge (☎ 233324; fax 233911), also in this area, was being vigorously renovated at the time of writing and should be open by now. Singles/doubles are expected to cost around Rs 700/800 with breakfast; Rs 800/1000 on half-board. Facilities will include a pool and restaurant.

Britannia (☎ 233215; fax 233944), close to the church in Grand Anse, is a whitewashed guesthouse and restaurant. The location is not crash hot, but the rooms are pleasant and the restaurant is good. Prices for a single/double/triple room are Rs 400/480/580 including breakfast. Air-con rooms go for a cool Rs 500/580/680 with breakfast. Meals cost an extra Rs 100.

Villas de Mer (☎ 233972; fax 233015) is a complex of six self-catering chalets, each with a separate verandah. Prices for single/double/triple occupancy are Rs 330/440/550 with breakfast; Rs 400/550/700 on half-board. A barbeque area is available for grill parties. The owner, Michel Gardette, runs Aldabra Cruise Pty Ltd & Aqua Diving Services, which offers yacht charters and diving trips – for full details refer to the Charters section in the Seychelles Getting Around chapter.

Villa Flamboyant (☎/fax 233036), in a serene and secluded setting by the beach, is a lovely place to stay and warmly recommended by many travellers. Owned by the hospitable Cresswell family, this homey guesthouse has comfortable singles/doubles/triples for Rs 500/660/900 (half-board). Meals are taken together at the long dining room table. There are plans to also open

some self-catering chalets. Ask Verney Cresswell (a keen English artist) to show you his paintings, created in the villa's relaxing art studio. Ecotourism is high on the Cresswell's agenda – a refreshing change in today's commercially-driven world.

Laurier Guest House (☎ 232241; fax 232362), in the centre of Anse Volbert, is a guesthouse and bungalow complex with three rooms and two chalets. Rates for a single/double room are Rs 300/400 – the single rate only applies if you stay longer than one night. The rate for double occupancy of a chalet is Rs 450 – no discount for single occupancy (maximum of three people). The complex includes a restaurant.

Duc de Praslin (☎ 232252; fax 232355), nearby, is a similar complex containing three chalets, eight rooms and a restaurant. Rates for single/double occupancy are Rs 500/580 (B&B); Rs 650/780 (half-board). This place is not right on the water, but very close to a good beach.

Café des Arts (☎ 232170; fax 232155) is in a pleasant setting by the beach and is a hotel, restaurant and art gallery all in one. The rooms (all doubles) cost Rs 700 (B&B). Meals are taken at the restaurant, which is open daily, except Monday, from 12.30 to 3.30 pm and 7.30 to 9.30 pm. Main courses at lunch cost from around Rs 50 to Rs 120; at dinner they're from Rs 90 to Rs 180. The art gallery exhibits paintings by artists such as Christine Harter (sold for between Rs 75 and Rs 600), and Michael Adams (for between Rs 1000 and Rs 3000).

Islanders (☎ 233224; fax 233154) is a complex set under coconut trees, which includes a restaurant, boutique, two self-catering chalets and four self-catering apartments. The owners, Miet and Patrick Godley, are happy to accommodate families with extra beds for children. Rates for single/double occupancy start at Rs 420/500 (self-catering); Rs 490/600 (B&B); Rs 600/800 (half-board). There are also two-bedroom apartments for Rs 800 per night; Rs 1000 (B&B) and Rs 1400 (half-board). There's a nice beach nearby.

Places to Stay – top end If luxury is more your style then there is no shortage of top end accommodation.

Berjaya Praslin Beach Resort (☎ 232222; fax 232244) has 79 rooms, a swimming pool, tennis court, the usual water activities and is near a good beach. The rates for a comfortable single/double/triple room are Rs 955/1000/1120 (B&B); Rs 1120/1330/1615 (half-board). If you feel like lashing out, there are also more luxurious suites. The service can be a little lacklustre at this hotel.

Chauve Souris Island Lodge (☎ 232200; fax 232130) is a five-suite lodge on a tiny island opposite Anse Volbert village. The charge is Rs 1200 per person per day, including all meals and some water activities.

Village du Pêcheur (☎ 232224; fax 232273), diagonally opposite the Berjaya Praslin Beach Resort at Anse Volbert, offers 13 good rooms. Rates for a pleasant 'beach' single/double are Rs 770/815 with breakfast; Rs 910/1060 on half-board. The 'garden' rooms are cheaper at Rs 640/695 (B&B); Rs 780/905 (half-board). The bar and restaurant are also open to nonresidents (see Places to Eat).

Paradise Sun Hotel (☎ 232255; fax 232019), at the west end of Anse Volbert beach, is a popular 80-room hotel on a very nice stretch of beach. A single/double/triple costs Rs 1300/1650/2200 on half-board only. It runs a range of excursions to nearby islands and has its own diving centre (see Diving in the Seychelles Facts for the Visitor chapter).

L'Archipel (☎ 232242; fax 232072) is at the other end of the beach. Good singles/doubles in the 24 well-spaced and well-situated bungalows cost Rs 1410/1500 with breakfast; Rs 1615/1910 on half-board (the rates increase from late December to early January). The hotel has lots of tropical vegetation, a secluded pool, can organise many water sports and is a delightful place to stay. There's a good restaurant that's also open to nonresidents (advance bookings essential). On some nights they have a special buffet; a fish buffet is Rs 205 per person.

Acajou (☎ 232400; fax 232401) is a fairly new complex of chalet-style accommodation made from South African acajou wood. Squeaky clean and comfortable singles/doubles/triples cost Rs 1140/1340/1600 (B&B); Rs 1340/1740/2140 (half-board). The price varies through the year, so make sure you ask when booking. Facilities include a swimming pool, bar and restaurant.

La Réserve (☎ 232211; fax 232166), at Anse Petite Cour, is a fine choice and is the closest hotel to the beautiful Anse Lazio beach (see Beaches earlier in this chapter for a description). It has three rooms in the main building, 14 bungalows, 12 villas and four suites. The single/double/triple rooms in the bungalows and villas cost Rs 1230/1450/1850 with breakfast (air-con is an extra Rs 100 per day). A half-board standard single/double/triple room is yours for Rs 1400/1800/2350; Rs 1500/2000/2650 on full-board. If you have an appetite for pure luxury, go for a suite – a double will set you back Rs 2300 (B&B), Rs 2650 on half-board and Rs 2850 on full-board. This hotel also has a very good restaurant that's open to nonresidents (with advance reservations).

Hotel Maison des Palmes (☎ 233411; fax 233880), on the beach at the western end of Grand Anse, is a wonderful place to stay – book well ahead as this place is a favourite with travellers. There is thatched bungalow-style accommodation with pleasant single/double/triple rooms for Rs 851/918/1046 (B&B); Rs 999/1212/1445 (half-board). There's a good restaurant (see Places to Eat). Facilities include a swimming pool, tennis court, pool table, table tennis and various water toys such as windsurfers and canoes. They also do boat excursions – see Charters in the Seychelles Getting Around chapter.

Hotel Marechiaro (☎ 233337; fax 233993) is also at the western end of Grand Anse, but is not as impressive as the Hotel Maison des Palmes. Rates for single/double/triple occupancy are Rs 1180/1430/1730 (B&B); Rs 1350/1770/2240 (half-board). More salubrious deluxe rooms cost Rs 2150/2540 a double/triple (B&B); Rs 2490/3010 (half-board). There's a pool, tennis court, restaurant and water activities.

Coco de Mer (☎ 233900; fax 233919) has 30 chalets set in gardens fronting the beach (the beach is not great though). Single/double rates are Rs 1040/1150 (B&B); Rs 1150/1400 (half-board). Rates rise from late December to early January. Hotel guests have free use of windsurfers, canoes, bicycles, tennis courts, gym and a pool. There are two bars and a good restaurant (see Places to Eat). Excursions to other islands can be arranged. The Savuka Diving & Fishing Centre is based here (Rs 250 per dive), and is also open to nonresidents. It also offers snorkelling, deep-sea fishing and boat charters.

Black Parrot Hotel (bookings through Coco de Mer hotel, above) has 12 exclusive rooms for Rs 1600/2000 on half-board. There's a swimming pool, bar and restaurant.

Château de Feuilles (☎ 233316; fax 233916), on the Pointe Cabris estate south of Baie Ste Anne, has rooms, apartments, bungalows, and suites at prices ranging from Rs 1000 for a double room, including breakfast, to Rs 2400 for four people sharing a suite, including breakfast.

Emerald Cove Hotel (☎ 232323; fax 232300) is an upmarket hotel in an isolated location. The hotel is reached by a short boat ride (included in the room tariff) which leaves from the Baie Ste Anne jetty. Singles/doubles cost Rs 1200/1400 including breakfast; Rs 1400/1750 on half-board. If you want a room with a sea view, it costs a bit more. Facilities include a swimming pool and restaurant.

Places to Eat

Most of the guesthouses and hotels on Praslin are open to nonresidents for meals (book ahead).

Bon Bon Plume (☎ 232136) is a palm-thatched restaurant ideally located by the delectable Anse Lazio beach (see Beaches earlier in this chapter for a description). House specials include fish, lobster and sorbets. Expect to pay from around Rs 100 to Rs 175 for a main dish; the set menu is Rs 155. It's open for lunch daily from 12.30 to 3 pm. From 10.30 am to 5.30 pm, you can get drinks here; a cold beer is Rs 15, orange juice is Rs 10 and a vanilla milkshake is a cool Rs 30.

Berjaya Pizzeria (☎ 232222), run by the Berjaya Praslin Beach Resort (see Places to Stay), is in a great position by the seaside at Anse Volbert, with its own sandy floor. It's popular with beach goers in search of a light lunch or dinner. This laid back place cooks up pizzas (around Rs 55) and pastas (around Rs 35). It's open daily from 12.30 to 10.30 pm – you can eat in or takeaway.

Village du Pêcheur (☎ 232224) (see Places to Stay), also at Anse Volbert, has a pleasant restaurant which is open daily to nonresidents. Lunch is served from 12.30 to 2.30 pm and dinner is from 7.30 to 9.30 pm. There are cocktails for around Rs 45, grilled fish for Rs 70, pasta for Rs 55 and desserts for around Rs 25. On Saturdays, there's a barbeque for Rs 150 per person. Book ahead.

Laurier Guest House (☎ 233241) (see Places to Stay), Anse Volbert, has a restaurant which serves Créole food. It opens for dinner daily from 7.30 pm; the set menu is Rs 90. They do lunch during the busy season only.

Hotel Maison des Palmes (☎ 233411) (see Places to Stay) has a charming restaurant which is open daily for lunch and dinner – there's a snack menu during the rest of the day. There's an à la carte menu at lunch (from noon to 2 pm) with main dishes from Rs 75 to Rs 120; fish curry in coconut milk is Rs 75 and coconut nougat is Rs 40. Dinner (from 7.30 to 9.30 pm) is a set menu which costs Rs 150 per person. On Wednesdays there's a grill night with music, and on Saturdays there's a Créole buffet with music – nonresidents may be admitted for a charge of Rs 150. Book ahead.

Britannia (☎ 233215) (see Places to Stay), at Grand Anse, does decent lunches and dinners. Main dishes range from Rs 70 to Rs 110; prawn curry is Rs 95, chicken curry is Rs 75, and pepper steak is Rs 95. It's open daily, except Sunday, for lunch (noon to 2 pm), and every night for dinner (7.30 to 9.30 pm). Ring ahead for a reservation.

Steve's Café (☎ 233215), near Britannia, is ideal for cheap eats on the run, with prices ranging from Rs 20 to Rs 45. You can also get soft drinks and ice cream. It's open Monday to Saturday from 8 am to 10.30 pm and you can eat in or takeaway.

Hibiscus (☎ 233900), at the Coco de Mer hotel (see Places to Stay), is open to nonresidents if they book ahead. Dinner costs Rs 180 per person.

Tante Mimi (☎ 232500), is a very swish restaurant above the Casino Des Îles (see Entertainment, following). It's open every night from 7.30 pm to 11 pm and has an à la carte menu specialising in seafood. It's the place to go for a full on splurge – be prepared to fork out around Rs 145 to Rs 225 for a main dish and around Rs 60 for a dessert.

Self-Catering Providing your own meals on Praslin will require a visit to the supermarket in Grand Anse or to the small stores in Grand Anse and Baie Ste Anne, which are stocked with a limited variety of imported tinned and packaged foods. To give self-caterers some idea about costs, a packet of spaghetti costs Rs 6, biscuits are from Rs 7, a loaf of sliced bread is Rs 7, milk is Rs 5 and a small packet of coffee is Rs 12. Fresh vegetables and fruit are hard to come by, as the people only tend to grow enough for their own needs.

Some stores have a selection of pastries and cakes for a few rupees. La Réserve hotel (see Places to Stay) has a little bakery which sells bread (Rs 7 per loaf); croissants and cakes are available on advance order.

You can meet the fishermen coming in near the police station at Baie Ste Anne. A horn announces their arrival.

Entertainment

Most of the large hotels have their own entertainment programs, usually on the weekend. Nightlife is pretty limited on Praslin and most people seem to like it that way.

Bars & Discos *First & Last Bar* (☎ 232344) is at the end of the pier at Baie Ste Anne and is a simple, down-to-earth joint, mainly a hangout for the locals. Run by Mr Gappy, it opens on Friday, Saturday and Sunday nights as a disco.

Lost Horizon Bar (☎ 232032) can be found at Baie Ste Anne. It also runs discos on Friday, Saturday and Sunday nights.

Casino *Casino Des Îles* (☎ 232500) is the major entertainment venue on Praslin and was opened in 1996. This grand casino is eager to attract customers, offering free transfers between your hotel and the casino. The slot machines are open daily from noon to 2 am, while the games rooms (blackjack, roulette, poker etc) is open from 7.30 pm to 3 am. There's also a small bar (open from noon to 3 am) where you can guzzle an icy beer (Rs 15), or stylishly sip a Cointreau on ice (Rs 20). Upstairs, there's a super snazzy restaurant (see Places to Eat, earlier). A late night snack menu is available downstairs; a club sandwich costs Rs 65. If you plan visiting the casino, smart casual dress is expected – no thongs, T-shirts or shorts.

Getting There & Away

Air The airport terminal is 3km from Grand Anse. See the Seychelles Getting Around chapter for flight details.

Boat You can get to the island by schooner from Mahé and La Digue. See the Seychelles Getting Around chapter for details of routes, times and prices for these schooner ferries.

Apart from the schooner ferries, all island-hopping, for example to Curieuse, Cousin, St Pierre and Aride is done by boat charter, either privately or through the hotels and tour operators. For more details, see the separate sections in this chapter for each of these islands.

The tour operators TSS, Mason's Travel, and NTA all have representatives on the island. Quite a few hotels conduct their own boat tours – for details see Charters in the Seychelles Getting Around chapter. For deep-sea fishing trips see Activities in the Seychelles Facts for the Visitor chapter.

Getting Around

Bus There is a decent bus service on the island; see the Seychelles Getting Around chapter for details.

Taxi Details about taxi services and prices are provided in the Seychelles Getting Around chapter.

Car Rental For car hire, try Solace Car Hire (☎ 233525), Prestige Car Hire (☎ 233226) or Austral Car Rental (☎ 232015). There are

petrol stations at Baie Ste Anne and Grand Anse. Car rental costs the same as on Mahé – see the Seychelles Getting Around chapter for details.

Bicycle Bikes are popular on Praslin and a fun way to get around. Some of the Praslin roads, however, can be heavy going on a bike, so you may get a bit saddle-sore after one day. You can rent bikes from Côte d'Or Bicycle Hire (☎ 232071), at the entry road to the Berjaya Praslin Beach Resort at Anse Volbert village. It rents out bikes for Rs 20/30/50 per hour/half day/full day; children's bikes go for Rs 20/40 for a half/full day. Special discounts are offered for long rentals; Rs 40/35/30/25/20 per day for three days/five days/eight days/two weeks/one month. Most hotels should be able to arrange bicycle hire for their guests or recommend a bike hire place.

Boat Most hotels, guesthouses and tour operators can arrange boat hire – Hotel Maison des Palmes (☎ 233411; fax 233880) is one possibility (see Charters in the Seychelles Getting Around chapter for details). You can also contact Mr Louis Bédier (☎ 232192; fax 232356), who operates regular boat excursions to neighbouring islands. Other good options include Michel Gardette's Aldabra Cruise Pty Ltd & Aqua Diving Services (☎ 233972; fax 233015), and Diving in Paradise (☎ 232148; fax 232244) – for full details see Charters in the Seychelles Getting Around chapter.

Walking A fabulous way of exploring this beautiful island is by foot. For details about various walks, see Walking Routes earlier in this chapter.

Travel Services Seychelles (TSS) (see Travel Agencies, earlier) can arrange guided walking tours of Praslin on request.

CURIEUSE ISLAND

This island, just 1.5km off the north coast of Praslin, was a leper colony from 1833 until 1965. The ruins of the leprosarium still stand

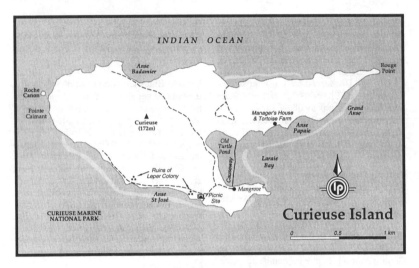

on the south coast around Anse St José, like rows of gutted pit cottages or an early holiday village.

At Anse St José itself, and still very much intact, is the old doctor's house, a Créole home with a spacious verandah looking across to Praslin. It has been declared a national monument by the government. It houses an information centre which is open daily from 9 am to 5 pm.

The only inhabitants of Curieuse at present are the island manager and his family, who live in a large house on Laraie Bay, and several park wardens. Roaming the island are a couple of hundred giant tortoises, each marked with a number and a yellow cross. Attempts to preserve and increase this colony of giant land tortoise introduced from Aldabra have been hampered by poaching. The island and surrounding waters are now an official marine national park and visitors are given a guided tour by wardens.

From the picnic site on Anse St José, you are guided over a rise and through a mangrove swamp before crossing the causeway to the manager's house.

There are some stunning granite rock sculptures en route. Look for the 'clash of the dinosaurs' at Laraie Bay and the 'pig' at Anse St José (where there is also a good beach). Beware of tiny blood-sucking seaweed gnats, which leave masses of spots on your legs.

There is also a track leading around the side of Curieuse hill (172m) to Anse Badamier on the north coast.

Getting There & Away

Most visitors to Curieuse arrive on a 'Three Islands' day trip (Cousin, Curieuse and St Pierre) organised by NTA (☎ 233233), Mason's Travel (☎ 233211) and TSS (☎ 233441). This trip costs around Rs 450 per person (almost half price for children) including lunch. For tour operators' office hours, see Travel Agencies earlier in this chapter.

COUSIN ISLAND

Approximately 1km in diameter and about 2km off the south-west coast of Praslin is Cousin Island, which used to be a coconut and cotton plantation, and is now one of the major highlights for visitors to the Seychelles – not to be missed! There's no hotel for tourists, but you can visit on a day trip (see Getting There & Away, following).

Noddies

Cousin hosts around 100,000 pairs of black (lesser) noddies during the south east monsoon. They prefer to nest in pisonia trees, but will make do with casuarina and other forest trees. At the height of the nesting season their smell pervades the island and their droppings drop so regularly that at this time of year you're strongly advised to wear a wide brimmed hat while walking the island's foot trails.

When mating season approaches, noddies go through an elaborate courtship ritual. The female bird sits in the tree where the nest will be built while the male carefully selects an appropriate leaf to use for building the nest. Having checked the leaf from every perspective he reverently hands it to his potential mate who disdainfully discards it. This process is repeated until a pile of discarded leaves litters the ground. Finally he hands her the right leaf, and she defecates on it! This leaf then forms the keystone of the nest, constructed from the previously discarded leaves cemented together with droppings.

The ritual far exceeds the quality of the resulting nest, however. No way about it, noddies build a shoddy nest. Into the shallow depression on this grotty little nest a single egg is laid and incubated for an average of 35 days. That is if the egg doesn't simply fall out of the nest. If that happens they just start all over again. Unfortunately chicks are also prone to falling out of the noddies' slipshod nest and in that case they, too, are simply abandoned. A storm during nesting time can wreak havoc upon a noddy colony.

Once the chicks are old enough to leave the nest they wander around in groups known as creches. During the day their parents venture far out to sea hunting small fish which swim close to the surface. When they return at night they call to their offspring, which recognise their parents' call and break away from the creche to be fed on regurgitated stomach contents. ∎

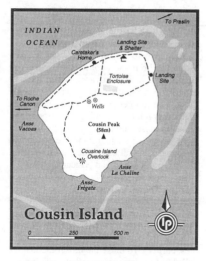

Cousin Island

The island was purchased by the International Council for Bird Preservation (now Bird Life International) in 1968 and turned into a nature reserve, which is supported by the World Wide Fund for Nature and the Seychelles government. It is the home of several endangered species, and it's also a breeding site for seabirds and turtles. It's an amazing experience to walk through thick forest with birds seemingly nesting on every branch. Undaunted by humans, birds create a constant flurry while gathering twigs, leaves and anything else that looks suitable for nesting material.

A small booklet, sold for Rs 3 on the island, explains the different species of birds, reptiles, insects and vegetation. There are thousands of skink and gecko, and plenty of guano. The rarest birds are the brush warbler and magpie robin. The most common birds are the black noddies.

You may also have the opportunity to see the *paille en queue*, or white-tailed tropic bird, at close quarters. This long-tailed bird graces the emblems of Réunion and Mauritius, but is not often seen on those islands. The island is also home to the oldest giant tortoise outside Aldabra, although Esmeralda on Bird Island also claims that distinction. Keep an eye open for George and Georgina, carapaces spotted with guano, who diligently plod after visitors in the hope of having their leathery necks stroked.

About six volunteer ICBP staff live on the island and take turns conducting guided tours. Roby Bresson, a lively local character, has spent much of his life on the island and has amassed a wealth of knowledge about the fauna and flora as well as a bunch of anecdotes. He walks with a slight limp, the result of almost losing a leg to an irate needlefish which he'd unintentionally rammed while windsurfing across to Praslin!

You have to go on a tour, which takes about 1½ hours at a comfortable rate. You cannot visit without advance notice and you cannot do your own thing when you get there. You can get close enough to the birds to photograph them nesting, but tripods and close-up lenses are not allowed.

At the end of the tour it may be possible to go for a dip, but official regulations forbid this. There are soft drinks and postcards on sale.

Getting There & Away

You can make arrangements to visit Cousin on a half day or full day tour through any of the hotels, or through TSS, Mason's Travel or NTA (for contact details see Travel Agencies, earlier). To make the most of Cousin, a full day tour is recommended, which costs Rs 395/210 for adults/children with lunch. A half-day tour costs Rs 315/170 (no lunch), or you can take a 'Three Island' (Cousin, Curieuse, and St Pierre) tour for around Rs 450 per person (about half price for children). Several tour operators also conduct trips from Mahé to Cousin – expect to pay around Rs 890/625 per adult/child, including lunch and transfers. A day trip to Cousin, Curieuse and St Pierre from Mahé will set you back around Rs 940/650 per adult/child, including transfers and lunch.

If you charter a boat or arrange a private visit, you will have to pay a landing fee of Rs 100 per boat. This fee is included in the price of group tours. In addition there is an admission fee of Rs 100 per person, also included in the cost of group tours. A private tour operator, Michel Gardette (☎ 233972; fax 233015), can arrange a day tour to Cousin for Rs 400 per person (daily except Sunday and Monday). It includes a guided tour of the bird sanctuary, a visit to Curieuse Island (where you have a barbequed fish and salad lunch) and a visit to St Pierre for snorkelling.

The boat ride from Grand Anse to Cousin takes about 15 minutes, but the landing sites vary depending on the time of the year. There is no jetty and often visitors have to be ferried from the launch to shore in a Zodiac dinghy. This can be amusing or harrowing, depending on the size of the swells.

COUSINE ISLAND

From the modest heights of Cousin you can see across to Cousine, a privately owned island which is not open to the public. The present owner is a South African millionaire who shelled out about US$5 million for the island.

ARIDE ISLAND

Aride Island lies 10km to the north of Praslin. The island was purchased for the Royal Society for Nature Conservation in 1973 by Christopher Cadbury (of chocolate fame).

Aride, the most northerly of the granite islands, rises to 135m and is partly surrounded by a coral reef. It has been declared a nature reserve, as it has the greatest concentration of seabirds in the area, including large colonies of lesser noddy, roseate terns and frigatebird (noted for its giant wing span). The strangely perfumed, white and purple-spotted Wright's

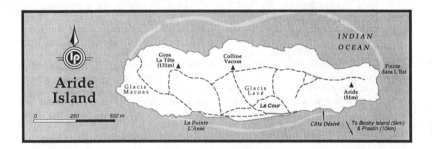

Wedge-tailed Shearwaters

While the noddies nest in trees, wedge-tailed shearwaters breed in burrows, from October to March. The male shearwaters return first to exactly the same burrow as in previous years, and clean things up in preparation for the arrival of their mates.

Shearwaters mate for life and when their companion, unseen for the past year, turns up all hell breaks loose. From dawn to dusk they shriek, wail, groan and howl to each other. The whole colony seems to get together on this and the noise builds up to an absolute crescendo then suddenly ceases. A single groan will recommence the whole symphony. It's said that sailors became convinced that certain islands were haunted. All night long this horrible, almost human-like noise would be heard, but come dawn the island would be found empty. The shearwaters had set out just before dawn to spend the day fishing.

Wedge-tailed shearwaters have a disproportionately large wingspan compared to their body size. This makes for easy flying but difficult takeoffs and landings. The birds have well-defined 'runways' where they line up to make their pre-dawn departure. When coming in to land, once they're committed on their final approach they have great difficulty in making changes of direction and have been known to collide with objects in their path.

A single egg is incubated for about 50 days and the chick is fed so energetically that it may eventually grow to be bigger than its parents! Then the parents abandon their offspring and fly off, leaving their well-fed chick to survive on its body fat, learn to fly and follow its parents. It's been suggested that shearwaters' lousy takeoff and landing abilities is not unrelated to the fact that their parents leave them to learn this vital skill by trial and error! ■

---

gardenia, grows nowhere else in the world and is also found here.

It can be reached by boat between April and October only. The rest of the year the winds and seas make landing difficult and dangerous on the island's southern coast, Côte Désiré. Problems with management and poor weather have hampered access for visitors.

Booby Island, just off the coast of Aride, is reputed to have received its name because of an anatomical resemblance! (Well, it might have been named for the bird...)

Getting There & Away

Between April and October, the larger hotels on Praslin and TSS, Mason's Travel, and NTA tour agencies run day trips several times a week. The price per person is around Rs 400 including lunch (children are charged about half price). If you want to visit from Mahé, the cost is Rs 890/625 per adult/child, including transfers and a barbeque lunch. Michel Gardette (☎ 233972; fax 233015) also conducts day tours to Aride, which cost Rs 350 per person including a barbeque lunch and snorkelling.

SEYCHELLES

La Digue & Other Inner Islands

HIGHLIGHTS

- La Digue Island, virtually unspoilt, an easy going tropical paradise
- Walk from La Passe to Grand Anse and, if you're feeling energetic, to Anse Fourmis
- Excellent diving, snorkelling and deep-sea fishing
- Bird Island, home for millions of feathery creatures

LA DIGUE

La Digue Island is truly beautiful and remains virtually unspoilt by either the local inhabitants, who number only around 2000, or the tourists, whose numbers remain low thanks to the sprinkling of hotels. If you thought the pace of life on Praslin was relaxed, you'll find La Digue even more easy going. It's a mellow place with friendly people and tremendous beaches – ideal for recharging your batteries. More and more travellers are discovering this paradise retreat, so getting a room can be tough at times – book well ahead. Alternatively, you can stay on nearby Praslin and visit La Digue on a day trip (see Boat in the Seychelles Getting Around chapter).

The island, which is only about 4km east of Praslin, was once a big coconut plantation. The main settlement stretches from the harbour area at La Passe down the west coast to L'Union.

The central granite ridge of the island reaches an altitude of 300m. Surrounding the island is a profusion of giant, naturally sculpted granite boulders which would do credit to Henry Moore. Together with the brilliant white sand, the azure sea and the greenery of the palms, the scenes are some of the most picturesque in the Seychelles.

Information

Tourist Office There's a tourist office (☎/fax 234393) in the Social Security building, near La Digue Island Lodge, however it may be shifting to near the pier. It provides all the usual tourist information, and stocks some glossy brochures and a map of the island. The office is open Monday to Friday from 8 am to noon and 1 to 4 pm; on Saturday from 9 am to noon.

Money Barclays Bank (☎ 234148) has a branch opposite La Island Lodge Hotel, next to Gregoire's. It is open on Monday, Wednesday and Friday from 10.30 am to 2 pm. There is also a Seychelles Savings Bank (☎ 234135), opposite the hospital, which is open Monday to Friday from 8.30 am to 2.30 pm and on Saturday from 9 to 11 am. You can change money at both banks.

Post The post office (☎ 234036) is next to the police station, near the pier at La Passe. It is open Monday to Friday from 8 am to noon and 1 to 4 pm. There is one mail collection per day. Although there is no official poste restante here, they will be happy to hold your letters with advance notice.

Travel Agency The only travel agent currently on La Digue is Mason's Travel (☎ 234227; fax 234266), near Gregoire's. The office is open Monday to Friday from 8 am to noon and 1 to 4 pm; on Saturday from 8 am to noon. They can arrange various activities including fishing trips, helicopter flights and inter-island trips – see Organised Tours later in this chapter.

Scenic Flights For information about scenic helicopter tours, visit the Helicopter Seychelles office (☎ 375400), which is located in the Social Security building. It's open daily from 9 am to noon and 2 to 5 pm. For more information see Helicopter in the Seychelles Getting Around chapter.

Library The National Library on La Digue is open Monday to Friday from 10.30 am to 4.30 pm and on Saturday from 9 am to noon.

Medical Services See Health in the Seychelles Facts for the Visitor chapter.

Dangers & Annoyances Refer to the Seychelles Facts for the Visitor chapter.

Beaches

On the south-eastern shore of La Digue are several white sandy bay beaches, swept by waves which have broken past the reef. Beware of dangerous undercurrents. A 3.5km road crosses the island from La Passe to Grand Anse, the largest and one of the busiest beaches – if you can call any place on La Digue busy. Look carefully and you may see the rock formation known as Le Roi Triste (sad king). To continue from there to the next cove, Anse Cocos, requires a little effort to find the path (a full description is given under Grand Anse & East Coast Walk later in this chapter).

Near La Passe, there is a nice path from L'Union down the coast to Anse Source d'-Argent. The track leads through variously shaped granite boulders – look out for the 'turtle's head' and the 'big fort' rocks – to the splendid beach at Anse Source d'Argent, the setting for many of the sets for the film

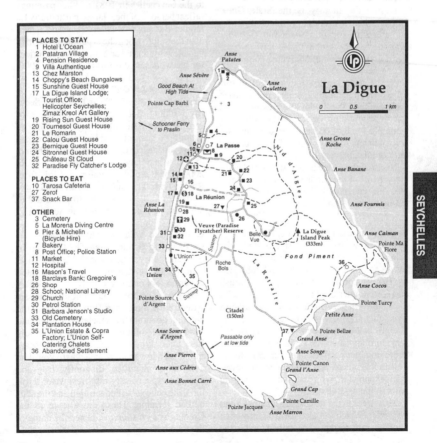

PLACES TO STAY
1 Hotel L'Ocean
2 Patatran Village
4 Pension Residence
9 Villa Authentique
13 Chez Marston
14 Choppy's Beach Bungalows
15 Sunshine Guest House
17 La Digue Island Lodge;
   Tourist Office;
   Helicopter Seychelles;
   Zimaz Kreol Art Gallery
19 Rising Sun Guest House
20 Tournesol Guest House
21 Le Romarin
22 Calou Guest House
23 Bernique Guest House
24 Sitronnel Guest House
25 Château St Cloud
32 Paradise Fly Catcher's Lodge

PLACES TO EAT
10 Tarosa Cafeteria
27 Zerof
37 Snack Bar

OTHER
3 Cemetery
5 La Morena Diving Centre
6 Pier & Michelin
   (Bicycle Hire)
7 Bakery
8 Post Office; Police Station
11 Market
12 Hospital
16 Mason's Travel
18 Barclays Bank; Gregoire's
26 Shop
28 School; National Library
29 Church
30 Petrol Station
31 Barbara Jenson's Studio
33 Old Cemetery
34 Plantation House
35 L'Union Estate & Copra
   Factory; L'Union Self-
   Catering Chalets
36 Abandoned Settlement

La Digue

0   0.5   1 km

Anse Patates
Anse Sévère
Good Beach At High Tide
Pointe Cap Barbi
Schooner Ferry to Praslin
Anse Gaulettes
La Passe
Anse Grosse Roche
Anse Banane
Anse La Réunion
La Réunion
Veuve (Paradise Flycatcher) Reserve
Anse Fourmis
Belle Vue
La Digue Island Peak (333m)
Anse Caiman
Pointe Ma Flore
L'Union
Anse Union
Roche Bois
Fond Piment
Pointe Source d'Argent
Citadel (150m)
Passable only at low tide
Anse Cocos
Pointe Turcy
Petite Anse
Anse Source d'Argent
Grand Anse
Pointe Bellze
Anse Pierrot
Anse Songe
Anse aux Cèdres
Pointe Canon
Grand l'Anse
Anse Bonnet Carré
Grand Cap
Pointe Jacques
Pointe Camille
Anse Marron

SEYCHELLES

Crusoe. During high tide, the trail can be impassable.

Anse Patates in the north of the island must rate as one of the Seychelles' finest and most beautiful beaches, and further down the east coast is another magical stretch of beach at Anse Gaulettes.

L'Union Estate & Copra Factory

The estate management charges Rs 10 to visit the copra factory and grounds at L'-Union. L'Union estate is open daily from 7 am to 5 pm. The factory still operates between 7 am and 3 pm every day.

Beside the factory is the State Guest House, which is used for presidential guests, and was also a location for the film *Goodbye Emanuelle*. The grounds also have a boat-yard, a vanilla plantation, tennis court (free of charge, but no rackets or balls available!), several Créole houses and some giant tortoises which naturally live near a giant rock (you can feed these adorable creatures with the vegetation provided). Horse riding is available for Rs 100 per hour and there are some chalets to stay in (see Places to Stay, later in this chapter).

North of the estate is an old colonial cemetery. Most of the headstones are now illegible, but you can still make out a couple dating to the 19th century.

Veuve (Paradise Flycatcher) Reserve

This narrow strip of forest alongside the central road into the interior of the island serves as a bird sanctuary. It was established by British conservationists Tony Beamish and Christopher Cadbury.

The bird in question is the black paradise flycatcher *(Terpsiphone corvina)*, which the Créoles call the *veuve* (widow) because the male bird appears to be in mourning with its streaming black tail feathers. Endemic to the Seychelles, there are thought to be fewer than 50 pairs left, with just five or six nesting pairs in the reserve itself.

Most trees in the reserve are takamaka and badamier. Watch out also for frog, moorhen and the rare terrapin, described under the

Grand Anse and East Coast walk later in this chapter.

Entry to the reserve is free. There's an information centre near the entrance of the reserve which sells a leaflet for Rs 10 and arranges a guided tour (free). The centre is open Monday to Friday from 8 am to 4 pm, but the reserve is open daily.

Barbara Jenson's Studio

North of L'Union Estate & Copra Factory is Barbara Jenson's studio (☎ 234406; fax 376356), which is open daily from 9 am to 6 pm. Originally from England, Barbara came to the Seychelles in 1984 and her paintings reflect her love of the islands, particularly La Digue. Barbara is a lovely lady and if you visit the studio when she is painting, you may be able to observe her being creative. Prices for her work range from Rs 100 to Rs 8000.

Zimaz Kreol Art Gallery

This gallery (☎ 234322), in the Social Security building, houses a small collection of wildly colourful paintings by George Camille. It's an interesting place to browse, and if you want to take a painting back home, expect to pay anywhere from Rs 65 to Rs 2000. There are also some nice cards from Rs 2 to Rs 6. The gallery is open Monday to Friday from 9.30 am to 12.30 pm and 2 to 5.30 pm; on Saturday from 9 am to 1 pm.

Grand Anse & East Coast Walk

La Passe to Grand Anse The first part of the walk, between La Passe and Grand Anse, follows the road and may be negotiated either on foot or bicycle.

Begin by walking south out of La Passe. After a little more than 1km, just before the colonial government cemetery, bear left and head inland through the copra plantation. Less than 1km later, you'll reach the Mare Soupape, a low marshy area where you'll be able to see moorhen, dragonfly, frog and even a couple of very rare freshwater terra-pins, the yellow-bellied terrapin and the star-bellied terrapin. These are known to the Créoles as *torti soupape*, hence the name of the marsh.

Past the marsh, follow the bend around to the left, then to the right, and continue to a T-junction. Here, take a right and follow the road as it slowly climbs up and across the spine of the island. After less than 2km, you'll reach the east coast at Grand Anse, which is a great place for a picnic but isn't really ideal for swimming because of high surf and dangerous currents, although a lot of people do take a dip. The beach at Grand Anse is truly magical, with turquoise waters and a soft sandy beach. From Grand Anse there's a path which leads to a rocky hill.

At Grand Anse, you can either decide to return to La Passe the way you came or continue to Petite Anse, Anse Cocos and beyond. Remember to bring along sun protection (sunscreen, sunglasses, T-shirt), as there are not many shady places to park yourself. There is a small snack bar at Grand Anse (see Places to Eat).

You can get a lorry ride to Grand Anse for around Rs 40 (return) – ask someone at the pier for details. A one-way ride by taxi from the pier costs around Rs 60 – share with other people to split the cost. For something more economical and environmentally friendly, ride there by bicycle – be prepared for a few minor (but strenuous) ascents which will really test your fitness. It's worth the effort though – the beach is a dream. Walking is the other alternative.

Grand Anse to Anse Fourmis If you're going on, follow the prominent track north along the coast, past the marshy areas. It will then turn inland and climb a short steep route over a rocky ridge before descending to the beautiful Petite Anse. This has less tourists than Grand Anse, but like Grand Anse, the currents can be strong here too, making swimming hazardous (especially from around June to October). Nonetheless, it's a fantastic place to lie on the soft sand and watch the wild waves crashing on the shore.

From there the track continues slightly inland behind the front row of trees and scrub along the beach, emerging at a track intersection near the northern end of Petite Anse. Here, you should turn left and cross two small bridges into a cattle pasture. Beyond it is a small farmstead (to be avoided – the owners don't appreciate being asked directions!).

About 15m to 20m beyond the second bridge (into the cattle pasture), you'll see a very faint track leading off to the right and into a clump of trees. Once among the trees, the track becomes quite prominent – good solid stone steps – and climbs over another small, rocky ridge. Near the top of the ridge, you'll pass through a gate and descend along a very well-defined track.

At the foot of the hill it turns seaward and leads out to the shore at Anse Cocos. Follow the beach northward towards the cluster of abandoned buildings and old rotting wooden boats. This was once a lively spot and served as an agricultural enterprise as well as a storage and transport point for copra from surrounding plantations. At the northern end of Anse Cocos is an enclosed rock pool which provides a calmer dip than the strong waves on the open beach.

From here the route becomes rougher and more difficult so if you aren't up for an adventure, return to Grand Anse the way you came. Otherwise, continue to the end of the beach, but avoid the fairly obvious track leading out to the rocky point (keep seaward of the swamp of bulrushes) and search among the trees for the track which climbs to the summit of the ridge. Once you're on the track, it'll be obvious, but at times you may have to search around in the grass to locate the route. Once over the ridge, the track drops to an abandoned building at the south end of Anse Caiman.

Here, strike off through the vegetation along a very faint track leading north along the coast. Resist any temptations to venture inland, especially at a muddy area where the track seems to disappear. Instead, search in the boulders ahead; the route is marked by splotches of white paint, placed at intervals of about 5m. You'll have to scramble a bit, but the route is marked.

At the north end of Anse Caiman, you'll arrive at a formidable-looking barrier of granite boulders. The route from here across to Anse Fourmis is very difficult so don't attempt it unless you're an agile scrambler. The only possible route through is marked by splotches of white paint on boulders, and keeps to within about 10m of the sea (at high tide). Again, don't be tempted inland – there's no way across the ridge higher up! After about 150m of rock-hopping and scrambling on all fours, you'll arrive at Anse Fourmis and will see the road about 50m away, straight ahead.

If you're trying to reach this route from the north, don't follow the faint track leading uphill, inland from the end of the road; it's a dead end. Instead, walk straight ahead (parallel to the coast). You'll see an opening in the trees ahead and just beyond, the first white paint splotch (a very large one, like a bull's-eye) on the boulder marking the route's beginning.

La Digue Island Peak

To reach the highest point on La Digue, head up to 333m La Digue Island Peak in the centre of the island. Take the only road leading uphill from the main route near Château St Cloud and follow it to its end. From there, you'll find a track leading up to and along Nid d'Aigles ridge. A right turn at the ridge will eventually get you to the peak but the going can get tough and the view obscured because of the profusion of French plum trees. There are a few isolated properties in the area.

Activities

For details about diving, snorkelling and deep-sea fishing possibilities on La Digue, see Activities in the Seychelles Facts for the Visitor chapter. For information about horse riding, see L'Union Estate & Copra Factory, earlier in this chapter.

Organised Tours

Many hotels can arrange a tour of the island, as well as fishing trips (see also Activities in the Seychelles Facts for the Visitor chapter) and boat charters to other islands (see Charters in the Seychelles Getting Around chapter).

Mason's Travel (☎ 234227; fax 234266) (see Travel Agency, earlier) offers various tours (some on request). A two-hour guided tour of the island is Rs 115 per person. For tours to other islands, see individual islands later in this chapter.

Michelin (☎ 234043), the bicycle hire place near the pier, can organise a tailor-made lorry tour of the island – speak to them for details about the cost and itinerary.

For information about scenic helicopter tours, see Scenic Flights earlier in this chapter.

Places to Stay – bottom end

Places to stay on La Digue are limited and the island is becoming increasingly popular with travellers, so don't leave hotel/guest-house bookings to the last minute. Often there is a vacancy for a short time only. If you do get stuck, some of the small hotel owners have friends who can put you up temporarily (and unofficially) for around the same fee, but don't rely on that. Quite a few of the cheaper places are inland from the seaside, but as the island is small, it doesn't take long to get to a beach. However, if you just *have* to stay by the water, there are a few options – see accommodation locations on the La Digue map.

Château St Cloud (☎/fax 234346), inland from La Passe, is owned by Myriam St Ange and is a former plantation house which hasn't changed much since it was built. It has 10 comfortable rooms which go for Rs 250/400 a single/double with breakfast; Rs 300/500 on half-board. The atmosphere is relaxed and informal – buffet meals are eaten together at a long table. Boat excursions can be arranged, there are bicycles for hire (Rs 25 per day) and a pool was being planned at the time of writing. Check out the centenarian tortoises – crusty old guys!

Bernique Guest House (☎ 234229; fax 234288), just along the road from Château St Cloud, is run by Mme Jeanne Legge. The guesthouse has three rooms and nine bungalows. The three rooms cost Rs 175/250/350 for single/double/triple occupancy including breakfast; Rs 250/350/500 on half-board. Bungalow prices are Rs 310/420/540 a single/double/triple including breakfast; Rs 400/570/800 on half-board. The restaurant (see Places to Eat) serves hearty food and is a pleasant place to relax and watch vivid green geckos beside the lights patiently waiting for the arrival of their insect dinner.

Sitronnel Guest House (☎ 234230), just south of Bernique, is an unpretentious guesthouse run by Madame Adrienne. She offers four double rooms for Rs 300 with breakfast; Rs 400 on half-board.

Le Romarin (☎ 234115), just north of Bernique, is run by the jolly Madame Bailey. This very modest guesthouse has three rooms and the rate is Rs 150 per person with breakfast, or Rs 200 per person on a half-board basis. If you fall hopelessly in love with La Digue (as many indeed do) and decide to stay for a month, Madame Bailey offers a sympathetic deal – have a chat to her about it.

Tournesol Guest House (☎ 234155; fax 234364), nearby, has six plain but comfortable rooms set in three bungalows which cost Rs 250/450 a single/double with breakfast; Rs 350/560 on half-board. There's a pleasant restaurant (see Places to Eat).

Calou Guest House (☎/fax 234083), in the same area, has five rooms for Rs 400/500 a single/double on a half-board basis only.

Chez Marston (☎/fax 234023), not far from the hospital, is one of the cheapest places to stay – ideal if you're strapped for cash. Small, but neat rooms (all with a kitchenette and on a half-board basis) cost Rs 250/400 a single/double. There's a boutique which sells clothes, souvenirs and some toiletries.

Choppy's Beach Bungalows (☎ 234224; fax 234088), on the shore near La Passe, has various room categories – garden, sea-facing and beach. Rates (half board) for the peak season (late December to early January, late March to mid April, late July to late August and early October to late November) are Rs 605/755/965 a single/double/triple for garden rooms; Rs 700/825/1060 for a sea-facing room, and Rs 775/925/1190 for a beach room. The tariff drops by roughly Rs 75 to Rs 100 during the non-peak season. You can hire bicycles here for a rather steep Rs 25/45 per half/full day. They can also organise boat tours and diving trips. The restaurant is an open, thatched shelter near the shore which is open for lunch from noon to 3 pm and for dinner from 7 to 9.30 pm. There's a Créole buffet twice a week (ring to check when) which costs Rs 110 per person. Nonresidents should book ahead.

Sunshine Guest House (☎ 234033), not far from Choppy's Beach Bungalows, is nothing fancy, but fairly cheap. There are rooms with communal bath for Rs 190/280 a single/double including breakfast; Rs 275/450 on half-board. If you prefer singing in the shower without an audience, ask for a private bathroom, which costs Rs 300 a

double (breakfast/dinner is an extra Rs 40/85 per person).

Paradise Fly Catcher's Lodge (☎/fax 234015), at Anse Union, is a fabulous place to stay with its eight rooms set in four well spaced bungalows. Large, squeaky clean singles/doubles cost Rs 400/500 with breakfast; Rs 450/700 on half-board. There are two rooms per bungalow which share a common living room and fully-equipped kitchen. There's a restaurant (for residents only), which is open daily for lunch and dinner. At lunch only sandwiches are available (Rs 25 to Rs 35).

Pension Residence (☎/fax 234304), just north of the pier, has six self-catering two-bedroom bungalows for Rs 600 per night. An extra bed is Rs 100 and breakfast/dinner is available for Rs 40/80 per person.

Rising Sun Guest House (☎/fax 234017), inland from Anse La Réunion, isn't really wonderful value for money compared to other places in this price range. Singles/doubles with breakfast go for Rs 225/325; Rs 325/525 on half-board.

Villa Authentique (☎/fax 234413), inland from La Passe, is a very homey place run by a friendly couple, Bertine and James. This is a down-to-earth family house with just three guest rooms – the floral curtains may make you feel like you're back at Grandma's, but hey, it's part of this villa's charm. A single/double/triple costs Rs 340/425/535 including breakfast. On half-board they go for Rs 425/595/790.

Vanilla Guest House (☎ 234125), also inland, is a simple, homey place in its own lush garden, run by Madame Symti Bibi. There are two standard rooms for Rs 250 per person per night, a larger room for Rs 300 and one small (slightly stuffy) room for Rs 200. All rooms are on a half-board basis. Guests have use of a communal kitchen.

Places to Stay – top end

Patatran Village (☎ 234333; fax 234344) is a spiffy complex of 12 chalets overlooking the sea at Anse Patates. The chalets, named after flowers, are clean, bright and enjoy good views across to the Soeurs islands and Félicité. Just a couple of metres away is one of the Seychelles' most picturesque beaches – Anse Patates. Rates for a standard single/double room are Rs 660/940 (half-board), or Rs 750/1120 (full-board). Superior bungalows cost Rs 780/1060 a single/double on half-board; Rs 870/1240 on full-board. The restaurant serves snacks, set meals and à la carte dishes (see Places to Eat).

Hotel L'Ocean (☎ 234180; fax 234308), near Patatran Village, offers singles/doubles/triples for Rs 575/700/920 (B&B); Rs 700/950/1295 (half-board). Facilities include a restaurant and bar.

SEYCHELLES

La Digue Island Lodge (☎ 234232; fax 234100), Anse La Réunion, is a large, resort-style hotel, which is certainly luxurious enough but a little lacking in warm service. The cheapest single/double rooms (no air-con) are in the lodge's annex at a cost of Rs 675/945 (half-board); Rs 755/1095 (full-board). For air-con, you'll pay Rs 765/1025 (half-board); Rs 840/1180 (full-board). For something with more character, there are singles/doubles in the garden chalets for Rs 890/1290 (half-board); Rs 955/1410 (full-board). If you can afford it, go for a beach chalet which has singles/doubles for Rs 1090/1490 (half-board); Rs 1155/1610 (full-board). There are also swanky suites available. The restaurant offers a good set menu or you can order a snack at the poolside bar (the pool is exclusively for residents). The hotel also has a small beach and a diving centre (see Activities in the Seychelles Facts for the Visitor chapter), and can organise a variety of tours around La Digue or to neighbouring islands. The hotel arranges day trips to Félicité several times a week for Rs 300 per person, including a barbeque lunch and time for snorkelling. They also offer exclusive accommodation packages – see Félicité Island later in this chapter.

L'Union Self-Catering Chalets (☎ 234240; fax 234005), in the L'Union Estate & Copra Factory grounds, offers four modern self-catering chalets fronting the beach. Each chalet has a dining room, fully-equipped kitchen and two air-con bedrooms. The cost is Rs 1650 per night (maximum of four people) and Rs 100 for an extra bed (maximum of two). Half/full board is an additional Rs 225/325 per person. Meals are provided at La Digue Island Lodge and if you take a half/full-board meal plan, you can also use facilities (such as the pool) at La Digue Island Lodge.

Places to Eat

There is a dearth of independent restaurants on La Digue. Most of the places to stay with their own restaurant will take reservations from nonresidents for meals (book ahead).

Tarosa Cafeteria (☎ 234250), near the pier, is not bad for a cheap feed. This small, unpretentious place has seating outdoors and is open every day from 10 am to 6 pm. Menu items include octopus salad (Rs 35), sandwiches (from Rs 20 to Rs 35), salads (from Rs 25 to Rs 35) and ice cream (Rs 5).

Zerof (☎ 234067), opposite the Veuve Reserve, has an emphasis on Créole cuisine and is open daily for lunch (noon to 3 pm) and dinner (7 to 10 pm). The à la carte menu offers a variety of dishes including grilled fish with Créole sauce (Rs 45),

sandwiches (Rs 35) and even pizzas (Rs 25). The set menu is Rs 75. There's a pool table for those interested.

Snack Bar (no phone), at the beautiful Grand Anse, is a life-saver for ravenous beach goers. There's only a small selection of things to munch on – expect to pay anywhere between Rs 25 and Rs 150. This little eatery mainly sells snacks and soft drinks and is open daily from 9 am to 6 pm.

La Digue Island Lodge (☎ 234232) (see Places to Stay) has a decent restaurant where you can order grilled fish for around Rs 70.

Bernique Guest House (☎ 234229) (see Places to Stay) serves an à la carte lunch from noon to 2 pm; main courses range from Rs 35 to Rs 85 – a favourite is the octopus in coconut milk (Rs 85). Dinner is from 7.30 pm and is a set meal (Rs 105 per person).

PatatranVillage (☎ 234333) (see Places to Stay) is recommended for a treat. You can get inexpensive light meals such as omelettes (Rs 35), pickled fish (Rs 45) and sandwiches (Rs 45), as well as more elaborate creations such as grilled lobster (Rs 175). The set meal is Rs 120 per person. Lunch is daily from noon to 2.30 pm and dinner is from 7 to 10 pm.

Tournesol Guest House (☎ 234155) (see Places to Stay) has a limited menu but is good for a reasonably cheap and cheerful feed. The set meal is Rs 100, while dishes on the à la carte menu range from Rs 20 to Rs 75. Octopus curry is Rs 50, fish and chips is Rs 50 and sandwiches are around Rs 20. The restaurant is open daily for lunch and dinner.

Self-Catering There are a couple of places to stock up on grocery items.

Gregoire's, near La Digue Island Lodge, is the largest shop on the island and sells the usual groceries, including wine, beer and spirits. A carton of juice is Rs 9.75, a loaf of bread is Rs 6, a small tin of Milo is Rs 6.15, a packet of biscuits is around Rs 8, a jar of jam is Rs 9.50, a packet of spaghetti is Rs 7.15 and a small tube of toothpaste is Rs 3.90. You can also pick up snacks such as samosas (Rs 1 each). For those after a tropical treat at sunset, a bottle of Malibu is Rs 134. Gregoire's is open Monday to Saturday from 8 am to 6.30 pm.

Bakery is a little place close to the pier (just behind Michelin) where self-caterers can buy a loaf of bread for Rs 6. They also have a small selection of cakes; coconut cake is Rs 2 per slice; banana cake is Rs 3 per slice.

Getting There & Away

You can get to La Digue by boat or helicopter

from either Mahé or Praslin. See the Seychelles Getting Around chapter for details.

Getting Around

Taxi There are only about three taxis on La Digue, as most people get around by bicycle or on foot. The scarcity of motorised vehicles means that the island is blissfully serene. Taxis charge about Rs 120/700 per hour/day on La Digue (to cut the cost share with other people). If you intend hiring a taxi for an hour or so, it's worth negotiating a discount. A one-way ride from the pier to Grand Anse is around Rs 60. A seat on a lorry is Rs 40 per person (return) – ask someone at the pier for details.

If you have a lot of luggage, you may want to hire a taxi to transport it to your hotel – book ahead as it can be difficult getting a taxi during certain times of the day. The virtues of backpacks and light packing pay off here. Alternatively you could plonk your luggage and yourself on an ox-cart (see Ox Cart, following, for details).

Bicycle Almost everyone walks or cycles on La Digue. Only essential vehicles are permitted on the island. Bicycle is a tremendous way of exploring this island paradise, largely because of the scarcity of traffic. However, beware of the occasional speeding biker – there have been a few nasty collisions in the past. The beauty about travelling by bike is that you can stop whenever you desire – to check out an art gallery, or stop for a picnic on a secluded beach. If you get lost, the locals will happily point you in the right direction. Keep in mind that there are no sealed roads and some wicked potholes, so you may be a bit saddle-sore by the end of the day.

There are loads of bikes to rent, with several operators offering rates of Rs 10/25 per hour/day. A good place to rent is at Michelin (☎ 234043), right near the pier, which is owned by Michelin Ladouce. Apart from standard bikes (Rs 10/25 per hour/day), they have tandems for Rs 10/40 per hour/day, as well as children's bikes and bikes with attached baby seats. Mason's Travel (see

Travel Agency) rents out bikes for a more expensive Rs 35 per day. Some hotels also rent out bikes, but often at a premium price – you're better off hiring from an independent operator if that's the case.

Check the bikes carefully, many are in poor condition and the gears sometimes don't work. If you hire for more than one day, ask for a discount. Don't lose your bike – you'll have to shell out an agonising Rs 1800 if you do!

Walking If you can't ride a bike don't despair, the island is small enough to cover comfortably on foot. It's a great place to ramble around at leisure, with plenty of alluring beaches to stop at for a cool dip if you work up a sweat. Several walks and hikes are described earlier in this chapter.

Ox Cart The ox carts are for pleasure trips and are not a particularly practical or cheap alternative. Michelin (☎ 234043) runs the ox carts and charges Rs 25 for one short trip, say from the pier to La Digue Island Lodge. Tours of the island lasting two to four hours cost around Rs 300 for two to four people.

Boat See Charters in the Seychelles Getting Around chapter. Your hotel may be able to recommend a reputable private boat operator.

FÉLICITÉ ISLAND

This mountainous island, 3.5km north-east of La Digue, has good walking trails and excellent snorkelling sites.

The island's main entrepreneur, Gregoire Payet (who runs the supermarket and La Digue Island Lodge), has renovated two French plantation houses for use as luxurious accommodation, complete with air-con and deluxe bathrooms. Each house has two bedrooms and can accommodate up to four. Close to the houses is the beach of La Penice – a motor cruiser is provided for fishing or snorkelling excursions. Walking tracks lead guests to discover the fauna and flora, including giant land tortoise and many bird species. A tennis court is also available. For evening entertainment you can either soak in the peace and quiet or watch TV.

The island is rented out according to the motto, 'own your island package'. The minimum number of guests is two and the maximum is eight. Once a reservation has been confirmed, no other reservation is allowed to overlap with the confirmed stay of the guests on the island. Group bookings are accepted only for families and groups of friends wishing to spend their holiday together.

The minimum length of stay is three days. The price is inclusive of full-board, all drinks, snorkelling gear and use of the yacht. Also included in the rates are the transfer – 30 minutes by boat – from La Digue or Praslin. Children under 12 years of age are charged half price; kids under six years old stay free of charge. Rates start at around Rs 4,800 for two people per night and peak at Rs 14,000 for eight people per night.

Alternatively, you can opt for a cheaper 'share your island package', which costs Rs 1950 for a double room per night, on full-board. An extra bed is Rs 975 including full-board. The tariff includes boat transfers. For bookings contact La Digue Island Lodge (☎ 234232; fax 234100), which also arranges day trips to Félicité at Rs 300 per person with lunch. Mason's Travel (☎ 234227; fax 234266) charges Rs 310/155 for adults/children for a day tour to Félicité including lunch.

FRÉGATE ISLAND

This privately-owned granite island, 56km east of Mahé and about 20km south of La Digue, was once reputed to be a pirate lair – today it's a stronghold for the birds.

Where La Digue has the only black paradise flycatchers, Praslin the only black parrots and Cousin the only brush warblers, Frégate has the rare magpie robin. It is also the last home of a species of tenebrionid

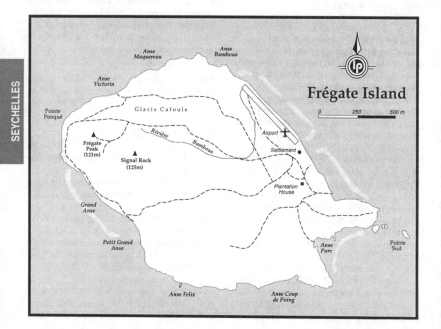

beetle! There once were Java deer on the island, which the French introduced from Mauritius, but these died out in the 1950s. The giant land tortoises are still around.

Attractions include superb beaches, such as Anse Victorin (considered one of the best beaches in the Seychelles), birdwatching, hiking along wooded paths and treasure hunting. There are caves around the island and, as at Bel Ombre, some rocks bear mysterious markings awaiting someone to decipher them.

Place to Stay
At the time of writing, the hotel on this island was under renovation and is scheduled to open by 1998. There were no details about the room tariffs, but the hotel is likely to be of five-star standard. Your best bet is to contact the Frégate Island office (☎ 323123; fax 324169), on Revolution Ave in Victoria, or ask a tour operator.

Getting There & Away
Flight costs were not confirmed at the time of writing, however a return ticket is expected to cost around Rs 415. For further details inquire at the Frégate Island office or ask a tour operator.

COCOS ISLAND
This is a tiny island just to the north of Félicité Island and closer to La Digue than to Praslin. It was once considered to be the best place for snorkelling in the area. However, the government closed it to visitors in 1987 because coral and shells were being damaged and pilfered at an alarming rate by tourists and locals. The island will continue to remain off limits until the coral has recovered.

PETITE SOEUR & GRANDE SOEUR ISLANDS
These two peaceful islands are north of Félicité and Cocos islands. Grande Soeur has good beaches, a forest of coconut palms, and dramatic outcrops of huge granite boulders. Mason's Travel (☎ 234227; fax 234266) arranges trips to Grande Soeur and Petite

Soeur Islands from La Digue for Rs 350 per person (less for children), including snorkelling and a barbeque lunch.

BIRD ISLAND
In contrast to the central granite islands of the Seychelles, this is a coral island – flat, covered in palms and ringed by a white coral beach. As the name implies, the entire island is dominated by birds, birds, birds. For most visitors it's an awesome and immensely enjoyable experience, but it takes a while to become accustomed to the sights, smells and noises of the bird world.

The privately-owned island, 96km north of Mahé, is 1km long and 2km wide. Apart from being an obvious magnet for ornithologists, Bird Island is also good for snorkelling, swimming, diving, windsurfing, deep-sea fishing and simply lazing around. Check where you swim, as there are dangerous currents in some parts.

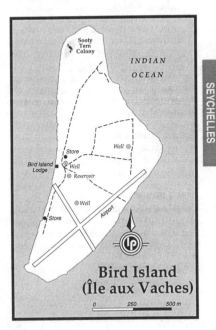

Bird Island (Île aux Vaches)

0   250   500 m

Bird Island is also called Île aux Vaches (Cow Island), probably derived from the local name for 'sea cows' or dugongs. The island takes its present name from the vast colonies of fairy tern, common noddy and millions of sooty tern which nest at one end. The sooty terns arrive between April and May and breed around October.

Large numbers of turtle also breed on the island. Out of 500 baby turtle born to each female, only 30 may survive to adulthood.

Bird Island claims to have the oldest tortoise in the Seychelles, if not the world. Esmeralda is believed to be more than 150 years old, weighs around 300kg, and, despite the name, is a male. The Cousin Island people maintain that their resident giant tortoise is older, but Esmeralda officially topped the weight stakes when he made it into the 1990 Guinness Book of Records.

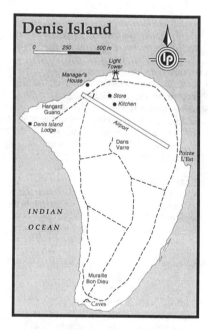

Denis Island

Places to Stay

Bird Island Lodge (☎ 323322; fax 323335) has 24 wooden bungalows with twin-bed rooms and verandahs facing the sea. Room prices were not confirmed at the time of writing, but should cost around Rs 990 per person for the first night on an obligatory full-board basis, including the flights. Rates for rooms become less expensive when booked for longer stays. For example, the rates per person for two/four/seven days are around Rs 1405/2555/4280 with full-board and including return flights. Contact the Bird Island office (☎ 224925; fax 225074) in Victoria for the latest information on tariffs.

Getting There & Away

For details about flight schedules and costs, contact the Bird Island office (☎ 224925; fax 225074) in Victoria.

DENIS ISLAND

Denis Island is similar in size and everything else to Bird Island, but is more exclusive. The island was named after the French navigator Denis de Trobriand, who discovered it in 1773.

Now Denis supports a population of around 50 and belongs to French couple Pierre and Suzanne Burkhardt, who bought it in 1975. Their brochure says, 'Denis Island is a privately owned island, we are not, nor

do we wish to be a hotel. Our sole ambition is to enable you to accomplish a dream.'

The coral island is south-east of Bird Island and about 80km from Mahé. The vegetation is thicker here than on Bird Island.

Places to Stay

Denis Island Lodge (for reservations, call ☎ 323392; fax 324192) has luxuriously thatched and secluded bungalows. The minimum booking is two days – day trippers are not allowed – and you must deposit 30% of the fee within eight days of making a reservation. Excursion packages are available from travel agents for a minimum of two nights, including the flights and full-board, for Rs 3080/4440 a single/double.

Getting There & Away

The price given under Place to Stay includes the return flight and accommodation. There are flights on Tuesday, Thursday, Sunday and sometimes on Friday. Contact the Denis Island office (☎ 323392; fax 324192), in Victoria, for further details and reservations.

Outer Islands

HIGHLIGHTS

- Water sports, fishing and diving on Desroches Island
- Aldabra Atoll, home to about 200,000 giant tortoise
- The amazing underwater world around Assomption Island

The majority of the Seychelles islands (all of them are coral) are scattered around over hundreds of km to the south-west of the main Mahé group and fall into three main groups – the Amirantes, Farquhar and Aldabra groups.

Let's face it, you would need to have a lot of time and money to go to these islands as a visitor. Or you would need to have a special scientific interest and authoritative or financial backing to persuade the Seychelles government to let you ride along with the workers and supply boats. For private boat charter, contact the Marine Charter Association (MCA) (☎ 322126; fax 224679) in Victoria (see also the Seychelles Getting Around chapter).

Only a few of the 70 islands are inhabited, by about 500 fishermen, research and agricultural workers employed by the Islands Development Company (IDC). The rest of the islands are too small to be productive, although one day some may end up as Maldives-style resorts.

The main industry of these islands is copra. More than 2500 tonnes are produced annually. Livestock has also been introduced.

The IDC is responsible for managing Coétivy, Desroches, Marie-Louise, Desnoeufs, Plate and Alphonse in the Amirantes group; Providence and Farquhar in the Farquhar group; and Cosmolédo and Astove in the Aldabra group.

Seven of the IDC islands have airstrips and the company also operates a few schooners, including *Lady Esme*. For prices and permission to visit the islands contact the IDC (☎ 224640; fax 224467) at New Port, Victoria.

AMIRANTES GROUP

The largest of the three groups, the Amirantes, lies 200km to 330km south-west of Mahé. The islands were named Ilhas do Amirante (Admiral Islands) in 1501 by Vasco da Gama, the Portuguese explorer.

To charter a boat to the Amirantes, contact the Marine Charter Association (☎ 322126; fax 224679), in Victoria (Mahé). They charge approximately Rs 4000 per boat (maximum of eight people), including lunch and soft drinks.

Desroches Island

The main island in the group is Desroches which, having been exploited for timber, is

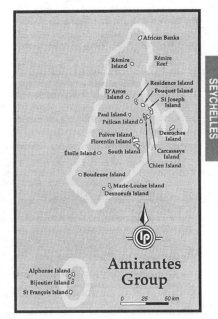

SEYCHELLES

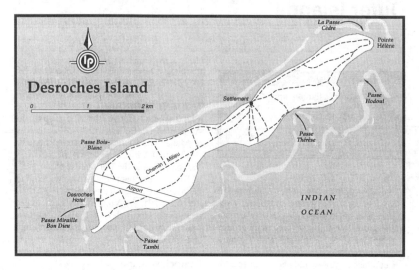

Desroches Island

0   1   2 km

now a tourist destination with a resort offering water sports, fishing, diving, and excursions to other islands in the Amirantes. The best time for diving is from September to May.

Desroches Hotel (☎ 229003; fax 229002) is back in action after copping quite a battering from very strong winds in 1990. It has 20 chalets and excursion packages only are available for a minimum of two nights, including the flights and full-board, for Rs 2207/2630 a single/double.

There are flights four times a week (Monday,

Wednesday, Friday and Sunday) between Mahé and Desroches. The trip takes one hour.

Poivre Island

Poivre Island is named after Pierre Poivre, the French governor of Mauritius from 1763 to 1772, who later introduced spices to Mahé. Poivre is accessible on yacht charters for up to eight people for around Rs 3500 per boat per day. Contact the Marine Charter Association (☎ 322126; fax 224679) in Victoria for more information.

D'Arros Island – Yours for just US$18 million

Fed up with life in the big smoke? Always dreamt of possessing your own little slice of paradise ... sipping champagne on one of the world's most beautiful beaches ... splashing in warm lagoons from sunrise to sunset? Dream no longer. The privately-owned tropical island of D'Arros, about 40km to the north of Poivre, is up for grabs ... for a mere US$18 million (negotiable).

This 170 hectare island was bought by an eminent Iranian family who now wish to sell it, preferably to someone who will retain the island as a private residence. Prince Chahram Pahlevi, current owner of D'Arros, does not want to see his remote and idyllic island destroyed by development. Very wise.

If you're beginning to think that this island has your name written all over it, negotiations for its purchase should be made through Mr Glynn Burridge, P.O Box 195, Victoria, Mahé, Seychelles (☎ 323960; fax 324011).

Visitors can holiday on D'Arros at certain times of the year. There is accommodation for up to 14 people; the island 'rent' is a mind-blowing US$7500 per night, on a full-board basis. You can get to D'Arros by chartering a plane or yacht – ask for details when booking.

Oh, and if you do end up buying the island, drop us a postcard! ■

Boat transfer from Desroches takes two hours, but the crossing has to be made at high tide when the reef surrounding Poivre is covered with sufficient water.

FARQUHAR GROUP

This group of islands – Farquhar Atoll, Providence and St Pierre – is another 400km south-west of the Amirantes. The lagoon of Farquhar Atoll is a popular resting point for yachts and schooners. Copra production and fishing are carried out by the few inhabitants. Île du Nord has an airstrip.

ALDABRA GROUP

This is the best known, most remote and most interesting of the outer island groups. Aldabra lies more than 1000km from Mahé – in fact it's closer to Madagascar (400km) and Africa (650km) than its own capital. There are no hotels on the Aldabra Group.

It is thought to have been discovered around the 9th century by Arab seafarers who called it Al Khadra, and through the centuries and various European pronunciations this became Aldabra.

When it was part of the British Indian Ocean Territory (along with Farquhar), Aldabra was fancied by the Americans for a military base, but fears of a run-in with conservationists put them off and they eventually decided on Diego García. (The poor Diego Garcíans had no powerful lobby to protect them.)

Aldabra Atoll

Aldabra Atoll is one of the world's largest coral atolls. It stretches for 22km east to west and contains four major islands – Picard (west), Polymnieli, Malabar (middle) and Grand Terre (south) – which enclose a huge tidal lagoon. Grand Passe, the main entrance to the lagoon, can be dangerous, particularly after low tide when the incoming tide rushes in at eight to 10 knots. Tiger sharks and manta rays also enter with the tide and water activities are not recommended at this time! Aldabra is the original habitat of the giant

land tortoises. There are about 200,000 of them on the atoll now, although at the turn of the century they were almost killed off. Marine turtles lay their eggs on the atoll and flocks of migratory birds, including flamingo, ibis, heron and frigatebirds, fly in and out in their thousands. The white-throated rail is the sole remaining species of flightless bird in the Indian Ocean. Aldabra was declared a nature reserve some years ago by the Seychelles government and is now listed as a World Heritage site.

Aldabra Atoll is inhabited only by scientists, and only for three months of the year. There is a scientific station, with generator-powered electricity, situated there. The Seychelles government is keen to see more scientists making use of the station.

The fishing settlement huts on West Island can be used by visiting scientists. There is no electricity. One major problem is the presence of giant 'robber' coconut crabs which scuttle about pinching anything they can lay their claws on and have been known to run off down burrows with cameras and clocks. If you catch a coconut crab, they are tasty to eat, but make sure you get rid of the poisonous large intestine.

SEYCHELLES

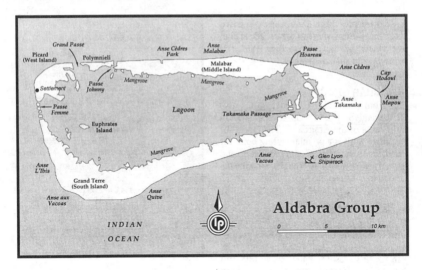

Aldabra Group

INDIAN OCEAN

0   5   10 km

Cosmolédo Atoll

The Cosmolédo Atoll (which includes Astove Island) is a ring of 12 tiny islands, 110km east of Assumption Island in the Aldabra Group. The largest of these islands is Wizard Island (Grand Île) which covers less than 2 sq km.

The islands have been more or less ignored by outsiders and still serve as nesting sites for tern, booby and the rare red-tailed tropicbird. Cosmolédo is managed by the Island Development Company.

Assumption Island

Sausage-shaped Assumption Island, 27km south of Aldabra, was once one of only two islands in the world with a population of the Abbot's booby (the other is Christmas Island in the Eastern Indian Ocean). It was also a stronghold of the flightless rail, but both these slow-moving birds were wiped out early on. Rich in guano, the island was exploited for its wealth in fertiliser but in the process it was stripped of vegetation and, as a result, was rendered uninhabitable to the birds which

Stingrays & Manta Rays

Rays are essentially flattened sharks but their feeding habits are quite unsharklike. Stingrays are bottom feeders, equipped with crushing teeth to grind the molluscs and crustaceans they sift out of the sand. They are often found lying motionless on the sandy bottom of shallow bays. It's fun to wade across such a bay, watching them suddenly rise up from the bottom and glide smoothly away. Just make certain you do scare them up, for stingrays are less than impressed when a human foot pins them down to the bottom, and that barbed and poisonous tail can then swing up and into your leg with painful efficiency.

Manta rays are among the largest fish found in the Indian Ocean, and a firm favourite of scuba divers. There's nothing quite like the feeling of sensing a shadow passing over the sun and looking up to see a huge manta ray swooping smoothly through the water above you. They are quite harmless, feeding only on plankton and small fish, and in some places seem quite relaxed about divers approaching them closely. Manta rays are sometimes seen to leap completely out of the water, landing back with a tremendous splash.

Despite their shy nature rays do have one shark-like characteristic in that they give birth to live young. A baby manta ray is born neatly wrapped up in its bat-like wings. ■

produced the guano. By the 1920s, it was practically bereft of plant or animal life. Furthermore, the green turtles which nested regularly on the island had been hunted to the brink of extinction and today, fewer than 200 females come ashore annually to lay their eggs.

Underwater, however, it's a different world and it was here that Jacques Cousteau came to film much of his documentary, *The Silent World*. Although he'd dived throughout the world, he reported that he'd never seen any other place on earth with the same clarity of water or such colourful and extensive reef life.

Assomption has an airstrip, so tourists can fly from Mahé, then take a three-hour boat trip to Aldabra.

Getting There & Away

If you wish to go to Aldabra as a tourist, contact the Marine Charter Association (☎ 322126; fax 224679) or the Islands Development Company (☎ 224640; fax 224467), both in Victoria (Mahé). A popular alternative to the long yacht trips from Mahé is to fly to Desroches and pick up a schooner or yacht charter from there.

Index

TEXT

LONELY PLANET PHRASEBOOKS

Building bridges,
Breaking barriers,
Beyond babble-on

Nepali phrasebook

Ethiopian Amharic phrasebook

Latin American Spanish phrasebook

Ukrainian phrasebook

Greek phrasebook

Vietnamese phrasebook

Listen for the gems

Speak your own words

Ask your own questions

Master of your own image

- handy pocket-sized books
- easy to understand Pronunciation chapter
- clear and comprehensive Grammar chapter
- romanisation alongside script to allow ease of pronunciation
- script throughout so users can point to phrases
- extensive vocabulary sections, words and phrases for every situation
- full of cultural information and tips for the traveller

'...vital for a real DIY spirit and attitude in language learning' – Backpacker

'the phrasebooks have good cultural backgrounders and offer solid advice for challenging situations in remote locations' – San Francisco Examiner

'...they are unbeatable for their coverage of the world's more obscure languages' – The Geographical Magazine

---

Arabic (Egyptian)
Arabic (Moroccan)
Australia
 Australian English, Aboriginal and Torres Strait languages
Baltic States
 Estonian, Latvian, Lithuanian
Bengali
Brazilian
Burmese
Cantonese
Central Asia
Central Europe
 Czech, French, German, Hungarian, Italian and Slovak
Eastern Europe
 Bulgarian, Czech, Hungarian, Polish, Romanian and Slovak
Ethiopian (Amharic)
Fijian
French
German
Greek

Hindi/Urdu
Indonesian
Italian
Japanese
Korean
Lao
Latin American Spanish
Malay
Mandarin
Mediterranean Europe
 Albanian, Croatian, Greek, Italian, Macedonian, Maltese, Serbian and Slovene
Mongolian
Nepali
Papua New Guinea
Pilipino (Tagalog)
Quechua
Russian
Scandinavian Europe
 Danish, Finnish, Icelandic, Norwegian and Swedish

South-East Asia
 Burmese, Indonesian, Khmer, Lao, Malay, Tagalog (Pilipino), Thai and Vietnamese
Spanish (Castilian)
 Basque, Catalan and Galician
Sri Lanka
Swahili
Thai
Thai Hill Tribes
Tibetan
Turkish
Ukrainian
USA
 US English, Vernacular, Native American languages and Hawaiian
Vietnamese
Western Europe
 Basque, Catalan, Dutch, French, German, Irish, Italian, Portuguese, Scottish Gaelic, Spanish (Castilian) and Welsh

---

LONELY PLANET TRAVEL ATLASES

Lonely Planet has long been famous for the number and quality of its guidebook maps. Now we've gone one step further and produced a handy companion series: Lonely Planet travel atlases – maps of a country produced in book form.

Unlike other maps, which look good but lead travellers astray, our travel atlases have been researched on the road by Lonely Planet's experienced team of writers. All details are carefully checked to ensure the atlas corresponds with the equivalent Lonely Planet guidebook.

The handy atlas format means no holes, wrinkles, torn sections or constant folding and unfolding. These atlases can survive long periods on the road, unlike cumbersome fold-out maps. The comprehensive index ensures easy reference.

- full-colour throughout
- maps researched and checked by Lonely Planet authors
- place names correspond with Lonely Planet guidebooks
  – no confusing spelling differences
- legend and travelling information in English, French, German, Japanese and Spanish
- size: 230 x 160 mm

Available now:
Chile & Easter Island • Egypt • India & Bangladesh • Israel & the Palestinian Territories •Jordan, Syria & Lebanon • Kenya • Laos • Portugal • South Africa, Lesotho & Swaziland • Thailand • Turkey • Vietnam • Zimbabwe, Botswana & Namibia

---

LONELY PLANET TV SERIES & VIDEOS

Lonely Planet travel guides have been brought to life on television screens around the world. Like our guides, the programmes are based on the joy of independent travel, and look honestly at some of the most exciting, picturesque and frustrating places in the world. Each show is presented by one of three travellers from Australia, England or the USA and combines an innovative mixture of video, Super-8 film, atmospheric soundscapes and original music.

Videos of each episode – containing additional footage not shown on television – are available from good book and video shops, but the availability of individual videos varies with regional screening schedules.

Video destinations include: Alaska • American Rockies • Australia – The South-East • Baja California & the Copper Canyon • Brazil • Central Asia • Chile & Easter Island • Corsica, Sicily & Sardinia – The Mediterranean Islands • East Africa (Tanzania & Zanzibar) • Ecuador & the Galapagos Islands • Greenland & Iceland • Indonesia • Israel & the Sinai Desert • Jamaica • Japan • La Ruta Maya • Morocco • New York • North India • Pacific Islands (Fiji, Solomon Islands & Vanuatu) • South India • South West China • Turkey • Vietnam • West Africa • Zimbabwe, Botswana & Namibia

The Lonely Planet TV series is produced by:
Pilot Productions
The Old Studio
18 Middle Row
London W10 5AT UK

For video availability and ordering information contact your nearest Lonely Planet office.

Music from the TV series is available on CD & cassette.

PLANET TALK

Lonely Planet's FREE quarterly newsletter

We love hearing from you and think you'd like to hear from us.

When...is the right time to see reindeer in Finland?
Where...can you hear the best palm-wine music in Ghana?
How...do you get from Asunción to Areguá by steam train?
What...is the best way to see India?

For the answer to these and many other questions read PLANET TALK.

Every issue is packed with up-to-date travel news and advice including:

- a letter from Lonely Planet co-founders Tony and Maureen Wheeler
- go behind the scenes on the road with a Lonely Planet author
- feature article on an important and topical travel issue
- a selection of recent letters from travellers
- details on forthcoming Lonely Planet promotions
- complete list of Lonely Planet products

To join our mailing list contact any Lonely Planet office.

Also available: Lonely Planet T-shirts. 100% heavyweight cotton.

LONELY PLANET ONLINE

Get the latest travel information before you leave or while you're on the road

Whether you've just begun planning your next trip, or you're chasing down specific info on currency regulations or visa requirements, check out Lonely Planet Online for up-to-the minute travel information.

As well as travel profiles of your favourite destinations (including maps and photos), you'll find current reports from our researchers and other travellers, updates on health and visas, travel advisories, and discussion of the ecological and political issues you need to be aware of as you travel.

There's also an online travellers' forum where you can share your experience of life on the road, meet travel companions and ask other travellers for their recommendations and advice. We also have plenty of links to other online sites useful to independent travellers.

And of course we have a complete and up-to-date list of all Lonely Planet travel products including guides, phrasebooks, atlases, Journeys and videos and a simple online ordering facility if you can't find the book you want elsewhere.

www.lonelyplanet.com
or
AOL keyword: lp

LONELY PLANET PRODUCTS

Lonely Planet is known worldwide for publishing practical, reliable and no-nonsense travel information in our guides and on our web site. The Lonely Planet list covers just about every accessible part of the world. Currently there are nine series: *travel guides, shoestring guides, walking guides, city guides, phrasebooks, audio packs, travel atlases, Journeys – a unique collection of travel writing and Pisces Books - diving and snorkeling guides.*

EUROPE

Amsterdam • Andalucia • Austria • Baltic States phrasebook • Berlin • Britain • Canary Islands • Central Europe on a shoestring • Central Europe phrasebook • Czech & Slovak Republics • Denmark • Dublin • Eastern Europe on a shoestring • Eastern Europe phrasebook • Estonia, Latvia & Lithuania • Europe • Finland • France • French phrasebook • Germany • German phrasebook • Greece • Greek phrasebook • Hungary • Iceland, Greenland & the Faroe Islands • Ireland • Italian phrasebook • Italy • Lisbon • London • Mediterranean Europe on a shoestring • Mediterranean Europe phrasebook • Paris • Poland • Portugal • Portugal travel atlas • Prague • Romania & Moldova • Russia, Ukraine & Belarus • Russian phrasebook • Scandinavian & Baltic Europe on a shoestring • Scandinavian Europe phrasebook • Slovenia • Spain • Spanish phrasebook • St Petersburg • Switzerland • Trekking in Spain • Ukrainian phrasebook • Vienna • Walking in Britain • Walking in Italy • Walking in Switzerland • Western Europe on a shoestring • Western Europe phrasebook

Travel Literature: The Olive Grove: Travels in Greece

NORTH AMERICA

Alaska • Backpacking in Alaska • Baja California • California & Nevada • Canada • Chicago • Deep South • Florida • Hawaii • Honolulu • Los Angeles • Mexico • Mexico City • Miami • New England • New Orleans • New York City • New York, New Jersey & Pennsylvania • Pacific Northwest USA • Rocky Mountain States • San Francisco • Seattle • Southwest USA • USA phrasebook • Washington, DC & the Capital Region

Travel Literature: Drive thru America

CENTRAL AMERICA & THE CARIBBEAN

• Bahamas and Turks & Caicos • Bermuda • Central America on a shoestring • Costa Rica • Cuba • Eastern Caribbean • Guatemala, Belize & Yucatán: La Ruta Maya • Jamaica • Panama

Travel Literature Green Dreams: Travels in Central America

SOUTH AMERICA

Argentina, Uruguay & Paraguay • Bolivia • Brazil • Brazilian phrasebook • Buenos Aires • Chile & Easter Island • Chile & Easter Island travel atlas • Colombia Ecuador & the Galápagos Islands • Latin American Spanish phrasebook • Peru • Quechua phrasebook • Rio de Janeiro • South America on a shoestring • Trekking in the Patagonian Andes • Venezuela

Travel Literature: Full Circle: A South American Journey

ISLANDS OF THE INDIAN OCEAN

Madagascar & Comoros • Maldives • Mauritius, Réunion & Seychelles

AFRICA

Africa - the South • Africa on a shoestring • Arabic (Moroccan) phrasebook • Cairo • Cape Town • Central Africa • East Africa • Egypt • Egypt travel atlas • Ethiopian (Amharic) phrasebook • The Gambia & Senegal • Kenya • Kenya travel atlas • Malawi, Mozambique & Zambia • Morocco • North Africa • South Africa, Lesotho & Swaziland • South Africa, Lesotho & Swaziland travel atlas • Swahili phrasebook • Tunisia • Trekking in East Africa • West Africa • Zimbabwe, Botswana & Namibia • Zimbabwe, Botswana & Namibia travel atlas

Travel Literature: Mali Blues • The Rainbird: A Central African Journey • Songs to an African Sunset: A Zimbabwean Story

MAIL ORDER

Lonely Planet products are distributed worldwide. They are also available by mail order from Lonely Planet, so if you have difficulty finding a title please write to us. North American and South American residents should write to 150 Linden St, Oakland CA 94607, USA; European and African residents should write to 10a Spring Place, London NW5 3BH; and residents of other countries to PO Box 617, Hawthorn, Victoria 3122, Australia.

NORTH-EAST ASIA

Beijing • Bhutan • Cantonese phrasebook • China • Hong Kong • Hong Kong, Macau & Guangzhou • Japan • Japanese phrasebook • Japanese audio pack • Korea • Korean phrasebook • Kyoto • Mandarin phrasebook • Mongolia • Mongolian phrasebook • North-East Asia on a shoestring • Seoul • South-West China • Taiwan • Tibet • Tibet phrasebook • Tokyo

Travel Literature: Lost Japan

MIDDLE EAST & CENTRAL ASIA

Arab Gulf States • Arabic (Egyptian) phrasebook • Central Asia • Central Asia phrasebook • Iran • Israel & the Palestinian Territories • Israel & the Palestinian Territories travel atlas • Istanbul • Jerusalem • Jordan & Syria • Jordan, Syria & Lebanon travel atlas • Lebanon • Middle East • Turkey • Turkish phrasebook • Turkey travel atlas • Yemen

Travel Literature: The Gates of Damascus • Kingdom of the Film Stars: Journey into Jordan

ALSO AVAILABLE:

Brief Encounters • Travel with Children • Traveller's Tales • Not the Only Planet

INDIAN SUBCONTINENT

Bangladesh • Bengali phrasebook • Bhutan • Delhi • Goa • Hindi/Urdu phrasebook • India • India & Bangladesh travel atlas • Indian Himalaya • Karakoram Highway • Nepal • Nepali phrasebook • Pakistan • Rajasthan • South India • Sri Lanka • Sri Lanka phrasebook • Trekking in the Indian Himalaya • Trekking in the Karakoram & Hindukush • Trekking in the Nepal Himalaya

Travel Literature: In Rajasthan • Shopping for Buddhas

SOUTH-EAST ASIA

Bali & Lombok • Bangkok • Burmese phrasebook • Cambodia • Ho Chi Minh City • Indonesia • Indonesian phrasebook • Indonesian audio pack • Indonesia's Eastern Islands • Jakarta • Java • Laos • Lao phrasebook • Laos travel atlas • Malay phrasebook • Malaysia, Singapore & Brunei • Myanmar (Burma) • Philippines • Pilipino phrasebook • Singapore • South-East Asia on a shoestring • South-East Asia phrasebook • South-West China • Thailand • Thailand's Islands & Beaches • Thailand travel atlas • Thai phrasebook • Thai audio pack • Thai Hill Tribes phrasebook • Vietnam • Vietnamese phrasebook • Vietnam travel atlas

AUSTRALIA & THE PACIFIC

Australia • Australian phrasebook • Bushwalking in Australia • Bushwalking in Papua New Guinea • Fiji • Fijian phrasebook • Islands of Australia's Great Barrier Reef • Melbourne • Micronesia • New Caledonia • New South Wales • New Zealand • Northern Territory • Outback Australia • Papua New Guinea • Papua New Guinea phrasebook • Queensland • Rarotonga & the Cook Islands • Samoa • Solomon Islands • South Australia • Sydney • Tahiti & French Polynesia • Tasmania • Tonga • Tramping in New Zealand • Vanuatu • Victoria • Western Australia

Travel Literature: Islands in the Clouds • Sean & David's Long Drive

ANTARCTICA

Antarctica

THE LONELY PLANET STORY

Lonely Planet published its first book in 1973 in response to the numerous 'How did you do it?' questions Maureen and Tony Wheeler were asked after driving, busing, hitching, sailing and railing their way from England to Australia.

Written at a kitchen table and hand collated, trimmed and stapled, *Across Asia on the Cheap* became an instant local bestseller, inspiring thoughts of another book.

Eighteen months in South-East Asia resulted in their second guide, *South-East Asia on a shoestring*, which they put together in a backstreet Chinese hotel in Singapore in 1975. The 'yellow bible', as it quickly became known to backpackers around the world, soon became *the* guide to the region. It has sold well over half a million copies and is now in its 9th edition, still retaining its familiar yellow cover.

Today there are over 350 titles, including travel guides, walking guides, language kits & phrasebooks, travel atlases and travel literature. The company is the largest independent travel publisher in the world. Although Lonely Planet initially specialised in guides to Asia, today there are few corners of the globe that have not been covered.

The emphasis continues to be on travel for independent travellers. Tony and Maureen still travel for several months of each year and play an active part in the writing, updating and quality control of Lonely Planet's guides.

They have been joined by over 80 authors and 200 staff at our offices in Melbourne (Australia), Oakland (USA), London (UK) and Paris (France). Travellers themselves also make a valuable contribution to the guides through the feedback we receive in thousands of letters each year and on our web site.

The people at Lonely Planet strongly believe that travellers can make a positive contribution to the countries they visit, both through their appreciation of the countries' culture, wildlife and natural features, and through the money they spend. In addition, the company makes a direct contribution to the countries and regions it covers. Since 1986 a percentage of the income from each book has been donated to ventures such as famine relief in Africa; aid projects in India; agricultural projects in Central America; Greenpeace's efforts to halt French nuclear testing in the Pacific; and Amnesty International.

'I hope we send people out with the right attitude about travel. You realise when you travel that there are so many different perspectives about the world, so we hope these books will make people more interested in what they see. Guidebooks can't really guide people. All you can do is point them in the right direction.'

– Tony Wheeler

LONELY PLANET PUBLICATIONS

Australia
PO Box 617, Hawthorn 3122, Victoria
tel: (03) 9819 1877 fax: (03) 9819 6459
e-mail: talk2us@lonelyplanet.com.au

USA
150 Linden St
Oakland, CA 94607
tel: (510) 893 8555 TOLL FREE: 800 275-8555
fax: (510) 893 8572
e-mail: info@lonelyplanet.com

UK
10a Spring Place,
London NW5 3BH
tel: (0171) 428 4800 fax: (0171) 428 4828
e-mail: go@lonelyplanet.co.uk

France:
1 rue du Dahomey, 75011 Paris
tel: 01 55 25 33 00 fax: 01 55 25 33 01
e-mail: bip@lonelyplanet.fr

World Wide Web: http://www.lonelyplanet.com
or *AOL keyword: lp*